2014 GUIDE TO LITERARY AGENTS

includes a 1-year online subscription to **Guide to Literary Agents** on

WritersMarket.com

Where & How to Sell What You Write

THE ULTIMATE MARKET RESEARCH TOOL FOR WRITERS

To register your *2014 Guide to Literary Agents* book and **start your 1-year online genre-only subscription**, scratch off the block below to reveal your activation code, then go to www.WritersMarket.com. Find the box that says "Have an Activation Code?" then click on "Sign Up Now" and enter your contact information and activation code. It's that easy!

UPDATED MARKET LISTINGS FOR YOUR INTEREST AREA
EASY-TO-USE SEARCHABLE DATABASE • RECORD-KEEPING TOOLS
PROFESSIONAL TIPS & ADVICE • INDUSTRY NEWS

Your purchase of *Guide to Literary Agents* gives you access to updated listings related to this genre of writing (valid through 12/31/14). For just $9.99, you can upgrade your subscription and get access to listings from all of our best-selling Market Books. Visit **www.WritersMarket.com** for more information.

WritersMarket.com
Where & How to Sell What You Write

Activate your WritersMarket.com subscription to get instant access to:

- **UPDATED LISTINGS IN YOUR WRITING GENRE:** Find additional listings that didn't make it into the book, updated contact information and more. WritersMarket.com provides the most comprehensive database of verified markets available anywhere.

- **EASY-TO-USE SEARCHABLE DATABASE:** Looking for a specific magazine or book publisher? Just type in its name. Or widen your prospects with the Advanced Search. You can also search for listings that have been recently updated!

- **PERSONALIZED TOOLS:** Store your best-bet markets, and use our popular recording-keeping tools to track your submissions. Plus, get new and updated market listings, query reminders, and more—every time you log in!

- **PROFESSIONAL TIPS & ADVICE:** From pay rate charts to sample query letters, and from how-to articles to Q&A's with literary agents, we have the resources writers need.

YOU'LL GET ALL OF THIS WITH YOUR INCLUDED SUBSCRIPTION TO

23RD ANNUAL EDITION

2014
GUIDE TO
LITERARY AGENTS

Chuck Sambuchino, Editor

WD
WRITER'S DIGEST
BOOKS
WritersDigest.com
Cincinnati, Ohio

Publisher & Editorial Director, Writing Community: Phil Sexton

Writer's Market website: www.writersmarket.com
Writer's Digest website: www.writersdigest.com
Writer's Digest Bookstore: www.writersdigestshop.com
Guide to Literary Agents Blog: www.guidetoliteraryagents.com/blog

Distributed in Canada by Fraser Direct
100 Armstrong Avenue
Georgetown, Ontario, Canada L7G 5S4
Tel: (905) 877-4411

Distributed in the U.K. and Europe by F&W Media International
Brunel House, Newton Abbot, Devon, TQ12 4PU, England
Tel: (+44) 1626-323200, Fax: (+44) 1626-323319
E-mail: postmaster@davidandcharles.co.uk

Distributed in Australia by Capricorn Link
P.O. Box 704, Windsor, NSW 2756 Australia
Tel: (02) 4577-3555

ISSN: 1078-6945
ISBN-13: 978-1-59963-728-0

Attention Booksellers: This is an annual directory of F+W Media, Inc. Return deadline for this edition is December 31, 2014.

Edited by: Chuck Sambuchino
Cover designed by: Claudean Wheeler
Interior designed by: Claudean Wheeler
Page layout by: Geoff Raker
Production coordinated by: Greg Nock

media

CONTENTS

RESOURCES

MARKETS

INDEXES

FROM THE EDITOR

If you examine today's publishing industry, on one hand, you'll find a business in an exciting time of change—with the rise of digital opportunities for writers. But with a closer look, you'll also see how (like with many things in life) the more things change, the more they stay the same.

So what *hasn't* changed in the writing world? Namely the fact that getting a literary agent to represent your writing is still a critical step to seeing your book in bookstores everywhere. And another constant is the undeniable value of a great manuscript and a dynamite query letter to attract the attention of agents. That's why we've added new, back-to-basics articles on both topics in this completely updated edition of the *Guide to Literary Agents*. Start with new articles from story gurus Donald Maass (an agent and author) and James Scott Bell (an author and writing coach) on crafting an excellent manuscript. Then get your tricky submission questions answered with our a new piece on 19 Query Letter FAQs.

After you're done, it's time to peruse through our agent listings—the biggest agent database you will find anywhere, online or in print. And while you're perusing through agencies to query, check out our "New Agent Spotlights" to focus in on hungry reps.

Please stay in touch with me through my blog (guidetoliteraryagents.com/blog) or Twitter (@chucksambuchino) and continue to pass along feedback and success stories. Until we next meet, good luck on your writing journey!

Chuck Sambuchino
Editor, *Guide to Literary Agents / Children's Writer's & Illustrator's Market*
Author, *How to Survive a Garden Gnome Attack* (2010); *Create Your Writer Platform* (2012)

HOW TO USE
GUIDE TO
LITERARY AGENTS

///

Searching for a literary agent can be overwhelming, whether you've just finished your first book or you have several publishing credits on your résumé. More than likely, you're eager to start pursuing agents and anxious to see your name on the spine of a book. But before you go directly to the listings of agencies in this book, take time to familiarize yourself with the way agents work and how you should approach them. By doing so, you will be more prepared for your search, and ultimately save yourself effort and unnecessary grief.

Read the articles

This book begins with feature articles that explain how to prepare for representation, offer strategies for contacting agents, and provide perspectives on the author/agent relationship. The articles are organized into three sections appropriate for each stage of the search process: **Getting Started** and **Contacting Agents**. You may want to start by reading through each article, and then refer back to relevant articles during each stage of your search.

Because there are many ways to make that initial contact with an agent, we've also provided a section called **Perspectives**. These personal accounts from agents and published authors offer information and inspiration for any writer hoping to find representation.

Decide what you're looking for

A literary agent will present your work directly to editors or producers. It's the agent's job to get her client's work published or sold, and to negotiate a fair contract. In the **Literary Agents** section, we list each agent's contact information and explain what type of work the agency represents as well as how to submit your work for consideration.

1. **WHY DO YOU INCLUDE AGENTS WHO ARE NOT SEEKING NEW CLIENTS?** Some agents ask that their listings indicate they are currently closed to new clients. We include them so writers know the agents exist and know not to contact them at this time.

2. **WHY DO YOU EXCLUDE FEE-CHARGING AGENTS?** We have received a number of complaints in the past regarding fees, and therefore have chosen to list only those agents who do not charge reading fees.

3. **WHY ARE SOME AGENTS NOT LISTED?** Some agents may not have responded to our requests for information. We have taken others out of the book after receiving serious complaints about them.

4. **DO I NEED MORE THAN ONE AGENT IF I WRITE IN DIFFERENT GENRES?** It depends. If you have written in one genre and want to switch to a new style of writing, ask your agent if she is willing to represent you in your new endeavor. Most agents will continue to represent clients no matter what genre they choose to write. Occasionally, an agent may feel she has no knowledge of a certain genre and will recommend an appropriate agent to her client. Regardless, you should always talk to your agent about any potential career move.

5. **WHY DON'T YOU LIST MORE FOREIGN AGENTS?** Most American agents have relationships with foreign co-agents in other countries. It is more common for an American agent to work with a co-agent to sell a client's book abroad than for a writer to work directly with a foreign agent. We do list agents in the United Kingdom, Australia, Canada and other countries who sell to publishers both internationally and in the United States. If you decide to query a foreign agent, make sure they represent American writers (if you're American). Some may request to only receive submissions from Canadians, for example, or UK residents.

6. **DO AGENTS EVER CONTACT A SELF-PUBLISHED WRITER?** If a self-published author attracts the attention of the media or if his book sells extremely well, an agent might approach the author in hopes of representing him.

7. **WHY WON'T THE AGENT I QUERIED RETURN MY MATERIAL?** An agent may not answer your query or return your manuscript for several reasons. Perhaps you did not include a self-addressed, stamped envelope (SASE). Many agents will discard a submission without a SASE. Or, the agent may have moved. To avoid using expired addresses, use the most current edition of *Guide to Literary Agents* or access the information online at WritersMarket.com. Another possibility is that the

agent is swamped with submissions. An agent can be overwhelmed with queries, especially if the agent recently has spoken at a conference or has been featured in an article or book. Also, some agents specify in their listings that they never return materials of any kind.

For face-to-face contact, many writers prefer to meet agents at **Conferences**. By doing so, writers can assess an agent's personality, attend workshops and have the chance to get more feedback on their work than they get by mailing submissions and waiting for a response. The conferences section lists conferences agents and/or editors attend. In many cases, private consultations are available, and agents attend with the hope of finding new clients to represent.

Utilize the extras

Aside from the articles and listings, this book offers a section of **Resources**. If you come across a term with which you aren't familiar, check out the Resources section for a quick explanation. Also, note the gray tabs along the edge of each page. The tabs block off each section so they are easier to flip to as you conduct your search.

Finally—and perhaps most importantly—are the **Indexes** in the back of the book. These can serve as an incredibly helpful way to start your search because they categorize the listings according to different criteria. For example, you can look for literary agents according to their specialties (fiction/nonfiction genres).

LISTING POLICY AND COMPLAINT PROCEDURE

Listings in *Guide to Literary Agents* are compiled from detailed questionnaires, phone interviews and information provided by agents. The industry is volatile, and agencies change frequently. We rely on our readers for information on their dealings with agents, as well as changes in policies or fees that differ from what has been reported to the editor of this book. Write to us (Guide to Literary Agents, F+W Media, 10151 Carver Road, Suite 200, Cincinnati, OH 45242) or e-mail us (literaryagent@fwmedia.com) if you have new information, questions or problems dealing with the agencies listed.

Listings are published free of charge and are not advertisements. Although the information is as accurate as possible, the listings are not endorsed or guaranteed by the editor or publisher of *Guide to Literary Agents*. If you feel you have not been treated fairly by an agent or representative listed in *Guide to Literary Agents*, we advise you to take the following steps:

- First try to contact the agency. Sometimes one letter or e-mail can clear up the matter. Politely relate your concern.
- Document all your correspondence with the agency. When you write to us with a complaint, provide the name of your manuscript, the date of your first contact with the agency and the nature of your subsequent correspondence.
- We will keep your letter on file and attempt to contact the agency. The number, frequency and severity of complaints will be considered when we decide whether or not to delete an agency's listing from the next edition.
- *Guide to Literary Agents* reserves the right to exclude any agency for any reason.

WHAT AN AGENT DOES

The scoop on day-to-day agent responsibilities.

//

A writer's job is to write. A literary agent's job is to find publishers for her clients' books. Because publishing houses receive more and more unsolicited manuscripts each year, securing an agent is becoming increasingly necessary. But finding an eager and reputable agent can be a difficult task. Even the most patient writer can become frustrated or disillusioned. As a writer seeking agent representation, you should prepare yourself before starting your search. Learn when to approach agents, as well as what to expect from an author/agent relationship. Beyond selling manuscripts, an agent must keep track of the ever-changing industry, writers' royalty statements, fluctuating market trends—and the list goes on.

So, once again, you face the question: Do I need an agent? The answer, much more often than not, is yes.

WHAT CAN AN AGENT DO FOR YOU?

For starters, today's competitive marketplace can be difficult to break into, especially for unpublished writers. Many larger publishing houses will only look at manuscripts from agents—and rightfully so, as they would be inundated with unsatisfactory writing if they did not. In fact, approximately 80 percent of books published by the six major houses are acquired through agents.

But an agent's job isn't just getting your book through a publisher's door. The following describes the various jobs agents do for their clients, many of which would be difficult for a writer to do without outside help.

AGENTS KNOW EDITORS' TASTES AND NEEDS

An agent possesses information on a complex web of publishing houses and a multitude of editors to ensure her clients' manuscripts are placed in the right hands. This knowledge is gathered through relationships she cultivates with acquisitions editors—the people who decide which books to present to their publisher for possible publication. Through her industry connections, an agent becomes aware of the specializations of publishing houses and their imprints, knowing that one publisher wants only contemporary romances while another is interested solely in nonfiction books about the military. By networking with editors, an agent also learns more specialized information—which editor is looking for a crafty Agatha Christie–style mystery for the fall catalog, for example.

AGENTS TRACK CHANGES IN PUBLISHING

Being attentive to constant market changes and shifting trends is another major requirement of an agent. An agent understands what it may mean for clients when publisher A merges with publisher B and when an editor from house C moves to house D. Or what it means when readers—and therefore editors—are no longer interested in Westerns, but can't get their hands on enough thriller and suspense novels.

AGENTS GET YOUR WORK READ FASTER

Although it may seem like an extra step to send your work to an agent instead of directly to a publishing house, the truth is an agent can prevent you from wasting months sending manuscripts that end up in the wrong place or buried in someone's slush pile. Editors rely on agents to save them time, as well. With little time to sift through the hundreds of unsolicited submissions arriving weekly in the mail, an editor is naturally going to prefer a work that has already been approved by a qualified reader (i.e., the agent) who knows the editor's preferences. For this reason, many of the larger publishers accept agented submissions only.

AGENTS UNDERSTAND CONTRACTS

When publishers write contracts, they are primarily interested in their own bottom line rather than the best interests of the author. Writers unfamiliar with contractual language may find themselves bound to a publisher with whom they no longer want to work. Or, they may find themselves tied to a publisher that prevents them from getting royalties on their first book until subsequent books are written. Agents use their experiences and knowledge to negotiate a contract that benefits the writer while still respecting the publisher's needs. After all, more money for the author will almost always mean more money for the agent— another reason they're on your side.

BEFORE YOU SUBMIT YOUR FICTION BOOK:

1. Finish your novel manuscript or short-story collection. An agent can do nothing for fiction without a finished product. Never query with an incomplete novel.
2. Revise your manuscript. Seek critiques from other writers or an independent editor to ensure your work is as polished as possible.
3. Proofread. Don't ruin a potential relationship with an agent by submitting work that contains typos or poor grammar.
4. Publish short stories or novel excerpts in literary journals, which will prove to prospective agents that editors see quality in your writing.
5. Research to find the agents of writers whose works you admire or are similar to yours.
6. Use the Internet and resources like *Guide to Literary Agents* to construct a list of agents who are open to new writers and looking for your category of fiction. (Jump to the listings sections of this book to start now.)
7. Rank your list according to the agents most suitable for you and your work.
8. Write your novel synopsis.
9. Write your query letter. As an agent's first impression of you, this brief letter should be polished and to the point.
10. Educate yourself about the business of agents so you will be prepared to act on any offer. This guide is a great place to start.

AGENTS NEGOTIATE—AND EXPLOIT—SUBSIDIARY RIGHTS

Beyond publication, a savvy agent keeps in mind other opportunities for your manuscript. If your agent believes your book also will be successful as an audio book, a Book-of-the-Month-Club selection or even a blockbuster movie, she will take these options into consideration when shopping your manuscript. These additional opportunities for writers are called subsidiary rights. Part of an agent's job is to keep track of the strengths and weaknesses of different publishers' subsidiary rights offices to determine the deposition of these rights regarding your work. After contracts are negotiated, agents will seek additional moneymaking opportunities for the rights they kept for their clients.

AGENTS GET ESCALATORS

An escalator is a bonus an agent can negotiate as part of the book contract. It is commonly given when a book appears on a bestseller list or if a client appears on a popular television show. For example, a publisher might give a writer a $30,000 bonus if he is picked for a book club. Both the agent and the editor know such media attention will sell more books, and the agent negotiates an escalator to ensure the writer benefits from this increase in sales.

AGENTS TRACK PAYMENTS

Because an agent receives payment only when the publisher pays the writer, it's in the agent's best interest to make sure the writer is paid on schedule. Some publishing houses are notorious for late payments. Having an agent distances you from any conflict regarding payment and allows you to spend time writing instead of making phone calls.

AGENTS ARE ADVOCATES

Besides standing up for your right to be paid on time, agents can ensure your book gets a better cover design, more attention from the publisher's marketing department or other benefits you may not know to ask for during the publishing process. An agent also can provide advice during each step of the way, as well as guidance about your long-term writing career.

ARE YOU READY FOR AN AGENT?

Now that you know what an agent is capable of, ask yourself if you and your work are at a stage where you need an agent. Look at the to-do lists for fiction and nonfiction writers in this article, and judge how prepared you are for contacting an agent. Have you spent enough time researching or polishing your manuscript? Does your nonfiction book proposal include everything it should? Is your novel completely finished? Sending an agent an incomplete project not only wastes your time, but also may turn off the agent in the process. Is the work thoroughly revised? If you've finished your project, set it aside for a few weeks, then examine it again with fresh eyes. Give your novel or proposal to critique group partners ("beta readers") for feedback. Join up with writing peers in your community or online.

Moreover, your work may not be appropriate for an agent. Most agents do not represent poetry, magazine articles, short stories or material suitable for academic or small presses; the agent's commission does not justify spending time submitting these types of works. Those agents who do take on such material generally represent authors on larger projects first, and then adopt the smaller items as a favor to the client.

If you believe your work is ready to be placed with an agent, make sure you're personally ready to be represented. In other words, consider the direction in which your writing career is headed. Besides skillful writers, agencies want clients with the ability to produce more than one book. Most agents say they're looking to represent careers, not books.

WHEN DON'T YOU NEED AN AGENT?

Although there are many reasons to work with an agent, some authors can benefit from submitting their own work directly to book publishers. For example, if your project focuses on a very specific area, you may want to work with a small or specialized press. These houses usually are open to receiving material directly from writers. Small presses often can give more attention to writers than large houses can, providing editorial help, marketing expertise and other advice. Academic books or specialized nonfiction books (such as a book about the history of Rhode Island) are good bets for unagented writers.

Beware, though, as you will now be responsible for reviewing and negotiating all parts of your contract and payment. If you choose this path, it's wise to use a lawyer or entertainment attorney to review all contracts. Lawyers who specialize in intellectual property can help writers with contract negotiations. Instead of earning a commission on resulting book sales, lawyers are paid for their time only.

And, of course, some people prefer working independently instead of relying on others. If you're one of these people, it's probably better to submit your own work instead of constantly butting heads with an agent. Let's say you manage to sign with one of the few literary agents who represent short-story collections. If the collection gets shopped around to publishers for several months and no one bites, your agent may suggest retooling the work into a novel or novella(s). Agents suggest changes—some bigger than others—and not all writers think their work is malleable. It's all a matter of what you're writing and how you feel about it.

BEFORE YOU SUBMIT YOUR NONFICTION BOOK:

1. Formulate a concrete idea for your book. Sketch a brief outline, making sure you'll have enough material for a book-length manuscript.

2. Research works on similar topics to understand the competition and determine how your book is unique.

3. Write sample chapters. This will help you estimate how much time you'll need to complete the work, and determine whether or not your writing will need editorial help. You will also need to include 1–4 sample chapters in the proposal itself.

4. Publish completed chapters in journals and/or magazines. This validates your work to agents and provides writing samples for later in the process.

5. Polish your nonfiction book proposal so you can refer to it while drafting a query letter—and you'll be prepared when agents contact you.

6. Brainstorm three to four subject categories that best describe your material.

7. Use the Internet and resources like *Guide to Literary Agents* to construct a list of agents who are open to new writers and looking for your category of nonfiction.

8. Rank your list. Research agent websites and narrow your list further, according to your preferences.

9. Write your query. Give an agent an excellent first impression by professionally and succinctly describing your premise and your experience.

10. Educate yourself about the business of agents so you can act on any offer.

AGENT STRAIGHT TALK

Leading literary reps answer some of writers' most frequently asked questions.

by Chuck Sambuchino, Ricki Schultz, Donna Gambale & Cris Freese

ON QUERIES & PITCHING

What are common problems you see in a query letter?

First, mistakes in grammar, spelling, word usage or sentence structure. Anything like that is going to put me right off. Second, not saying what the book is about right away. I am only able to spend a minute at most reading your query letter—tell me exactly what I should know immediately. Third, being boring or unoriginal—writers don't seem to realize how many query letters we read in a day or a week. We've seen everything and are looking, more than anything, for our attention to be caught. Be surprising!

—**ELLEN PEPUS**, *co-founder,
Signature Literary*

Let's say you're looking through the slush pile at query letters. What are common elements you see in a query letter that don't truly need to be there?

If your query letter is more than one page long, there are things in there that are superfluous. The most common unnecessary addition is a description of the writer's family/personal life if the book is not a memoir. Some personal background is good, but I would much prefer to know about the amazing novel you wrote. The personal information can come later. The other most common misstep is listing weak qualifications for writing the book. What I mean by that is when someone says, "I have a daughter, so I am qualified to write this very general book about how to raise daughters." In today's very crowded book market, you must have a strong platform to write nonfiction.

—**ABIGAIL KOONS**, *literary agent,
The Park Literary Group*

Do you see many query letters that come in too long?

Length is an issue. Even though I accept online queries, I still want the query to come in somewhere close to one page. I think that writers often think that because it's online, I have no way of knowing that it's more than a page. Believe me, I do. Queries that are concise and compelling are the most intriguing.

—REGINA BROOKS, *founder,*
Serendipity Literary Agency

ON FICTION & GENRES

With literary fiction, what do you look for? What gets you to keep reading?

With literary fiction, I often look for a track record of previous publications. If you've been published in *Tin House* or *McSweeney's* or *GlimmerTrain*, I want to know. It tells me that the writer is, in fact, committed to their craft and building an audience out there in the journals. But if you have a good story and are a brilliant writer, I wouldn't mind if you lived in a cave in the Ozarks. For the record, I have yet to sign anyone who lives in a cave in the Ozarks.

—MICHELLE BROWER, *literary agent,*
Folio Literary

How does a writer know if her writing falls into the category of women's fiction, as opposed to perhaps literary fiction?

I think I have a fairly good definition of women's fiction. These are not simply stories with female characters but stories that tell us the female journey. Women's fiction is a way for women to learn and grow, and to relate to others what it is to be a woman. When I think of literary fiction, the emphasis is placed more on the telling of a good story instead of making the female journey the centerpiece.

—SCOTT EAGAN, *founder,*
Greyhaus Literary

ON NONFICTION & MEMOIR

A lot of people want to write a memoir, but few are good. What do you look for in a memoir?

Memoir is such a tricky genre. Everyone has a story (when I go to writing conferences, memoir writers are usually the overwhelming majority), and, unfortunately, you are right—few are good and many are overly sentimental. I look for two main things: a unique story and great writing. Memoirs should read like novels; they should have suspense, conflict, emotion, character development, dialogue and narrative arc. On top of all that, it's a tough question to ask about one's own story, but authors should ask it: Why will people be interested in me?

—**Taryn Fagerness**, *founder,*
Taryn Fagerness Literary Agency

What's the most important advice you can give for writing nonfiction book proposals?
Three things. 1) Spill the beans. Don't try to tantalize and hold back the juice. 2) No BS! We learn to see right through BS, or we fail rapidly. 3) Get published small. Local papers, literary journals, websites, anything. The more credits you have, the better. And list them all (although not to the point of absurdity) in your query. Why does everyone want to pole-vault from being an unpublished author to having a big book contract? It makes no sense. You have to learn to drive before they'll let you pilot the Space Shuttle.

—**Gary Heidt**, *co-founder,*
Signature Literary

Nonfiction writers are always hearing about the importance of building a platform. What does that really mean?
Build your base. I've given workshops at writers' conferences about establishing an author platform, and it all boils down to one basic concept: Develop a significant following before you go out with your nonfiction book. If you build it, they (publishers) will come. Think about that word *platform*. What does it mean? If you are standing on a physical platform, it gives you greater visibility. And that's what it's all about: visibility. How visible are you to the world? That's what determines your level of platform. Someone with real platform is the "go-to" person in their area of expertise. If a reporter from the *New York Times* is doing a story on what you know about most, they will want to go to you for an interview first. But if you don't make yourself known to the world as the expert in your field, then how will the *NYT* know to reach out to you? RuPaul used to say, "If you don't love yourself, how the hell else is anybody else gonna love you?" I'm not saying be egotistical. I'm just saying, know your strengths, and learn to toot your own horn. Get out there. Make as many connections as you possibly can. We live in a celebrity-driven world. Love it or hate it, either way we all have to live with it. So, celebrate what you have to offer, and if it's genuine and enough people respond to it, then you will become a celebrity in your own right. Get out there and prove to the world that you are the be-all and end-all when it comes to what you know about most. Publishers don't expect you to be as big as Oprah, or Martha, or the Donald, but they do expect you to be the next Oprah, or Martha, or the next Donald in your own field.

—**Jeffery McGraw**, *literary agent,*
The August Agency

Your bio says you seek "travel narrative nonfiction." Can you help define this category for writers?
Travel and adventure narrative nonfiction is the type of book that takes you away to another place. It is often a memoir, but can be a journalistic story of a particular

event or even a collection of essays. The key here is that it tells an interesting and engaging story. It is also very important these days that the story is fresh and new—you'd be surprised at how many people have had the exact same experience with the rickshaw in Bangkok that you had. Some successful examples of this genre are Jon Krakauer's *Into Thin Air*, Elizabeth Gilbert's *Eat, Pray, Love*, and most things by Paul Theroux and Bill Bryson.

—ABIGAIL KOONS, *literary agent,*
The Park Literary Group

What stands out for you in a nonfiction book proposal? What immediately draws you into a project?

There are several factors that can help a book's ultimate prospects: great writing, great platform or great information, and ideally all three. For narrative works, the writing should be gorgeous, not just functional. For practical works, the information should be insightful, comprehensive and preferably new. And for any work of nonfiction, of course, the author's platform is enormously important.

—TED WEINSTEIN, *founder,*
Ted Weinstein Literary

What's a common mistake writers make when composing book proposals?

Nonfiction proposals should be fairly easy to write. There's a lot of information available to writers on how to write "the greatest," "the most compelling," "the no-fail" nonfiction proposal, so I'm often surprised when authors fail to mention their reasons and credentials for writing the work. Like publishers, I often jump to the credentials section of the proposal before getting to the meat of the proposal. I need to know why an author is qualified to write what they're writing and how their work differs from what has already been published on the topic they've chosen.

—JANET BENREY, *founder,*
Benrey Literary

ON CHILDREN'S & YOUNG ADULT

Can you offer some basic tips for writing children's nonfiction?

You can write about almost anything when it comes to children's nonfiction, even if it's been done before. But you need to come at the subject from a different angle. If there is already a book on tomatoes and how they grow, then try writing about tomatoes from a cultural angle. There are a ton of books on slavery, but not many on slaves in Haiti during the Haitian Revolution (Is there even one? There's an idea—someone take it and query me!). Another thing to always consider is your audience. Kids already have textbooks at school, so you shouldn't write your book like one. Come at the subject in a way that kids can relate to and find interesting. Humor is always a useful tool in nonfiction for kids.

—**JOANNA VOLPE**, *founder,*
New Leaf Literary

Where are writers going wrong in picture book submissions?

Rhyming! So many writers think picture books need to rhyme. There are some editors who won't even look at books in rhyme, and a lot more who are extremely wary of them, so it limits an agent on where it can go and the likelihood of it selling. It's also particularly hard to execute perfectly. Aside from rhyming, I see way too many picture books about a family pet or bedtime.

—**KELLY SONNACK**, *literary agent,*
Andrea Brown Literary Agency

I've heard that nothing is taboo anymore in young adult books, and you can write about topics such as sex and drugs. Is this true?

I would say this: Nothing is taboo if it's done well. Each scene needs to matter in a novel. I've read a number of "edgy" young adult books where writers seem to add in scenes just for shock value, and it doesn't work with the flow of the rest of the novel. "Taboo" subjects need to have a purpose in the progression of the novel. Taboo topics do, however, affect whether the school and library market will pick up the book—and this can have an effect on whether a publisher feels they can sell enough copies.

—**JESSICA REGEL**, *literary agent,*
Jean V. Naggar Literary Agency

In young adult manuscripts, what are some page-one clichés you come across?

The most common problem I see is a story that's been told a million times before, without any new twists to make it unique enough to stand out. Same plot, same situations, same set up = the same ol' story. For example: abusive parents/kid's a rebel; family member(s) killed tragically/kid's a loner; divorced parents/kid acts out. Another problem I often see is when the protagonist/main characters don't have an age-appropriate voice. For example: if your main character is 14, let him talk like a 14-year-old. And lastly, being unable to "connect" with the main character(s). For example: Characters are too whiny or bratty, or character shows no emotion/angst.

—**CHRISTINE WITTHOHN**, *founder,*
Book Cents Literary

What are some reasons you stop reading a young adult manuscript?

Once I've determined that the writing is strong enough, it's usually a question of plot (we receive many works that are derivative or otherwise unoriginal) or voice. As we know from the young adults in our lives, anything that sounds even vaguely parental will not be well received. And there's nothing worse than narration that reads like a text message from a grandmother. In the past month, I've received 29 YA partials. Looking back on my notes, I see that I rejected eight for writing, seven for voice, six for derivative or unoriginal plots, four because they were inappropriate for the age group and two that simply weren't a good fit for the agency but may find a home elsewhere. Then there were two I liked and passed them on to others in my office. Also, I think a lot of writers, seeing the success of *Twilight*, have tried to force their manuscripts into this genre. I know you've heard it before, but it's so true: Write what you love—don't write what you think will sell.

—JESSICA SINSHEIMER, *literary agent,*
Sarah Jane Freymann Literary Agency

What can writers do to enhance their chances of getting a picture book published?

I know it sounds simplistic, but write the very best picture books you can. I think the market contraction has been a good thing, for the most part. I'm only selling the very best picture books my clients write—but I'm definitely selling them. Picture books are generally skewing young, and have been for some time, so focus on strong read-alouds and truly kid-friendly styles. I'm having a lot of luck with projects that have the feel of being created by an author-illustrator even if the author is not an artist, in that they're fairly simple, have all kinds of room for fun and interpretation in the illustrations, and have a lot of personality. I see a lot of picture book manuscripts that depend too heavily on dialogue, which tends to give them the feel of a chapter book or middle grade novel. The style isn't a picture book style.

—ERIN MURPHY, *founder,*
Erin Murphy Literary Agency

ON OTHER AGENT MATTERS

Do agents usually hold out for a good deal on a book, or do they take the first acceptable offer that comes along?

Well, an offer in your pocket is always better than none. Certainly, if an agent feels she can demand more for a book, she should hold out; however, usually the editor who makes the first offer is the most enthusiastic and thoroughly understands the book, and may turn out to be the best editor and in-house advocate for that book. The most money is not necessarily the best deal for an author. That enthusiasm, commitment and support from all divisions within a publishing house often means more than those dollars in your bank account. An agent's experience regarding what editors are looking to buy, what publishers are currently paying and what the marketplace is like should lead that agent to advise her client regarding whether or not an offer on the table is the *best* (whatever its true meaning) that can be expected. We do *see* editors on a regular basis. Again, working from experience, an agent helps her client make the best possible decision. We all want our authors to accomplish their goals.

—**LAURA LANGLIE**, *founder,*
Laura Langlie, Literary Agent

What advice would you give writers who have had work rejected by agents?

It still surprises me how many writers are angry or defensive when agents reject their work. It's a wasted opportunity. We invest countless hours reading book proposals and giving each proposal careful thought. We have firsthand knowledge of what's selling (or easy to sell) and what's not. Rather than firing off a counter-response (which has probably never convinced an agent in the history of agenting), authors should use the opportunity to find out why they were rejected and improve their future chances of success. It is not rude to ask for more detailed feedback following a rejection, as long as the request is polite. We may be able to give advice or point out character, dialogue, pacing, pitch or structural issues that you might have missed. It could also lead to a referral or a request to resubmit.

—**BRANDI BOWLES**, *literary agent,*
Foundry Literary + Media

A week from now, my self-published novel will come rolling off the presses. Can I use the finished product as bait to hook a reputable agent?

Frankly, my sense is that providing an agent or editor with an already produced book only reduces its attractiveness as a potential property. First, the extra effort and expense smacks of trying too hard. And second, it conveys the sense that the material may already have made the rounds before—else why the desperation to self-publish? Agents, in particular, want the sense that they are discovering something precious and unknown. And to that end, less really is more, in terms of presentation. A simple and straightforward cover letter without any cheesy come-ons, complete with an appropriately modest listing of awards or other writing credentials, is all that should accompany a manuscript. The rest is up to the work itself.

—**ROB MCQUILKIN**, *literary agent,*
Lippincott Massie McQuilkin

I'm talking with an agent who politely refused to share a list of who he represents and what he's recently sold. Is this normal?

I understand agencies that don't list clients in directories and public access places. That's a personal choice. Hartline (my agency) lists authors and books sold right on their website. To get down to the point of considering representation, however, not knowing anything about who they have represented and what success they've had would, to me, be like agreeing to surgery without knowing for sure that my doctor has a medical degree. If someone applies for a job, they have to provide a résumé and show their experience and qualifications. An agent is not going to take on a client without knowing the critical details about them, and I believe the client is entitled to the same consideration. Before you sign with an agent, know who they are, who they represent and what titles they've sold.

—TERRY W. BURNS, *literary agent,*
Hartline Literary Agency

What are the most common things you see writers do wrong during an in-person pitch at a writers' conference?

Two things: One, some authors don't seem to understand their true "hook," or most interesting aspect of their work. One writer I met spoke about his young adult fantasy novel, but it wasn't until the end of his pitch that he mentioned how his book was inspired by Japanese folklore and myths. How cool! That is what I would have wanted to hear first. Two: Some authors over-praise their work. Coming from the author, such statements make me a bit skeptical. Of course the writer thinks his or her own work is amazing, but what is it about your work that makes it so fabulous? Why is it wonderful? I want more concrete information about an author's work so I can really think about where the book might fit in the market.

—TARYN FAGERNESS, *founder,*
Taryn Fagerness Literary Agency

Let's say an acquaintance calls you and says, "An agent wants to represent me, but she's new to the scene and has no sales. Is that OK?" How would you answer that?

An agent with little or no sales who has been an assistant at a leading agency will have just as much clout getting to an editor perhaps as an established agent, at least initially. One of the things I always advise writers to do is to ask an interested agent—that is, one who's made an offer of representation—"Why do you want to be my agent?" They will then hear a very clear thumbnail sketch of how that agent will sound agenting.

—KATHARINE SANDS, *literary agent,*
Sarah Jane Freymann Literary Agency

RICKI SCHULTZ (rickischultz.com, @rickischultz) is an Ohio-based freelance writer and a recovering high school English teacher. She writes young adult fiction and, as coordinator of The Write-Brained Network (writebrainednetwork.com), she enjoys connecting with other writers.

DONNA GAMBALE works an office job by day, writes young adult novels by night, and travels when possible. She is a contributing editor for the Guide to Literary Agents Blog, and freelances as a copyeditor and proofreader of both fiction and nonfiction. She is the author of a mini kit, *Magnetic Kama Sutra* (Running Press, 2009). You can find her online at firstnovelsclub.com, where she and her critique group blog about writing, reading, and the rest of life.

CHUCK SAMBUCHINO (chucksambuchino.com, @chucksambuchino) edits the *Guide to Literary Agents* (guidetoliteraryagents.com/blog) as well as the *Children's Writer's & Illustrator's Market*. His pop-humor books include *How to Survive a Garden Gnome Attack* (film rights optioned by Sony) and *Red Dog / Blue Dog: When Pooches Get Political*. Chuck's other writing books include *Formatting & Submitting Your Manuscript, 3rd. Ed.*, as well as *Create Your Writer Platform* (fall 2012). Besides that, he is a husband, sleep-deprived new father, guitarist, dog owner, and cookie addict.

CRIS FREESE is currently an undergrad at Xavier University majoring in English Literature and interning with Writer's Digest Books. He also interned with IMPACT and North Light Books, both of F+W Media, while also writing for the Xavier *Newswire* and covering the men's basketball team. Upon graduating in May 2013, he hopes to find a job in publishing or start his Master's in Professional Writing.

ASSESSING CREDIBILITY

Check out agents before you query.

Many people wouldn't buy a used car without at least checking the odometer, and savvy shoppers would consult the blue books, take a test drive and even ask for a mechanic's opinion. Much like the savvy car shopper, you want to obtain the best possible agent for your writing, so you should do some research on the business of agents before sending out query letters. Understanding how agents operate will help you find an agent appropriate for your work, as well as alert you about the types of agents to avoid.

Many writers take for granted that any agent who expresses interest in their work is trustworthy. They'll sign a contract before asking any questions and simply hope everything will turn out all right. We often receive complaints from writers regarding agents *after* they have lost money or have work bound by contract to an ineffective agent. If writers put the same amount of effort into researching agents as they did writing their manuscripts, they would save themselves unnecessary grief.

The best way to educate yourself is to read all you can about agents and other authors. Organizations such as the Association of Authors' Representatives (AAR; aar-online.org), the National Writers Union (NWU; nwu.org), American Society of Journalists and Authors (ASJA; asja.org) and Poets & Writers, Inc. (pw.org), all have informational material on finding and working with an agent.

Publishers Weekly (publishersweekly.com) covers publishing news affecting agents and others in the publishing industry. The Publishers Lunch newsletter (publishersmarketplace.com) comes free via e-mail every workday and offers news on agents and editors, job postings, recent book sales and more.

Even the Internet has a wide range of sites where you can learn basic information about preparing for your initial contact, as well as specific details on individual agents. You can also find online forums and listservs, which keep authors connected and allow them to share experiences they've had with different editors and agents. Keep in mind, however, that not everything printed on the Web is solid fact; you may come across the site of a writer who is bitter because an agent rejected his manuscript. Your best bet is to use the Internet to supplement your other research.

Once you've established what your resources are, it's time to see which agents meet your criteria. Below are some of the key items to pay attention to when researching agents.

LEVEL OF EXPERIENCE

Through your research, you will discover the need to be wary of some agents. Anybody can go to the neighborhood copy center and order business cards that say "literary agent," but that title doesn't mean she can sell your book. She may lack the proper connections with others in the publishing industry, and an agent's reputation with editors can be a major strength or weakness.

Agents who have been in the business awhile have a large number of contacts and carry the most clout with editors. They know the ins and outs of the industry and are often able to take more calculated risks. However, veteran agents can be too busy to take on new clients or might not have the time to help develop an author. Newer agents, on the other hand, may be hungrier, as well as more open to unpublished writers. They probably have a smaller client list and are able to invest the extra effort to make your book a success.

If it's a new agent without a track record, be aware that you're taking more of a risk signing with her than with a more established agent. However, even a new agent should not be new to publishing. Many agents were editors before they were agents, or they worked at an agency as an assistant. This experience is crucial for making contacts in the publishing industry, and learning about rights and contracts. The majority of listings in this book explain how long the agent has been in business, as well as what she did before becoming an agent. You could also ask the agent to name a few editors off the top of her head who she thinks may be interested in your work and why they sprang to mind. Has she sold to them before? Do they publish books in your genre?

If an agent has no contacts in the business, she has no more clout than you do. Without publishing prowess, she's just an expensive mailing service. Anyone can make photocopies, slide them into an envelope and address them to "Editor." Unfortunately, without a contact name and a familiar return address on the envelope, or a phone call from a trusted colleague letting an editor know a wonderful submission is on its way, your work will land in the slush pile with all the other submissions that don't have representation. You can do your own mailings with higher priority than such an agent could.

PAST SALES

Agents should be willing to discuss their recent sales with you: how many, what type of books and to what publishers. Keep in mind, though, that some agents consider this information confidential. If an agent does give you a list of recent sales, you can call the publishers' contracts department to ensure the sale was actually made by that agent. While it's true that even top agents are not able to sell every book they represent, an inexperienced agent who proposes too many inappropriate submissions will quickly lose her standing with editors.

You can also find out details of recent sales on your own. Nearly all of the listings in this book offer the titles and authors of books with which the agent has worked. Some of them also note to which publishing house the book was sold. Again, you can call the publisher and affirm the sale. If you don't have the publisher's information, simply go to your local library or bookstore to see if they carry the book. Consider checking to see if it's available on websites like Amazon.com, too. You may want to be wary of the agent if her books are nowhere to be found or are only available through the publisher's website. Distribution is a crucial component to getting published, and you want to make sure the agent has worked with competent publishers.

TYPES OF FEES

Becoming knowledgeable about the different types of fees agents may charge is vital to conducting effective research. Most agents make their living from the commissions they receive after selling their clients' books, and these are the agents we've listed. Be sure to ask about any expenses you don't understand so you have a clear grasp of what you're paying for. Described below are some types of fees you may encounter in your research.

Office fees

Occasionally, an agent will charge for the cost of photocopies, postage and long-distance phone calls made on your behalf. This is acceptable, so long as she keeps an itemized account of the expenses and you've agreed on a ceiling cost. The agent should only ask for office expenses after agreeing to represent the writer. These expenses should be discussed up front, and the writer should receive a statement accounting for them. This money is sometimes returned to the author upon sale of the manuscript. Be wary if there is an upfront fee amounting to hundreds of dollars, which is excessive.

Reading fees

Agencies that charge reading fees often do so to cover the cost of additional readers or the time spent reading that could have been spent selling. Agents also claim that charging reading fees cuts down on the number of submissions they receive. This practice can save the agent time and may allow her to consider each manuscript more extensively. Whether such promises are kept depends upon the honesty of the agency. You may pay a fee and never receive a response from the agent, or you may pay someone who never submits your manuscript to publishers.

Officially, the Association of Authors' Representatives' (AAR) Canon of Ethics prohibits members from directly or indirectly charging a reading fee, and the Writers Guild of America (WGA) does not allow WGA signatory agencies to charge a reading fee to WGA members, as stated in the WGA's Artists' Manager Basic Agreement. A signatory may charge you a fee if you are not a member, but most signatory agencies do not charge a reading fee as an across-the-board policy.

WARNING SIGNS! BEWARE OF . . .

- Excessive typos or poor grammar in an agent's correspondence.

- A form letter accepting you as a client and praising generic things about your book that could apply to any book. A good agent doesn't take on a new client very often, so when she does, it's a special occasion that warrants a personal note or phone call.

- Unprofessional contracts that ask you for money up front, contain clauses you haven't discussed or are covered with amateur clip-art or silly borders.

- Rudeness when you inquire about any points you're unsure of. Don't employ any business partner who doesn't treat you with respect.

- Pressure, by way of threats, bullying or bribes. A good agent is not desperate to represent more clients. She invites worthy authors but leaves the final decision up to them.

- Promises of publication. No agent can guarantee you a sale. Not even the top agents sell everything they choose to represent. They can only send your work to the most appropriate places, have it read with priority and negotiate you a better contract if a sale does happen.

- A print-on-demand book contract or any contract offering you no advance. You can sell your own book to an e-publisher any time you wish without an agent's help. An agent should pursue traditional publishing routes with respectable advances.

- Reading fees from $25–$500 or more. The fee is usually nonrefundable, but sometimes agents agree to refund the money if they take on a writer as a client, or if they sell the writer's manuscript. Keep in mind, however, that payment of a reading fee does not ensure representation.

- No literary agents who charge reading fees are listed in this book. It's too risky of an option for writers, plus non-fee-charging agents have a stronger incentive to sell your work. After all, they don't make a dime until they make a sale. If you find that a literary agent listed in this book charges a reading fee, please contact the editor at literaryagent@fwmedia.com.

Critique fees

Sometimes a manuscript will interest an agent, but the agent will point out areas requiring further development and offer to critique it for an additional fee. Like reading fees, payment of a critique fee does not ensure representation. When deciding if you will benefit from having someone critique your manuscript, keep in mind that the quality and quantity of comments varies from agent to agent. The critique's usefulness will depend on the agent's knowledge of the market. Also be aware that agents who spend a significant portion of their time commenting on manuscripts will have less time to actively market work they already represent.

In other cases, the agent may suggest an editor who understands your subject matter or genre, and has some experience getting manuscripts into shape. Occasionally, if your story is exceptional, or your ideas and credentials are marketable but your writing needs help, you will work with a ghostwriter or co-author who will share a percentage of your commission, or work with you at an agreed-upon cost per hour.

An agent may refer you to editors she knows, or you may choose an editor in your area. Many editors do freelance work and would be happy to help you with your writing project. Of course, before entering into an agreement, make sure you know what you'll be getting for your money. Ask the editor for writing samples, references or critiques he's done in the past. Make sure you feel comfortable working with him before you give him your business.

An honest agent will not make any money for referring you to an editor. We strongly advise writers not to use critiquing services offered through an agency. Instead, try hiring a freelance editor or joining a writer's group until your work is ready to be submitted to agents who don't charge fees.

RESEARCHING AGENTS

Get personal and establish a connection.

....

by C. Hope Clark

I clicked from website to website, one blog to another, all telling me my chances of finding an agent were slim in the current publishing environment. Statistics spouted success rates of one half of one percent. One agent read 8,000 queries in a year and only signed five new clients. Some agents even posted the number of queries they received each week versus the number of manuscripts requested. All too often the percentage equaled zero. Hellbent on beating the odds, I devised a plan to find my agent.

Throughout the course of 20 months, I submitted 72 queries, opened 55 rejections and received invitations for seven complete manuscripts. I landed an 88 percent response rate, and finally, a contract with an agent. How did I do it? I got personal.

WHERE TO FIND AGENTS

Many writers cringe at the thought of researching the publishing business. You must be better than that. Embrace the research, especially if it leads to representation. The more you analyze the rules, the players, the successes and failures, the more you increase your chances of signing a contract with a representative. Set aside time (i.e., days, weeks) to educate yourself about these professionals. You have your manuscript, your synopsis, a list of published books like yours and a biography. You've edited and re-edited your query so it's tight as a drum. Now focus. Whom do you see as your handler, your mentor, your guide through the publishing maze? And where do you find him or her?

Agency websites

Most literary houses maintain a website. They post guidelines and books they've pushed into the marketplace. They also inform you about the individual agents on staff—including bios, favorite reads, writing styles they prefer, photos and maybe where they attended school. Read all the website has to offer, taking notes. If any agent represents your type of work, record what they prefer in a query and move on to their blog, if they keep one.

Blogs

Agent blogs reveal clues about what agents prefer. While websites are static in design, blogs allow comments. Here agents offer information about publishing changes, new releases—even their vacations and luncheons with movers and shakers in the industry. Some agents solicit feedback with dynamic dilemmas or ethical obstacles. Kristin Nelson of Nelson Literary, Mary Kole of Movable Type Literary, and Rachelle Gardner of Books & Such Literary have been known to post short contests for their blog readers, if for no other reason than to emphasize what they seek in a client. For a complete list of agent blogs, go to the GLA Blog (guidetoliteraryagents.com/blog) and see them on the right.

Guidebooks and databases

The *Guide to Literary Agents* is a premier example of a guidebook resource. Use it to cull the agents who seek writers just like you. PublishersMarketplace.com and WritersMarket.com offer online, fingertip access to the websites, addresses and desires of most agents—and also point you in other directions to learn more.

Facebook and Twitter

Social networking has enabled writers to see yet another side of agents. These mini-versions of agents' lives can spark ideas for you to use in a query as well as help you digest the publishing world through professional eyes.

Conferences

Margot Starbuck, author of *The Girl in the Orange Dress* and *Unsqueezed: Springing Free from Skinny Jeans*, met her agent at a writers conference. "He had given a seminar that was essentially themed, 'My Perfect Client,' describing the type of writer he'd want to represent. When I got home, I crafted my letter to his own specs!"

It's easier to query an agent you've met, whom you've heard, who has articulated what he likes. That subtle Midwestern accent you would not have heard otherwise might trigger you to pitch about your travel book or romance set in Nebraska. A one-hour class might empower you to query a particular agent after hearing her pet peeves and desires.

Online interviews

Google an agent's name and the word "interview." Authors, writers' organizations, magazines and commercial writing sites post such interviews to attract readers. A current Q&A

might prompt you to reword that query opening and pique an agent's interest. The agent might express a wish to read less women's fiction and more young adult novels these days—information not spelled out on her website profile. She might reveal a weakness for Southern writing. Reps also hop from agency to agency, and a timely interview might let you know she's changed location.

THE PLAN

Not wanting to collaborate with a complete stranger, I began dissecting agents' information to get a better feel for them. After noting 1) name, 2) agency, 3) query preferences, and 4) an address for each potential agent on a spreadsheet column, I dug down more for what I deemed the "zing" factor—the human factor. As a previous human resource director, I knew the power of connection. An applicant attending the same university as the manager often warranted a second glance. A first-time interviewee who played golf might reap a return invitation. Why couldn't this concept apply to literary agents? I was a job seeker; they were hiring. How could I make them take a second look at me and the fabulous writing I offered?

I reread bios and Googled deeper; I studied interviews and deciphered blogs. I read between the lines, earnestly seeking what made these people more than agents. Just like I canvassed the doctors and hairdressers in my life, I investigated these people for characteristics that bridged their preferences with mine.

Zing factors

The human connection between you and an agent is what I call the "zing" factor. These agents receive hundreds of queries per week, most skimmed or unread. You never know when an agent has been up all night with a sick child or arrived at work fighting the flu. You have no control over the timing that places your query in an agent's hands. What you can control is a creative opening that doesn't echo like the 30 before it and the 20 after, and rises to the top even if the reader hasn't had his coffee.

Agents hate to be taken for granted or treated like an anonymous personality (i.e., "Dear Agent"). The attention you give to zing factors will demonstrate that you respect the agent as a person. Suddenly you have that magical connection that holds his attention at least long enough to read your dead-on synopsis.

What makes for a great conduit between you and your agent? Anything and everything.

CLIENTELE—Signing good authors and landing great contracts make an agent proud. If you intend to become part of an agency's stable of authors, become familiar with who occupies the neighboring stalls. Recognize agents for what they have accomplished.

Author Tanya Egan Gibson not only emphasized her knowledge of Susan Golomb's clients, but she contacted one of the authors and asked permission to use him as a reference after meeting at a conference. The query won her representation and, later, a contract with Dutton Publishers.

Christine Chitnis introduced herself to other authors at a retreat where they shared critiques and ideas. Once she completed her manuscript, she pitched to the agents of those authors, knowing they could vouch for the quality of her work. She acquired an agent after two attempts.

PREVIOUS MEETINGS—A dinner table discussion with an agent at a conference could provide the lead for your next query. Make a point to meet and greet agents at these functions. They expect it. Give and take in the conversations. Don't smother them with your views. Listen for advice. Be polite. Afterward, before the experience evaporates, record notes about the topics discussed, the locale, maybe even the jokes or awkward speaker. The zing factor becomes instant recall when you remind an agent you met over dinner, during a fast-pitch or over drinks. You evolve into a person instead of another faceless query.

RECOGNITION—In your query, include where you found the agent's name. Congratulate him or her on recent contracts for books that sound similar to yours. You'll find this information through a website called Publishers Marketplace, or on the agency's website, blog, tweets or Facebook page.

FAVORITE READS—Agents are voracious readers, and, like any word geeks, they have favorite genres, authors and styles. Website bios often mention what sits on their nightstand, and blogs might post writers they admire. Note where you uncovered this information and marvel at your similarities.

GEOGRAPHY—All agents aren't born and reared in New York. With the ease of communication these days, agents live everywhere and telecommute. They also come from other places, and those roots might mirror yours. A New York agent who grew up in Georgia might have a soft spot for Civil War nonfiction.

PERSONAL INTERESTS—Agents have lives and off-duty pastimes. When author Nina Amir first contacted her agent, she also noted a mutual love of horses—in particular, a desire to save ex-racehorses from slaughter. The agent immediately called her.

In pitching to literary agent Verna Dreisbach, I revealed a common interest in mentoring teenage writers, knowing Verna founded Capitol City Young Writers, a nonprofit for youth interested in writing and publishing. Because my proposal was a mystery and I married a federal agent, I also admired her past work in law enforcement. Later, when asked if those initial items caught her attention, Verna responded in the positive. "Of course it made an impact. Writing with a degree of expertise in any field is crucial, including law enforcement. I looked forward to reading your work. I choose to represent authors that

I have a connection with, and your interests and aspirations certainly fit well with mine. As I expected, we hit it off immediately."

PASSION

Nothing, however, replaces the ability to show passion in your work. Genuine excitement over your book is contagious, and agents spot it in an instant. Carole Bartholomeaux unknowingly personalized her query through her passion. Her agent, an expectant father at the time, was touched by her story about a small town putting their lives on the line to save a group of Jewish children during World War II. You are the biggest advocate for your book, with your agent a close second. Everyone in your path should feel that energy. When agents sense it, they jump on your bandwagon knowing that readers will do the same.

When asked which grabbed her attention more, the personalization or the writing, Dreisbach replied diplomatically yet succinctly: "Both are equally important—authors who are personal and professional. Just as in any business, it is important to stand out from the crowd. I do not mean by being bizarre or unusual, but through the expression of a writer's passion, honesty and talent."

Don't cheapen yourself, though. Nathan Bransford, former agent and current award-winning blogger, gives his opinion about personalizing a query: "The goal of personalization isn't to suck up to the agent and score cheap points. As much as some people think we agents just want people to suck up to us, it's really not true. There is an art to personalization. Dedication and diligence are important, so if you query me, I hope you'll do your homework, and sure, if you've read books by my clients, mention that. Just don't try and trick me."

So be genuine. Be your passionate self and the person who obviously has done the research. A relationship with an agent is to be entered seriously and practically, with both parties sharing excitement for a common goal.

C. HOPE CLARK is the founder of FundsforWriters.com, chosen by *Writer's Digest* for its 101 Best Websites for Writers for the past 10 years. Her newsletters reach 40,000 readers weekly. She's published in numerous online and print publications, including *Writer's Digest, The Writer Magazine* and many Chicken Soups. Currently, she's preparing for the first release in her Carolina Slade suspense series, expected in winter 2011/2012 from Bell Bridge Books. Hope speaks at several writers conferences each year, and you can find her at hopeclark.blogspot. com, twitter.com/hopeclark, and facebook.com/chopeclark. She writes from the banks of Lake Murray, S.C.

AGENT SPOTLIGHTS

A close look at 6 established agents seeking clients right now.

....

by Kara Gebhart Uhl

Due to the fact that *Guide to Literary Agents* lists so many agencies and agents in its listings, the amount of personal attention given to individual agents is, understandably, scant. With that in mind, it's time to get up close and personal with six literary agents who are actively building their client lists right now. Meet six reps and get to know a little more about them, their opinion of what a dream client is like, and much more.

VICTORIA MARINI (GELFMAN SCHNEIDER LITERARY AGENTS)

ABOUT VICTORIA: After joining Gelfman Schneer as an agent assistant, Victoria Marini began taking on clients in 2010, and she's already racked up an impressive list of writers, including Corey Ann Haydu (*OCD Love Story*), Hannah Sternberg (*Queens of All the Earth*) and Meredith Zeitlin (*Freshman Year & Other Unnatural Disasters*). Marini is eager for submissions and on the hunt for a variety of young adult genres—thriller, suspense, mystery, sci-fi, and "super-fresh" paranormal—alongside adult works of romantic suspense and literary fiction with a great hook.

SUBMISSION GUIDELINES: gelfmanschneider.com

DREAM CLIENT: "I have so many. My dream clients are creative, shockingly talented, responsive, intelligent, passionate, professional people. Also, friendly."

FAVORITE CONVERSATION WHEN AGREEING TO WORK WITH A NEW CLIENT: "There's no particular dialogue that occurs, but rather a sense of connection. We just click. We share the same vision and get along and feel comfortable talking with one another."

BIGGEST PET PEEVE: "It's a toss-up between passive-aggressive behavior and being ignored. I think both are unproductive and foolish. So, maybe, it's really foolishness or a lack of productivity?"

MOST UNCOMFORTABLE WRITING CONFERENCE ENCOUNTER: "I accidentally yawned at someone's pitch. It wasn't actually at the book. I yawned at the worst possible moment. I couldn't stifle it any more. Poor guy was clearly offended and hurt, but didn't want to get into it with me. I felt terrible. I tried to reassure him of my interest, but he didn't believe me."

HARDEST LESSON FOR WRITERS TO LEARN: "There will always be someone better than you. It's the hardest lesson for anyone to learn, I think."

BEST PUBLISHING ADVICE RECEIVED: "I've been lucky to have a community of supportive superiors and peers, so I get great advice on a daily basis. Some of the gems have been: 'If you're not willing to lose sleep over it, turn it down,' and, 'Just because a book is great, doesn't mean it's great for you.' In fact, a lot of it is really smart relationship advice, but instead of love and men, it's books and authors."

BIGGEST CAREER SURPRISE: "How good it feels when something nice happens. I really do love this job—even when I whine about its shortcomings or my failures, I love it. And I wanted this job because I expected I'd love it. But the sense of fulfillment, those moments when the fantastic happens—finding a good manuscript in the slush pile, offers, an author loves your idea—I didn't expect that part to be as awesome as it is."

MARCIA WERNICK (WERNICK & PRATT AGENCY)

ABOUT MARCIA: Marcia Wernick and her business partner, Linda Pratt, opened their agency dedicated to children's books in January 2011. An industry vet, Wernick brought with her an impressive client list, including Mo Willems (*Don't Let the Pigeon Drive the Bus!*) and Elizabeth Cody Kimmel (the Suddenly Supernatural series), from her work at the Sheldon Fogelman Agency—but she's still eager for new submissions. "I'd be thrilled to find a compelling middle-grade novel with a great character, and maybe even a bit of magic thrown in for good measure," she says. "I'm particularly drawn to a strong main character with lots of heart. ... I'm also a sucker for a Southern voice."

SUBMISSION GUIDELINES: wernickpratt.com/submissions-policy

BEST WRITING CONFERENCE ENCOUNTER: "Many years ago I met Jackie Urbanovic at a conference. We agreed that she wasn't ready for representation, but we kept in touch, exchanging ideas, feedback and developing a lovely relationship. Ten years later, when she sent me her [submission] for *Duck at the Door,* it was a real treat to be able to get it sold, published and on The

New York Times bestseller list, all in just over one year. This story is [one of many examples] of an "overnight success" that was really 10 years in the making!"

DREAM CLIENT: "A prolific, literary client who writes proficiently for various ages and across genres within the children's market. I find the variation exciting, [and] on a practical basis it gives more flexibility to [my clients]: They can publish more than one book at a time if the books are for a different age group or genre, because they will not be competing with themselves."

BEST QUERY: "From Mo Willems for *Don't Let the Pigeon Drive the Bus!* The query was short, informative [and] humorous. … It seemed to capture the essence of what working with Mo would be like, and 13 years later, I can say that impression was correct."

WORST QUERY: "A novel from a 15-year-old who I took great care to reply to in a kind way, yet her mother called me afterward to berate me for not taking on her daughter as a client. That was quite a few years ago, but I can still tell you that young woman's name."

HARDEST LESSON FOR WRITERS TO LEARN: "Everything takes longer than one expects, including the time from final delivery of a work until it's published. Once delivered, it can be hard to move on to the next project, but that's the best thing to do if you haven't already begun doing so. I do not recommend [immediately] working on a prequel, sequel or companion book, as the sale of one is too dependent on the success of the prior project. It's better to move on to a separate, stand-alone project, especially when early in one's career."

BEST PUBLISHING ADVICE RECEIVED: "A publishing agent friend of mine once shared the following: 'If you're only looking for big, you might miss out on great.' "

BRIAN DEFIORE (DeFIORE AND COMPANY)

ABOUT BRIAN: Brian DeFiore has worked in publishing since 1981, having served as an editor, editor-in-chief and publisher at several major publishing houses—including St. Martin's Press, Dell Publishing, Delacorte Press and Hyperion—before founding DeFiore and Company in Manhattan in 1999. In addition to his role as literary agent, DeFiore serves on the board of directors of the Association of Authors Representatives, and is on the faculty of The Center for Publishing at New York University.

SUBMISSION GUIDELINES: DeFiore is looking for "something that will amaze me—no other qualification is nearly as important." He accepts queries at querybrian@defioreandco.com; for complete guidelines, visit defioreandco.com.

BIGGEST CAREER SURPRISE: "When I was an editor I believed that when an agent sent me something and I thought it was terrific, that my response was an absolute—and that every editor who had it also must have thought it was terrific. Now that I'm an agent I see that even when a book is one that turns out to be a bestseller, at the time of submission, of 10 editors, four may love it, two may hate it and the rest are indifferent."

BEST QUERY: "It was a very short one- or two-sentence query that said, basically: 'I'm a graduate of the Iowa Writers' Workshop, and have written a comic novel narrated by a chimpanzee. Would you like to see it?' How could you say no to that? I always use that example as a bit of advice when talking to writers: Keep it direct, simple, surprising. (It turned out to be the wonderful award-winning novel *The Evolution of Bruno Littlemore* by Benjamin Hale.)"

DREAM CLIENT/PROJECT: "A dream client is one whose talent continually surprises me, and my belief in it is what keeps me on my toes to make sure I'm doing right by his or her work. And similarly, the dream project is one I can't possibly describe in advance: It could be fiction or nonfiction, but it will be surprising in its freshness."

FAVORITE CONVERSATION WHEN AGREEING TO WORK WITH A NEW CLIENT: "It's always a little awkward when you want to take a new client on, but you think the book needs some editorial work. As an agent, I'm nervous that if the client is talking to other agents, and those others are saying that the book is perfect as is, I'll lose the client. But ultimately I think I can't do my job with integrity without saying what I think needs to be said—and the greatest conversation is when the client says, 'I knew that aspect wasn't working. You have good insight and you see what I'm trying to do.' That's when I know it's really right."

WORST QUERY: "By definition it was unmemorable, but no doubt it was for a 'fictional novel.' "

BEST PUBLISHING ADVICE RECEIVED: "That the authors are our stars and that we must never forget that; we are nothing without them. Interestingly, that was taught to me by a publisher—a former boss of mine, Carole Baron—not an agent."

HARDEST LESSON FOR WRITERS TO LEARN: "That the industry doesn't always—in fact, it rarely—makes perfect sense, and good books often don't find the readers or get the attention that they should, and it's often not anyone's fault. It can be as random as life itself."

JOHN RUDOLPH (DYSTEL & GODERICH LITERARY)

ABOUT JOHN: John Rudolph spent 12 years as an acquiring children's book editor for Simon & Schuster Books for Young Readers and the G.P. Putnam's Sons imprint of the Penguin Young Readers Group before joining Dystel & Goderich as a literary agent in 2010. Now, with a strong track record of deals in the young adult, memoir, picture book and pop culture genres, he is expanding his client list in other areas, too. "I'm looking for any and all narrative nonfiction," Rudolph says. "Thrillers and other commercial men's fiction are up my alley as well. On the children's side, I'm on the hunt for character-based middle-grade and young adult fiction, and I would dearly love to find the next great picture book writer/illustrator."

SUBMISSION GUIDELINES: dystel.com/submission-requirements

HARDEST LESSON FOR WRITERS TO LEARN: "On the writing side, regardless of genre, just about every project involves a 'show, don't tell' discussion. Publishing-wise, I think it's the waiting—no matter how well versed authors are in the publishing process, there's almost always a 'Why the @%$! is this taking so long?' moment."

BEST/WORST QUERY: "Not sure if it's the worst or best, but the greatest query I got was the picture book about talking poop—fully illustrated, of course. That gem arrived my very first week as an editorial assistant at Simon & Schuster—a suitably auspicious way to start a publishing career."

PERFECT DAY: "Any day that I sell a book!"

BIGGEST PET PEEVE: "You would think that with the enduring popularity of a certain Christmas song, it wouldn't be that difficult to send a letter to John Rudolph—not Randolph, Rudolf, or my all-time favorite, Rudlof."

DREAM CLIENT: "Since Keith Richards is taken, I'll have to go with Springsteen. Give me a call, Boss …"

BEST PUBLISHING ADVICE RECEIVED: "That at the end of the day, it's the author's name that's on the jacket."

STRANGEST WRITING CONFERENCE ENCOUNTER: "Luckily, I've been spared any major conference craziness so far—never had anyone pass me a manuscript in the restroom or anything like that. The *best* experience was about a year ago, when I actually signed up a writer as a client—first time that ever happened!"

BIGGEST CAREER SURPRISE: "That I'm an agent! And that, after 12 years as a children's book editor, half my list now consists of adult titles."

FAVORITE CONVERSATION WHEN AGREEING TO WORK WITH A NEW CLIENT: "Short of learning that an author already has an offer on the table, the best conversations end with the revelation that a client loves to bake—and that treats are in the mail."

EDDIE SCHNEIDER (JABBERWOCKY LITERARY AGENCY)

ABOUT EDDIE: A former magazine editor, computer salesman, short-order cook, freelance graphic designer and archery instructor, Eddie Schneider joined JABberwocky in 2008. He previously worked as an agent at Folio Literary Management. Schneider seeks literary fiction, science fiction and narrative nonfiction, and maintains an interest in young adult and middle-grade. He's currently on the hunt for plot-driven literary fiction: "I've seen it and therefore know it exists, but it's my white whale," he says.

SUBMISSION GUIDELINES: awfulagent.com/submissions-2

BEST PUBLISHING ADVICE EVER RECEIVED: " 'Keep your stick on the ice.' I can't tell you how many times that's saved me from the penalty box."

PERFECT DAY IN THE OFFICE: "I'm afraid I wouldn't be in the office the day I had to attend a client's Nobel acceptance speech."

BIGGEST PET PEEVE: "Sentence fragments, left unedited and desultory, in novels. Attention-grabbing? Lyrical? Lazy."

BIGGEST CAREER SURPRISE: "Even though I know better, even though I shouldn't be, I'm always surprised when something appallingly written blows up and sells tens of millions of copies. These books are a blast of unmitigated id, and a cultural letting off of steam, so there's a point, but it's always a shock to see these become the ambassadors of literary culture to people who otherwise don't read."

DREAM CLIENT: "Of the people I don't already represent, the author I'd most like to might be David Mitchell (*Ghostwritten*). I'm most interested in authors with a lot of range who can write at a very high level throughout that range."

HARDEST LESSON FOR AUTHORS TO LEARN: "It's hardest to put aside the starter novel and write something new. Doing that is like having to put your own dog to sleep, and you can only comfort yourself with the idea that maybe you can take the pelt and stitch together a new, better dog."

FAVORITE CONVERSATION WHEN AGREEING TO WORK WITH A CLIENT: "We have a provision in our retainer agreement whereby we agree to kitchen-test dessert recipes for the Pillsbury Bake-Off (really), and finally had a client take us up on that."

LAST AMAZING THING READ: "Although it wanders a bit, I really enjoyed Keith Richards' *Life*. Most lives do that, now that I think about it."

BEST/STRANGEST WRITING CONFERENCE EXPERIENCE: "I could tell you about the time we went to a rodeo, or poked around in an abandoned building, or what happened when we sat in a hot tub in a snowstorm (these are all things I've done at writing conferences), but I'm afraid I've run out of space."

CARLY WATTERS (P.S. LITERARY AGENCY)

ABOUT CARLY: At the Canada-based P.S. Literary Agency, Carly Watters doesn't confine her work to any borders—she represents authors in the U.S. and beyond. And her literary background is equally international: Watters received her master's in publishing studies at City University London, and began her career there at the Darley Anderson Literary, TV and Film Agency, as well as Bloomsbury Publishing PLC. Currently, she's on the hunt for high-concept commercial fiction, world lit, young adult, high-concept picture books and platform-based nonfiction. She blogs at agentcarlywatters.wordpress.com.

SUBMISSION GUIDELINES: psliterary.com/submissions.html

DREAM CLIENT: "My dream project would be the next women's fiction 'book-club book' ... a book that connects with women, makes them reflect on their lives, makes them want to share it with all their friends, and makes readers fiercely loyal to it because of their emotional connection to it. Some examples for me are *Revolutionary Road, The Good Daughter, The Help* and *Room*. So if you are querying with this type of book, please send it to me!"

BEST QUERY: "The best query I've received is one of my most recent clients' query letters. It was passionate, understanding of her abilities and her place in her genre, captivating in plot and emotion, backed with a curious biography, and listed her impressive previous publications. ... [My advice is to] inject your personality into your query while sticking to guidelines."

WORST QUERY: "The worst query can be summed up by a few traits: spelling mistakes, genres I don't represent, overconfidence, mass-emailing to dozens of agents, zero fact checking—and yes, some queries contain all of these things."

BEST PUBLISHING ADVICE EVER RECEIVED: "Talent-spotting and trusting your instincts is a big part of being an agent. ... I was trained to always talent-spot with a commercial angle, and it's never failed me, because agents want to represent writers who will connect with readers and sell copies."

FAVORITE CONVERSATION WHEN AGREEING TO WORK WITH A NEW CLIENT: "I love telling them how much I love [their book]! I know writing is a solitary activity, so when I gush about my connection to their work, it solidifies our working relationship and lets them trust me that I'll take care of their baby—the book."

HARDEST LESSON FOR AUTHORS TO LEARN: "Some of the best writers I work with are flexible, adaptable, and resourceful. However, in general, aspiring authors need to learn that publishing is not creative writing. It's the merger of art and commerce, and you can't be up in arms with the business side of publishing just because you think your creative writing work 'deserves' to be published. The books that 'deserve' to be published are the ones that publishers inevitably invest in based on their market research and sales histories."

BIGGEST CAREER SURPRISE: "People tell you that this industry is full of great people, but you don't comprehend it until you're really in it. You will meet the most creative, intelligent and hardest-working people in the publishing business."

KARA GEBHART UHL, formerly a managing editor at *Writer's Digest* magazine, now freelance writers and edits in Fort Thomas, KY. She also blogs about parenting at pleiadesbee.com. Her essays have appeared on The Huffington Post, *The New York Times*' Motherlode and *TIME: Healthland*. Her parenting essay, "Apologies to the Parents I Judged Four Years Ago" was named one of *TIME*'s "Top 10 Opinions of 2012."

REVISION AND SELF-EDITING

Polish your work before submitting.

....

by James Scott Bell

Submitting a novel without rewriting is like playing hockey naked. You're just not equipped to put your best, um, face on things. And sooner rather than later a well-placed puck is going to hit you where it hurts most.

That puck is the editor's or agent's built-in prejudice against weak material. They are tuned to say *No*. That's why you rewrite. You want to take out all those *No* reasons.

THE TIME TO REVISE

So you have a completed manuscript. This is a crucial time. What you must avoid is any temptation to stop and do wholesale revisions before you have read the entire manuscript once.

Think of this process as Google Earth. You want to get a complete overview of your "earth." Your novel. Your story as a whole. You can spin the earth a little here and there to get a better view, but stay up top. You'll tag a few places to visit later, to zoom in on. That'll be the nuts and bolts of revision.

First, it's essential to give yourself a break from the first draft. At least two weeks. During this "cooling phase," try to forget about your book completely.

Then try to read the complete manuscript in a couple of sittings—three or four at the most. What you want to create is the feeling of being a fresh reader, getting into this book for the first time.

Don't stop to make changes at this point. You may jot a few things down, notes to yourself and the like, but keep going to get the overall impression of the book. Too many writers just sit down and read a manuscript page by page, making changes as they come up. Big or small, each item is dealt with the moment it's seen.

Much better is to go from large to small. To start with the most crucial aspects and work your way down to the final step, which is The Polish.

MAKING BIG-PICTURE REVISIONS

When it comes to revision, I've found that most writers need a systematic approach. Think of this, then, as your ultimate revision checklist. Apply these questions to every manuscript you write.

Lead Character

- Is my Lead worth following for a whole novel? Why?
- How can I make my Lead "jump off the page" more?
- Do my characters sufficiently contrast? Are they interesting enough on their own?
- Will readers bond to my Lead because he …
- … cares for someone other than himself?
- … is funny, irreverent, or a rebel with a cause?
- … is competent at something?
- … is an underdog facing long odds without giving up?
- … has a dream or desire readers can relate to?
- … has undeserved misfortune, but doesn't whine about it?
- … is in jeopardy or danger?

Opposition Character

- Is the opposition character just as fully realized as the Lead?
- Is his behavior justified (in his own mind)?
- Are you being "fair" with the opposition?
- Is he as strong or (preferably) stronger than the Lead, in terms of ability to win the fight?

Plot

- Is there any point where a reader might feel like putting the book down?
- Does the novel feel like it's about people doing things?
- Does the plot feel forced or unnatural?
- Is the story out of balance? Too much action? Too much reaction?

The Opening

- Do I open with some part of the story engine running? Or am I spending too much time warming up?

- How do my opening pages conform to Hitchcock's axiom ("A good story is life with the dull parts taken out")?
- What is the story world I'm trying to present? What mood descriptions bring that story world to life for the reader?
- What is the tone of my novel going to be? Are the descriptions consistent with that mood?
- What happens in Act I that's going to compel the reader to keep reading? What danger to the Lead?
- Is there enough conflict in the setup to run through the whole book?

Middles

- Do I deepen character relationships?
- Why should the reader care what's happening?
- Have I justified the final battle or final choice that will wrap things up at the end?
- Is there a sense of death (physical, professional, or psychological) that overhangs?
- Is there a strong adhesive keeping the characters together (such as moral or professional duty; physical location; other reasons characters can't just walk away)?

Endings

- Are there loose threads left dangling? (You must either resolve these in a way that doesn't distract from the main plotline, or go back and snip them.)
- Do I give a feeling of resonance? (The best endings leave a sense of something beyond the confines of the book covers.)
- Will the readers feel the way I want them to feel?

Scenes

- Is there conflict or tension in every scene?
- Do I establish a viewpoint character?
- If the scene is action, is the objective clear?
- If the scene is reaction, is the emotion clear?
- Exposition: Do I have large chunks of information dumped in one spot?
- Is my exposition doing double duty? Cut any exposition that doesn't also add to the mood or tone of your novel.

Voice, Style, & Point of View

- Are there sections where the style seems forced or stilted? (Try reading it out loud. Hearing it will often help identify places to be cut or modified.)
- Is the POV consistent in every scene?

- If writing in first person, can the character see and feel what it is I describe?
- If writing in third person, do I slip into the thoughts of other characters rather than the POV character in the scene? Do I describe something the character can't see or feel?

Setting & Description

- Have I brought the setting to life for the reader?
- Does the setting operate as a "character"?
- Are my descriptions of places and people too generic?
- Are my descriptions doing "double duty" by adding to the mood or tone?

Dialogue

- Can I put in non sequiturs, or answer a question with a question, and so on?
- Can I change some attributions—he said, she said—to action beats?
- Does my dialogue have conflict or tension, even between allies?

Theme

- Do I know what my theme is?
- Has a different theme emerged in the writing? Am I fighting it?
- Have I woven in thematic elements naturally?
- Have I avoided "the lecture"?

THE POLISH

Now, before you send off the manuscript, give it one more read. This won't take long in comparison, but it will add that extra sparkle that could make all the difference.

Chapter Openings

- Can I begin a little further in?
- Does the opening grab? Have a hint of conflict or action?
- Do most of my chapters begin the same way? (Vary them.)

Chapter Endings

- Can I find a place to end a chapter earlier? How does it feel? (It may be better, it may not. If it is, use it.)

Dialogue

- Is there plenty of "white space" in my dialogue exchanges? Can I cut any words to make the dialogue tighter?

Word Search

- Do a word search for those repeated words and phrases you tend to overuse. Then modify them accordingly.
- In addition, look for:
    1. *Very*. This is almost always a useless adjective. Cut it.
    2. *Suddenly*. Again, mostly not needed.
    3. *Adverbs*. Cut them unless absolutely necessary.

Big Moments

- Identify five big moments in your manuscript. After each moment, make a list of ten ways you can heighten that moment, make it more intense, give it more juice.

WHAT THE PROCESS LOOKS LIKE

Below are two versions of a section from my novel, *Sins of the Fathers*. The first is my original. The second shows a little of the thinking process that goes into self-editing.

Original Version

First came the children.

In Lindy's dream they were running and screaming, dozens of them, in some sunlit field. A billowing surge of terrified kids, boys and girls, some in baseball garb, others in variegated ragtag clothes that gave the impression of a Dickens novel run amok.

What was behind them, what was causing the terror, was something dark, unseen. In the hovering over visions that only dreams afford, Lindy sought desperately the source of the fear.

There was a black forest behind the field, like you'd see in fairy tales. Or nightmares.

She moved toward the forest, knowing who it was, who was in there, and she'd meet him coming out. It would be Darren DiCinni, and he would have a gun, and in the dream she kept low to avoid being shot herself.

Moving closer and closer now, the screams of the scattering children fading behind her. Without having to look behind she knew that a raft of cops was pulling up to the scene.

She wondered if she was going to warn DiCinni, or was she just going to look at him?

Would he say anything to her, or she to him?

The dark forest had the kind of trees that come alive at night, with gnarly arms and knotted trunks. It was the place where the bad things lived.

Lindy didn't want to go in, but she couldn't stop herself.

That's when the dark figure started to materialize, from deep within the forest, and he was running toward her.

Edited Version

First came the children.

In Lindy's dream they were running and screaming, dozens of them, in some sunlit field. A billowing surge of terrified kids, boys and girls, some in baseball garb, others in variegated ragtag clothes that gave the impression of a Dickens novel run amok.

~~What was behind them, what was causing the terror, was something dark, unseen~~. [Weak sentence structure. Rethink. Check "dark." I use it a lot!] In the hovering over visions [Confusing.] that only dreams afford, Lindy sought desperately the source of the fear.

~~There was~~ [Sentences starting with "There" are generally weak. Rethink.] a black forest behind the field, like you'd see [Using "you" in this way can be effective in some places, but overuse is not good. Rethink.] in fairy tales. Or nightmares.

She moved toward the forest, ~~knowing who it was, who was in there~~, [Awkward.] and she'd meet him coming out. ~~It would be Darren DiCinni, and he would have a gun, and in the dream she kept low to avoid being shot herself~~. [See if I can strengthen this dramatic image.]

Moving closer and closer now, the screams of the scattering children fading behind her. Without having to look behind she knew that a raft of cops was pulling up to the scene.

She wondered if she was going to warn DiCinni, or was she just going to look at him? [Tighten.]

Would he say anything to her, or she to him?

~~The dark forest had the kind of trees that come alive at night, with gnarly arms and knotted trunks. It was the place where the bad things lived~~. [Rethink. There's "dark" again.]

Lindy didn't want to go in, but she couldn't stop herself.

~~That's when~~ [Unneeded verbiage.] the dark figure started to materialize, from deep within the forest, and he [How do we know it's he?] was running toward her.

LEARNING TO BE A REAL WRITER

Self-editing is the ability to know what makes fiction work. You learn to be your own guide so you may, as Renni Browne and Dave King put it in *Self-Editing for Fiction Writers*, "See your manuscript the way an editor might see it—to do for yourself what a publishing house editor once might have done."

By self-editing and revising your work, you'll be operating on all cylinders. This is how you become a real writer. Cutting, shaping, adding, subtracting, working it, making it better—that's what real writing is all about. This is how unpublished writers become published.

Excerpted with permission (Writer's Digest Books) from *Write Great Fiction: Revision and Self-Editing* by **JAMES SCOTT BELL** (jamesscottbell.com).

CRAFTING A QUERY

How to write a great letter that gets agents' attention.

by Kara Gebhart Uhl

So you've written a book. And now you want an agent. If you're new to publishing, you probably assume that the next step is to send your finished, fabulous book out to agents, right? Wrong. Agents don't want your finished, fabulous book. In fact, they probably don't even want *part* of your finished, fabulous book—at least, not yet. First, they want your query.

A query is a short, professional way of introducing yourself to an agent. If you're frustrated by the idea of this step, imagine yourself at a cocktail party. Upon meeting someone new, you don't greet them with a boisterous hug and kiss and, in three minutes, reveal your entire life story including the fact that you were late to the party because of some gastrointestinal problems. Rather, you extend your hand. You state your name. You comment on the hors d'oeuvres, the weather, the lovely shade of someone's dress. Perhaps, after this introduction, the person you're talking to politely excuses himself. Or, perhaps, you become best of friends. It's basic etiquette, formality, professionalism—it's simply how it's done.

Agents receive hundreds of submissions every month. Often they read these submissions on their own time—evenings, weekends, on their lunch break. Given the number of writers submitting, and the number of agents reading, it would simply be impossible for agents to ask for and read entire book manuscripts off the bat. Instead, a query is a quick way for you to, first and foremost, pitch your book. But it's also a way to pitch yourself. If an agent is intrigued by your query, she may ask for a partial (say, the first three chapters of your manuscript). Or she may ask for the entire thing.

As troublesome as it may first seem, try not to be frustrated by this process. Because, honestly, a query is a really great way to help speed up what is already a monumentally slow-paced industry. Have you ever seen pictures of slush piles—those piles of unread queries on many well-known agents' desks? Imagine the size of those slush piles if they held full manuscripts instead of one-page query letters. Thinking of it this way, query letters begin to make more sense.

Here we share with you the basics of a query, including its three parts and a detailed list of dos and don'ts.

PART I: THE INTRODUCTION

Whether you're submitting a 100-word picture book or a 90,000-word novel, you must be able to sum up the most basic aspects of it in one sentence. Agents are busy. And they constantly receive submissions for types of work they don't represent. So upfront they need to know that, after reading your first paragraph, the rest of your query is going to be worth their time.

An opening sentence designed to "hook" an agent is fine—if it's good and if it works. But this is the time to tune your right brain down and your left brain up—agents desire professionalism and queries that are short and to-the-point. Remember the cocktail party and always err on the side of formality. Tell the agent, in as few words as possible, what you've written, including the title, genre and length.

In the intro, you also must try to connect with the agent. Simply sending 100 identical query letters out to "Dear Agent" won't get you published. Instead, your letter should be addressed not only to a specific agency but a specific agent within that agency. (And double, triple, quadruple check that the agent's name is spelled correctly.) In addition, you need to let the agent know why you chose her specifically. A good author-agent relationship is like a good marriage. It's important that both sides invest the time to find a good fit that meets their needs. So how do you connect with an agent you don't know personally? Research.

1. Make a connection based on an author or book the agent already represents.
Most agencies have websites that list who and what they represent. Research those sites. Find a book similar to yours and explain that, because such-and-such book has a similar theme or tone or whatever, you think your book would be a great fit. In addition, many agents will list specific genres/categories they're looking for, either on their websites or in interviews. If your book is a match, state that.

2. Make a connection based on an interview you read.
Search agents' names online and read any and all interviews they've participated in. Perhaps they mentioned a love for X and your book is all about X. Perhaps they mentioned that they're looking for Y and your book is all about Y. Mention the specific interview. Prove that you've invested as much time researching them as they're about to spend researching you.

3. Make a connection based on a conference you both attended.
Was the agent you're querying the keynote speaker at a writing conference you were recently at? If so, mention it, and comment on an aspect of his speech you liked. Even better, did you meet the agent in person? Mention it, and if there's something you can say to jog her memory about the meeting, say it. Better yet, did the agent specifically ask you to send your manuscript? Mention it.

Finally, if you're being referred to a particular agent by an author that agent already represents—that's your opening sentence. That referral is guaranteed to get your query placed at the top of the stack.

PART II: THE PITCH

Here's where you really get to sell your book—but in only three to 10 sentences. Consider a book's jacket flap and its role in convincing readers to plunk down $24.95 to buy what's in between those flaps. Like a jacket flap, you need to hook an agent in the confines of very limited space. What makes your story interesting and unique? Is your story about a woman going through a mid-life crisis? Fine, but there are hundreds of stories about women going through mid-life crises. Is your story about a woman who, because of a mid-life crisis, leaves her life and family behind to spend three months in India? Again, fine, but this story, too, already exists—in many forms. Is your story about a woman who, because of a mid-life crisis, leaves her life and family behind to spend three months in India, falls in love with someone new while there and starts a new life—and family? And then has to deal with everything she left behind upon her return? *Now* you have a hook.

Practice your pitch. Read it out loud, not only to family and friends, but to people willing to give you honest, intelligent criticism. If you belong to a writing group, workshop your pitch. Share it with members of an online writing forum. Know anyone in the publishing industry? Share it with them. Many writers spend years writing their books. We're not talking about querying magazines here; we're talking about querying an agent who could become a lifelong partner. Spend time on your pitch. Perfect it. Turn it into jacket-flap material so detailed, exciting and clear that it would be near impossible to read your pitch and not want to read more. Use active verbs. Write your pitch, put it aside for a week, then look at it again. Don't send a query simply because you finished a book. Send a query because you finished your pitch and are ready to take the next steps.

PART III: THE BIO

If you write fiction, unless you're a household name or you've recently been a guest on some very big TV or radio shows, an agent is much more interested in your pitch than in who you are. If you write nonfiction, who you are—more specifically, your platform and publicity—is much more important. Regardless, these are key elements that must be present in every bio:

1. Publishing credits

If you're submitting fiction, focus on your fiction credits—previously published works and short stories. That said, if you're submitting fiction and all your previously published work is nonfiction—magazine articles, essays, etc.—that's still fine and good to mention. Don't be overly long about it. Mention your publications in bigger magazines or well-known literary journals. If you've never had anything published, don't say you lack official credits. Simply skip this altogether and thank the agent for his time.

2. Contests and awards

If you've won many, focus on the most impressive ones and those that most directly relate to your work. Don't mention contests you entered and weren't named in. Also, feel free to leave titles and years out of it. If you took first place at the Delaware Writers Conference for your fiction manuscript, that's good enough. Mentioning details isn't necessary.

3. MFAs

If you've earned or are working toward a Master of Fine Arts in writing, say so and state the program. Don't mention English degrees or online writing courses.

4. Large, recognized writing organizations

Agents don't want to hear about your book club and the fact that there's always great food, or the small critique group you meet with once a week. And they really don't want to hear about the online writing forum you belong to. But if you're a member of something like the Romance Writers of America (RWA), the Mystery Writers of America (MWA), the Society of Children's Book Writers and Illustrators (SCBWI), the Society of Professional Journalists (SPJ), the American Medical Writers, etc., say so. This shows you're serious about what you do and you're involved in groups that can aid with publicity and networking.

5. Platform and publicity

If you write nonfiction, who you are and how you're going to help sell the book once it's published becomes very important. Why are you the best person to write it and what do you have now—public speaking engagements, an active website or blog, substantial cred in your industry—that will help you sell this book?

Finally, be cordial. Thank the agent for taking the time to read your query and consider your manuscript. Ask if you may send more, in the format she desires (partial, full, etc.).

Think of the time you spent writing your book. Unfortunately, you can't send your book to an agent for a first impression. Your query *is* that first impression. Give it the time it deserves. Keep it professional. Keep it formal. Let it be a firm handshake—not a sloppy kiss. Let it be a first meeting that evolves into a lifelong relationship—not a rejection slip. But expect those slips. Just like you don't become best friends with everyone you meet at a cocktail party, you can't expect every agent you pitch to sign you. Be patient. Keep pitching. And in the meantime, start writing that next book.

DOS AND DON'TS FOR QUERYING AGENTS

DO:

- Keep the tone professional.

- Query a specific agent at a specific agency.

- Proofread. Double-check the spelling of the agency and the agent's name.

- Keep the query concise, limiting the overall length to one page (single space, 12-point type in a commonly used font).

- Focus on the plot, not your bio, when pitching fiction.

- Pitch agents who represent the type of material you write.

- Check an agency's submission guidelines to see how to query—for example, via e-mail or mail—and whether or not to include a SASE.

- Keep pitching, despite rejections.

DON'T:

- Include personal info not directly related to the book. For example, stating that you're a parent to three children doesn't make you more qualified than someone else to write a children's book.

- Say how long it took you to write your manuscript. Some bestselling books took 10 years to write—others, six weeks. An agent doesn't care how long it took—an agent only cares if it's good. Same thing goes with drafts—an agent doesn't care how many drafts it took you to reach the final product.

- Mention that this is your first novel or, worse, the first thing you've ever written aside from grocery lists. If you have no other publishing credits, don't advertise that fact. Don't mention it at all.

- State that your book has been edited by peers or professionals. Agents expect manuscripts to be edited, no matter how the editing was done.

- Bring up screenplays or film adaptations—you're querying an agent about publishing a book, not making a movie.

- Mention any previous rejections.

- State that the story is copyrighted with the U.S. Copyright Office or that you own all rights. Of course you own all rights. You wrote it.

- Rave about how much your family and friends loved it. What matters is that the agent loves it.

- Send flowers or anything else except a self-addressed stamped envelope (and only if the SASE is required), if sending through snail mail.

- Follow up with a phone call. After the appropriate time has passed (many agencies say how long it will take to receive a response), follow up in the manner you queried— via e-mail or mail.

KARA GEBHART UHL, formerly a managing editor at *Writer's Digest* magazine, now freelance writers and edits in Fort Thomas, KY. She also blogs about parenting at pleiadesbee.com. Her essays have appeared on The Huffington Post, *The New York Times*' Motherlode and *TIME: Healthland*. Her parenting essay, "Apologies to the Parents I Judged Four Years Ago" was named one of *TIME*'s "Top 10 Opinions of 2012."

① SAMPLE QUERY 1: LITERARY FICTION
Agent's Comments: Jeff Kleinman (Folio Literary)

From: Garth Stein
To: Jeff Kleinman
Subject: Query: "The Art of Racing in the Rain" ①

Dear Mr. Kleinman:

② Saturday night I was participating in a fundraiser for the King County Library System out here in the Pacific Northwest, and I met your client Layne Maheu. He spoke very highly of you and suggested that I contact you.

③ I am a Seattle writer with two published novels. I have recently completed my third novel, *The Art of Racing in the Rain*, and I find myself in a difficult situation: My new book is narrated by a dog, and my current agent ④ told me that he cannot (or will not) sell it for that very reason. Thus, I am seeking new representation.

⑤ *The Art of Racing in the Rain* is the story of Denny Swift, a race car driver who faces profound obstacles in his life, and ultimately overcomes them by applying the same techniques that have made him successful on the track. His story is narrated by his "philosopher dog," Enzo, who, having a nearly human soul (and an obsession with opposable thumbs), believes he will return as a man in his next lifetime.

⑥ My last novel, *How Evan Broke His Head and Other Secrets*, won a 2006 Pacific Northwest Booksellers Association Book Award, and since the award ceremony a year ago, I have given many readings, workshops and lectures promoting the book. When time has permitted, I've read the first chapter from *The Art of Racing in the Rain*. Audience members have been universally enthusiastic and vocal in their response, and the first question asked is always: "When can I buy the book about the dog?" Also very positive.

⑦ I'm inserting, below, a short synopsis of *The Art of Racing in the Rain*, and my biography. Please let me know if the novel interests you; I would be happy to send you the manuscript.

Sincerely,
Garth Stein

① Putting the word "Query" and the title of the book on the subject line of an e-mail often keeps your e-mail from falling into the spam folder. ② One of the best ways of starting out correspondence is figuring out your connection to the agent. ③ The author has some kind of track record. Who's the publisher, though? Were these both self-published novels, or were there reputable publishers involved? (I'll read on, and hope I find out.) ④ This seems promising, but also know this kind of approach can backfire, because we agents tend to be like sheep—what one doesn't like, the rest of us are wary of, too (or, conversely, what one likes, we all like). But in this case getting in the "two published novels" early is definitely helpful. ⑤ The third paragraph is the key pitch paragraph and Garth gives a great description of the book—he sums it up, gives us a feel for what we're going to get. This is the most important part of your letter. ⑥ Obviously it's nice to see the author's winning awards. Also good: The author's not afraid of promoting the book. ⑦ The end is simple and easy—it doesn't speak of desperation, or doubt, or anything other than polite willingness to help.

Dear Mr. Malawer:

I would like you to represent my 65,000-word contemporary teen novel *My Big Nose & Other Natural Disasters*.

① Seventeen-year-old Jory Michaels wakes up on the first day of summer vacation with her same old big nose, no passion in her life (in the creative sense of the word), and all signs still pointing to her dying a virgin. Plus, her mother is busy roasting a chicken for Day #6 of the Dinner For Breakfast Diet.

② In spite of her driving record (it was an accident!), Jory gets a job delivering flowers and cakes to Reno's casinos and wedding chapels. She also comes up with a new summer goal: saving for a life-altering nose job. She and her new nose will attract a fabulous boyfriend. Nothing like the shameless flirt Tyler Briggs, or Tom who's always nice but never calls. Maybe she'll find someone kind of like Gideon at the Jewel Café, except better looking and not quite so different. Jory survives various summer disasters like doing yoga after sampling Mom's Cabbage Soup Diet, Enforced Mother Bonding With Crazy Nose Obsessed Daughter Night, and discovering Tyler's big secret. But will she learn to accept herself and maybe even find her passion, in the creative (AND romantic!) sense of the word?

③ I have written for *APPLESEEDS, Confetti, Hopscotch, Story Friends, Wee Ones Magazine,* the *Deseret News, Children's Playmate* and Blooming Tree Press' *Summer Shorts* anthology. I won the Utah Arts Council prize for *Not-A-Dr. Logan's Divorce Book*. My novels *Jungle Crossing* and *Going Native!* each won first prize in the League of Utah Writers contest. I currently serve as an SCBWI Regional Advisor.

④ I submitted *My Big Nose & Other Natural Disasters* to Krista Marino at Delacorte because she requested it during our critique at the summer SCBWI conference (no response yet).

Thank you for your time and attention. I look forward to hearing from you.

Sincerely,
Sydney Salter Husseman

① With hundreds and hundreds of queries each month, it's tough to stand out. Sydney, however, did just that. First, she has a great title that totally made me laugh. Second, she sets up her main character's dilemma in a succinct and interesting way. In one simple paragraph, I have a great idea of who Jory is and what her life is about—the interesting tidbits about her mother help show the novel's sense of humor, too. **②** Sydney's largest paragraph sets up the plot and the conflict, and introduces some exciting potential love interests and misadventures that I was excited to read about. Again, Sydney really shows off her fantastic sense of humor, and she leaves me hanging with a question that I needed an answer to. **③** She has writing experience and has completed other manuscripts that were prize-worthy. Her SCBWI involvement—while not a necessity—shows me that she has an understanding of and an interest in the children's publishing world. **④** The fact that an editor requested the manuscript is always a good sign. That I knew Krista personally and highly valued her opinion was, as Sydney's main character Jory would say, "The icing on the cake."

③ SAMPLE QUERY 3: NONFICTION (SELF-HELP)
Agent's Comments: Michelle Wolfson (Wolfson Literary)

Dear Ms. Wolfson:

① Have you ever wanted to know the best day of the week to buy groceries or go out to dinner? Have you ever wondered about the best time of day to send an e-mail or ask for a raise? What about the best time of day to schedule a surgery or a haircut? What's the best day of the week to avoid lines at the Louvre? What's the best day of the month to make an offer on a house? What's the best time of day to ask someone out on a date? ②

My book, *Buy Ketchup in May and Fly at Noon: A Guide to the Best Time to Buy This, Do That, and Go There*, has the answers to these questions and hundreds more.

③ As a long-time print journalist, I've been privy to readership surveys that show people can't get enough of newspaper and magazine stories about the best time to buy or do things. This book puts several hundreds of questions and answers in one place—a succinct, large-print reference book that readers will feel like they need to own. Why? Because it will save them time and money, and it will give them valuable information about issues related to health, education, travel, the workplace and more. In short, it will make them smarter, so they can make better decisions. ④

Best of all, the information in this book is relevant to anyone, whether they live in Virginia or the Virgin Islands, Portland, Oregon, or Portland, Maine. In fact, much of the book will find an audience in Europe and Australia.

⑤ I've worked as a journalist since 1984. In 1999, the Virginia Press Association created an award for the best news writing portfolio in the state—the closest thing Virginia had to a reporter-of-the-year award. I won it that year and then again in 2000. During the summer of 2007, I left newspapering to pursue book projects and long-form journalism.

⑥ I saw your name on a list of top literary agents for self-help books, and I read on your website that you're interested in books that offer practical advice. *Buy Ketchup in May and Fly at Noon* offers plenty of that. Please let me know if you'd like to read my proposal.

Sincerely,
Mark Di Vincenzo

① I tend to prefer it when authors jump right into the heart of their book, the exception being if we've met at a conference or have some other personal connection. Mark chose clever questions for the opening of the query. All of those questions are, in fact, relevant to my life—with groceries, dinner, e-mail and a raise—and yet I don't have a definitive answer to them. ② He gets a little more offbeat and unusual with questions regarding surgery, the Louvre, buying a house and dating. This shows a quirkier side to the book and also the range of topics it is going to cover, so I know right away there is going to be a mix of useful and quirky information on a broad range of topics. ③ By starting with "As a long-time print journalist," Mark immediately establishes his credibility for writing on this topic. ④ This helps show that there is a market for this book, and establishes the need for such a book. ⑤ Mark's bio paragraph offers a lot of good information. ⑥ It's nice when I feel like an author has sought me out specifically and thinks we would be a good fit.

Dear Ms. Weed:

① Natalie Miller had a plan. She had a goddamn plan. Top of her class at Dartmouth. Even better at Yale Law. Youngest aide ever to the powerful Senator Claire Dupris. Higher, faster, stronger. This? Was all part of the plan. True, she was so busy ascending the political ladder that she rarely had time to sniff around her mediocre relationship with Ned, who fit the three Bs to the max: basic, blond and boring, and she definitely didn't have time to mourn her mangled relationship with Jake, her budding rock star ex-boyfriend.

The lump in her right breast that Ned discovers during brain-numbingly bland morning sex? That? Was most definitely not part of the plan. And Stage IIIA breast cancer? Never once had Natalie jotted this down on her to-do list for conquering the world. When her (tiny-penised) boyfriend has the audacity to dump her on the day after her diagnosis, Natalie's entire world dissolves into a tornado of upheaval, and she's left with nothing but her diary to her ex-boyfriends, her mornings lingering over "The Price is Right," her burnt-out stubs of pot that carry her past the chemo pain, and finally, the weight of her life choices—the ones in which she might drown if she doesn't find a buoy.

② *The Department of Lost and Found* is a story of hope, of resolve, of digging deeper than you thought possible until you find the strength not to crumble, and ultimately, of making your own luck, even when you've been dealt an unsteady hand.

③ I'm a freelance writer and have contributed to, among others, *American Baby, American Way, Arthritis Today, Bride's, Cooking Light, Fitness, Glamour, InStyle Weddings, Men's Edge, Men's Fitness, Men's Health, Parenting, Parents, Prevention, Redbook, Self, Shape, Sly, Stuff, USA Weekend, Weight Watchers, Woman's Day, Women's Health,* and ivillage.com, msn.com and women.com. I also ghostwrote *The Knot Book of Wedding Flowers.*

If you are interested, I'd love to send you the completed manuscript. Thanks so much! Looking forward to speaking with you soon.

Allison Winn Scotch

① The opening sentence reads like great jacket copy, and I immediately know who our protagonist is and what the conflict for her will be. (And it's funny, without being silly.) **②** The third paragraph tells me where this book will land: upmarket women's fiction. (A great place to be these days!) **③** This paragraph highlights impressive credentials. While being able to write nonfiction does not necessarily translate over to fiction, it shows me that she is someone worth paying more attention to. And her magazine contacts will help when it comes time to promote the book.

⑤ SAMPLE QUERY 5: MAINSTREAM/COMEDIC FICTION
Agent's Comments: Michelle Brower (Folio Literary)

Dear Michelle Brower:

❶ "I spent two days in a cage at the SPCA until my parents finally came to pick me up. The stigma of bringing your undead son home to live with you can wreak havoc on your social status, so I can't exactly blame my parents for not rushing out to claim me. But one more day and I would have been donated to a research facility."

Andy Warner is a zombie.

After reanimating from a car accident that killed his wife, Andy is resented by his parents, abandoned by his friends, and vilified by society. Seeking comfort and camaraderie in Undead Anonymous, a support group for zombies, Andy finds kindred souls in Rita, a recent suicide who has a taste for consuming formaldehyde in cosmetic products, and Jerry, a 21-year-old car crash victim with an artistic flair for Renaissance pornography.

❷ With the help of his new friends and a rogue zombie named Ray, Andy embarks on a journey of personal freedom and self-discovery that will take him from his own casket to the SPCA to a media-driven, class-action lawsuit for the civil rights of all zombies. And along the way, he'll even devour a few Breathers.

Breathers is a contemporary dark comedy about life, or undeath, through the eyes of an ordinary zombie. In addition to *Breathers*, I've written three other novels and more than four dozen short stories—a dozen of which have appeared in small press publications. Currently, I'm working on my fifth novel, also a dark comedy, about fate.

Enclosed is a two-page synopsis and the first chapter of *Breathers*, with additional sample chapters or the entire manuscript available upon request. I appreciate your time and interest in considering my query and I look forward to your response.

Sincerely,
Scott G. Browne

❶ What really draws me to this query is the fact that it has exactly what I'm looking for in my commercial fiction—story and style. Scott includes a brief quote from the book that manages to capture his sense of humor as an author and his uniquely relatable main character (hard to do with someone who's recently reanimated). I think this is a great example of how query letters can break the rules and still stand out in the slush pile. I normally don't like quotes as the first line, because I don't have a context for them, but this quote both sets up the main concept of the book *and* gives me a sense of the character's voice. This method won't necessarily work for most fiction, but it absolutely is successful here. ❷ The letter quickly conveys that this is an unusual book about zombies, and being a fan of zombie literature, I'm aware that it seems to be taking things in a new direction. I also appreciate how Scott conveys the main conflict of his plot and his supporting cast of characters—we know there is an issue for Andy beyond coming back to life as a zombie, and that provides momentum for the story.

QUERY LETTER FAQS

Here are answers to 19 of the most tricky and confusing query questions around.

....

by Chuck Sambuchino

Readers and aspiring writers often find querying literary agents to be intimidating and terrifying. Here are some important questions and answers to consider as you craft your query letter.

When contacting agents, the query process isn't as simple as, "Just keep e-mailing until something good happens." There are ins, outs, strange situations, unclear scenarios, and plenty of what-have-you that block the road to signing with a rep. In short, there are plenty of murky waters out there in the realm of submissions. Luckily, writers have plenty of questions to ask. Here are some of the most interesting (and important) questions and answers regarding protocol during the query process.

When should you query? When is your project ready?

There is no definitive answer, but here's what I suggest. Get other eyes on the material—"beta readers"—people who can give you feedback that is both honest and helpful. These beta readers (usually members of a critique group) will give you feedback. You do not want major concerns, such as, "It starts too slow" or "This character is not likeable." Address these problems through revisions. After rewriting, give it to more beta readers. If they come back with no major concerns, the book is ready, or at least very close.

How should you start your query? Should you begin with a paragraph from the book?

I would not include a paragraph from the book nor would I write the letter in the "voice" of one your characters—those are gimmicks. If you choose, you can just jump right into the pitch—there's nothing wrong with that. But what I recommend is laying out the details of your book in one easy sentence: "I have a completed 78,000-word thriller titled *Dead Cat Bounce*." I suggest this because jumping into a pitch can be jarring and confusing. Think about it. If you started reading an e-mail and the first sentence was simply "Billy has a problem," you don't know if Billy is an adult or a child, or if he is being held captive by terrorists versus being nervous because his turtle is missing. In other words, the agent doesn't know whether to laugh or be worried. He's confused. And when an agent gets confused, he may just stop reading.

Can you query multiple agents at the same agency?

Generally, no. A rejection from one literary agent usually means a rejection from the entire agency. If you query one agent and she thinks the work isn't right for her but still has promise, she will pass it on to fellow agents in the office who can review it themselves.

Should you mention that the query is a simultaneous submission?

You can, but you don't have to. If you say it's exclusive, they understand no other eyes are on the material. If you say nothing, they will assume multiple agents must be considering it. However, some agents will specifically request in their guidelines to be informed if it's a simultaneous submission.

Even if an agent doesn't request it, should you include a few sample pages with your query letter?

This is up to you. When including sample pages, though, remember to paste the pages below the query letter. Do not attach them in a document. Also, do not include much—perhaps 1–5 pages. Most people asking this question probably have more faith in their opening pages than in their query. That's understandable, but keep in mind that while including sample pages may help with an occasional agent who checks out your writing, it doesn't solve the major problem of your query being substandard. Keep working on the query until you have faith in it, regardless of whether you sneak in unsolicited pages or not.

Can your query be more than one page long?

The rise of e-queries removed the dreaded page break, so now it's easy to have your query go over one page. This does not necessarily mean it's a wise move. Going a few sentences over one page is likely harmless, but you don't need a query that trends long. Lengthy letters are a sign of a rambling pitch, which will probably get you rejected. Edit and trim your pitch down as need be. Find beta readers or a freelance query editor to give you ideas and notes. Remember that a succinct letter is preferred, and oftentimes more effective. An exception to this, however, is querying for nonfiction books. Nonfiction queries have to be heavy on author platform, and those notes (with proper names of publications and organizations and websites, etc.) can get long. Feel free to go several sentences over one page if you have to list out platform and marketing notes, as long as the pitch itself is not the item making your letter too long.

How do you follow up with an agent who hasn't responded to your submission?

This is a complicated question, and I'll try to address its many parts.

First, check the agency website for updates and their latest formal guidelines. They might have gone on leave, or they might have switched agencies. They may also have submission guidelines that state how they only respond to submissions if interested. So keep in mind there might be a very good reason as to why you shouldn't follow up or rather why you shouldn't follow up right now.

However, let's say an agent responds to submissions "within three months" and it's been three and a half months with no reply. A few weeks have passed since the "deadline," so now it's time to nicely follow up. All you do is paste your original query into a new e-mail and send it to the agent with a note above the query that says, "Dear [agent], I sent my query below to you [length of time] ago and haven't heard anything. I'm afraid my original note got lost in a spam filter, so I am pasting it below in the hopes that you are still reviewing queries and open to new clients. Thank you for considering my submission. Sincerely, [name]." That's it. Be polite and simply resubmit. If an agent makes it sound like he does indeed respond to submissions but doesn't have a time frame for his reply, I say follow up after three months.

But before you send that follow up, make sure you are not to blame for getting no reply. Perhaps your previous e-mail had an attachment when the agent warned, "No attachments." Perhaps your previous e-mail did not put "Query" in the subject line even though the agent requested just that. Or perhaps your previous e-mail misspelled the agent's e-mail address and the query truly got lost in cyberspace. In other words, double-check everything. If you send that follow up and the agent still doesn't reply, it's probably time to move on.

Can you re-query an agent after she rejects you?

You can, though I'd say you have about a 50/50 shot of getting your work read. Some agents seem to be more than open to reviewing a query letter if it's undergone serious editing. Other agents, meanwhile, believe that a no is a no—period. In other words, you really don't know, so you might as well just query away and hope for the best.

How many query rejections would necessitate a major overhaul of the query?

Submit no more than 10 queries to start. If only 0–1 respond with requests for more, then you've got a problem. Go back to the drawing board and overhaul the query before the next wave of 6–10 submissions. Doing this ensures that you can try to identify where you're going wrong in your submission.

Should you mention that you've self-published books in the past?

In my opinion, you don't have to. If you self-published a few e-books that went no-where, you don't have to list every one and their disappointing sales numbers. The re-lease of those books should not affect your new novel that you're submitting to agents. However, if your self-published projects experienced healthy sales (5,000+ print books, 20,000+ e-books), mention it. Only talk about your self-published projects if they will help your case. Otherwise, just leave them out of the conversation and focus on the new project at hand.

Should you mention your age in a query? Do agents have a bias against older writers and teenagers?

I'm not sure any good can come from mentioning your age in a query. Usually the peo-ple who ask this question are either younger than 20 or older than 70. Some literary agents may be hesitant to sign older writers because reps are looking for career clients, not simply individuals with one memoir/book to sell. If you're older, write multiple books to convince an agent that you have several projects in you, and do not mention your age in the query to be safe.

Should you mention in the query that your work is copyrighted and/or has had book editing?

No. All work is copyrighted the moment you write it down in any medium, so saying something that is obvious only comes off as amateurish. On the same note, all work should be edited, so saying that the work is edited (even by a professional editor) also comes off as amateurish.

Is it better to send a query over snail mail or e-mail?

If you have a choice, do not send a snail mail query. They're more of a hassle to physi-cally produce, and they cost money to send. Ninety percent (or more) of queries are sent over e-mail for two very good reasons. E-mail is quicker, in terms of sending sub-missions and agents' response time, and it's free. Keep in mind that almost all agents have personal, detailed submission guidelines in which they say exactly what they want to receive in a submission and how they want to receive it. So you will almost always not have a choice in how to send materials. Send the agent what they asked for, exactly how they asked for it.

What happens when you're writing a book that doesn't easily fall into one specific genre? How do you handle that problem in a query letter?

Know that you have to bite the bullet and call it *something*. Even if you end up calling it a "middle grade adventure with supernatural elements," then you're at least call-ing it something. Writers really get into a pickle when they start their pitches with an intro such as, "It's a sci-fi western humorous fantastical suspense romance, set in steampunk Britain … with erotic werewolf transvestite protagonists." Fundamentally, it must be something, so pick its core genre and just call it that—otherwise your query might not even get read. I'm not a huge fan of writers comparing their work to other projects (saying, "It's X meets Z"—that type of thing), but said strategy—comparing your book to others in the marketplace—is most useful for those authors who have a hard time describing the plot and tone of their tale.

If you're writing a memoir, do you pitch it like a fiction book (complete the whole manuscript) or like a nonfiction book (a complete book proposal with a few sample chapters)?

I'd say 80 percent of agents review memoir like they would a novel. If interested, they ask for the full book and consider it mostly by how well it's written. I have met several agents, however, who want to see a nonfiction book proposal—either with some sample chapters, or sometimes in addition to the whole book. So to answer the question, you can choose to write only the manuscript, and go from there. Or you can choose to complete a proposal, as well, so you have as many weapons as possible as you move forward. (In my opinion, a writer who has both a complete memoir manuscript and nonfiction book proposal seems like a professional who is ahead of the curve and wise to platform matters—and, naturally, people in publishing are often attracted to writers who are ahead of the curve and/or can help sell more books.)

If you're pitching a novel, should the topics of marketing and writer platform be addressed in the query?

Concerning query letters for novels, the pitch is what's paramount, and any mention of marketing or platform is just gravy. If you have some promotional credentials, these skills will definitely be beneficial in selling more books when your title is released. But a decent platform will not get a mediocre novel published. Feel free to list worthwhile, impressive notes about your platform and marketing skills, but don't let them cloud your writing. Remember, the three most crucial elements to a novel selling are *the writing, the writing, the writing.*

Do you need to query conservative agents for a conservative book? A liberal agent for a liberal book?

I asked a few agents this question and some said they were willing to take on any political slant if the book was well written and the author had a great writer platform. A few agents, on the other hand, said they needed to be on the same page politically with the author for a political/religious book, and would only take on books they agreed with. Bottom line: Some will be open-minded; some won't. Look for reps who have taken on books similar to yours, and feel free to query other agents, too. The worst any agent can say is no.

If you're writing a series, does an agent want you to say that in the query?

The old mentality for this was no, you should not discuss a series in the query, and instead just pitch one book and let any discussion naturally progress to the topic of more books, if the agent so inquires. However, I've overheard more and more literary agents say that they do want to know if your book is the potential start of the series. So, the correct answer, it appears, depends on who you ask. In circumstances like these, I recommend crafting an answer to cover all bases: "This book could either be a standalone project or the start of a series." When worded like this, you disclose the series potential, but don't make it sound like you're saying, "I want a 5-book deal or NOTHING." You'll sound like an easy-to-work-with writing professional and leave all options open.

Can you query an agent for a short story collection?

I'd say 95 percent of agents do not accept short story collection queries. The reason? Collections just don't sell well. If you have a collection of short stories, you can do one of three things:

1) Repurpose some or all of the stories into a novel, which is much easier to sell;

2) Write a new book—a novel—and sell that first to establish a reader base. That way, you can have a base that will purchase your next project—the collection—ensuring the publisher makes money on your short stories.

3) Query the few agents who do take collections and hope for the best. If you choose this third route, I suggest you get some of the stories published to help the project gain some momentum. A platform and/or media contacts would help your case, as well.

....

CHUCK SAMBUCHINO (chucksambuchino.com, @chucksambuchino on Twitter) edits the *Guide to Literary Agents* (guidetoliteraryagents.com/blog) as well as the *Children's Writer's & Illustrator's Market*. His pop humor books include *How to Survive a Garden Gnome Attack* (film rights optioned by Sony) and *Red Dog / Blue Dog: When Pooches Get Political* (reddog-bluedog.com). Chuck's other writing books include *Formatting & Submitting Your Manuscript, 3rd. Ed.*, and *Create Your Writer Platform* (fall 2012). Besides that, he is a husband, guitarist, sleep-deprived new father, dog owner, and cookie addict.

....

NONFICTION BOOK PROPOSALS IN THE DIGITAL AGE

....

by Jane Friedman

If you wrote a nonfiction* book 20 years ago, your greatest competition was probably other books on the same topic.

If you're writing a nonfiction book today, your greatest competition is probably the immediate gratification of websites and online communities that offer diverse information and services.

Your first step, of course, in pursuing the publication of a nonfiction book is not to write the manuscript, but to create a proposal you'll use to pitch the book to agents or publishers before you write it. The writer's goal in crafting the proposal has always been to comprehensively address these three key questions:

- **So what?** What evidence can you offer that your book is needed? How does it fill a gap in the market? What's unique about it?
- **Who cares?** Who's the target audience? What size is the market for this book? What do we know about those readers?
- **Who are you?** What combination of expertise, credentials and platform makes you the absolute perfect person to write this book?

In today's digital world, though, you have to take your proposal a step further. You must show how you will compete effectively in book form. Because a book, even a book on a marketable topic, can now sometimes be seen as a less desirable way to deliver information—especially information that goes out of date quickly, is effectively found online or offers more value when personalized.

Think of your book proposal as a business plan that must make a strong case that your book will sell. As such, there are key elements you must include (see the sidebar on the opposite page for a complete list). But to make that case most effectively in today's world, you'll need to give three primary areas extra consideration up front, before you even begin crafting the proposal itself: 1) the competitive analysis, 2) the evidence of need for the book (which you'll reflect in your market overview) and 3) your online content strategy (which will become part of your platform and marketing plan).

Note: For the purposes of this article, nonfiction book refers primarily to non-narrative works—e.g., prescriptive (self-help, etc.) and informational (reference, etc.) books.

1. COMPETITIVE ANALYSIS

An essential part of every book proposal has always been the analysis of competitive book titles. But today, you can't stop there; you have to go far beyond addressing your competition on the shelves. Here are the different aspects to assess.

Print Book Titles

Visit at least one major chain bookstore, and study what's on the shelves where your book would belong. You need to see specifically what's being distributed to stores, and which books have multiple copies on the shelf (which indicates popularity and a faster pace of sale). You can't find this in an online search.

Then, in your proposal, list at least three to five (if not more) of the most relevant or popular competing titles, with specs (price, page count, format, ISBN) and a 100–200 word description of what makes each book distinctive as a competitor. Don't overlook the need to assess each author's platform, too.

E-book Titles

Repeat the process, studying e-book offerings through sites like Amazon and Barnes & Noble. Search by category (the same category that applies to your book) and by keyword. Look for the most highly ranked titles and the most reviewed. Determine if the titles are e-book originals or also available in print, and indicate available formats in your analysis. Again, don't forget to analyze the authors.

Top Blogs

There are millions of blogs out there, but not all blogs are created equal. Identify major blogs associated with your topic that target your audience. If you're active online and savvy about your subject, you should already know what these blogs are. (If you don't, popular tech blog ReadWriteWeb offers advice for uncovering highly ranked blogs: readwriteweb.com/archives/identify_top_blogs_redux.php.)

Websites, Multimedia & Apps

When you have a question or problem, what's the first thing you do? You probably type it into a search engine. Go through this process for your competitive analysis. What will potential readers of your book find if they turn to Google first? Or an app store on their smartphones? Or YouTube?

Determine how easy it is to find online information on your topic, and whether that information is trustworthy. Also note: Is it free, or do you need to pay for it? Is it customized or personalized? How well known are the authors or organizations behind the information? Consider all of the following mediums:

- Websites
- Community sites, forums and message boards
- Online classes, webinars and self-study courses
- Mobile and tablet applications
- Podcasts and videocasts
- Electronic newsletters or downloads
- Presentations and slides (e.g., SlideShare).

As a final step, ask a few librarians (or other experts on your topic) what online resources they use or recommend.

When you're ready to write your proposal, the most visible and competitive online and multimedia offerings should be described in the competitive analysis section, right alongside the books. Discuss how your book compares and why it is needed. Later, your research into online competitors can also be used to spark and develop marketing and promotional ideas for your book.

2. EVIDENCE OF NEED FOR THE BOOK

The availability of online information can kill the potential for some types of print books. Publishers of reference, cooking and travel books especially are transforming their products to stay relevant. (You may even realize, in the process of researching the online competition, that what you should do isn't write a book, but get started with a blog or community site instead—more on this later.)

However, there are still ways you can make a case for a print book as you compile the market overview and/or platform statement in your proposal. Here are three of the best:

Prove that your target audience prefers books.

This is tough to do, but it's good research to conduct in any case. Begin educating yourself by talking to booksellers and librarians about books in your category. Have they seen shelf space stay the same, expand or shrink? Are they seeing a move to digital information, or not? Then, try these strategies to seek out more concrete positive indicators:

- Locate major bloggers or websites that are selling books that offer even more in-depth or valuable information.
- Find industry articles (e.g., in *Publishers Weekly* or on publishersmarketplace.com) that discuss the health/growth of book publishing in your particular category.
- Identify recent successful publication of books in your category, especially those authored by noncelebrities.

Reference your most positive findings in your proposal. Keep in mind that any good editor or agent will probably already know—or at least have preconceived ideas—about market trends in each category. Still, the more you can reflect your own market savvy, the better.

Demonstrate you're writing something that isn't more effectively delivered through online media.

Not all information or content is appropriate for online consumption or multimedia adaptation. For example, when it comes to certain types of college textbooks, complex formatting and design issues (as well as student preferences) still drive demand for print editions.

This is an area where you need to be honest with yourself and your analysis of where your category/topic seems to be flourishing. You also need to pay attention to trends and new tech developments, because things are moving fast. That said, as far as your proposal is concerned, don't discuss format (mass-market, paperback, hardcover, electronic, etc.) unless it's one of the unique selling points of your proposed book. If you have ideas and material for multi-media features—either as marketing and promotional tools, or for an enhanced e-book edition or app—create a section in your proposal that addresses those opportunities. Otherwise, formats shouldn't affect your proposal, because the same concerns apply to them all: Books, whether print or digital, still have to compete against other types of online and informational media. Let your publisher lead the discussion on the best format for your book when the time comes.

Show that you already reach an online market of readers who are clamoring for a book.

If you have a platform—or visibility to readers—you can argue that you have a captive audience for books you author. People with social media impact, influence through popular online tools and services, or proven track records of self-published e-book sales all have online platforms that can lead to the successful launch of a print book. This is how most popular bloggers land book deals. But your captive audience probably needs to be at least 50,000 visitors per month to merit the interest of a commercial publisher.

If you have an online platform worth discussing, include the following in your proposal's platform section:

- Detail your stats across all channels: visitors/month, followers, subscribers, sales numbers, etc., and how long you've been active on each channel.
- Describe your growth trajectory. Do you gain 1,000 blog readers every two months? Do you attract 100 new Twitter followers every day?
- Quantify the impact your online activity has, or what your influence is. A good starting point for doing this is klout.com, a free tool for anyone using Facebook and Twitter. If you blog, consider how many comments you average per post, or how many people subscribe to your blog via e-mail or RSS feeds.
- If you offer free or paid downloads, share those essential numbers—they show how many of your followers are really listening, and how many you can spark to action.

Here is an example of an effective statement about the impact of your online activity:

"I have 60,000 followers on Twitter, and Twitter is the No. 2 source of traffic to my blog (2,000 visits per month). More than half the links that I share on Twitter get at least 100 clicks each."

This shows a highly engaged audience, rather than one of superficial followings that hold little meaning for marketing purposes.

3. YOUR ONLINE CONTENT STRATEGY

Many book ideas I see shopped at conferences should really have started out as blogs or interactive websites, even if only to test-market the ideas, learn more about the target audiences, and ultimately produce more successful print products—ones that have significant value because they were created with awareness of and in collaboration with what exists online.

The book cannot be the be-all, end-all of what you do in today's nonfiction market. Agents and editors want to see that your book is not the beginning or the end of the road—that it is merely one aspect of your much larger purpose and strategy for developing content and serving a readership, online and off.

So, think creatively about what can be done outside the book format. What are you already doing that can support the book and give it a presence or companion online? How can the content in your book be divided or reworked? Could it be customized or personalized? Have you thought about audio or video versions or supplements? Could you create an online class? How about an e-newsletter?

An effective and holistic content strategy combines print, online and multimedia channels to:

- Market and promote yourself and your work. You can lure new audiences with free bits of information and eventually interest them in paying for the most valuable content—which may or may not be in book form.

- Keep your readers engaged and your brand visible. What happens when people finish your book? They should have a place where they can continue the conversation online—with you and other readers—and receive updates. The people who are most talented at content strategy know how to build scarcity into their most valuable offerings. Usually this means customizing content for your most loyal fans, or offering gated or one-time experiences or products. Your time and attention is a limited resource, and can be turned into premium content.

Reflect your ability to do all of this in the platform and marketing plan elements of your book proposal, and agents and publishers will have a clear picture of your value both on and off the page.

We're still experiencing a revolution in how we find, use and share information—and authors who recognize the increasing need to demonstrate why their books will be the most viable ways to deliver information will already have a leg up on the competition. Incorporate this knowledge into your proposal, and you'll increase its chances of hitting your mark.

....

JANE FRIEDMAN (janefriedman.com), a former publisher of WD, is an industry authority on publishing. As of 2012, she is the online editor for the *Virginia Quarterly Review*.

....

ESSENTIAL ELEMENTS OF A NONFICTION BOOK PROPOSAL

HOOK
Start by simply giving a brief description of your book, including its title.

MARKET OVERVIEW
Address the "So what?" and "Who cares?" questions. Never claim that anyone or everyone can benefit from your book. Instead, identify the specific demographic your book primarily targets—e.g., married women over 40 who want to feel younger and more energetic. Then, demonstrate the evidence of need for your book within that target market.

AUTHOR BIO & PLATFORM
Answer the "Who are you?" question. There are two critical aspects to this: expertise and platform.

Expertise is related to your credentials and experience. Are you considered authoritative or trusted on the topic? Why are you qualified to write this book?

In addition to having some expertise, you also need a platform. Platform is your visibility and reach to your intended audience or market. Platform includes your online efforts, your online content strategy, and how you're visible offline, and can involve speaking engagements, publication credits, websites/blogs, social media presence and media mentions. It encompasses relationships, networks and influence you have in the field of your topic.

Don't expect to succeed by being the "outsider" or "everyday" person who's going to break the mold. Nonfiction publishers today want recognized writers who already reach readers, especially online.

COMPETITIVE ANALYSIS

List the key resources (in print and online) that already target your specific market. Be sure the analysis supports and strengthens the evidence of need for your book that you've established in your market overview.

MARKETING PLAN

Your marketing plan is one of the most essential components of your proposal. Do not write this plan in a tentative fashion, describing things you are "willing" to do, or how you will "try" to contact people for publicity. Eliminate all wishful thinking. Ground it on what you can accomplish today. Make it concrete and realistic, and include as many numbers as you can.

Weak: I plan to contact bloggers for guest blogging opportunities.

Better: I have been a guest blogger at [list great blogs], which on average brings my site 10,000 new visitors each month. I have invitations to return again, plus I've made contact with 10 other bloggers for future guest posts.

Weak: I plan to contact conferences and speak on [book topic].

Better: I am in contact with organizers at XYZ conferences, and have spoken at three events within the past year, reaching 5,000 people in my target audience.

Your plan should be executable without the help of a publisher. You should also mention if you'll be investing a portion of your advance (or a particular dollar amount) on marketing or a publicist.

OUTLINE

Include a short description of every chapter you plan to include in your book.

SAMPLE CHAPTER

This is your chance to demonstrate to publishers that you can successfully execute what you are proposing. Include a complete, well-written and well-researched chapter that will leave them hungry to read more.

PUTTING IT ALL TOGETHER

This all is a very cursory overview of a complex topic. For more information on how to craft a full book proposal, consult a resource such as *How to Write a Book Proposal: 4th Edition* by literary agent Michael Larsen (WD Books).

CONFERENCES

Make the most out of writing conferences by meeting agents, editors and peers.

....

by Ricki Schultz

If you've picked up this book, chances are, you're serious about writing and want to know how to advance to the next level. That said, no matter what the stage of your writing career, as a serious professional, you should attend writers' conferences.

Writers' conferences are events where writers gather together to see presentations and seminars from accomplished people in the industry. Some events last a day; others last a weekend. Others still may even last a week—but those are most likely *retreats*, which focus on sitting down to relax and write, rather than conferences, which are about mingling and learning. This article will address conferences—and all the reasons you should think about heading out to one this year.

REASONS TO ATTEND

Networking

First off, writing is a business. If you're looking to land an agent or sign a book deal with such-and-such a publisher, the chances of that happening without networking are slim to nonexistent; you have to get out there and make things happen. Conferences are golden opportunities to connect not only with industry professionals but with other writers as well.

Second, writing can be a *lonely* business. Although you might start out on a roll, you can also lose your flow in an instant. It's during those times that writers most need the advice, ideas, and companionship of other writers. Conferences are chock-full of people—just like you—who know what it's like to consider setting their manuscripts ablaze after yet another revision. If you've ever been rereading your manuscript and wished you had a friend who could give a critique, consider attending a conference because that is where you can meet such people—and critique partners are invaluable.

Seminars

Other than providing you with a place to rub elbows with industry professionals and other write-minded folks, writers' conferences offer myriad opportunities for you to learn more about the craft and business of writing. Published authors, as well as editors and agents, teach seminars and sit on panels. Presentation schedules vary, but they usually include sessions on everything from drafting query letters to developing characters.

Some presenters assign in-class exercises or homework; some divulge secrets on how they structure plot; but every conference is packed with tips on how to shape your writing. In addition, most offer group or one-on-one critique sessions with authors, agents and editors, so you can get specific feedback on how to attack your current project.

HOW TO CHOOSE AN EVENT

If you've made up your mind that you want to attend a conference but have no idea which one, it's all a matter of asking yourself some simple questions.

Do you want a general event, a specialized conference or a retreat?

General conferences are just what you think they are—events that are general in nature and geared toward all categories and levels of writers. There are hundreds of these nationwide every year, and most of the biggest fall under this category. However, just as there are plenty of general events, there are also conferences that focus on a particular category of writing. If you are writing children's books, romance, Christian themes or mystery/thriller, there are specialized conferences out there for you. Lastly, retreats are longer events designed to let writers write, rather than sit in on seminars or pitch agents.

What do you want to get out of the experience?

This question, obviously, is key. If you want to just focus and write—maybe finally finish that novel—then an intensive retreat is just what you need. Do you want to sit down and learn? Are you ready to pitch agents? If so, then you want to look for conferences that not only have agents in attendance, but that have agents in attendance who represent the category you're writing. This is where a specialized conference comes in handy. If you're writing Christian fiction, then all agents at a Christian conference should listen to your pitch. Bigger conferences often have a slew of editors and agents on the roster—but they also cost more. Start by looking local. You may find an event nearby that has a solid list of seminars and professionals as part of the conference.

MAXIMIZE THE EXPERIENCE

Here are some tips on how to maximize your conference experience and make a lasting impression on the industry's finest.

Be prepared

This involves doing some homework before the conference; however, it's worth the time and effort.

1. BUSINESS CARDS. Cards are a quick, inexpensive way to assert professionalism. Don't hand them out to literary agents, editors or authors (unless someone specifically asks), but do distribute them whenever you make a connection with another writer. Agents and editors will generally hand you a card if they're interested, and they will quickly give instructions on what to send them and how.

2. HAVE WORK HANDY. Even though it's extremely rare for agents and editors to request material from you (outside a pitch session), you want to be prepared for anything and everything—which means having your work handy at a moment's notice. Because agents vary in terms of preferences, print out a few hard copies of your first chapter and synopsis and stick them on your person at all times. For a more "green" option, carry a thumb drive with your first chapter and synopsis on it. That way, you can raid your hotel's business center and print or e-mail your work, should the need arise.

3. STUDY THE FACULTY. Another way to stand out from the crowd is to read up on the presenters. Not only will this prior knowledge aid you in choosing which sessions to attend, but it will also help you identify those individuals with whom you want to schmooze. Likewise, having studied up on the industry pros will ease the daunting task of talking to them. When you run into the editor from Your Dream Publishers, you will have something more to say than just an awkward hello.

IN PRACTICE: The second day of one of the conferences I attended, I sat with some faculty members—one being an editor who didn't represent my genre. This relieved me, as I was just looking for a friendly dinner that night. No pitching. Someone else asked what I was working on, so I gave a short synopsis of my manuscript. Later, the editor at our table approached me and requested some pages. She said that she had recently worked on a young adult book and was interested in building her list in that area. Even though I wasn't planning to pitch, I had one ready—and I had brought my work on a flash drive—so I was able to e-mail her with a partial right there. Score!

Dress the part

It's the oldest business advice in the world, but this simple cliché can help you stand out at writing conferences: Dress for success. As much as we might resist it because we're writers (and, therefore, averse to anything as cold and unfeeling as the business world), writing is a business. You have to be able to sell your writing—and the first way to do that at a conference is to sell people on you. You want to stand out in a positive way—and if you achieve that from something as simple as not wearing jeans, good for you. Your attire won't get you a book deal, but dressing in professional garb will make you pop against all the schlubs who didn't.

IN PRACTICE: At a conference, an agent who'd read some of my pages struck up a conversation, saying she liked my look in addition to the premise of my manuscript, and she thought I'd be marketable. This led to several other conversations throughout the conference—some about my manuscript and some about where I wanted my writing career to take me. And she wanted to see the rest of my manuscript.

As well, at a different writers' workshop, the agent who later became *my* agent approached me because she liked my dress (we had quite a funny conversation about it). Two years later, I mentioned said conversation in my query letter to her, and she remembered—and requested the full.

These opportunities did not present themselves *all* because of what I wore—but it definitely opened up the lines of communication and, with some follow-through, worked to my advantage. Plus, both agents had been to my website, my blog and my online community. I not only "dressed the part" in terms of actual clothing, but in building a platform as well.

Be visible

Sign up for any and all extras the conference offers, such as critiques, pitch sessions, slush fests and contests. Some of these things cost extra money, but they make the experience that much more worth it. Think of them as your takeaways, because you can gain much in terms of feedback, networking, and experience from each of them. Go to as many sessions as possible while you're there. You can't go to everything, but the more activities you attend, the more people you'll meet, the more you'll learn and the more visible you'll become. After all, how can those agents fall in love with you if they never see you? You can sleep when you get home. In addition, don't hide in the corner during sessions. Ask questions. You've got a unique opportunity to pick this pro's brain, so take advantage of it.

IN PRACTICE: I signed up for a query workshop at one conference I attended. Although I wasn't querying with my manuscript then, I had a query letter written. Always one for free feedback (sans a rejection), I read my pitch ... and the agent gave me a referral to one of her colleagues—all because I took advantage of a conference "extra" and had the guts to be "visible" within the class.

Be open

No one said going to these things isn't scary at first, but the more assertive you are, the more you'll get out of a conference.

ATTENDEES

Walking up to complete strangers may threaten your comfort levels—particularly because you might fear everyone there is more accomplished than you—but you need to do it anyway. If you can't think of a conversation starter, simply ask, "What do you write?" Every attendee fears the same things you do, and they're all dying to talk about what they're writing, what they're reading, whom they've queried, etc. If you overcome your initial nervousness, you'll stand out from the wallflowers and make connections.

Furthermore, talk to anyone and everyone. No matter where you are in your writing journey, be just as open to meeting folks with less experience as you are to meeting those with more. Who knows? The guy who just asked you what a literary agent is might be the next Stephen King. If you blow him off to schmooze some big-name agent, that will make just as much of an impression on him as if you'd been friendly; it just won't make the kind of impression you want.

IN PRACTICE: With conferences hosting agents, editors and bestselling authors, I always do my homework before arriving. At a recent conference, I approached some fellow writers at a cocktail hour. Because I'd done my research, I was able to give my new pals the scoop on the who's who around the patio.

INDUSTRY PROFESSIONALS

Even more frightening than chatting up conference attendees is approaching the agents, editors and authors of the faculty. Some of these people are famous; some of these people are from—gasp—New York City, and they all hold your publishing career in the palms of their hands.

One common misconception is that these people do not want to be bothered; on the contrary, agents and editors expect to field questions and hear pitches at conferences. If there is an opportunity to sit with one of them, take it. Don't stalk the person; just use your best judgment about appropriate times. Often at meals, the faculty will distribute themselves among the conference-goers, so these are perfect opportunities to get to know them.

IN PRACTICE: When researching presenters for a previous conference I attended, I saw that Chuck Sambuchino (editor of this book) and I actually shared a mutual friend. I used this fact to start up a conversation. That led to an invitation to dinner with other presenters and attendees. That dinner led to talk of freelance work (and this article you're now reading!). As well, at dinner, I ended up sitting next to an agent with whom I had scheduled a pitch session for the next day (eek!). Sharing that meal with her actually helped take the edge off when it came time for my pitch.

FOLLOW THROUGH

A last way you can stand out and make the most of a writers' conference happens after you return home—and it lies in the follow-through. If you got to know someone well enough to exchange information, take a few minutes to shoot your conference buddy an e-mail, saying how much you enjoyed chatting with her. Not only is this important in terms of fostering those sanity-saving writer groups, but you never know: The lady from Wichita, with whom you split the last sugar cookie, might snag an agent before you do—and if you stay in touch with her, you might have a potential referral to her agency within your grasp.

Ultimately, however, to start making splashes at writers' conferences, you first need to scrape together the dough and get to one. You already consider yourself to be a serious writer—now prove it.

IN PRACTICE: In the time since attending several recent events and conferences, I have followed up with many of the people I met. Some have become beta readers, critique partners—and friends. What's more, I blogged about the events, and some agents even commented on my posts!

RICKI SCHULTZ (rickischultz.com, @rickischultz) is an Ohio-based freelance writer and a recovering high school English teacher. She writes young adult fiction and, as coordinator of The Write-Brained Network (writebrainednetwork.com), she enjoys connecting with other writers. Ricki is represented by agent Barbara Poelle of the Irene Goodman Literary Agency.

DEBUT AUTHORS

14 first-time authors explain how they got published, and how you can, too.

compiled by Chuck Sambuchino

There's something fresh, inspiring, and amazing about debut novels. It's with that in mind that we collected 14 successful debuts from the past two years and sat down to ask the authors questions about how they broke in, what they did right and what advice they have for scribes who are trying to follow in their footsteps. These are writers of adult fiction, adult nonfiction, memoir and books for children—same as you—who saw their work come to life through hard work and determination. Read on to learn more about their individual journeys.

MEMOIR

❶ WENDY WELCH

WENDYWELCHBIGSTONEGAP.WORDPRESS.COM

The Little Bookstore of Big Stone Gap (OCT. 2012, ST. MARTIN'S)

QUICK TAKE: Two bibliophiles with no retail experience set in motion a comedy of errors when they move to the Appalachian Coalfields and start a used books shop, just as the economy tanks and e-readers debut—and manage to build a community.

WRITES FROM: Big Stone Gap, Va.

TIME FRAME: The draft of the book was about five months in the making, then working with my literary agent on the proposal was another two months.

ENTER THE AGENT: Pamela Malpas at Harold Ober Agency represents me. I sent a polite and carefully constructed letter, and Pamela asked to see the manuscript, then asked me to call.

BIGGEST SURPRISE: Bookstores are not dead in the public imagination and interest, no matter what anyone says. And second, as much as one hears about how the whole publishing industry turns on money and fame and who's bigger than who, suddenly here was this little silly story about a tiny bookshop and people were so happy for us.

DO DIFFERENT NEXT TIME: Work faster and more steadily on the edits instead of procrastinating.

PLATFORM: I had assets and resources to bring to a platform, but I didn't know what they were. St. Martin's Press taught me the value of Twitter and Pinterest (I was already a Facebook addict).

ADVICE FOR WRITERS: Be yourself. That way, if you do find someone interested in publishing what you have to say, it will be your voice and not a made-up person you feel trapped into being for the whole rest of the process. And celebrate every step from your first draft through hunting the agent, through hooking a publisher, through editing and marketing to publication day. Not only is publishing fickle, but the world is a pretty random place; you never know what will or won't happen tomorrow.

MAINSTREAM FICTION

② Jennifer Zobair
JENNIFERZOBAIR.COM

Painted Hands (JUNE 2013, THOMAS DUNNE BOOKS)

QUICK TAKE: A book about young, successful Muslim women in Boston, and the difficult choices they face when relationships with unlikely men shatter their friendship, and the current political climate threatens their careers.

WRITES FROM: Boston, Mass.

PRE-BOOK: I spent about a year writing short stories before I began *Painted Hands.* I have a real affection for short fiction, but my stories tended to span months or years. Eventually, I realized that what I really wanted to do was write a novel.

TIME FRAME: I started the book in the fall of 2009 and had a solid draft by Thanksgiving of 2010.

ENTER THE AGENT: I found my agent, Kent D. Wolf of Lippincott Massie McQuilkin through querying. I was looking for agents who were interested in multicultural and/or book club women's fiction, and Kent responded to my e-mail in less than an hour.

BIGGEST SURPRISE: That this is even happening is an incredible surprise. In that sense, the biggest surprises were when Kent offered representation, and spoke about the issues in the novel so respectfully and knowledgably, and when Toni Plummer from Thomas Dunne Books offered to acquire it and called it beautiful.

WHAT YOU DID RIGHT: I revised the manuscript many times and sought feedback from people I trust, both writers and non-writers. I worked just as hard on my query letter.

PLATFORM: I had a website, a connected blog, and a Twitter account (@jazobair) when I started querying.

ADVICE FOR WRITERS: Write the story you are passionate about, not what you think is trendy. You're going to live with your manuscript for a long time, you're going to have to revise and revisit and rethink, and you'd better love it and be committed to it. Trust your gut, but also listen to people who know more than you do.

GRIT LIT

 **③ FRANK BILL**

FRANKBILLSHOUSEOFGRIT.BLOGSPOT.COM

Donnybrook (MARCH 2012)

QUICK TAKE: "The Donnybrook" is a three-day bare-knuckle tournament in the sticks of southern Indiana. Twenty fighters. One wire-fence ring. Fight until only one man is left standing while rowdy onlookers bet on the fighters.

WRITES FROM: Southern Indiana

PRE-BOOK: I'd written two previous books. I found my voice by writing these two books—teaching myself how to write, focusing on style, form, structure and movement.

TIME FRAME: I wrote *Donnybrook* in about a 3–6 month span. This includes sending it to my agent, getting her notes, and me adding or cutting things.

ENTER THE AGENT: My mentor and a good friend mentioned the same agent, and told me to send my manuscript of stories to her. I did. Her name is Stacia Decker. She liked the stories and wanted to see a novel. I sent what I had on a story, and she signed me. The rest is history.

WHAT YOU LEARNED: Editors are your best friends and biggest fans. I'd heard so many horror stories about editors and publishing houses. I haven't had that. But then again they're the best and they're very passionate about their writers, and it shows.

WHAT YOU DID RIGHT: No matter how many rejection slips I got, I kept writing, reading and learning. I pushed myself to be better and better every time I put words on the page.

PLATFORM: After 2008, I had a small online following through Twitter, Facebook and my blog. And I still have all of that, but I also have a publisher and they give that extra reach and it's growing bit by bit.

ADVICE FOR WRITERS: Don't give up. Editors at the journals get thousands upon thousands of stories, and they only have maybe five or ten spots each quarter. That means as a writer, you have to write something different, moving and more active than anyone else. That also means developing your voice and your craft as a writer.

LITERARY FICTION

④ RYAN MCILVAIN
RYANMCILVAIN.COM
Elders (MARCH 2013, HOGARTH)

QUICK TAKE: A novel about two young Mormon missionaries in Brazil and the mental binds that their friendship and faith enforce on them.

WRITES FROM: Los Angeles, Calif.

PRE-BOOK: I was writing semiautobiographical short stories about doubters, people working hard at faith and having little to show for it. When one of the longer ones appeared in *The Paris Review*, I got excited about the stories and cobbled them together into a novel.

TIME FRAME: It took me six years, all told. From the first groping attempts at a book to the edited galleys of one. The successive drafts of my novel, and the tough reads from friends, had taught me that I was a fallen and deeply imperfect writer. All that mattered anymore was the product, the thing itself: I learned to slash whole chapters if they didn't work, my tender ego be damned.

ENTER THE AGENT: I met P.J. Mark of Janklow & Nesbit at the Bread Loaf Writers' Conference in Vermont and through the introduction of another friend, Stuart Nadler.

WHAT YOU LEARNED: I used to be skeptical when I heard about writers tossing complete drafts and starting "control-N" new, but now I'm less so. I still doubt that anybody truly trashes whole drafts in the age of hard drives, but to start from a blank page and with all the terror that entails? I believe it. I've done it myself.

DO DIFFERENT NEXT TIME: I think I might have saved two years of my writing life if I'd done the "control-N" new draft upfront—this instead of trying to cobble the short stories into a novel.

ADVICE FOR WRITERS: From the essayist and polymath Pat Madden: "Just keep on keeping on. That's the game."

MYSTERY

⑤ SUSAN SPANN
TWITTER.COM/SUSANSPANN
Claws of the Cat: A Shinobi Mystery **(MINOTAUR, JULY 2013)**

QUICK TAKE: When a samurai is murdered in a Kyoto teahouse, master ninja Hiro Hattori has three days to find the killer in order to save both the beautiful geisha accused of the crime and the Jesuit priest that Hiro has pledged his own life to protect.

WRITES FROM: Fair Oaks, Calif.

PRE-BOOK: In early 2011, I was standing in the bathroom preparing for work when an idea popped into my head: "Most ninjas commit murders, but Hiro Hattori solves them." I'd written some unpublished fiction before that, and published several nonfiction articles (in my role as a publishing attorney), but the minute Hiro popped into my mind, I knew I'd found my fiction niche—historical mystery. I studied medieval Japan in college, and I'm a lifelong fan of Japanese history and culture, so writing a mystery set in the samurai era seemed like a perfect fit—though I admit it took me a very long time to think of it.

TIME FRAME: I wrote the first draft in 30 days. (The editing took much longer.)

ENTER THE AGENT: I met my fantastic agent, Sandra Bond of Bond Literary Agency, at the Rocky Mountain Fiction Writers' Colorado Gold Conference.

WHAT YOU LEARNED: The biggest lesson I learned from the process? Keep writing, keep learning, and never stop improving your skills. Hard work and perseverance will eventually bring success, but the road isn't short, and it isn't paved with unicorns and rainbows.

WHAT YOU DID RIGHT: I never gave up and I kept moving forward instead of stalling out on a single story. When I had the next manuscript finished and polished, I put the older one in a digital drawer and started to query the new one. If I'd spent all those years revising my very first story, I never would have improved enough to write a mystery novel like *Claws of the Cat*.

DO DIFFERENT NEXT TIME: I'd have learned to accept real criticism sooner. Like most novice authors, I didn't seek out honest critique—or learn to appreciate its value—early enough.

ADVICE FOR WRITERS: Never give up; never surrender.

PICTURE BOOK

⑥ JESSE KLAUSMEIER

JESSEKLAUSMEIER.COM

Open This Little Book (**CHRONICLE, JAN. 2013**)

QUICK TAKE: *Open This Little Book* is my love letter to books; a conceptual and interactive book that takes readers on an unexpected journey of friendship and celebrates the love of reading.

WRITES FROM: Los Angeles, Calif.

PRE-BOOK: I worked for a small independent production studio and wrote and/or edited TV series treatments for network pitches, and copy for commercials, infomercials, and instructional/corporate videos. Later, at Nickelodeon, I worked on promos and series launches for their animated shows. I've always loved children's literature, so I joined the Society of Children's Book Authors and Illustrators (SCBWI) and that group played an instrumental role in me finding my publisher and my agent.

TIME FRAME: I first had the idea of a book about books-inside-of-books when I was five years old. About 4 pages in, I got distracted and quit. The idea of books within books stuck with me though, and I wrote the first draft of *Open This Little Book* 20 years later. Now, I'm so happy to be able to show young readers that their ideas are important, and their books could get published, too.

ENTER THE AGENT: I met my agent, Steve Fraser (Jennifer De Chiara Literary), at a SCBWI writing retreat in Encino. A year later, at that very same SCBWI writing retreat, I shared another manuscript (*Open This Little Book*) with editor Victoria Rock from Chronicle, who ended up acquiring it. When Victoria expressed interest, I got back in touch with Steve, and he signed me on.

WHAT YOU LEARNED: I sold the manuscript at the end of 2008, and it came out in January 2013.

WHAT YOU DID RIGHT: I think the best things I did were becoming an active member of SCBWI, getting the annual *Children's Writer's & Illustrator's Market* books, and really committing to learning the craft of writing for children. I read and studied hundreds of picture books.

PLATFORM: I'm on Facebook, Twitter (@jesseklausmeier), Pinterest, and I try to interact with people on all platforms.

WOMEN'S FICTION

⑦ AMY SUE NATHAN

AMYSUENATHAN.COM

The Glass Wives (MAY 2013, ST. MARTIN'S GRIFFIN)

QUICK TAKE: A single mom is compelled to take in her ex-husband's young widow and baby, causing secrets to be revealed as she redefines the meaning of family.

WRITES FROM: Near Chicago.

PRE-NOVEL: I started blogging and writing articles in 2006, and began freelancing for *The Chicago Tribune*. [Writing] short-form pieces left me wanting more—to dig deeper than a few thousand words allowed. I knew that if I wanted to write a story that addressed an important question such as "What makes a family?" I was going to need to write a novel.

TIME FRAME: The first words of what became *The Glass Wives* go back to 2007. For the first two years, the novel was written in first person. One day I had a hunch that if I rewrote in third person, the book would be more personal and intimate. I was right. What I learned from this was that it's never too late to make big changes.

ENTER THE AGENT: My agent is Jason Yarn of The Paradigm Agency, and we met through a QueryTracker contest.

WHAT YOU LEARNED: Writers I knew were landing book deals and experiencing other things I was working toward, so I made a decision to learn from them instead of begrudging them. I learned that another author's success doesn't infringe on mine.

WHAT YOU DID RIGHT: I know it's cliché, but I maintained a positive attitude (whenever possible) and kept writing through divorce, death, raising two kids alone, and starting a new career. Instead of having it all work against me, I put it to work for me. I also said a few prayers and crossed my fingers.

PLATFORM: My platform evolved because I really enjoyed blogging and social media right from the start. Now my platform includes Women's Fiction Writers, a Facebook page, and a few multi-author blogs such as The Debutante Ball and Book Pregnant. I'm also on Twitter and Facebook.

NEXT UP: I'm writing my next novel. It's about the trouble it all can get you into if you're not careful. Or even if you are.

TRAVEL / MEMOIR

⑧ MOSES GATES

MOSESGATES.COM

Hidden Cities: Travels to the Secret Corners of the World's Great Metropolises (**TARCHER, MARCH 2013**)

QUICK TAKE: A book of worldwide urban exploration and adventure.

WRITES FROM: New York City.

PRE-BOOK: I spent 2006 and 2007 doing a lot of crazy stuff. At the end of 2007, I climbed up the Notre Dame and got arrested. And I remember thinking, You know, I could totally write a book about all this.

TIME FRAME: By the time I got the deal, I had a bunch of essays written. I thought I'd put them together and knock it out in three months. It took me almost a year to write my first draft. Maybe 10 percent of it was stuff I'd written before. Somehow, the few new stories became the whole book.

ENTER THE AGENT: My agent is the talented and tenacious Alyssa Reuben of the Paradigm Agency. Yes—cold pitching to the slush pile does actually work on occasion.

WHAT YOU LEARNED: Deals are sealed on a handshake. After I got the deal, my agent told me I wouldn't get the contract for a few months. It took some convincing before I accepted that this meant I was 100 percent getting published.

WHAT YOU DID RIGHT: Just wrote well. What I really learned was that even though everyone's always talking about platform and marketing, good writing and voice still matter. The people that become literary agents and editors are people who believe in good writing and good storytelling.

DO DIFFERENT NEXT TIME: Ask for more time to review copy edits, which is where your voice and rhythm can really get screwed up.

NEXT UP: I worked as a double-decker tour bus guide for a while. There's something in there—maybe another memoir, maybe a novel.

FANTASY / SCIENCE FICTION

⑨ MICHAEL J. MARTINEZ

MICHAELJMARTINEZ.NET

The Daedalus Incident **(NIGHT SHADE BOOKS, MAY 2013)**

QUICK TAKE: In 2132, astronauts at a Martian mining colony face an incursion from another dimension—one in which 18th century sailing ships ply the void between worlds.

WRITES FROM: Northern New Jersey.

PRE-NOVEL: I've been in journalism for two decades, including stints at ABCNEWS.com and The Associated Press. Yet the idea for this book was always floating in the back of my mind, despite having zero experience writing fiction.

TIME FRAME: Back in 2003, I saw a poster for Disney's *Treasure Planet*. I was taken with the visual of a sailing ship in space and quickly rented the film. It wasn't good, so I figured I could do better, and soon I had 40,000 words of setting notes. I figured I would try it as a novel. The first draft was done in about three months.

ENTER THE AGENT: [After I queried her,] Sara Megibow of the Nelson Literary Agency asked for a partial—and then rejected it. However, she left the door open for me to work on it and re-submit. We ended up going back and forth three or four times over an eight-month period before she took me on.

WHAT YOU LEARNED: Publishing is a very subjective business. I was very surprised by comments from publishers who passed on the book before Night Shade Books acquired it. No two comments were the same, and some were diametrically opposed.

WHAT YOU DID RIGHT: My reporting experience compelled me to do my research in terms of getting an agent. I did my due diligence on each agent, making sure they represented my genre and had a good track record of placing authors with great publishers. And I followed their submissions guidelines exactly. It's an imperfect system, but it does work. I'm a slush pile find, after all.

DO DIFFERENT NEXT TIME: More revisions! Looking back, my book was nowhere near ready for submission. The book that Sara and I finally submitted to publishers was the eighth full revision.

NEXT UP: A second novel, which is the sequel to *The Daedalus Incident*.

CRIME FICTION

⑩ ROBERT LEWIS

ROBERTKLEWIS.COM

Untold Damage (APRIL 2013, MIDNIGHT INK)

QUICK TAKE: A former narcotics officer who is also a recovering junkie tries to find the answer to the mystery of his best friend's death.

WRITES FROM: Berkeley, Calif.

PRE-BOOK: I had written the original first Mark Mallen novel, but it didn't sell. During the time it was out to editors, I wrote a first draft of what I thought would be the second Mallen book. Well, when the first one didn't sell, I put the second book aside and figured I'd try something different—with a different protagonist, etc. That didn't work out so well. So, there I was, feeling incredibly desperate, when I came across this second book in my desk drawer. I had really forgotten all about it. I read it, and it worked me, so I went to work and banged it out fairly quickly. I'll never forget getting the e-mail from my agent saying, "YAY! I love it!"

ENTER THE AGENT: My agent is Barbara Poelle of the Irene Goodman Literary Agency, and I'm very lucky to have her in my corner. I would have like 10,000 of her babies if she asked me. Seriously though, she's been a great mentor, sounding board, and advocate.

WHAT YOU LEARNED: The biggest learning experience was adapting to the fact that my book was no longer really an artistic endeavor but was now a product that needed to sell units. It becomes a business, and you need to conduct yourself accordingly.

WHAT YOU DID RIGHT: I believe that having patience, never giving up, and working on my craft all went together to help me break in. I mean, heck, I had been trying to get published for over seven years! I worked on my writing six days a week after coming home from my day job.

PLATFORM: When I got together with Barbara, she told me to start blogging. She also hooked me up with a blogging job over at the place for fans of crime fiction: CriminalElement.com. And I'm on Twitter.

NEXT UP: I'm at work on the second Mallen book.

YOUNG ADULT

11 AMANDA SUN
AMANDASUNBOOKS.COM
Ink: The Paper Gods Series **(JUNE 2013, HARLEQUIN TEEN)**

QUICK TAKE: After her mother's death, 16-year-old Katie moves to Japan, where she crosses paths with her new school's kendo star, whose drawings come to life in dangerous ways.

WRITES FROM: Toronto

PRE-NOVEL: I had a few short stories published in anthologies—one literary fiction set in Japan, and two YA Fantasy stories—but I really wanted to write something that combined my interests. The Paper Gods series is inspired by my own time living in Japan, and is a way to write both what I love and what I know.

TIME FRAME: The first half was written in the fall of 2009 and the second half in the spring of 2010. I posted an excerpt of *Ink* in an online blog contest, where it was spotted by an agent who asked me to query her as soon as the project was ready. I didn't end up signing with that agent, but her belief in the project helped give me the courage to keep going.

ENTER THE AGENT: I queried Melissa Jeglinski of The Knight Agency through the recommendation of a mutual friend. Melissa was a dream agent to me, and I'd queried her before with earlier projects.

BIGGEST SURPRISE: The glowing rejections I received. Who knew agents and editors could praise your work and still turn you down? It turns out rejections aren't so much about "no" as about finding the right person for your work. You need an agent and editor who get your vision and can push you. It takes time for the stars to align.

WHAT YOU DID RIGHT: I was aware of the market. I started following 50 YA blogs and reading every novel I could get my hands on. Then I wrote *Ink*, and it sold quickly.

DO DIFFERENT NEXT TIME: I think it's easy to get hung up on querying a novel and forget to keep writing new ones. The second novel I wrote is the one that sold, and I held back that success by focusing too much on the first project.

PLATFORM: I spend a healthy dose of time on social media every day. My book is set in Japan, so I also like to go to anime conventions and chat with readers there.

NEXT UP: Book Two of The Paper Gods series, out in 2014.

HISTORICAL FICTION

⑫ ALISON ATLEE

ALISONATLEE.COM

The Typewriter Girl (JAN. 2013, GALLERY BOOKS)

QUICK TAKE: Scandalous, "ruined" Betsey Dobson fights to make an independent living among the upper class at an 1890s seaside resort.

WRITES FROM: Kentucky.

PRE-BOOK: I'd been trying to break into the romance genre, but was told several times that my voice wasn't "right" for romance. I didn't quite understand or believe that until the person who became my agent said, "There's more to this story and place you've created; let's bring it out."

TIME FRAME: This book was really about the revisions, which took about two years with my agent, and then even more with my editor. I'd always thought of myself as a writer who worked meticulously on a first draft, and thus avoided heavy revisions. Learning I don't have to work that way was both tough and valuable.

ENTER THE AGENT: I made an initial query list by looking at agent rosters for smaller regional writing conferences, thinking those agents were seeking new clients more actively. A valid rationale? I don't know, but Emmanuelle Morgen [of Stonestong Literary] was in that first list.

WHAT YOU LEARNED: How long the contract takes. I knew of things going horribly wrong even after the deal, so I was eager to have the actual contract in my hand.

WHAT YOU DID RIGHT: One, studied craft. Two, never quit. Three, risked leaving one agent to find a better fit for me.

DO DIFFERENT NEXT TIME: I do wonder if taking time off from my day job would have led to selling earlier.

NEXT UP: I'm working on another historical novel.

LITERARY FICTION

⓭ TARA CONKLIN

TARACONKLIN.COM

The House Girl (LITERARY FICTION, WILLIAM MORROW, 2013)

QUICK TAKE: The lives of two indomitable young women—a slave in antebellum Virginia and a lawyer in modern-day New York—intersect in a story about truth, love and justice.

WRITES FROM: Seattle, Wash.

PRE-BOOK: I had written stories ever since childhood, but I considered it a hobby and never tried seriously to have anything published. When I began *The House Girl*, I didn't think I was writing a novel, but I couldn't get the characters out of my head, so I kept writing.

TIME FRAME: It was about four years from first word until I sent the manuscript off to agents.

ENTER THE AGENT: My agent is the fabulous Michelle Brower of Folio Literary Management. I found her the old-fashioned way: with a cold query. On the Folio website, her description of the fiction she was looking to represent summarized exactly the book that I had written.

BIGGEST SURPRISE: After hearing so many horror stories about big publishing houses, I've been wonderfully surprised by the warmth and enthusiasm of everyone I've been lucky enough to work with.

WHAT YOU DID RIGHT: First, I worked very hard. I wrote, rewrote, and rewrote again before sending the manuscript off to agents. Second, I carefully researched agents and only contacted those whom I felt certain would love the book.

DO DIFFERENT NEXT TIME: I probably should have believed in myself earlier. I always wanted to be a writer, but it took many years before I had the confidence and chutzpah to really give it a go.

PLATFORM: I'm a regular contributor to popcorntheblog.wordpress.com, a blog about all things writing. I have a website, Facebook author page, and Twitter feed.

NEXT UP: I'm working on my second novel, tentatively titled *This is the Sea*.

NONFICTION / SPIRITUALITY

14 ANNIE KAGAN AFTERLIFEOFBILLYFINGERS.COM

The Afterlife of Billy Fingers: How My Bad-Boy Brother Proved to Me That There's Life After Death (**HAMPTON ROADS**, **MARCH 2013**)

QUICK TAKE: The true story of how my brother Billy began communicating with me several weeks after he died.

WRITES FROM: East Hampton, New York.

PRE-BOOK: I was a successful chiropractor in New York City when I began a serious meditation practice. Without knowing what the future held, I gave up being a chiropractor, moved to a secluded house by the water and began writing songs. Soon, my brother Billy, who had a problem with addiction, came back into my life and although I tried to save him, it was too late. When he woke me a few weeks after his death to describe his journey through the afterlife, I wrote down every word.

TIME FRAME: The book happened on Billy's schedule. It took about three years to have a complete draft, and strange as it sounds, Billy edited it with me from the other side.

ENTER THE AGENT: My agent is Claire Gerus who has her own boutique agency. I chose her over an agent at a much larger agency because Claire knew the genre and was passionate.

ALONG THE WAY: Even though it wasn't easy, I said "no" to people who knew a lot more about writing than I did. During my music career, I had put the artistic sensibilities of the guy with the Grammys over my own, and I didn't like the way my album turned out. I vowed never to do that again.

WHAT YOU DID RIGHT: I got great endorsements from other writers in the field. I had no platform at all starting out. I remedied that by asking the great Raymond Moody, author of the international bestseller *Life After Life*, to write the foreword to my book.

CHUCK SAMBUCHINO (chucksambuchino.com, @chucksambuchino on Twitter) edits the *Guide to Literary Agents* (guidetoliteraryagents.com/blog) as well as the *Children's Writer's & Illustrator's Market*. His pop humor books include *How to Survive a Garden Gnome Attack* (film rights optioned by Sony) and *Red Dog / Blue Dog: When Pooches Get Political* (reddog-bluedog.com). Chuck's other writing books include *Formatting & Submitting Your Manuscript, 3rd. Ed.*, and *Create Your Writer Platform* (fall 2012). Besides that, he is a husband, guitarist, sleep-deprived new father, dog owner, and cookie addict.

THE MEMOIR MARKET

*Top agents get real about what you
need to know to break in.*

....

by Jessica Strawser

Objectivity can be hard for even the most skilled writers to achieve—particularly when the stories they're writing are, by definition, personal. Still, if we want our work to be read, we need to be able to view it from the perspective of a reader. Does the story get your attention right away? Does the language carry you smoothly from one scene to the next? Is this something you would relate to, stay up late reading, recommend to your friends?

When your story is one you've lived rather than imagined, honest assessments like these can be tougher than ever to make—and understandably so. But if you're writing a memoir— one you want to publish for an audience beyond your family and friends, that is—it's imperative to understand where your work fits in. Will there be a market for a book like yours? If no one knows who you are, will anyone care about your story? Can you really transform your own remarkable (or not so remarkable) experiences into a work with appeal to a broad audience? The earlier you can answer these questions, the better off you'll be.

To help you get started, we've assembled a round table of agents in the genre to reveal the inside story on the market for memoir. We didn't hesitate to ask the tough questions— and they didn't hold back on answering. The bad news: Sometimes it seems like everyone is writing a memoir—and not everyone's story warrants one. The good news: Demand for the genre doesn't seem to be fading, so that means there's still room to break in. And, as with everything else in publishing, knowing how to increase your chances really can put you ahead of the game.

Read on to find out how.

THE ROUND TABLE

1. Laney Katz Becker (laney@marksonthoma.com) is an agent at Markson Thoma Literary Agency in New York. Prior to becoming an agent, Becker was an advertising copywriter, freelance journalist and award-winning author of fiction and nonfiction. Today, she uses her writing skills to help her authors shape their projects. She loves a great memoir, especially if it teaches her something new, exposes her to a different culture/country or has a great voice. Becker specializes in debut authors; her "newbies" have made both national and international bestseller lists.

2. Mollie Glick is an agent at Foundry Literary + Media (foundrymedia. com) specializing in literary fiction, memoir and narrative nonfiction. Her recent projects include Ellen Bryson's *The Transformation of Bartholomew Fortuno*, Zoe Klein's *Drawing in the Dust* and Jonathan Evison's *All About Lulu*. She also recently closed a seven-figure sale for Josephine Angelini's young adult series, *Starcrossed*.

3. Jeff Kleinman (foliolit.com) is a literary agent, intellectual property attorney and founding partner of Folio Literary Management. As an agent, Kleinman feels privileged to have the chance to learn an incredible variety of new subjects, meet an extraordinary range of people and feel, at the end of the day, that he's helped to build something—a wonderful book, perhaps, or an author's career. His authors include Garth Stein, Robert Hicks, Charles Shields, Bruce Watson, Neil White and Philip Gerard.

4. Byrd Leavell, a graduate of the University of Virginia and the Radcliffe Publishing Program, began his career at Carlisle & Company and then served as an agent at InkWell Management and Venture Literary. He is now in his fifth year as an agent at The Waxman Literary Agency (waxmanagency.com). His clients include Justin Halpern, John Parker Jr., Scott Sigler, Patrick McEnroe, Mark Frauenfelder and Tucker Max; he has represented several bestsellers.

5. Sharlene Martin founded Martin Literary Management (martinliterarymanagement.com) in 2003. She has since represented several *New York Times* bestselling nonfiction books, including Jane Velez-Mitchell's *iWant*, Mary Jo Buttafuocco's *Getting It Through My Thick Skull*, Brooke and Keith Desserich's *Notes Left Behind* and Suzanne Hansen's *You'll Never Nanny in This Town Again*. She is the co-author, with Anthony Flacco, of *Publish Your Nonfiction Book: Strategies for Learning the Industry, Selling Your Book and Building a Successful Career.*

What characteristics can make a memoir from an unknown writer marketable?

SHARLENE MARTIN: First of all, it needs a solid concept for the book that invites the reader's concerns into the experience of reading it, instead of just saying, "Let me tell you all about wonderful me." [It also needs] great writing, which means an identifiable narrative voice, a tone that is appropriate to the subject, an awareness of the need to keep a reader turning pages, and a thorough demonstration of spelling, grammar and syntax.

JEFF KLEINMAN: No. 1: Voice. More and more these days, the writer's voice—its memorability, the distinctiveness with which the author describes scenes, characters, events—really can make it stand apart. There are lots of potential factors that can make a memoir "unputdownable" (and therefore marketable), but these days that voice seems absolutely critical. No. 2: Premise. Books need to be able to distinguish themselves from the others. It's really tough—for an agent, editor or bookseller—to sell a book that sounds like all the others, that makes the reader think, "Yeah, I've read that kind of book before." So having a truly unique, special, compelling premise can make a huge difference. No. 3: The author's platform. The author may be "unknown," but having published materials in well-known, preferably national, forums can provide a useful link to the buyer: *I may not know who this writer is, but I know the paper she writes for, and I love/like/trust it*, is what you want your buyer thinking.

LANEY KATZ BECKER: Unknown is the key word in that question. Platform is more important than ever when it comes to previously unpublished authors. If you can bring a readership with you—[say,] because of your huge following on Facebook, Twitter or other social media—that counts for a lot. Previously published essays and/or articles are also enticing, especially if the magazine or journal will commit to running more of your work once the memoir pubs. And, of course, any broadcast media appearances help prove that your story is marketable and appealing to a wide audience.

BYRD LEAVELL: The easy answer is of course the writing. But if the story doesn't sound extremely interesting and/or unique, the writer is pretty much going to have to be Faulkner to get editors excited. Of course, "writing" and "story" are not exactly brain-busting answers to this question. Maybe the best way to [answer this] is to walk through the steps of a memoir submission. Usually, an agent and author will work for months to put together a 30–50 page proposal that lays the book out in detail. The agent will then get on the phone and call a carefully assembled list of editors (the submission list) and will describe (sell) each one over the phone on the strengths of this particular memoir. For me, this is usually going to involve some combination of the following: the strength or power of the narrative, the emotional impact it creates, and then the potential audience—because these are all the things that draw me to a good memoir in the first place. Basically, if you're *unknown*, you need a great story, and then you need to hit a 450-foot home run with your proposal that blows editors out of their chairs and has them visualizing tens or even hundreds of thousands of sales.

Which popular types of memoirs do you see as approaching a saturation point? Which do you see as areas to watch that could turn into the next memoir trend?

MARTIN: On some days it seems as though every therapist in the country who is dealing with addicts of one kind or another has told them to journal their recovery and then turn it into a book. Quitting booze or drugs is a good thing to do, but it isn't the triumph of the human spirit.

MOLLIE GLICK: I'm sick of dysfunctional family stories, but I'm a big fan of memoirs by people who have lived lives the rest of us only dream of.

KLEINMAN: Memoirs about a guy (or woman) and his dog seem particularly challenging in this post–*Marley & Me* universe. Publishers keep cranking them out, and the public seems to keep buying them, but at, I suspect, lower levels than before. Another area that seems a bit challenging is war memoirs—from Afghanistan or Iraq—by either embedded journalists or service personnel. Finally, though books by cancer/disease survivors are prevalent, I find them very tough to sell to publishers (unless the survivor has some kind of name recognition). As for the "next big thing," I only wish I knew. I keep expecting Vietnam War memoirs to make a huge resurgence, but it hasn't happened yet.

LEAVELL: I guess I approach the entire genre as though it's already completely saturated. The key is finding a story, or a way to tell it, that separates your book from everything out there. When I'm working with a client, I try to steer them away from, "I was born in a big/small town, and I liked listening to punk music, and I hated my mother and blahdee blahda blah blah." If you want to separate your story, find a way to tell it that focuses 100 percent on the reader and cuts out all the writing that is just there for your own ego. What do people want to read? I think they want to read one great story after another, with all the usual navel-gazing exposition cut out. And this is exactly what I try and get my clients to write.

What factors in a query or in the opening pages of a memoir will make you want to read more?

BECKER: For me, it's all about a fresh story, told in a unique voice. I want the writer's personality to ooze through the pages. I expect the writing to come to life. I especially enjoy a story that has the same page-turning momentum I look for in compelling fiction.

LEAVELL: Aggressive, confident, well-written prose that immediately finds a way to show the reader this is a book that is going to be one "unputdownable"—straight from their keyboard to your brain—story that you are going to enjoy every minute of.

KLEINMAN: Premise—above all, the premise. I read that one- or two-sentence description of what the book is about and I think, "Wow, what an *amazing* story!" That almost never happens, but when it does, it really makes me pay attention. [Then], I can get a sense, immediately, from the query and/or opening pages, whether I'm in the hands of a master craftsman—a writer who really can describe, entertain, absorb me in her world. So many times I read an intriguing premise and then I'm disappointed in its execution. The writing just doesn't hold up: Descriptions are trite, dialogue seems invented or clumsy, characters don't come alive on the page, and so on.

GLICK: Wanting to turn the page! I really look for the same thing in a memoir that I do in a novel. If I have a manuscript with me on the subway, would I rather read the submission than whatever book I'm lugging around that day?

What are the most common mistakes you see in queries?

GLICK: Assuming that readers have background knowledge about an author's life. Assuming that we want to hear everything that ever happened to them. Neglecting to tell a story with a narrative arc.

KLEINMAN: It always boils down to a failure of the same issues, again and again: tired-sounding premise ("This is a story of my growing up in Brooklyn in the 1950s") or weak writing ("Dear Mr. Kleinman: I am writing my story. It is a good story. You should read it."), or both.

BECKER: Everyone thinks his/her story is interesting, but that doesn't mean it should be published. Think about whether your story has universal appeal, and if it doesn't, figure out whether it could be refocused so it does. Also, I sell all memoir by proposal *only*, so if I ask authors for a proposal and they write back telling me they have a full manuscript so they don't need a proposal, that's not good. What's worse? When they say they don't have a proposal, but will get me one next week. Writing a good proposal takes time—months, even—so I prefer authors not query me until they already have a solid, polished proposal. I also hate it when queries from writers tell me that they've given the manuscript to their: a) students; b) book club; c) friends; d) family; or e) all of the above. These writers say that they've given their manuscript to a bunch of people I don't know and *everyone* loves it—like that should mean something to me. It doesn't. Unless of course any of those people is a bestselling author, major celebrity, book reviewer—in which case, their endorsement is worth a mention—you're better off to omit the praise from the peanut gallery.

MARTIN: Many new memoirists mistakenly think that just because they are writing it, the world is hungry to read it. They want to begin with their day of birth and slowly roll us all up the long hill of their childhood, when their actual story does not begin until many years later. In a memoir, write your life as if it's an action movie, even if there is no action in it. Constantly pull the reader's attention back to the book.

LEAVELL: Think about the reader and, even more so, about John Q. Bookbrowser spending 10 minutes in the Barnes & Noble in Wichita. Why on God's green earth is he going to spend $25 and then commit hours of his life to reading about you? Answer that question, and you're golden.

How much can memoirists blur the line between fact and fiction?

BECKER: They can't. Unless of course they lead with an author's note letting readers know that what they're reading is actually a fictionalized memoir.

LEAVELL: If your book is a memoir, it has to be 100 percent true. End of story. If you slightly dramatize the story to make it read better, I have no problem with that. Find me someone who doesn't do that every time they tell a story at a bar.

GLICK: I don't believe memoirists should be making things up. Period. That said, a memoir is obviously a writer's subjective take on what happened in his/her life. And I also think it's totally fine to edit out events or periods of time to build a narrative arc. In other words, I think it's fine to edit events out, I just don't believe in adding events in.

KLEINMAN: Yikes, I don't want to know. In general, I'm OK with some invented dialogue—if it seems realistic and believable—but I'm not OK with inventing scenes, combining characters and so forth. This is really a tricky issue, and will absolutely depend on the book and the writer's style, talent and voice. It may make sense for writers to get a subscription to the magazine *Creative Nonfiction*, which wrestles often with this issue.

MARTIN: If you are talking about a memoir, then you cannot. It makes no difference if a few other crooks have done it. Memoir by definition is supposed to be factual.

How can writers with memoirs-in-progress make honest, objective determinations about whether or not their books are viable candidates for traditional publication, or might be better suited for self-publication?

GLICK: That's a good question! I think one way to evaluate this is: Can you do a quick, one-line elevator pitch describing the topic of your memoir? What angle does it take? Unless you're very famous, no one wants to hear your life story, and a memoir isn't a summary of everything that's ever happened to you. It's a book that follows the line of one of the major threads in your life.

LEAVELL: Imagine how hard you think the market is for a completely unknown writer trying to sell their memoir. OK, now multiply that by a gazillion, and put St. Peter at the gate, and he's in a very bad mood. That's how hard the market is. Don't get me wrong: All of that can be overcome if you have a proposal that delivers on all the points that I mentioned above. If you don't, it probably isn't going to happen for you. But then, the best thing about publishing today is that it's possible for writers to go out and, entirely on their own, show what their books are capable of in the marketplace. There isn't an editor in all of publishing who isn't going to be interested in an author who's single-handedly sold 10,000–15,000 copies of their book—which is becoming more and more doable with each passing day.

BECKER: The category of memoir, like fiction, is very subjective, so there's not a good answer to this question. *But*, some questions that might help you sort out whether your memoir is viable for traditional publication include:

1. If the reader doesn't know you, would they care? Why?
2. Is there a universal story/theme? What is it? (Is it a transformation story? An inspirational tale? A cautionary tale? Coming of age?)
3. If you summed up your story in one to two sentences, would my response be, "Wow!"?
4. How truly different is your story—and is it different enough to warrant publishing yet another book on the topic?

KLEINMAN: Step 1: Go to your local bookstore. (If your local bookstore is small, find the closest "big" bookstore, because they'll have more books than many independents.) Find the shelf where your memoir will go. Are there a lot of other similar books? If so, that may be an indicator that the area's pretty overpublished. Similarly, if there are no other books, that may indicate that it's not an area that's done particularly well. Step 2: Assess your book. Assess: a) Its message—is this a message that will appeal to a large group of people, nationwide? Or a specific group of people, or a specific region? Then assess: b) Your writing—how well, honestly, do you write? If you think you write very well, find a local writers' group and get someone else's opinion. A client of mine often says to me, "Just because you dance at your friend's wedding doesn't mean you're ready for a national ballroom dancing competition." That dancing champion is pretty much what agents (and publishers) are looking for. Step 3: Send your query out to 10 agents. If none of them respond, rewrite your query letter, focusing on the writing and making the premise more memorable. Send to another 10. If you still don't have a positive response, really take a hard look at the writing and premise, to see if they fall into any of the traps I mentioned before. If you send out the manuscript to 50 publishing professionals (agents, editors at smaller presses, etc.) and you don't have any bites, you might want to look very seriously into self-publishing.

MARTIN: Anyone who can complete a memoir deserves to see it in print, as far as I'm concerned, but that may not mean mainstream commercial publication. Self-publishing is now available to anyone at very little cost.

What is the best thing aspiring memoir writers can do to begin to establish platforms for their work? How important is it for them to do so?

GLICK: If you've got an amazing story to tell and you write well, that's enough for me. That said, having a popular blog and/or publishing personal essays in national magazines won't hurt your case!

BECKER: The platform is super important right now. Publishers often pass on projects they love because they can't get enough in-house support. Why? Because the author didn't have a strong enough platform! Writers could start with the Internet to build their readership through social networking sites and blogging. They should find a way to capture e-mail addresses whenever possible. Writers should also work on getting their writing published, online and off. Try to get speaking gigs in front of audiences that would be likely readers. Forget, "If you build it/publish it they will come," and shift your focus toward figuring out how you can bring readers with you. Agents and publishers will love you for it—and you'll find your path to publishing is much, much easier.

KLEINMAN: An Internet presence is often very helpful. If you have 300,000 followers, you'll find it much easier to get a book deal than if you have three. The higher your profile, the less strong the premise and the writing have to be—we can always find you a ghostwriter, if you have a significant national presence.

LEAVELL: The tools are out there. Put great content up on a website, and then find a way to start drawing people to read it. It's no secret that publishers want writers who are adept at creating fans. Prove that you are one of them.

QUERIES VS. PROPOSALS

Because memoirs are narrative stories that, though nonfiction, flow much the way a novel does, some agents prefer that you send a query letter for your memoir just as you would for a novel. Other agents treat memoirs like other nonfiction submissions and prefer that you send a book proposal up front.

This means you'll need to pay special attention to the guidelines of any given agent before you submit. It also means you'll likely need to do double duty in preparing your submissions materials before you send out anything at all. You don't want to find yourself in a situation where an agent requests materials you don't have at the ready. This is especially tricky when it comes to the manuscript itself. Agents who require queries will expect the full manuscript to already be completed (and revised, and polished). The agents who require proposals, on the other hand, may be expecting to have input into the shape of your story before it's written.

Frustrating? Yes. Avoidable? No. Your best course of action is to err on the side of being as prepared as you can, and trust that all your hard work will pay off later.

CREATE YOUR WRITER PLATFORM

8 fundamental rules for author visibility.

....

by Chuck Sambuchino

The chatter about the importance of a writer platform builds each year. Having an effective platform has never been more important than right now. With so many books available and few publicists left to help promote, the burden now lies upon the author to make sure copies of their book fly off bookshelves. In other words, the pressure is on for writers to act as their own publicist and chief marketer, and very few can do this successfully.

Know that if you're writing nonfiction, a damn good idea won't cut it. You need to prove that people will buy your book by showing a comprehensive ability to market yourself through different channels such as social networking sites and traditional media. If you can't do that, a publisher won't even consider your idea.

WHAT IS PLATFORM?

Platform, simply put, is your visibility as an author. In other words, platform is your personal ability to sell books right this instant. Better yet, I've always thought of platform like this: When you speak, who listens? In other words, when you have a something to say, what legitimate channels exist for you to release your message to audiences who will consider buying your books/services?

Platform will be your key to finding success as an author, especially if you're writing nonfiction. Breaking the definition down, realize that platform is your personal ability to sell books through:

1. Who you are
2. Personal and professional connections you have
3. Any media outlets (including personal blogs and social networks) that you can utilize to sell books

In my opinion, the following are the most frequent building blocks of a platform:

1. A blog of impressive size
2. A newsletter of impressive size
3. Article/column writing (or correspondent involvement) for the media—preferably for larger publications, radio, and TV shows
4. Contributions to successful websites, blogs and periodicals helmed by others
5. A track record of strong past book sales that ensures past readers will buy your future titles
6. Networking, and your ability to meet power players in your community and subject area
7. Public speaking appearances—especially national ones; the bigger the better
8. An impressive social media presence (such as on Twitter or Facebook)
9. Membership in organizations that support the successes of their own
10. Recurring media appearances and interviews—in print, on the radio, on TV, or online
11. Personal contacts (organizational, media, celebrity, relatives) who can help you market at no cost to yourself, whether through blurbs, promotion or other means.

Not all of these methods will be of interest/relevance to you. As you learn more about to how to find success in each one, some will jump out at you as practical and feasible, while others will not. And to learn what constitutes "impressive size" in a platform plank, check out this article: **tinyurl.com/8d2hnrj**.

"PLATFORM" VS. "PUBLICITY"

Platform and publicity are interconnected yet very different. Platform is what you do before a book comes out to make sure that when it hits shelves, it doesn't stay there long. Publicity is an active effort to acquire media attention for a book that already exists. In other words, platform falls upon the author, whereas (hopefully) publicity will be handled by a publicist, either in-house or contracted for money.

Do something right now: Go to Amazon.com and find a book for sale that promises to teach you how to sell more books. Look at the comparable titles below it and start scrolling left to right using the arrows. (Do it now. I'll wait.) Tons of them, aren't there? It's because so many authors are looking for any way possible to promote their work, especially the many self-published writers out there. They've got a book out—and now they realize copies aren't selling. Apparently having your work online to buy at places like Amazon isn't enough to have success as a writer. That's why we must take the reins on our own platform and marketing.

> As a last thought, perhaps consider it like this: Publicity is about asking and wanting: gimme gimme gimme. Platform is about giving first, then receiving because of what you've given and the goodwill it's earned you.

THE FUNDAMENTAL PRINCIPLES OF PLATFORM

1. It is in giving that we receive.

In my experience, this concept—*it is in giving that we receive*—is the fundamental rule of platform, and it will rear its head in every chapter of this book, over and over again. Building a platform means that people follow your updates, listen to your words, respect and trust you, and, yes, will consider buying whatever it is you're selling. But they will only do that if they like you—and the way you get readers to like you is by legitimately helping them. Answer their questions. Give them stuff for free. Share sources of good, helpful information. Make them laugh and smile. Inform them and make their lives easier and/or better. Do what they cannot: cull together information or entertainment of value. Access people and places they want to learn more about. Help them achieve their goals. Enrich their lives. After they have seen the value you provide, they will want to stay in contact with you for more information. They begin to like you, and become a follower. And the more followers you have, the bigger your platform becomes.

2. You don't have to go it alone.

Creating a large and effective platform from scratch is, to say the least, a daunting task. But you don't have to swim out in the ocean alone; you can—and are encouraged to—work with others. There are many opportunities to latch on to bigger publications and groups in getting your words out. And when your own platform outlets—such as a blog—get large enough, they will be a popular source for others seeking to contribute guest content. You will find yourself constantly teaming with others on your way up, and even after you've found some success.

3. Platform is what you are *able* to do, not what you are *willing* to do.

I review nonfiction book proposals for writers, and in each of these proposals there is a marketing section. Whenever I start to read a marketing section and see bullet points such as "I am happy to go on a book tour" or "I believe that Fox News and MSNBC will be interested in this book because it is controversial," then I stop reading—because the proposal has a big problem. Understand this immediately: Your platform is not pie-in-the-sky thinking. It is not what you hope will happen or maybe could possibly hopefully happen sometime if you're lucky and all the stars align when your publicist works really hard. It's also not what you are willing to do, such as "be interviewed by the media" or "sign books at trade events."

(Everyone is willing to do these things, so by mentioning them, you are making no case for your book because you're demonstrating no value.) The true distinction for writer platform is that it must be absolutely what you can make happen right now.

4. You can only learn so much about writer platform by instruction, which is why you should study what others do well and learn by example.

I don't know about you, but, personally, I learn from watching and doing better than I learn from reading. On that note, don't be afraid to study and mimic what others are doing. If you are looking for totally original ideas on how to blog and build your platform, I'll just tell you right now there likely are few or none left. So if you want to see what's working, go to the blogs and websites and Twitter feeds and newspaper columns of those you admire—then take a page from what they're doing. If you start to notice your favorite large blogs include all their social networking links at the top ("Find me on Twitter," "Find me on Facebook"), then guess what? Do the same. If people are getting large followings doing book reviews of young adult fantasy novels, why not do the same?

5. You must make yourself easy to contact.

I have no idea why people make themselves difficult to contact without a website and/or e-mail listed online. Besides "visibility," another way to think about platform is to examine your reach. And if your goal is reach, you do not want to limit people's abilities to find and contact you much if at all. You want people to contact you. You want other writers to e-mail from out of the blue. I love it when a member of the media finds my info online and writes me. I don't even mind it when a writer sends me an e-mail with a random question. I've made long-term friends that way—friends who have bought my book and sung my praises to others. It's called networking—and networking starts by simply making yourself available, and taking the next step to encourage people with similar interests or questions to contact you.

6. Start small and start early.

A true writer platform is something that's built before your book comes out, so that when the book hits your hands, you will be above the masses for all to see. I won't lie—the beginning is hard. It's full of a lot of effort and not a whole lot of return. Fear not; this will pass. Building a platform is like building a structure—every brick helps. Every brick counts. Small steps are not bad. You must always be considering what an action has to offer and if it can lead to bigger and better things. "What frustrates most people is that they want to have platform now," says literary agent Roseanne Wells of the Marianne Strong Literary Agency. "It takes time and a lot of effort, and it builds on itself. You can always have more platform, but trying to sell a book before you have it will not help you."

7. Have a plan, but feel free to make tweaks.

At first, uncertainty will overwhelm you. What are you going to blog about? How should you present yourself when networking? Should your Twitter handle be your name or the title of your book/brand? All these important questions deserve careful thought early on. The earlier you have a plan, the better off you will be in the long run—so don't just jump in blind. The more you can diagram and strategize at the beginning, the clearer your road will be.

As you step out and begin creating a writer platform, make sure to analyze how you're doing, then slowly transition so you're playing to your strengths and eliminating your weakest elements. No matter what you want to write about, no matter what platform elements you hone in on, don't ignore the importance of analysis and evolution in your journey. Take a look at what you're doing right and wrong to make sure you're not throwing good money after bad. And feel free to make all kinds of necessary tweaks and changes along the way to better your route.

8. Numbers matter—so quantify your platform

If you don't include specific numbers or details, editors and agents will be forced to assume the element of platform is unimpressive, which is why you left out the crucial detail of its size/reach. Details are sexy; don't tease us. Try these right and wrong approaches below:

WRONG: "I am on Twitter and just love it."
CORRECT: "I have more than 10,000 followers on Twitter."

WRONG: "I do public speaking on this subject."
CORRECT: "I present to at least 10 events a year—sometimes as a keynote. The largest events have up to 1,200 attendees."

WRONG: "I run a blog that has won awards from other friendly bloggers."
CORRECT: "My blog averages 75,000 page views each month and is growing at a rate of 8 percent each month over the past year."

Also, analyzing numbers will help you see what's working and not working in your platform plan—allowing you to make healthy changes and let the strategy evolve. Numbers reflect the success you're having, and it's up to you to figure out why you're having that success.

CHUCK SAMBUCHINO (chucksambuchino.com, @chucksambuchino on Twitter) edits the *Guide to Literary Agents* (guidetoliteraryagents.com/blog) as well as the *Children's Writer's & Illustrator's Market*. His pop humor books include *How to Survive a Garden Gnome Attack* (film rights optioned by Sony) and *Red Dog / Blue Dog: When Pooches Get Political* (reddog-bluedog.com). Chuck's other writing books include *Formatting & Submitting Your Manuscript, 3rd. Ed.*, and *Create Your Writer Platform* (fall 2012). Besides that, he is a husband, guitarist, sleep-deprived new father, dog owner, and cookie addict.

"PLATFORM" VS. "CREDENTIALS"

Like we discussed, the most important question you will be asked as you try to get your nonfiction book published is: "Why are you the best person to write this book?" This question is two-fold, as it speaks to both your credentials and your platform. To be a successful author, you will need both, not just the former.

Your credentials encompass your education and experience to be considered as an expert in your category. For example, if you want to write a book called *How to Lose 10 Pounds in 10 Weeks*, then my first thought would be to wonder if you are a doctor or a dietician. If not, what position do you hold that would give you solid authority to speak on your subject and have others not question the advice you're presenting? Or maybe you want to write a book on how to sell real estate in a challenging market. To have the necessary gravitas to compose such a book, you would likely have to have worked as an agent for decades and excelled in your field—likely winning awards over the years and acting in leadership roles within the real estate agent community.

Would you buy a book on how to train a puppy from someone whose only credential was that they owned a dog? I wouldn't. I want to see accolades, leadership positions, endorsements, educational notes and more. I need to make sure I'm learning from an expert before I stop questioning the text and take it as helpful fact.

All this—all your authority—comes from your credentials. That's why they're so necessary. But believe it or not, credentials are often easier to come by than platform.

Platform, as we now know, is your ability to sell books and market yourself to target audience(s). There are likely many dieticians out there who can teach people interesting ways to lower their weight. But a publishing company is not interested in the 90 percent of them who lack any platform. They want the 10 percent of experts who have the ability to reach readers. Publishing houses seek experts who possess websites, mailing lists, media contacts, a healthy number of Twitter followers and a plan for how to grow their visibility.

It's where credentials meet platform—*that's* where book authors are born.

CRAFTING A NOVEL AGENTS WILL LOVE

How to hook an agent with voice and flair.

....

by Donald Maass

You'll never meet an author who admits to publishing a "failed" novel. You will, though, encounter authors in bars and on blogs who will loudly tell you what's wrong with the book industry. They'll chronicle in detail how their titles languished on the shelves because their publishers screwed up and failed *them*.

But accept blame? No way. If sales were disappointing or an option was dropped, it's the fault of weak "support," a lousy cover, awful back-panel copy, bad timing, distribution mistakes, lack of subsidiary rights sales, or a host of other common publishing woes.

How can it be the author's fault? After all, he wrote a book that was *good enough*. It was published. It met the standard—one that sometimes seems impossibly high. Any poor performance was therefore not the author's doing but someone else's, right?

But if that's true, then why do some novels become successful *in spite of* the sting of small deals, minimal press runs, little promotion, forgettable covers, bland copy, distribution snafus, and the absence of movie deals or translation sales?

Take timing and distribution troubles, for instance. In a recent interview right here in *Writer's Digest*, British author Chris Cleave related that due to a terrorist attack in London on the publication day of his first novel, *Incendiary*—which happened to be about a terrorist attack in London—the book was yanked from bookshop shelves after only about 90 minutes on sale. Talk about disasters! Yet that book later found its audience and was successful, even becoming a feature film. Cleave went on to write the mega-sellers *Little Bee* and *Gold*.

And what about awful covers? Do you remember what was on the covers of *Mystic River* or *Empire Falls*? I didn't think so. It didn't matter. In fact, think about any great novel you read in the last decade and ask yourself this: Was the reason you bought or loved that novel the flap copy, the Italian edition, the movie option, the author's Twitter feed, or the news of her honking big advance? Probably not.

I'm not saying that the industry is perfect, or that authors can't help their sales with smart self-promotion. (Although my experience has been that the boost is typically smaller than evangelists would like you to believe.) If you want to distract yourself with those issues, go ahead. I won't stop you. But you'll be missing a critical point.

As a literary agent who's helped guide fiction careers for more than 30 years, here's what I've learned: Runaway success comes from great fiction, period. The publishing industry may help or hinder but cannot stop a powerful story from being powerful. Conversely, the book business cannot magically transform an adequate novel into a great one.

You may not like every bestseller (*Fifty Shades of Grey*, anyone?), but if a book is selling well then it's doing things right for many readers. By the same token, less commercially successful novels are not doing enough of those things, even if they were good enough to get into print.

What are those critical factors, then? Let's take a look at some of the most common.

CULPRIT NO. 1: TIMID VOICES

Great novels not only draw us in immediately but command our attention. They not only hold our interest but hold us rapt. They cast a spell. A snappy premise and meaty plot can hook us and keep us reading but cannot by themselves work that magic. It takes something extra: voice.

What is voice, anyway? Narrative style? Character diction? A set of subject matter or a singular setting? All of the above? Pinning it down can be difficult, but start with this: We primarily experience stories through point-of-view characters.

To put it differently, voice in a novel is not the author's thoughts or vocabulary but the sum total of what her characters observe, think, feel and express in their own unique ways.

First-person narrators automatically have a voice, but that doesn't necessarily mean it's strong. Victims, whiners and passive daughters often have weak voices. On the flip side, snappy narrators who fire off zingers every page or so don't always leave a lasting impression, either. Have you ever met a government-issue alpha male or central-casting kick-ass heroine whose name you forgot as soon as you turned the final page? Then you know what I mean.

Lorrie Moore's bestselling literary novel *A Gate at the Stairs* is the coming-of-age story of Tassie Keltjin, a 20-year-old student and daughter of a potato farmer. As the novel opens, Tassie is on a term break and needs money. She is looking for babysitting jobs.

I was looking in December for work that would begin at the start of the January term. I'd finished my exams and was answering ads from the student job board, ones for "childcare provider." I liked children—I did!—or rather, I liked them OK. They were sometimes interesting.

Tassie is about as ordinary as characters get. She's a student. She needs a job. She has no odd talent, paranormal ability or backstory secret. The only reason we're compelled to read about her is her voice, her take on things. Her take on herself is wry. She's a future babysitter trying to talk herself into liking kids. That wry voice makes her engaging enough to lure us forward into the rest of her tragi-comic story.

Third-person narrators are a step removed from the reader, true enough, but when their inner experiences are both vivid and different, then their voices can become strong. It's not just language. It's not only getting into a character's head. It's how you use both of those things to create a strong voice.

Erin Morgenstern's bestselling literary fantasy *The Night Circus* is a three-ring carnival of voice that's all the more remarkable for using not only the third person but the often icy present tense. Open her novel at random and see. Here's Lefèvre, the circus manager, practicing knife throwing by aiming at the byline of a reviewer in a newspaper clipping:

> *The sentence that holds his name is the particular one that has incensed M. Lefèvre to the point of knife throwing. A single sentence that reads thusly: "M. Chandresh Christophe Lefèvre continues to push the boundaries of the modern stage, dazzling his audiences with spectacle that is almost transcendent."*
>
> *Most theatrical producers would likely be flattered by such a remark. They would clip the article for a scrapbook of reviews, quote it for references and referrals.*
>
> *But not this particular theatrical producer. No, M. Chandresh Christophe Lefèvre instead focuses on that penultimate word. Almost.* **Almost***.*

How often do you use the words *thusly* and *penultimate* in your fiction? Not often? That's OK. I'm not saying that stuffy diction is the way to craft a strong voice. But in this case, it makes the repressed anger and obsessive perfectionism of M. Chandresh Christophe Lefèvre wonderfully distinctive.

STRENGTHEN THAT HARD-TO-DEFINE VOICE:

- What's your protagonist's initial view of the main story problem? Evolve that understanding in three steps. How is it different at the end? Put each stage on the page.
- What's your protagonist's opening opinion of a secondary character, the story's locale, or era? Open with that ... then change it by the end.
- Pick anything ordinary in the world of your story: for example, a vehicle, a sport, or a topic of public debate. Give your protagonist a fanatic view. Write his rant.

CULPRIT NO. 2: UNTESTED CHARACTERS

If voice comes from a character's way of looking at the world, a character's continuing grip on the reader comes from what she does, why she does it, and who she is. It's not enough for your characters to simply have actions, motives and principles. Those drivers can be weak or they can be strong.

Let's start with actions. The weakest action is inaction. You'd think this is obvious, yet many scenes, indeed whole novels (yes, even published ones), can pass without a character actually doing something. Reacting, observing, and bearing what is hard or painful are not actions. Running away is active, technically speaking, but it isn't as strong as facing up, confronting and fighting.

More compelling are actions that show spine, take courage, spring from high principles or bring characters face to face with their deepest fears. Strongest of all are self-sacrifice, forgiveness and other actions that demonstrate growth, grace and love.

What about motives? In life our motives are many, deep and intertwined. Unfortunately, in many novels characters are motivated in ways that are single-minded and simplistic. Generic motives make for cartoonish characters.

You can see that in some genre novels. Detectives have codes, romance heroines seek love, and fantasy heroes fight evil. Is that bad? No. Codes, yearning for love and fighting evil are good—but as characters' lone motives they're also generic.

What makes characters' motivations genuinely gripping, then? There's a hierarchy. Mixed motives make characters real. Conflicting motives make characters complex. Most gripping of all are motives that reveal to us characters' innermost cores. We're shaped by our hurts. When a character's hurts are unique and specific, what propels them on their journeys—motivates them—paradoxically becomes universal.

Think of it this way: The deeper you dig into what drives your protagonist, the more readers will be able to connect.

What about principles? They are the rules we live by and the beliefs we hold. These too can be weak or strong. Generic principles are common and obvious. *Do unto others* is a fine but commonplace rule for living. Compelling principles are personal, a twist on what's familiar. *Build a bridge to everyone you meet—then walk across it*, is somewhat more personal. That's especially true if the protagonist who lives by that rule is a bridge inspector.

When actions, motives and principles come together the effect can be profound. Jamie Ford's longtime bestseller *Hotel on the Corner of Bitter and Sweet* is set largely in Seattle in 1942. It's the story of Henry Lee, a sixth-grade Chinese-American boy who falls in love with Keiko Okabe, a Japanese-American girl in his class. When Keiko and her family are removed to an internment camp, Henry is distraught. That would be enough for many literary novels. The romantic tragedy has happened. The political point is made.

But Ford has his protagonist *do something*: Henry gets a job as a kitchen assistant to the school cook who has been contracted to feed the prisoners at the internment camp. He goes looking for Keiko.

Another language barrier Henry ran into was within Camp Harmony. Just seeing a Chinese kid standing on an apple crate behind the serving counter was strange enough. But the more he questioned those who came through his chow line about the Okabes, the more frustrated he became. Few cared, and those who did never seemed to understand. Still, like a lost ship occasionally sending out an SOS, Henry kept peppering those he served with questions.

"Okabes? Does anyone know the Okabes?"

Henry's search poignantly shows the strength of his character. He rejects his father (who tries to force a Chinese Nationalist identity on Henry), ignores social prejudice and defies the odds. His actions, motives and principles are high, more so because he's only a kid.

PUT YOUR PROTAGONIST TO THE TEST:

- What's the biggest thing your protagonist could possibly do, but can't? By the end of the story, have her do it.
- The story problem bugs your protagonist like it bugs no one else. The real reason connects back to something from childhood—what? Build that into a dramatic, character-defining backstory event. Let it underlie every scene, but reveal what happened only late in the story.
- In what way are your protagonist's operating principles unlike anyone else's? Boil them down to one precept. Drop that in early, and then depict, challenge and deepen that axiom at least three times by the story's end.

CULPRIT NO. 3: OVERLY INTERIOR OR EXTERIOR STORIES

You're the god of your story world. So there's no reason not to play god with your story.

Certain story patterns are pretty much guaranteed to lead to fiction of underwhelming force. That's often true of novels built on delay, suffering and being stuck. Even plot-heavy yarns can leave us yawning. Stupendous plot turns don't necessarily have a stupendous effect.

Quiet authors need to create a disturbance in church. At the other end of the spectrum, razzle-dazzle storytellers need to recognize that a burst of flash powder doesn't cause the audience to feel deeply. More simply, interior stories need more dramatic outward events; by the same token, dramatic outward events need to create a more devastating interior impact.

If you shy away from that cheap gimmick called plot, I applaud your integrity—but try focusing on the inner state of your main character at any given moment and finding a way to externalize it. Make something happen. If, conversely, you focus on keeping your pages turning at a mile a minute, good for you—but try sending your protagonist on a mission not just to save the world but also to save himself.

In a practical sense, playing god with your story means making your characters do bigger things and, conversely, *feel* bigger things when they experience something small.

Earlier I mentioned *Fifty Shades of Grey*. It's hard to find anyone who thinks this mainstream erotica is especially well written, yet its blockbuster status suggests that millions nevertheless find it easy to surrender to it. Why is that, then?

The novel's heroine, student Anastasia Steele, falls under the spell of a man with a dark sexual side, entrepreneur Christian Grey. Anastasia at first resists his magnetic appeal. The slow breakdown of that resistance generates the tension in the novel's early chapters. It's an internal tension, though, and to work it must infuse every routine encounter.

In an early scene Grey comes into the hardware store where Anastasia works and he buys cable ties, masking tape and rope. Anastasia renders polite customer service, but inside is intrigued, confused and quivering. When he leaves, she narrates her feelings in this passage:

> *Okay, I like him. There, I've admitted it to myself. I cannot hide from my feelings anymore. I've never felt like this before. I find him attractive, very attractive. But it's a lost cause, I know, and I sigh with bittersweet regret. It was just a coincidence, his coming here. But still, I can admire him from afar, surely. No harm can come of that.*

While the prose may not be the most artful ever written, notice in this passage the push-pull of Anastasia's feelings. She submits to her attraction but immediately rejects it. She dismisses his visit to the hardware store as a fluke. (Really? Masking tape?) Her decision to admire him from afar is an amusing piece of foreshadowing. Most significantly, her response to Grey's hardware shopping is overly large, as if a godlike master has dropped into a humble hardware store from on high—which for Anastasia is true.

PLAY GOD WITH YOUR STORY:

- Your character is stymied, suffering and stuck. She phones a crisis hotline. You answer. You're trained to convince callers to get help. What should your protagonist do? Make her do it ... then make it fail.
- Your action hero races ahead at top speed. Throw up a roadblock. Force a one-hour delay. During that hour, ask your hero the following: Why are you racing? Why does it matter? You're racing but also running from—what? Write it down. Fold it in. There's time to deepen your character.
- Rain a punishment on your protagonist, and simultaneously test his inner conviction. What's the hardest possible test for him? Add it. What's being tested? Make that clear.

A MEASURE OF SUCCESS

If there are no pink slips for published authors, how do you know you've "failed"? The fact is that there is no failure per se; there are only disappointing sales, dropped options, unreturned calls, panic and anger. A bruised self-image is painful.

Recovery starts with examining first how it is that you define success. If it's by *selling a lot of copies*, then you're setting yourself up for failure, because you'll always lose to the heavy hitters like Harlan Coben. Indeed, I've found that focusing on selling a lot of copies is almost a guarantee that you won't.

Likewise, blaming the publishing industry for your disappointment will not heal or strengthen you. It's a mental trap. Book publishing is a big industry. It's dominated by a handful of big conglomerates that put out roughly 6,000 new works of fiction every year. Things are bound to go wrong.

While the industry isn't without blame, the fact is that you can't change the business. You can only change your writing.

When you make it to that happy place called *published*, remember that as a writer you have the same strengths and weaknesses that you did before. Your strengths have grown strong enough to get you over the first hurdle; your weaknesses have lessened enough that they didn't stop you from jumping over the bar. But you still have growing to do.

If you encounter disappointments in your publishing career, don't despair. That happens to pretty much every author. The trick is not to simmer but to learn. Learn what? How to become a more powerful storyteller.

The good news is that when you do, industry flaws become less bothersome. In fact, you'll run into fewer of them and finally none at all. Your books will succeed—not because you've beat the odds but because you've become a great novelist.

DONALD MAASS' literary agency sells more than 150 novels every year to major publishers in the U.S. and overseas. He is the author of several books on writing, most recently *Writing 21st Century Fiction* (WD Books).

"HOW I GOT MY AGENT"

Five stories told by agented writers.

....

by Chuck Sambuchino

Merit Badges

Once I knew I was writing a novel, I also knew it would help to have published work when I was ready to find an agent. With the dreamy optimism of the inexperienced, I submitted stories and essays to the mountaintops: *The Atlantic*, *The Paris Review* and *Granta*. And thus began a decade-long process of manuscript revision paralleled with humbling self-revision. A few pieces did manage to fill some pages in anthologies and regional literary

journals, and I gathered these little recognitions like scout merit badges, pinning them to the sash I'd show to prospective agents.

During the years of schooling, reading, writing and revising, I'd collected a fistful of agents' names from book acknowledgments, industry articles and seminars, and—the golden fleece in the agent search—referral promises from author friends. I had learned about the mechanics of the process: the query letter with its pithy opening sentence, the snappy synopsis, the bio (adorned with my merit badges), the strict compliance to submission guidelines, the helmet for the barrage of rejections. Patient and perhaps too-kind friends had read my novel and delivered thumbs-ups. I began querying literary agents partly because I couldn't face revising the manuscript yet again. Instead, I wrote and repeatedly revised the query letter, synopsis and bio. I should have paid more attention to the lessons that rose from boiling down a manuscript into a one-page description. I was seeing my novel in a different light, its themes shifting in emphasis as I tried to write the kind of copy that would sell the book. Like any loving mother, I believed that no one but I could see the flaws in my 500-page child.

Queries and Setbacks

After so many years working on the novel, the relative speed of creating the query package prodded the impetus to send it out. I mailed it to my best hope, careful to give her an exclusive submission. As a fail-safe measure I bought the latest *Guide to Literary Agents*, checked who might be a good fit for my novel and verified their submission guidelines online. The stars shone brightly the day the agent's assistant called asking for the first 50 pages, and I barely slept—until the rejection came. It included a generous paragraph pointing to the weaknesses that I continued to rationalize away. As a salve, I sharpened the query and sent it out again, and yet again, until I'd burnt through the precious commodity of the half-dozen agents with whom I had a meaningful connection. With each rejection came a revision of my writerly worth, a meek reshaping of the image of big-name agents fighting over my pages flying in scattered delight.

Rather than work on my manuscript, I created a detailed list of agent prospects coded by cold-query acceptance levels, for affinity of their represented books to mine, and charted to date-track the process. About 30 queries in, I received an offer, but the agent's request to radically refocus the novel didn't feel right, nor did the tone of the conversation we had. I agonized over this decision, finally choosing to trust my gut over my eagerness to sign. That experience, along with 40 rejections in nine months, made it impossible to deny that my child wasn't communicating properly. I devoted time to rehabilitate her. Plus, there were only 10 more names on my prospective agent list.

An Unexpected Call

A month later, I knew I had a better product. Even the query felt simple to revise and sounded fresh and clear. And as the winter holidays approached, I had better results.

Three agents requested the complete manuscript. I nurtured hope that my novel would have a little fireside attention in a comfortable home setting.

Then came a call from Nat Sobel. The strange thing was: I'd heard of Nat but he was not one of the many agents I queried. He actually called to say that he had admired my short story in a small literary journal and asked if I had anything book-length. I described the novel and, my brain going clickity-clack, told him that three other agents had the full manuscript.

I sent it overnight to his holiday vacation home—the fireside!—and the next day he said Sobel Weber Associates was interested if I was open to revising the material. This time, knowing that revision had improved my "finished" novel and could only make it better, and with all my expectations thoroughly revised after the year-long querying process, it felt completely right.

---

② DELILAH MARVELLE
Author of historical romance novels.

PHOTO: Cynthia O'Donnell

A Setback

A few months before the release of my second book, *Lord of Pleasure*, I discovered that my publisher, Kensington, was not going to be renewing contracts. It's a writer's worst nightmare to be rejected by your own publisher once you thought you've made it. What could possibly be worse than being rejected by your own publisher? Letting go of your agent beforehand, which, yes, I'd unfortunately just done. Right after my agent and I parted ways, I got the bad news from Kensington.

So without a contract and without an agent, I basically started over. I queried 15 agents and every single one of them came back with the same answer: "Love the writing but it's a tough market. We can't take on this project right now." Considering that it had originally taken me 11 years to get published and that during those 11 years, I had garnered more than 200 rejections, I knew I needed to keep trudging onward. So I did the one thing I could do. I submitted to publishers on my own. Or at least those that would let me query without an agent (which isn't very many). I queried Avon, HQN and Sourcebooks, and waited.

A Life-changing Event

Two weeks later, I went to the National Romance Writers of America Conference, which I attend every year. It's an amazing writing haven where connections and education abound for all romance writers, published or not. I went with no expectations, just the high hopes that I could push my upcoming book and make some friends.

At one of the luncheons, I sat at a table with a group of lovely women I didn't know and we all started to talk. About the same time, a gentleman nabbed the last empty seat at the table and quietly sat there listening to our conversation. I happened to touch upon the topic of my blog, which I post to every first of the month on topics of sex in the context of history. That is exactly when the gentleman spoke up and said, "That sounds very fascinating. Might I have a card?" Seeing I was discussing my blog, I thought "Perve" (because I seem to attract them), so I drawled, "And you *are*?" He paused, then graciously replied, "Donald Maass." Needless to say, after recognizing the name of this top agent, I choked, gave him my card (feeling much like a dolt) and thought, "Well there goes *that* chance." Then, the night before the conference was over, my life completely changed.

Although there are usually tons of desserts available after the event's Golden Heart and Rita Ceremony, for some reason, this year, there were none to be had as the staff wasn't refilling the platters. Being a chef, I immediately flagged down a waiter, handed him an empty plate and kindly asked him to go into the kitchen and bring me whatever dessert he could find. While I waited by the kitchen door, the editor from Sourcebooks approached me and on the spot offered me a four-book contract based on the proposal for the new series I had submitted. As I stood there in complete shock, the waiter came back and delivered a huge piece of chocolate cake. All for me. So yes, I had my cake and ate it, too. I hardly got home and immediately called up the two other publishers who had my series to let them know I had an offer. Avon passed with glowing compliments, but HQN counteroffered. And that's when I realized, "Holy cow, I need an agent."

A Clean Slate

My good writing buddies, Lisa Hendrix and Kristina McMorris, quickly offered up their fabulous agents, whom I called immediately. My husband, however, kept pestering me and saying, "Why don't you call Donald Maass?" I cringed. After I had insulted the man? I think not. My husband, however, kept pressing, and needless to say, I caved and called. Lo and behold, Donald not only offered representation, but assistance in honing my writing. To get an agent and writing coach all in one? A complete dream! I signed with him and he helped me through the daunting process of choosing which publisher was best for me.

To receive two offers from two amazing publishers may be what every writer dreams about, but it's not quite as fun filled as you might think when you're actually living it. After some back and forth between the two publishers, I eventually decided on HQN, who offered me a three-book deal.

So what did I learn from my roller-coaster experience? Trust your gut and don't ever, ever let an agent decide your career for you.

> ③ **COLIN BRODERICK** ·
> Author of *Orangutan*, a memoir.

PHOTO: Renta Broderick

Rock Bottom

On the sixth day of the sixth month in 2006, I left my apartment in Hells Kitchen with the last of my belongings in a small U-Haul truck to drive to farmhouse up north and try to save my life. It might sound like I'm fabricating the facts here for dramatic effect, but as I started the truck and headed north, I glanced at the dash clock and it read 6:06. It occurred to me then, and I still believe it now, that there was some Dante-esque connection at play here; my life had spiraled to its lowest point. I was a 38-year-old, twice-divorced alcoholic weighing in at an astonishing 115 pounds. I was broke and now I had lost my apartment. It was time to start the long crawl out of the hole I had dug for myself. I had witnessed the depths of the inferno and it held little of the allure it once did for me. I wanted nothing more to do with it.

Within three days, I had started writing what was to become my memoir, *Orangutan*. I had been writing for 20 years since moving to New York from Northern Ireland at the age of 20 to work construction. I'd completed a couple of novels, plays, short stories and notebooks full of poetry—but I had managed to get only one short story published, and that had been 10 years before. I'd spent my 20s convinced that I would be "discovered." An agent or editor would read one page of my manuscript and run to the nearest phone to dial my number with an offer that would catapult me into the waiting arms of the Nobel Prize Committee. It didn't happen. I did send my early manuscripts out to a few agents and agencies, but I can't remember even receiving a rejection letter. It seemed finding an agent was more difficult than finding a publisher. I used to say that you needed an agent to get one in this town.

The Referral

After spending a year on *Orangutan*—a year that saw me back on the bottle for a brief but productive period that added a stint in an upstate jail to my résumé—I started dating a girl who had been a bartender of mine once upon a time. She was a writer, also. She read what I had written and was convinced that this was the manuscript that would finally get me published. She took me back to the city and gave me a place to stay and a desk for my work. I married her for her efforts and quit drinking to devote my time and energy to creating a career for myself in the only profession that has ever made any sense to me: writing.

I was at a meeting one night way downtown—one of those meetings you hear about where the alcoholics gather to drink coffee and smoke their cigarettes—when I heard a guy about my age tell his story. He'd escaped from a locked ward at Bellevue Mental Hospital, and had been the first to escape from the institution since the early 1970s. He'd sobered up and written a book about it, and with the help of his wonderful agent had just nailed down a book deal. I lurked around outside the meeting afterward waiting for my moment. He was quite popular and had a lot of goodbyes to say, but I was patient. This was my guy—I was sure of it. When he finally turned to leave, I followed him around the corner and stopped him with a tap on the shoulder.

"Excuse me, my name's Colin. I just heard your story in there, and it was great. Here's the deal: I heard you say you have an agent. Well, I'm a writer myself and I have this manuscript almost finished that could really use an agent." Here he started mumbling some line about how he had introduced someone to his agent already and it hadn't really worked out for him, but I didn't let him finish. "I can assure you," I told him, "that if you introduce me to your agent, you will always remember this as the night you discovered Colin Broderick." He smiled. I had appealed to his cooky sense of happenstance. He laughed and eyed me skeptically.

"I promise," I said. "I will not embarrass you."

The Pitch

Three days later (thanks to a phone call from this nice man), I was seated in the office of Dystel and Goderich down on Union Square. I was on one couch, and two agents, Jane and Miriam, were on another facing me. "OK, shoot," Jane said, clasping her hands in her lap. The two women glared at me with raised eyebrows.

"What?" I had no idea what to do next.

"Well, why are we sitting here with you? Shoot."

This was the moment I had been waiting for my entire adult life. Here was an honest-to-goodness shot at the hoop. I jumped right in with my story, and within a few minutes I could tell they were warming up. We had made a connection. They asked me if I'd brought anything with me for them to read. I had. I gave them a disc with what I had of the manuscript so far, and within three days I was back in their office signing a contract. I had my agent!—the same agency who represented Barack Obama, a Hemingway, Judge Judy and a Bellevue escapee. I had found my home.

It took six months for them to sell *Orangutan* to Three Rivers Press (Random House, no less). Over the past two years, both Jane and Miriam have been working closely with me helping me refine my next book proposal. They have just submitted it to the publishers. It's been a long hard road, but it's been well worth the wait. And that Bellevue escapee (author Chris Campion) and I became fast friends into the bargain.

4 KRISTYN CROW
Author of several children's picture books.

PHOTO: Steven Crow

Sneaking In

Carving out time to attend a week-long writing conference wasn't easy for a mother of seven. I had to arrange baby-sitting, swap car-pool shifts, stock the refrigerator and leave a trail of reminder notes for my husband. But the dream of getting a children's picture book published had nagged at me since I was a kid, and I couldn't ignore it any longer. I had been writing stories for 20 years.

When I arrived at the conference registration desk, the secretary told me that Rick Walton's workshop—the one I really wanted—had "no spaces available." She insisted I select another. But Rick Walton was the local guru of picture books, having authored more than 50. I wanted to learn from him. So I snuck into his class, finding an open chair in the corner. Gratefully, nobody shooed me out the door.

I'm One of "Those People"?

Soon manuscript critiques were underway, and after a dozen or so it was my turn. "Who will volunteer to read this one?" Rick asked. A hand went up, and as my story was read aloud, I tried to pretend my guts weren't twisting into knots. I had written a rhyming, jazzy tale of a rat in the city, told in scat. Admittedly, the thing was odd. Would anybody get it? When the reader finished, there was an awkward silence, then a wave of positive comments. Rick seemed enthusiastic. "There's a literary agent here at the conference you should show this to," he said. I was ecstatic.

A meeting was arranged. I remember entering a small classroom and sitting across from the classy-looking agent in high heels. It was the Dollar Store meets Saks Fifth Avenue. I smiled, introduced myself and gave her my manuscript. She looked it over, then got a confused expression and began to chuckle. "Who sent you to me?" she asked. Before I could answer, she looked up at the ceiling, speaking aloud to some invisible force in the universe: "Why do they always send *these people* to me?" I blinked, dumb-struck. I didn't know who "these people" were, but they sounded pitiful. She handed back my story with a verbal pat on the head, and pointed to the door. Needless to say, I was crushed.

Back in workshops, I privately shared the agent's reaction. Rick shook his head. "She's wrong," he said. "Here. Try this agent." He wrote down the name and address of Kendra Marcus of Bookstop Literary Agency. "Send her your manuscript and a few more of your best things. See what happens." I tucked the piece of paper into my purse, thanking him, but wasn't sure I was ready to set myself up for more rejection.

The conference ended, and I returned to my life of refereeing kid-squabbles, finding missing socks in potted plants, and experimenting with macaroni and cheese. It took several months of prodding from my husband before I had the courage to send off "a few of my best things" to the mysterious agent scrawled on the paper in my purse. Yet finally, I did. And I waited. Then tragedy struck. The United States was attacked on September 11th. Everyone was in an awful state of shock, rage and mourning. Church and synagogue attendance was on the rise as our troops prepared for war. Suddenly my whimsical rat story about—of all places—New York City, which mentioned—of all things—the Twin Towers, seemed ridiculous. It was all bad karma. I put my dream away for good.

The Call

Several weeks after the dust had cleared (both literally and figuratively), I was looking through my pantry when the telephone rang. The voice on the line said, "Kristyn, this is Kendra Marcus from Bookstop Literary Agency. And if you're interested, I'd like to represent you." I dropped the can of chili I was holding. She continued: "I've been reading over your manuscripts and they're very good. If you're willing to make some revisions, I think I can sell these stories."

A year later, Kendra sold *Cool Daddy Rat* to G.P. Putnam's sons. It received starred reviews, and Mike Lester won the Rueben award for his illustrations. Since then, she's sold other picture books for me, including *Bedtime at the Swamp* (HarperCollins), *The Middle-Child Blues* (G.P. Putnam's Sons) and *Skeleton Cat* (Scholastic). Kendra and her perceptive associate, Minju Chang, have been more than agents; they've been mentors, advocates and friends. I am thrilled to be represented by Bookstop.

Sure, one agent didn't connect with my work, but the next enthusiastically signed me on as a client. I'm often haunted by the question, "What if I hadn't tried again?"

5 **A.C. ARTHUR**
Author of almost two dozen books, mostly romance.

PHOTO: RW Phtography

Not on the Same Page

Since my first book was published in 2003, my search for an agent has been a long and tedious one. One of the first obstacles I faced was that I didn't really know what the job of an agent was, and therefore, didn't have a clue what I was looking for. Of course that led to my first choice not necessarily being the right one (meaning I signed with the first agent who showed any interest in my work). And three years and three additional contracts later, I released that agent. Why? Because we wanted different things from my writing career—and that is a recipe for disaster in an agent/writer relationship.

I continued to get publishing contracts and to write books, all the while knowing there was something or someone missing from taking my career to the next level.

Referral and Rejection

One day in 2006, during a routine rant about not having an agent, an editor friend of mine suggested Christine Witthohn of Book Cents Literary Agency. My friend's exact words were, "She's a new agent, but she's smart. She knows what she's doing and how to work for you." This sounded fantastic, so I sent Christine an e-mail and she, in turn, asked for a proposal.

The phone call I received from her about two weeks later was not what I'd been expecting. You see, I thought that because I had a referral and because Christine had immediately responded by requesting material, I was a sure thing. Not so!

Christine's exact words were, "You don't need me." I was devastated, but had to respect her honesty. Besides, she was so nice to talk to, the fact that she was actually rejecting me stung just a little less. I couldn't really figure out why she said I didn't need her, because I was convinced I did. But I accepted her decision and tried to move on. This meant the search was still on, and I sent out numerous queries to more agents—some I'd queried in the past and other new ones. This is a very subjective industry; it all depends on the right editor seeing the right manuscript at the right time. I'm persistent, if nothing else.

A Fated Connection

In early 2008 when a very reputable agent expressed interest in my work, I was overjoyed. Again, I was convinced I'd found the right agent. Again, I was wrong. What was it about me that I just couldn't find the right person to represent my work? The funny thing was, after only a couple of months with this agent, I had a feeling I'd once again missed the mark. There was no real connection. And while I thought I'd done a good job of explaining what I wanted, where I wanted my career to go, we still came out on opposite sides. That's not to say that this agent wasn't good; he just wasn't the one for me.

At this point I still had the same problem; I was sans agent. The publishing houses that I wanted to write for accepted only agented submissions. Besides that, the contracts were changing—the language becoming increasingly more technical—and I knew I wasn't getting the best deals for myself. So on this agent search, I researched and researched and sent only material that I thought specific agents would be interested in. Meanwhile, in April 2009, I finally got to meet Christine at the Romantic Times Booklovers Convention. I didn't pitch her; I just wanted to meet her.

A little while later, I had another proposal and needed some honest feedback—so I called on Christine again for advice. Again, she responded immediately, which I'd always been impressed by because I know how busy agents are. And her response was more like a friend would reply to another friend's message, rather than an agent to an author, so that was very cool! Two months later, I was signing a Book Cents Literary Agency contract. We finally decided we were right for each other. It had taken three years, but I firmly believe in timing, especially in this industry. I also believe in fated connections.

CHUCK SAMBUCHINO (chucksambuchino.com, @chucksambuchino on Twitter) edits the *Guide to Literary Agents* (guidetoliteraryagents.com/blog) as well as the *Children's Writer's & Illustrator's Market*. His pop humor books include *How to Survive a Garden Gnome Attack* (film rights optioned by Sony) and *Red Dog / Blue Dog: When Pooches Get Political* (reddog-bluedog.com). Chuck's other writing books include *Formatting & Submitting Your Manuscript, 3rd. Ed.*, and *Create Your Writer Platform* (fall 2012). Besides that, he is a husband, guitarist, sleep-deprived new father, dog owner, and cookie addict.

GLA SUCCESS STORIES

Those who came before and succeeded.

I realize there are other places you can turn to for information on agents, but the *Guide to Literary Agents* has always prided itself as being the biggest (we list almost every agent) and the most thorough (guidelines, sales, agent-by-agent breakdowns, etc.). That's why it's sold more than 250,000 copies. It *works*—and if you keep reading, I'll prove it to you. Here are testimonials from a handful of writers who have used this book to find an agent and publishing success.

❶ MARISHA CHAMBERLAIN, *The Rose Variations* (Soho)
"*Guide to Literary Agents* oriented me, the lowly first-time novelist, embarking on an agent search. The articles and the listings gave insight into the world of literary agents that allowed me to comport myself professionally and to persist. And I did find a terrific agent."

2 **EUGENIA KIM**, *The Calligrapher's Daughter* (Holt)

"After so many years working on the novel, the relative speed of creating the query package prodded the impetus to send it out ... As a fail-safe measure, I bought the *Guide to Literary Agents* [and] checked who might be a good fit for my novel..."

3 **EVE BROWN-WAITE**, *First Comes Love, Then Comes Malaria* (Broadway)

"I bought the *Guide To Literary Agents* ... and came across Laney Katz Becker. So I sent off a very funny query. On March 15, 2007, Laney called. 'I love your book,' she said. 'I'd like to represent you.' Three months later, Laney sold my book—at auction—in a six-figure deal."

4 **MARA PURNHAGEN**, *Tagged* (Harlequin Teen)

"I trusted the *Guide to Literary Agents* to provide solid, up-to-date information to help me with the process. I now have a wonderful agent and a four-book deal."

5 **RICHARD HARVELL**, *The Bells* (Crown)

"*Guide to Literary Agents* contains a wealth of information and advice, and was crucial in my successful search for an agent. My book has now sold in 11 [countries] and counting."

6 **PATRICK LEE**, *The Breach* (Harper)

"The *GLA* has all the info you need for narrowing down a list of agencies to query."

7 **KAREN DIONNE**, *Freezing Point* and *Boiling Point* (Jove)

"I'm smiling as I type this, because I actually got my agent via the *Guide to Literary Agents*. I certainly never dreamed that I'd tell my [success] story in the same publication!"

8 **HEATHER NEWTON**, *Under the Mercy Trees* (Harper)

"I found my literary agent through the *Guide to Literary Agents*!"

⑨ Michael Wiley, *The Last Striptease* and *The Bad Kitty Lounge* (Minotaur)
"*GLA* was very useful to me when I started. I always recommend it to writers."

⑩ Les Edgerton, *Hooked* and 11 more books
"Just signed with literary agent Chip MacGregor and I came upon him through the *Guide to Literary Agents*. If not for *GLA*, I'd probably still be looking."

⑪ Jennifer Cervantes, *Tortilla Sun* (Chronicle)
"Within 10 days of submitting, I found an amazing agent—and it's all thanks to *GLA*."

⑫ Carson Morton, *Stealing Mona Lisa* (St. Martin's / Minotaur)
"I wanted to thank you for the *Guide to Literary Agents*. After contacting 16 literary agencies, number 17 requested my historical novel. Within a few weeks, they offered to represent me. Hard work and good, solid, accurate information makes all the difference. Thanks again."

⑬ Darien Gee, *Friendship Bread: A Novel* (Ballantine)
"The *Guide to Literary Agents* was an indispensable tool for me when I was querying agents. I highly recommend it for any aspiring author."

⑭ lexi george, *Demon Hunting in Dixie* (Brava)
"The *Guide to Literary Agents* is an invaluable resource for writers."

⑮ stephanie barden, *Cinderella Smith* (HarperCollins)
"When I felt my book was finally ready for eyes other than mine to see it, I got some terrific advice: Go buy the *Guide to Literary Agents*. By the time I was through with it, it looked like it had gone to battle—it was battered and dog-eared and highlighted and Post-It-Noted. But it was victorious; I had an agent. Huge thanks, *GLA*—I couldn't have done it without you!"

16 **BILL PESCHEL,** *Writers Gone Wild: The Feuds, Frolics, and Follies of Literature's Great Adventurers, Drunkards, Lovers, Iconoclasts, and Misanthropes* (Perigee)

"The *Guide to Literary Agents* gave me everything I needed to sell *Writers Gone Wild*. It was the personal assistant who found me the right agents to pitch, the publicist who suggested conferences to attend and the trusted adviser who helped me negotiate the path to publication."

17 **LAURA GRIFFIN,** *Unforgivable* (Pocket Books)

"Writing the book is only the first step. Then it's time to find a home for it. The *Guide to Literary Agents* is filled with practical advice about how to contact literary agents who can help you market your work."

18 **DEREK TAYLOR KENT (A.K.A. DEREK THE GHOST),** *Scary School* (HarperCollins)

"The *Guide to Literary Agents* was absolutely instrumental to my getting an agent and subsequent three-book deal with HarperCollins."

19 **TAMORA PIERCE,** *Alanna: The First Adventure: The Song of the Lioness* (Atheneum)

"The best guide to literary agents is the *Guide to Literary Agents*, published by Writer's Market Books … These listings will tell you the names and addresses of the agencies; if an agency is made up of more than one agent, they will list the different agents and what kinds of book they represent; they will include whether or not the agent will accept simultaneous submissions (submitting a manuscript to more agents than one)."

20 **WADE ROUSE,** *It's All Relative: Two Families, Three Dogs, 34 Holidays, and 50 Boxes of Wine: A Memoir* (Crown)

"And when you think you're done writing your book? Write some more. And when you think you're finished? Set it aside for a while, go back, redraft, edit, rewrite, and redraft … Then pick up the Writer's Digest *Guide to Literary Agents*."

㉑ DIANNA DORISI WINGET, *A Smidgen of Sky* (Harcourt)

"*Guide to Literary Agents* is simply the best writing reference book out there. I don't think I would have landed an agent without it."

㉒ CAROLE BRODY FLEET, *Happily Even After: A Guide to Getting Through (and Beyond!) the Grief of Widowhood* (Viva Editions)

"I am not overstating it when I say that *Guide to Literary Agents* was absolutely instrumental in my landing an agent. Moreover, I wound up with numerous agents from which to choose—how often does *that* happen to an unknown and unpublished author? Thank you again for this book. It not only changed my life forever, but it led to our being able to serve the widowed community around the world."

㉓ GUINEVERE DURHAM, *Teaching Test-Taking Skills: Proven Techniques to Boost Your Student's Scores* (R&L Education)

"I was looking for an agent for my book. I had been trying for 7 years. I have enough rejection letters to wallpaper my office. Finally, I researched the *Guide to Literary Agents*. Three months later I had a contract."

㉔ ADAM BROWNLEE, *Building a Small Business That Warren Buffett Would Love* (John Wiley and Sons)

"The *Guide to Literary Agents* was invaluable for me in many ways. Specifically, the sections on 'Write a Killer Query Letter' and 'Nonfiction Book Proposals' enabled me to put together a package that led to the publication of my book."

㉕ KIM BAKER, *Pickle: The (Formerly) Anonymous Prank Club of Fountain Point Middle School* (Roaring Brook)

"I read the *Guide to Literary Agents* religiously when I was planning submissions."

26 JERI WESTERSON, *Blood Lance: A Medieval Noir* (Pocket Books)
"The whole writing industry is so confusing. Where to start? I started with the Writer's Digest *Guide to Literary Agents,* where I not only created my list of agents and game plan, I received all sorts of excellent information in crafting my winning query letter. I recommend it to anyone starting out. And yes, I did get an agent through the Guide."

27 NOELLE STERNE, *Trust Your Life: Forgive Yourself and Go After Your Dreams* (Unity)
"Your *Guide to Literary Agents* and the features from authors on the often-hard lessons learned from the dream of publishing have helped me immensely to keep my feet on the ground, butt in the chair, and fingers on the keyboard. Thank you, Chuck, for taking all the time and effort and for caring."

28 LYNNE RAIMONDO, *Dante's Wood: A Mark Angelotti Novel* (Seventh Street Books)
"*Guide to Literary Agents* is how I found my agent, so I owe you one."

29 GENNIFER ALBIN, *Crewel* (Pocket Books)
"I'm very familiar with the *Guide to Literary Agents*! I used it a lot as I was prepping to query."

GLOSSARY OF INDUSTRY TERMS

Your guide to every need-to-know term.

#10 ENVELOPE. A standard, business-size envelope.

ACKNOWLEDGMENTS PAGE. The page of a book on which the author credits sources of assistance—both individuals and organizations.

ACQUISITIONS EDITOR. The person responsible for originating and/or acquiring new publishing projects.

ADAPTATION. The process of rewriting a composition (novel, story, film, article, play) into a form suitable for some other medium, such as TV or the stage.

ADVANCE. Money a publisher pays a writer prior to book publication, usually paid in installments, such as one-half upon signing the contract and one-half upon delivery of the complete, satisfactory manuscript. An advance is paid against the royalty money to be earned by the book. Agents take their percentage off the top of the advance as well as from the royalties earned.

ADVENTURE. A genre of fiction in which action is the key element, overshadowing characters, theme and setting.

AUCTION. Publishers sometimes bid for the acquisition of a book manuscript with excellent sales prospects. The bids are for the amount of the author's advance, guaranteed dollar amounts, advertising and promotional expenses, royalty percentage, etc. Auctions are conducted by agents.

AUTHOR'S COPIES. An author usually receives about 10 free copies of his hardcover book from the publisher; more from a paperback firm. He can obtain additional copies at a price that has been reduced by an author's discount (usually 50 percent of the retail price).

AUTOBIOGRAPHY. A book-length account of a person's entire life written by the subject himself.

BACKLIST. A publisher's list of books that were not published during the current season, but that are still in print.

BACKSTORY. The history of what has happened before the action in your story takes place, affecting a character's current behavior.

BIO. A sentence or brief paragraph about the writer; includes work and educational experience.

BIOGRAPHY. An account of a person's life (or the lives of a family or close-knit group) written by someone other than the subject(s). The work is set within the historical framework (i.e., the unique economic, social and political conditions) existing during the subject's life.

BLURB. The copy on paperback book covers or hardcover book dust jackets, either promoting the book and the author or featuring testimonials from book reviewers or well-known people in the book's field. Also called flap copy or jacket copy.

BOILERPLATE. A standardized publishing contract. Most authors and agents make many changes on the boilerplate before accepting the contract.

BOOK DOCTOR. A freelance editor hired by a writer, agent or book editor who analyzes problems that exist in a book manuscript or proposal, and offers solutions to those problems.

BOOK PACKAGER. Someone who draws elements of a book together—from initial concept to writing and marketing strategies—and then sells the book package to a book publisher and/or movie producer. Also known as book producer or book developer.

BOUND GALLEYS. A prepublication, often paperbound, edition of a book, usually prepared from photocopies of the final galley proofs. Designed for promotional purposes, bound galleys serve as the first set of review copies to be mailed out. Also called bound proofs.

CATEGORY FICTION. A term used to include all types of fiction. See *genre*.

CLIMAX. The most intense point in the story line of a fictional work.

CLIPS. Samples, usually from newspapers or magazines, of your published work. Also called tearsheets.

COMMERCIAL FICTION. Novels designed to appeal to a broad audience. These are often broken down into categories such as western, mystery and romance. See *genre*.

CONFESSION. A first-person story in which the narrator is involved in an emotional situation that encourages sympathetic reader identification, concluding with the affirmation of a morally acceptable theme.

CONFLICT. A prime ingredient of fiction that usually represents some obstacle to the main character's (i.e., the protagonist's) goals.

CONTRIBUTOR'S COPIES. Copies of the book sent to the author. The number of contributor's copies is often negotiated in the publishing contract.

CO-PUBLISHING. Arrangement where author and publisher share publication costs and profits of a book. Also called co-operative publishing.

COPYEDITING. Editing of a manuscript for writing style, grammar, punctuation and factual accuracy.

COPYRIGHT. A means to protect an author's work. A copyright is a proprietary right designed to give the creator of a work the power to control that work's reproduction, distribution and public display or performance, as well as its adaptation to other forms.

COVER LETTER. A brief letter that accompanies the manuscript being sent to an agent or publisher.

CREATIVE NONFICTION. Type of writing where true stories are told by employing the techniques usually reserved for novelists and poets, such as scenes, character arc, a three-act structure and detailed descriptions. This category is also called narrative nonfiction or literary journalism.

CRITIQUING SERVICE. An editing service offered by some agents in which writers pay a fee for comments on the salability or other qualities of their manuscript. Sometimes the critique includes suggestions on how to improve the work. Fees vary, as does the quality of the critique.

CURRICULUM VITAE (CV). Short account of one's career or qualifications.

DEADLINE. A specified date and/or time that a project or draft must be turned into the editor. A deadline factors into a preproduction schedule, which involves copyediting, typesetting and production.

DEAL MEMO. The memorandum of agreement between a publisher and author that precedes the actual contract and includes important issues such as royalty, advance, rights, distribution and option clauses.

DEUS EX MACHINA. A term meaning "God from the machine" that refers to any unlikely, contrived or trick resolution of a plot in any type of fiction.

DIALOGUE. An essential element of fiction. Dialogue consists of conversations between two or more people, and can be used heavily or sparsely.

DIVISION. An unincorporated branch of a publishing house/company.

ELECTRONIC RIGHTS. Secondary or subsidiary rights dealing with electronic/multimedia formats (the Internet, CD-ROMs, electronic magazines).

EL-HI. Elementary to high school. A term used to indicate reading or interest level.

EROTICA. A form of literature or film dealing with the sexual aspects of love. Erotic content ranges from subtle sexual innuendo to explicit descriptions of sexual acts.

ETHNIC. Stories and novels whose central characters are African American, Native American, Italian American, Jewish, Appalachian or members of some other specific cultural group. Ethnic fiction usually deals with a protagonist caught between two conflicting ways of life: mainstream American culture and his ethnic heritage.

EVALUATION FEES. Fees an agent may charge to simply evaluate or consider material without further guarantees of representation. Paying upfront evaluation fees to agents is never recommended and strictly forbidden by the Association of Authors' Representations. An agent makes money through a standard commission—taking 15 percent of what you earn through advances and, if applicable, royalties.

EXCLUSIVE. Offering a manuscript, usually for a set period of time such as one month, to just one agent and guaranteeing that agent is the only one looking at the manuscript.

EXPERIMENTAL. Type of fiction that focuses on style, structure, narrative technique, setting and strong characterization rather than plot. This form depends largely on the revelation of a character's inner being, which elicits an emotional response from the reader.

FAMILY SAGA. A story that chronicles the lives of a family or a number of related or interconnected families over a period of time.

FANTASY. Stories set in fanciful, invented worlds or in a legendary, mythic past that rely on outright invention or magic for conflict and setting.

FILM RIGHTS. May be sold or optioned by the agent/author to a person in the film industry, enabling the book to be made into a movie.

FLOOR BID. If a publisher is very interested in a manuscript, he may offer to enter a floor bid when the book goes to auction. The publisher sits out of the auction, but agrees to take the book by topping the highest bid by an agreed-upon percentage (usually 10 percent).

FOREIGN RIGHTS. Translation or reprint rights to be sold abroad.

FOREIGN RIGHTS AGENT. An agent who handles selling the rights to a country other than that of the first book agent. Usually an additional percentage (about 5 percent) will be added on to the first book agent's commission to cover the foreign rights agent.

GENRE. Refers to either a general classification of writing, such as a novel, poem or short story, or to the categories within those classifications, such as problem novels or sonnets.

GENRE FICTION. A term that covers various types of commercial novels, such as mystery, romance, Western, science fiction, fantasy, thriller and horror.

GHOSTWRITING. A writer puts into literary form the words, ideas or knowledge of another person under that person's name. Some agents offer this service; others pair ghostwriters with celebrities or experts.

GOTHIC. Novels characterized by historical settings and featuring young, beautiful women who win the favor of handsome, brooding heroes while simultaneously dealing with some life-threatening menace—either natural or supernatural.

GRAPHIC NOVEL. Contains comic-like drawings and captions, but deals more with everyday events and issues than with superheroes.

HIGH CONCEPT. A story idea easily expressed in a quick, one-line description.

HI-LO. A type of fiction that offers a high level of interest for readers at a low reading level.

HISTORICAL. A story set in a recognizable period of history. In addition to telling the stories of ordinary people's lives, historical fiction may involve political or social events of the time.

HOOK. Aspect of the work that sets it apart from others and draws in the reader/viewer.

HORROR. A story that aims to evoke some combination of fear, fascination and revulsion in its readers—either through supernatural or psychological circumstances.

HOW-TO. A book that offers the reader a description of how something can be accomplished. It includes both information and advice.

IMPRINT. The name applied to a publisher's specific line of books.

IN MEDIAS RES. A Latin term, meaning "into the midst of things," that refers to the literary device of beginning a narrative at a dramatic point in a story well along in the sequence of events to immediately convey action and capture reader interest.

IRC. International Reply Coupon. Buy at a post office to enclose with material sent outside the country to cover the cost of return postage. The recipient turns them in for stamps in their own country.

ISBN. This acronym stands for International Standard Book Number. ISBN is a tool used for both ordering and cataloging purposes.

JOINT CONTRACT. A legal agreement between a publisher and two or more authors that establishes provisions for the division of royalties their co-written book generates.

JUVENILE. Category of children's writing that can be broken down into easy-to-read books (ages 7–9), which run 2,000–10,000 words, and middle-grade books (ages 9–12), which run 20,000–40,000 words.

LIBEL. A form of defamation, or injury to a person's name or reputation. Written or published defamation is called *libel*, whereas spoken defamation is known as *slander*.

LITERARY. A book where style and technique are often as important as subject matter. In literary fiction, character is typically more important than plot, and the writer's voice and skill with words are both very essential. Also called serious fiction.

LOGLINE. A one-sentence description of a plot.

MAINSTREAM FICTION. Fiction on subjects or trends that transcend popular novel categories like mystery or romance. Using conventional methods, this kind of fiction tells stories about people and their conflicts.

MARKETING FEE. Fee charged by some agents to cover marketing expenses. It may be used to cover postage, telephone calls, faxes, photocopying or any other legitimate expense incurred in marketing a manuscript. Recouping expenses associated with submissions and marketing is the one and only time agents should ask for out-of-pocket money from writers.

MASS MARKET PAPERBACKS. Softcover books, usually 4×7 inches, on a popular subject directed at a general audience and sold in groceries, drugstores and bookstores.

MEMOIR. An author's commentary on the personalities and events that have significantly influenced one phase of his life.

MIDLIST. Those titles on a publisher's list expected to have limited sales. Midlist books are mainstream, not literary, scholarly or genre, and are usually written by new or relatively unknown writers.

MULTIPLE CONTRACT. Book contract that includes an agreement for a future book(s).

MYSTERY. A form of narration in which one or more elements remain unknown or unexplained until the end of the story. Subgenres include: amateur sleuth, caper, cozy, heist, malice domestic, police procedural, etc.

NET RECEIPTS. One method of royalty payment based on the amount of money a book publisher receives on the sale of the book after the booksellers' discounts, special sales discounts and returned copies.

NOVELIZATION. A novel created from the script of a popular movie and published in paperback. Also called a movie tie-in.

NOVELLA. A short novel or long short story, usually 20,000–50,000 words. Also called a novelette.

OCCULT. Supernatural phenomena, including ghosts, ESP, astrology, demonic possession, paranormal elements and witchcraft.

ONE-TIME RIGHTS. This right allows a short story or portions of a fiction or nonfiction book to be published again without violating the contract.

OPTION. The act of a producer buying film rights to a book for a limited period of time (usually six months or one year) rather than purchasing said rights in full. A book can be optioned multiple times by different production companies.

OPTION CLAUSE. A contract clause giving a publisher the right to publish an author's next book.

OUTLINE. A summary of a book's content (up to 15 double-spaced pages); often in the form of chapter headings with a descriptive sentence or two under each one to show the scope of the book.

PICTURE BOOK. A type of book aimed at ages 2–9 that tells the story partially or entirely with artwork, with up to 1,000 words. Agents interested in selling to publishers of these books often handle both artists and writers.

PLATFORM. A writer's speaking experience, interview skills, website and other abilities that help form a following of potential buyers for his book.

PROOFREADING. Close reading and correction of a manuscript's typographical errors.

PROPOSAL. An offer to an editor or publisher to write a specific work, usually a package consisting of an outline and sample chapters.

PROSPECTUS. A preliminary written description of a book, usually one page in length.

PSYCHIC/SUPERNATURAL. Fiction exploiting—or requiring as plot devices or themes—some contradictions of the commonplace natural world and materialist assumptions about it (including the traditional ghost story).

QUERY. A letter written to an agent or a potential market to elicit interest in a writer's work.

READER. A person employed by an agent or buyer to go through the slush pile of manuscripts and scripts, and select those worth considering.

REGIONAL. A book faithful to a particular geographic region and its people, including behavior, customs, speech and history.

RELEASE. A statement that your idea is original, has never been sold to anyone else, and that you are selling negotiated rights to the idea upon payment. Some agents may ask that you sign a release before they request pages and review your work.

REMAINDERS. Leftover copies of an out-of-print or slow-selling book purchased from the publisher at a reduced rate. Depending on the contract, a reduced royalty or no royalty is paid to the author on remaindered books.

REPRINT RIGHTS. The right to republish a book after its initial printing.

ROMANCE. A type of category fiction in which the love relationship between a man and a woman pervades the plot. The story is told from the viewpoint of the heroine, who meets a man (the hero), falls in love with him, encounters a conflict that hinders their relationship, and then resolves the conflict with a happy ending.

ROYALTIES. A percentage of the retail price paid to the author for each copy of the book that is sold. Agents take their percentage from the royalties earned and from the advance.

SASE. Self-addressed, stamped envelope. It should be included with all mailed correspondence.

SCHOLARLY BOOKS. Books written for an academic or research audience. These are usually heavily researched, technical and often contain terms used only within a specific field.

SCIENCE FICTION. Literature involving elements of science and technology as a basis for conflict, or as the setting for a story.

SERIAL RIGHTS. The right for a newspaper or magazine to publish sections of a manuscript.

SIMULTANEOUS SUBMISSION. Sending the same query or manuscript to several agents or publishers at the same time.

SLICE OF LIFE. A type of short story, novel, play or film that takes a strong thematic approach, depending less on plot than on vivid detail in describing the setting and/or environment, and the environment's effect on characters involved in it.

SLUSH PILE. A stack of unsolicited submissions in the office of an editor, agent or publisher.

STANDARD COMMISSION. The commission an agent earns on the sales of a manuscript. The commission percentage (usually 15 percent) is taken from the advance and royalties paid to the writer.

SUBAGENT. An agent handling certain subsidiary rights, usually working in conjunction with the agent who handled the book rights. The percentage paid the book agent is increased to pay the subagent.

SUBSIDIARY. An incorporated branch of a company or conglomerate (for example, Crown Publishing Group is a subsidiary of Random House, Inc.).

SUBSIDIARY RIGHTS. All rights other than book publishing rights included in a book publishing contract, such as paperback rights, book club rights and movie rights. Part of an agent's job is to negotiate those rights and advise you on which to sell and which to keep.

SUSPENSE. The element of both fiction and some nonfiction that makes the reader uncertain about the outcome. Suspense can be created through almost any element of a story, including the title, characters, plot, time restrictions and word choice.

SYNOPSIS. A brief summary of a story, novel or play. As a part of a book proposal, it is a comprehensive summary condensed in a page or page-and-a-half, single-spaced. Unlike a query letter or logline, a synopsis is a front-to-back explanation of the work—and will give away the story's ending.

TERMS. Financial provisions agreed upon in a contract, whether between writer and agent, or writer and editor.

TEXTBOOK. Book used in school classrooms at the elementary, high school or college level.

THEME. The point a writer wishes to make. It poses a question—a human problem.

THRILLER. A story intended to arouse feelings of excitement or suspense. Works in this genre are highly sensational, usually focusing on illegal activities, international espionage, sex and violence.

TOC. Table of Contents. A listing at the beginning of a book indicating chapter titles and their corresponding page numbers. It can also include chapter descriptions.

TRADE BOOK. Either a hardcover or softcover book sold mainly in bookstores. The subject matter frequently concerns a special interest for a more general audience.

TRADE PAPERBACK. A soft-bound volume, usually 5×8 inches, published and designed for the general public; available mainly in bookstores.

TRANSLATION RIGHTS. Sold to a foreign agent or foreign publisher.

UNSOLICITED MANUSCRIPT. An unrequested full manuscript sent to an editor, agent or publisher.

VET. A term used by editors when referring to the procedure of submitting a book manuscript to an outside expert (such as a lawyer) for review before publication. Memoirs are frequently vetted to confirm factually accuracy before the book is published.

WESTERNS/FRONTIER. Stories set in the American West, almost always in the 19th century, generally between the antebellum period and the turn of the century.

YOUNG ADULT (YA). The general classification of books written for ages 12–15. They run 40,000–80,000 words and include category novels—adventure, sports, paranormal, science fiction, fantasy, multicultural, mysteries, romance, etc.

NEW AGENT SPOTLIGHTS

Learn about new reps seeking clients.

....

by Chuck Sambuchino

One of the most common recurring blog items I get complimented on is my "New Agent Alerts," a series where I spotlight new/newer literary reps who are open to queries and looking for clients right now.

This is due to the fact that newer agents are golden opportunities for aspiring authors because they are actively building their client lists. They're hungry to sign new clients and start the ball rolling with submissions to editors and get books sold. Whereas an established agent with 40 clients may have little to no time to consider new writers' work (let alone help them shape it), a newer agent may be willing to sign a promising writer whose work is not a guaranteed huge payday.

THE CONS AND PROS OF NEWER AGENTS

At writing conferences, a frequent question I get is "Is it OK to sign with a new agent?" The question comes about because people value experience and wonder about the skill of someone who's new to the scene. The concern is an interesting one, so let me try to list the downsides and upsides to choosing a rep who's in her first few years agenting.

Probable cons
- They are less experienced in contract negotiations.
- They know fewer editors at this point than a rep who's been in business a while, meaning there is a less likely chance they can help you get published. This is a big, justified point—and writers' foremost concern.
- They are in a weaker position to demand a high advance for you.

- New agents come and some go. This means if your agent is in business for a year or two and doesn't find the success for which they hoped, they could bail on the biz altogether. That leaves you without a home. If you sign with an agent who's been in business for 14 years, however, chances are they won't quit tomorrow.

Probable pros

- They are actively building their client lists—and that means they are anxious to sign new writers and lock in those first several sales.
- They are willing to give your work a longer look. They may be willing to work with you on a project to get it ready for submission, whereas a more established agent has lots of clients and no time—meaning they have no spare moments to help you with shaping your novel or proposal.
- With fewer clients under their wing, you will get more attention than you would with an established rep.
- If they've found their calling and don't seem like they're giving up any time soon (and keep in mind, most do continue on as agents), you can have a decades-long relationship that pays off with lots of books.
- They have little going against them. An established agent once told me that a new agent is in a unique position because they have no duds under their belt. Their slates are clean.

HOW CAN YOU DECIDE FOR YOURSELF?

1. Factor in if they're part of a larger agency. Agents share contacts and resources. If your agent is the new girl at an agency with five people, those other four agents will help her (and you) with submissions. In other words, she's new, but not alone.

2. Learn where the agent came from. Has she been an apprentice at the agency for two years? Was she an editor for seven years and just switched to agenting? If they already have a few years in publishing under their belt, they're not as green as you may think. Agents don't become agents overnight.

3. Ask where she will submit the work. This is a big one. If you fear the agent lacks proper contacts to move your work, ask straight out: "What editors do you see us submitting this book to, and have you sold to them before?" The question tests their plan for where to send the manuscript and get it in print.

4. Ask them, "Why should I sign with you?" This is another straight-up question that gets right to the point. If she's new and has little/no sales at that point, she can't respond with "I sell tons of books and I make it rain cash money!! Dolla dolla bills, y'all!!!" She can't rely on her track record to entice you. So what's her sales pitch? Weigh her enthusiasm, her plan for the book, her promises of hard work and anything else she tells you. In the publishing business, you want communication and enthusiasm from agents (and editors). Both are invaluable. What's the point of signing with a huge agent when they don't return your e-mails and consider your book last on their list of priorities for the day?

5. If you're not sold, you can always say no. It's as simple as that. Always query new/newer agents because, at the end of the day, just because they offer representation doesn't mean you have to accept.

NEW AGENT SPOTLIGHTS

Peppered throughout this book's large number of agency listings are sporadic "New Agent Alert" sidebars. Look them over to see if these newer reps would be a good fit for your work. Always read personal information and submission guidelines carefully. Don't let an agent reject you because you submitted work incorrectly. Wherever possible, we have included a website address for their agency, as well as their Twitter handle for those reps that tweet.

Also please note that as of when this book went to press in 2013, all these agents were still active and looking for writers. That said, I cannot guarantee every one is still in their respective position when you read this, nor that they have kept their query inboxes open. I urge you to visit agency websites and double check before you query. (This is always a good idea in any case.) Good luck!

....

CHUCK SAMBUCHINO (chucksambuchino.com, @chucksambuchino on Twitter) edits the *Guide to Literary Agents* (guidetoliteraryagents.com/blog) as well as the *Children's Writer's & Illustrator's Market.* His pop-humor books include *How to Survive a Garden Gnome Attack* (film rights optioned by Sony) and *Red Dog / Blue Dog: When Pooches Get Political* (reddog-bluedog.com). Chuck's other writing books include *Formatting & Submitting Your Manuscript, 3rd. Ed.,* as well as *Create Your Writer Platform* (fall 2012). Besides that, he is a husband, sleep-deprived new father, guitarist, dog owner, and cookie addict.

....

LITERARY AGENTS

Agents listed in this section generate 98-100 percent of their income from commission on sales. They do not charge for reading, critiquing or editing your manuscript or book proposal. It's the goal of an agent to find salable manuscripts: Her income depends on finding the best publisher for your manuscript.

Since an agent's time is better spent meeting with editors, she will have little or no time to critique your writing. Agents who don't charge fees must be selective and often prefer to work with established authors, celebrities or those with professional credentials in a particular field.

Some agents in this section may charge clients for office expenses such as photocopying, foreign postage, long-distance phone calls or express mail services. Make sure you have a clear understanding of what these expenses are before signing any agency agreement.

SUBHEADS

Each agency listing is broken down into subheads to make locating specific information easier. In the first section, you'll find contact information for each agency. You'll also learn if the agents within the agency belong to any professional organizations; membership in these organizations can tell you a lot about an agency. For example, members of the Association of Authors' Representatives (AAR) are prohibited from charging reading or evaluating fees. Additional information in this section includes the size of each agency, its willingness to work with new or unpublished writers, and its general areas of interest.

Member Agents: Agencies comprised of more than one agent list member agents and their individual specialties. This information will help you determine the appropriate person to whom you should send your query letter.

Represents: This section allows agencies to specify what nonfiction and fiction subjects they represent. Make sure you query only those agents who represent the type of material you write.

Look for the key icon to quickly learn an agent's areas of specialization. In this portion of the listing, agents mention the specific subject areas they're currently seeking, as well as those subject areas they do not consider.

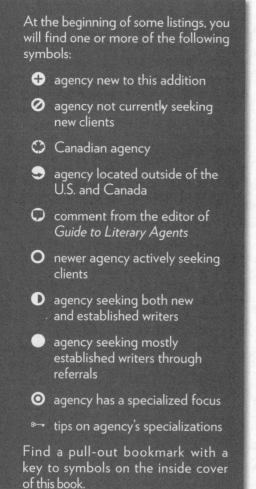

At the beginning of some listings, you will find one or more of the following symbols:

➕ agency new to this addition

⊘ agency not currently seeking new clients

🍁 Canadian agency

🌏 agency located outside of the U.S. and Canada

💬 comment from the editor of *Guide to Literary Agents*

◯ newer agency actively seeking clients

◐ agency seeking both new and established writers

⬤ agency seeking mostly established writers through referrals

◎ agency has a specialized focus

✎ tips on agency's specializations

Find a pull-out bookmark with a key to symbols on the inside cover of this book.

How to Contact: Most agents open to submissions prefer an initial query letter that briefly describes your work. While some agents may ask for an outline and a specific number of sample chapters, most don't. You should send these items only if the agent requests them. In this section, agents also mention if they accept queries by fax or e-mail, if they consider simultaneous submissions, and how they prefer to obtain new clients.

Recent Sales: To give you a sense of the types of material they represent, the agents list specific titles they've sold, as well as a sampling of clients' names. Note that some agents consider their client list confidential and may only share client names once they agree to represent you.

Terms: Provided here are details of an agent's commission, whether a contract is offered and for how long, and what additional office expenses you might have to pay if the agent agrees to represent you. Standard commissions range from 10-15 percent for domestic sales and 15-20 percent for foreign or dramatic sales (with the difference going to the co-agent who places the work).

Writers' Conferences: A great way to meet an agent is at a writers' conference. Here agents list the conferences they usually attend. For more information about a specific conference, check the Conferences section in this book.

Tips: In this section, agents offer advice and additional instructions for writers.

SPECIAL INDEXES

Literary Agents Specialties Index: This index organizes agencies according to the subjects they are interested in receiving. This index should help you compose a list of agents specializing in your areas. Cross-referencing categories and concentrating on agents interested in two or more aspects of your manuscript might increase your chances of success.

Agents Index: This index provides a list of agents' names in alphabetical order, along with the name of the agency for which they work. Find the name of the person you would like to contact, and then check the agency listing.

2M COMMUNICATIONS LTD.

33 W. 17 St., Penthouse, New York NY 10011. (212)741-1509. **Fax:** (212)691-4460. **E-mail:** morel@2mcommunications.com. **Website:** www.2mcommunications.com. **Contact:** Madeleine Morel. Member of AAR. Represents 100 clients. 20% of clients are new/unpublished writers. Currently handles: nonfiction books 100%.

Prior to becoming an agent, Ms. Morel worked at a publishing company.

REPRESENTS Nonfiction books. **Considers these nonfiction areas:** autobiography, biography, child guidance, cooking, cultural interests, diet/nutrition, ethnic, foods, health, history, medicine, music, parenting, self-help, women's issues, women's studies, cookbooks.

Only represents ghostwriters and works with major literary agents and publishing houses whose "platformed" authors require help.

HOW TO CONTACT Query with SASE. Submit outline, 3 sample chapters. Accepts simultaneous submissions. Responds in 1 week to queries. Responds in 1 month to mss. Obtains most new clients through recommendations from others, solicitations.

TERMS Agent receives 15% commission on domestic sales. Agent receives 20% commission on foreign sales. Offers written contract, binding for 2 years. Charges clients for postage, photocopying, long-distance calls, faxes.

A+B WORKS

E-mail: query@aplusbworks.com. **Website:** http://aplusbworks.com. **Contact:** Amy Jameson, Brandon Jameson. Estab. 2004.

Prior to her current position, Ms. Jameson worked at Janklow & Nesbit Associates.

REPRESENTS Nonfiction books, novels. **Considers these fiction areas:** young adult and middle-grade fiction, women's fiction, and select narrative nonfiction.

HOW TO CONTACT Query via e-mail only. "Please review our submissions policies first. Send queries to query@aplusbworks.com."

DOMINICK ABEL LITERARY AGENCY, INC.

146 W. 82nd St., #1A, New York NY 10024. (212)877-0710. **Fax:** (212)595-3133. **E-mail:** dominick@dalainc.com. Member AAR. Represents 100 clients. Currently handles: adult fiction and nonfiction.

HOW TO CONTACT Query via e-mail.

TERMS Agent receives 15% commission on domestic sales. Agent receives 20% commission on foreign sales.

ABOUT WORDS AGENCY

E-mail: query@aboutwords.org. **Website:** http://aboutwords.org. **Contact:** Felice Gums. Currently handles: nonfiction books 40%, novels 60%.

About Words Agency is looking for commercial fiction and nonfiction. Does not want true crime, religious/Christian market, poetry.

HOW TO CONTACT Only accepts e-mail queries. Send via e-mail with the subject: Query - [title of your book].

TERMS Agent receives 15% commission on domestic sales. Agent receives 20% commission on foreign sales. Offers written contract.

ADAMS LITERARY

7845 Colony Rd., C4 #215, Charlotte NC 28226. (704)542-1440. **Fax:** (704)542-1450. **E-mail:** info@adamsliterary.com. **E-mail:** submissions@adamsliterary.com. **Website:** www.adamsliterary.com. **Contact:** Tracey Adams, Josh Adams, Quinlan Lee. Member of AAR. Other memberships include SCBWI and WNBA. Currently handles: juvenile books.

MEMBER AGENTS Tracey Adams, Josh Adams, Quinlan Lee.

Represents "the finest children's book authors and artists."

HOW TO CONTACT Contact through online form on website only. Send e-mail if that is not operating correctly. "All submissions and queries must be made through the online form on our website. We will not review—and will promptly recycle—any unsolicited submissions or queries we receive by post. Before submitting your work for consideration, please carefully review our complete guidelines." Responds in 6 weeks. "While we have an established client list, we do seek new talent—and we accept submissions from both published and aspiring authors and artists."

TERMS Agent receives 15% commission on domestic sales; 20% on foreign sales. Offers written contract.

TIPS "Guidelines are posted (and frequently updated) on our website."

BRET ADAMS LTD. AGENCY

448 W. 44th St., New York NY 10036. (212)765-5630. **E-mail:** literary@bretadamsltd.net. **Website:** http://bretadamsltd.net. **Contact:** Colin Hunt, Mark Orsini. Member of AAR. Currently handles: movie scripts, TV scripts, stage plays.

MEMBER AGENTS Bruce Ostler, Mark Orsini.

REPRESENTS Movie scripts, TV scripts, TV movie of the week, theatrical stage play.

☞ Handles theatre/film and TV projects. No books. Cannot accept unsolicited material.

HOW TO CONTACT Professional recommendation.

● THE AGENCY GROUP, LLC

142 W 57th St., 6th Floor, New York NY 10019. (212)581-3100. **E-mail:** sarahstephens@theagencygroup.com. **Website:** www.theagencygroup.com. **Contact:** Marc Gerald, agent. Represents 50 clients. 10% of clients are new/unpublished writers. Currently handles: nonfiction books 60%, novels 30%, multimedia 10%.

○ Prior to becoming an agent, Mr. Gerald owned and ran an independent publishing and entertainment agency.

MEMBER AGENTS Marc Gerald, Sarah Stephens, Caroline Greeven.

REPRESENTS Nonfiction books, novels. **Considers these nonfiction areas:** anthropology, archeology, architecture, art, autobiography, biography, business, child guidance, cooking, cultural interests, dance, decorating, design, economics, environment, ethnic, finance, foods, government, health, history, how-to, humor, interior design, investigative, law, medicine, memoirs, money, nature, nutrition, parenting, personal improvement, popular culture, politics, psychology, satire, self-help, sports, true crime. **Considers these fiction areas:** action, adventure, cartoon, comic books, commercial, confession, contemporary issues, crime, detective, erotica, ethnic, experimental, family saga, feminist, frontier, gay, glitz, hi-lo, historical, horror, humor, inspirational, juvenile, lesbian, literary, mainstream, metaphysical, military, multicultural, multimedia, mystery, New Age, occult, picture books, plays, poetry, poetry in translation, police, psychic, regional, religious, romance, satire, short story collections, spiritual, sports, supernatural, suspense, thriller, translation, war, Westerns, women's, young adult.

☞ "While we admire beautiful writing, we largely represent recording artists, celebrities, authors, and pop culture and style brands with established platforms. When we represent fiction, we work almost exclusively in genre and in areas of expertise. We tend to take a non-linear approach to content—many of our projects ultimately have a TV/film or digital component." This agency is only taking on new clients through referrals.

HOW TO CONTACT "We are currently not accepting submissions except by referral." Accepts simultaneous submissions. Responds in 1 month to queries. Responds in 3 months to mss. Obtains most new clients through recommendations from others.

TERMS Agent receives 15% commission on domestic sales. Agent receives 20% commission on foreign sales. Offers written contract. Charges clients for office fees (only for mss that have been sold).

◑ THE AHEARN AGENCY, INC.

2021 Pine St., New Orleans LA 70118. **E-mail:** pahearn@aol.com. **Website:** www.ahearnagency.com. **Contact:** Pamela G. Ahearn. Other memberships include MWA, RWA, ITW. Represents 35 clients. 20% of clients are new/unpublished writers. Currently handles: novels 100%.

○ Prior to opening her agency, Ms. Ahearn was an agent for 8 years and an editor with Bantam Books.

REPRESENTS Considers these fiction areas: action, adventure, contemporary issues, crime, detective, ethnic, family saga, feminist, glitz, historical, humor, literary, mainstream, mystery, police, psychic, regional, romance, supernatural, suspense, thriller.

☞ Handles women's fiction and suspense fiction only. Does not want to receive category romance, science fiction or fantasy.

HOW TO CONTACT Query with SASE or via e-mail. Accepts simultaneous submissions. Responds in 8 weeks to queries. Responds in 10 weeks to mss. Obtains most new clients through recommendations from others, solicitations, conferences.

TERMS Agent receives 15% commission on domestic sales. Agent receives 20% commission on foreign sales. Offers written contract, binding for 1 year; renewable by mutual consent.

RECENT SALES *The Ronin's Mistress*, by Laura Joh Rowland; *How to Woo a Reluctant Lady*, Jeffies; *The Things That Keep Us Here*, by Carla Buckley.

WRITERS CONFERENCES Moonlight & Magnolias; RWA National Conference; Thriller Fest; Florida Romance Writers; Bouchercon; Malice Domestic.

TIPS "Be professional! Always send in exactly what an agent/editor asks for—no more, no less. Keep query letters brief and to the point, giving your writing credentials and a very brief summary of your book. If one agent rejects you, keep trying—there are a lot of us out there!"

AITKEN ALEXANDER ASSOCIATES

18-21 Cavaye Place, London England SW10 9PT United Kingdom. (020)7373-8672. **Fax:** (020)7373-6002. **E-mail:** reception@aitkenalexander.co.uk. **Website:** www.aitkenalexander.co.uk. Estab. 1976. Represents 300+ clients. 10% of clients are new/unpublished writers.

MEMBER AGENTS Gillon Aitken, agent; Clare Alexander, agent; Andrew Kidd, agent.

REPRESENTS Nonfiction books, novels. **Considers these nonfiction areas:** current affairs, government, history, law, memoirs, popular culture, politics. **Considers these fiction areas:** historical, literary.

⌐ "We specialize in literary fiction and nonfiction." Does not represent illustrated children's books, poetry, or screenplays.

HOW TO CONTACT Query with SASE. Submit synopsis, first 30 pages, and SASE. Aitken Alexander Associates. Address submission to an individual agent or to the Submissions Department. Responds in 6-8 weeks to queries. Obtains most new clients through recommendations from others, solicitations.

TERMS Agent receives 15% commission on domestic sales. Agent receives 20% commission on foreign sales. Offers written contract; 28-day notice must be given to terminate contract. Charges for photocopying and postage.

RECENT SALES Sold 50 titles in the last year. *My Life with George*, by Judith Summers (Voice); *The Separate Heart*, by Simon Robinson (Bloomsbury); *The Fall of the House of Wittgenstein*, by Alexander Waugh (Bloomsbury); *Shakespeare's Life*, by Germane Greer (Picador); *Occupational Hazards*, by Rory Stewart.

TIPS "Before submitting to us, we advise you to look at our existing client list to establish whether your work will be of interest. Equally, you should consider whether the material you have written is ready to submit to a literary agency. If you feel your work qualifies, then send us a letter introducing yourself. Keep it relevant to your writing (e.g., tell us about any previously published work, be it a short story or journalism; you may be studying or have completed a post graduate qualification in creative writing; when it comes to nonfiction, we would want to know what qualifies you to write about the subject)."

ALIVE COMMUNICATIONS, INC.

7680 Goddard St., Suite 200, Colorado Springs CO 80920. (719)260-7080. **Fax:** (719)260-8223. **E-mail:** submissions@alivecom.com. **Website:** www.alivecom.com. **Contact:** Rick Christian. Member of AAR. Other memberships include Authors Guild. Represents 100+ clients. 5% of clients are new/unpublished writers. Currently handles: nonfiction books 50%, novels 40%, juvenile books 10%.

MEMBER AGENTS Rick Christian, president (blockbusters, bestsellers); Lee Hough (popular/commercial nonfiction and fiction, thoughtful spirituality, children's); Andrea Heinecke (thoughtful/inspirational nonfiction, women's fiction/nonfiction, popular/commercial nonfiction & fiction); Joel Kneedler popular/commercial nonfiction and fiction, thoughtful spirituality, children's).

REPRESENTS Nonfiction books, novels, short story collections, novellas. **Considers these nonfiction areas:** autobiography, biography, business, child guidance, economics, how-to, inspirational, parenting, personal improvement, religious, self-help, women's issues, women's studies. **Considers these fiction areas:** adventure, contemporary issues, crime, family saga, historical, humor, inspirational, literary, mainstream, mystery, police, religious, satire, suspense, thriller.

⌐ This agency specializes in fiction, Christian living, how-to and commercial nonfiction. Actively seeking inspirational, literary and mainstream fiction, and work from authors with established track records and platforms. Does not want to receive poetry, scripts or dark themes.

HOW TO CONTACT Query via e-mail. "Be advised that this agency works primarily with well-established, bestselling, and career authors. Always looking for a breakout, blockbuster author with genuine talent." New clients come through recommendations from others.

TERMS Agent receives 15% commission on domestic sales. Offers written contract; 2-month notice must be given to terminate contract.

RECENT SALES Sold 300+ titles in the last year. Alive's bestselling titles include: *Heaven is for Real*, by Todd Burpo with Lynn Vincent (Nelson); *Loving*, by Karen Kingsbury (Zondervan); *A Hole in our Gospel*, by Rich Stearns (Nelson); *The Chance*, by Karen Kingsbury (Howard); *Unfinished*, by Rich Stearns

NEW AGENT SPOTLIGHT

STEVE KASDIN (CURTIS BROWN LTD)
curtisbrown.com

ABOUT STEVE: Steve Kasdin joined Curtis Brown in 2012. He has more than 20 years' experience in books and publishing, beginning his career as the mystery buyer at Barnes & Noble. He has been a Marketing executive at St. Martin's Press, Scholastic and Harcourt, an agent at the Sandra Dijkstra Agency and worked on Content Acquisition in the Kindle group at Amazon.com. In addition to representing clients at Curtis Brown, he is also the agency's Director of Digital Strategy, advising clients on all aspects of electronic publishing.

HE IS SEEKING: "Interesting, well-drawn characters thrown into unpredictable situations. I'm looking for: commercial fiction, including mysteries/thrillers, romantic suspense (emphasis on the suspense), and historical fiction); narrative nonfiction, including biography, history and current affairs; and young adult fiction, particularly if it has adult crossover appeal. I am *not* interested in SF/fantasy, memoirs, vampires and writers trying to capitalize on trends."

HOW TO SUBMIT: skasdin@cbltd.com. Responds in 4-6 weeks. Please send a query letter about what makes your book unique, a 1-3 page plot synopsis, a brief bio (including a description of your publishing history, if you have one), and the first 40-50 pages of your manuscript as a Word attachment to the email. "Let me know in your query letter if I am reading your work exclusively, in which case, I shall give it priority. If the book has been self-published or previously published, please let me know all the details—publisher, date, etc."

(Nelson); *The Pastor: A Memoir*, by Eugene Peterson (Harper One); *The Bridge*, by Karen Kingsbury (Howard); *Adapt or Die*, by Lt. Gen. (ret) Rick Lynch with Mark Dagostino (Baker); *C.S. Lewis: A Life*, by Alister McGrath (Tyndale); *7*, by Jen Hatmaker (B&H); *Successful Women Think Differently*, by Valorie Burton (Harvest House); *Same Kind of Different as Me*, by Ron Hall and Denver Moore (Nelson); *Lifelong Love Affair*, by Jimmy Evans with Frank Martin (Baker);

Days of War, by Cliff Graham (Zondervan); *Realm Walkers*, by Donita K. Paul (Zondervan).

TIPS Rewrite and polish until the words on the page shine. Endorsements and great connections may help, provided you can write with power and passion. Network with publishing professionals by making contacts, joining critique groups, and attending writers' conferences in order to make personal connections and to get feedback. Alive Communications, Inc., has established itself as a premiere literary agency. We serve an elite group of authors who are critically acclaimed and commercially successful in both Christian and general markets.

❶ ALLEN O'SHEA LITERARY AGENCY

615 Westover Rd., Stamford CT 06902. (203)359-9965. **Fax:** (203)357-9909. **E-mail:** marilyn@allen-oshea.com; coleen@allenoshea.com. **Website:** www.allenoshea.com. **Contact:** Marilyn Allen. Represents 100 clients. 20% of clients are new/unpublished writers. Currently handles: nonfiction books 99%.

○ Prior to becoming agents, both Ms. Allen and Ms. O'Shea held senior positions in publishing.

MEMBER AGENTS Marilyn Allen; Coleen O'Shea.
REPRESENTS Nonfiction books. **Considers these nonfiction areas:** biography, business, cooking, current affairs, health, history, how-to, humor, military, money, popular culture, psychology, sports, interior design/decorating.

⚷ "This agency specializes in practical nonfiction including cooking, sports, business, pop culture, etc. We look for clients with strong marketing platforms and new ideas coupled with strong writing." Actively seeking narrative nonfiction, health and history writers; very interested in writers who have large blog following and interesting topics. Does not want to receive fiction, memoirs, poetry, textbooks or children's.

HOW TO CONTACT Query via e-mail or mail with SASE. Submit outline, author bio, marketing page. No phone or fax queries. Accepts simultaneous submissions. Responds in 1 week to queries; 1-2 months to mss. Obtains most new clients through recommendations from others, conferences.

TERMS Agent receives 15% commission on domestic sales. Offers written contract, binding for 2 years; 1-month notice must be given to terminate contract. Charges for photocopying large mss, and overseas postage—"typically minimal costs."

RECENT SALES Sold 45 titles in the last year. "This agency prefers not to share information about specific sales, but see our website."

WRITERS CONFERENCES ASJA, Publicity Submit for Writers, Connecticut Authors and Publishers, Mark Victor Hansen Mega Book Conference.

TIPS "Prepare a strong overview, with competition, marketing and bio. We will consider when your proposal is ready."

❶ MIRIAM ALTSHULER LITERARY AGENCY

53 Old Post Rd. N, Red Hook NY 12571. (845)758-9408. **E-mail:** query@maliterary.com. **Website:** www.miriamaltshulerliteraryagency.com. **Contact:** Miriam Altshuler. Estab. 1994. Member of AAR. Represents 40 clients. Currently handles: nonfiction books 45%, novels 45%, story collections 5%, juvenile books 5%.

○ Ms. Altshuler has been an agent since 1982.

REPRESENTS Nonfiction books, novels, short story collections, juvenile. **Considers these nonfiction areas:** biography, ethnic, history, language, memoirs, multicultural, music, nature, popular culture, psychology, sociology, film, women's. **Considers these fiction areas:** literary, mainstream, multicultural, some selective children's books.

⚷ Literary commercial fiction and nonfiction. Does not want self-help, mystery, how-to, romance, horror, spiritual, fantasy, poetry, screenplays, science fiction or techno-thriller, western.

HOW TO CONTACT Query. "If we want to see your ms we will respond via e-mail (if you do not have an e-mail address, please send an SASE). We will only respond if interested in materials. Submit contact info with e-mail address." Prefers to read materials exclusively. Accepts simultaneous submissions. Responds in 3 weeks to mss. Obtains most new clients through recommendations from others.

TERMS Agent receives 15% commission on domestic sales. Agent receives 20% commission on foreign sales. Charges clients for overseas mailing, photocopies, overnight mail when requested by author.

WRITERS CONFERENCES Bread Loaf Writers' Conference; Washington Independent Writers Conference; North Carolina Writers' Network Conference.

TIPS See the website for specific submission details.

❶ AMBASSADOR LITERARY AGENCY

P.O. Box 50358, Nashville TN 37205. (615)370-4700. **E-mail:** wes@ambassadoragency.com; info@ambassadoragency.com. **Website:** www.ambassadoragency.com. **Contact:** Wes Yoder. Represents 25-30 clients. 10% of clients are new/unpublished writers. Currently handles: nonfiction books 95%, novels 5%.

○ Prior to becoming an agent, Mr. Yoder founded a music artist agency in 1973; he established a speakers bureau division of the company in 1984.

REPRESENTS Nonfiction books, novels. **Considers these nonfiction areas:** biography, current affairs, ethnic, government, history, how to, memoirs, popular culture, religion, self help, womens.

✎ "This agency specializes in religious market publishing dealing primarily with A-level publishers." Actively seeking popular nonfiction themes, including the following: practical living; Christian spirituality; literary fiction. Does not want to receive short stories, children's books, screenplays, or poetry.

HOW TO CONTACT Ambassador Literary's department represents a growing list of best-selling authors. We represent select authors and writers who are published by the leading religious and general market publishers in the United States and Europe, and represent television and major motion picture rights for our clients. Authors should e-mail a short description of their manuscript with a request to submit their work for review. Guidelines for submission will be sent if we agree to review a manuscript. Accepts simultaneous submissions. Responds in 2-4 weeks to queries. Obtains most new clients through recommendations from others.

TERMS Agent receives 15% commission on domestic sales. Agent receives 20% commission on foreign sales. Offers written contract.

RECENT SALES Sold 20 titles in the last year. *The Death and Life of Gabriel Phillips*, by Stephen Baldwin (Hachette); *Amazing Grace: William Wilberforce and the Heroic Campaign to End Slavery*, by Eric Mataxas (Harper San Francisco); *Life@The Next Level*, by Courtney McBath (Simon and Schuster); *Women, Take Charge of Your Money*, by Carolyn Castleberry (Random House/Multnomah).

ⓘ MARCIA AMSTERDAM AGENCY

41 W. 82nd St., Suite 9A, New York NY 10024-5613. (212)873-4945. **Contact:** Marcia Amsterdam. Signatory of WGA. Currently handles: nonfiction books 15%, novels 70%, movie scripts 5%, TV scripts 10%.

○ Prior to opening her agency, Ms. Amsterdam was an editor.

REPRESENTS Novels, movie scripts, feature film, sitcom. **Considers these fiction areas:** adventure, detective, horror, mainstream, mystery, romance (contemporary, historical), science, thriller, young adult. **Considers these script areas:** comedy, romantic comedy.

HOW TO CONTACT Query with SASE. Responds in 1 month to queries.

TERMS Agent receives 15% commission on domestic sales. Agent receives 20% commission on foreign sales. Agent receives 10% commission on film sales. Offers written contract, binding for 1 year. Charges clients for extra office expenses, foreign postage, copying, legal fees (when agreed upon).

RECENT SALES *Hidden Child* by Isaac Millman (FSG); *Lucky Leonardo*, by Jonathan Canter (Sourcebooks).

TIPS "We are always looking for interesting literary voices."

ⓘ BETSY AMSTER LITERARY ENTERPRISES

6312 SW Capitol Hwy #503, Portland OR 97239. **Website:** www.amsterlit.com. **Contact:** Betsy Amster (adult); Mary Cummings (children's and YA). Estab. 1992. Member of AAR. Represents more than 65 clients. 35% of clients are new/unpublished writers. Currently handles: nonfiction books 65%, novels 35%.

○ Prior to opening her agency, Ms. Amster was an editor at Pantheon and Vintage for 10 years, and served as editorial director for the Globe Pequot Press for 2 years.

REPRESENTS Nonfiction books, novels. **Considers these nonfiction areas:** art & design, biography, business, child guidance, cooking/nutrition, current affairs, ethnic, gardening, health/medicine, history, memoirs, money, parenting, popular culture, psychology, science/technology, self-help, sociology, travelogues, social issues, women's issues. **Considers these fiction areas:** ethnic, literary, women's, high quality.

✎ "Actively seeking strong narrative nonfiction, particularly by journalists; outstanding literary fiction (the next Jennifer Haigh or Jess Walter); witty, intelligent commerical women's fiction (the next Elinor Lipman); mysteries that open new worlds to us; and high-profile self-help and psychology, preferably research based." Does not want to receive poetry, children's books, romances, western, science fiction, action/adventure, screenplays, fantasy, techno-thrillers, spy capers, apocalyptic scenarios, or political or religious arguments.

HOW TO CONTACT For adult titles: b.amster.as sistant@gmail.com. "For fiction or memoirs, please embed the first three pages in the body of your e-mail. For nonfiction, please embed your proposal." For children's and YA: b.amster.kidsbooks@gmail.com. See submission requirements online at website. "For picture books, please embed the entire text in the body of your e-mail. For novels, please embed the first three pages." Accepts simultaneous submissions. Responds in 1 month to queries. Responds in 2 months to mss. Obtains most new clients through recommendations from others, solicitations, conferences.

TERMS Agent receives 15% commission on domestic sales. Agent receives 20% commission on foreign sales. Offers written contract, binding for 1 year; 3-month notice must be given to terminate contract. Charges for photocopying, postage, messengers, galleys/books used in submissions to foreign and film agents and to magazines for first serial rights.

WRITERS CONFERENCES Los Angeles Times Festival of Books; USC Masters in Professional Writing; San Diego State University Writers' Conference; UCLA Extension Writers' Program; The Loft Literary Center; Willamette Writers Conference.

⊙ THE ANDERSON LITERARY AGENCY

435 Convent Ave., Suite 5, New York NY 10031. (646)783-9736. **E-mail:** contact@andersonliterary-agency.com. **Website:** www.andersonliteraryagency.com. **Contact:** Giles Anderson.

REPRESENTS Nonfiction books. **Considers these nonfiction areas:** biography, memoirs, religious, science, true crime.

☛ Biography, business/investing/finance, history, religious, mind/body/spirit, science.

HOW TO CONTACT Send brief query via e-mail.

⊙ ANDERSON LITERARY MANAGEMENT, LLC

12 W. 19th St., New York NY 10011. (212)645-6045. **Fax:** (212)741-1936. **E-mail:** info@andersonliterary.com; kathleen@andersonliterary.com; claire@andersonliterary.com. **Website:** www.andersonliterary.com. **Contact:** Kathleen Anderson. Estab. 2006. Member of AAR. Represents 100+ clients. 20% of clients are new/unpublished writers. Currently handles: nonfiction books 50%, novels 50%.

MEMBER AGENTS Kathleen Anderson, Claire Wheeler.

REPRESENTS Nonfiction books, novels, short story collections, juvenile. **Considers these nonfiction areas:** anthropology, archeology, architecture, art, autobiography, biography, cultural interests, current affairs, dance, design, education, environment, ethnic, gay, government, history, law, lesbian, memoirs, music, nature, politics, psychology, women's issues, women's studies. **Considers these fiction areas:** action, adventure, ethnic, family saga, feminist, frontier, gay, historical, lesbian, literary, mystery, suspense, thriller, westerns, women's, young adult.

☛ "Specializes in adult and young adult literary and commercial fiction, narrative nonfiction, American and European history, literary journalism, nature and travel writing, memoir, and biography. We do not represent science fiction, cookbooks, gardening, craft books or children's picture books. While we love literature in translation, we cannot accept samples of work written in languages other than English."

HOW TO CONTACT Query with SASE. Submit synopsis, first 3 sample chapters, proposal (for nonfiction). Snail mail queries only. Accepts simultaneous submissions. Responds in 6 weeks to queries. Obtains most new clients through recommendations from others, solicitations, conferences.

TERMS Agent receives 15% commission on domestic sales. Offers written contract.

WRITERS CONFERENCES Squaw Valley Conference.

TIPS "We do not represent plays or screenplays."

⊙ ARCADIA

31 Lake Place N., Danbury CT 06810. **E-mail:** arcadialit@sbcglobal.net. **Contact:** Victoria Gould Pryor. Member of AAR.

REPRESENTS Nonfiction books, literary and commercial fiction. **Considers these nonfiction areas:** biography, business, current affairs, health, history, psychology, science, true crime, women's, investigative journalism; culture; classical music; life transforming self-help.

☛ "I'm a very hands-on agent, which is necessary in this competitive marketplace. I work with authors on revisions until whatever we present to publishers is as strong as possible. Arcadia represents talented, dedicated, intelligent and ambitious writers who are looking for a long-term relationship based on professional success and mutual respect." Does not want to receive science fiction/fantasy, horror, memoirs about addiction or abuse, humor or children's/YA. "We are only able to read fiction submissions from previously published authors."

HOW TO CONTACT No unsolicited submissions. Query with SASE. This agency accepts e-queries (no attachments).

⊘ EDWARD ARMSTRONG LITERARY AGENCY

Fayville MA 01745. (401)569-7099. **Contact:** Edward Armstrong.

REPRESENTS Novels, short story collections, novellas. **Considers these fiction areas:** mainstream, romance, science, thriller, suspense.

🔑 Does not want to receive nonfiction or textbooks.

HOW TO CONTACT Obtains most new clients through solicitations.

TERMS Agent receives 5% commission on domestic sales. Agent receives 5% commission on foreign sales. This agency charges for photocopying and postage.

● THE AXELROD AGENCY

55 Main St., P.O. Box 357, Chatham NY 12037. (518)392-2100. **E-mail:** steve@axelrodagency.com. **Website:** www.axelrodagency.com. **Contact:** Steven Axelrod. Member of AAR. Represents 15-20 clients. 1% of clients are new/unpublished writers. Currently handles: novels 95%.

💬 Prior to becoming an agent, Mr. Axelrod was a book club editor.

REPRESENTS Novels. **Considers these fiction areas:** mystery, romance, women's.

HOW TO CONTACT Query with SASE. Accepts simultaneous submissions. Responds in 3 weeks to queries. Responds in 6 weeks to mss. Obtains most new clients through recommendations from others.

TERMS Agent receives 15% commission on domestic sales. Agent receives 20% commission on foreign sales. No written contract.

WRITERS CONFERENCES RWA National Conference.

● BARER LITERARY, LLC

20 W. 20th St., Suite 601, New York NY 10011. (212)691-3513. **E-mail:** submissions@barerliterary.com. **Website:** www.barerliterary.com. **Contact:** Julie Barer. Estab. 2004. Member of AAR.

💬 Before becoming an agent, Julie worked at Shakespeare & Co. Booksellers in New York City. She is a graduate of Vassar College.

MEMBER AGENTS Julie Barer; William Boggess (mainstream, literary, southern, short story collections, literary memoir, popular science, narrative history, and smart sportswriting).

REPRESENTS Nonfiction books, novels, short story collections., Julie Barer is especially interested in working with emerging writers and developing long-term relationships with new clients. **Considers these nonfiction areas:** biography, ethnic, history, memoirs, popular culture, women's. **Considers these fiction areas:** contemporary issues, ethnic, historical, literary, mainstream.

🔑 This agency no longer accepts young adult submissions. No health/fitness, business/investing/finance, sports, mind/body/spirit, reference, thrillers/suspense, military, romance, children's books/picture books, screenplays.

HOW TO CONTACT Query with SASE; no attachments if query by e-mail. "We do not respond to queries via phone or fax."

TERMS Agent receives 15% commission on domestic sales. Agent receives 20% commission on foreign sales. Offers written contract. Charges for photocopying and books ordered.

RECENT SALES *The Unnamed*, by Joshua Ferris (Reagan Arthur Books); *Tunneling to the Center of the Earth*, by Kevin Wilson (Ecco Press); *A Disobedient Girl*, by Ru Freeman (Atria Books); *A Friend of the Family*, by Lauren Grodstein (Algonquin); *City of Veils*, by Zoe Ferraris (Little, Brown).

⊕ BARONE LITERARY AGENCY

385 North St., Batavia OH 45103. (513)732-6740. **Fax:** (513)297-7208. **E-mail:** baroneliteraryagency@roadrunner.com. **Website:** www.baroneliteraryagency.com. **Contact:** Denise Barone. Estab. 2010. RWA Represents 7 clients. 100% of clients are new/unpublished writers.

💬 Denise Barone still maintains an active law degree, but is "hoping, increasingly, to focus [my] efforts more on agenting."

REPRESENTS Considers these nonfiction areas: memoirs. **Considers these fiction areas:** action, adventure, cartoon, comic books, commercial, confession, contemporary issues, crime, detective, erotica, ethnic, experimental, family saga, fantasy, feminist, frontier, gay, glitz, hi-lo, historical, horror, humor, inspirational, juvenile, lesbian, literary, mainstream, metaphysical, military, multicultural, multimedia, mystery, New Age, occult, plays, psychic, regional, religious, romance, science fiction, sports, thriller, women's, young adult. **Considers these script areas:** action, adventure, animation, cartoon, comedy, contemporary issues, crime, detective, erotica, ethnic, experimental, family saga, fantasy, feminist, gay, glitz, historical, horror, juvenile, lesbian, mainstream, mystery, police, psychic, religious, romantic comedy, romantic drama, science fiction, sports, supernatural, teen, thriller, western.

⚐ Actively seeking adult contemporary romance. Does not want textbooks.

HOW TO CONTACT Submit query letter, SASE and synopsis. Accepts simultaneous submissions. Obtains new clients by queries/submissions, Facebook, recommendations from others.

TERMS 15% commission on domestic sales, 20% on foreign sales. Offers written contract.

RECENT SALES *The Cinderella Files,* by Rebekah Purdy (Astrea Press); *The Trouble with Charlie,* by Cathy Bennett (Astrea Press).

TIPS "In the immortal words of Sir Winston Churchill, if you want to get published, you must never give up!"

◑ LORETTA BARRETT BOOKS, INC.

220 E. 23rd St., 11th Floor, New York NY 10010. (212)242-3420. **E-mail:** query@lorettabarrettbooks. com. **Website:** www.lorettabarrettbooks.com. **Contact:** Loretta A. Barrett; Nick Mullendore; Gabriel Davis. Estab. 1990. Member of AAR. Currently handles: nonfiction books 50%, novels 50%.

◖ Prior to opening her agency, Ms. Barrett was vice president and executive editor at Doubleday and editor-in-chief of Anchor Books.

MEMBER AGENTS Loretta A. Barrett; Nick Mullendore.

REPRESENTS Nonfiction books, novels. **Considers these nonfiction areas:** biography, child guidance, current affairs, ethnic, government, health/nutrition, history, memoirs, money, multicultural, nature, popular culture, psychology, religion, science, self help, sociology, spirituality, sports, women's, young adult, creative nonfiction. **Considers these fiction areas:** contemporary, psychic, adventure, detective,

ethnic, family, historical, literary, mainstream, mystery, thriller, young adult.

⚐ "The clients we represent include both fiction and nonfiction authors for the general adult trade market. The works they produce encompass a wide range of contemporary topics and themes including commercial thrillers, mysteries, romantic suspense, popular science, memoirs, narrative fiction and current affairs." No children's, juvenile, cookbooks, gardening, science fiction, fantasy novels, historical romance.

HOW TO CONTACT See guidelines online. Use e-mail (no attachments) or if by post, query with SASE. For hardcopy queries, please send a 1-2 page query letter and a synopsis or chapter outline for your project. In your letter, please include your contact information, any relevant background information on yourself or your project, and a paragraph of description of your project. If you are submitting electronically, then all of this material may be included in the body of your e-mail. Accepts simultaneous submissions. Responds in 3-6 weeks to queries.

TERMS Agent receives 15% commission on domestic sales. Agent receives 20% commission on foreign sales. Offers written contract. Charges clients for shipping and photocopying.

● BARRON'S LITERARY MANAGEMENT

4615 Rockland Dr., Arlington TX 76016. **E-mail:** barronsliterary@sbcglobal.net. **Contact:** Adele Brooks, president.

REPRESENTS Nonfiction books, novels. **Considers these nonfiction areas:** business/investing/finance, health/exercise/nutrition, history, cook books, psychology, science, true crime. **Considers these fiction areas:** historical, horror, all mysteries, detective/pi/police, romance: suspense, paranormal, historical, chick lit and lady lit, science fiction, thriller, crime thriller, medical thriller.

⚐ Barron's Literary Management is a small Dallas/Fort Worth-based agency with good publishing contacts. Seeks tightly written, fast moving fiction, as well as authors with a significant platform or subject area expertise for nonfiction book concepts.

HOW TO CONTACT Contact by e-mail initially. Send bio and a brief synopsis of story or a nonfiction proposal. Obtains most new clients through e-mail submissions.

TIPS "Have your book tightly edited, polished, and ready to be seen before contacting agents. I respond quickly and if interested may request an electronic or hard copy mailing."

⚫⚫ LORELLA BELLI LITERARY AGENCY (LBLA)

54 Hartford House, 35 Tavistock Crescent, Notting Hill, London England W11 1AY United Kingdom. (44)(207)727-8547. **Fax:** (44)(870)787-4194. **E-mail:** info@lorellabelliagency.com. **Website:** www.lorella belliagency.com. **Contact:** Lorella Belli. Membership includes AAA

REPRESENTS Nonfiction books, novels. **Considers these nonfiction areas:** business, current affairs, economics, history, personal improvement, politics, science, self-help, technology, travel, women's issues, women's studies, food/wine; popular music; lifestyle. **Considers these fiction areas:** historical, literary, genre fiction; women's; crime.

⚫➤ "We are interested in first-time novelists, journalists, multicultural and international writing, and books about Italy." Does not want children's books, fantasy, science fiction, screenplays, short stories, or poetry.

HOW TO CONTACT For fiction, send query letter, first 3 chapters, synopsis, brief CV, SASE. For nonfiction, send query letter, full proposal, chapter outline, 2 sample chapters, SASE.

TERMS Agent receives 15% commission on domestic sales. Agent receives 20% commission on foreign sales.

TIPS "Please send an initial inquiry letter or e-mail before submitting your work to us."

⚫ FAYE BENDER LITERARY AGENCY

19 Cheever Place, Brooklyn NY 11231. **E-mail:** info@ fbliterary.com. **Website:** www.fbliterary.com. **Contact:** Faye Bender. Estab. 2004. Member of AAR.

MEMBER AGENTS Faye Bender.

REPRESENTS Nonfiction books, novels, juvenile. **Considers these nonfiction areas:** biography, memoirs, popular culture, women's issues, women's studies, young adult, narrative; health; popular science. **Considers these fiction areas:** commercial, literary, women's, young adult (middle-grade).

⚫➤ "I choose books based on the narrative voice and strength of writing. I work with previously published and first-time authors." Faye does

not represent picture books, genre fiction for adults (western, romance, horror, science fiction, fantasy), business books, spirituality, or screenplays.

HOW TO CONTACT Query with SASE and 10 sample pages via mail or e-mail (no attachments). Guidelines online. "Please do not send queries or submissions via registered or certified mail, or by FedEx or UPS requiring signature. We will not return unsolicited submissions weighing more than 16 ounces, even if an SASE is attached. We do not respond to queries via phone or fax."

TIPS "Please keep your letters to the point, include all relevant information, and have a bit of patience."

THE BENT AGENCY

Bent Agency, The, 204 Park Place, Number 2, Brooklyn NY 11238. **E-mail:** info@thebentagency.com. **Website:** www.thebentagency.com. **Contact:** Jenny Bent; Susan Hawk; Molly Ker Hawn; Nicole Steen; Gemma Cooper. Estab. 2009.

⚫ Prior to forming her own agency, Ms. Bent was an agent and vice president at Trident Media.

MEMBER AGENTS Jenny Bent (all adult fiction, except for science fiction); Susan Hawk (young adult and middle grade books; within the realm of kids stories, she likes fantasy, science fiction, historical fiction, and mystery); Molly Ker Hawn (young adult and middle grade books, including contemporary, historical science fiction, fantasy, thrillers, mystery; Nicole Steen (literary and commercial fiction, narrative nonfiction, and memoir); Gemma Cooper (all ages of children's and young adult books, including picture books, likes historical, contemporary, thrillers, mystery, humor, and science fiction).

REPRESENTS Considers these fiction areas: commercial, crime, historical, horror, mystery, picture books, romance, suspense, thriller, women's, young adult literary.

HOW TO CONTACT For Jenny Bent, e-mail: queries@thebentagency.com; for Susan Hawk, e-mail: kidsqueries@thebentagency.com; for Molly Ker Hawn, e-mail: hawnqueries@thebentagency.com; for Nicole Steen, e-mail: steenqueries@thebentagency.com; for Gemma Cooper, e-mail: cooperqueries@ thebentagency.com. "Tell us briefly who you are, what your book is, and why you're the one to write it. Then include the first 10 pages of your material in the body of your e-mail. We respond to all queries; please resend your query if you haven't had a response within 4 weeks." Accepts simultaneous submissions.

RECENT SALES *The Ghost Bride*, by Yangsze Choo (Morrow); *The Life List*, by Lori Nelson Spielman (Bantam); *17 First Kisses*, by Rachael Allen (Harper); *Starter House*, by Sonja Condit (Morrow); *Disalmanac*, by Scott Bateman (Perigee); *Moms Who Drink and Swear*, by Nicole Knepper (NAL); *Movies R Fun*, by Josh Cooley (Chronicle); *Lark Rising*, by Sandra Waugh (Random House); *Chickens in the Road*, by Suzanne McMinn (HarperOne); *The Secret Diamond Sisters*, by Michelle Maddow (HarlequinTeen).

DAVID BLACK LITERARY AGENCY

335 Adams St., Suite 2707, Brooklyn NY 11201. (718)852-5500. **Website:** www.davidblackagency. com. **Contact:** David Black, owner. Member of AAR. Represents 150 clients. Currently handles: nonfiction books 90%, novels 10%.

MEMBER AGENTS David Black; Susan Raihofer (general nonfiction, literary fiction); Gary Morris (commercial fiction, psychology); Joy E. Tutela (general nonfiction, literary fiction); Linda Loewenthal (general nonfiction, health, science, psychology, narrative); Antonella Iannarino (commerial and literary fiction, YA/middle-grade fiction, nonfiction); David M. Larabell (nonfiction); Susan Raihofer (commerical fiction and nonfiction);Sarah Smith (nonfiction).

REPRESENTS Nonfiction books, novels. **Considers these nonfiction areas:** autobiography, biography, business, economics, finance, government, health, history, inspirational, law, medicine, military, money, multicultural, psychology, religious, sports, war, women's issues, women's studies. **Considers these fiction areas:** literary, mainstream, commercial.

→ This agency specializes in business, sports, politics, and novels.

HOW TO CONTACT Query with SASE. For nonfiction works, send a formal proposal that includes an overview, author bio, chapter outline, a marketing/publicity section, a competition section, and at least 1 sample chapter. Also include writing samples, such as newspaper or magazine clips if relevant. (See questions in Guidelines online.) When submitting fiction, include a synopsis, author bio, and the first 3 chapters of the book (25-50 pages). Accepts simultaneous submissions. Responds in 2 months to queries.

TERMS Agent receives 15% commission on domestic sales. Charges clients for photocopying and books purchased for sale of foreign rights.

RECENT SALES SOME of the agency's best-selling authors include: Mitch Albom, Erik Larson, Ken Davis, Bruce Feiler, Dan Coyle, Jane Leavy, Randy Pausch, Steve Lopez, Jenny Sanford, David Kidder and Noah Oppenheim.

BLEECKER STREET ASSOCIATES, INC.

217 Thompson St., #519, New York NY 10012. (212)677-4492. **Fax:** (212)388-0001. **E-mail:** bleeckerst@hotmail.com. **Contact:** Agnes Birnbaum. Member of AAR. Other memberships include RWA, MWA. Represents 60 clients. 20% of clients are new/unpublished writers. Currently handles: nonfiction books 75%, novels 25%.

⚬ Prior to becoming an agent, Ms. Birnbaum was a senior editor at Simon & Schuster, Dutton/Signet, and other publishing houses.

REPRESENTS Nonfiction books, novels. **Considers these nonfiction areas:** New Age, animals, biography, business, child, computers, cooking, current affairs, ethnic, government, health, history, how to, memoirs, military, money, nature, popular culture, psychology, religion, science, self help, sociology, sports, true crime, women's. **Considers these fiction areas:** ethnic, historical, literary, mystery, romance, thriller, women's.

→ "We're very hands-on and accessible. We try to be truly creative in our submission approaches. We've had especially good luck with first-time authors." Does not want to receive science fiction, westerns, poetry, children's books, academic/scholarly/professional books, plays, scripts, or short stories.

HOW TO CONTACT Query with SASE. No e-mail, phone, or fax queries. Accepts simultaneous submissions. Responds in 2 weeks to queries. Responds in 1 month to mss. "Obtains most new clients through recommendations from others, solicitations, conferences, plus, I will approach someone with a letter if his/her work impresses me."

TERMS Agent receives 15% commission on domestic sales. Agent receives 25% commission on foreign sales. Offers written contract; 1-month notice must be given to terminate contract. Charges for postage, long distance, fax, messengers, photocopies (not to exceed $200).

RECENT SALES Sold 14 titles in the last year. *Following Sarah*, by Daniel Brown (Morrow); *Biology of the Brain*, by Paul Swingle (Rutgers University Press); *Santa Miracles*, by Brad and Sherry Steiger (Adams); *Surviving the College Search*, by Jennifer Delahunt (St. Martin's).

TIPS "Keep query letters short and to the point; include only information pertaining to the book or background as a writer. Try to avoid superlatives in description. Work needs to stand on its own, so how much editing it may have received has no place in a query letter."

BOOK CENTS LITERARY AGENCY, LLC

P.O. Box 11826, Charleston WV 25339. **E-mail:** cw@bookcentsliteraryagency.com. **Website:** www.bookcentsliteraryagency.com. **Contact:** Christine Witthohn. Member of AAR. RWA, MWA, SinC, KOD

MEMBER AGENTS Christine Witthohn (Christine represents both published and unpublished authors.).

"Single-title romance (contemporary, romantic comedy, paranormal, mystery/suspense), women's lit (must have a strong hook), mainstream mystery/suspense, thrillers (high octane, psychological), literary fiction and new adult. For nonfiction, seeking women's issues/experiences, fun/quirky topics (particularly those of interest to women), cookbooks (fun, ethnic, etc.), gardening (herbs, plants, flowers, etc.), books with a 'save-the-planet' theme, how-to books, travel and outdoor adventure." Does not want to receive category romance, erotica, inspirational, historical, sci-fi/fantasy, horror/dark thrillers (serial killers), short stories/novella, children's picture books, poetry, screenplays.

HOW TO CONTACT "We are closed to unsolicited queries at this time. We only accept referrals from clients and other industry pros and manuscripts we've requested from writers who have pitched us at conferences we've attended. Please note, we are a green company and only accept e-mail submissions."

TIPS "Sponsors *International Women's Fiction Festival* in Matera, Italy. See: www.womensfictionfestival.com for more information. Christine is also the U.S. rights and licensing agent for leading French publisher, Bragelonne, Egmont-Germany. For a list of up coming publications, leading clients and sales, visit: www.publishersmarketplace.com/members/BookCents."

BOOKENDS, LLC

136 Long Hill Rd., Gillette NJ 07933. **Website:** www.bookends-inc.com. **Contact:** Kim Lionetti, Jessica Alvarez. Member of AAR. RWA, MWA Represents 50+ clients. 10% of clients are new/unpublished writers. Currently handles: nonfiction books 50%, novels 50%.

MEMBER AGENTS Jessica Faust (**no longer accepting unsolicited material**) (fiction: romance, erotica, women's fiction, mysteries and suspense; nonfiction: business, finance, career, parenting, psychology, women's issues, self-help, health, sex); Kim Lionetti (only currently considering romance, women's fiction, and young adult queries. "If your book is in any of these 3 categories, please be sure to specify 'Romance,' 'Women's Fiction,' or 'Young Adult' in your e-mail subject line. Any queries that do not follow these guidelines will not be considered."); Jessica Alvarez (romance, women's fiction, erotica, romantic suspense).

REPRESENTS Nonfiction books, novels. **Considers these nonfiction areas:** business, child, ethnic, gay, health, how-to, money, psychology, religion, self-help, sex, true crime, women's. **Considers these fiction areas:** detective, cozies, mainstream, mystery, romance, thrillers, women's.

"BookEnds is currently accepting queries from published and unpublished writers in the areas of romance (and all its sub-genres), erotica, mystery, suspense, women's fiction, and literary fiction. We also do a great deal of nonfiction in the areas of self-help, business, finance, health, pop science, psychology, relationships, parenting, pop culture, true crime, and general nonfiction." BookEnds does not want to receive children's books, screenplays, science fiction, poetry, or technical/military thrillers.

HOW TO CONTACT Review website for guidelines, as they change. BookEnds is no longer accepting unsolicited proposal packages or snail mail queries. Send query in the body of e-mail to only 1 agent.

THE BOOKER ALBERT LITERARY AGENCY

P.O Box 20931, York, PA 17402. **E-mail:** brittany@thebookeralbertagency.com; jordy@thebookeralbertagency.com. **Website:** www.thebookeralbertagency.com.

MEMBER AGENTS Brittany Booker (contemporary romances, fantasies, YA and New Adult, middle grade, erotica); Jordy Albert (middle grade, young adult, romance, new adult romance, women's fiction).

○ Prior to opening the agency, both Ms. Booker and Ms. Albert were agents at the Corvisiero Literary Agency.

HOW TO CONTACT E-mail only (no attachments). Include genre and word count at the beginning of your query. Responds within 8 weeks if interested.

TERMS Agent receives 15% commission on domestic sales.

● **BOOKS & SUCH LITERARY AGENCY**

52 Mission Circle, Suite 122, PMB 170, Santa Rosa CA 95409. **E-mail:** representation@booksandsuch.com. **Website:** www.booksandsuch.biz. **Contact:** Janet Kobobel Grant, Wendy Lawton, Rachel Kent, Mary Keeley, Rachelle Gardner. Member of AAR. Member of CBA (associate), American Christian Fiction Writers. Represents 150 clients. 5% of clients are new/unpublished writers. Currently handles: nonfiction books 50%, novels 50%.

○ Prior to becoming an agent, Ms. Grant was an editor for Zondervan and managing editor for *Focus on the Family*; Ms. Lawton was an author, sculptor, and designer of porcelein dolls. Ms. Keeley accepts both nonfiction and adult fiction. She previously was an acquisition editor for Tyndale publishers.

REPRESENTS Nonfiction books, novels. **Considers these nonfiction areas:** humor, religion, self help, women's. **Considers these fiction areas:** contemporary, family, historical, mainstream, religious, romance.

⚷ This agency specializes in general and inspirational fiction, romance, and in the Christian booksellers market. Actively seeking well-crafted material that presents Judeo-Christian values, if only subtly.

HOW TO CONTACT Query via e-mail only; no attachments. Accepts simultaneous submissions. Responds in 1 month to queries. "If you don't hear from us asking to see more of your writing within 30 days after you have sent your e-mail, please know that we have read and considered your submission but determined that it would not be a good fit for us." Obtains most new clients through recommendations from others, conferences.

TERMS Agent receives 15% commission on domestic sales. Agent receives 20% commission on foreign sales. Offers written contract; 2-month notice must be given to terminate contract. No additional charges.

RECENT SALES Sold 125 titles in the last year. *One Perfect Gift*, by Debbie Macomber (Howard Books); *Greetings from the Flipside*, by Rene Gutteridge and Cheryl Mckay (B&H Publishing); *Key on the Quilt*, by Stephanie Grace Whitson (Barbour Publishing); *Annotated Screwtape Letters, Annotations*, by Paul Mccusker, (Harper One). Other clients include: Lauraine Snelling, Lori Copeland, Rene Gutteridge, Dale Cramer, BJ Hoff, Diann Mills.

WRITERS CONFERENCES Mount Hermon Christian Writers' Conference; Writing for the Soul; American Christian Fiction Writers' Conference; San Francisco Writers' Conference.

TIPS "The heart of our agency's motivation is to develop relationships with the authors we serve, to do what we can to shine the light of success on them, and to help be a caretaker of their gifts and time."

BOOKSTOP LITERARY AGENCY

67 Meadow View Rd., Orinda CA 94563. (925)254-2664. **Fax:** (925)254-2668. **E-mail:** kendra@bookstopliterary.com; info@bookstopliterary.com. **Website:** www.bookstopliterary.com. Estab. 1983.

⚷ "Special interest in Hispanic, Asian American, and African American writers; quirky picture books; clever adventure/mystery novels; and authentic and emotional young adult voices."

HOW TO CONTACT Send: cover letter, entire ms for picture books; first 30 pages of novels; proposal and sample chapters OK for nonfiction. E-mail submissions: Paste cover letter and first 10 pages of ms into body of e-mail, send to info@bookstopliterary.com. Send sample illustrations only if you are an illustrator.

TERMS Agent receives 15% commission on domestic sales. Offers written contract, binding for 1 year.

● **THE BARBARA BOVA LITERARY AGENCY**

3951 Gulf Shore Blvd. N., Unit PH 1-B, Naples FL 34103. (239)649-7263. **Fax:** (239)649-7263. **E-mail:** michaelburke@barbarabovaliteraryagency.com. **Website:** www.barbarabovaliteraryagency.com. **Contact:** Ken Bova, Michael Burke. Represents 30 clients. Currently handles: nonfiction books 20%, fiction 80%.

REPRESENTS Nonfiction books, novels. **Considers these nonfiction areas:** biography, history, science, self help, true crime, women's, social sciences. **Considers these fiction areas:** adventure, crime, detective, mystery, police, science fiction, suspense, thriller, women's, young adult, teen lit.

8—✒ This agency specializes in fiction and nonfiction, hard and soft science. "We also handle foreign, movie, television, and audio rights." No scripts, poetry, or children's books.

HOW TO CONTACT Query through website. No attachments. "We accept short (3-5 pages) e-mail queries. All queries should have the word 'Query' in the subject line. Include all information as you would in a standard, snail mail query letter, such as pertinent credentials, publishing history, and an overview of the book. Include a word count of your project. You may include a short synopsis. We're looking for quality fiction and nonfiction." Obtains most new clients through recommendations from others.

TERMS Agent receives 15% commission on domestic sales. Agent receives 20% commission on foreign sales. Charges clients for overseas postage, overseas calls, photocopying, shipping.

RECENT SALES Sold 24 titles in the last year. *The Green Trap* and *The Aftermath*, by Ben Bova; *Empire and a War of Gifts*, by Orson Scott Card; *Radioman*, by Carol E. Hipperson.

◐ BRADFORD LITERARY AGENCY

5694 Mission Center Rd., #347, San Diego CA 92108. (619)521-1201. **E-mail:** queries@bradfordlit.com. **Website:** www.bradfordlit.com. Member of AAR. RWA, SCBWI, ALA Represents 50 clients. 20% of clients are new/unpublished writers. Currently handles: nonfiction books 5%, novels 95%.

MEMBER AGENTS Laura Bradford, Natalie Lakosil, Sarah LaPolla.

REPRESENTS Nonfiction books, novels, novellas, stories within a single author's collection, anthology. **Considers these nonfiction areas:** business, child care, current affairs, health, history, how-to, memoirs, money, popular culture, psychology, self-help, women's interest. **Considers these fiction areas:** adventure, detective, erotica, ethnic, historical, humor, mainstream, mystery, romance, thriller, psychic/supernatural.

8—✒ Actively seeking romance (historical, romantic suspense, paranormal, category, contemporary, erotic), urban fantasy, women's fiction, mystery, thrillers, children's (Natalie Lakosil only), and young adult. Does not want to receive poetry, screenplays, short stories, westerns, horror, new age, religion, crafts, cookbooks, gift books.

HOW TO CONTACT Accepts e-mail queries only; send to queries@bradfordlit.com. The entire submission must appear in the body of the e-mail and not as an attachment. The subject line should begin as follows: QUERY: (the title of the ms or any short message that is important should follow). For fiction: e-mail a query letter along with the first chapter of ms and a synopsis. Include the genre and word count in cover letter. Nonfiction: e-mail full nonfiction proposal including a query letter and a sample chapter. Accepts simultaneous submissions. Responds in 2-4 weeks to queries. Responds in 10 weeks to mss. Obtains most new clients through solicitations.

TERMS Agent receives 15% commission on domestic sales. Agent receives 20% commission on foreign sales. Offers written contract, non-binding for 2 years; 45-day notice must be given to terminate contract. Charges for extra copies of books for foreign submissions.

RECENT SALES Sold 68 titles in the last year. *All Fall Down*, by Megan Hart (Mira Books); *Body and Soul*, by Stacey Kade (Hyperion Children's); *All Things Wicked*, by Karina Cooper (Avon); *Circle Eight: Matthew*, by Emma Lang (Kensington Brava); *Midnight Enchantment*, by Anya Bast (Berkley Sensation); *Outpost*, by Ann Aguirre (Feiwel and Friends); *The One That I Want*, by Jennifer Echols (Simon Pulse); *Catch Me a Cowboy*, by Katie Lane (Grand Central); *Back in a Soldier's Arms*, by Soraya Lane (Harlequin); *Enraptured*, by Elisabeth Naughton (Sourcebooks); *Wicked Road to Hell*, by Juliana Stone (Avon); *Master of Sin*, by Maggie Robinson (Kensington Brava); *Chaos Burning*, by Lauren Dane (Berkley Sensation); *If I Lie*, by Corrine Jackson (Simon Pulse); *Renegade*, by J.A. Souders (Tor).

WRITERS CONFERENCES RWA National Conference; Romantic Times Booklovers Convention.

◐ BRANDT & HOCHMAN LITERARY AGENTS, INC.

1501 Broadway, Suite 2310, New York NY 10036. (212)840-5760. **Fax:** (212)840-5776. **Contact:** Gail Hochman. Member of AAR. Represents 200 clients.

MEMBER AGENTS Carl Brandt; Gail Hochman; Marianne Merola; Charles Schlessiger; Bill Contardi; Joanne Brownstein, Emily Forland; Emma Patterson (literary and commercial fiction, upmarket women's fiction, historical fiction, narrative nonfiction, pop culture, memoir, food writing, and YA and MG fiction and nonfiction); Jody Klein (literary and commercial fiction, crime/suspense, historical fiction, graphic novels/memoirs, and magical realism, as well as narrative nonfiction (especially related to sports, science, or history), and prescriptive nonfiction).

REPRESENTS Nonfiction books, novels, short story collections, juvenile, journalism. **Considers these nonfiction areas:** autobiography, biography, cultural interests, current affairs, ethnic, government, history, law, politics, women's issues, women's studies. **Considers these fiction areas:** contemporary issues, ethnic, historical, literary, mystery, romance, suspense, thriller, young adult.

HOW TO CONTACT Does not accept e-mail submissions. Send one-page query letter with SASE. Accepts simultaneous submissions. Responds in 1 month to queries. Obtains most new clients through recommendations from others.

TERMS Agent receives 15% commission on domestic sales. Agent receives 20% commission on foreign sales. Charges clients for ms duplication or other special expenses agreed to in advance.

TIPS "Write a letter which will give the agent a sense of you as a professional writer—your long-term interests as well as a short description of the work at hand."

THE JOAN BRANDT AGENCY

788 Wesley Dr., Atlanta GA 30305. (404)351-8877. **Contact:** Joan Brandt.

Prior to her current position, Ms. Brandt was with Sterling Lord Literistic.

REPRESENTS Nonfiction books, novels, short story collections. **Considers these nonfiction areas:** investigative, true crime. **Considers these fiction areas:** family saga, historical, literary, mystery, suspense, thriller, women's.

HOW TO CONTACT Query letter with SASE. Accepts simultaneous submissions.

TERMS Agent receives 15% commission on domestic sales. Agent receives 20% commission on foreign sales. No written contract.

THE BRATTLE AGENCY

P.O. Box 380537, Cambridge MA 02238. (617)721-5375. **E-mail:** christopher.vyce@thebrattleagency.com. **E-mail:** submissions@thebrattleagency.com. **Contact:** Christopher Vyce.

Prior to being an agent Mr. Vyce worked for the Beacon Press in Boston as an acquisitions editor.

MEMBER AGENTS Christopher Vyce.

HOW TO CONTACT Query by e-mail. Include cover letter, brief synopsis, brief CV. "Once you have queried the agency and we have asked to see your manuscript, please submit: first 3 chapters of ms, a synopsis, brief bio or resume, SASE. Responds in 2 days. If asked to see mss, responds in 6-8 weeks.

BARBARA BRAUN ASSOCIATES, INC.

7 E. 14th St., Suite 19F, New York NY 10003. **Fax:** (212)604-9023. **E-mail:** bbasubmissions@gmail.com. **Website:** www.barbarabraunagency.com. **Contact:** Barbara Braun. Member of AAR.

MEMBER AGENTS Barbara Braun; John F. Baker.

REPRESENTS Nonfiction books, novels. **Considers these nonfiction areas:** "We represent literary and commercial fiction, as well as serious nonfiction, including psychology, biography, history, women's issues, social and political issues, cultural criticism, as well as art, architecture, film, photography, fashion and design." **Considers these fiction areas:** literary and commercial.

"Our fiction is strong on women's stories, historical and multicultural stories, as well as mysteries and thrillers. We're interested in narrative nonfiction and books by journalists. We do not represent poetry, science fiction, fantasy, horror, or screenplays. Look online for more details."

HOW TO CONTACT "E-mail submissions only, marked 'query' in subject line. We no longer accept submissions by regular mail. Your query should include: a brief summary of your book, word count, genre, any relevant publishing experience, and the first 5 pages of your ms pasted into the body of the e-mail. (No attachments—we will not open these.)"

TERMS Agent receives 15% commission on domestic sales. Agent receives 20% commission on foreign sales.

RECENT SALES *Clara and Mr. Tiffany*, by Susan Vreeland.

TIPS "Our clients' books are represented throughout Europe, Asia, and Latin America by various sub-agents. We are also active in selling motion picture rights to the books we represent, and work with various Hollywood agencies."

NEW AGENT SPOTLIGHT

ETHAN VAUGHAN
(KIMBERLEY CAMERON & ASSOCIATES)

Kimberleycameron.com

ABOUT ETHAN: Ethan has worked in journalism since 2007, but his first introduction to publishing came with a 2011 summer internship at Folio Literary Management in New York, where he worked under the redoubtable Jeff Kleinman and got a crash course in agenting. Ethan graduated from George Mason University with a degree in government and international politics in December 2011 and began interning with Kimberley Cameron & Associates the same month.

HE IS SEEKING: "Fantasy/sci-fi (particularly of the young adult variety) has long been my default, but I also appreciate and am actively looking for women's fiction, literary fiction, historical fiction, and historical nonfiction. While I love escaping into an incredible new world, I'm a big sucker for really well-done literary fiction (something like *A Tree Grows in Brooklyn*, which sheds light on who we are as humans). As regards my first love, fantasy, I am very selective. I strongly prefer fantasy that is somehow grounded in the real world, be that through the integration of mythology (as in the Percy Jackson series) or through a fantasy universe being hidden inside our own (as in the Harry Potter and Chronicles of Narnia series). A fantasy that takes place in a standalone or alternate world has to be exceptionally well executed to work for me."

HOW TO SUBMIT: Please send your query with synopsis and first 50 pages attached to ethan@kimberleycameron.com.

M. COURTNEY BRIGGS

Derrick & Briggs, LLP, 100 N. Broadway Ave., 28th Floor, Oklahoma City OK 73102-8806. (405)235-1900. **Fax:** (405)235-1995. **Website:** www.derrickandbriggs.com.

○ Prior to becoming an agent, Ms. Briggs was in subsidiary rights at Random House for 3 years; an associate agent and film rights associate with Curtis Brown, Ltd.; and an attorney for 16 years.

REPRESENTS Nonfiction books, novels, juvenile. **Considers these nonfiction areas:** young adult.

⊶ "I work primarily, but not exclusively, with children's book authors and illustrators. I will also consult or review a contract on an hourly basis." Actively seeking children's fiction, children's picture books (illustrations and text), young adult novels, fiction, nonfiction.

HOW TO CONTACT Query with SASE. Only published authors should submit queries. Obtains most new clients through recommendations from others.

TERMS Agent receives 15% commission on domestic sales. Agent receives 25% commission on foreign sales. Offers written contract; 60-day notice must be given to terminate contract.
WRITERS CONFERENCES SCBWI Annual Winter Conference.

BROWNE & MILLER LITERARY ASSOCIATES, LLC

410 S. Michigan Ave., Suite 460, Chicago IL 60605. (312)922-3063. **Fax:** (312)922-1905. **E-mail:** mail@browneandmiller.com. **Website:** www.browneandmiller.com. Estab. 1971. Member of AAR. RWA, MWA Represents 85+ clients. 5% of clients are new/unpublished writers.

○ Prior to opening the agency, Danielle Egan-Miller worked as an editor.

⊶ Considers primarily YA fiction, fiction, young adult. "We love great writing and have a wonderful list of authors writing YA in particular." Not looking for picture books, middle-grade.

HOW TO CONTACT Query with SASE. Accepts queries by e-mail. Responds in 2-4 weeks to queries; 4-6 months to mss. Obtains clients through recommendations from others.

TERMS Agent receives 15% commission on domestic sales; 20% on foreign sales. Offers written contract. Offers written contract, binding for 2 years. 30 days notice must be given to terminate contract.

RECENT SALES Sold 10 books for young readers in the last year.

TIPS "We are very hands-on and do much editorial work with our clients. We are passionate about the books we represent and work hard to help clients reach their publishing goals."

① ANDREA BROWN LITERARY AGENCY, INC.

1076 Eagle Dr., Salinas CA 93905. (831)422-5925. **Fax:** (831)422-5915. **E-mail:** andrea@andreabrownlit.com; caryn@andreabrownlit.com; lauraqueries@gmail.com; jennifer@andreabrownlit.com; kelly@andreabrownlit.com; jennL@andreabrownlit.com; jamie@andreabrownlit.com; jmatt@andreabrownlit.com; lara@andreabrownlit.com. **Website:** www.andreabrownlit.com. **Contact:** Andrea Brown, president. Member of AAR. 10% of clients are new/unpublished writers.

○ Prior to opening her agency, Ms. Brown served as an editorial assistant at Random House and Dell Publishing and as an editor with Knopf.

MEMBER AGENTS Andrea Brown (President); Laura Rennert (Senior Agent); Caryn Wiseman (Senior Agent); Kelly Sonnack (Agent); Jennifer Rofé (Agent); Jennifer Laughran (Agent); Jamie Weiss Chilton (Agent); Jennifer Mattson (Associate Agent); Lara Perkins (Associate Agent, Digital Manager).

REPRESENTS Nonfiction, fiction, juvenile books. **Considers these nonfiction areas:** juvenile nonfiction, memoirs, young adult, narrative. **Considers these fiction areas:** juvenile, literary, picture books, women's, young adult, middle-grade, all juvenile genres.

⊶ Specializes in "all kinds of children's books—illustrators and authors." 98% juvenile books. Considers: nonfiction, fiction, picture books, young adult.

HOW TO CONTACT For picture books, submit complete ms. For fiction, submit query letter, first 10 pages. For nonfiction, submit proposal, first 10 pages. Illustrators: submit a query letter and 2-3 illustration samples (in jpeg format), link to online portfolio, and text of picture book, if applicable. "We only accept queries via e-mail. No attachments, with the exception of jpeg illustrations from illustrators." Visit the agents' bios on our website and choose only one agent to whom you will submit your e-query. Send a short e-mail query letter to that agent with QUERY in the subject field. Accepts simultaneous submissions. If we are interested in your work, we will certainly follow up by e-mail or by phone. However, if you haven't heard from us within 6 to 8 weeks, please assume that we are passing on your project. Obtains most new clients through referrals from editors, clients and agents. Check website for guidelines and information.

TERMS Agent receives 15% commission on domestic sales. Agent receives 25% commission on foreign sales. Offers written contract.

RECENT SALES *The Scorpio Races*, by Maggie Stiefvater (Scholastic); *The Raven Boys*, by Maggie Stiefvater (Scholastic); *Wolves of Mercy Falls* series, by Maggie Stiefvater (Scholastic); *The Future of Us*, by Jay Asher; *Triangles*, by Ellen Hopkins (Atria); *Crank*, by Ellen Hopkins (McElderry/S&S); *Burned*, by Ellen Hopkins (McElderry/S&S); *Impulse*, by Ellen Hopkins (McElderry/S&S); *Glass*, by Ellen Hopkins (McElderry/S&S); *Tricks*, by Ellen Hopkins (McElderry/S&S); *Fallout*, by Ellen Hopkins (McElderry/S&S); *Perfect*, by Ellen Hopkins (McElderry/S&S); *The Strange Case of Origami Yoda*, by Tom Angleberger (Amulet/Abrams); *Darth Paper Strikes Back*, by Tom Angleberger (Amulet/Abrams); Becoming Chloe, by Catherine Ryan Hyde (Knopf); Sasha Cohen autobiography (HarperCollins); *The Five Ancestors*, by Jeff Stone (Random House); *Thirteen Reasons Why*, by Jay Asher (Penguin); *Identical*, by Ellen Hopkins (S&S).

WRITERS CONFERENCES SCBWI; Asilomar; Maui Writers' Conference; Southwest Writers' Conference; San Diego State University Writers' Conference; Big Sur Children's Writing Workshop; William Saroyan Writers' Conference; Columbus Writers' Conference; Willamette Writers' Conference; La Jolla Writers' Conference; San Francisco Writers' Conference; Hilton Head Writers' Conference; Pacific Northwest Conference; Pikes Peak Conference.

TIPS "ABLA is consistently ranked #1 in juvenile sales in Publishers Marketplace. Several clients have placed in the top 10 of the NY Times Bestseller List in the last year, including Tom Angleberger, Jay Asher, Ellen Hopkins, and Maggie Stiefvater. Awards recently won by ABLA clients include the Michael L. Printz Honor, the APALA Asian/Pacific Award and Honor, Charlotte Zolotow Honor, Cybils Award, EB White Read Aloud Award and Honor, Edgar Award Nominee, Indies Choice Honor Award, Jack Ezra Keats New Writer Award, Odyssey Honor Audiobook, Orbis PIctus Honor, Pura Belpré Illustrator Honor Book; SCBWI Golden Kite Award; Stonewall Honor; Texas Bluebonnet Award; Theodore Seuss Geisel Honor; William C. Morris YA Debut Award."

☾☻◉ THE BUKOWSKI AGENCY

14 Prince Arthur Ave., Suite 202, Toronto Ontario M5R 1A9 Canada. (416)928-6728. **Fax:** (416)963-9978. **E-mail:** assistant@thebukowskiagency.com; info@thebukowskiagency.com. **Website:** www.thebukowskiagency.com. **Contact:** Denise Bukowski. Represents 70 clients.

○ Prior to becoming an agent, Ms. Bukowski was a book editor.

REPRESENTS Nonfiction books, novels.

⚷ "The Bukowski Agency specializes in international literary fiction and upmarket nonfiction for adults. Bukowski looks for Canadian writers whose work can be marketed in many media and territories, and who have the potential to make a living from their work." Actively seeking nonfiction and fiction works from Canadian writers. Does not want submissions from American authors, nor genre fiction, poetry, children's literature, picture books, film scripts, or TV scripts.

HOW TO CONTACT Query with SASE. Submit proposal package, outline/proposal, synopsis, publishing history, author bio. Send submissions by snail mail only. See online guidelines for nonfiction and fiction specifics. No unsolicited fiction. "The Bukowski Agency is currently accepting nonfiction submissions from prospective authors who are residents in Canada. We ask for exclusivity for 6 weeks after receipt to allow time for proper consideration. Please see our nonfiction submission guidelines for more details on submitting proposals for nonfiction. Submissions should be sent by mail, in hard copy only." Responds in 6 weeks to queries.

☺ BURKEMAN & SERAFINA CLARKE LTD, BRIE

14 Neville Ct., Abbey Road, London England NW8 9DD United Kingdom. (44)(870)199-5002. **Fax:** (44)(870)199-1029. **E-mail:** info@burkemanandclarke.com. **Website:** www.burkemanandclarke.com.

REPRESENTS **Considers these nonfiction areas:** , narrative history, popular science, celebrity memoirs, popular culture. **Considers these fiction areas:** , commercial literary fiction, psychological thrillers, historial, children's.

⚷ No academic text, poetry, short stories, musicals, or short films

HOW TO CONTACT Not accepting submissions at present. Please see website for details and updates.

● KIMBERLEY CAMERON & ASSOCIATES

1550 Tiburon Blvd., #704, Tiburon CA 94920. **Fax:** (415)789-9191. **E-mail:** info@kimberleycameron.com. **Website:** www.kimberleycameron.com. **Contact:** Kimberley Cameron. Member of AAR. 30% of clients are new/unpublished writers.

○ Kimberley Cameron & Associates (formerly The Reece Halsey Agency) has had an illustrious client list of established writers, including the estate of Aldous Huxley, and has represented Upton Sinclair, William Faulkner, and Henry Miller.

MEMBER AGENTS Kimberley Cameron, Elizabeth Kracht, Pooja Menon, Amy Cloughley, and Ethan Vaughan.

REPRESENTS Nonfiction, fiction. **Considers these nonfiction areas:** biography, current affairs, foods, humor, language, memoirs, popular culture, science, true crime, women's issues, women's studies, lifestyle,. **Considers these fiction areas:** adventure, contemporary issues, ethnic, family saga, historical, horror, mainstream, mystery, interlinked short story collections, thriller, women's, and sophisticated/crossover young adult.

⌘ "We are looking for a unique and heartfelt voice that conveys a universal truth."

HOW TO CONTACT Query via e-mail. "See our website for submission guidelines." Obtains new clients through recommendations from others, solicitations.

TERMS Agent receives 15% on domestic sales; 10% on film sales. Offers written contract, binding for 1 year.

WRITERS CONFERENCES Pacific Northwest Writers Association Conference; Women's Fiction Festival in Matera, Italy; Willamette Writers Conference; San Francisco Writers Conference; Book Passage Mystery and Travel Writers Conferences; Chuckanut Writers Conference; many others.

TIPS "Please consult our submission guidelines and send a polite, well-written query to our e-mail address."

⊙ CASTIGLIA LITERARY AGENCY

1155 Camino Del Mar, Suite 510, Del Mar CA 92014. **E-mail:** castigliaagency-query@yahoo.com. **Website:** www.castigliaagency.com. Member of AAR. Other memberships include PEN. Represents 65 clients. Currently handles: nonfiction books 55%, novels 45%.

MEMBER AGENTS Julie Castiglia (not accepting queries at this time); Win Golden (fiction: thrillers, mystery, crime, science fiction, YA, commercial/literary fiction; nonfiction: narrative nonfiction, current events, science, journalism.

REPRESENTS Nonfiction books, novels. **Considers these nonfiction areas:** animals, anthropology, archeology, autobiography, biography, business, child guidance, cooking, cultural interests, current affairs, economics, environment, ethnic, finance, foods, health, history, inspirational, language, literature, medicine, money, nature, nutrition, psychology, religious, science, technology, women's issues, women's studies. **Considers these fiction areas:** contem-

porary issues, ethnic, literary, mainstream, mystery, suspense, women's.

⌘ Does not want to receive horror, screenplays, poetry, or academic nonfiction.

HOW TO CONTACT Query via e-mail. No unsolicited submissions. No snail mail submissions accepted. Obtains most new clients through recommendations from others, solicitations, conferences.

TERMS Agent receives 15% commission on domestic sales. Agent receives 25% commission on foreign sales. Offers written contract; 6-week notice must be given to terminate contract.

RECENT SALES *Germs Gone Wild*, by Kenneth King (Pegasus); *The Insider* by Reece Hirsch (Berkley/Penguin); *The Leisure Seeker*, by Michael Zadoorian (Morrow/HarperCollins); *Beautiful: The Life of Hedy Lamarr*, by Stephen Shearer (St. Martin's Press); *American Libre*, by Raul Ramos y Sanchez (Grand Central); *The Two Krishnas*, by Ghalib Shiraz Dhalla (Alyson Books).

WRITERS CONFERENCES Santa Barbara Writers' Conference; Southern California Writers' Conference; Surrey International Writers' Conference; San Diego State University Writers' Conference; Willamette Writers' Conference.

TIPS "Be professional with submissions. Attend workshops and conferences before you approach an agent."

⊕ CHALBERG & SUSSMAN

115 West 29th St, Third Floor, New York, NY 10001. (917)261-7550. **Website:** www.chalbergsussman.com.

MEMBER AGENTS Terra Chalberg (terra@chalbergsussman.com), Rachel Sussman (rachel@chalbergsussman.com).

◉ Prior to her current position, Ms. Chalber was an agent with The Susan Golomb Literary Agency. Ms. Sussman was previously wth Zachary Shuster Harmsworth Agency

HOW TO CONTACT Query via e-mail or snail mail. Include SASE if by smail mail. Responds if interested.

TERMS Agent receives 15% commission on domestic sales.

RECENT SALES *The Marrowbone Marble Company*, by Glenn Taylor; *Tiger, Tiger*, by Margaux Fragoso; *Fires of Our Choosing*, by Eugene Cross; *Young House Love*, by Sherry and John Petersik.

⊙ CHASE LITERARY AGENCY

236 W. 26th St., Suite 801, New York NY 10001. (212)477-5100. **E-mail:** farley@chaseliterary.com.

Website: www.chaseliterary.com. **Contact:** Farley Chase.

MEMBER AGENTS Farley Chase.

☞ Wants: General fiction, reference, biography, business/investing/finance, history, health, travel, lifestyle, cookbooks, sports, African-American, science, humor, pop-culture, popular science, natural history, military history, memoir. "I'm interested in humor books and pop culture projects, photo, graphic, and otherwise illustrated books; books that can be adapted out of blogs or websites." No YA, romance, or science fiction.

HOW TO CONTACT Query. Include first few pages of ms with query.

RECENT SALES *Loopers*, by John Dunn; *The Afrika ReichHE AFRIKA REICH*, by Guy Saville; *Top of the First: The End of Word War II*, by Robert Weintraub.

JANE CHELIUS LITERARY AGENCY

548 Second St., Brooklyn NY 11215. (718)499-0236. **Fax:** (718)832-7335. **E-mail:** queries@janechelius.com. **Website:** www.janechelius.com. Member of AAR.

REPRESENTS Nonfiction books, novels. **Considers these nonfiction areas:** biography, humor, medicine, parenting, popular culture, satire, women's issues, women's studies, natural history; narrative. **Considers these fiction areas:** literary, mystery, suspense.

☞ Does not want to receive fantasy, science fiction, children's books, stage plays, screenplays, or poetry.

HOW TO CONTACT Please see website for submission procedures. Does not consider e-mail queries with attachments. No unsolicited sample chapters or mss. Responds in 3-4-weeks usually.

ELYSE CHENEY LITERARY ASSOCIATES, LLC

78 Fifth Avenue, 3rd Floor, New York NY 10011. **Website:** www.cheneyliterary.com. **Contact:** Elyse Cheney; Adam Eaglin; Alex Jacobs.

○ Prior to her current position, Ms. Cheney was an agent with Sanford J. Greenburger Associates. Mr. Eaglin was previously at The Wylie Agency.

REPRESENTS Nonfiction, novels. **Considers these nonfiction areas:** autobiography, biography, business, cultural interests, current affairs, finance, history, memoirs, multicultural, politics, science, sports, women's issues, women's studies, narrative nonfiction

and journalism. **Considers these fiction areas:** , upmarket commercial fiction, historical fiction, literary, suspense, upmarket women's fiction.

HOW TO CONTACT Query this agency with a referral. Include SASE or IRC. No fax queries. Snail mail or e-mail (submissions@cheneyliterary.com) only.

RECENT SALES *Moonwalking with Einstein: The Art and Science of Remembering Everything*, by Joshua Foer; *The Possessed: Adventures with Russian Books and the People Who Read Them*, by Elif Batuman (Farrar, Strauss & Giroux); *The Coldest Winter Ever*, by Sister Souljah (Atria); *A Heartbreaking Work of Staggering Genius*, by Dave Eggers (Simon and Schuster); *No Easy Day*, by Mark Owen; *Malcom X: A Life of Reinvention*, by Manning Marable.

◑◉ THE CHUDNEY AGENCY

72 North State Rd., Suite 501, Briarcliff Manor NY 10510. (201)758-8739. **E-mail:** steven@thechudneyagency.com. **Website:** www.thechudneyagency.com. **Contact:** Steven Chudney. Estab. 2001. Other memberships include SCBWI. 90% of clients are new/unpublished writers.

○ Prior to becoming an agent, Mr. Chudney held various sales positions with major publishers.

REPRESENTS Novels, juvenile. **Considers these nonfiction areas:** juvenile. **Considers these fiction areas:** historical, juvenile, literary, mystery, suspense, young adult.

☞ This agency specializes in children's and teens books, and wants to find authors who are illustrators as well. "At this time, the agency is only looking for author/illustrators (one individual), who can both write and illustrate wonderful picture books. The author/illustrator must really know and understand the prime audience's needs and wants of the child reader! Storylines should be engaging, fun, with a hint of a life lessons and cannot be longer than 800 words. With chapter books, middle grade and teen novels, I'm primarily looking for quality, contemporary literary fiction: novels that are exceedingly well-written, with wonderful settings and developed, unforgettable characters. I'm looking for historical fiction that will excite me, young readers, editors, and reviewers, and will introduce us to unique characters in settings and situations, countries, and eras we haven't encountered too often yet in children's and teen literature." Does not want to receive any fantasy or science fiction; board books or lift-the-flap books, fables, folklore, or traditional fairytales, poetry or mood pieces, stories for all ages (as these ultimately are too adult oriented), message-driven stories that are heavy-handed, didactic or pedantic.

HOW TO CONTACT No snail-mail submissions. Queries only. Submit proposal package, 4-6 sample chapters. For children's, submit full text and 3-5 illustrations. Accepts simultaneous submissions. Responds in 2-3 weeks to queries. Responds in 3-4 weeks to mss.

TERMS Agent receives 15% commission on domestic sales. Agent receives 20% commission on foreign sales. Offers written contract, binding for 1 year; 30-day notice must be given to terminate contract.

TIPS "If an agent has a website, review it carefully to make sure your material is appropriate for that agent. Read lots of books within the genre you are writing; work hard on your writing; don't follow trends—most likely, you'll be too late."

CINE/LIT REPRESENTATION

P.O. Box 802918, Santa Clarita CA 91380-2918. (661)513-0268. **Fax:** (661)513-0915. **Contact:** Mary Alice Kier. Member of AAR.

MEMBER AGENTS Mary Alice Kier; Anna Cottle.

REPRESENTS Nonfiction books, novels.

8⊸ "Looking for nonfiction books: mainstream, thrillers, mysteries, supernatural, horror, narrative nonfiction, environmental, adventure, biography, travel, and pop culture." Does not want to receive Westerns, sci-fi, or romance.

HOW TO CONTACT Send query letter with SASE.

● EDWARD B. CLAFLIN LITERARY AGENCY, LLC

128 High Ave., Suite #2, Nyack NY 10960. (845)358-1084. **E-mail:** edclaflin@aol.com. **Contact:** Edward Claflin. Represents 30 clients. 10% of clients are new/unpublished writers.

○ Prior to opening his agency, Mr. Claflin worked at Banbury Books, Rodale, and Prentice Hall Press. He is the co-author of 13 books.

REPRESENTS Nonfiction books. **Considers these nonfiction areas:** business, cooking, current affairs, economics, finance, food, health, history, how-to, medicine, military, money, nutrition, psychology, sports, war.

8⊸ This agency specializes in consumer health, narrative history, psychology/self-help, and business. Actively seeking compelling and authoritative nonfiction for specific readers. Does not want to receive fiction.

HOW TO CONTACT Query with synopsis, bio, SASE or e-mail attachment in Word. Responds in 1 month to queries. Obtains most new clients through recommendations from others.

TERMS Agent receives 15% commission on domestic sales.

● FRANCES COLLIN, LITERARY AGENT

P.O. Box 33, Wayne PA 19087-0033. **E-mail:** queries@francescollin.com. **Website:** www.francescollin.com. **Contact:** Sarah Yake, associate agent. Member of AAR. Represents 90 clients. 1% of clients are new/unpublished writers. Currently handles: nonfiction books 50%, fiction 50%.

REPRESENTS Nonfiction books, fiction, young adult.

8⊸ Does not want to receive cookbooks, craft books, poetry, screenplays, or books for young children.

HOW TO CONTACT Query via e-mail describing project (text in the body of the e-mail only, no attachments) to queries@francescollin.com. "Please note that all queries are reviewed by both agents." No phone or fax queries. Accepts simultaneous submissions.

TERMS Agent receives 15% commission on domestic sales. Agent receives 20% commission on foreign sales. Offers written contract.

● DON CONGDON ASSOCIATES INC.

110 William St., Suite 2202, New York NY 10038. (212)645-1229. **Fax:** (212)727-2688. **E-mail:** dca@doncongdon.com. **Website:** http://doncongdon.com. **Contact:** Michael Congdon, Susan Ramer, Cristina Concepcion, Maura Kye Casella, Katie Kotchman, Katie Grimm. Member of AAR. Represents 100 clients. Currently handles: nonfiction books 60%, other 40% fiction.

REPRESENTS Nonfiction books, fiction. **Considers these nonfiction areas:** anthropology, archeology, autobiography, biography, child guidance, cooking, current affairs, dance, environment, film, foods, government, health, history, humor, language, law, literature, medicine, memoirs, military, music, nature, nutrition, parenting, popular culture, politics, psychology, satire, science, technology, theater, travel, true crime, war, women's issues, women's studies, creative nonfiction. **Considers these fiction areas:** action, adventure, contemporary issues, crime, detective, literary, mainstream, mystery, police, short story collections, suspense, thriller, women's.

Ⅾ— Especially interested in narrative nonfiction and literary fiction.

HOW TO CONTACT Query with SASE or via e-mail (no attachments). Responds in 3 weeks to queries. Responds in 1 month to mss. Obtains most new clients through recommendations from other authors.

TERMS Agent receives 15% commission on domestic sales. Agent receives 19% commission on foreign sales. Charges client for extra shipping costs, photocopying, copyright fees, book purchases.

TIPS "Writing a query letter with an SASE is a must. We cannot guarantee replies to foreign queries via standard mail. No phone calls. We never download attachments to e-mail queries for security reasons, so please copy and paste material into your e-mail."

CONNOR LITERARY AGENCY

2911 W. 71st St., Minneapolis MN 55423. (612)866-1486. **E-mail:** connoragency@aol.com; coolmkc@aol.com. **Website:** www.connorliteraryagency.webs.com. **Contact:** Marlene Connor Lynch. Represents 50 clients. 30% of clients are new/unpublished writers. Currently handles: nonfiction books 50%, novels 50%.

💬 Prior to opening her agency, Ms. Connor served at the Literary Guild of America, Simon & Schuster, and Random House. She is author of *Welcome to the Family: Memories of the Past for a Bright Future* (Broadway Books) and *What is Cool: Understanding Black Manhood in America* (Crown).

MEMBER AGENTS Marlene Connor Lynch (all categories of mainstream nonfiction and fiction); Deborah Coker (mainstream and literary fiction, multicultural fiction, children's books, humor, politics, memoirs, narrative nonfiction, true crime/investigative).

REPRESENTS Nonfiction books, novels.

Ⅾ— "We are currently accepting mss, and we are expanding our interest to include more mainstream and multicultural fiction."

HOW TO CONTACT Query with 1 page and synopsis; include SASE. All unsolicited mss returned unopened. Obtains most new clients through recommendations from others, conferences, grapevine.

TERMS Agent receives 15% commission on domestic sales. Agent receives 25% commission on foreign sales. Offers written contract, binding for 1 year.

RECENT SALES *Beautiful Hair at Any Age*, by Lisa Akbari; *12 Months of Knitting*, by Joanne Yordanou; *The Warrior Path: Confessions of a Young Lord* by Felipe Luciano.

WRITERS CONFERENCES National Writers Union, Midwest Chapter; Agents, Agents, Agents; Texas Writers' Conference; Detroit Writers' Conference; Annual Gwendolyn Brooks Writers' Conference for Literature and Creative Writing; Wisconsin Writers' Festival.

TIPS "Previously published writers are preferred; new writers with national exposure or potential to have national exposure from their own efforts preferred."

◉ THE DOE COOVER AGENCY

P.O. Box 668, Winchester MA 01890. (781)721-6000. **E-mail:** info@doecooveragency.com. **Website:** www.doecooveragency.com. Represents 150+ clients. Currently handles: nonfiction books 80%, novels 20%.

MEMBER AGENTS Doe Coover (general nonfiction, including business, cooking/food writing, health andscience); Colleen Mohyde (literary and commercial fiction, general nonfiction); Associate: Frances Kennedy.

REPRESENTS Considers these nonfiction areas: autobiography, biography, business, cooking, economics, foods, gardening, health, history, nutrition, science, technology, social issues, narrative nonfiction. **Considers these fiction areas:** commercial, literary.

Ⅾ— The agency specializes in narrative nonfiction, particularly biography, business, cooking and food writing, health, history, popular science, social issues, gardening, and humor; literary and commercial fiction. The agency does not represent poetry, screenplays, romance, fantasy, science fiction or unsolicited children's books.

HOW TO CONTACT Accepts queries by e-mail only. Check website for submission guidelines. No unsolicited mss. Accepts simultaneous submissions. Responds within 4-6 weeks, only if additional material is required. Obtains most new clients through solicitation and recommendation.

TERMS Agent receives 15% commission on domestic sales, 10% of original advance commission on foreign-sales. No reading fees.

RECENT SALES *Vegetable Literacy*, by Deborah Madison (Ten Speed Press); *Frontera: Margaritas, Guacamoles, and Snacks*, by Rick Bayless and Deann Groen Bayless (W.W. Norton); *Silvana's Gluten-Free Kitchen*, by Silvana Nardone (Houghton Mifflin Harcourt); *The Essay*, by Robin Yocum (Arcade Publishing); *The Flower of Empire*, by Tatiana Holway (Oxford University Press); *Confederates Don't Wear Couture*, by Stephanie Strohm (Houghton Mifflin Harcourt); Dulcie Schwartz mystery series, by Clea Simon (Severn House UK), *Gourmet Weekday* and *Gourmet Italian*, by Conde Nast Publications (Houghton Mifflin Harcourt); Untitled Biography of Eunice Kennedy Shriver, by Eileen McNamara (Simon & Schuster); Movie/TV MOW scripts optioned: Keeper of the House, by Rebecca Godwin. Other clients include: WGBH, New England Aquarium, Duke University, Blue Balliett, David Allen, Jacques Pepin, Cindy Pawlcyn, Joann Weir, Suzanne Berne, Paula Poundstone, Anita Silvey, Marjorie Sandor, Tracy Daugherty, Carl Rollyson, and Joel Magnuson.

ⓞ CORVISIERO LITERARY AGENCY

275 Madison Ave., 14th Floor, New York NY 10016. (646)942-8396. **Fax:** (646)217-3758. **E-mail:** contact@corvisieroagency.com. **E-mail:** query@corvisieroagency.com. **Website:** www.corvisieroagency.com. **Contact:** Marisa A. Corvisiero, senior agent and literary attorney.

MEMBER AGENTS Marisa A. Corvisiero, senior agent and literary attorney (romance, thrillers, adventure, paranormal, fantasy, science fiction, young adult, middle grade, nonfiction); Saritza Hernandez (all genres of romance and erotica; GLBT young adult); Stacey Donaghy; Brittany Howard; Doreen MacDonald; Sarah Negovetich (young adult and middle grade).

HOW TO CONTACT Accepts submissions via e-mail only. Include 5 pages of complete and polished ms pasted into the body of an e-mail, and a 1-2 page synopsis. For nonfiction, include a proposal instead of the synopsis. All sample pages must be properly formatted into 1 inch margins, double-spaced lines, Times New Roman black font size 12.

TIPS "For tips and discussions on what we look for in query letters and submissions, please take a look at Marisa A. Corvisiero's blog: Thoughts From A Literary Agent."

CRAWFORD LITERARY AGENCY

92 Evans Rd., Barnstead NH 03218. (603)269-5851. **E-mail:** crawfordlit@att.net. **Contact:** Susan Crawford. Winter Office: 3920 Bayside Rd., Fort Myers Beach FL 33931. (239)463-4651. **Fax:** (239)463-0125.

REPRESENTS Nonfiction books, commercial fiction.

8→ Actively seeking action/adventure stories; medical, legal, and psychological thrillers; true crime; romance and romantic suspense; self-help; inspirational; how-to; women's issues. No short stories, or poetry.

HOW TO CONTACT Query with cover letter, SASE. Accepts simultaneous submissions. Responds in 3-6 weeks. Obtains most new clients through recommendations from others and conferences.

TERMS Agent receives 15% commission on domestic sales. Agent receives 20% commission on foreign sales. Offers written contract.

RECENT SALES *Sexy Star Cooking: An Astrology Cookbook for Lovers*, by Sabra Ricci; *Date with the Devil*, by Don Lasseter; *Petals from the Sky*, by Mingmei Yip.

WRITERS CONFERENCES Hawaii Spellbinders Conference; Love is Murder Mystery Conference; Puerto Villarta Writers Conference; International Film & Television Workshops; Maui Writers Conference; Emerson College Conference; Suncoast Writers Conference; San Diego Writers Conference; Simmons College Writers Conference; Cape Cod Writers Conference; Maui-Writers Alaskan Cruise; Western Caribbean Cruise and Fiji Island Writers Retreat.

TIPS "Keep learning to improve your craft. Attend conferences and network."

ⓞ THE CREATIVE CULTURE, INC.

47 E. 19th St., 3rd Floor, New York NY 10003. (212)680-3510. **Fax:** (212)680-3509. **E-mail:** submissions@thecreativeculture.com. **Website:** www.thecreativeculture.com. **Contact:** Debra Goldstein. Estab. 1998. Member of AAR.

ⓞ Prior to opening her agency, Ms. Goldstein and Ms. Gerwin were agents at the William Morris Agency; Ms. Naples was a senior editor at Simon & Schuster.

MEMBER AGENTS Debra Goldstein (self-help, creativity, fitness, inspiration, lifestyle); Mary Ann Naples (health/nutrition, lifestyle, narrative nonfiction, practical nonfiction, literary fiction, animals/vegetarianism); Laura Nolan (literary fiction, parenting, self-help, psychology, women's studies, current affairs, science); Karen Gerwin (pop culture, lifestyle, parenting, humor, memoir/narrative nonfiction, women's interests, and a very limited selection of fiction [no genre categories, i.e. thrillers, romance, sci-fi/fantasy, etc.]); Matthew Elblonk (literary fiction, humor, pop culture, music and young adult; interests also include commercial fiction, narrative nonfiction, science, and he is always on the lookout for something slightly quirky or absurd).

REPRESENTS Nonfiction books, novels.

➤ "We are known for our emphasis on lifestyle books that enhance readers' overall well-being—be it through health, inspiration, entertainment, thought-provoking ideas, life management skills, beauty and fashion, or food. Does not want to receive children's books, poetry, screenplays, or science fiction."

HOW TO CONTACT Query with bio, book description, 4-7 sample pages (fiction only), SASE. "We only reply if interested. Please see the titles page to get a sense of the books we represent." Responds in 2 months to queries.

CREATIVE TRUST, INC.

5141 Virginia Way, Suite 320, Brentwood TN 37027. (615)297-5010. **Fax:** (615)297-5020. **E-mail:** info@ creativetrust.com. **Website:** www.creativetrust.com. New York Office: 39 Broadway, 3rd Floor, New York NY 10006. Currently handles: novella Graphic Novels, movie scripts, multimedia, other Video Scripts.

HOW TO CONTACT "Creative Trust Literary Group does not accept unsolicited mss or book proposals from unpublished authors. We do accept unsolicited inquiries from previously published authors under the following requisites: e-mail inquiries only, which must not be accompanied by attachments of any kind. If we're interested, we'll e-mail you an invitation to submit additional materials and instructions on how to do so."

⬤ CRICHTON & ASSOCIATES

6940 Carroll Ave., Takoma Park MD 20912. (301)495-9663. **Fax:** (202)318-0050. **E-mail:** query@crichton-associates.com. **Website:** www.crichton-associates.com. **Contact:** Sha-Shana Crichton. 90% of clients are new/unpublished writers. Currently handles: nonfiction books 50%, fiction 50%.

◔ Prior to becoming an agent, Ms. Crichton did commercial litigation for a major law firm.

REPRESENTS Nonfiction books, novels. **Considers these nonfiction areas:** child guidance, cultural interests, ethnic, gay, government, investigative, law, lesbian, parenting, politics, true crime, women's issues, women's studies, African-American studies. **Considers these fiction areas:** ethnic, feminist, inspirational, literary, mainstream, mystery, religious, romance, suspense, chick lit.

➤ Actively seeking women's fiction, romance, and chick lit. Looking also for multicultural fiction and nonfiction. Does not want to receive poetry, children's, YA, science fiction, or screenplays.

HOW TO CONTACT "In the subject line of e-mail, please indicate whether your project is fiction or nonfiction. Please do not send attachments. Your query letter should include a description of the project and your biography. If you wish to send your query via snail mail, please include your telephone number and e-mail address. We will respond to you via e-mail. For fiction, include short synopsis and first 3 chapters with query. For nonfiction, send a book proposal." Responds in 3-5 weeks to queries.

TERMS Agent receives 15% commission on domestic sales. Agent receives 20% commission on foreign sales. Offers written contract, binding for 45 days. Only charges fees for postage and photocopying.

RECENT SALES *The African American Entrepreneur*, by W. Sherman Rogers (Praeger); *The Diversity Code*, by Michelle Johnson (Amacom); *Secret & Lies*, by Rhonda McKnight (Urban Books); *Love on the Rocks*, by Pamela Yaye (Harlequin). Other clients include Kimberly White, Beverley Long, Jessica Trap, Altonya Washington, Cheris Hodges.

WRITERS CONFERENCES Silicon Valley RWA; BookExpo America.

⊘ THE MARY CUNNANE AGENCY

PO Box 336, Bermagui, NSW 2546, Australia. **E-mail:** christine@cunnaneagency.com. **E-mail:** mary@cunnaneagency.com. **Website:** www.cunnaneagency.com. Membership includes the Australian Literary Agents Association.

MEMBER AGENTS Mary Cunnane: mary@cunnaneagency.com.

➤ "We do not represent science fiction, fantasy, romance novels, new age/spiritual books, or children's books."

HOW TO CONTACT "We prefer an initial inquiry by phone, e-mail, or letter telling us something about the project and prospective author. If e-mailing, then please address your inquiry to Mary Cunnane and copy Christine Poulton. Please do not send files in excess of 10 megabytes. If we are interested, we will ask you to send the entire ms along with an SASE sufficiently large to post the ms back to you. We strive to read and respond within 4-6 weeks of receipt of the ms. Our server and Hotmail accounts do not work well together, so please try to avoid such accounts."

RICHARD CURTIS ASSOCIATES, INC.

171 E. 74th St., New York NY 10021. (212)772-7363. **Fax:** (212)772-7393. **Website:** www.curtisagency.com. Memberships include RWA, MWA, ITW, SFWA. Represents 100 clients. 1% of clients are new/unpublished writers. Currently handles: nonfiction books 50%, other 50% genre fiction.

○ Mr. Curtis authored more than 50 published books.

REPRESENTS Considers these nonfiction areas: autobiography, biography, business, economics, health, history, medicine, science, technology. **Considers these fiction areas:** , YA fantasy, contemporary romance.

HOW TO CONTACT Considers only authors published by National Houses.

TERMS Agent receives 15% commission on domestic sales. Agent receives 25% commission on foreign sales. Offers written contract. Charges for photocopying, express mail, international freight, book orders.

RECENT SALES Sold 100 titles in the last year: *Sylo*, by DJ MacHale; *War Dogs*, by Greg Bear; *Ever After*, by Kim Harrison.

WRITERS CONFERENCES RWA National Conference.

CURTIS BROWN, LTD.

10 Astor Place, New York NY 10003-6935. (212)473-5400. **E-mail:** gknowlton@cbltd.com. **Website:** www. curtisbrown.com. **Contact:** Ginger Knowlton. Alternate address: Peter Ginsberg, president at CBSF, 1750 Montgomery St., San Francisco CA 94111; (415)954-8566. Member of AAR. Signatory of WGA.

MEMBER AGENTS Ginger Clark; Katherine Fausset; Holly Frederick; Emilie Jacobson; Elizabeth Hardin; Ginger Knowlton, executive vice president; Timothy Knowlton, CEO; Laura Blake Peterson; Steve Kasdin; Mitchell Waters. San Francisco office: Peter Ginsberg (president).

REPRESENTS Nonfiction books, novels, short story collections, juvenile. **Considers these nonfiction areas:** agriculture horticulture, americana, crafts, interior, juvenile, New Age, young, animals, anthropology, art, biography, business, child, computers, cooking, current affairs, education, ethnic, gardening, gay, government, health, history, how-to, humor, language, memoirs, military, money, multicultural, music, nature, philosophy, photography, popular culture, psychology, recreation, regional, religion, science, self-help, sex, sociology, software, spirituality, sports, film, translation, travel, true crime, women's, creative nonfiction. **Considers these fiction areas:** contemporary, glitz, New Age, psychic, adventure, comic, confession, detective, erotica, ethnic, experimental, family, fantasy, feminist, gay, gothic, hi lo, historical, horror, humor, juvenile, literary, mainstream, military, multicultural, multimedia, mystery, occult, picture books, plays, poetry, regional, religious, romance, science, short, spiritual, sports, thriller, translation, western, youn, women's.

HOW TO CONTACT Prefers to read materials exclusively. *No unsolicited mss.* Query with SASE. If a picture book, send only 1 picture book ms. Considers simultaneous queries, "but please tell us." Returns material only with SASE. Responds in 3 weeks to queries; 5 weeks to mss. Obtains most new clients through recommendations from others, solicitations, conferences.

TERMS Agent receives 15% commission on domestic sales; 20% on foreign sales. Offers written contract. 75-day notice must be given to terminate contract. Offers written contract. Charges for some postage (overseas, etc.).

RECENT SALES This agency prefers not to share information on specific sales.

CURTIS BROWN (AUST) PTY LTD

P.O. Box 19, Paddington NSW 2021 Australia. (+61)(2)9361-6161; (+61)(2)9331-5301. **Fax:** (+61)(2)9360-3935. **E-mail:** reception@curtisbrown.com.au. **Website:** www.curtisbrown.com.au. 10% of clients are new/unpublished writers. Currently handles: nonfiction books 30%, novels 30%, juvenile books 25%, other 15% other.

○ "Prior to joining Curtis Brown, most of our agents worked in publishing or the film/theatre industries in Australia and the United Kingdom."

MEMBER AGENTS Fiona Inglis (managing director/agent); Fran Moore (deputy managing director / agent); Tara Wynne (agent); Pippa Masson (agent); Clare Forster (agent); Annabel Blay (rights manager).

☞ "We are Australia's oldest and largest literary agency representing a diverse range of Australian and New Zealand writers and Estates."

HOW TO CONTACT "Please refer to our website for information regarding ms submissions, permissions, theatre rights requests, and the clients and Estates we represent. We are not currently looking to represent poetry, short stories, stage/screenplays, picture books, or translations. We do not accept e-mailed or faxed submissions. No responsibility is taken for the receipt or loss of mss."

CYNTHIA CANNELL LITERARY AGENCY

833 Madison Ave., New York NY 10021. (212)396-9595. **Website:** www.cannellagency.com. **Contact:** Cynthia Cannell. Estab. 1997. Member of AAR. Other memberships include the Women's Media Group.

○ Prior to forming the Cynthia Cannell Literary Agency, Ms. Cannell was, for 12 years, vice president of Janklow & Nesbit Associates.

☞ Does not represent screenplays, children's books, illustrated books, cookbooks, romance, category mystery, or science fiction.

HOW TO CONTACT "Please query us with an e-mail or letter. If querying by e-mail, send a brief description of your project with relevant biographical information including publishing credits (if any) to info@cannellagency.com. Do not send attachments. If querying by conventional mail, enclose an SASE."

D4EO LITERARY AGENCY

7 Indian Valley Rd., Weston CT 06883. (203)544-7180. **Fax:** (203)544-7160. **E-mail:** bob@d4eo.com; mandy.hubbard.queries@gmail.com; kristin.d4eo@gmail.com; bree@d4eo.com; samantha@d4eo.com. **Website:** www.d4eoliteraryagency.com. **Contact:** Bob Diforio. Represents 100+ clients. 50% of clients are new/unpublished writers. Currently handles: nonfiction books 70%, novels 25%, juvenile books 5%.

○ Prior to opening his agency, Mr. Diforio was a publisher.

MEMBER AGENTS Bob Diforio, Many Hubbard, Kristin Miller-Vincent, Bree Odgen, Samantha Dighton, Joyce Holland (currently closed to submissions).

REPRESENTS Nonfiction books, novels. **Considers these nonfiction areas:** juvenile, art, biography, business, child, current affairs, gay, health, history, how-to, humor, memoirs, military, money, psychology, religion, science, self help, sports, true crime, women's. **Considers these fiction areas:** adventure, detective, erotica, historical, horror, humor, juvenile, literary, mainstream, mystery, picture books, romance, science, sports, thriller, western, young adult.

HOW TO CONTACT Query with SASE. Accepts and prefers e-mail queries. Prefers to read material exclusively. Responds in 1 week to queries. Obtains most new clients through recommendations from others.

TERMS Agent receives 15% commission on domestic sales. Agent receives 25% commission on foreign sales. Offers written contract, binding for 2 years; 60-day notice must be given to terminate contract. Charges for photocopying and submission postage.

● LAURA DAIL LITERARY AGENCY, INC.

350 Seventh Ave., Suite 2003, New York NY 10001. (212)239-7477. **Fax:** (212)947-0460. **E-mail:** queries@ldlainc.com. **Website:** www.ldlainc.com. Member of AAR.

MEMBER AGENTS Laura Dail; Tamar Rydzinski.

REPRESENTS Nonfiction books, novels.

☞ Specializes in historical, literary and some young adult fiction, as well as both practical and idea-driven nonfiction. "Due to the volume of queries and mss received, we apologize for not answering every e-mail and letter. None of us handles children's picture books or chapter books. No New Age. We do not handle screenplays or poetry."

HOW TO CONTACT Query with SASE or e-mail. This agency prefers e-queries. Include the word "query" in the subject line. If mailing your query, include an SASE.

◐ DANIEL LITERARY GROUP

1701 Kingsbury Dr., Suite 100, Nashville TN 37215. (615)730-8207. **E-mail:** submissions@danielliterarygroup.com. **Website:** www.danielliterarygroup.com. **Contact:** Greg Daniel. Represents 45 clients. 30% of clients are new/unpublished writers. Currently handles: nonfiction books 85%, novels 15%.

○ Prior to becoming an agent, Mr. Daniel spent 10 years in publishing—6 at the executive level at Thomas Nelson Publishers.

REPRESENTS Nonfiction books, novels. **Considers these nonfiction areas:** autobiography, biography, business, child guidance, current affairs, economics, environment, film, health, history, how-to, humor, inspirational, medicine, memoirs, nature, parenting, personal improvement, popular culture, religious, satire, self-help, sports, theater, women's issues, women's studies. **Considers these fiction areas:** action, adventure, contemporary issues, crime, detective, family saga, historical, humor, inspirational, literary, mainstream, mystery, police, religious, satire, suspense, thriller.

8—→ The agency currently accepts all fiction topics, except for children's, romance, and sci-fi. "We take pride in our ability to come alongside our authors and help strategize about where they want their writing to take them in both the near and long term. Forging close relationships with our authors, we help them with such critical factors as editorial refinement, branding, audience, and marketing." The agency is open to submissions in almost every popular category of nonfiction, especially if authors are recognized experts in their fields. No screenplays, poetry, science fiction/fantasy, romance, children's, or short stories.

HOW TO CONTACT Query via e-mail only. Submit publishing history, author bio, brief synopsis of work, key selling points; no attachments. For fiction, send first 5 pages pasted in e-mail. Check Submissions Guidelines before querying or submitting. "Please do not query via telephone." Responds in 2-3 weeks to queries.

● DARHANSOFF & VERRILL LITERARY AGENTS

236 W. 26th St., Suite 802, New York NY 10001. (917)305-1300. **Fax:** (917)305-1400. **E-mail:** submissions@dvagency.com. **Website:** www.dvagency.com. Member of AAR. Represents 120 clients. 10% of clients are new/unpublished writers. Currently handles: nonfiction books 25%, novels 60%, story collections 15%.

MEMBER AGENTS Liz Darhansoff, Chuck Verrill, Michele Mortimer.

REPRESENTS Novels, juvenile books, narrative nonfiction, literary fiction, mystery & suspense, young adult.

HOW TO CONTACT Send queries via e-mail or by snail mail with SASE. Obtains most new clients through recommendations from others.

●● CAROLINE DAVIDSON LITERARY AGENCY

5 Queen Anne's Gardens, London England W4 1TU United Kingdom. (44)(208)995-5768. **Fax:** (44)(208)994-2770. **E-mail:** enquiries@cdla.co.uk. **Website:** www.cdla.co.uk. **Contact:** Caroline Davidson.

REPRESENTS Nonfiction books, serious material only, novels.

8—→ Does not consider autobiographies, chick lit, children's, crime, erotica, fantasy, horror, local history, murder mysteries, occult, self-help, short stories, sci-fi, thrillers, individual short stories, or memoir.

HOW TO CONTACT Send e-mail or query with SASE. See website for additional details and what to include for fiction and nonfiction. Responds in 2 weeks to queries. Obtains most new clients through recommendations from others, solicitations.

TIPS "Visit our website before submitting any work to us."

● LIZA DAWSON ASSOCIATES

350 Seventh Ave., Suite 2003, New York NY 10001. (212)465-9071. **Fax:** (212)947-0460. **E-mail:** queryliza@lizadawsonassociates.com. **Website:** www.lizadawsonassociates.com. **Contact:** Anna Olswanger. Member of AAR. Other memberships include MWA, Women's Media Group. Represents 50+ clients. 30% of clients are new/unpublished writers. Currently handles: nonfiction books 60%, novels 40%.

Prior to becoming an agent, Ms. Dawson was an editor for 20 years, spending 11 years at William Morrow as vice president and 2 years at Putnam as executive editor. Ms. Blasdell was a senior editor at HarperCollins and Avon. Ms. Olswanger is an author.

MEMBER AGENTS Liza Dawson (plot-driven literary fiction, historicals, thrillers, suspense, parenting books, history, psychology [both popular and clinical], politics, narrative nonfiction and memoirs); Caitlin Blasdell (science fiction, fantasy (both adult and young adult), parenting, business, thrillers and women's fiction); Anna Olswanger (gift books for adults, young adult fiction and nonfiction, children's illustrated books, and Judaica); Havis Dawson (business books, how-to and practical books, spirituality, fan-

NEW AGENT SPOTLIGHT

BRITTANY HOWARD (CORVISIERO LITERARY)

Corvisieroagency.com
@brittanydhoward

ABOUT BRITTANY: Brittany Howard of Corvisiero Literary is all about experiences. She's lived in small towns, big cities, and traveled the world. She has a degree in theatre and is currently pursuing a MFA in Creative Writing. When reading, she loves to be introduced to new and interesting people and places. She looks for strong voice, good storytelling, and fascinating relationships between characters. More than anything, she loves when a book surprises her.

SHE IS SEEKING: Her first love is YA fiction—from high fantasy to paranormal to soft sci-fi to contemporary—she loves all young adult. She also likes high concept, adventure themed, and funny middle grade fiction, but a strong voice is must for her in MG. She's willing to look at picture books, but is very selective. For adult fiction, she prefers stories that are a romance at heart—contemporary, paranormal, fantasy, sci-fi, and historical are all genres she's been known to enjoy. Anything with theatrical or artistic or interesting historical elements will probably catch her eye, too. She's tends to steer clear of adult epic fantasy, hardcore Sci-fi, YA issue books, chapter books, or books with multiple points of view.

HOW TO SUBMIT: Brittany prefers that you paste the 1-2 page synopsis and the first 5 pages directly into the query e-mail. Do not send Brittany attachments. E-mail your query with pasted material to query@corvisieroagency.com with "Query For Brittany" in the subject line.

tasy, Southern-culture fiction and military memoirs); Hannah Bowman (commercial fiction, especially science fiction and fantasy; women's fiction; cozy mysteries; romance; young adult; also nonfiction in the areas of mathematics, science, and spirituality); Judith Engracia (all types of fiction, especially middle-grade, young adult, urban fantasy, steampunk, and paranormal romance).
REPRESENTS Nonfiction books, novels and gift books (Olswanger only). **Considers these nonfiction areas:** autobiography, biography, business, health,

history, medicine, memoirs, parenting, politics, psychology, sociology, women's issues, women's studies. **Considers these fiction areas:** literary, mystery, regional, suspense, thriller, fantasy and science fiction (Blasdell only).
○──▪ This agency specializes in readable literary fiction, thrillers, mainstream historicals, women's fiction, academics, historians, business, journalists, and psychology.
HOW TO CONTACT Query by e-mail only. No phone calls. Responds in 4 weeks to queries; 8 weeks

to mss. Obtains most new clients through recommendations from others, conferences.

TERMS Agent receives 15% commission on domestic sales. Agent receives 20% commission on foreign sales. Offers written contract. Charges clients for photocopying and overseas postage.

THE JENNIFER DECHIARA LITERARY AGENCY

31 East 32nd St., Suite 300, New York NY 10016. (212)481-8484. **Fax:** (212)481-9582. **E-mail:** jenndec@aol.com; stephenafraser@verizon.net. **Website:** www.jdlit.com. **Contact:** Jennifer DeChiara, Stephen Fraser. Represents 100 clients. 50% of clients are new/unpublished writers. Currently handles: nonfiction books 25%, novels 25%, juvenile books 50%.

○ Prior to becoming an agent, Ms. DeChiara was a writing consultant, freelance editor at Simon & Schuster and Random House, and a ballerina and an actress.

MEMBER AGENTS Jennifer DeChiara, Stephen Fraser (stephenafraser@verizon.net); Marie Lamba (young adult, middle grade, general fiction, some memoir, marie.jdlit@gmail.com); Linda Epstein (literary fiction, upscale commercial fiction, narrative nonfiction, memoir, Jewish themes, middle grade, young adult, health and parenting, cookbooks, LGBTQ community subjects, linda.p.epstein@gmail.com), Roseanne Wells (queryroseanne@gmail.com, narrative nonfiction, memoir, science, history, travel humor, food, literary fiction, middle grade, smart detective novels).

REPRESENTS Nonfiction books, novels, juvenile. **Considers these nonfiction areas:** autobiography, biography, child guidance, cooking, crafts, criticism, cultural interests, current affairs, dance, decorating, education, environment, ethnic, film, finance, foods, gay, government, health, history, hobbies, how-to, humor, interior design, investigative, juvenile nonfiction, language, law, lesbian, literature, medicine, memoirs, military, money, music, nature, nutrition, parenting, personal improvement, photography, popular culture, politics, psychology, satire, science, self-help, sociology, sports, technology, theater, true crime, war, women's issues, women's studies, celebrity biography. **Considers these fiction areas:** confession, crime, detective, ethnic, family saga, fantasy, feminist, gay, historical, horror, humor, juvenile, lesbian, literary, mainstream, mystery, picture books, police, regional, satire, sports, suspense, thriller, young adult, chick lit, psychic/supernatural, glitz.

☛ "We represent both children's and adult books in a wide range of ages and genres. We are a full-service agency and fulfill the potential of every book in every possible medium—stage, film, television, etc. We help writers every step of the way, from creating book ideas to editing and promotion. We are passionate about helping writers further their careers, but are just as eager to discover new talent, regardless of age or lack of prior publishing experience. This agency is committed to managing a writer's entire career. For us, it's not just about selling books, but about making dreams come true. We are especially attracted to the downtrodden, the discouraged, and the downright disgusted." Actively seeking literary fiction, chick lit, young adult fiction, self-help, pop culture, and celebrity biographies. Does not want Westerns, poetry, or short stories.

HOW TO CONTACT E-query one agent only and put "Query" in the subject line. Accepts simultaneous submissions. Responds in 3-6 months to queries. Responds in 3-6 months to mss.

TERMS Agent receives 15% commission on domestic sales. Agent receives 20% commission on foreign sales. Offers written contract.

RECENT SALES Sold more than 100 titles in the past year. PEN Award-winner YA novel: *Glimpse*, by Carol LynchWilliams (St. Martin's) ; PEN and Edgar Award-winning middle-grade: *Icefall*, by Matthew Kirby (Scholastic); Newbery Honor Medal-winner and *New York Times* bestselling middle-grade: *Heart of a Samurai*, by Margi Preus (Abrams); Lambda Award-winner YA novel: *Split Screen*, by Brent Hartinger (HarperCollins); *A Moose That Says Moo*, by Jennifer Hamburg (Farrar, Straus & Giroux); *Naptime for Barney*, by Danny Sit (Sterling); *The 30-Day Heartbreak Cure*, by Catherine Hickland (Simon & Schuster); *The One-Way Bridge*, by *New York Times* bestselling author Cathie Pelletier (Sourcebooks); *New York Times* bestselling: *Not Young, Still Restless*, by Jeanne Cooper (HarperCollins). Other clients include *New York Times* bestselling author Sylvia Browne, Sonia Levitin, Susan Anderson.

❶ DEFIORE & CO.

47 E. 19th St., 3rd Floor, New York NY 10003. (212)925-7744. **Fax:** (212)925-9803. **E-mail:** info@defioreandco.com; submissions@defioreandco.com. **Website:** www.defioreandco.com. **Contact:** Lauren Gilchrist. Member of AAR. Represents 75 clients. 50% of clients are new/unpublished writers. Currently handles: nonfiction books 70%, novels 30%.

- Prior to becoming an agent, Mr. DeFiore was publisher of Villard Books (1997-1998), editor-in-chief of Hyperion (1992-1997), and editorial director of Delacorte Press (1988-1992).

MEMBER AGENTS Brian DeFiore (popular nonfiction, business, pop culture, parenting, commercial fiction); Laurie Abkemeier (memoir, parenting, business, how-to/self-help, popular science); Kate Garrick (literary fiction, memoir, popular nonfiction); Matthew Elblonk (young adult, popular culture, narrative nonfiction); Caryn Karmatz-Rudy (popular fiction, self-help, narrative nonfiction); Adam Schear (commercial fiction, humor, YA, smart thrillers, historical fiction, and quirky debut literary novels. For nonfiction: popular science, politics, popular culture, and current events); Meredith Kaffel (smart upmarket women's fiction, literary fiction [especially debut] and literary thrillers, narrative nonfiction, nonfiction about science and tech, sophisticated pop culture/humor books); Rebecca Strauss (literary and commercial fiction, women's fiction, urban fantasy, romance, mystery, YA, memoir, pop culture, and select nonfiction).

REPRESENTS Nonfiction books, novels. **Considers these nonfiction areas:** autobiography, biography, business, child guidance, cooking, economics, foods, how-to, inspirational, money, multicultural, parenting, popular culture, psychology, religious, self-help, sports, young adult, middle-grade. **Considers these fiction areas:** ethnic, literary, mainstream, mystery, suspense, thriller.

- "Please be advised that we are not considering children's picture books, poetry, adult science fiction and fantasy, romance, or dramatic projects at this time."

HOW TO CONTACT Query with SASE or e-mail to submissions@defioreandco.com. "Please include the word "Query" in the subject line. All attachments will be deleted; please insert all text in the body of the e-mail. For more information about our agents, their individual interests, and their query guidelines, please visit our 'About Us' page." Accepts simultaneous submissions. Responds in 3 weeks to queries. Responds in 2 months to mss. Obtains most new clients through recommendations from others.

TERMS Agent receives 15% commission on domestic sales. Agent receives 20% commission on foreign sales. Offers written contract; 10-day notice must be given to terminate contract. Charges clients for photocopying and overnight delivery (deducted only after a sale is made).

WRITERS CONFERENCES Maui Writers Conference; Pacific Northwest Writers Conference; North Carolina Writers' Network Fall Conference.

● JOELLE DELBOURGO ASSOCIATES, INC.

101 Park St., 3rd Floor, Montclair NJ 07042. (973)773-0836. **Fax:** (973)783-6802. **E-mail:** info@delbourgo.com. **Website:** www.delbourgo.com. **Contact:** Joelle Delbourgo, Jacquie Flynn. Represents more than 100 clients. Currently handles: nonfiction books 75%, novels 25%.

- Prior to becoming an agent, Ms. Delbourgo was an editor and senior publishing executive at HarperCollins and Random House.

MEMBER AGENTS Joelle Delbourgo (narrative nonfiction, serious "expert-driven" nonfiction, self-help, psychology, business, history, science, medicine, quality fiction); Jacquie Flynn (thought-provoking and practical business, parenting, education, personal development, current events, science and other select nonfiction and fiction titles); Carrie Cantor (current events, politics, history, popular science and psychology, memoir, and narrative nonfiction).

REPRESENTS Nonfiction books, novels. **Considers these nonfiction areas:** autobiography, biography, business, child guidance, cooking, cultural interests, current affairs, decorating, diet/nutrition, economics, education, environment, ethnic, foods, gay/lesbian, government, health, history, how-to, inspirational, interior design, investigative, law, medicine, metaphysics, money, New Age, popular culture, politics, psychology, religious, science, sociology, technology, true crime, women's issues, women's studies, New Age/metaphysics, interior design/decorating. **Considers these fiction areas:** historical, literary, mainstream, mystery, suspense.

- "We are former publishers and editors with deep knowledge and an insider perspective. We have a reputation for individualized attention to clients, strategic management of authors' careers, and creating strong partnerships with publishers for our clients." Actively seeking history, narrative nonfiction, science/medicine, memoir, literary fiction, psychology, parenting, biographies, current affairs, politics, young adult fiction and nonfiction. Does not want to receive genre fiction, science fiction, fantasy, or screenplays.

HOW TO CONTACT Query by mail with SASE. Accepts simultaneous submissions. Responds in 3 weeks to queries. Responds in 2 months to mss.

TERMS Agent receives 15% commission on domestic sales. Agent receives 20% commission on foreign sales. Offers written contract. Charges clients for postage and photocopying.

RECENT SALES *Alexander the Great*, by Philip Freeman; *The Big Book of Parenting Solutions*, by Dr. Michele Borba; *The Secret Life of Ms. Finkelman*, by Ben H. Wintners; *Not Quite Adults*, by Richard Settersten Jr. and Barbara Ray; *Tabloid Medicine*, by Robert Goldberg, PhD; *Table of Contents*, by Judy Gerlman and Vicky Levi Krupp.

TIPS "Do your homework. Do not cold call. Read and follow submission guidelines before contacting us. Do not call to find out if we received your material. No e-mail queries. Treat agents with respect, as you would any other professional, such as a doctor, lawyer or financial advisor."

SANDRA DIJKSTRA LITERARY AGENCY

1155 Camino del Mar, PMB 515, Del Mar CA 92014. (858)755-3115. **Fax:** (858)794-2822. **E-mail:** elise@dijkstraagency.com. **Website:** www.dijkstraagency.com. Member of AAR. Other memberships include Authors Guild, PEN West, Poets and Editors, MWA. Represents 100+ clients. 30% of clients are new/unpublished writers. Currently handles: nonfiction books 50%, novels 45%, juvenile books 5%.

MEMBER AGENTS Sandra Dijkstra, president (adult only). Acquiring Sub-agents: Elise Capron (adult only), Jill Marr (adult only), Thao Le (adult and YA), Jennifer Azantian (YA only). Sub-rights agent: Andrea Cavallaro; Roz Foster (associate agent).

REPRESENTS Nonfiction books, novels. **Considers these nonfiction areas:** biography, business, history, memoirs, psychology, science, self-help, narrative. **Considers these fiction areas:** contemporary issues, fantasy, literary, science fiction, suspense, thriller, women's, young adult.

HOW TO CONTACT "Please see guidelines on our website, and please note that we now only accept e-mail submissions. Due to the large number of unsolicited submissions we receive, we are only able to respond those submissions in which we are interested." Accepts simultaneous submissions. Responds to queries of interest within 6 weeks.

TERMS Works in conjunction with foreign and film agents. Agent receives 15% commission on domestic sales and 20% commission on foreign sales. Offers written contract. No reading fee.

TIPS "Be professional and learn the standard procedures for submitting your work. Be a regular patron of bookstores, and study what kind of books are being published and will appear on the shelves next to yours. You'll also find lots of books on writing and the publishing industry that will help you. At conferences, ask published writers about their agents. Don't believe the myth that an agent has to be in New York to be successful. We've already disproved it!"

DONADIO & OLSON, INC.

121 W. 27th St., Suite 704, New York NY 10001. (212)691-8077. **Fax:** (212)633-2837. **E-mail:** mail@donadio.com. **Website:** http://donadio.com. **Contact:** Neil Olson. Member of AAR.

MEMBER AGENTS Neil Olson (no queries); Edward Hibbert (no queries); Carrie Howland (represents literary fiction and nonfiction as well as young adult fiction. She can be reached at **carrie@donadio.com**.).

REPRESENTS Nonfiction books, novels.

This agency represents mostly fiction, and is very selective.

HOW TO CONTACT Query by snail mail is preferred; for e-mail use mail@donadio.com; only send submissions to open agents. Obtains most new clients through recommendations from others.

JANIS A. DONNAUD & ASSOCIATES, INC.

525 Broadway, Second Floor, New York NY 10012. (212)431-2664. **Fax:** (212)431-2667. **E-mail:** jdonnaud@aol.com; donnaudassociate@aol.com. **Contact:** Janis A. Donnaud. Member of AAR. Signatory of WGA. Represents 40 clients. 5% of clients are new/unpublished writers. Currently handles: nonfiction books 100%.

Prior to opening her agency, Ms. Donnaud was vice president and associate publisher of Random House Adult Trade Group.

REPRESENTS Nonfiction books. **Considers these nonfiction areas:** autobiography, African-American, biography, business, celebrity, child guidance, cooking, current affairs, diet/nutrition, foods, health, humor, medicine, parenting, psychology, satire, women's issues, women's studies, lifestyle.

This agency specializes in health, medical, cooking, humor, pop psychology, narrative nonfiction, biography, parenting, and current affairs. We give a lot of service and attention to clients. Does not want to receive "fiction, poetry, mysteries, juvenile books, romances, science fiction, young adult, religious or fantasy."

HOW TO CONTACT Query with SASE. Submit description of book, 2-3 pages of sample material. Prefers to read materials exclusively. No phone calls. Responds in 1 month to queries and mss. Obtains most new clients through recommendations from others.

TERMS Agent receives 15% commission on domestic and film sales; 20% commission on foreign sales. Offers written contract; 1-month notice must be given to terminate contract.

RECENT SALES *50 Shades of Chicken*, by F.L. Fowler; *From Mama's Table to Mine*, by Bobby Deen; *Fat Chance*, by Robert Lustig, M.D., *30 Lessons for Living*, by Karl Pillemer, Ph. D.; *Mumbai, New York, Scranton*, by Tamara Shopsin.

JIM DONOVAN LITERARY

5635 SMU Blvd., Suite 201, Dallas TX 75206. **E-mail:** jdliterary@sbcglobal.net. **Contact:** Melissa Shultz, agent. Represents 30 clients. 10% of clients are new/unpublished writers. Currently handles: nonfiction books 75%, novels 25%.

MEMBER AGENTS Jim Donovan (history—particularly American, military and Western; biography; sports; popular reference; popular culture; fiction—literary, thrillers and mystery); Melissa Shultz (parenting, women's issues, memoir).

REPRESENTS Nonfiction books, novels. **Considers these nonfiction areas:** autobiography, biography, business, child guidance, current affairs, economics, environment, health, history, how-to, investigative, law, medicine, memoirs, military, money, music, parenting, popular culture, politics, sports, true crime, war, women's issues, women's studies. **Con**-siders these fiction areas: action, adventure, crime, detective, literary, mainstream, mystery, police, suspense, thriller.

This agency specializes in commercial fiction and nonfiction. "Does not want to receive poetry, children's, short stories, inspirational or anything else not listed above."

HOW TO CONTACT "For nonfiction, I need a well-thought query letter telling me about the book: What it does, how it does it, why it's needed now, why it's better or different than what's out there on the subject, and why the author is the perfect writer for it. For fiction, the novel has to be finished, of course; a short (2 to 5 page) synopsis—not a teaser, but a summary of all the action, from first page to last—and the first 30-50 pages is enough. This material should be polished to as close to perfection as possible." Accepts simultaneous submissions. Responds in 3 weeks to queries. Responds in 1 month to mss. Obtains most new clients through recommendations from others.

TERMS Agent receives 15% commission on domestic sales. Agent receives 20% commission on foreign sales. Offers written contract, binding for 1 year; 30-day notice must be given to terminate contract. This agency charges for things such as overnight delivery and manuscript copying. Charges are discussed beforehand.

RECENT SALES Sold 31 titles in the past year. *Manson: The Life and Times of Charles Manson*, by Jeff Guinn (Simon and Schuster); *Shot All to Hell*, by Mark Lee Gardner (Morrow); *Grant and Lee*, by William C. Davis (Da Capo); *Below*, by Ryan Lockwood (Kensington); *The Dead Lands*, by Joe McKinney (Kensington); *Perfect: Don Larsen's Miraculous World Series Game and the Men Who Made It Happen*, by Lew Paper (NAL); *Untouchable: The Life and Times of Elliott Ness, America's Greatest Crime Fighter* (Viking); *Undefeated: America's Heroic Fight for Bataan and Corregidor*, by Bill Sloan (Simon and Schuster).

TIPS "Get published in short form—magazine reviews, journals, etc.—first. This will increase your credibility considerably, and make it much easier to sell a full-length book."

DOYEN LITERARY SERVICES, INC.

1931-660th St., Newell IA 50568-7613. **E-mail:** bestseller@barbaradoyen.com. **Website:** www.barbaradoyen.com. **Contact:** (Ms.) B.J. Doyen, president. Represents over 100 clients. 20% of clients are new/

unpublished writers. Currently handles: nonfiction books 100%.

○ Prior to opening her agency, Ms. Doyen worked as a published author, teacher, guest speaker, and wrote and appeared in her own weekly TV show airing in 7 states. She is also the coauthor of *The Everything Guide to Writing a Book Proposal* (Adams 2005) and *The Everything Guide to Getting Published* (Adams 2006).

REPRESENTS Nonfiction for adults, no children's. **Considers these nonfiction areas:** agriculture, Americana, animals, anthropology, archeology, architecture, art, autobiography, biography, business, child guidance, computers, cooking, crafts, cultural interests, current affairs, diet/nutrition, design, economics, education, environment, ethnic, film, foods, gardening, government, health, history, hobbies, horticulture, language, law, medicine, memoirs, metaphysics, military, money, multicultural, music, parenting, photography, popular culture, politics, psychology, recreation, regional, science, self-help, sex, sociology, software, technology, theater, true crime, women's issues, women's studies, creative nonfiction, computers, electronics.

8—¬ This agency specializes in nonfiction. Actively seeking business, health, science, how-to, self-help—all kinds of adult nonfiction suitable for the major trade publishers. Does not want to receive pornography, screenplays, children's books, fiction, or poetry.

HOW TO CONTACT Send a **query letter** initially. "Do not send us any attachments. Your text must be in the body of the e-mail. Please read the website before submitting a query. Include your background information in a bio. Send no unsolicited attachments." Accepts simultaneous submissions. Responds immediately to queries. Responds in 3 weeks to mss.

TERMS Agent receives 15% commission on domestic sales. Agent receives 20% commission on foreign sales. Offers written contract, binding for 2 years.

RECENT SALES *Stem Cells For Dummies*, by Lawrence S.B. Goldstein and Meg Schneider; *The Complete Idiot's Guide to Country Living*, by Kimberly Willis; *The Complete Illustrated Pregnancy Companion* by Robin Elise Weiss; *The Complete Idiot's Guide to Playing the Fiddle*, by Ellery Klein; *Healthy Aging for Dummies*, by Brent Agin, MD and Sharon Perkins, RN.

TIPS "Our authors receive personalized attention. We market aggressively, undeterred by rejection. We get the best possible publishing contracts. We are very interested in nonfiction book ideas at this time and will consider most topics. Many writers come to us from referrals, but we also get quite a few who initially approach us with query letters. Do not call us regarding queries. It is best if you do not collect editorial rejections prior to seeking an agent, but if you do, be upfront and honest about it. Do not submit your manuscript to more than 1 agent at a time—querying first can save you (and us) much time. We're open to established or beginning writers—just send us a terrific letter!"

DREISBACH LITERARY MANAGEMENT

PO Box 5379, El Dorado Hills CA 95762. (916)804-5016. **E-mail:** verna@dreisbachliterary.com. **Website:** www.dreisbachliterary.com. **Contact:** Verna Dreisbach. Estab. 2007.

REPRESENTS **Considers these nonfiction areas:** animals, biography, business, health, multicultural, parenting, travel, true crime, women's issues. **Considers these fiction areas:** commercial, literary, mystery, thriller, young adult.

8—¬ The agency has a particular interest in books with a political, economic, or social context. Open to most types of nonfiction. Fiction interests include literary, commercial, and YA. Verna's first career as a law enforcement officer gives her a genuine interest and expertise in the genres of mystery, thriller, and true crime. Does not want to receive sci-fi, fantasy, horror, poetry, screenplay, Christian, or children's books.

HOW TO CONTACT E-mail queries only. No attachments in the query; they will not be opened. No unsolicited mss.

RECENT SALES *How to Blog a Book* (Writer's Digest Books); *Quest for Justice* (New Horizon Press); *Walnut Wine and Truffle Groves* (Running Press); *Coming to the Fire* (BenBella Books); *Off the Street* (Behler Publications); *Lowcountry Bribe* (Bell Bridge Books).

◑ DUNHAM LITERARY, INC.

110 William St., Suite 2202, New York NY 10038. (212)929-0994. **E-mail:** dunhamlit@yahoo.com. **E-mail:** query@dunhamlit.com. **Website:** www.dunhamlit.com. **Contact:** Jennie Dunham. Member of AAR. SCBWI Represents 50 clients. 15% of clients are

new/unpublished writers. Currently handles: nonfiction books 25%, novels 25%, juvenile books 50%.

○ Prior to opening her agency, Ms. Dunham worked as a literary agent for Russell & Volkening. The Rhoda Weyr Agency is now a division of Dunham Literary, Inc.

REPRESENTS Nonfiction books, novels, short story collections, juvenile. **Considers these nonfiction areas:** anthropology, archeology, autobiography, biography, cultural interests, environment, ethnic, government, health, history, language, law, literature, medicine, popular culture, politics, psychology, science, technology, women's issues, women's studies. **Considers these fiction areas:** ethnic, juvenile, literary, mainstream, picture books, young adult.

HOW TO CONTACT Query with SASE. Responds in 1 week to queries; 2 months to mss. Obtains most new clients through recommendations from others, solicitations.

TERMS Agent receives 15% commission on domestic sales. Agent receives 20% commission on foreign sales.

RECENT SALES Sold 30 books for young readers in the last year. *Peter Pan*, by Robert Sabuda (Little Simon); *Flamingos on the Roof*, by Calef Brown (Houghton); *Adele and Simon in America*, by Barbara McClintock (Farrar, Straus & Giroux); *Caught Between the Pages*, by Marlene Carvell (Dutton); *Waiting For Normal*, by Leslie Connor (HarperCollins), *The Gollywhopper Games*, by Jody Feldman (Greenwillow); *America the Beautiful*, by Robert Sabuda; *Dahlia*, by Barbara McClintock; *Living Dead Girl*, by Tod Goldberg; *In My Mother's House*, by Margaret McMulla; *Black Hawk Down*, by Mark Bowden; *Look Back All the Green Valley*, by Fred Chappell; *Under a Wing*, by Reeve Lindbergh; *I Am Madame X*, by Gioia Diliberto.

● DUNOW, CARLSON, & LERNER AGENCY

27 W. 20th St., Suite 1107, New York NY 10011. **E-mail:** mail@dclagency.com. **Website:** www.dclagency.com. **Contact:** Jennifer Carlson, Henry Dunow, Betsy Lerner. Member of AAR.

MEMBER AGENTS Jennifer Carlson (young adult and middle grade, some fiction and nonfiction); Henry Dunow (quality fiction—literary, historical, strongly written commercial—and with voice-driven nonfiction across a range of areas—narrative history, biography, memoir, current affairs, cultural trends and criticism, science, sports); Erin Hosier (nonfiction:

popular culture, music, sociology and memoir); Betsy Lerner (nonfiction writers in the areas of psychology, history, cultural studies, biography, current events, business; fiction: literary, dark, funny, voice driven); Yishai Seidman (broad range of fiction: literary, postmodern, and thrillers; nonfiction: sports, music, and pop culture); Amy Hughes (nonfiction in the areas of history, cultural studies, memoir, current events, wellness, health, food, pop culture, and biography; also literary fiction; Julia Kenny

REPRESENTS Nonfiction books, novels, juvenile.

HOW TO CONTACT Query with SASE or by e-mail. No attachments. Unable to respond to queries except when interested.

◑ DUPREE/MILLER AND ASSOCIATES INC. LITERARY

100 Highland Park Village, Suite 350, Dallas TX 75205. (214)559-BOOK. **Fax:** (214)559-PAGE. **Website:** www.dupreemiller.com. Member of ABA. Represents 200 clients. 20% of clients are new/unpublished writers. Currently handles: nonfiction books 90%, novels 10%.

MEMBER AGENTS Jan Miller, president/CEO; Shannon Miser-Marven, senior executive VP; Annabelle Baxter; Nena Madonia; Cheri Gillis.

REPRESENTS Nonfiction books, novels, scholarly, syndicated, religious.inspirational/spirituality. **Considers these nonfiction areas:** animals, anthropology, archeology, architecture, art, autobiography, biography, business, child guidance, cooking, crafts, current affairs, dance, diet/nutrition, design, economics, education, environment, ethnic, film, foods, gardening, government, health, history, how-to, humor, language, literature, medicine, memoirs, money, multicultural, music, parenting, philosophy, photography, popular culture, psychology, recreation, regional, satire, science, self-help, sex, sociology, sports, technology, theater, translation, true crime, women's issues, women's studies. **Considers these fiction areas:** action, adventure, crime, detective, ethnic, experimental, family saga, feminist, glitz, historical, humor, inspirational, literary, mainstream, mystery, picture books, police, psychic, religious, satire, sports, supernatural, suspense, thriller.

⚸ This agency specializes in commercial fiction and nonfiction.

HOW TO CONTACT Submit 1-page query, summary, bio, how to market, SASE through U.S. postal service.

Obtains most new clients through recommendations from others, conferences, lectures.

TERMS Agent receives 15% commission on domestic sales. Offers written contract.

WRITERS CONFERENCES Aspen Summer Words Literary Festival.

TIPS "If interested in agency representation, it is vital to have the material in the proper working format. As agents' policies differ, it is important to follow their guidelines. Work on establishing a strong proposal that provides sample chapters, an overall synopsis (fairly detailed), and some biographical information on yourself. Do not send your proposal in pieces; it should be complete upon submission. Your work should be in its best condition."

DYSTEL & GODERICH LITERARY MANAGEMENT

1 Union Square W., Suite 904, New York NY 10003. (212)627-9100. **Fax:** (212)627-9313. **Website:** www.dystel.com. **Contact:** Michael Bourret; Jim McCarthy. Member of AAR. Other membership includes SCBWI. Represents 617 clients. 50% of clients are new/unpublished writers. Currently handles: nonfiction books 65%, novels 35%.

Dystel & Goderich Literary Management recently acquired the client list of Bedford Book Works.

MEMBER AGENTS Jane Dystel; Miriam Goderich; Stacey Kendall Glick; Michael Bourret; Jim McCarthy; Jessica Papin; Lauren E. Abramo; John Rudolph; Brenna Barr; Rachel Stout; Yassine Belkacemi.

REPRESENTS Nonfiction books, novels, cookbooks. **Considers these nonfiction areas:** animals, anthropology, archeology, autobiography, biography, business, child guidance, cultural interests, current affairs, economics, ethnic, gay/lesbian, health, history, humor, inspirational, investigative, medicine, metaphysics, military, New Age, parenting, popular culture, psychology, religious, science, technology, true crime, women's issues, women's studies. **Considers these fiction areas:** action, adventure, crime, detective, ethnic, family saga, gay, lesbian, literary, mainstream, mystery, police, suspense, thriller.

"This agency specializes in cookbooks and commercial and literary fiction and nonfiction." "We are actively seeking fiction for all ages, in all genres. We're especially interested in quality young adult fiction, from realistic to paranormal, and all kinds of middle-grade, from funny boy books to more sentimental fare. Though we are open to author/illustrators, we are not looking for picture book mss. And, while we would like to see more YA memoir, nonfiction is not something we usually handle." No plays, screenplays, or poetry.

HOW TO CONTACT Query with SASE. "Please include the first 3 chapters in the body of the e-mail. Email queries preferred (Michael Bourret only accepts e-mail queries); will accept mail. See website for full guidelines." Accepts simultaneous submissions. Responds in 6 to 8 weeks to queries; within 8 weeks to mss. Obtains most new clients through recommendations from others, solicitations, conferences.

TERMS Agent receives 15% commission on domestic sales. Agent receives 19% commission on foreign sales. Offers written contract.

WRITERS CONFERENCES Backspace Writers' Conference; Pacific Northwest Writers' Association; Pike's Peak Writers' Conference; Writers League of Texas; Love Is Murder; Surrey International Writers Conference; Society of Children's Book Writers and Illustrators; International Thriller Writers; Willamette Writers Conference; The South Carolina Writers Workshop Conference; Las Vegas Writers Conference; Writer's Digest; Seton Hill Popular Fiction; Romance Writers of America; Geneva Writers Conference.

TIPS "DGLM prides itself on being a full-service agency. We're involved in every stage of the publishing process, from offering substantial editing on mss and proposals, to coming up with book ideas for authors looking for their next project, negotiating contracts and collecting monies for our clients. We follow a book from its inception through its sale to a publisher, its publication, and beyond. Our commitment to our writers does not, by any means, end when we have collected our commission. This is one of the many things that makes us unique in a very competitive business."

EAST/WEST LITERARY AGENCY, LLC

1158 26th St., Suite 462, Santa Monica CA 90403. (310)573-9303. **Fax:** (310)453-9008. **E-mail:** dwarren@eastwestliteraryagency.com; rpfeffer@eastwestliteraryagency.com. Estab. 2000. Currently handles: juvenile books 90%, adult books 10%.

MEMBER AGENTS Deborah Warren, founder; Rubin Pfeffer, partner content agent and digital media strategist.

HOW TO CONTACT By referral only. Submit proposal and first 3 sample chapters, table of contents (2 pages or fewer), synopsis (1 page). For picture books, submit entire ms. Requested submissions should be sent by mail as a Word document in Courier, 12-pt., double-spaced with 1.20-inch margin on left, ragged right text, 25 lines per page, continuously paginated, with all your contact info on the first page. Only responds if interested, no need for SASE. Responds in 60 days. Obtains new clients through recommendations from others.

TERMS Agent receives 15% commission on domestic sales. Agent receives 25% commission on foreign sales. Offers written contract; 30-day notice must be given to terminate contract. Charges for out-of-pocket expenses, such as postage and copying.

◑ THE EBELING AGENCY

P.O. Box 2529, Lyons CO 80540. (303)823-6963. E-mail: Michael@EbelingAgency.com. **Website:** www.ebelingagency.com. **Contact:** Michael Ebeling. Represents 6 clients. 50% of clients are new/unpublished writers. Currently handles: nonfiction books 100%.

Prior to becoming an agent, Mr. Ebeling established a career in the publishing industry through long-term author management. He has expertise in sales, platforms, publicity and marketing.

MEMBER AGENTS Michael Ebeling, Michael@EbelingAgency.com.

REPRESENTS Nonfiction books. **Considers these nonfiction areas:** animals, business, cooking, diet/nutrition, environment, foods, history, how-to, humor, inspirational, medicine, money, music, parenting, psychology, religious, satire, self-help, spirituality, sports, food/fitness.

⚬━ "We accept very few clients for representation. To be considered, an author needs a very strong platform and a unique book concept. We represent nonfiction authors, most predominantly in the areas of business and self-help. We are very committed to our authors and their messages, which is a main reason we have such a high placement rate. We are always looking at new ways to help our authors gain the exposure they need to not only get published, but develop a successful literary career." Actively seeking well-written nonfiction material with fresh perspectives written by writers with established platforms. Does not want to receive fiction, poetry or children's lit.

HOW TO CONTACT E-mail query and proposal to Mr. Ebeling. E-queries only. Accepts simultaneous submissions. Responds in 4-6 weeks to queries. Obtains most new clients through referrals and queries.

TERMS Agent receives 15% commission on domestic sales. Agent receives 20% commission on foreign sales. Offers written contract; 60-day notice must be given to terminate contract. There is a charge for normal out-of-pocket fees, not to exceed $200 without client approval.

WRITERS CONFERENCES BookExpo America; San Francisco Writers' Conference.

TIPS "Approach agents when you're already building your platform, you have a well-written book, you have a firm understanding of the publishing process, and you have come up with a complete competitive proposal. Know the name of the agent you are contacting. You're essentially selling a business plan to the publisher. Make sure you've made a convincing pitch throughout your proposal, as ultimately, publishers are taking a financial risk by investing in your project."

● ANNE EDELSTEIN LITERARY AGENCY

404 Riverside Dr., #12D, New York NY 10025. (212)414-4923. **Fax:** (212)414-2930. **E-mail:** info@aeliterary.com. **E-mail:** submissions@aeliterary.com. **Website:** www.aeliterary.com. Member of AAR.

MEMBER AGENTS Anne Edelstein; Krista Ingebretson.

REPRESENTS Nonfiction, fiction. **Considers these nonfiction areas:** history, memoirs, psychology, cultural history. **Considers these fiction areas:** literary.

⚬━ This agency specializes in fiction and narrative nonfiction.

HOW TO CONTACT E-mail queries only; consult website for submission guidelines.

RECENT Sales *Amsterdam*, by Russell Shorto (Doubleday); *The Story of Beautiful Girl*, by Rachel Simon (Grand Central).

EDUCATIONAL DESIGN SERVICES LLC

5750 Bou Ave, Suite 1508, N. Bethesda MD 20852. **E-mail:** blinder@educationaldesignservices.com. **Website:** www.educationaldesignservices.com. **Contact:**

B. Linder. Estab. 1981. 80% of clients are new/unpublished writers.

8➤ "We specialize in educational materials to be used in classrooms (in class sets), for staff development or in teacher education classes." Actively seeking educational, text materials. Not looking for picture books, story books, fiction; no illustrators.

HOW TO CONTACT Query by e-mail or with SASE or send outline and 1 sample chapter. Considers simultaneous queries and submissions if so indicated. Returns material only with SASE. Responds in 6-8 weeks to queries/mss. Obtains clients through recommendations from others, queries/solicitations, or through conferences.

TERMS Agent receives 15% commission on domestic sales; 25% on foreign sales. Offers written contract, binding until any party opts out. Terminate contract through certified letter.

RECENT SALES *How to Solve Word Problems in Mathematics*, by Wayne (McGraw-Hill*); Preparing for the 8th Grade Test in Social Studies*, by Farran-Paci (Amsco); *Minority Report*, by Gunn-Singh (Scarecrow Education); *No Parent Left Behind*, by Petrosino & Spiegel (Rowman & Littlefield); *Teaching Test-taking Skills* (R&L Education); *10 Languages You'll Need Most in the Classroom*, by Sundem, Krieger, Pickiewicz (Corwin Press*); Kids, Classrooms & Capital Hill*, by Flynn (R&L Education); *Bully Nation*, by Susan Eva Porter (Paragon House).

◐ JUDITH EHRLICH LITERARY MANAGEMENT, LLC

880 Third Ave., 8th Floor, New York NY 10022. (646)505-1570. **Fax:** (646)505-1570. **E-mail:** jehrlich@judithehrlichliterary.com. **Website:** www.judithehrlichliterary.com. Member of include Author's Guild, the American Society of Journalists and Authors.

○ Prior to her current position, Ms. Ehrlich was an award-winning journalist; she is the co-author of *The New Crowd: The Changing of the Jewish Guard on Wall Street* (Little, Brown).

MEMBER AGENTS Judith Ehrlich; Sophia Seidner: sseidner@judithehrlichliterary.com (strong literary fiction and nonfiction including self-help, narrative nonfiction, memoir, and biography. Areas of special interest include medical and health-related topics, science [popular, political and social], animal welfare, current events, politics, law, history, ethics, parody and humor, sports, art and business self-help).

REPRESENTS Nonfiction books, novels.

8➤ "Special areas of interest include compelling narrative nonfiction, outstanding biographies and memoirs, lifestyle books, works that reflect our changing culture, women's issues, psychology, science, social issues, current events, parenting, health, history, business, and prescriptive books offering fresh information and advice." Does not want to receive children's or young adult books, novellas, poetry, textbooks, plays, or screenplays.

HOW TO CONTACT Query with SASE. Queries should include a synopsis and some sample pages. Send e-queries to jehrlich@judithehrlichliterary.com. The agency will respond only if interested.

RECENT SALES Fiction: *Breaking the Bank*, by Yona Zeldis McDonough (Pocket); *Sinful Surrender*, by Beverley Kendall (Kensington); Nonfiction: *Strategic Learning: How to be Smarter Than Your Competition and Turn Key Insights Into Competitive Advantage*, by William Pieterson (Wiley); *Paris Under Water: How the City of Light Survived the Great Flood of 1910*, by Jeffrey Jackson (Palgrave Macmillan); *When Growth Stalls: How It Happens, Why You're Stuck & What to Do About It*, by Steve McKee (Jossey-Bass); *I'm Smarter Than My Boss. Now What?* by Diane Garnick (Bloomberg Press).

◉ THE LISA EKUS GROUP, LLC

57 North St., Hatfield MA 01038. (413)247-9325. **Fax:** (413)247-9873. **E-mail:** lisaekus@lisaekus.com. **Website:** www.lisaekus.com. **Contact:** Lisa Ekus-Saffer. Member of AAR.

REPRESENTS Nonfiction books. **Considers these nonfiction areas:** cooking, diet/nutrition, foods, occasionally health/well-being and women's issues.

HOW TO CONTACT Submit a one-page query via e-mail or submit complete hard copy proposal with title page, proposal contents, concept, bio, marketing, TOC, etc. Include SASE for the return of materials.

RECENT SALES "Please see the regularly updated client listing on our website."

TIPS "Please do not call. No phone queries."

◑ ETHAN ELLENBERG LITERARY AGENCY

548 Broadway, #5-E, New York NY 10012. (212)431-4554. **Fax:** (212)941-4652. **E-mail:** agent@ethanellen

berg.com. **Website:** http://ethanellenberg.com. **Contact:** Ethan Ellenberg. Estab. 1984. Represents 80 clients. 10% of clients are new/unpublished writers. Currently handles: nonfiction books 25%, novels 75%.

○ Prior to opening his agency, Mr. Ellenberg was contracts manager of Berkley/Jove and associate contracts manager for Bantam.

MEMBER AGENTS Denise Little: deniselitt@aol. com. (accepts romance, paranormal, YA, science fiction, fantasy, Christian fiction, and commercial nonfiction. Send a short query letter telling about your writing history, and including the first 15 pages of the work you want her to represent. If she is interested in your work, she'll reply to you within four weeks); Evan Gregory (accepting clients).

REPRESENTS Nonfiction books, novels, children's books. **Considers these nonfiction areas:** biography, current affairs, health, history, medicine, military, science, technology, war, narrative. **Considers these fiction areas:** commercial, fantasy, mystery, romance, science fiction, suspense, thriller, young adult, children's (all types).

⌖ "This agency specializes in commercial fiction—especially thrillers, romance/women's, and specialized nonfiction. We also do a lot of children's books. Actively seeking commercial fiction as noted above—romance/fiction for women, science fiction and fantasy, thrillers, suspense and mysteries. Our other two main areas of interest are children's books and narrative nonfiction. We are actively seeking clients, follow the directions on our website." Does not want to receive poetry, short stories, or screenplays.

HOW TO CONTACT For fiction, send introductory letter, outline, first 3 chapters, SASE. For nonfiction, send query letter, proposal, 1 sample chapter, SASE. For children's books, send introductory letter, up to 3 picture book mss, outline, first 3 chapters, SASE. Accepts simultaneous submissions. Responds in 2 weeks to queries (no attachments); 4-6 weeks to mss.

TERMS Agent receives 15% commission on domestic sales. Agent receives 10% commission on foreign sales. Offers written contract. Charges clients (with their consent) for direct expenses limited to photocopying and postage.

WRITERS CONFERENCES RWA National Conference; Novelists, Inc.; and other regional conferences.

TIPS We do consider new material from unsolicited authors. Write a good, clear letter with a succinct description of your book. We prefer the first 3 chapters when we consider fiction. For all submissions, you must include a SASE or the material will be discarded. It's always hard to break in, but talent will find a home. Check our website for complete submission guidelines. We continue to see natural storytellers and nonfiction writers with important books.

THE NICHOLAS ELLISON AGENCY

Affiliated with Sanford J. Greenburger Associates, 55 Fifth Ave., 15th Floor, New York NY 10003. (212)206-5600. **Fax:** (212)463-8718. **E-mail:** nellison@sjga.com. **Website:** www.greenburger.com. **Contact:** Nicholas Ellison. Represents 70 clients. Currently handles: nonfiction books 50%, novels 50%.

○ Prior to becoming an agent, Mr. Ellison was an editor at Minerva Editions and Harper & Row, and editor-in-chief at Delacorte.

MEMBER AGENTS Nicholas Ellison; Chelsea Lindman.

REPRESENTS Nonfiction books, novels literary, mainstream children's books. **Considers these fiction areas:** literary, mainstream.

HOW TO CONTACT Submit query in the body of an e-mail; no attachments. Responds in 6 weeks to queries.

TERMS Agent receives 15% commission on domestic sales. Agent receives 20% commission on foreign sales.

◑ THE ELAINE P. ENGLISH LITERARY AGENCY

4710 41st St. NW, Suite D, Washington DC 20016. (202)362-5190. **Fax:** (202)362-5192. **E-mail:** queries@ elaineenglish.com. **E-mail:** elaine@elaineenglish. com. **Website:** www.elaineenglish.com/literary.php. **Contact:** Elaine English, Lindsey Skouras. Member of AAR. Represents 20 clients. 25% of clients are new/ unpublished writers. Currently handles: novels 100%.

○ Ms. English has been working in publishing for more than 20 years. She is also an attorney specializing in media and publishing law.

MEMBER AGENTS Elaine English (novels).

REPRESENTS Novels. **Considers these fiction areas:** historical, multicultural, mystery, suspense, thriller, women's, romance (single title, historical, contemporary, romantic, suspense, chick lit, erotic), general women's fiction. The agency is slowly but steadily acquiring in all mentioned areas.

☞ Actively seeking women's fiction, including single-title romances. Does not want to receive any science fiction, time travel, or picture books.

HOW TO CONTACT Generally prefers e-queries sent to queries@elaineenglish.com. If requested, submit synopsis, first 3 chapters, SASE. "Please check our website for further details." Responds in 4-8 weeks to queries; 3 months to requested submissions. Obtains most new clients through recommendations from others, conferences, submissions.

TERMS Agent receives 15% commission on domestic sales. Agent receives 20% commission on foreign sales. Offers written contract; 30-day notice must be given to terminate contract. Charges only for shipping expenses; generally taken from proceeds.

RECENT SALES Have been to Sourcebooks, Tor, Harlequin.

WRITERS CONFERENCES RWA National Conference; Novelists, Inc.; Malice Domestic; Washington Romance Writers Retreat, among others.

○ THE EPSTEIN LITERARY AGENCY

P.O. Box 484, Kensington MD **E-mail:** kate@epstein literary.com. **Website:** www.epsteinliterary.com. **Contact:** Kate Epstein. Member of AAR. Currently handles: nonfiction books 70%; 30% fiction.

◑ Prior to opening her literary agency, Ms. Epstein was an acquisitions editor at Adams Media. Ms. Epstein has been a literary agent since 2005.

MEMBER AGENTS Kate Epstein.

REPRESENTS Nonfiction books for adults. **Considers these nonfiction areas:** crafts (how-to and reference).

☞ "My background as an editor means that I'm extremely good at selling to them. It also means I'm a careful and thorough line editor. I'm particularly skilled at hardening concepts to make them sellable and proposing the logical follow-up for any book." Actively seeking commercial nonfiction for adults. Does not want scholarly works.

HOW TO CONTACT Query via e-mail (no attachments). Accepts simultaneous submissions. Responds in 3 months to queries. Obtains most new clients through solicitations.

TERMS Agent receives 25% commission on domestic sales. Agent receives 20% commission on foreign sales. Offers written contract; 30-day notice must be given to terminate contract.

RECENT SALES *Silver Like Dust*, by Kimi Cunningham Grant (Pegasus); *Knits For Nerds*, by Toni Carr (Andrews McMeel); *Chasing the Jaguar*, by Peter Allison (Globe Pequot Press/Allen & Unwin).

◑ FELICIA ETH LITERARY REPRESENTATION

555 Bryant St., Suite 350, Palo Alto CA 94301-1700. (650)375-1276. **Fax:** (650)401-8892. **E-mail:** feliciaeth. literary@gmail.com. **Website:** http://ethliterary.com. **Contact:** Felicia Eth. Member of AAR. Represents 25-35 clients. Currently handles: nonfiction books 75%, novels 25% adult.

REPRESENTS Nonfiction books, novels. **Considers these nonfiction areas:** animals, anthropology, autobiography, biography, business, child guidance, cultural interests, current affairs, economics, ethnic, gay/lesbian, government, health, history, investigative, law, medicine, parenting, popular culture, politics, psychology, science, sociology, technology, true crime, women's issues, women's studies. **Considers these fiction areas:** literary, mainstream.

☞ This agency specializes in high-quality fiction (preferably mainstream/contemporary) and provocative, intelligent, and thoughtful nonfiction on a wide array of commercial subjects.

HOW TO CONTACT Query with SASE. Accepts simultaneous submissions. Responds in 3 weeks to queries. Responds in 4-6 weeks to mss.

TERMS Agent receives 15% commission on domestic sales. Agent receives 20% commission on foreign sales. Agent receives 20% commission on film sales. Charges clients for photocopying and express mail service.

RECENT SALES Sold 70-10 titles in the last year. *Bumper Sticker Philosophy*, by Jack Bowen (Random House); *Boys Adrift* by Leonard Sax (Basic Books); *A War Reporter*, by Barbara Quick (HarperCollins); *Pantry*, by Anna Badkhen (Free Press/S&S).

WRITERS CONFERENCES "Wide array—from Squaw Valley to Mills College."

TIPS "For nonfiction, established expertise is certainly a plus—as is magazine publication—though not a prerequisite. I am highly dedicated to those projects I represent, but highly selective in what I choose."

⬥ FAIRBANK LITERARY REPRESENTATION

P.O. Box 6, Hudson NY 12534-0006. (617)576-0030. **Fax:** (617)576-0030. **E-mail:** queries@fairbankliterary.com. **Website:** www.fairbankliterary.com. **Contact:** Sorche Fairbank. Member of AAR. Represents 45 clients. 20% of clients are new/unpublished writers. Currently handles: nonfiction books 60%, novels 22%, story collections 3%, other 15% illustrated.

MEMBER AGENTS Sorche Fairbank (narrative nonfiction, commercial and literary fiction, memoir, food and wine); Matthew Frederick, matt@fairbankliterary.com (scout for sports nonfiction, architecture, design).

REPRESENTS Nonfiction books, novels, short story collections. **Considers these nonfiction areas:** agriculture, architecture, art, autobiography, biography, cooking, crafts, cultural interests, current affairs, decorating, diet/nutrition, design, environment, ethnic, foods, gay/lesbian, government, hobbies, horticulture, how-to, interior design, investigative, law, memoirs, photography, popular culture, politics, science, sociology, sports, technology, true crime, women's issues, women's studies. **Considers these fiction areas:** action, adventure, feminist, gay, lesbian, literary, mainstream, mystery, sports, suspense, thriller, women's, Southern voices.

⚞ "I have a small agency in Harvard Square, where I tend to gravitate toward literary fiction and narrative nonfiction, with a strong interest in women's issues and women's voices, international voices, class and race issues, and projects that simply teach me something new about the greater world and society around us. We have a good reputation for working closely and developmentally with our authors and love what we do." Actively seeking literary fiction, international and culturally diverse voices, narrative nonfiction, topical subjects (politics, current affairs), history, sports, architecture/design and pop culture. Does not want to receive romance, poetry, science fiction, pirates, vampire, young adult, or children's works.

HOW TO CONTACT Query with SASE. Submit author bio. Accepts simultaneous submissions. Responds in 6 weeks to queries. Responds in 10 weeks to mss. Obtains most new clients through recommendations from others, solicitations, conferences, ideas generated in-house.

TERMS Agent receives 15% commission on domestic sales. Agent receives 20% commission on foreign sales. Offers written contract, binding for 12 months; 45-day notice must be given to terminate contract.

WRITERS CONFERENCES San Francisco Writers' Conference, Muse and the Marketplace/Grub Street Conference, Washington Independent Writers' Conference, Murder in the Grove, Surrey International Writers' Conference.

TIPS "Be professional from the very first contact. There shouldn't be a single typo or grammatical flub in your query. Have a reason for contacting me about your project other than I was the next name listed on some website. Please do not use form query software! Believe me, we can get a dozen or so a day that look identical—we know when you are using a form. Show me that you know your audience—and your competition. Have the writing and/or proposal at the very, very best it can be before starting the querying process. Don't assume that if someone likes it enough they'll 'fix' it. The biggest mistake new writers make is starting the querying process before they—and the work—are ready. Take your time and do it right."

⬥ THE FIELDING AGENCY, LLC

269 S. Beverly Dr., No. 341, Beverly Hills CA 90212. (323)461-4791. **E-mail:** wlee@fieldingagency.com; query@fieldingagency.com. **Website:** www.fieldingagency.com. **Contact:** Whitney Lee. Currently handles: nonfiction books 25%, novels 35%, juvenile books 35%, other 5% other.

◔ Prior to her current position, Ms. Lee worked at other agencies in different capacities.

REPRESENTS Nonfiction books, novels, short story collections, juvenile. **Considers these nonfiction areas:** animals, anthropology, archeology, architecture, art, autobiography, biography, business, child guidance, cooking, crafts, cultural interests, current affairs, decorating, diet/nutrition, design, economics, education, environment, ethnic, foods, gay/lesbian, government, health, history, hobbies, how-to, humor, investigative, juvenile nonfiction, language, law, literature, medicine, memoirs, military, money, parenting, popular culture, politics, psychology, satire, science, self-help, sociology, sports, technology, translation, true crime, war, women's issues, women's studies. **Considers these fiction areas:** action, adventure, cartoon, comic books, crime, detective, ethnic, family saga, fantasy, feminist, gay, glitz, historical, horror, humor, juvenile, lesbian, literary, mainstream, mystery, picture books, police, romance, satire, suspense, thriller, women's, young adult.

☛ "We specialize in representing books published abroad and have strong relationships with foreign co-agents and publishers. For books we represent in the U.S., we have to be head-over-heels passionate about it because we are involved every step of the way." Does not want to receive scripts for TV or film.

HOW TO CONTACT Query with SASE. Submit synopsis, author bio. Accepts queries by e-mail and snail mail. Accepts simultaneous submissions. Obtains most new clients through recommendations from others.

TERMS Agent receives 15% commission on domestic sales. Agent receives 20% commission on foreign sales. Offers written contract, binding for 9-12 months.

WRITERS CONFERENCES London Book Fair; Frankfurt Book Fair; Bologna Book Fair.

◑ DIANA FINCH LITERARY AGENCY

116 W. 23rd St., Suite 500, New York NY 10011. **E-mail:** diana.finch@verizon.net. **Website:** http://dianafinchliteraryagency.blogspot.com. **Contact:** Diana Finch. Member of AAR. Represents 40 clients. 20% of clients are new/unpublished writers. Currently handles: nonfiction books 85%, novels 15%, juvenile books 5%, multimedia 5%.

○ Seeking to represent books that change lives. Prior to opening her agency in 2003, Ms. Finch worked at Ellen Levine Literary Agency for 18 years.

REPRESENTS Nonfiction books, novels, scholarly. **Considers these nonfiction areas:** autobiography, biography, business, child guidance, computers, cultural interests, current affairs, dance, economics, environment, ethnic, film, government, health, history, how-to, humor, investigative, juvenile nonfiction, law, medicine, memoirs, military, money, music, parenting, photography, popular culture, politics, psychology, satire, science, self-help, sports, technology, theater, translation, true crime, war, women's issues, women's studies, computers, electronic. **Considers these fiction areas:** action, adventure, crime, detective, ethnic, historical, literary, mainstream, police, thriller, young adult.

☛ Actively seeking narrative nonfiction, popular science, memoir and health topics. "Does not

want romance, mysteries, or children's picture books."

HOW TO CONTACT Query with SASE or via e-mail (no attachments). Accepts simultaneous submissions. Obtains most new clients through recommendations from others.

TERMS Agent receives 15% commission on domestic sales. Agent receives 20% commission on foreign sales. Offers written contract. "I charge for photocopying, overseas postage, galleys, and books purchased, and try to recoup these costs from earnings received for a client, rather than charging outright."

RECENT SALES *Heidegger's Glasses*, by Thaisa Frank; *Genetic Rounds*, by Robert Marion, MD (Kaplan); *Honeymoon in Tehran*, by Azadeh Moaveni (Random House); *Darwin Slept Here* by Eric Simons (Overlook); *Black Tide,* by Antonia Juhasz (HarperCollins); *Stalin's Children,* by Owen Matthews (Bloomsbury); *Radiant Days,* by Michael Fitzgerald (Shoemaker & Hoard); *The Queen's Soprano,* by Carol Dines (Harcourt Young Adult); *What to Say to a Porcupine,* by Richard Gallagher (Amacom); *The Language of Trust,* by Michael Maslansky et al.

TIPS "Do as much research as you can on agents before you query. Have someone critique your query letter before you send it. It should be only 1 page and describe your book clearly—and why you are writing it—but also demonstrate creativity and a sense of your writing style."

◑ FINEPRINT LITERARY MANAGEMENT

115 W. 29th, 3rd Floor, New York NY 10001. (212)279-1282. **E-mail:** stephany@fineprintlit.com. **Website:** www.fineprintlit.com. Member of AAR.

MEMBER AGENTS Peter Rubie, CEO (nonfiction interests include narrative nonfiction, popular science, spirituality, history, biography, pop culture, business, technology, parenting, health, self help, music, and food; fiction interests include literate thrillers, crime fiction, science fiction and fantasy, military fiction and literary fiction, middle grade and YA fiction and nonfiction for boys); **Stephany Evans**, Nonfiction: health and wellness, especially women's health; spirituality, environment/sustainability, food and wine, memoir, and narrative nonfiction; Fiction: stories with a strong and interesting female protagonist, both literary and upmarket commercial/book club fiction, romance—all sub genres; mysteries; **Janet Reid**, Nonfiction: narrative nonfiction, history and biography; Fiction: thrillers. **Brooks Sherman**, Nonfiction: narrative nonfiction, history, pop culture, and food; Fiction: literary, upmarket, crime, science fiction grounded in realistic settings, high/contemporary/dark fantasy, magical realism, middle grade, young adult, and picture books; **Becky Vinter**, Nonfiction: travel, food, health, wellness, business/management, environment, current events, memoir; Fiction: women's fiction, romance, mysteries, literary, book club, young adult; **Laura Wood**, Nonfiction: nonfiction books, business, dance, economics, history, humor, law,science, narrative nonfiction, popular science; Fiction: fantasy, science fiction, suspense.

HOW TO CONTACT Query with SASE. Submit synopsis and first 3-5 pages of ms embedded in an e-mail proposal for nonfiction. Do not send attachments or manuscripts without a request. See contact page onilne at website for e-mails. Obtains most new clients through recommendations from others, solicitations.

TERMS Agent receives 15% commission on domestic sales. Agent receives 20% commission on foreign sales.

JAMES FITZGERALD AGENCY

118 Waverly Place #1B, New York NY 10011. (212)308-1122. **E-mail:** submissions@jfitzagency.com. **Website:** www.jfitzagency.com. **Contact:** James Fitzgerald.

○ Prior to his current position, Mr. Fitzgerald was an editor at St. Martin's Press, Doubleday, and the New York Times.

MEMBER AGENTS James Fitzgerald.

REPRESENTS Books that reflect the popular culture of today being in the forms of fiction, nonfiction, graphic and packaged books.

☛ Does not want to receive poetry or screenplays.

HOW TO CONTACT Query with SASE. Submit proposal package, outline/proposal, publishing history, author bio, overview.

RECENT SALES *Gimme Something Better: The Profound, Progressive, and Occasionally Pointless History of Punk in the Bay Area*, by Jack Boulware and Silke Tudor (Viking/Penguin); *Black Dogs: The Possibly Story of Classic Rock's Greatest Robbery*, by Jason Buhrmester (Three Rivers/Crown); *Theo Gray's Med Science: Experiments You Can Do at Home — But Probably Shouldn't* (Black Dog and Loenthal).

TIPS "Please submit all information in English, even if your manuscript is in Spanish."

FLAMING STAR LITERARY ENTERPRISES

11 Raup Rd., Chatham NY 12037. **E-mail:** flamingstarlit@aol.com; janvall@aol.com. **Website:** www.flamingstarlit.com for Joseph Vallely; www.janisvallely.com for Janis Vallely. **Contact:** Joseph B. Vallely, Janis C. Vallely. Represents 100 clients. 25% of clients are new/unpublished writers. Currently handles: nonfiction books 100%.

○ Prior to opening the agency, Mr. Vallely served as national sales manager for Dell; Ms. Vallely was V.P. and Associate Publisher of Doubleday.

REPRESENTS Nonfiction books. **Considers these nonfiction areas:** current affairs, diet/nutrition, government, health, law, memoirs, politics, psychology, self-help, Health, science, memoir and psychology are represented through our separate offices at www.janisvallely.com.

☛ This agency specializes in upscale commercial nonfiction. No poetry, screenplays, fiction, YA, children's lit

HOW TO CONTACT E-mail only (no attachments). Responds in one week to queries. Obtains most new clients through recommendations from others, solicitations.

TERMS Agent receives 15% commission on domestic sales. Agent receives 20% commission on foreign sales. Offers written contract.

RECENT SALES *Diabetes Without Drugs*, by Suzy Cohen (Rodale).

TIPS "See website."

FLANNERY LITERARY

1140 Wickfield Ct., Naperville IL 60563. (630)428-2682. **Fax:** (630)428-2683. **E-mail:** FlanLit@aol.com. **Contact:** Jennifer Flannery. Represents 40 clients. 50% of clients are new/unpublished writers. Currently handles: juvenile books 100%.

☛ This agency specializes in children's and young adult fiction and nonfiction. It also accepts picture books. 100% juvenile books.

HOW TO CONTACT Query by mail with SASE or e-mail query. Responds in 2 weeks to queries; 1 month to mss. Obtains new clients through referrals and queries.

TERMS Agent receives 15% commission on domestic sales. Agent receives 20% commission on foreign sales. Offers written contract, binding for life of book in print; 1-month notice must be given to terminate contract.

TIPS "Write an engrossing, succinct query describing your work. We are always looking for a fresh new voice."

FLETCHER & COMPANY

78 Fifth Ave., 3rd Floor, New York NY 10011. (212)614-0778. **Fax:** (212)614-0728. **E-mail:** info@fletcherand co.com. **Website:** www.fletcherandco.com. **Contact:** Christy Fletcher. Member of AAR.

MEMBER AGENTS See http://fletcherandco.com/staff for current agent list.

REPRESENTS Nonfiction books, novels. **Considers these nonfiction areas:** biography, business, current affairs, health, history, memoirs, science, sports, travel, African American, narrative, lifestyle. **Considers these fiction areas:** literary, young adult, commercial. ☛ Does not want genre fiction.

HOW TO CONTACT Query with SASE or e-mail according to guidelines on website; no attachments. Responds in 6 weeks to queries.

● THE FOLEY LITERARY AGENCY

34 E. 38th St., New York NY 10016-2508. (212)686-6930. **Contact:** Joan Foley, Joseph Foley. Estab. 1956. Represents 10 clients. Currently handles: nonfiction books 75%, novels 25%.

REPRESENTS Nonfiction books, novels. **Considers these nonfiction areas:** business services.

HOW TO CONTACT Query with letter, brief outline, SASE. Responds promptly to queries. Obtains most new clients through recommendations from others (rarely taking on new clients).

TERMS Agent receives 10% commission on domestic sales. Agent receives 15% commission on foreign sales.

◑ FOLIO LITERARY MANAGEMENT, LLC

The Film Center Building, 630 Ninth Ave., Suite 1101, New York NY 10036. (212)400-1494. **Fax:** (212)967-0977. **Website:** www.foliolit.com. Member of AAR. Represents 100+ clients.

💬 Prior to creating Folio Literary Management, Mr. Hoffman worked for several years at another agency; Mr. Kleinman was an agent at Graybill & English; Ms. Wheeler was an agent at Creative Media Agency.

MEMBER AGENTS Scott Hoffman; Jeff Kleinman; Paige Wheeler; Jonathan Lyons; Michelle Brower; Claudia Cross; Jita Fumich; Michael Harriot; Molly Jaffa; Shawna Morey; Erin Niumata; Marcy Posner; Steve Troha; Emily van Beek, Erin Harris, Melissa Sarver.

REPRESENTS nonfiction books, novels, short story collections. **Considers these nonfiction areas:** animals, art, biography, business, child guidance, economics, environment, health, history, how-to, humor, inspirational, memoirs, military, parenting, popular culture, politics, psychology, religious, satire, science, self-help, technology, war, women's issues, women's studies, animals (equestrian), narrative nonfiction, espionage; fitness, lifestyle, relationship, culture, cookbooks. **Considers these fiction areas:** erotica, fantasy, literary, mystery, religious, romance, science, thriller, psychological, young, womens, Southern; legal; edgy crime, young adult, middle grade, women's nonfiction, popular sociology.

☛ No poetry, stage plays, or screenplays.

HOW TO CONTACT Query via e-mail only (no attachments). Read agent bios online for specific submission guidelines and email addresses. Responds in 1 month to queries.

TIPS "Please do not submit simultaneously to more than one agent at Folio. If you're not sure which of us is exactly right for your book, don't worry. We work closely as a team, and if one of our agents gets a query that might be more appropriate for someone else, we'll always pass it along. It's important that you check each agent's bio page for clear directions as to how to submit, as well as when to expect feedback."

✚ FOREWORD LITERARY

Silicon Valley, CA. **Website:** www.forewordliterary.com.

MEMBER AGENTS Laurie McLean (adult genre fiction (romance, fantasy, science fiction, mystery, thrillers, suspense, horror, etc.) plus middle-grade and young adult children's books; querylaurie@forewordliterary.com. Gordon Warnock (nonfiction and fiction, querygordon@forewordliterary.com). Pam van Hylckama Vlieg (young adult, middle grade, new adult, romance, urban fantasy, paranormal, and epic/high fantasy; querypam@forewordliterary.com). Jen Karsbaek (women's fiction, upmarket commercial fiction, historical fiction, and literary fiction, mystery, fantasy, and occasionally romance approaches to any of the genres listed; queryjen@forewordliterary.com). Danielle Smith (middle grade, picture books, chapter books; querydanielle@forewordliterary.com). x.

HOW TO CONTACT Query only one agent at this agency. Send a query letter only to start.

◐ FOUNDRY LITERARY + MEDIA

33 West 17th St., PH, New York NY 10011. (212)929-5064. **Fax:** (212)929-5471. **Website:** www.foundry media.com.

MEMBER AGENTS Peter H. McGuigan (smart, off-beat nonfiction, particularly works of narrative nonfiction on pop culture, niche history, biography, music and science; fiction interests include commercial and literary, across all genres, especially first-time writers); Yfat Reiss Gendell (favors nonfiction books focusing on all manners of prescriptive: how-to, science, health and well-being, memoirs, adventure, travel stories and lighter titles appropriate for the gift trade genre. Yfat also looks for commercial fiction highlighting the full range of women's experiences—young and old—and also seeks science fiction, thrillers and historical fiction); Stéphanie Abou (in fiction and nonfiction alike, Stéphanie is always on the lookout for authors who are accomplished storytellers with their own distinctive voice, who develop memorable characters, and who are able to create psychological conflict with their narrative. She is an across-the-board fiction lover, attracted to both literary and smart upmarket commercial fiction. In nonfiction she leans towards projects that tackle big topics with an unusual approach. Pop culture, health, science, parenting, women's and multicultural issues are of special interest); Chris Park (memoirs, narrative nonfiction, Christian nonfiction and character-driven fiction); David Patterson (outstanding narratives and/or idea-driven works of nonfiction); Hannah Brown Gordon (fiction, YA, memoir, narrative nonfiction, history, current events, science, psychology and pop culture); Mollie Glick (literary fiction, narrative nonfiction, YA, and a bit of practical nonfiction); Stephen Barbara (all categories of books for young readers in addition to servicing writers for the adult market); Brandi Bowles (idea and platform-driven nonfiction in all categories, including music and pop culture, humor, business, sociology, philosophy, health, and relationships. Quirky, funny, or contrarian proposals are always welcome in her in-box, as are big-idea books that change the way we think about the world. Brandi also represents fiction in the categories of literary fiction, women's fiction, urban fantasy, and YA); Rachel Hecht (upmarket, commercial, mainstream,

children's books); Anthony Mattero (smart, platform-driven, nonfiction particularly in the genres of pop-culture, humor, music, sports, and pop-business).

REPRESENTS Considers these nonfiction areas: biography, child, health, memoirs, multicultural, music, popular culture, science. **Considers these fiction areas:** literary, religious.

HOW TO CONTACT Query with SASE. Should be addressed to one agent only. Submit synopsis, 3 sample chapters, author bio, For nonfiction, submit query, proposal, sample chapter, TOC, bio. Put submissions on your snail mail submission.

TIPS "Consult website for each agent's submission instructions."

● ◉ FOX CHASE AGENCY, INC.

701 Lee Road, Suite 102, Chesterbrook Corporate Center, Chesterbrook PA 19087. Member of AAR.
MEMBER AGENTS A.L. Hart; Jo C. Hart.
REPRESENTS Nonfiction books, novels.
HOW TO CONTACT No unsolicited mss. Query with SASE.

FOX LITERARY

110 W. 40th St., Suite 410, New York NY 10018. **E-mail:** submissions@foxliterary.com. **Website:** www.foxliterary.com.

REPRESENTS Considers these nonfiction areas: memoirs, biography, pop culture, narrative nonfiction, history, science, spirituality, self-help, celebrity, dating/relationships, women's issues, psychology, film and entertainment, cultural/social issues, journalism. **Considers these fiction areas:** erotica, fantasy, literary, romance, science, young adult, science fiction, thrillers, historical fiction, literary fiction, graphic novels, commercial fiction, women's fiction, gay and lesbian, erotica, historical romance.

⚷ Does not want to receive screenplays, poetry, category westerns, horror, Christian/inspirational, or children's picture books.

HOW TO CONTACT E-mail query and first 5 pages in body of e-mail. E-mail queries preferred. For snail mail queries, must include an e-mail address for response and no response means NO. Do not send SASE.

LYNN C. FRANKLIN ASSOCIATES, LTD.

1350 Broadway, Suite 2015, New York NY 10018. (212)868-6311. **Fax:** (212)868-6312. **E-mail:** agency@fsainc.com. **E-mail:** agency@franklinandsiegal.com. **Contact:** Lynn Franklin, president; Claudia Nys, foreign rights. Other memberships include PEN America. Represents 30-35 clients. 50% of clients are new/unpublished writers. Currently handles: nonfiction books 90%, novels 10%.

REPRESENTS Nonfiction books, novels. **Considers these nonfiction areas:** New Age, biography, current affairs, health, history, memoirs, psychology, religion, self help, spirituality. **Considers these fiction areas:** literary, mainstream, commercial; juvenile, middle-grade, and young adult.

☞ "This agency specializes in general nonfiction with a special interest in self-help, biography/memoir, alternative health, and spirituality."

HOW TO CONTACT Query via e-mail to agency@franklinandsiegal.com. No unsolicited mss. No attachments. For nonfiction, query letter with short outline and synopsis. For fiction, query letter with short synopsis and a maximum of 10 sample pages (in the body of the e-mail). Please indicate "query adult" or "query children's" in the subject line. Accepts simultaneous submissions. Responds in 2 weeks to queries. Responds in 6 weeks to mss. Obtains most new clients through recommendations from others, solicitations.

TERMS Agent receives 15% commission on domestic sales. Agent receives 20% commission on foreign sales. Offers written contract.

RECENT SALES Adult: *Made for Goodness*, by Archbishop Desmond Tutu and Reverend Mpho Tutu (HarperOne); *Children of God Storybook Bible*, by Archbishop Desmond Tutu (Zondervan for originating publisher Lux Verbi); *Playing Our Game: Why China's Economic Rise Doesn't Threaten the West*, by Edward Steinfeld (Oxford University Press); *The 100 Year Diet*, by Susan Yager (Rodale); Children's/YA: *I Like Mandarin*, by Kirsten Hubbard (Delacorte/Random House); *A Scary Scene in a Scary Movie*, by Matt Blackstone (Farrar, Straus & Giroux).

◑ JEANNE FREDERICKS LITERARY AGENCY, INC.

221 Benedict Hill Rd., New Canaan CT 06840. (203)972-3011. **Fax:** (203)972-3011. **E-mail:** jeanne.fredericks@gmail.com. **Website:** www.jeannefredericks.com. **Contact:** Jeanne Fredericks. Member of AAR. Other memberships include Authors Guild. Represents 90 clients. 10% of clients are new/unpublished writers. Currently handles: nonfiction books 100%.

● Prior to opening her agency in 1997, Ms. Fredericks was an agent and acting director with the Susan P. Urstadt, Inc. Agency.

REPRESENTS Nonfiction books. **Considers these nonfiction areas:** animals, autobiography, biography, child guidance, cooking, decorating, foods, gardening, health, history, how-to, interior design, medicine, parenting, photography, psychology, self-help, women's issues.

☞ This agency specializes in quality adult nonfiction by authorities in their fields. Does not want to receive children's books or fiction.

HOW TO CONTACT Query first with SASE, then send outline/proposal, 1-2 sample chapters, SASE, or by e-mail, if requested. See submission guidelines online first. Accepts simultaneous submissions. Responds in 3-5 weeks to queries. Responds in 2-4 months to mss. Obtains most new clients through recommendations from others, solicitations, conferences.

TERMS Agent receives 15% commission on domestic sales. Agent receives 25% commission on foreign sales with co-agent. Offers written contract, binding for 9 months; 2-month notice must be given to terminate contract. Charges client for photocopying of whole proposals and mss, overseas postage, priority mail, express mail services.

RECENT SALES *The Creativity Cure*, by Carrie Alton, M.D., and Alton Barron, M.D. (Scribner); *Lilias! Yoga*, by Lilias Folan (Skyhorse); *The Epidural Book,* by Rich Siegenfeld, M.D. (Johns Hopkins University Press); *A Place in the Sun*, by Stephen Snyder (Rizzoli); *Margaret Mitchell's Gone with the Wind*, by Ellen F. Brown and John Wiley, Jr. (Taylor); *World Class Marriage*, by Patty Howell and Ralph Jones (Rowman and Littlefield); *Teenage as a Second Language*, by Barbara Greenberg, Ph.D. and Jennifer Powell-Lunder, Psy.D.; *The Small Budget Gardener*, by Maureen Gilmer (Cool Springs Press); *Palm Beach Gardens and Terraces,* by Kathleen Quigley (Rizzoli); *Step Ahead of Autism*, by Anne Burnett (Sunrise River); *Electrified*, by Bob Shaw (Sterling); *The Green Market Baking Book* by Laura Martin (Sterling); Tales of the Seven Seas, by Dennis Powers (Taylor); *The Generosity Plan* by Kathy LeMay (Beyond Words/Atria); *Canadian Vegetable Gardening* by Doug Green (Cool Springs).

WRITERS CONFERENCES Connecticut Authors and Publishers Association-University Conference; ASJA Writers' Conference; BookExpo America; Garden Writers' Association Annual Symposium; Harvard Medical School CME Course in Publishing.

TIPS "Be sure to research competition for your work and be able to justify why there's a need for your book. I enjoy building an author's career, particularly if he/she is professional, hardworking, and courteous. Aside from 20 years of agenting experience, I've had 10 years of editorial experience in adult trade book publishing that enables me to help an author polish a proposal so that it's more appealing to prospective editors. My MBA in marketing also distinguishes me from other agents."

GRACE FREEDSON'S PUBLISHING NETWORK

375 N. Broadway, Suite 102, Jericho NY 11753. (516)931-7757. **Fax:** (516)931-7759. **E-mail:** gfreed son@worldnet.att.net. **Contact:** Grace Freedson. 17 Center Dr., Syosset NY 11791. Represents 100 clients. 10% of clients are new/unpublished writers. Currently handles: nonfiction books 90%, juvenile books 10%.

○ Prior to becoming an agent, Ms. Freedson was a managing editor and director of acquisition for Barron's Educational Series.

REPRESENTS Nonfiction books, juvenile. **Considers these nonfiction areas:** animals, business, cooking, crafts, current affairs, diet/nutrition, economics, education, environment, foods, health, history, hobbies, how-to, humor, medicine, money, popular culture, psychology, satire, science, self-help, sports, technology.

☞ "In addition to representing many qualified authors, I work with publishers as a packager of unique projects—mostly series." Does not want to receive fiction.

HOW TO CONTACT Query with SASE. Submit synopsis, SASE. Responds in 2-6 weeks to queries. Obtains most new clients through recommendations from others.

TERMS Agent receives 15% commission on domestic sales. Offers written contract; 30-day notice must be given to terminate contract.

RECENT SALES Sold 50 titles in the last year. *The Dangers Lurking Beyond the Glass Ceiling*, by D. sherr bourierg Carter (Prometheus); *Threats, Lies and Intimidation: Inside Debt Collection*, by Fred Williams (FT Press); *Plastic Planet*, by Kathryn Jones (FT Press).

WRITERS CONFERENCES BookExpo of America.

TIPS "At this point, I am only reviewing proposals on nonfiction topics by credentialed authors with platforms."

FRESH BOOKS LITERARY AGENCY

231 Diana St., Placerville CA 95667. **E-mail:** matt@fresh-books.com. **Website:** www.fresh-books.com. **Contact:** Matt Wagner. Represents 30+ clients. 5% of clients are new/unpublished writers. Currently handles: nonfiction books 95%, multimedia 5%.

○ Prior to becoming an agent, Mr. Wagner was with Waterside Productions for 15 years.

REPRESENTS Nonfiction books. **Considers these nonfiction areas:** animals, anthropology, archeology, architecture, art, business, child guidance, computers, cooking, crafts, cultural interests, current affairs, dance, design, economics, education, environment, ethnic, gay/lesbian, government, health, history, hobbies, humor, law, medicine, military, money, music, parenting, photography, popular culture, politics, psychology, satire, science, sports, technology.

☞ "I specialize in tech and how-to. I love working with books and authors, and I've repped many of my clients for upwards of 15 years now." Actively seeking popular science, natural history, adventure, how-to, business, education and reference. Does not want to receive fiction, children's books, screenplays, or poetry.

HOW TO CONTACT Electronic submissions only. Consult website for guidelines. No phone calls or snail mail submissions. Accepts simultaneous submissions. Responds in 1-4 weeks to queries. Responds in 1-4 weeks to mss. Obtains most new clients through recommendations from others.

TERMS Agent receives 15% commission on domestic sales. Agent receives 20% commission on foreign sales.

RECENT SALES *The Myth of Multitasking: How Doing It All Gets Nothing Done* (Jossey-Bass); *Wilderness Survival for Dummies* (Wiley); and *The Zombie Combat Manual* (Berkley).

TIPS "Do your research. Find out what sorts of books and authors an agent represents. Go to conferences. Make friends with other writers—most of my clients come from referrals."

SARAH JANE FREYMANN LITERARY AGENCY

59 W. 71st St., Suite 9B, New York NY 10023. (212)362-9277. **E-mail:** sarah@sarahjanefreymann.com; Submissions@SarahJaneFreymann.com. **Website:** www.

sarahjanefreymann.com. **Contact:** Sarah Jane Freymann, Steve Schwartz. Represents 100 clients. 20% of clients are new/unpublished writers. Currently handles: nonfiction books 75%, novels 23%, juvenile books 2%.

MEMBER AGENTS Sarah Jane Freymann; (nonfiction books, novels, illustrated books); Jessica Sinsheimer, Jessica@sarahjanefreymann.com (young adult fiction); Steven Schwartz, steve@sarahjane freymann.com; Katharine Sands (general fiction and nonfiction).

REPRESENTS Considers these nonfiction areas: animals, anthropology, architecture, art, autobiography, biography, business, child guidance, cooking, current affairs, decorating, diet/nutrition, design, economics, ethnic, foods, health, history, interior design, medicine, memoirs, parenting, psychology, self-help, women's issues, women's studies, lifestyle. **Considers these fiction areas:** ethnic, literary, mainstream.

HOW TO CONTACT Query with SASE. Responds in 2 weeks to queries. Responds in 6 weeks to mss. Obtains most new clients through recommendations from others.

TERMS Agent receives 15% commission on domestic sales. Agent receives 20% commission on foreign sales. Offers written contract. Charges clients for long distance, overseas postage, photocopying. 100% of business is derived from commissions on ms sales.

RECENT SALES *How to Make Love to a Plastic Cup: And Other Things I Learned While Trying to Knock Up My Wife*, by Greg Wolfe (Harper Collins); *I Want to Be Left Behind: Rapture Here on Earth*, by Brenda Peterson (a Merloyd Lawrence Book); *That Bird Has My Name: The Autobiography of an Innocent Man on Death Row*, by Jarvis Jay Masters with an Introduction by Pema Chodrun (HarperOne); *Perfect One-Dish Meals*, by Pam Anderson (Houghton Mifflin); *Birdology*, by Sy Montgomery (Simon & Schuster); *Emptying the Nest: Launching Your Reluctant Young Adult*, by Dr. Brad Sachs (Macmillan); *Tossed & Found*, by Linda and John Meyers (Steward, Tabori & Chang); *32 Candles*, by Ernessa Carter; *God and Dog*, by Wendy Francisco.

TIPS "I love fresh, new, passionate works by authors who love what they are doing and have both natural talent and carefully honed skill."

◐ FREDRICA S. FRIEDMAN AND CO., INC.

136 E. 57th St., 14th Floor, New York NY 10022. (212)829-9600. **Fax:** (212)829-9669. **E-mail:** info@ fredricafriedman.com; submissions@fredricafried man.com. **Website:** www.fredricafriedman.com. **Contact:** Ms. Chandler Smith. Represents 75+ clients. 50% of clients are new/unpublished writers. Currently handles: nonfiction books 95%, novels 5%.

REPRESENTS Nonfiction books, novels, anthologies. **Considers these nonfiction areas:** art, biography, business, child, cooking, current affairs, education, ethnic, gay, government, health, history, how to, humor, language, memoirs, money, music, photography, popular culture, psychology, self help, sociology, film, true crime, women's, interior design/decorating. **Considers these fiction areas:** literary.

⌐☞ "We represent a select group of outstanding nonfiction and fiction writers. We are particularly interested in helping writers expand their readership and develop their careers." Does not want poetry, plays, screenplays, children's books, sci-fi/fantasy, or horror.

HOW TO CONTACT Submit e-query, synopsis; be concise, and include any pertinent author information, including relevant writing history. If you are a fiction writer, we also request a one-page sample from your manuscript to provide its voice. We ask that you keep all material in the body of the e-mail. Accepts simultaneous submissions. Responds in 4-6 weeks to queries. Responds in 4-6 weeks to mss. Obtains most new clients through recommendations from others.

TERMS Agent receives 15% commission on domestic sales. Agent receives 25% commission on foreign sales. Offers written contract. Charges for photocopying and messenger/shipping fees for proposals.

RECENT SALES *A World of Lies: The Crime and Consequences of Bernie Madoff*, by Diana B. Henriques (Times Books/Holt); *Polemic and Memoir: The Nixon Years* by Patrick J. Buchanan (St. Martin's Press); *Angry Fat Girls: Five Women, Five Hundred Pounds, and a Year of Losing It . . . Again*, by Frances Kuffel (Berkley/Penguin); *Life with My Sister Madonna*, by Christopher Ciccone with Wendy Leigh (Simon & Schuster Spotlight); *The World Is Curved: Hidden Dangers to the Global Economy*, by David Smick (Portfolio/Penguin); *Going to See the Elephant*, by Rodes Fishburne (Delacorte/Random House); *Seducing the Boys Club: Uncensored Tactics from a Woman at the Top*, by Nina DiSesa (Ballantine/Random House); *The Girl from*

Foreign: A Search for Shipwrecked Ancestors, Forgotten Histories, and a Sense of Home, by Sadia Shepard (Penguin Press).

TIPS "Spell the agent's name correctly on your query letter."

THE FRIEDRICH AGENCY

19 W. 21st St., Suite 201, New York NY 10010. **E-mail:** mfriedrich@friedrichagency.com; lcarson@friedrichagency.com; mschulman@friedrichagency.com; nichole@friedrichagency.com. **Website:** www.friedrichagency.com. **Contact:** Molly Friedrich; Lucy Carson. Member of AAR. Signatory of WGA. Represents 50+ clients.

Prior to her current position, Ms. Friedrich was an agent at the Aaron Priest Literary Agency.

MEMBER AGENTS Molly Friedrich, founder and agent (open to queries); Lucy Carson, foreign rights director and agent (open to queries); Molly Schulman, assistant; Nichole LeFebvre, foreign rights assistant.

REPRESENTS Full-length fiction and nonfiction.

HOW TO CONTACT Query by e-mail (strongly preferred), or by mail with SASE. See guidelines on website.

RECENT SALES *V is for Vengeance*, by Sue Grafton; *Don't Go*, by Lisa Scottoline; *Olive Kitteridge,* by Elizabeth Strout. Other clients include Frank McCourt, Jane Smiley, Esmeralda Santiago, Terry McMillan, Cathy Schine, and more.

FULL CIRCLE LITERARY, LLC

7676 Hazard Center Dr., Suite 500, San Diego CA 92108. **E-mail:** submissions@fullcircleliterary.com. **Website:** www.fullcircleliterary.com. **Contact:** Stefanie Von Borstel. Represents 55 clients. 60% of clients are new/unpublished writers. Currently handles: nonfiction books 70%, novels 10%, juvenile books 20%.

Before forming Full Circle, Ms. Von Borstel worked in both marketing and editorial capacities at Penguin and Harcourt; Ms. Ghahremani received her law degree from UCLA, and has experience in representing authors on legal affairs.

MEMBER AGENTS Lilly Ghahremani (Lilly is only taking referrals: young adult, pop culture, crafts, "green" living, narrative nonfiction, business, relationships, Middle Eastern interest, multicultural); Stefanie Von Borstel (Latino interest, crafts, parenting, wedding/relationships, how-to, self help, middle grade/teen fiction/YA, green living, multicultural/

bilingual picture books); Adriana Dominguez (fiction areas of interest: children's books—picture books, middle grade novels, and {literary} young adult novels; on the adult side, she is looking for literary, women's, and historical fiction. Nonfiction areas of interest: multicultural, pop culture, how-to, and titles geared toward women of all ages); Sara Sciuto (middle grade, young adult, picture books).

REPRESENTS Nonfiction books, juvenile. **Considers these nonfiction areas:** animals, autobiography, biography, business, child guidance, crafts, cultural interests, current affairs, dance, diet/nutrition, ethnic, foods, health, hobbies, how-to, humor, juvenile nonfiction, medicine, parenting, popular culture, satire, self-help, women's issues, women's studies. **Considers these fiction areas:** ethnic, literary, young adult.

"Our full-service boutique agency, representing a range of nonfiction and children's books (limited fiction), provides a one-stop resource for authors. Our extensive experience in the realms of law and marketing provide Full Circle clients with a unique edge. Actively seeking nonfiction by authors with a unique and strong platform, projects that offer new and diverse viewpoints, and literature with a global or multicultural perspective. We are particularly interested in books with a Latino or Middle Eastern angle and books related to pop culture." Does not want to receive screenplays, poetry, commercial fiction or genre fiction (horror, thriller, mystery, Western, sci-fi, fantasy, romance, historical fiction).

HOW TO CONTACT Agency accepts e-queries. See website for fiction guidelines, as they are in flux. For nonfiction, send full proposal. Accepts simultaneous submissions. Responds in 1-2 weeks to queries. Responds in 4-6 weeks to mss. Obtains most new clients through recommendations from others, solicitations, conferences.

TERMS Agent receives 15% commission on domestic sales. Agent receives 20% commission on foreign sales. Offers written contract; up to 30-day notice must be given to terminate contract. Charges for copying and postage.

TIPS "Put your best foot forward. Contact us when you simply can't make your project any better on your own, and please be sure your work fits with what the agent you're approaching represents. Little things count, so copyedit your work. Join a writing group and attend conferences to get objective and constructive feedback before submitting. Be active about building your platform as an author before, during, and after publication. Remember this is a business and your agent is a business partner."

◑ THE G AGENCY, LLC

P.O. Box 374, Bronx NY 10471. (718)664-4505. **E-mail:** gagencyquery@gmail.com. **Contact:** Jeff Gerecke. Estab. 2012.

MEMBER AGENTS Jeff Gerecke.

✎➝ General fiction, mystery, biography, computers/technology, business/investing/finance, history, sports, military history, pop culture.

RECENT SALES *Killing The Cranes,* by Edward Girardet (Chelsea Green); *Islam Without Extremes,* by Mustafa Akyol (Norton); *The Race to the New World,* by Douglas Hunter (Palgrave); *Intelligence and US Foreign Policy,* by Paul Pillar (Columbia UP); *Transforming Darkness to Light,* by Travis Vining (Bella Rosa); *Faith Misplaced: The Broken Promise of US-Arab Relations,* by Ussama Makdisi (Public Affairs); *Drinking Arak Off An Ayatollah's Beard,* by Nick Jubber (DaCapo); *The Rule of Empires,* by Tim Parsons (Oxford).

TIPS "I am interested in commercial and literary fiction, as well as serious nonfiction and pop culture. My focus as an agent has always been on working with writers to shape their work for its greatest commercial potential. I provide lots of editorial advice in sharpening manuscripts and proposals before submission. I've been a member of the Royalty Committee of the Association of Authors Representatives since its founding and am always keen to challenge publishers for their willfully obscure royalty reporting. Also I have recently taken over the position of Treasurer of the A.A.R. My publishing background includes working at the University of California Press so I am always intrigued by academic subjects which are given a commercial spin to reach an audience outside academia. I've also worked as a foreign scout for publishers like Hodder & Stoughton in England and Wilhelm Heyne in Germany, which gives me a good sense of how American books can be successfully translated overseas."

◎ NANCY GALLT LITERARY AGENCY

273 Charlton Ave., South Orange NJ 07079. (973)761-6358. **Fax:** (973)761-6318. **Website:** www.nancygallt. com. **Contact:** Nancy Gallt. Represents 40 clients.

30% of clients are new/unpublished writers. Currently handles: juvenile books 100%.

◑ Prior to opening her agency, Ms. Gallt was subsidiary rights director of the children's book division at Morrow, Harper and Viking.

MEMBER AGENTS Nancy Gallt; Marietta Zacker.
REPRESENTS Juvenile.

✎➝ "I only handle children's books." Actively seeking picture books, middle grade, and young adult novels. Does not want to receive rhyming picture book texts.

HOW TO CONTACT Submit a novel or chapter book by copying and pasting the first 5 pages onto the body of the e-mail and attach the first three chapters to submissions@nancygallt.com. Do not send to individual e-mail address, but do address submission to specific agent. If submitting a picture book: please copy and paste the entire manuscript into the body of the e-mail and attach it, as well. A response from one agent is a response from the entire company. Please see website for more submission details. Accepts simultaneous submissions. Responds in 3 months to queries. Responds in 3 months to mss. Obtains most new clients through recommendations from others, solicitations.

TERMS Agent receives 15% commission on domestic sales. Agent receives 20% commission on foreign sales. Offers written contract; 30-day notice must be given to terminate contract.

RECENT SALES Sold 50 titles in the last year. *Kane Chronicles* series, by Rick Riordan (Hyperion); *Nightshade City,* by Hilary Wagner (Holiday House); *Cinderella Smith,* by Stephanie Barden (HarperCollins); *The Square Cat,* by Elizabeth Schoonmaker (Simon & Schuster); *Granddaughter's Necklace,* illustrated by Bagram Ibatoulline (Scholastic).

TIPS "Writing and illustrations stand on their own, so submissions should tell the most compelling stories possible—whether visually, in words, or both."

◎ THE GARAMOND AGENCY, INC.

1840 Columbia Rd. NW, #503, Washington DC 20009. **E-mail:** query@garamondagency.com. **Website:** www.garamondagency.com. Other memberships include Author's Guild.

MEMBER AGENTS Lisa Adams; David Miller.
REPRESENTS Nonfiction books. **Considers these nonfiction areas:** business, current affairs, economics,

NEW AGENT SPOTLIGHT

SAMANTHA DIGHTON (D4EO LITERARY)

D4eoliteraryagency.com
@SamanthaDighton

ABOUT SAMANTHA: Samantha Dighton joined D4EO Literary in September 2012. She graduated Summa Cum Laude from Hobart and William Smith Colleges with degrees in Writing & Rhetoric and Dance Theory & Performance Studies. Prior to joining D4EO, she worked at The Sagalyn Agency and as a reader for Curtis Brown. She is based in Washington, D.C.

SHE IS SEEKING: Sam is looking for character-driven stories with strong voice. She likes characters who are relatable yet flawed, vibrant settings that take on a life of their own, and a story that lasts well beyond the final page. She is generally looking at the following categories: literary fiction, historical fiction, mystery/suspense, magical realism, psychological thrillers, young adult (realistic) and narrative nonfiction. Please no science fiction, paranormal/urban fantasy, or bodice-ripping romances (though romantic subplots are always welcome!).

HOW TO SUBMIT: E-queries only. Send to samantha@d4eo.com. Paste the first 10 pages in the body of the e-mail, below your query. Please include "Query: [Title]" in the subject line.

---

history, law, politics, psychology, science, technology, social science, narrative nonfiction.

8—☛ "We work closely with our authors through each stage of the publishing process, first in developing their books and then in presenting themselves and their ideas effectively to publishers and to readers. We represent our clients throughout the world in all languages, media, and territories through an extensive network of subagents." No proposals for children's or young adult books, fiction, poetry, or memoir.

HOW TO CONTACT Queries sent by e-mail may not make it through the spam filters on our server. Please e-mail a brief query letter only, we do not read unsolicited manuscripts submitted by e-mail under any circumstances. See website.

RECENT SALES *Big Data*, by Viktor Mayer-Schoenberger and Kenneth Cukier (Houghton Mifflin Harcourt); *Nature's Fortune*, by Mark R Tercek and Jonathan S. Adams (Basic Books); *Forecast*, by Mark Buchanan (Bloomsbury); *Fever Season*, by Jeanette Keith (Bloomsbury); *Martha Jefferson Randolph*, by Cynthia Kierner (UNC Press). See website for other clients.

TIPS "Query us first if you have any questions about whether we are the right agency for your work."

MAX GARTENBERG LITERARY AGENCY

912 N. Pennsylvania Ave., Yardley PA 19067. (215)295-9230. **Website:** www.maxgartenberg.com. **Contact:** Anne Devlin (fiction and nonfiction). Estab. 1954. Represents 100 clients. 20% of clients are new/unpublished writers. Currently handles: nonfiction books 80%, novels 20%.

MEMBER AGENTS Anne G. Devlin (current events, politics, true crime, women's issues, sports, parenting, biography, environment, narrative nonfiction, health, lifestyle, literary fiction, romance, and celebrity); Dirk Devlin (thrillers, science fiction, mysteries, and humor).

REPRESENTS Nonfiction books, novels. **Considers these nonfiction areas:** agriculture horticulture, animals, art, biography, child, current affairs, health, history, money, music, nature, psychology, science, self help, sports, film, true crime, women's.

HOW TO CONTACT Writers desirous of having their work handled by this agency may query by e-mail to agdevlin@aol.com. Accepts simultaneous submissions. Responds in 2 weeks to queries. Responds in 6 weeks to mss. Obtains most new clients through recommendations from others, following up on good query letters.

TERMS Agent receives 15% commission on domestic sales. Agent receives 20% commission on foreign sales.

RECENT SALES *Blazing Ice: Pioneering the 21st Century's Road to the South Pole*, by John H. Wright; *Beethoven for Kids: His Life and Music*, by Helen Bauer; *Slaughter on North LaSalle*, by Robert L. Snow; *What Patients Taught Me*, by Audrey Young, MD (Sasquatch Books); *Unorthodox Warfare: The Chinese Experience*, by Ralph D. Sawyer (Westview Press); *Encyclopedia of Earthquakes and Volcanoes*, by Alexander E. Gates (Facts on File); *Homebirth in the Hospital*, by Stacey Kerr, M.D. (Sentient Publications).

TIPS "We have recently expanded to allow more access for new writers."

DON GASTWIRTH & ASSOCIATES

265 College St., New Haven CT 06510. (203)562-7600. **Fax:** (203)562-4300. **E-mail:** Donlit@snet.net. **Contact:** Don Gastwirth. Signatory of WGA. Represents 26 clients. 10% of clients are new/unpublished writers. Currently handles: nonfiction books 30%, scholarly books 60%, other 10% other.

○ Prior to becoming an agent, Mr. Gastwirth was an entertainment lawyer and law professor.

REPRESENTS Nonfiction books, scholarly. **Considers these nonfiction areas:** business, current affairs, history, military, money, music, nature, popular culture, psychology, translation, true crime. **Considers these fiction areas:** mystery, thriller.

8—⚷ This is a selective agency and is rarely open to new clients that do not come through a referral.

HOW TO CONTACT Query with SASE.

TERMS Agent receives 15% commission on domestic sales. Agent receives 10% commission on foreign sales.

ⓓ GELFMAN SCHNEIDER LITERARY AGENTS, INC.

250 W. 57th St., Suite 2122, New York NY 10107. (212)245-1993. **Fax:** (212)245-8678. **E-mail:** mail@gelfmanschneider.com. **Website:** www.gelfmanschneider.com. **Contact:** Jane Gelfman, Deborah Schneider. Member of AAR. Represents 300+ clients. 10% of clients are new/unpublished writers.

MEMBER AGENTS Jane Gelfman, Deborah Schneider, Victoria Marini.

REPRESENTS Fiction and nonfiction books. **Considers these fiction areas:** literary, mainstream, mystery, women's, young adult.

8—⚷ Does not want to receive romance, science fiction, westerns, or children's books.

HOW TO CONTACT Query with SASE. Send queries via snail mail only. No unsolicited mss. Please send a query letter, a synopsis, and a sample chapter only. Consult website for each agent's submission requirements. Responds in 1 month to queries. Responds in 2 months to mss.

TERMS Agent receives 15% commission on domestic sales. Agent receives 20% commission on foreign sales. Agent receives 15% commission on film sales. Offers written contract. Charges clients for photocopying and messengers/couriers.

⬤ GEORGES BORCHARDT, INC.

136 E. 57th St., New York NY 10022. **Website:** www.gbagency.com. Member of AAR.

MEMBER AGENTS Anne Borchardt; Georges Borchardt; Valerie Borchardt.

8—⚷ This agency specializes in literary fiction and outstanding nonfiction.

HOW TO CONTACT *No unsolicited mss.* Obtains most new clients through recommendations from others.

TERMS Agent receives 15% commission on domestic sales. Agent receives 20% commission on foreign sales. Offers written contract.

⬤ THE GERNERT COMPANY

136 East 57th St., 18th Floor, New York NY 10022. (212)838-7777. **Fax:** (212)838-6020. **E-mail:** info@thegernertco.com. **Website:** www.thegernertco.com. **Contact:** Sarah Burnes.

○ Prior to her current position, Ms. Burnes was with Burnes & Clegg, Inc.

MEMBER AGENTS Sarah Burnes (commercial fiction, adventure and true story); Stephanie Cabot (literary fiction, commercial fiction, historical fiction); Chris Parris-Lamb; Seth Fishman; Logan Garrison; Will Roberts; Erika Storella; Anna Worrall. At this time, Courtney Gatewood and Rebecca Gardner are closed to queries.

REPRESENTS Nonfiction books, novels.

HOW TO CONTACT Queries should be addressed to a specific agent via the e-mail subject line. Please send a query letter, either by mail or e-mail, describing the work you'd like to submit, along with some information about yourself and a sample chapter if appropriate. Please do not send e-mails to individual agents; use info@thegernertco.com and indicate which agent you're querying. See company website for more instructions. Obtains most new clients through recommendations from others, solicitations.

RECENT SALES *House of Joy*, by Sarah-Kate Lynch (Plume); *Mudbound*, by Hillary Jordan (Algonquin); *The Reluctant Diplomat: Peter Paul Rubens and His Secret Mission to Save Europe From Itself*, by Mark Lamster (Talese).

BARRY GOLDBLATT LITERARY LLC

320 Seventh Ave. #266, Brooklyn NY 11215. (718)832-8787. **E-mail:** query@bgliterary.com. **Contact:** Barry Goldblatt. Estab. 2000.

MEMBER AGENTS Barry Goldblatt, Joe Monti.

8→ "Please see our website for specific submission guidelines and information on agents' particular tastes."

HOW TO CONTACT Obtains clients through referrals, queries, and conferences.

TERMS Agent receives 15% commission on domestic sales; 20% on foreign and dramatic sales. Offers written contract. 60 days notice must be given to terminate contract.

RECENT SALES *Ambassador*, by Will Alexander; *Dangerous*, by Shannon Hale; *Glad Rags*, by Genevieve Valentine; *The Retribution of Mara Dyer*, by Michelle Hodkin.

TIPS "We're a hands-on agency, focused on building an author's career, not just making an initial sale. We don't care about trends or what's hot; we just want to sign great writers."

● FRANCES GOLDIN LITERARY AGENCY, INC.

57 E. 11th St., Suite 5B, New York NY 10003. (212)777-0047. **Fax:** (212)228-1660. **E-mail:** agency@goldinlit.com. **Website:** www.goldinlit.com. Estab. 1977. Member of AAR. Represents over 100 clients.

MEMBER AGENTS Frances Goldin, principal/agent; Ellen Geiger, agent (commercial and literary fiction and nonfiction, cutting-edge topics of all kinds); Matt McGowan, agent/rights director (innovative works of fiction and nonfiction); Sam Stoloff, agent (literary fiction, memoir, history, accessible sociology and philosophy, cultural studies, serious journalism, narrative and topical nonfiction with a progressive orientation); Sarah Bridgins, agent/office manager (literary fiction and nonfiction).

REPRESENTS Nonfiction books, novels.

8→ "We are hands on and we work intensively with clients on proposal and manuscript development." Does not want anything that is racist, sexist, agist, homophobic, or pornographic. No screenplays, children's books, art books, cookbooks, business books, diet books, romance, self-help, or genre fiction.

HOW TO CONTACT Query with SASE. No unsolicited mss or work previously submitted to publishers. Prefers hard-copy queries. If querying by e-mail, put word "query" in subject line. For queries to Sam Stoloff or Ellen Geiger, please use online submission form. Responds in 4-6 weeks to queries.

❶ THE SUSAN GOLOMB LITERARY AGENCY

540 President St., 3rd Floor, Brooklyn NY 11215. **Fax:** (212)239-9503. **E-mail:** susan@sgolombagency.com; krista@sgolombagency.com. **Contact:** Susan Golomb; Krista Ingebretson. Currently handles: nonfiction books 50%, novels 40%, story collections 10%.

MEMBER AGENTS Susan Golomb (accepts queries); Krista Ingebretson (accepts queries).

REPRESENTS Novels, short story collections. **Considers these nonfiction areas:** animals, anthropology, biography, business, current affairs, economics, environment, health, history, law, memoirs, military, money, popular culture, politics, psychology, science, sociology, technology, women's issues, women's studies. **Considers these fiction areas:** ethnic, historical, humor, literary, mainstream, satire, thriller, women's, young adult, chick lit.

"We specialize in literary and upmarket fiction and nonfiction that is original, vibrant and of excellent quality and craft. Nonfiction should be edifying, paradigm-shifting, fresh and entertaining." Actively seeking writers with strong voices. Does not want to receive genre fiction.

HOW TO CONTACT Query via mail with SASE or by e-mail. Will respond if interested. Submit outline/proposal, synopsis, 1 sample chapter, author bio. Obtains most new clients through recommendations from others, solicitations, and unsolicited queries.

TERMS Offers written contract.

RECENT SALES *The Kraus Project*, by Jonathan Franzen (FSG); *The Word Exchange*, by Alena Graedon (Doubleday); *The Flamethrowers*, by Rachel Kushner (Scribner); *The Book of Jonah*, by Joshua Feldman (Holt); *Last Stories* and *Other Stories* and *The Dying Grass*, by William T. Vollmann (Viking)

IRENE GOODMAN LITERARY AGENCY

27 W. 24th St., Suite 700B, New York NY 10010. **E-mail:** irene.queries@irenegoodman.com. **Website:** www.irenegoodman.com. **Contact:** Irene Goodman, Miriam Kriss. Member of AAR.

MEMBER AGENTS Irene Goodman; Miriam Kriss; Barbara Poelle; Rachel Ekstrom.

REPRESENTS Nonfiction, novels. **Considers these nonfiction areas:** narrative nonfiction dealing with social, cultural and historical issues; an occasional memoir and current affairs book, parenting, social issues, francophilia, anglophilia, Judaica, lifestyles, cooking, memoir. **Considers these fiction areas:** historical, intelligent literary, modern urban fantasies, mystery, romance, thriller, women's.

"Specializes in the finest in commercial fiction and nonfiction. We have a strong background in women's voices, including mysteries, romance, women's fiction, thrillers, suspense. Historical fiction is one of Irene's particular passions and Miriam is fanatical about modern urban fantasies. In nonfiction, Irene is looking for topics on narrative history, social issues and trends, education, Judaica, Francophilia, Anglophilia, other cultures, animals, food, crafts, and memoir." Barbara is looking for commercial thrillers with strong female protagonists; Miriam is looking for urban fan-

tasy and edgy sci-fi/young adult. No children's picture books, screenplays, poetry, or inspirational fiction.

HOW TO CONTACT Query. Submit synopsis, first 10 pages. E-mail queries only! See the website submission page. No e-mail attachments. Responds in 2 months to queries. Consult website for each agent's submission guidelines.

RECENT SALES *The Ark*, by Boyd Morrison; *Isolation*, by C.J. Lyons; *The Sleepwalkers*, by Paul Grossman; *Dead Man's Moon*, by Devon Monk; *Becoming Marie Antoinette*, by Juliet Grey; *What's Up Down There*, by Lissa Rankin; *Beg for Mercy*, by Toni Andrews; *The Devil Inside*, by Jenna Black.

TIPS "We are receiving an unprecedented amount of e-mail queries. If you find that the mailbox is full, please try again in two weeks. E-mail queries to our personal addresses will not be answered. E-mails to our personal inboxes will be deleted."

GOUMEN & SMIRNOVA LITERARY AGENCY

Nauki pr., 19/2 fl. 293, St. Petersburg 195220 Russia. **E-mail:** info@gs-agency.com. **Website:** www.gs-agency.com. **Contact:** Julia Goumen, Natalia Smirnova. Represents 20 clients. 10% of clients are new/unpublished writers. Currently handles: nonfiction books 10%, novels 80%, story collections 5%, juvenile books 5%.

Prior to becoming agents, both Ms. Goumen and Ms. Smirnova worked as foreign rights managers with an established Russian publisher selling translation rights for literary fiction.

MEMBER AGENTS Julia Goumen (translation rights, Russian language rights, film rights); Natalia Smirnova (translation rights, Russian language rights, film rights).

REPRESENTS Nonfiction books, novels, short story collections, novellas, movie, TV, TV movie, sitcom. **Considers these nonfiction areas:** biography, current affairs, ethnic, humor, memoirs, music. **Considers these fiction areas:** adventure, experimental, family, historical, horror, literary, mainstream, mystery, romance, thriller, young, womens. **Considers these script areas:** action, comedy, detective, family, mainstream, romantic comedy, romantic drama, teen, thriller.

"We are the first full-service agency in Russia, representing our authors in book publishing, film, television, and other areas. We are also the first agency, representing Russian authors worldwide, based in Russia. The agency also represents international authors, agents and publishers in Russia. Our philosophy is to provide an individual approach to each author, finding the right publisher both at home and across international cultural and linguistic borders, developing original marketing and promotional strategies for each title." Actively seeking manuscripts written in Russian, both literary and commercial; and foreign publishers and agents with the high-profile fiction and general nonfiction lists to represent in Russia. Does not want to receive unpublished manuscripts in languages other than Russian, or any information irrelevant to our activity.

HOW TO CONTACT Submit synopsis, author bio. Accepts simultaneous submissions. Responds in 14 days to mss. Obtains most new clients through recommendations from others, solicitations.

TERMS Agent receives 20% commission on domestic sales. Agent receives 20% commission on foreign sales. Offers written contract, binding for 1 year; 2-month notice must be given to terminate contract.

DOUG GRAD LITERARY AGENCY, INC.

156 Prospect Park West, Brooklyn NY 11215. (718)788-6067. **E-mail:** doug.grad@dgliterary.com. **E-mail:** query@dgliterary.com. **Website:** www.dglit erary.com. **Contact:** Doug Grad. Estab. 2008.

Prior to being an agent, Doug Grad spent the last 22 years as an editor at 4 major publishing houses.

HOW TO CONTACT Query by e-mail first at query@ dgliterary.com. No sample material unless requested.

RECENT SALES *Drink the Tea*, by Thomas Kaufman (St. Martin's); *15 Minutes: The Impossible Math of Nuclear War*, by L. Douglas Keeney (St. Martin's).

GRAHAM MAW CHRISTIE LITERARY AGENCY

19 Thornhill Crescent, London England N1 1BJ United Kingdom. (44)(207)812-9937; 0(207) 609 1326. **E-mail:** enquiries@grahammawchristie.com; info@ grahammawchristie.com. **E-mail:** submissions@ grahammawchristie.com. **Website:** www.graham mawchristie.com. Represents 40 clients. 30% of clients are new/unpublished writers. Currently handles: nonfiction books 100%.

Prior to opening her agency, Ms. Graham Maw was a publishing director at HarperCollins and worked in rights, publicity and editorial. She has ghostwritten several nonfiction books, which gives her an insider's knowledge of both the publishing industry and the pleasures and pitfalls of authorships. Ms. Christie has a background in advertising and journalism.

MEMBER AGENTS Jane Graham Maw; Jennifer Christie.

REPRESENTS Nonfiction books. **Considers these nonfiction areas:** autobiography, biography, child guidance, cooking, diet/nutrition, foods, health, how-to, medicine, memoirs, parenting, popular culture, psychology, self-help.

"We aim to make the publishing process easier and smoother for authors. We work hard to ensure that publishing proposals are watertight before submission. We aim for collaborative relationships with publishers so that we provide the right books to the right editor at the right time. We represent ghostwriters as well as authors." Actively seeking work from UK writers only. Does not want to receive fiction, poetry, children's books, plays or e-mail submissions.

HOW TO CONTACT "Our books are currently full. We will open them again: please check the website for updates." Query with synopsis, chapter outline, bio, SASE. Responds in 2 weeks to queries. Obtains most new clients through recommendations from others.

TERMS Agent receives 15% commission on domestic sales. Agent receives 20% commission on foreign sales. Offers written contract; 30-day notice must be given to terminate contract.

WRITERS CONFERENCES London Book Fair, Frankfurt Book Fair.

TIPS "UK clients only!"

ASHLEY GRAYSON LITERARY AGENCY

1342 W. 18th St., San Pedro CA 90732. **Fax:** (310)514-1148. **E-mail:** graysonagent@earthlink.net. **Website:** www.graysonagency.com/blog. Estab. 1976. Member of AAR. Represents 100 clients. 5% of clients are new/unpublished writers. Currently handles: nonfiction books 20%, novels 50%, juvenile books 30%.

MEMBER AGENTS Ashley Grayson (fantasy, mystery, thrillers, young adult); Carolyn Grayson (chick lit, mystery, children's, nonfiction, women's fiction, romance, thrillers); Denise Dumars (mind/body/spirit, women's fiction, dark fantasy/horror); Lois Winston (women's fiction, chick lit, mystery).

REPRESENTS Nonfiction books, novels. **Considers these nonfiction areas:** business, computers, economics, history, investigative, popular culture, science, self-help, sports, technology, true crime, mind/body/spirit, lifestyle. **Considers these fiction areas:** fantasy, juvenile, multicultural, mystery, romance, science fiction, suspense, women's, young adult, chick lit.

☛ "We prefer to work with published (traditional print), established authors. We will give first consideration to authors who come recommended to us by our clients or other publishing professionals. We accept a very small number of new, previously unpublished authors. The agency is temporarily closed to queries from writers who are not published at book length (self published or print-on-demand do not count). There are only three exceptions to this policy: (1) Unpublished authors who have received an offer from a reputable publisher, who need an agent before beginning contract negotiations; (2) Authors who are recommended by a published author, editor or agent who has read the work in question; (3) Authors whom we have met at conferences and from whom we have requested submissions. Authors who are recognized within their field or area may still query with proposals. We are seeking more mysteries and thrillers."

HOW TO CONTACT As of early 2008, the agency was only open to fiction authors with publishing credits (no self-published). For nonfiction, only writers with great platforms will be considered. Responds to queries in 1 month; mss in 2-3 months.

TERMS Agent receives 15% commission on domestic sales. Agent receives 20% commission on foreign sales.

RECENT SALES Sold 25+ books last year. *Juliet Dove, Queen of Love*, by Bruce Coville (Harcourt); *Alosha*, by Christopher Pike (TOR); *Sleeping Freshmen Never Lie*, by David Lubar (Dutton); *Ball Don't Lie*, by Matt de la Peña (Delacorte); *Wiley & Grampa's Creature Features*, by Kirk Scroggs (10-book series, Little Brown); *Snitch*, by Allison van Diepen (Si-

mon Pulse). Also represents: J.B. Cheaney (Knopf), Bruce Wetter (Atheneum).

TIPS "We do request revisions as they are required. We are long-time agents, professional and known in the business. We perform professionally for our clients and we ask the same of them."

● SANFORD J. GREENBURGER ASSOCIATES, INC.

55 Fifth Ave., New York NY 10003. (212)206-5600. **Fax:** (212)463-8718. **E-mail:** queryHL@sjga.com. **Website:** www.greenburger.com. Member of AAR. Represents 500 clients.

MEMBER AGENTS Heide Lange; Faith Hamlin; Nicolas Ellison; Dan Mandel; Matthew Bialer; Courtney Miller-Callihan, Brenda Bowen (authors and illustrators of children's books for all ages as well as graphic novelists); Lisa Gallagher; Chelsea Lindman (literary fiction, crime fiction and YA/children's, as well as nonfiction in the areas of pop culture, politics, health, and science); Lindsay Ribar (young adult and middle grade fiction); Rachael Dillon Fried (unique literary voices, women's fiction, narrative nonfiction, memoir, and comedy).

REPRESENTS Nonfiction books and novels. **Considers these nonfiction areas:** Americana, animals, anthropology, archeology, architecture, art, biography, business, computers, cooking, crafts, current affairs, decorating, diet/nutrition, design, education, environment, ethnic, film, foods, gardening, gay/lesbian, government, health, history, horticulture, how-to, humor, interior design, investigative, juvenile nonfiction, language, law, literature, medicine, memoirs, metaphysics, military, money, multicultural, music, New Age, philosophy, photography, popular culture, psychology, recreation, regional, romance, science, sex, sociology, software, sports, theater, translation, travel, true crime, women's issues, women's studies, young adult, software. **Considers these fiction areas:** action, adventure, crime, detective, ethnic, family saga, feminist, gay, glitz, historical, humor, lesbian, literary, mainstream, mystery, police, psychic, regional, satire, sports, supernatural, suspense, thriller.

☛ No Westerns. No screenplays.

HOW TO CONTACT Submit query, first 3 chapters, synopsis, brief bio, SASE. Consult website for submission guidelines. Accepts simultaneous submissions. Responds in 2 months to queries and mss.

Responds to mss. Obtains most new clients through recommendations from others.

TERMS Agent receives 15% commission on domestic sales. Agent receives 20% commission on foreign sales. Charges for photocopying and books for foreign and subsidiary rights submissions.

THE GREENHOUSE LITERARY AGENCY

11308 Lapham Dr., Oakton VA 22124. **E-mail:** submissions@greenhouseliterary.com. **Website:** www.greenhouseliterary.com. **Contact:** Sarah Davies, vice president; John M. Cusick, agent (US); Julia Churchill, agent (UK). Member of AAR. Other memberships include SCBWI. Represents 20 clients. 100% of clients are new/unpublished writers. Currently handles: juvenile books 100%.

○ Sarah Davies has had an editorial and management career in children's publishing spanning 25 years; for 5 years prior to launching the Greenhouse she was Publishing Director of Macmillan Children's Books in London, and publishing leading authors from both sides of the Atlantic.

REPRESENTS Juvenile. **Considers these fiction areas:** juvenile, young adult.

○→ "We exclusively represent authors writing fiction for children and teens. The agency has offices in both the US and UK, and Sarah Davies (who is British) personally represents authors to both markets. The agency's commission structure reflects this—taking 15% for sales to both US and UK, thus treating both as 'domestic' market." All genres of children's and YA fiction—ages 5+. Does not want to receive nonfiction, poetry, picture books (text or illustration) or work aimed at adults; short stories, educational or religious/inspirational work, pre-school/novelty material, or screenplays.

HOW TO CONTACT E-mail queries only; short letter containing a brief outline, biography and any writing 'credentials'. The first five pages of text should be pasted into the e-mail. All submissions are answered. Responds in 2-6 week to queries; 6-8 weeks to requested mss. Obtains most new clients through recommendations from others, solicitations, conferences.

TERMS Agent receives 15% commission on domestic sales. Agent receives 25% commission on foreign sales. Offers written contract. This agency occasion-ally charges for submission copies to film agents or foreign publishers.

RECENT SALES *Fracture*, by Megan Miranda (Walker); *Paper Valentine*, by Brenna Yovanff (Razorbill); *Uses for Boys*, by Erica L. Scheidt (St Martin's); *Dark Inside*, by Jeyn Roberts (Simon & Schuster); *Breathe*, by Sarah Crossan (HarperCollins); *After the Snow*, by SD Crockett (Feiwel/Macmillan); *Sean Griswold's Head*, by Lindsey Leavitt (Hyperion).

WRITERS CONFERENCES Bologna Children's Book Fair, ALA and SCBWI conferences, BookExpo America.

TIPS "Before submitting material, authors should read the Greenhouse's 'Top 10 Tips for Authors of Children's Fiction' and carefully follow our submission guidelines which can be found on the website."

KATHRYN GREEN LITERARY AGENCY, LLC

250 West 57th St., Suite 2302, New York NY 10107. (212)245-4225. **Fax:** (212)245-4042. **E-mail:** query@kgreenagency.com. **Contact:** Kathy Green. Other memberships include Women's Media Group. Represents approximately 20 clients. 50% of clients are new/unpublished writers. Currently handles: nonfiction books 50%, novels 25%, juvenile books 25%.

○ Prior to becoming an agent, Ms. Green was a book and magazine editor.

REPRESENTS Nonfiction books, novels, short story collections, juvenile, middle grade and young adult. **Considers these nonfiction areas:** autobiography, biography, business, child guidance, cooking, current affairs, diet//nutrition, economics, education, foods, history, how-to, humor, interior design, investigative, juvenile nonfiction, memoirs, parenting, popular culture, psychology, satire, self-help, sports, true crime, women's issues, women's studies, juvenile. **Considers these fiction areas:** crime, detective, family saga, historical, humor, juvenile, literary, mainstream, mystery, police, romance, satire, suspense, thriller, women's, young adult, women's.

○→ Keeping the client list small means that writers receive my full attention throughout the process of getting their project published. Does not want to receive science fiction or fantasy.

HOW TO CONTACT Query to query@kgreenagency.com. Send no samples unless requested. Accepts simultaneous submissions. Responds in 1-2 months to mss. Obtains most new clients through recommendations from others, solicitations, conferences.

TERMS Agent receives 15% commission on domestic sales. Agent receives 20% commission on foreign sales. No written contract.

RECENT SALES The Touch Series by Laurie Stolarz; *How Do You Light a Fart*, by Bobby Mercer; *Creepiosity*, by David Bickel; *Hidden Facets: Diamonds for the Dead* by Alan Orloff; *Don't Stalk the Admissions Officer*, by Risa Lewak; *Designed Fat Girl*, by Jennifer Joyner.

TIPS "This agency offers a written agreement."

🌑 ⦿ GREGORY & CO. AUTHORS' AGENTS

3 Barb Mews, Hammersmith, London W6 7PA England. (44)(207)610-4676. **Fax:** (44)(207)610-4686. **E-mail:** info@gregoryandcompany.co.uk. **E-mail:** maryjones@gregoryandcompany.co.uk. **Website:** www.gregoryandcompany.co.uk. **Contact:** Jane Gregory. Other memberships include AAA. Represents 60 clients. Currently handles: nonfiction books 10%, novels 90%.

MEMBER AGENTS Stephanie Glencross.

REPRESENTS Nonfiction books, novels. **Considers these nonfiction areas:** autobiography, biography, history. **Considers these fiction areas:** crime, detective, historical, literary, mainstream, police, thriller, contemporary women's fiction.

⚷ As a British agency, we do not generally take on American authors. Actively seeking well-written, accessible modern novels. Does not want to receive horror, science fiction, fantasy, mind/body/spirit, children's books, screenplays, plays, short stories or poetry.

HOW TO CONTACT Query with SASE. Submit outline, first 10 pages by e-mail or post, publishing history, author bio. Send submissions to Mary Jones, submissions editor: maryjones@gregoryandcompany. co.uk. Accepts simultaneous submissions. Returns materials only with SASE. Obtains most new clients through recommendations from others, conferences.

TERMS Agent receives 15% commission on domestic sales. Agent receives 20% commission on foreign sales. Offers written contract; 1-month notice must be given to terminate contract. Charges clients for photocopying of whole typescripts and copies of book for submissions.

RECENT SALES *Ritual*, by Mo Hader (Bantam UK/ Grove Atlantic); *A Darker Domain*, by Val McDermid (HarperCollins UK); *The Chameleon's Shadow*, by Minette Walters (Macmillan UK/Knopf Inc); *Stratton's War*, by Laura Wilson (Orion UK/St. Martin's).

WRITERS CONFERENCES CWA Conference; Bouchercon.

⚫ BLANCHE C. GREGORY, INC.

2 Tudor City Place, New York NY 10017. (212)697-0828. **E-mail:** info@bcgliteraryagency.com. **Website:** www.bcgliteraryagency.com. Member of AAR.

REPRESENTS Nonfiction books, novels, juvenile.

⚷ This agency specializes in adult fiction and nonfiction; children's literature is also considered. Does not want to receive screenplays, stage plays or teleplays.

HOW TO CONTACT Submit query, brief synopsis, bio, SASE. No e-mail queries. Online submission form available at website. Obtains most new clients through recommendations from others.

⦿ GREYHAUS LITERARY

3021 20th St., PL SW, Puyallup WA 98373. **E-mail:** scott@greyhausagency.com. **Website:** www.greyhausagency.com. **Contact:** Scott Eagan, member RWA. Estab. 2003.

⚷ "Greyhaus only focuses on romance and women's fiction. Please review submission information found on the website to know exactly what Greyhaus is looking for. Stories should be 75,000-120,000 words in length or meet the word count requirements for the Harlequin series lines found on the Harlequin website." Does not want sci-fi, fantasy, literary, futuristic, erotica, writers targeting e-pubs, young adult, nonfiction, memoirs, how-to books, self-help, screenplays, novellas, poetry.

HOW TO CONTACT Send a query, the first 3 pages and a synopsis of no more than 3 pages. There is also a submission form on this agency's website.

⦿ JILL GRINBERG LITERARY AGENCY

16 Court St., Suite 3306, Brooklyn NY 11241. (212)620-5883. **Fax:** (212)627-4725. **E-mail:** info@grinberglit erary.com. **Website:** www.jillgrinbergliterary.com.

💬 Prior to her current position, Ms. Grinberg was at Anderson Grinberg Literary Management.

MEMBER AGENTS Jill Grinberg; Kirsten Wolf (foreign rights).

REPRESENTS Nonfiction books, novels. **Considers these nonfiction areas:** autobiography, biography, business, current affairs, economics, government, health, history, law, medicine, multicultural, politics, psychology, science, spirituality, technology, travel, women's issues, women's studies. **Considers these fiction areas:** commercial, fantasy, historical, juvenile, literary, romance, science fiction, women's, young adult, middle grade.

HOW TO CONTACT Query with SASE. Send a proposal and author bio for nonfiction; send a query, synopsis and the first 50 pages for fiction.

TIPS "We prefer submissions by mail."

JILL GROSJEAN LITERARY AGENCY

1390 Millstone Rd., Sag Harbor NY 11963. (631)725-7419. **E-mail:** JillLit310@aol.com. **Contact:** Jill Grosjean.

Prior to becoming an agent, Ms. Grosjean managed an independent bookstore. She also worked in publishing and advertising.

Actively seeking literary novels and mysteries.

HOW TO CONTACT E-mail queries preferred, no attachments. No cold calls, please. Accepts simultaneous submissions, though when manuscript requested, requires exclusive reading time. Accepts simultaneous submissions. Responds in 1 week to queries; month to mss. Obtains most new clients through recommendations and solicitations.

TERMS Agent receives 15% commission on domestic sales; 20% commission on foreign and film sales.

RECENT SALES *A Spark of Death*, *Fatal Induction*, and *Capacity for Murder*, by Bernadette Pajer (Poison Pen Press); *Neutral Ground*, by Greg Garrett (Bondfire Books); *Threading the Needle*, by Marie Bostwick (Kensington Publishing).

WRITERS CONFERENCES Thrillerfest; Texas Writer's League; Book Passage Mystery's Writer's Conference.

LAURA GROSS LITERARY AGENCY

P.O. Box 610326, Newton Highlands MA 02461. (617)964-2977. **Fax:** (617)964-3023. **E-mail:** query@lg-la.com. **Website:** www.lg-la.com. **Contact:** Laura Gross. Estab. 1988. Represents 30 clients. Currently handles: nonfiction books 40%, novels 50%, scholarly books 10%.

Prior to becoming an agent, Ms. Gross was an editor.

REPRESENTS Nonfiction books, novels. **Considers these nonfiction areas:** autobiography, biography, child guidance, cultural interests, current affairs, ethnic, government, health, history, law, medicine, memoirs, parenting, popular culture, politics, psychology, sports, women's issues, women's studies. **Considers these fiction areas:** historical, literary, mainstream, mystery, suspense, thriller.

HOW TO CONTACT Submit online using submissions manager. Query with SASE or by e-mail. Submit author bio. Responds in several days to queries. Obtains most new clients through recommendations from others.

TERMS Agent receives 15% commission on domestic sales. Agent receives 20% commission on foreign sales. Offers written contract.

THE MITCHELL J. HAMILBURG AGENCY

149 S. Barrington Ave., #732, Los Angeles CA 90049. (310)471-4024. **Fax:** (310)471-9588. **Contact:** Michael Hamilburg. Estab. 1937. Signatory of WGA. Represents 70 clients. Currently handles: nonfiction books 70%, novels 30%.

REPRESENTS Nonfiction books, novels. **Considers these nonfiction areas:** anthropology, biography, business, child, cooking, current affairs, education, government, health, history, memoirs, military, money, psychology, recreation, regional, self help, sex, sociology, spirituality, sports, travel, women's, creative nonfiction; romance; architecture; inspirational; true crime. **Considers these fiction areas:** glitz, New Age, adventure, experimental, feminist, humor, military, mystery, occult, regional, religious, romance, sports, thriller, crime; mainstream; psychic.

HOW TO CONTACT Query with outline, 2 sample chapters, SASE. Responds in 1 month to mss. Obtains most new clients through recommendations from others, conferences, personal search.

TERMS Agent receives 10-15% commission on domestic sales.

THE JOY HARRIS LITERARY AGENCY, INC.

381 Park Avenue S, Suite 428, New York NY 10016. (212)924-6269. **Fax:** (212)725-5275. **E-mail:** submissions@jhlitagent.com; contact@jhlitagent.com. **Website:** joyharrisliterary.com. **Contact:** Joy Harris. Member of AAR. Represents more than 100 clients. Currently handles: nonfiction books 50%, novels 50%.

REPRESENTS Nonfiction books, novels, and young adult. **Considers these fiction areas:** ethnic, experimental, family saga, feminist, gay, glitz, hi-lo, historical, humor, lesbian, literary, mainstream, multicultural, multimedia, mystery, regional, satire, short story collections, spiritual, suspense, translation, women's, young adult.

⊶ We do not accept unsolicited manuscripts, and are not accepting poetry, screenplays, or self-help submissions at this time.

HOW TO CONTACT Visit our website for guidelines. Query with sample chapter, outline/proposal, SASE. Accepts simultaneous submissions. Responds in 2 months to queries. Obtains most new clients through recommendations from clients and editors.

TERMS Agent receives 15% commission on domestic sales. Agent receives 20% commission on foreign sales. Charges clients for some office expenses.

⊙ HARTLINE LITERARY AGENCY

123 Queenston Dr., Pittsburgh PA 15235-5429. (412)829-2483. **Fax:** (412)829-2432. **E-mail:** joyce@hartlineliterary.com. **Website:** www.hartlineliterary.com. **Contact:** Joyce A. Hart. Represents 40 clients. 20% of clients are new/unpublished writers. Currently handles: nonfiction books 40%, novels 60%.

MEMBER AGENTS Joyce A. Hart, principal agent; Terry Burns: terry@hartlineliterary.com; Tamela Hancock Murray: tamela@hartlineliterary.com; Diana Flegal: diana@hartlineliterary.com; Andy Scheer.

REPRESENTS Nonfiction books, novels. **Considers these nonfiction areas:** business, child guidance, cooking, diet/nutrition, economics, foods, inspirational, money, parenting, religious, self-help, women's issues, women's studies. **Considers these fiction areas:** action, adventure, contemporary issues, family saga, historical, inspirational, literary, mystery, regional, religious, suspense, thriller, amateur sleuth, cozy, contemporary, gothic, historical, and regency romances.

⊶ "This agency specializes in the Christian bookseller market." Actively seeking adult fiction, self-help, nutritional books, devotional, and business. Does not want to receive erotica, gay/lesbian, fantasy, horror, etc.

HOW TO CONTACT Submit summary/outline, author bio, 3 sample chapters. Accepts simultaneous submissions. Responds in 2 months to queries. Re-

sponds in 3 months to mss. Obtains most new clients through recommendations from others.

TERMS Agent receives 15% commission on domestic sales. Offers written contract.

RECENT SALES *Aurora, An American Experience in Quilt, Community and Craft,* and *A Flickering Light,* by Jane Kirkpatrick (Waterbrook Multnomah); *Oprah Doesn't Know My Name* by Jane Kirkpatric (Zondervan); *Paper Roses, Scattered Petals, and Summer Rains,* by Amanda Cabot (Revell Books); *Blood Ransom,* by Lisa Harris (Zondervan); *I Don't Want a Divorce,* by David Clark (Revell Books); *Love Finds You in Hope, Kansas,* by Pamela Griffin (Summerside Press); Journey to the Well, by Diana Wallis Taylor (Revell Books); *Paper Bag Christmas, The Nine Lessons* by Kevin Milne (Center Street); *When Your Aging Parent Needs Care* by Arrington & Atchley (Harvest House); *Katie at Sixteen* by Kim Vogel Sawyer (Zondervan); *A Promise of Spring,* by Kim Vogel Sawyer (Bethany House); *The Big 5-OH!,* by Sandra Bricker (Abingdon Press); A *Silent Terror & A Silent Stalker,* by Lynette Eason (Steeple Hill); Extreme Devotion series, by Kathi Macias (New Hope Publishers); *On the Wings of the Storm,* by Tamira Barley (Whitaker House); Tribute, by Graham Garrison (Kregel Publications); *The Birth to Five Book,* by Brenda Nixon (Revell Books); *Fat to Skinny Fast and Easy,* by Doug Varrieur (Sterling Publishers).

⊙⊙ ANTONY HARWOOD LIMITED

103 Walton St., Oxford OX2 6EB England. +44 01865 559 615. **Fax:** +44 01865 310 660. **E-mail:** mail@antonyharwood.com. **Website:** www.antonyharwood.com. **Contact:** Antony Harwood; James Macdonald Lockhart; Jo Williamson. Estab. 2000. Represents 52 clients.

◑ Prior to starting this agency, Mr. Harwood and Mr. Lockhart worked at publishing houses and other literary agencies.

MEMBER AGENTS Antony Harwood, James Macdonald Lockhart, Jo Williamson (children's).

REPRESENTS Nonfiction books, novels. **Considers these nonfiction areas:** Americana, animals, anthropology, archeology, architecture, art, autobiography, biography, business, child guidance, computers, cooking, current affairs, design, economics, education, environment, ethnic, film, gardening, gay/lesbian, government, health, history, horticulture, how-to, humor, language, memoirs, military, money, multi-

NEW AGENT SPOTLIGHT

JENNIFER UDDEN
(THE DONALD MAASS LITERARY AGENCY)

Maassagency.com
@suddenlyjen

ABOUT JENNIFER: Jennifer Udden joined the Donald Maass Literary Agency in 2010. She graduated from Mount Holyoke College and previously worked in nonprofit arts fundraising.

SHE IS SEEKING: Science fiction, fantasy, romance, and mysteries—and is particularly interested in finding works that combine aspects of these genres.

HOW TO CONTACT: Query judden@maassagency.com.

cultural, music, parenting, philosophy, photography, popular culture, psychology, recreation, regional, science, self-help, sex, sociology, software, spirituality, sports, technology, translation, travel, true crime, war, women's issues, women's studies. **Considers these fiction areas:** action, adventure, cartoon, comic books, confession, crime, detective, erotica, ethnic, experimental, family saga, fantasy, feminist, frontier, gay, hi-lo, historical, horror, humor, lesbian, literary, mainstream, military, multicultural, multimedia, mystery, occult, picture books, plays, police, regional, religious, romance, satire, science fiction, spiritual, sports, suspense, thriller, translation, war, westerns, young adult, gothic.

⚷ "We accept every genre of fiction and nonfiction except for children's fiction for readers ages 10 and younger." No poetry or screenplays.

HOW TO CONTACT Submit outline, 2-3 sample chapters via e-mail in a Word or RTF format or postal mail (include SASE or IRC). Responds in 2 months to queries.

TERMS Agent receives 15% commission on domestic sales. Agent receives 20% commission on foreign sales.

● JOHN HAWKINS & ASSOCIATES, INC.

71 W. 23rd St., Suite 1600, New York NY 10010. (212)807-7040. **Fax:** (212)807-9555. **E-mail:** jha@jhalit.com; moses@jhalit.com; Frazier@jhalit.com; Ahawkins@jhalit.com. **Website:** www.jhalit.com.

Contact: Moses Cardona (rights and translations); Liz Free (permissions); Warren Frazier, literary agent; Anne Hawkins, literary agent. Member of AAR. Represents over 100 clients. 5-10% of clients are new/unpublished writers. Currently handles: nonfiction books 40%, novels 40%, juvenile books 20%.

MEMBER AGENTS Moses Cardona; Liz Free; Warren Frazier; Anne Hawkins.

REPRESENTS Nonfiction books, novels. **Considers these nonfiction areas:** Americana, biography, business, cultural interests, current affairs, design, economics, education, ethnic, film, gardening, gay/lesbian, government, health, history, horticulture, memoirs, money, multicultural, popular culture, politics, psychology, recreation, science, self-help, sex, sociology, software, theater, travel, young adult, music, creative nonfiction. **Considers these fiction areas:** action, adventure, crime, detective, ethnic, experimental, family saga, gay, glitz, hi-lo, historical, inspirational, literary, mainstream, multicultural, multimedia, mystery, police, short story collections, sports, supernatural, suspense, thriller, translation, war, westerns, women's, young adult.

HOW TO CONTACT Submit query, proposal package, outline, SASE. Accepts simultaneous submissions. Responds in 1 month to queries. Obtains most new clients through recommendations from others.

TERMS Agent receives 15% commission on domestic sales. Agent receives 20% commission on foreign sales. Charges clients for photocopying.

RECENT SALES *The Doll*, by Taylor Stevens; *Flora*, by Gail Godwin; *The Affairs of Others*, by Amy Loyd.

● HEACOCK HILL LITERARY AGENCY, INC.

West Coast Office, 1020 Hollywood Way, #439, Burbank CA 91505. (505)585-0111. **E-mail:** agent@heacockhill.com. **Website:** www.heacockhill.com. **Contact:** Catt LeBaigue or Tom Dark. Member of AAR. Other memberships include SCBWI.

○ Prior to becoming an agent, Ms. LeBaigue spent 18 years with Sony Pictures and Warner Bros.

MEMBER AGENTS Tom Dark (adult fiction, nonfiction); Catt LeBaigue (juvenile fiction, adult nonfiction including arts, crafts, anthropolgy, astronomy, nature studies, ecology, body/mind/spirit, humanities, self-help).

REPRESENTS Nonfiction, fiction. **Considers these nonfiction areas:** hiking.

HOW TO CONTACT E-mail queries only. No unsolicited manuscripts. No e-mail attachments. Responds in 1 week to queries. Obtains most new clients through recommendations from others, solicitations.

TERMS Offers written contract.

TIPS "Write an informative original e-query expressing your book idea, your qualifications, and short excerpts of the work. No unfinished work, please."

◐ HELEN HELLER AGENCY INC.

4-216 Heath Street W, Toronto Ontario M5P 1N7 Canada. (416)489-0396. **E-mail:** info@helenhelleragency.com. **Website:** www.helenhelleragency.com. **Contact:** Helen Heller. Represents 30+ clients.

○ Prior to her current position, Ms. Heller worked for Cassell & Co. (England), was an editor for Harlequin Books, a senior editor for Avon Books, and editor-in-chief for Fitzhenry & Whiteside.

MEMBER AGENTS Helen Heller, helen@helenhelleragency.com; Daphne Hart, daphne.hart@sympatico.ca; Sarah Heller, sarah@helenhelleragency.com.

REPRESENTS Nonfiction books, novels.

⚷ Actively seeking adult fiction and nonfiction (excluding children's literature, screenplays or genre fiction). Does not want to receive screenplays, poetry, or young children's picture books.

HOW TO CONTACT Submit synopsis, publishing history, author bio. Online submission form available at website. Responds in 6 weeks. Obtains most new clients through recommendations from others, solicitations.

RECENT SALES *Break on Through*, by Jill Murray (Doubleday Canada); *Womankind: Faces of Change Around the World*, by Donna Nebenzahl (Raincoast Books); *One Dead Indian: The Premier, The Police, and the Ipperwash Crisis*, by Peter Edwards (McClelland & Stewart); a full list of deals is available online.

TIPS "Whether you are an author searching for an agent, or whether an agent has approached you, it is in your best interest to first find out who the agent represents, what publishing houses has that agent sold to recently and what foreign sales have been made. You should be able to go to the bookstore, or search online and find the books the agent refers to. Many authors acknowledge their agents in the front or back or their books."

◑ RICHARD HENSHAW GROUP

E-mail: submissions@henshaw.com. **Website:** www.richardhenshawgroup.com. **Contact:** Rich Henshaw. Member of AAR. Other memberships include SinC, MWA, HWA, SFWA, RWA. 20% of clients are new/unpublished writers. Currently handles: nonfiction books 35%, novels 65%.

○ Prior to opening his agency, Mr. Henshaw served as an agent with Richard Curtis Associates, Inc.

REPRESENTS Nonfiction books, novels. **Considers these nonfiction areas:** animals, autobiography, biography, business, child guidance, cooking, current affairs, dance, economics, environment, foods, gay/lesbian, health, humor, investigative, money, music, New Age, parenting, popular culture, politics, psychology, science, self-help, sociology, sports, technology, true crime, women's issues, women's studies, electronic. **Considers these fiction areas:** action, adventure, crime, detective, ethnic, family saga, historical, humor, literary, mainstream, mystery, police, psychic, romance, satire, science fiction, sports, supernatural, suspense, thriller.

⚷ This agency specializes in thrillers, mysteries, science fiction, fantasy and horror.

HOW TO CONTACT Query with SASE. Accepts multiple submissions. Responds in 3 weeks to queries. Responds in 6 weeks to mss. Obtains most new clients through recommendations from others, solicitations, conferences.

TERMS Agent receives 15% commission on domestic sales. Agent receives 20% commission on foreign sales. No written contract. Charges clients for photocopying and book orders.

RECENT SALES *Though Not Dead*, by Dana Stabenow; *The Perfect Suspect*, by Margaret Coel; *City of Ruins*, by Kristine Kathryn Rusch; *A Dead Man's Tale*, by James D. Doss, *Wickedly Charming*, by Kristine Grayson, History of the World series by Susan Wise Bauer; *Notorious Pleasures*, by Elizabeth Hoyt.

TIPS "While we do not have any reason to believe that our submission guidelines will change in the near future, writers can find up-to-date submission policy information on our website. Always include a SASE with correct return postage."

HERMAN AGENCY

350 Central Park West, New York NY 10025. (212)749-4907. **E-mail:** Ronnie@HermanAgencyInc.com. **Website:** www.hermanagencyinc.com. Estab. 1999. Currently handles: books for young readers.

MEMBER AGENTS Ronnie Ann Herman, Jill Corcoran.

REPRESENTS Children's. **Considers these fiction areas:** picture books, middle grade and young adult, fiction and nonfiction for all ages.

HOW TO CONTACT Submit via e-mail to one of the agents listed above. See website for specific agents' specialties.

TIPS "Check our website to see if you belong with our agency."

THE JEFF HERMAN AGENCY, LLC

P.O. Box 1522, Stockbridge MA 01262. (413)298-0077. **Fax:** (413)298-8188. **E-mail:** jeff@jeffherman.com. **Website:** www.jeffherman.com. **Contact:** Jeffrey H. Herman. Represents 100 clients. 10% of clients are new/unpublished writers. Currently handles: nonfiction books 85%, scholarly books 5%, textbooks 5%.

Prior to opening his agency, Mr. Herman served as a public relations executive.

MEMBER AGENTS Deborah Levine, vice president (nonfiction book doctor); Jeff Herman.

REPRESENTS Nonfiction books. **Considers these nonfiction areas:** business, economics, government, health, history, how-to, law, medicine, politics, psychology, self-help, spirituality, technology, popular reference.

This agency specializes in adult nonfiction.

HOW TO CONTACT Query with SASE. Accepts simultaneous submissions.

TERMS Agent receives 15% commission on domestic sales. Offers written contract. Charges clients for copying and postage.

RECENT SALES *Days of Our Lives* book series; *H&R Block* book series. Sold 35 titles in the last year.

HIDDEN VALUE GROUP

1240 E. Ontario Ave., Ste. 102-148, Corona CA 92881. **E-mail:** bookquery@hiddenvaluegroup.com. **Website:** www.hiddenvaluegroup.com. **Contact:** Nancy Jernigan. Represents 55 clients. 10% of clients are new/unpublished writers.

MEMBER AGENTS Jeff Jernigan, jjernigan@hiddenvaluegroup.com (men's nonfiction, fiction, Bible studies/curriculum, marriage and family); Nancy Jernigan, njernigan@hiddenvaluegroup.com (nonfiction, women's issues, inspiration, marriage and family, fiction).

REPRESENTS Nonfiction books and adult fiction; no poetry. **Considers these nonfiction areas:** autobiography, biography, business, child guidance, economics, history, how-to, inspirational, juvenile nonfiction, language, literature, memoirs, money, parenting, psychology, religious, self-help, women's issues, women's studies. **Considers these fiction areas:** action, adventure, crime, detective, fantasy, frontier, inspirational, literary, police, religious, thriller, westerns, women's.

"The Hidden Value Group specializes in helping authors throughout their publishing career. We believe that every author has a special message to be heard and we specialize in getting that message out." Actively seeking established fiction authors, and authors who are focusing on women's issues. Does not want to receive poetry or short stories.

HOW TO CONTACT Query with SASE. Submit synopsis, 2 sample chapters, author bio, and marketing and speaking summary. Accepts queries to bookquery@hiddenvaluegroup.com. No fax queries. Responds in 1 month to queries. Responds in 1 month to mss. Obtains most new clients through recommendations from others, solicitations.

TERMS Agent receives 15% commission on domestic sales. Agent receives 15% commission on foreign sales. Offers written contract.

WRITERS CONFERENCES Glorieta Christian Writers' Conference; CLASS Publishing Conference.

JULIE A. HILL AND ASSOCIATES, LLC

12997 Caminto del Pasaje, #530, Del Mar CA 92014. (858)259-2595. **Fax:** (858)259-2777. **E-mail:** Hillagent@aol.com. **Website:** www.publishersmarketplace/members/hillagent. **Contact:** Julie Hill. Represents 50+ clients. 20% of clients are new/unpublished writers. Currently handles: nonfiction books 90%, story collections 5%, other 5% books that accompany films.

MEMBER AGENTS Julie Hill, agent and principal.

REPRESENTS Nonfiction books. **Considers these nonfiction areas:** biography, cooking, ethnic, health, history, how-to, language, memoirs, music, New Age, popular culture, psychology, religious, self-help, travel, women's issues.

☞ Currently interested in finding memoir from wives and adult children of drug lords, known criminals, and those in polygamist marriages. Currently developing a memoir from one of the largest Mexican drug cartels. Actively seeking travel, health, and media tie-ins. Does not want to receive horror, juvenile, sci-fi, thrillers or autobiographies of any kind.

HOW TO CONTACT Snail mail: Query with SASE. Submit outline/proposal, SASE. Accepts simultaneous submissions: Yes. Responds in 4-6 weeks to queries. E-submissions, please send to: HIllagent@aol.com. Accepts simultaneous submissions. Responds in 4-6 weeks to queries. Obtains most new clients through recommendations from other authors, editors, and agents.

RECENT SALES Bestselling *Publish This Book,* by Stephen Markley (reviewed by *PW, Huffington Post* and many others; *Cracking Up,* from the book *The Happy Neurotic,* by David Granirer, to GRBTV. Travel: multiple titles to Frommers (Wiley) for kids travel and theme parks guides, including *Walt Disney World for Dummies,* by Laura Lea Miller, Barnes and Noble travel bestsellers. Falcon (Globe Pequot) hiking guides: *Best Easy Day Hikes to Long Island,* and others by Susan Finch. *Insiders Guides, Off the Beaten Path, Best Day Trips* to multiple US cities by multiple authors, including New York City, Chicago, Seattle, Houston, Palm Beaches (Fla) and many more.

◑ FREDERICK HILL BONNIE NADELL, INC.

8899 Beverly Blvd., Suite 805, Los Angeles CA 90048. (310)860-9605. **Fax:** (310)860-9672. **E-mail:** queries.hillnadell@gmail.com. **Website:** www.hillnadell.com. Represents 100 clients.

MEMBER AGENTS Bonnie Nadell; Elise Proulx, associate.

REPRESENTS Nonfiction books, novels. **Considers these nonfiction areas:** biography, current affairs, environment, government, health, history, language, literature, medicine, popular culture, politics, science, technology, biography; government/politics, narrative. **Considers these fiction areas:** literary, mainstream.

HOW TO CONTACT Query with SASE. Keep your query to one page. Send via snail mail or email. Do not send the same query to multiple locations. Accepts simultaneous submissions.

TERMS Agent receives 15% commission on domestic sales. Agent receives 20% commission on foreign sales. Agent receives 15% commission on film sales. Charges clients for photocopying and foreign mailings.

RECENT SALES *Living the Sweet Life in Paris* by David Lebovitz (memoir); *Next Stop, Reloville: Inside America's New Rootless Professional Class* by Peter Kilborn.

BARBARA HOGENSON AGENCY

165 West End Ave., Suite 19-C, New York NY 10023. (212)874-8084. **Fax:** (212)362-3011. **E-mail:** bhogenson@aol.com. **Contact:** Barbara Hogenson; Lori Styler, contract manager. Member of AAR.

HOW TO CONTACT Query with SASE. Obtains most new clients through recommendations from other clients only.

TIPS "We do not specialize in mystery."

➕◑ THE HOLMES AGENCY

1942 Broadway, Suite 314, Boulder CO 80302. (720)443-8550. **E-mail:** kristina@holmesliterary.com. **Website:** www.holmesliterary.com. **Contact:** Kristina A. Holmes.

MEMBER AGENTS Kristina A. Holmes.

☞ Health and wellness, spirituality, psychology, relationships, women's issues, sex, science, nature, environmental issues, business, cookbooks, gift books, literary nonfiction, memoir.

HOW TO CONTACT Query and proposal via e-mail.

RECENT SALES *Virtual Freedom: How To Work With Virtual Assistants To Create More Time, Increase Your Productivity, And Build Your Dream Business*, by Chris Ducker (Benbella Books 2014); *Recipes For A Sacred Life: True Stories And A Few Miracles*, by Rivvy Neshama (Divine Arts, Fall 2013); *50 Ways To Say You're Awesome*, by Alexandra Franzen (Sourcebooks, Fall 2013); *The Cosmic View Of Albert Einstein: His Reflections On Humanity And The Universe*, by Editors Walt Martin And Magda Ott (Sterling, Fall 2013); *Go Green, Spend Less, Live Better: The Ultimate Guide To Saving The Planet, Saving Money, And Protecting Your Health*, by Crissy Trask (Skyhorse, Spring 2013); *Pinfluence: The Complete Guide To Marketing Your Business With Pinterest*, by Beth Hayden (John Wiley & Sons, Summer 2012); *Stillpower: Excellence with Ease in Sports—and Life*, by Garret Kramer (Beyond Words/Atria/Simon & Schuster, Summer 2012); *Kissed by a Fox: And Other Stories of Friendship in Nature*, by Priscilla Stuckey (Counterpoint Press, Fall 2012); *The Mother's Wisdom Deck*, by Niki Dewart and Elizabeth Marglin (Sterling Publishing, Spring 2012).

TIPS "With seven years of experience as a literary agent, I have had the privilege of working with many gifted and inspiring writers. Some of them are bestselling authors and well-known experts in their field, but what makes them truly special, from my perspective, is their deep passion for their work, and their commitment to guiding, educating, and inspiring people around the world. At The Holmes Agency, I'm looking for considered and intelligent writing on a variety of nonfiction subjects. I am seeking authors focused on inspiring and helping positively transform readers' lives. I am open to queries, including from first time authors. However, please be aware that I don't generally represent authors without a platform."

HOPKINS LITERARY ASSOCIATES

2117 Buffalo Rd., Suite 327, Rochester NY 14624-1507. (585)352-6268. **Contact:** Pam Hopkins. Member of AAR. Other memberships include RWA. Represents 30 clients. 5% of clients are new/unpublished writers. Currently handles: novels 100%.

REPRESENTS Novels. **Considers these fiction areas:** mostly women's genre romance, historical, contemporary, category, women's.

This agency specializes in women's fiction, particularly historical, contemporary, and category romance, as well as mainstream work.

HOW TO CONTACT Regular mail with synopsis, 3 sample chapters, SASE. Accepts simultaneous submissions. Responds in 2 weeks to queries. Responds in 1 month to mss. Obtains most new clients through recommendations from others, solicitations, conferences.

TERMS Agent receives 15% commission on domestic sales. Agent receives 20% commission on foreign sales. No written contract.

RECENT SALES Sold 50 titles in the last year. *The Wilting Bloom Series* by Madeline Hunter (Berkley); *The Dead Travel Fast*, by Deanna Raybourn; *Baggage Claim*, by Tanya Michna (NAL).

WRITERS CONFERENCES RWA National Conference.

HORNFISCHER LITERARY MANAGEMENT

P.O. Box 50544, Austin TX 78763. **E-mail:** queries@ hornfischerlit.com. **Website:** www.hornfischerlit. com. **Contact:** James D. Hornfischer, president. Represents 45 clients. 10% of clients are new/unpublished writers. Currently handles: nonfiction books 100%.

Prior to opening his agency, Mr. Hornfischer held editorial positions at HarperCollins and McGraw-Hill. "My New York editorial background is useful in this regard. In 17 years as an agent, I've handled 12 *New York Times* nonfiction bestsellers, including 3 No. 1's."

REPRESENTS Nonfiction books. **Considers these nonfiction areas:** anthropology, archeology, autobiography, biography, business, child guidance, current affairs, economics, environment, government, health, history, how-to, humor, inspirational, investigative, law, medicine, memoirs, military, money, multicultural, parenting, popular culture, politics, psychology, religious, satire, science, self-help, sociology, sports, technology, true crime, war.

Actively seeking "the best work of terrific writers." Does not want poetry or genre fiction.

HOW TO CONTACT E-mail queries only. Submit proposal package, outline, 2 sample chapters. Accepts simultaneous submissions. Responds in 5-6 weeks to submissions. Obtains most new clients through referrals from clients, reading books and magazines, pursuing ideas with New York editors.

TERMS Agent receives 15% commission on domestic sales. Agent receives 25% commission on foreign sales. Offers written contract. Reasonable expenses deducted from proceeds after book is sold.

RECENT SALES *The Next 100 Years*, by George Friedman (Doubleday); *Traitor to His Class* by H. W. Brands (Doubleday); *Scent of the Missing,* by Susannah Charleson (Houghton Mifflin Harcourt); *Red November* by W. Craig Reed (Morrow); and *Abigail Adams,* by Woody Holton (Free Press). See agency website for more sales information.

TIPS "When you query agents and send out proposals, present yourself as someone who's in command of his material and comfortable in his own skin. Too many writers have a palpable sense of anxiety and insecurity. Take a deep breath and realize that — if you're good — someone in the publishing world will want you."

HSG AGENCY

287 Spring St., New York NY 10013. (646)442-5770. **E-mail:** channigan@hsagency.com; jsalky@hsagency.com; jgetzler@hsagency.com. **Website:** http://hsgagency.com. **Contact:** Carrie Hannigan; Jesseca Salky; Josh Getzler. Estab. 2011.

○ Prior to opening HSG Agency, Ms. Hannigan, Ms. Salky. and Mr. Getzler were agents at Russell & Volkening.

MEMBER AGENTS Carrie Hannigan, Jesseca Salky, Josh Getzler.

REPRESENTS Considers these nonfiction areas: business, child guidance, cooking, current affairs, education, foods, memoirs, politics, psychology, science, travel, women's issues. **Considers these fiction areas:** crime, historical, humor, literary, mystery, thriller, young adult.

○━ Ms. Hannigan is actively seeking adult books, both fiction and nonfiction. Some nonfiction areas she is currently interested in are social sciences, food, travel, women and children's issues, photography, and almost any kind of immersion journalism. Ms. Salky is actively seeking literary and commercial fiction that appeals to women and men; "all types of nonfiction, with a particular interest in memoir and narrative nonfiction in the areas of science, pop-psychology, politics, current affairs, business, education, food, and any other topic that

is the vehicle for a great story." Mr. Getzler is actively seeking nonfiction, crime-related fiction (mystery, thriller, creepy), adult, and YA/middle-grade books. He is particularly into foreign and historical thrillers and mysteries. No screenplays, romance fiction, science fiction, or religious fiction.

HOW TO CONTACT Prefers electronic submission. Will accept hard copy queries by mail with SASE, if necessary. Send query letter, first 5 pages of ms within e-mail to appropriate agent. Picture books: include entire ms. Responds in 4-6 weeks.

RECENT SALES *The Beginner's Goodbye*, by Anne Tyler (Knopf); *Rescue Matters!*, by Sheila Webster Boneham (Alpine); *All the News Unfit to Print*, by Eric Burns (Wiley); *Punching Out*, by Paul Clemens (Anchor).

ANDREA HURST & ASSOCIATES

P.O. Box 1467, Coupeville WA 98239. **E-mail:** andrea@andreahurst.com. **Website:** www.andreahurst.com. **Contact:** Andrea Hurst. Represents 100+ clients. 50% of clients are new/unpublished writers. Currently handles: nonfiction books 50%, novels 50%.

○ Prior to becoming an agent, Ms. Hurst was an acquisitions editor as well as a freelance editor and published writer.

MEMBER AGENTS Andrea Hurst, andrea@andreahurst.com (adult fiction, women's fiction, nonfiction—including personal growth, health and wellness, science, business, parenting, relationships, women's issues, animals, spirituality, women's issues, metaphysical, psychological, cookbooks, and self-help). Amberley Finnarelli.

REPRESENTS Nonfiction, novels, juvenile books. **Considers these fiction areas:** inspirational, juvenile, literary, mainstream, psychic, religious, romance, supernatural, thriller, women's, young adult.

○━ "We work directly with our signed authors to help them polish their work and their platform for optimum marketability. Our staff is always available to answer phone calls and e-mails from our authors and we stay with a project until we have exhausted all publishing avenues." Actively seeking "well written nonfiction by authors with a strong platform; superbly crafted fiction with depth that touches the mind and heart and all of our listed subjects." Does not want to receive sci-fi, horror, Western, poetry, or screenplays.

HOW TO CONTACT Email query with SASE. Submit outline/proposal, synopsis, 2 sample chapters, author bio. Query a specific agent after reviewing website. Use (agentfirstname)@andreahurst.com. Accepts simultaneous submissions. Obtains most new clients through recommendations from others, solicitations, conferences.

TERMS Agent receives 15% commission on domestic sales. Agent receives 20% commission on foreign sales. Offers written contract, binding for 6 to 12 months; 30-day notice must be given to terminate contract. This agency charges for postage. No reading fees.

RECENT SALES *No Buddy Left Behind,* by Terrir Crisp and Cindy Hurn, Lyons Press; *A Year of Miracles* Dr. Bernie Siegel, NWL; *Selling Your Crafts on Etsy* (St. Martin's); *The Underground Detective Agency* (Kensington); *Alaskan Seafood Cookbook* (Globe Pequot); *Faith, Hope and Healing,* by Dr. Bernie Siegel (Rodale); *Code Name: Polar Ice,* by Jean-Michel Cousteau and James Fraioli (Gibbs Smith); *How to Host a Killer Party,* by Penny Warner (Berkley/Penguin).

WRITERS CONFERENCES San Francisco Writers' Conference; Willamette Writers' Conference; PNWA; Whidbey Island Writers Conference.

TIPS "Do your homework and submit a professional package. Get to know the agent you are submitting to by researching their website or meeting them at a conference. Perfect your craft: Write well and edit ruthlessly over and over again before submitting to an agent. Be realistic: Understand that publishing is a business and be prepared to prove why your book is marketable and how you will market it on your own. Be persistent! Andrea Hurst is no longer accepting unsolicited query letters. Unless you have been referred by one of our authors, an agent or publisher, please check our website for another appropriate agent. www.andreahurst.com."

INKLINGS LITERARY

3419 Virginia Beach Blvd. #C-12, Virginia Beach, VA 23452. (757)340.1860. **E-mail:** michelle@inklingsliterary.com; jamie@inklingsliterary.com. **Website:** www.inklingsrliterary.com. Estab. 2012.

Ms. Johnson was formerly an agent at the Corvisiero Literary Agency. Ms. Bail was formerly an agent at Andrea Hurst & Associates.

MEMBER AGENTS Michelle Johnson (in adult, new adult and YA fiction, Michelle looks for contemporary, suspense, thriller, mystery, horror, fantasy, and also loves paranormal and supernatural elements within those genres); Dr. Jamie Brodnar Drowley (in adult, new adult and young adult fiction, Jamie is seeking fantasy, mystery, romance, paranormal, historical, contemporary, horror, light sci-fi and thrillers; she also reps middle grade); Margaret Bail (adult fiction only. Specifically, she seeks romance, science fiction, thrillers, action/adventure, historical fiction, Western, fantasy—think Song of Fire and Ice or Dark Tower, NOT Lord of the Rings or Chronicles of Narnia). .

REPRESENTS Novels, juvenile books.

HOW TO CONTACT Each agent's openness to queries varies from season to season. Check the website. When open to submissions, they ask for a query, first five pages, and a one page synopsis to query@inklings literary.com

INKWELL MANAGEMENT, LLC

521 Fifth Ave., 26th Floor, New York NY 10175. (212)922-3500. **Fax:** (212)922-0535. **E-mail:** info@inkwellmanagement.com. **Website:** www.inkwell management.com. Represents 500 clients. Currently handles: nonfiction books 60%, novels 40%.

MEMBER AGENTS Michael V. Carlisle; Richard Pine; Kimberly Witherspoon; George Lucas; Catherine Drayton; Lizz Blaise; David Forrer; Alexis Hurley; Nat Jacks; Lyndsey Blessing; Allison Hunter; Jacqueline Murphy; Charlie Olsen; David Hale Smith; Hannah Schwartz; Eliza Rothstein; Lauren Smythe; Monika Woods.

REPRESENTS Nonfiction books, novels.

HOW TO CONTACT Query with SASE or via e-mail to submissions@inkwellmanagement.com. Obtains most new clients through recommendations from others.

TERMS Agent receives 15% commission on domestic sales. Agent receives 20% commission on foreign sales. Offers written contract.

TIPS "We will not read mss before receiving a letter of inquiry."

ICM PARTNERS (INTERNATIONAL CREATIVE MANAGEMENT)

730 Fifth Ave., New York NY 10019. (212)556-5600. **Website:** www.icmtalent.com. **Contact:** Literary Department. 10250 Constellation Blvd. Los Angeles, CA 90067 t 310.550.4000; 3rd Floor, Marlborough House,

10 Earlham Street, London, WC2H 9LN, England. +44.0.20.7836.8564 Member of AAR. Signatory of WGA.

MEMBER AGENTS Lisa Bankoff, lbankoff@icmtalent.com (fiction interests include: literary fiction, family saga, historical fiction, offbeat/quirky; nonfiction interests include: history, biography, memoirs, narrative); Patrick Herold, pherold@icmtalent.com; Jennifer Joel, jjoel@icmtalent.com (fiction interests include: literary fiction, commercial fiction, historical fiction, thrillers/suspense; nonfiction interests include: history, sports, art, adventure/true story, pop culture); Esther Newberg; Sloan Harris; Amanda Binky Urban; Heather Schroder; Kristine Dahl; Andrea Barzvi, abarzvi@icmtalent.com (fiction interests include: chick lit, commercial fiction, women's fiction, thrillers/suspense; nonfiction interests include: sports, celebrity, self-help, dating/relationships, women's issues, pop culture, health and fitness); Tina Dubois Wexler, twexler@icmtalent.com (literary fiction, chick lit, young adult, middle grade, memoir, narrative nonfiction); Kate Lee, klee@icmtalent.com (mystery, commercial fiction, short stories, memoir, dating/relationships, pop culture, humor, journalism).

REPRESENTS Nonfiction books, novels.

☞ We do not accept unsolicited submissions.

HOW TO CONTACT Query with SASE. Send queries via snail mail and include an SASE. Target a specific agent. Obtains most new clients through recommendations from others.

TERMS Agent receives 15% commission on domestic sales. Agent receives 20% commission on foreign sales.

● **INTERNATIONAL TRANSACTIONS, INC.**

P.O. Box 97, Gila NM 88038-0097. (845)373-9696. **Fax:** (480)393-5162. **E-mail:** submissions@intltrans.com; submission-fiction@intltrans.com; submission-nonfiction@intltrans.com. **Website:** www.intltrans.com. **Contact:** Peter Riva. Represents 40+ clients. 10% of clients are new/unpublished writers. Currently handles: nonfiction books 60%, novels 25%, story collections 5%, juvenile books 5%, scholarly books 5%.

MEMBER AGENTS Peter Riva (nonfiction, fiction, illustrated; television and movie rights placement); Sandra Riva (fiction, juvenile, biographies); JoAnn Collins (fiction, women's fiction, medical fiction).

REPRESENTS Nonfiction books, novels, short story collections, juvenile, scholarly, illustrated books, anthologies. **Considers these nonfiction areas:** anthropology, archeology, architecture, art, autobiography, biography, computers, cooking, cultural interests, current affairs, diet/nutrition, design, ethnic, foods, gay/lesbian, government, health, history, humor, investigative, language, law, literature, medicine, memoirs, military, music, photography, politics, satire, science, sports, translation, true crime, war, women's issues, women's studies. **Considers these fiction areas:** action, adventure, crime, detective, erotica, experimental, family saga, feminist, gay, historical, humor, lesbian, literary, mainstream, mystery, police, satire, spiritual, sports, suspense, thriller, women's, young adult, chick lit.

☞ "We specialize in large and small projects, helping qualified authors perfect material for publication." Actively seeking intelligent, well-written innovative material that breaks new ground. Does not want to receive material influenced by TV (too much dialogue); a rehash of previous successful novels' themes, or poorly prepared material.

HOW TO CONTACT First, e-query with an outline or synopsis. E-queries only! Responds in 3 weeks to queries. Responds in 5 weeks to mss. Obtains most new clients through recommendations from others, solicitations.

TERMS Agent receives 15% (25% on illustrated books) commission on domestic sales. Agent receives 20% commission on foreign sales. Offers written contract; 120-day notice must be given to terminate contract.

TIPS 'Book'—a published work of literature. That last word is the key. Not a string of words, not a book of (TV or film) 'scenes,' and never a stream of consciousness unfathomable by anyone outside of the writer's coterie. A writer should only begin to get 'interested in getting an agent' if the work is polished, literate and ready to be presented to a publishing house. Anything less is either asking for a quick rejection or is a thinly disguised plea for creative assistance—which is often given but never fiscally sound for the agents involved. Writers, even published authors, have difficulty in being objective about their own work. Friends and family are of no assistance in that process either. Writers should attempt to get their work read by the most unlikely and stern critic as part of the editing process, months before any agent is approached. In another matter: the economics of our job have changed as well. As the publishing world goes through the transition

NEW AGENT SPOTLIGHT

YASSINE BELKACEMI
(DYSTEL & GODERICH LITERARY MANAGEMENT)

Dystel.com

ABOUT YASSINE: Yassine Belkacemi is an agent at Dystel & Goderich Literary Management. He grew up in Glasgow, Scotland, and studied American History and Literature at the University of Edinburgh before crossing the Atlantic to complete an M.A. in American Studies at Columbia University. In between studying and exploring New York, Yassine began interning at Dystel & Goderich in 2011 and soon became increasingly fascinated with the dynamic world of publishing.

HE IS SEEKING: Any literary fiction that has a transatlantic setting or deals with themes of immigration. He has a deep interest in fiction that is set in the contemporary American West, and is also on the lookout for historical and hard-boiled/noir fiction. On the nonfiction side, he is enthusiastic about projects that examine cultural politics, nationalism, pop culture and mass media.

HOW TO CONTACT: Query him at ybelkacemi@dystel.com.

to e-books (much as the music industry went through the change to downloadable music)—a transition we expect to see at 95% within 10 years—everyone is nervous and wants 'assured bestsellers' from which to eke out a living until they know what the new e-world will bring. This makes the sales rate and, especially, the advance royalty rates, plummet. Hence, our ability to take risks and take on new clients' work is increasingly perilous financially for us and all agents."

JABBERWOCKY LITERARY AGENCY

24-16 Queens Plaza S, Suite 505, Long Island City NY 11101. (718)392-5985. **Website:** www.awfulagent.com. **Contact:** Joshua Bilmes. Other memberships include SFWA. Represents 40 clients. 15% of clients are new/unpublished writers. Currently handles: nonfiction books 15%, novels 75%, scholarly books 5%, other 5% other.
MEMBER AGENTS (Check the agency website as different agents at this agency are closed to queries at different times) Joshua Bilmes; Eddie Schneider, Jessie Cammack, Lisa Rodgers.
REPRESENTS Novels. **Considers these nonfiction areas:** autobiography, biography, business, cooking, current affairs, diet/nutrition, economics, film, foods, gay/lesbian, government, health, history, humor, language, law, literature, medicine, money, popular culture, politics, satire, science, sociology, sports, theater, war, women's issues, women's studies, young adult. **Considers these fiction areas:** action, adventure, contemporary issues, crime, detective, ethnic, family saga, fantasy, gay, glitz, historical, horror, humor, lesbian, literary, mainstream, police, psychic, regional, satire, science fiction, sports, supernatural, thriller.
This agency represents quite a lot of genre fiction and is actively seeking to increase the amount of nonfiction projects. It does not handle children's or picture books. Book-length material only—no poetry, articles, or short fiction.

HOW TO CONTACT "We are currently open to un-solicited queries. No e-mail, phone, or fax queries, please. Query with SASE. Please check our website, as there may be times during the year when we are not accepting queries. Query letter only; no manu-script material unless requested." Accepts simulta-neous submissions. Responds in 3 weeks to queries. Obtains most new clients through solicitations, rec-ommendation by current clients.

TERMS Agent receives 15% commission on domestic sales. Agent receives 20% commission on foreign sales. Offers written contract, binding for 1 year. Charges clients for book purchases, photocopying, interna-tional book/ms mailing.

RECENT SALES Sold 30 US and 100 foreign titles in the last year. *Dead in the Family*, by Charlaine Harris; *The Way of Kings*, by Brandon Sanderson; *The Desert Spear*, by Peter V. Brett; *Oath of Fealty*, by Elizabeth Moon. Other clients include Tanya Huff, Simon Green, Jack Campbell, Kat Richardson, and Jon Sprunk.

TIPS "In approaching with a query, the most impor-tant things to us are your credits and your biographi-cal background to the extent it's relevant to your work. I (and most agents) will ignore the adjectives you may choose to describe your own work."

JAMES PETER ASSOCIATES, INC.

P.O. Box 358, New Canaan CT 06840. (203)972-1070. **E-mail:** gene_brissie@msn.com. **Website:** www.jamespeterassociates.com. **Contact:** Gene Brissie. Represents 75 individual and 6 corporate clients. 15% of clients are new/unpublished writers. Current-ly handles: nonfiction books 100%.

REPRESENTS Nonfiction books. **Considers these nonfiction areas:** anthropology, archeology, architec-ture, art, biography, business, current affairs, dance, design, ethnic, film, gay/lesbian, government, health, history, language, literature, medicine, military, money, music, popular culture, psychology, self-help, theater, travel, war, women's issues, women's studies, memoirs (political, business).

"We are especially interested in general, trade, and reference nonfiction." Does not want to receive children's/young adult books, poetry, or fiction.

HOW TO CONTACT Submit proposal package, out-line, SASE. Prefers to read materials exclusively. Re-sponds in 1 month to queries. Obtains most new cli-ents through recommendations from others, solicita-tions, contact with people who are doing interesting things.

TERMS Agent receives 15% commission on domestic sales. Agent receives 20% commission on foreign sales. Offers written contract.

J DE S ASSOCIATES, INC.

9 Shagbark Road, Wilson Point, South Norwalk CT 06854. (203)838-7571. **Website:** www.jdeassociates.com. **Contact:** Jacques de Spoelberch. Represents 50 clients. Currently handles: nonfiction books 50%, novels 50%.

Prior to opening his agency, Mr. de Spoelberch was an editor with Houghton Mifflin.

REPRESENTS Nonfiction books, novels. **Considers these nonfiction areas:** biography, business, cultur-al interests, current affairs, economics, ethnic, gov-ernment, health, history, law, medicine, metaphysics, military, New Age, personal improvement, politics, self-help, sociology, sports, translation. **Considers these fiction areas:** crime, detective, frontier, histor-ical, juvenile, literary, mainstream, mystery, New Age, police, suspense, westerns, young adult.

HOW TO CONTACT Query with SASE. "Kindly do not include sample proposals or other materials un-less specifically requested to do so." Responds in 2 months to queries. Obtains most new clients through recommendations from authors and other clients.

TERMS Agent receives 15% commission on domestic sales. Agent receives 20% commission on foreign sales. Charges clients for foreign postage and photocopying.

THE CAROLYN JENKS AGENCY

30 Cambridge Park Dr., #3150, Cambridge MA 02140. (617)354-5099. **E-mail:** queries@carolynjenksagency.com. **Website:** www.carolynjenksagency.com. **Con-tact:** Carolyn Jenks. Estab. 1987. Signatory of WGA Represents 30 clients. 50% of clients are new/unpub-lished writers. Currently handles: 10% nonfiction books; 25% juvenile books; 3% short story collec-tions; 40% novels; 10% movie scripts; 2% poetry; 5% TV scripts.

MEMBER AGENTS "See agency website for current member preferences.".

REPRESENTS **Considers these nonfiction areas:** ar-chitecture, art, autobiography, biography, business, cultural interests, current affairs, design, education, ethnic, gay/lesbian, government, history, juvenile nonfiction, language, law, literature, memoirs, metaphysics, military, money, music, New Age, religious, science, technology, translation, true crime, women's issues, women's studies. **Considers these fiction areas:** action, adventure, ethnic, experimental, family saga, fantasy, feminist, frontier, gay, historical, horror, humor, inspirational, juvenile, lesbian, literary, mainstream, mystery, psychic, regional, religious, science fiction, supernatural, thriller, westerns, women's, young adult. **Considers these script areas:** autobiography, biography, contemporary issues, ethnic, experimental, family saga, fantasy, feminist, frontier, gay, historical, horror, inspirational, lesbian, mainstream, mystery, psychic, religious, romantic comedy, romantic drama, science fiction, supernatural, suspense, thriller, western.

⚷━ Seeking literary/commercial science fiction, blockbuster novels, quality American plays, cinematic writing (novels that lend themselves to cinematic adaptation), character-driven novels. Does not want to receive children's picture books, how-to books, cookbooks, manga, erotica, humor books.

HOW TO CONTACT Submit query letter with bio. Responds in 1-5 days to queries; 1 week to 50 pages of ms; 3 weeks to full ms. Obtains new clients by recommendations from others, queries/submissions, agency outreach.

TERMS 15% commission on domestic; 15% commission on foreign (unless the agency handles the foreign sales, in which case a 15% fee is added to the coagent from said foreign country); 10% commission for TV or the amount designated by the WGA. Offers written contract, 1-3 years depending on the project. Requires 60 day notice before terminating contract.

RECENT SALES *The Red Tent*, by Anita Diamant (HBO); *The Dagger X*, by Brian Eames (Simon and Schuster); *The Sinners and the Sea*, by Rebecca Kanner (Howard Books/Simon and Schuster); *Apple Unplugged*, by Erin Kelly (Harper Collins Greenwillow).

WRITERS CONFERENCES Book Expo America (NYC); London Book Fair (London, UK).

TIPS "Do not make cold calls to the agency. E-mail contact only. Do not query for more than one property at a time."

◐ **JET LITERARY ASSOCIATES**
941 Calle Mejia, #507, Santa Fe NM 87501. (505)780-0721. **E-mail:** etp@jetliterary.com. **Website:** www.jetliterary.com. **Contact:** Liz Trupin-Pulli. Represents 75 clients. 35% of clients are new/unpublished writers.

MEMBER AGENTS Liz Trupin-Pulli (adult and YA fiction/nonfiction; romance, mysteries, parenting); Jim Trupin (adult fiction/nonfiction, military history, pop culture); Jessica Trupin, associate agent based in Seattle (adult fiction and nonfiction, children's and young adult, memoir, pop culture).

REPRESENTS Nonfiction books, novels, short story collections. **Considers these nonfiction areas:** autobiography, biography, business, child guidance, cultural interests, current affairs, economics, ethnic, gay/lesbian, government, humor, investigative, law, memoirs, military, parenting, popular culture, politics, satire, sports, true crime, war, women's issues, women's studies. **Considers these fiction areas:** action, adventure, crime, detective, erotica, ethnic, gay, glitz, historical, humor, lesbian, literary, mainstream, mystery, police, romance, suspense, thriller, women's, young adult.

⚷━ "JET was founded in New York in 1975, so we bring a wealth of knowledge and contacts, as well as quite a bit of expertise to our representation of writers." Actively seeking women's fiction, mysteries and narrative nonfiction. JET represents the full range of adult and YA fiction and nonfiction, including humor and cookbooks. Does not want to receive sci-fi, fantasy, horror, poetry, children's or religious.

HOW TO CONTACT An e-query only is accepted. Responds in 1 week to queries. Responds in 8 weeks to mss. Obtains most new clients through recommendations from others, solicitations, conferences.

TERMS Agent receives 15% commission on domestic sales. Agent receives 10% commission on foreign sales. Offers written contract, binding for 3 years. This agency charges for reimbursement of mailing and any photocopying.

WRITERS CONFERENCES Women Writing the West; Southwest Writers Conference; Florida Writers Association Conference.

TIPS Do not write cute queries—stick to a straightforward message that includes the title and what your book is about, why you are suited to write this particular book, and what you have written in the past (if anything), along with a bit of a bio.

●◎ KELLER MEDIA INC.

578 Washington Blvd., No. 745, Marina del Ray CA 90292. (800)278-8706. **E-mail:** query@KellerMedia.com. **Website:** www.KellerMedia.com. **Contact:** Wendy Keller, senior agent; Elise Howard, editorial assistant; Laura Rensing, editorial assistant. Estab. 1989. Member of the National Speakers Association. 25% of clients are new/unpublished writers. Currently handles: nonfiction books 100%.

○ Prior to becoming an agent, Ms. Keller was an award-winning journalist and worked for PR Newswire.

REPRESENTS Nonfiction. **Considers these nonfiction areas:** business, current affairs, finance, health, history, nature, politics, psychology, science, self-help, sociology, spirituality, women's issues.

⌐ "We focus a great deal of attention on authors who want to also become paid professional speakers, and current speakers who want to become authors. All of our authors are highly credible experts, who have or want a significant platform in media, academia, politics, paid professional speaking, syndicated columns, or regular appearances on radio/TV." Does not want (and "absolutely will not respond to) fiction, scripts, teleplays, poetry, juvenile, anything Christian, picture books, illustrated books, first-person stories of mental or physical illness, wrongful incarceration, abduction by aliens, books channeled by aliens, demons, or dead celebrities (I wish I was kidding!)."

HOW TO CONTACT "To query, just go to www.KellerMedia.com/query and fill in the simple form; it takes 1 minute or less. You'll get a fast, courteous response. Please do not mail us anything unless requested to do so by a staff member." Accepts simultaneous submissions. Responds in 7 days. Obtains most new clients through referrals.

TERMS Agent receives 15% commission on domestic sales. Agent receives 20% commission on foreign, dramatic, sponsorship, appearance fees, audio, and merchandising deals. "30% on speaking engagements we book for the author."

TIPS "Don't send a query to any agent unless you're certain they handle the type of book you're writing. 90% of all rejections happen because what you offered us doesn't fit our established, advertised, printed, touted and shouted guidelines. Be organized! Have your proposal in order before you query. Never

make apologies for 'bad writing' or sloppy content. Please just get it right before you waste your 1 shot with us. Have something new, different or interesting to say and be ready to dedicate your whole heart to marketing it. Marketing is everything."

◎ NATASHA KERN LITERARY AGENCY

P.O. Box 1069, White Salmon WA 98672. (509)493-3803. **E-mail:** agent@natashakern.com. **Website:** www.natashakern.com. **Contact:** Natasha Kern. Other memberships include RWA, MWA, SinC, The Authors Guild, and American Society of Journalists and Authors

○ Prior to opening her agency, Ms. Kern worked as an editor and publicist for Simon & Schuster, Bantam, and Ballantine. This agency has sold more than 700 books.

MEMBER AGENTS Natasha Kern.

REPRESENTS Considers these nonfiction areas: animals, child guidance, cultural interests, current affairs, environment, ethnic, gardening, health, inspirational, medicine, metaphysics, New Age, parenting, popular culture, psychology, religious, self-help, spirituality, women's issues, women's studies, investigative journalism. **Considers these fiction areas:** commercial, historical, inspirational, mainstream, multicultural, mystery, religious, romance, suspense, thriller, women's.

⌐ "This agency specializes in commercial fiction and nonfiction for adults. We are a full-service agency." Historical novels from any country or time period; contemporary fiction including novels with romance or suspense elements; and multi-cultural fiction. We are also seeking inspirational fiction in a broad range of genres including: suspense and mysteries, historicals, romance, and contemporary novels. Does not represent horror, true crime, erotica, children's books, short stories or novellas, poetry, screenplays, technical, photography or art/craft books, cookbooks, travel, or sports books.

HOW TO CONTACT See submission instructions online. Send query to queries@natashakern.com. Please include the word "QUERY" in the subject line. "We do not accept queries by snail mail or phone." Accepts simultaneous submissions. Responds in 3 weeks to queries.

TERMS Agent receives 15% commission on domestic sales. Agent receives 20% commission on foreign sales. Agent receives 15% commission on film sales.

RECENT SALES Sold 43 titles in the last year. *China Dolls*, by Michelle Yu and Blossom Kan (St. Martin's); *Bastard Tongues*, by Derek Bickerton (Farrar Strauss); *Bone Rattler*, by Eliot Pattison; *Wicked Pleasure*, by Nina Bangs (Berkley); *Inviting God In*, by David Aaron (Shambhala); *Unlawful Contact*, by Pamela Clare (Berkley); *Dead End Dating*, by Kimberly Raye (Ballantine); *A Scent of Roses*, by Nikki Arana (Baker Book House); *The Sexiest Man Alive*, by Diana Holquist (Warner Books).

WRITERS CONFERENCES RWA National Conference; MWA National Conference; ACFW Conference; and many regional conferences.

TIPS "Your chances of being accepted for representation will be greatly enhanced by going to our website first. Our idea of a dream client is someone who participates in a mutually respectful business relationship, is clear about needs and goals, and communicates about career planning. If we know what you need and want, we can help you achieve it. A dream client has a storytelling gift, a commitment to a writing career, a desire to learn and grow, and a passion for excellence. We want clients who are expressing their own unique voice and truly have something of their own to communicate. This client understands that many people have to work together for a book to succeed and that everything in publishing takes far longer than one imagines. Trust and communication are truly essential."

● VIRGINIA KIDD AGENCY, INC.

538 E. Harford St., P.O. Box 278, Milford PA 18337. (570)296-6205. **Fax:** (570)296-7266. **Website:** www. vk-agency.com. Other memberships include SFWA, SFRA. Represents 80 clients.

MEMBER AGENTS Christine Cohen.

REPRESENTS Novels. **Considers these fiction areas:** fantasy, historical, mainstream, mystery, science fiction, suspense, women's, speculative.

8—π This agency specializes in science fiction and fantasy.

HOW TO CONTACT *This agency is not accepting queries from unpublished authors at this time.* Submit synopsis (1-3 pages), cover letter, first chapter, SASE. Snail mail queries only. Responds in 6 weeks to queries.

TERMS Agent receives 15% commission on domestic sales. Agent receives 20-25% commission on foreign sales. Agent receives 20% commission on film sales. Offers written contract; 2-month notice must be given to terminate contract. Charges clients occasionally for extraordinary expenses.

RECENT SALES *Sagramanda*, by Alan Dean Foster (Pyr); *Incredible Good Fortune*, by Ursula K. Le Guin (Shambhala); *The Wizard and Soldier of Sidon*, by Gene Wolfe (Tor); *Voices and Powers*, by Ursula K. Le Guin (Harcourt); *Galileo's Children*, by Gardner Dozois (Pyr); *The Light Years Beneath My Feet* and *Running From the Deity*, by Alan Dean Foster (Del Ray); *Chasing Fire*, by Michelle Welch. Other clients include Eleanor Arnason, Ted Chiang, Jack Skillingstead, Daryl Gregory, Patricia Briggs, and the estates for James Tiptree, Jr., Murray Leinster, E.E. "Doc" Smith, R.A. Lafferty.

TIPS "If you have a completed novel that is of extraordinary quality, please send us a query."

◉ KIRCHOFF/WOHLBERG, INC.

897 Boston Post Rd., Madison CT 06443. (203)245-7308. **Fax:** (203)245-3218. **E-mail:** rzollshan@kirchoffwohlberg.com. **Website:** www.kirchoffwohlberg.com. **Contact:** Ronald Zollshan. Memberships include SCBWI, Society of Illustrators, SPAR, Bookbuilders of Boston, New York Bookbinders' Guild, AIGA.

○ Kirchoff/Wohlberg has been in business for more than 35 years.

8—π This agency specializes in juvenile fiction and nonfiction through young adult.

HOW TO CONTACT "Submit by mail to address above. We welcome the submission of mss from first-time or established children's book authors. Please enclose an SASE, but note that while we endeavor to read all submissions, we cannot guarantee a reply or their return." Accepts simultaneous submissions.

TERMS Offers written contract, binding for at least 1 year. Agent receives standard commission, depending upon whether it is an author only, illustrator only, or an author/illustrator.

◑ HARVEY KLINGER, INC.

300 W. 55th St., Suite 11V, New York NY 10019. (212)581-7068. **E-mail:** queries@harveyklinger.com. **Website:** www.harveyklinger.com. **Contact:** Harvey Klinger. Member of AAR. Represents 100 clients.

25% of clients are new/unpublished writers. Currently handles: nonfiction books 50%, novels 50%.

MEMBER AGENTS David Dunton (popular culture, music-related books, literary fiction, young adult, fiction, and memoirs); Sara Crowe (children's and young adult authors, adult fiction and nonfiction, foreign rights sales); Andrea Somberg (literary fiction, commercial fiction, romance, sci-fi/fantasy, mysteries/thrillers, young adult, middle grade, quality narrative nonfiction, popular culture, how-to, self-help, humor, interior design, cookbooks, health/fitness).

REPRESENTS Nonfiction books, novels. **Considers these nonfiction areas:** autobiography, biography, cooking, diet/nutrition, foods, health, investigative, medicine, psychology, science, self-help, spirituality, sports, technology, true crime, women's issues, women's studies. **Considers these fiction areas:** action, adventure, crime, detective, family saga, glitz, literary, mainstream, mystery, police, suspense, thriller.

⊶ This agency specializes in big, mainstream, contemporary fiction and nonfiction.

HOW TO CONTACT Use online e-mail submission form, or query with SASE. No phone or fax queries. Don't send unsolicited manuscripts or e-mail attachments. Responds in 2 months to queries and mss. Obtains most new clients through recommendations from others.

TERMS Agent receives 15% commission on domestic sales. Agent receives 25% commission on foreign sales. Offers written contract. Charges for photocopying mss and overseas postage for mss.

RECENT SALES *Woman of a Thousand Secrets*, by Barbara Wood; *I Am Not a Serial Killer*, by Dan Wells; untitled memoir, by Bob Mould; *Children of the Mist*; by Paula Quinn; *Tutored*, by Allison Whittenberg; *Will You Take Me As I Am*, by Michelle Mercer. Other clients include: George Taber, Terry Kay, Scott Mebus, Jacqueline Kolosov, Jonathan Maberry, Tara Altebrando, Alex McAuley, Eva Nagorski, Greg Kot, Justine Musk, Alex McAuley, Nick Tasler, Ashley Kahn, Barbara De Angelis.

● **KNEERIM, WILLIAMS & BLOOM**

90 Canal St., Boston MA 02114. **E-mail:** jill@kwlit.com; jtwilliams@kwlit.com. **E-mail:** submissions@kwlit.com. **Website:** www.kwlit.com. Also located in New York, Los Angeles, New Mexico and Washington D.C. Estab. 1990.

○ Prior to becoming an agent, Mr. Williams was a lawyer; Ms. Kneerim was a publisher and editor; Ms. Bloom worked in magazines; Ms. Flynn in academia.

MEMBER AGENTS John Taylor "Ike" Williams (accepts queries); Jill Kneerim (accepts queries); Brettne Bloom; Kathyrn Beaumont; Hope Denekamp; Katherine Flynn; Rasheed McWilliams; Carol Franco; Gerald Gross.

REPRESENTS Nonfiction books, novels. **Considers these nonfiction areas:** anthropology, archeology, autobiography, biography, business, child guidance, current affairs, economics, environment, government, health, history, inspirational, language, law, literature, medicine, memoirs, parenting, popular culture, politics, psychology, religious, science, sociology, sports, technology, women's issues, women's studies. **Considers these fiction areas:** historical, literary, mainstream.

⊶ "This agency specializes in narrative nonfiction, history, science, business, women's issues, commercial and literary fiction, film, and television. We have 5 agents and 4 scouts in Boston, New York, Washington DC and Santa Fe." Actively seeking distinguished authors, experts, professionals, intellectuals, and serious writers. Does not want to receive blanket multiple submissions, genre fiction or original screenplays.

HOW TO CONTACT Submit query via e-mail only at: submissions@kwlit.com. No hard copies will be accepted. Submissions should contain a cover letter explaining your book and why you are qualified to write it, a two-page synopsis of the book, one sample chapter, and your c.v. or a history of your publications. Accepts simultaneous submissions. Responds in 4-6 weeks to queries. Responds in 2 months to mss. Obtains most new clients through recommendations from others.

RECENT SALES *The Inner Circle*, by Brad Meltzer; *First Family*, by Joe Ellis; *Commencement*, by J. Courtney Sullivan; *Hitch-22*, by Christopher Hitchens.

● **THE KNIGHT AGENCY.**

E-mail: submissions@knightagency.net. **Website:** knightagency.net. Member of AAR.

MEMBER AGENTS Deidre Knight, Judson Knight, Pamela Harty (health, parenting, southern history, African-American interest, business, motivation, romance, young adult, children's, middle grade, and

Christian living); Lucienne Diver (fantasy, science fiction, romance, romantica, suspense and young adult); Elaine Spencer (romance, women's fiction, young adult and middle grade); Nephele Tempest (literary/commercial fiction, women's fiction, fantasy, science fiction, romantic suspense, paranormal romance, contemporary romance, historical fiction, young adult and middle grade fiction); Melissa Jeglinski (romance (contemporary, category, historical, inspirational) young adult, middle grade, women's fiction and mystery).

⚷ This agency specialized in romance and other areas of genre fiction.

HOW TO CONTACT Query via e-mail only. Address your query to a specific agent Responds within 2 months.

TERMS Agent receives standard 15% commission. Offers written contract.

RECENT SALES *Daylights*, by Rachel Caine (Tantor); *Dark Angel*, by TJ Bennett (Entangled); *Bride for a Night*, by Sandra Steffen (Harlequin Special Edition).

TIPS "Our agents are open to reviewing manuscripts and material from both first-time authors and publishing veterans. We receive thousands of query letters each year, so it is imperative that you read the guidelines outlined below before submitting your project. Your assistance in adhering to these standards will ensure that the agency can receive, evaluate and respond to your material as quickly and efficiently as possible."

⬤ LINDA KONNER LITERARY AGENCY

10 W. 15th St., Suite 1918, New York NY 10011. (212)691-3419. **E-mail:** ldkonner@cs.com. **Website:** www.lindakonnerliteraryagency.com. **Contact:** Linda Konner. Member of AAR. Signatory of WGA. Other memberships include ASJA. Represents 85 clients. 30-35% of clients are new/unpublished writers. Currently handles: nonfiction books 100%.

REPRESENTS Nonfiction books. **Considers these nonfiction areas:** diet/nutrition, gay/lesbian, health, medicine, money, parenting, popular culture, psychology, self-help, women's issues, biography (celebrity), African American and Latino issues, relationships.

⚷ This agency specializes in health, self-help, and how-to books. Authors/co-authors must be top experts in their field with a substantial media platform.

HOW TO CONTACT Query by e-mail or by mail with SASE, synopsis, author bio, sufficient return postage. Prefers to read materials exclusively for 2 weeks. Accepts simultaneous submissions. Obtains most new clients through recommendations from others, occasional solicitation among established authors/journalists.

TERMS Agent receives 15% commission on domestic sales. Agent receives 25% commission on foreign sales. Offers written contract. Charges one-time fee for domestic expenses; additional expenses may be incurred for foreign sales.

RECENT SALES *Organize Your Mind, Organize Your Life*, by Paul Hammerness, PhD, Margaret Moore and John Hanc, with the editors of Harvard Health Publications; *Southern Plate: Cherished Recipes and Stories From My Grandparents*, by Christy Jordan (Harper Studio); *Second Acts: Finding a Passionate New Career*, by Kerry Hannon (Chronicle Books); *Who Do You Think You Are?: Tracing Your Family History*, a tie-in to the NBC TV series, by Megan Smolenyak (Viking).

WRITERS CONFERENCES ASJA Writers Conference, Harvard Medical School's "Publishing Books, Memoirs and Other Creative Nonfiction" Annual Conference.

ⓞ KRAAS LITERARY AGENCY

E-mail: irenekraas@sbcglobal.net. **Website:** www.kraasliteraryagency.com. **Contact:** Irene Kraas. Represents 35 clients. 75% of clients are new/unpublished writers. Currently handles: novels 100%.

MEMBER AGENTS Irene Kraas, principal.

REPRESENTS Novels. **Considers these fiction areas:** literary, thriller, young adult.

⚷ This agency is interested in working with published writers, but that does not mean self-published writers. "The agency is ONLY accepting new manuscripts in the genre of adult thrillers and mysteries. Submissions should be the first ten pages of a completed manuscript embedded in an email. I do not open attachments or go to websites." Does not want to receive short stories, plays, or poetry. This agency no longer represents adult fantasy or science fiction.

HOW TO CONTACT Query and e-mail the first 10 pages of a completed ms. Requires exclusive read on mss. Attachments aren't accepted. Accepts simultaneous submissions.

TERMS Offers written contract.

TIPS "I am interested in material—in any genre—that is truly, truly unique."

STUART KRICHEVSKY LITERARY AGENCY, INC.

381 Park Ave. S., Suite 428, New York NY 10016. (212)725-5288. **Fax:** (212)725-5275. **E-mail:** query@skagency.com. **Website:** www.skagency.com. Member of AAR.

MEMBER AGENTS Stuart Krichevsky; Shana Cohen (science fiction, fantasy); Jennifer Puglisi (assistant).

REPRESENTS Nonfiction books, novels.

HOW TO CONTACT Submit query, synopsis, 1 sample page via e-mail (no attachments). Snail mail queries also acceptable. Attachments will not be opened for security reasons. Obtains most new clients through recommendations from others, solicitations.

EDITE KROLL LITERARY AGENCY, INC.

20 Cross St., Saco ME 04072. (207)283-8797. **Fax:** (207)283-8799. **E-mail:** ekroll@maine.rr.com. **Contact:** Edite Kroll. Represents 45 clients. 20% of clients are new/unpublished writers. Currently handles: nonfiction books 40%, novels 5%, juvenile books 40%, scholarly books 5%, other.

○ Prior to opening her agency, Ms. Kroll served as a book editor and translator.

REPRESENTS Nonfiction books, novels, very selective, juvenile, scholarly. **Considers these nonfiction areas:** juvenile, selectively, biography, current affairs, ethnic, gay, government, health, no diet books, humor, memoirs, selectively, popular culture, psychology, religion, selectively, self help, selectively, women's, issue-oriented nonfiction. **Considers these fiction areas:** juvenile, literary, picture books, young adult, middle grade, adult.

⚷ "We represent writers and writer-artists of both adult and children's books. We have a special focus on international feminist writers, women writers and artists who write their own books (including children's and humor books)." Actively seeking artists who write their own books and international feminists who write in English. Does not want to receive genre (mysteries, thrillers, diet, cookery, etc.), photography books, coffee table books, romance, or commercial fiction.

HOW TO CONTACT Query with SASE. Submit outline/proposal, synopsis, 1-2 sample chapters, author bio, entire ms if sending picture book. No phone queries. Responds in 2-4 weeks to queries. Responds in 4-8 weeks to mss. Obtains most new clients through recommendations from others.

TERMS Agent receives 15% commission on domestic sales. Agent receives 20% commission on foreign sales. Offers written contract; 30-day notice must be given to terminate contract. Charges clients for photocopying and legal fees with prior approval from writer.

RECENT SALES Sold 12 domestic/30 foreign titles in the last year. This agency prefers not to share information on specific sales. Clients include Shel Silverstein estate, Suzy Becker, Geoffrey Hayes, Henrik Drescher, Charlotte Kasl, Gloria Skurzynski, Fatema Mernissa.

TIPS "Please do your research so you won't send me books/proposals I specifically excluded."

KT LITERARY, LLC

9249 S. Broadway, #200-543, Highlands Ranch CO 80129. (720)344-4728. **Fax:** (720)344-4728. **E-mail:** contact@ktliterary.com. **Website:** http://ktliterary.com. **Contact:** Kate Schafer Testerman. Member of AAR. Other memberships include SCBWI. Represents 20 clients. 60% of clients are new/unpublished writers. Currently handles: nonfiction books 5%, novels 5%, juvenile books 90%.

○ Prior to her current position, Ms. Schafer was an agent with Janklow & Nesbit.

REPRESENTS Nonfiction books, novels, juvenile books. **Considers these nonfiction areas:** popular culture. **Considers these fiction areas:** action, adventure, fantasy, historical, juvenile, romance, science fiction, women's, young adult.

⚷ "I'm bringing my years of experience in the New York publishing scene, as well as my lifelong love of reading, to a vibrant area for writers, proving that great work can be found, and sold, from anywhere. Actively seeking brilliant, funny, original middle grade and young adult fiction, both literary and commercial; witty women's fiction (chick lit); and pop culture, narrative nonfiction. Quirky is good." Does not want picture books, serious nonfiction, and adult literary fiction.

HOW TO CONTACT E-mail queries only. Keep an eye on the KT Literary blog for updates. Responds in 2 weeks to queries. Responds in 2 months to mss. Obtains most new clients through recommendations from others, solicitations, conferences.

TERMS Agent receives 15% commission on domestic sales. Agent receives 20% commission on foreign sales. Offers written contract; 30-day notice must be given to terminate contract.

WRITERS CONFERENCES Various SCBWI conferences, BookExpo.

TIPS "If we like your query, we'll ask for (more). Continuing advice is offered regularly on my blog 'Ask Daphne,' which can be accessed from my website."

THE LA LITERARY AGENCY

P.O. Box 46370, Los Angeles CA 90046. (323)654-5288. **E-mail:** ann@laliteraryagency.com; mail@laliteraryagency.com. **Website:** www.laliteraryagency.com. **Contact:** Ann Cashman.

Prior to becoming an agent, Mr. Lasher worked in publishing in New York and Los Angeles.

MEMBER AGENTS Ann Cashman, Eric Lasher, Maureen Lasher.

REPRESENTS Nonfiction books, novels. **Considers these nonfiction areas:** animals, anthropology, archeology, architecture, art, autobiography, biography, business, child guidance, cooking, cultural interests, current affairs, diet/nutrition, design, economics, environment, ethnic, foods, government, health, history, how-to, investigative, law, medicine, parenting, popular culture, politics, psychology, science, self-help, sociology, sports, technology, true crime, women's issues, women's studies, narrative nonfiction. **Considers these fiction areas:** action, adventure, crime, detective, family saga, feminist, historical, literary, mainstream, police, sports, thriller.

HOW TO CONTACT Prefers submissions by mail, but welcomes e-mail submissions as well. Nonfiction: query letter and book proposal; fiction: query letter and first 50 (double-spaced) pages. Query with outline, 1 sample chapter.

RECENT SALES *Full Bloom: The Art and Life of Georgia O'Keeffe*, by Hunter Druhojowska-Philp (Norton); *And the Walls Came Tumbling Down*, by H. Caldwell (Scribner); *Italian Slow & Savory*, by Joyce Goldstein (Chronicle); *A Field Guide to Chocolate Chip Cookies*, by Dede Wilson (Harvard Common Press); *Teen Knitting Club* (Artisan); *The Framingham Heart Study*, by Dr. Daniel Levy (Knopf).

PETER LAMPACK AGENCY, INC.

The Empire State Building, 350 Fifth Ave., Suite 5300, New York NY 10118. (212)687-9106. **Fax:** (212)687-9109. **E-mail:** alampack@verizon.net. **E-mail:** submissions-andrew@peterlampackagency.com. **Website:** www.peterlampackagency.com. **Contact:** Andrew Lampack. Represents 50 clients. 10% of clients are new/unpublished writers. Currently handles: nonfiction books 20%, novels 80%.

MEMBER AGENTS Peter Lampack (president); Rema Delanyan (foreign rights); Andrew Lampack (new writers).

REPRESENTS Nonfiction books, novels. **Considers these fiction areas:** adventure, crime, detective, family saga, literary, mainstream, mystery, police, suspense, thriller, contemporary relationships.

"This agency specializes in commercial fiction, and nonfiction by recognized experts." Actively seeking literary and commercial fiction, thrillers, mysteries, suspense, and psychological thrillers. Does not want to receive horror, romance, science fiction, westerns, historical literary fiction or academic material.

HOW TO CONTACT Query via e-mail. *No unsolicited mss.* Responds within 2 months to queries. Obtains most new clients through referrals made by clients.

TERMS Agent receives 15% commission on domestic sales. Agent receives 20% commission on foreign sales.

RECENT SALES *Spartan Gold*, by Clive Cussler with Grant Blackwood; *The Wrecker*, by Clive Cussler with Justin Scott; *Medusa*, by Clive Cussler and Paul Kemprecos; *Silent Sea* by Clive Cussler with Jack Dubrul; *Summertime*, by J.M. Coetzee; *Dreaming in French*, by Megan McAndrew; *Time Pirate*, by Ted Bell.

WRITERS CONFERENCES BookExpo America; Mystery Writers of America.

TIPS "Submit only your best work for consideration. Have a very specific agenda of goals you wish your prospective agent to accomplish for you. Provide the agent with a comprehensive statement of your credentials— educational and professional accomplishments."

LAURA LANGLIE, LITERARY AGENT

63 Wyckoff St., Brooklyn NY 11201. (718)855-8102. **Fax:** (718)855-4450. **E-mail:** laura@lauralanglie.com. **Contact:** Laura Langlie. Represents 25 clients. 50% of clients are new/unpublished writers. Currently handles: nonfiction books 15%, novels 58%, story collections 2%, juvenile books 25%.

Prior to opening her agency, Ms. Langlie worked in publishing for 7 years and as an agent at Kidde, Hoyt & Picard for 6 years.

REPRESENTS Nonfiction books, novels, short story collections, novellas, juvenile. **Considers these nonfiction areas:** autobiography, biography, cultural interests, current affairs, environment, film, history, language, law, literature, memoirs, popular culture, politics, psychology, theater, women's issues, women's studies, history of medicine and science, animals (not how-to). **Considers these fiction areas:** crime, detective, ethnic, feminist, historical, humor, juvenile, literary, mainstream, mystery, police, suspense, thriller, young adult, mainstream.

⌐ "I'm very involved with and committed to my clients. Most of my clients come to me via recommendations from other agents, clients and editors. I've met very few at conferences. I've often sought out writers for projects, and I still find new clients via the traditional query letter." Does not want to receive how-to, children's picture books, hardcore science fiction, poetry, men's adventure, or erotica.

HOW TO CONTACT Query with SASE. Accepts queries via fax. Accepts simultaneous submissions. Responds in 1 week to queries. Responds in 1 month to mss. Obtains most new clients through recommendations, submissions.

TERMS Agent receives 15% commission on domestic sales. Agent receives 20% commission on foreign and dramatic sales. No written contract.

RECENT SALES Sold 15 titles in the last year. *As Close As Hands and Feet*, by Emily Arsenault (William Morrow); *The Aviator's Wife*, by Melanie Benjamin (Delacorte Press); *Free Verse* and *Ashes to Asheville*, by Sarah Dooley (G.P. Putnam's Son's/Penguin Young Reader's Group); *Miss Dimple Suspects*, by Mignon F. Ballard (St. Martin's Press); *Awaken*, by Meg Cabot (Scholastic, Inc.); *Size 12 and Ready to Rock*, by Meg Cabot (William Morrow); *Adaptation* and *Inheritance*, by Malinda Lo (Little, Brown & Co Books for Young Readers); *One Tough Chick*, by Leslie Margolis (Bloomsbury); *The Elite Gymnasts*, by Dominique Moceanu and Alicia Thompson (Disney/Hyperion); *The Lighthouse Road*, by Peter Geye (Unbridled Books); *The Nazi and the Psychiatrist*, by Jack El-Hai (Public Affairs Books); *The Last Animal*, by Abby Geni (Counterpoint Press); *Something Resembling Love*, by Mary Hogan (William Morrow); *Little Wolves*, by Thomas Maltman (Soho Press).

TIPS "Be complete, forthright and clear in your communications. Do your research as to what a particular agent represents."

LANGTONS INTERNATIONAL AGENCY

124 West 60th St., #42M, New York NY 10023. (646)344-1801. **E-mail:** langton@langtonsinternational@com; llangton@langtonsinternational.com. **Website:** www.langtonsinternational.com. **Contact:** Linda Langton, President.

○ Prior to becoming an agent, Ms. Langton was a co-founding director and publisher of the international publishing company, The Ink Group.

REPRESENTS Nonfiction books and literary fiction. **Considers these nonfiction areas:** biography, health, history, how-to, politics, self-help, true crime. **Considers these fiction areas:** literary, political thrillers, young adult, and middle grade books.

⌐ "Langtons International Agency is a multi-media literary and licensing agency specializing in nonfiction, inspirational, thrillers and children's middle grade and young adult books as well as the the visual world of photography."

HOW TO CONTACT Please submit all queries via hard copy to the address above or e-mail outline/proposal, synopsis, publishing history, author bio. Only published authors should query this agency. Accepts simultaneous submissions.

RECENT SALES *Talking with Jean-Paul Sartre: Conversations and Debates*, by Professor John Gerassi (Yale University Press); *The Obama Presidency and the Politics of Change*, by Professor Stanley Renshon (Routledge Press); *I Would See a Girl Walking*, by Diana Montane and Kathy Kelly (Berkley Books); *Begin 1913-1992*, by Avi Shilon (Yale University Press); *This Borrowed Earth*, by Robert Emmet Hernan (Palgrave McMillan); *The Perfect Square*, by Nancy Heinzen (Temple Uni Press); *The Honey Trail* by Grace Pundyk (St. Martin's Press); *Dogs of Central Park* by Fran Reisner (Rizzoli/Universe Publishing).

◐ MICHAEL LARSEN/ELIZABETH POMADA, LITERARY AGENTS

1029 Jones St., San Francisco CA 94109. (415)673-0939. **E-mail:** larsenpoma@aol.com. **Website:** www.larsenpomada.com. **Contact:** Mike Larsen, Elizabeth Pomada. Member of AAR. Other memberships include Authors Guild, ASJA, PEN, WNBA, California Writers Club, National Speakers Association. Represents 100

NEW AGENT SPOTLIGHT

LAURA BIAGI (JEAN V. NAGGAR LITERARY AGENCY)
Jvnla.com
@LauraJBiagi

ABOUT LAURA: Laura Biagi joined the Jean V. Naggar Literary Agency Inc. (JVNLA) in 2009. She is actively building her own client list, seeking adult literary fiction and young readers books. She also handles the sale of Australian and New Zealand rights for the agency. She has worked closely with Jean Naggar and Jennifer Weltz on their titles, as well as Jennifer Weltz on the submission of JVNLA's titles internationally. Laura's writing background has honed her editorial eye and has driven her enthusiasm for discovering and developing literary talent. She studied creative writing and anthropology at Northwestern University. As a writer, she has participated in workshops at the Squaw Valley Community of Writers, the Juniper Summer Writing Institute, and the New York State Summer Writers Institute. She is the recipient of a Kentucky Emerging Artist Award for fiction writing. Laura grew up in a small town in Kentucky and maintains a fondness for Southern biscuits and unobstructed views of the stars.

SHE IS SEEKING: In the adult fiction realm, she is particularly interested in literary fiction, magical realism, cultural themes, and debut authors. She is drawn to strong voices, complex narrative arcs, dynamic and well-developed characters, psychological twists, and dystopian/apocalyptic literary fiction.

In the young readers realm, she is seeking young adult novels, middle grade novels, and picture books. She loves young readers books that have a magical tinge to them and vivid writing. She also looks for titles that incorporate high concept, dark/edgy, and quirky elements, as well as titles that challenge the way we typically view the world.

HOW TO SUBMIT: Please e-mail your query to lbiagi@jvnla.com, or submit your query to her via the website. Please include the first page of your manuscript when submitting your query.

clients. 40-45% of clients are new/unpublished writers. Currently handles: nonfiction books 70%, novels 30%.

Prior to opening their agency, Mr. Larsen and Ms. Pomada were promotion executives for major publishing houses. Mr. Larsen worked for Morrow, Bantam, and Pyramid (now part of Berkley); Ms. Pomada worked at Holt, David McKay and Dial Press. Mr. Larsen is the author of the 4th edition of *How to Write a Book Proposal* and *How to Get a Literary Agent* as well as the coauthor of *Guerilla Marketing for Writers: 100 Weapons for Selling Your Work*, which was republished in September 2009.

MEMBER AGENTS Michael Larsen (nonfiction); Elizabeth Pomada (fiction & narrative nonfiction).

REPRESENTS Considers these nonfiction areas: anthropology, archeology, architecture, art, autobiography, biography, business, current affairs, diet//nutrition, design, economics, environment, ethnic, film, foods, gay/lesbian, health, history, how-to, humor, inspirational, investigative, law, medicine, memoirs, metaphysics, money, music, New Age, popular culture, politics, psychology, religious, satire, science, self-help, sociology, sports, travel, women's issues, women's studies, futurism. **Considers these fiction areas:** action, adventure, contemporary issues, crime, detective, ethnic, experimental, family saga, feminist, gay, glitz, historical, humor, inspirational, lesbian, literary, mainstream, mystery, police, religious, romance, satire, suspense, chick lit.

- We have diverse tastes. We look for fresh voices and new ideas. We handle literary, commercial and genre fiction, and the full range of nonfiction books. Actively seeking commercial, genre, and literary fiction. Does not want to receive children's books, plays, short stories, screenplays, pornography, poetry or stories of abuse.

HOW TO CONTACT Query with SASE. **Elizabeth Pomada** handles literary and commercial fiction, romance, thrillers, mysteries, narrative nonfiction and mainstream women's fiction. If you have completed a novel, **please e-mail the first 10 pages and 2-page synopsis to larsenpoma@aol.com**. Use 14-point typeface, double-spaced, as an e-mail letter with no attachments. For nonfiction, please read Michael's *How to Write a Book Proposal* book—available through your library or bookstore, and through our website—so you will know exactly what editors need. Then, before you start writing, send him the title, subtitle, and your promotion plan via conventional mail (with SASE) or e-mail. If sent as e-mail, please include the information in the body of your e-mail with NO attachments. Please allow up to 2 weeks for a response.

See each agent's page on the website for contact and submission information. Responds in 8 weeks to pages or submissions.

TERMS Agent receives 15% commission on domestic sales. Agent receives 20% (30% for Asia) commission on foreign sales. May charge for printing, postage for multiple submissions, foreign mail, foreign phone calls, galleys, books, legal fees.

RECENT SALES Sold at least 15 titles in the last year. *Secrets of the Tudor Court*, by D. Bogden (Kensington); *Zen & the Art of Horse Training*, by Allan Hamilton, MD (Storey Pub.); *The Solemn Lantern Maker* by Merlinda Bobis (Delta); *Bite Marks*, the fifth book in an urban fantasy series by J.D. Rardin (Orbit/Grand Central); *The Iron King*, by Julie Karawa (Harlequin Teen).

WRITERS CONFERENCES This agency organizes the annual San Francisco Writers' Conference (www.sfwriters.org).

TIPS "We love helping writers get the rewards and recognition they deserve. If you can write books that meet the needs of the marketplace and you can promote your books, now is the best time ever to be a writer. We must find new writers to make a living, so we are very eager to hear from new writers whose work will interest large houses, and nonfiction writers who can promote their books. For a list of recent sales, helpful info, and three ways to make yourself irresistible to any publisher, please visit our website."

⊙ THE STEVE LAUBE AGENCY

5025 N. Central Ave., #635, Phoenix AZ 85012. (602)336-8910. **E-mail:** krichards@stevelaube.com. **Website:** www.stevelaube.com. **Contact:** Steve Laube. Other memberships include CBA. Represents 60+ clients. 5% of clients are new/unpublished writers. Currently handles: nonfiction books 48%, novels 48%, novella 2%, scholarly books 2%.

- Prior to becoming an agent, Mr. Laube worked 11 years as a Christian bookseller and 11 years as editorial director of nonfiction with Bethany House Publishers.

REPRESENTS Nonfiction books, novels. **Considers these nonfiction areas:** religious. **Considers these fiction areas:** religious.

- Primarily serves the Christian market (CBA). Actively seeking Christian fiction and religious nonfiction. Does not want to receive children's picture books, poetry, or cookbooks.

HOW TO CONTACT Submit proposal package, outline, 3 sample chapters, SASE. For e-mail submissions, attach as Word doc or PDF. Consult website for guidelines. Accepts simultaneous submissions. Responds in 6-8 weeks to queries. Obtains most new clients through recommendations from others, solicitations, conferences.

TERMS Agent receives 15% commission on domestic sales. Agent receives 20% commission on foreign sales. Offers written contract; 30-day notice must be given to terminate contract.

RECENT SALES Sold 80 titles in the last year. Other clients include Deborah Raney, Allison Bottke, H. Norman Wright, Ellie Kay, Jack Cavanaugh, Karen Ball, Tracey Bateman, Susan May Warren, Lisa Bergren, John Rosemond, Cindy Woodsmall, Karol Ladd, Judith Pella, Michael Phillips, Margaret Daley, William Lane Craig, Tosca Lee, Ginny Aiken.

WRITERS CONFERENCES Mount Hermon Christian Writers' Conference; American Christian Fiction Writers' Conference.

LAUNCHBOOKS LITERARY AGENCY

566 Sweet Pea Place, Encinitas CA 92024. (760)944-9909. **E-mail:** david@launchbooks.com. **Website:** www.launchbooks.com. **Contact:** David Fugate. Represents 45 clients. 35% of clients are new/unpublished writers. Currently handles: nonfiction books 90%, fiction books 10%.

○ David Fugate has been an agent for 20 years and has successfully represented more than 1,000 book titles. He left another agency to found LaunchBooks in 2005.

REPRESENTS Novels. **Considers these nonfiction areas:** anthropology, archeology, autobiography, biography, business, computers, cultural interests, current affairs, diet/nutrition, economics, education, environment, ethnic, foods, government, health, history, how-to, humor, investigative, law, medicine, memoirs, military, money, music, parenting, popular culture, politics, satire, science, sociology, sports, technology, true crime, war.

⚷ Actively seeking a wide variety of nonfiction, including narrative nonfiction, business, technology, adventure, popular culture, science, creative nonfiction, current events, history, politics, reference, memoirs, health, how-to, lifestyle, parenting, and more. Also interested in seeing commercial fiction, thrillers, and

genre-breaking novels in science fiction, horror, and apocalyptic fiction.

HOW TO CONTACT Query via e-mail. Submit outline/proposal, synopsis, 1 sample chapter, author bio. Accepts simultaneous submissions. Responds in 1 week to queries. Responds in 4 weeks to mss. Obtains most new clients through recommendations from others, solicitations.

TERMS Agent receives 15% commission on domestic sales. Agent receives 25% commission on foreign sales. Offers written contract; 30-day notice must be given to terminate contract. Charges occur very seldom. This agency's agreement limits any charges to $50 unless the author gives a written consent.

RECENT SALES *Ex-Heroes and Ex-Patriots*, by Peter Clines (Crown); *We Are Anonymous*, by Parmy Olson (Little, Brown); *The $100 Startup*, by Chris Guillebeau (Crown); *Ghost in the Wires*, by Kevin Mitnick (Little, Brown); *Kingpin*, by Kevin Poulsen (Crown); *Powering the Dream*, by Alexis Madrigal (Da Capo); *Countdown to Zero Day*, by Kim Zetter (Crown); *Rogue Code*, by Mark Russinovich (Thomas Dunne Books); *Beyond Human*, by Mark McClusky (Hudson Street Press); *Mad Science*, by Wired Magazine (Little, Brown); *You Can Buy Happiness (And It's Cheap)*, by Tammy Strobel (New World Library); *The Automattic Year*, by Scott Berkun (Jossey-Bass); *The Big Tiny*, by Dee Williams (Blue Rider Press).

SARAH LAZIN BOOKS

121 W. 27th St., Suite 704, New York NY 10001. (212)989-5757. **Fax:** (212)989-1393. **E-mail:** manuela@lazinbooks.com; slazin@lazinbooks.com. **Website:** www.lazinbooks.com. **Contact:** Sarah Lazin. Member of AAR. Represents 75+ clients. Currently handles: nonfiction books 80%, novels 20%.

MEMBER AGENTS Sarah Lazin; Manuela Jessel.

REPRESENTS Nonfiction books, novels. **Considers these nonfiction areas:** narrative nonfiction, history, politics, contemporary affairs, popular culture, music, biography and memoir.

⚷ Works with companies who package their books; handles some photography.

HOW TO CONTACT Query with SASE. No e-mail queries. Only accepts queries on referral.

TERMS Agent receives 15% commission on domestic sales. Agent receives 20% commission on foreign sales.

⊙ THE NED LEAVITT AGENCY

70 Wooster St., Suite 4F, New York NY 10012. (212)334-0999. **Website:** www.nedleavittagency. com. **Contact:** Ned Leavitt; Jillian Sweeney. Member of AAR. Represents 40+ clients.

MEMBER AGENTS Ned Leavitt, founder and agent; Britta Alexander, agent.

REPRESENTS Nonfiction books, novels.

☞ "We are small in size, but intensely dedicated to our authors and to supporting excellent and unique writing."

HOW TO CONTACT This agency now only takes queries/submissions through referred clients. Do *not* cold query.

TIPS "Look online for this agency's recently changed submission guidelines." For guidance in the writing process we strongly recommend the following books: *Writing Down The Bones* by Nathalie Goldberg; *Bird By Bird* by Anne Lamott.

◑ ROBERT LECKER AGENCY

4055 Melrose Ave., Montreal QC H4A 2S5 Canada. (514)830-4818. **Fax:** (514)483-1644. **E-mail:** leckerlink@aol.com. **Website:** www.leckeragency.com. **Contact:** Robert Lecker. Represents 20 clients. 20% of clients are new/unpublished writers. Currently handles: nonfiction books 80%, novels 10%, scholarly books 10%.

○ Prior to becoming an agent, Mr. Lecker was the cofounder and publisher of ECW Press and professor of English literature at McGill University. He has 30 years of experience in book and magazine publishing.

MEMBER AGENTS Robert Lecker (popular culture, music); Mary Williams (travel, food, popular science).

REPRESENTS Nonfiction books, novels, scholarly, syndicated material. **Considers these nonfiction areas:** autobiography, biography, cooking, cultural interests, dance, diet/nutrition, ethnic, film, foods, how-to, language, literature, music, popular culture, science, technology, theater. **Considers these fiction areas:** action, adventure, crime, detective, erotica, literary, mainstream, mystery, police, suspense, thriller.

☞ RLA specializes in books about popular culture, popular science, music, entertainment, food, and travel. The agency responds to articulate, innovative proposals within 2 weeks. Actively seeking original book mss only after receipt of outlines and proposals.

HOW TO CONTACT Query first. Only responds to queries of interest. Discards the rest. Accepts simultaneous submissions. Responds in 2 weeks to queries. Responds in 1 month to mss. Obtains most new clients through recommendations from others, conferences, interest in website.

TERMS Agent receives 15% commission on domestic sales. Agent receives 15-20% commission on foreign sales. Offers written contract, binding for 1 year; 6-month notice must be given to terminate contract.

◑ THE LESHNE AGENCY

16 W. 23rd St., 4th Floor, New York NY 10010. **E-mail:** info@leshneagency.com. **E-mail:** submissions@leshneagency.com. **Website:** www.leshneagency.com. **Contact:** Lisa Leshne, agent and owner.

○ Prior to founding the Leshne Agency, Lisa was a literary agent at Larry Kirshbaum's, LJK Literary.

MEMBER AGENTS Lisa Leshne, agent and owner; Sandy Hodgman, director of foreign rights.

☞ Wants "authors across all genres. We are interested in narrative, memoir, and prescriptive nonfiction, with a particular interest in sports, wellness, business, political and parenting topics. We will also look at truly terrific commercial fiction and young adult and middle-grade books."

HOW TO CONTACT "Submit all materials in the body of an e-mail; no attachments. Be sure to include the word 'QUERY' and the title of your ms in the subject line. Include brief synopsis, TOC or chapter outline, 10 sample pages, bio, any previous publications, word count, how much of the ms is complete, and the best way to reach you."

⊙ LEVEL FIVE MEDIA, LLC

130 W. 42nd St., Suite 1901-02, New York NY 10036. (212)575-4600. **Fax:** (212)575-7797. **Contact:** Stephen Hanselman.

○ Prior to becoming an agent, Ms. Hemming served as president and publisher of HarperCollins General Books. Mr. Hanselman served as senior VP and publisher of HarperBusiness, HarperResource and HarperSanFrancisco.

MEMBER AGENTS Stephen Hanselman; Cathy Hemming.

REPRESENTS Nonfiction books, novels. **Considers these nonfiction areas:** business, cooking, diet/nutrition, economics, foods, health, history, how-to, inspirational, medicine, money, parenting, psychology, self-help, fitness/exercise, popular science, investigative journalism, lifestyle, popular reference, cultural studies.

☛ "Our commitment is to focus on fewer authors and to provide more of these missing services, including media development and marketing consultation, by building their benefits into each project that is offered to publishers. Given this choice of focus, we are not accepting submissions except from published authors, credentialed speakers, established journalists, media personalities, leading scholars and religious figures, prominent science and health professionals, and high-level business consultants."

HOW TO CONTACT Query with SASE. Submit synopsis, publishing history, author bio, cover letter. No snail mail queries. Qualified fiction authors must have a previously published book or be referred. Obtains most new clients through recommendations from others.

LEVINE GREENBERG LITERARY AGENCY, INC.

307 Seventh Ave., Suite 2407, New York NY 10001. (212)337-0934. **Fax:** (212)337-0948. **E-mail:** submit@levinegreenberg.com. **Website:** www.levinegreenberg.com. Member of AAR. Represents 250 clients. 33% of clients are new/unpublished writers. Currently handles: nonfiction books 70%, novels 30%.

○ Prior to opening his agency, Mr. Levine served as vice president of the Bank Street College of Education.

MEMBER AGENTS James Levine, Daniel Greenberg, Stephanie Kip Rostan, Lindsay Edgecombe, Danielle Svetcov, Elizabeth Fisher, Victoria Skurnick.

REPRESENTS Nonfiction books, novels. **Considers these nonfiction areas:** New Age, animals, art, biography, business, child, computers, cooking, gardening, gay, health, money, nature, religion, science, self help, sociology, spirituality, sports, women's. **Considers these fiction areas:** literary, mainstream, mystery, thriller, psychological, women's.

☛ This agency specializes in business, psychology, parenting, health/medicine, narrative nonfiction, spirituality, religion, women's issues, and commercial fiction.

HOW TO CONTACT See website for full submission procedure at "How to Submit." Or use our e-mail address if you prefer, or online submission form. Do not submit directly to agents. Prefers electronic submissions. Cannot respond to submissions by mail. Obtains most new clients through recommendations from others.

TERMS Agent receives 15% commission on domestic sales. Agent receives 20% commission on foreign sales. Offers written contract. Charges clients for out-of-pocket expenses—telephone, fax, postage, photocopying—directly connected to the project.

WRITERS CONFERENCES ASJA Writers' Conference.

TIPS "We focus on editorial development, business representation, and publicity and marketing strategy."

◑ PAUL S. LEVINE LITERARY AGENCY

1054 Superba Ave., Venice CA 90291. (310)450-6711. **Fax:** (310)450-0181. **E-mail:** paul@paulslevinelit.com. **Website:** www.paulslevinelit.com. **Contact:** Paul S. Levine. Other memberships include the State Bar of California. Represents over 100 clients. 75% of clients are new/unpublished writers. Currently handles: nonfiction books 60%, novels 10%, movie scripts 10%, TV scripts 5%, juvenile books 5%.

MEMBER AGENTS Paul S. Levine (children's and young adult fiction and nonfiction, adult fiction and nonfiction except sci-fi, fantasy, and horror); Loren R. Grossman (archaeology, art/photography/architecture, gardening, education, health, medicine, science).

REPRESENTS Nonfiction books, novels, episodic drama, movie, TV, movie scripts, feature film, TV movie of the week, sitcom, animation, documentary, miniseries, syndicated material, reality show. **Considers these nonfiction areas:** architecture, art, autobiography, biography, business, child guidance, computers, cooking, crafts, cultural interests, current affairs, diet/nutrition, design, economics, education, ethnic, film, foods, gay/lesbian, government, health, history, hobbies, how-to, humor, investigative, language, law, medicine, memoirs, military, money, music, New Age, parenting, photography, popular culture, politics, psychology, science, self-help, sociology, sports, theater, true crime, women's issues, women's studies, creative nonfiction, animation. **Considers these fiction areas:** action, adventure, comic books, confession, crime, detective, erotica, ethnic, experimental, family saga, feminist, frontier, gay, glitz, historical, humor, inspirational, lesbian, literary, mainstream, mystery, police, regional, religious, romance, satire, sports, suspense, thriller, westerns. **Considers these script areas:** action, biography, cartoon, comedy, contemporary, detective, erotica, ethnic, experimental, family, feminist, gay, glitz, historical, horror, juvenile, mainstream, multimedia, mystery, religious, romantic comedy, romantic drama, sports, teen, thriller, western.

✎➤ Does not want to receive science fiction, fantasy, or horror.

HOW TO CONTACT Query with SASE. Accepts simultaneous submissions. Responds in 1 day to queries. Responds in 6-8 weeks to mss. Obtains most new clients through conferences, referrals, listings on various websites, and in directories.

TERMS Agent receives 15% commission on domestic sales. Offers written contract. Charges for postage and actual, out-of-pocket costs only.

RECENT SALES Sold 8 books in the last year.

WRITERS CONFERENCES Willamette Writers Conference; San Francisco Writers Conference; Santa Barbara Writers Conference and many others.

TIPS "Write good, sellable books."

◑ LIPPINCOTT MASSIE MCQUILKIN

27 West 20th Street, Suite 305, New York NY 10011. **Fax:** (212)352-2059. **E-mail:** info@lmqlit.com. **Website:** www.lmqlit.com.

MEMBER AGENTS Maria Massie (fiction, memoir, cultural criticism); Will Lippincott (politics, current affairs, history); Rob McQuilkin (fiction, history, psychology, sociology, graphic material); Jason Anthony (young adult, pop culture, memoir, true crime, and general psychology); Ethan Bassoff (literary and crime fiction and narrative nonfiction including history, science, humor, and sports writing); Kent Wolf (literary fiction, upmarket women's fiction, memoir, pop culture, all types of narrative nonfiction, and select YA); Laney Katz Becker (nonfiction, fiction, memoir).

REPRESENTS Nonfiction books, novels, short story collections, scholarly, graphic novels. **Considers these nonfiction areas:** animals, anthropology, archeology, architecture, art, autobiography, biography, business, child guidance, cultural interests, current affairs, design, economics, ethnic, film, gay/lesbian, government, health, history, inspirational, language, law, literature, medicine, memoirs, military, money, music, parenting, popular culture, politics, psychology, religious, science, self-help, sociology, technol-

ogy, true crime, women's issues, women's studies, young adult. **Considers these fiction areas:** action, adventure, cartoon, comic books, confession, family saga, feminist, gay, historical, humor, lesbian, literary, mainstream, regional, satire.

✎➤ "LMQ focuses on bringing new voices in literary and commercial fiction to the market, as well as popularizing the ideas and arguments of scholars in the fields of history, psychology, sociology, political science, and current affairs. Actively seeking fiction writers who already have credits in magazines and quarterlies, as well as nonfiction writers who already have a media platform or some kind of a university affiliation." Does not want to receive romance, genre fiction, or children's material.

HOW TO CONTACT "We accepts electronic queries only. Only send additional materials if requested." Accepts simultaneous submissions. Responds in 1 week to queries. Responds in 1 month to mss. Obtains most new clients through recommendations from others, solicitations, conferences.

TERMS Agent receives 15% commission on domestic sales. Agent receives 20% commission on foreign sales. Offers written contract; 30-day notice must be given to terminate contract. Only charges for reasonable business expenses upon successful sale.

RECENT SALES Clients include: Peter Ho Davies, Kim Addonizio, Natasha Trethewey, Anne Carson, David Sirota, Katie Crouch, Uwen Akpan, Lydia Millet, Tom Perrotta, Jonathan Lopez, Chris Hayes, Caroline Weber.

● LITERARY AND CREATIVE ARTISTS, INC.

3543 Albemarle St., N.W., Washington D.C. 20008-4213. **E-mail:** lca9643@lcadc.com. **Website:** www.lcadc.com. **Contact:** Muriel Nellis. Member of AAR. Other memberships include Authors Guild, American Bar Association, American Booksellers Association. Currently handles: nonfiction books 50%, novels 50%.

MEMBER AGENTS Prior to becoming an agent, Mr. Powell was in sales and contract negotiation.

REPRESENTS Nonfiction books, novels, art, biography, business, photography, popular culture, religion, self help, literary, regional, religious, satire. **Considers these nonfiction areas:** autobiography, biography, business, cooking, diet/nutrition, economics, foods, government, health, how-to, law, medicine, memoirs, philosophy, politics, human drama; lifestyle.

8—☞ "Specializles in adult trade fiction and nonfiction. Currently, we are only accepting projects by established authors. Actively seeking quality projects by authors with a vision of where they want to be in 10 years and a plan of how to get there." We do not handle poetry, or purely academic/technical work.

HOW TO CONTACT Query via e-mail first and include a synopsis. No attachments. We do not accept unsolicited manuscripts, faxed manuscripts, manuscripts sent by email or manuscripts on computer disk. Accepts simultaneous submissions. Responds in 3 weeks to queries. Responds in 1 week to mss. Obtains new clients through recommendations from others.

TERMS Agent receives 15% commission on domestic sales. Agent receives 25% commission on foreign sales. Offers written contract. Charges clients for long-distance phone/fax, photocopying, shipping.

TIPS "If you are an unpublished author, join a writers group, even if it is on the Internet. You need good honest feedback. Don't send a manuscript that has not been read by at least five people. Don't send a manuscript cold to any agent without first asking if they want it. Try to meet the agent face to face before signing. Make sure the fit is right."

◑ THE LITERARY GROUP INTERNATIONAL

330 W. 38th St., Suite 408, New York NY 10018. (646)442-5896. **E-mail:** js@theliterarygroup.com. **Website:** www.theliterarygroup.com. **Contact:** Frank Weimann. 1900 Ave. of the Stars, 25 Fl., Los Angeles, CA 90067; Tel: (310)282-8961; **Fax:** (310) 282-8903 65% of clients are new/unpublished writers. Currently handles: nonfiction books 50%, 50% fiction.

MEMBER AGENTS Frank Weimann.

REPRESENTS Nonfiction books, novels, graphic novels. **Considers these nonfiction areas:** animals, anthropology, biography, business, child guidance, crafts, creative nonfiction, current affairs, education, ethnic, film, government, health, history, humor, juvenile nonfiction, language, memoirs, military, multicultural, music, nature, popular culture, politics, psychology, religious, science, self-help, sociology, sports, travel, true crime, women's issues, women's studies. **Considers these fiction areas:** adventure, contemporary issues, detective, ethnic, experimental, family saga, fantasy, feminist, historical, horror, humor, literary, multicultural, mystery, psychic, romance, sports, thriller, young adult, regional, graphic novels.

8—☞ This agency specializes in nonfiction (memoir, military, history, biography, sports, how-to).

HOW TO CONTACT Query with SASE. Prefers to read materials exclusively. Only responds if interested. Obtains most new clients through referrals, writers conferences, query letters.

TERMS Agent receives 15% commission on domestic sales. Agent receives 20% commission on foreign sales. Offers written contract; 30-day notice must be given to terminate contract.

RECENT SALES *One From the Hart*, by Stefanie Powers with Richard Buskin (Pocket Books); *Sacred Trust, Deadly Betrayal*, by Keith Anderson (Berkley); *Gotti Confidential*, by Victoria Gotti (Pocket Books); Anna Sui's illustrated memoir (Chronicle Books); *Mania*, by Craig Larsen (Kensington); *Everything Explained through Flowcharts*, by Doogie Horner (HarperCollins); *Bitch*, by Lisa Taddeo (TOR); film rights for *Falling Out of Fashion*, by Karen Yampolsky to Hilary Swank and Molly Smith for 2S Films.

WRITERS CONFERENCES San Diego State University Writers' Conference; Maui Writers' Conference; Agents and Editors Conference; NAHJ Convention in Puerto Rico, others.

● LITERARY MANAGEMENT GROUP, INC.

P.O. Box 40965, Nashville TN 37204. (615)812-4445. **E-mail:** brucebarbour@literarymanagementgroup. com; brb@brucebarbour.com. **Website:** http://liter arymanagementgroup.com; www.brucebarbour.com. **Contact:** Bruce Barbour.

◔ Prior to becoming an agent, Mr. Barbour held executive positions at several publishing houses, including Revell, Barbour Books, Thomas Nelson, and Random House.

REPRESENTS Nonfiction books, novels. **Considers these nonfiction areas:** biography, Christian living; spiritual growth; women's and men's issues; prayer; devotional; meditational; Bible study; marriage; business; family/parenting.

8—☞ "Although we specialize in the area of Christian publishing from an Evangelical perspective, we have editorial contacts and experience in general interest books as well." Does not want to receive gift books, poetry, children's books, short stories, or juvenile/young adult fiction. No unsolicited mss or proposals from unpublished authors.

HOW TO CONTACT Query with SASE. E-mail proposal as an attachment. Consult website for each agent's submission guidelines.

TERMS Agent receives 15% commission on domestic sales.

◑ LITERARY SERVICES, INC.

P.O. Box 888, Barnegat NJ 08005. **E-mail:** john@literaryservicesinc.com; shane@literaryservicesinc.com. **Website:** www.LiteraryServicesInc.com. **Contact:** John Willig. Other memberships include Author's Guild. Represents 90 clients. 25% of clients are new/unpublished writers. Currently handles: nonfiction books 100%. Beginning to accept and consider crime fiction projects.

MEMBER AGENTS John Willig (business, personal growth, narratives, history, health); Cynthia Zigmund (personal finance, investments, entrepreneurship).

REPRESENTS Nonfiction books. **Considers these nonfiction areas:** architecture, art, biography, business, child guidance, cooking, crafts, design, economics, health, history, politics, how-to, humor, language, literature, metaphysics, money, New Age, popular culture, psychology, satire, science, self-help, sports, technology, true crime.

8—➤ We work primarily with nonfiction and mystery/crime fiction authors. "Our publishing experience and 'inside' knowledge of how companies and editors really work sets us apart from many agencies; our specialties are noted above, but we are open to unique presentations in all nonfiction topic areas." Actively seeking business, work/life topics, story-driven narratives. Does not want to receive fiction (except crime fiction), children's books, science fiction, religion or memoirs.

HOW TO CONTACT Query with SASE. For starters, a one-page outline sent via e-mail is acceptable. See our website and our Submissions section to learn more about our questions. Do not send mss unless requested. Accepts simultaneous submissions. Responds in 3-4 weeks to queries. Responds in 4 weeks to mss. Obtains most new clients through recommendations from others, solicitations, conferences.

TERMS Agent receives 15% commission on domestic sales. Agent receives 20% commission on foreign sales. Offers written contract. This agency charges administrative fees for copying, postage, etc.

RECENT SALES Sold 32 titles in the last year. *In Pursuit of Elegance* (Doubleday/Currency). A full list of new books is noted on the website.

WRITERS CONFERENCES Author 101; Publicity Summit; Writer's Digest.

TIPS "Be focused. In all likelihood, your work is not going to be of interest to 'a very broad audience' or 'every parent,' so I appreciate when writers put aside their passion and do some homework, i.e., positioning, special features and benefits of your work. Be a marketer. How have you tested your ideas and writing (beyond your inner circle of family and friends)? Have you received any key awards for your work or endorsements from influential persons in your field? What steps, especially social media, have you taken to increase your presence in the market?"

◑ LIVING WORD LITERARY AGENCY

P.O. Box 40974, Eugene OR 97414. **E-mail:** livingwordliterary@gmail.com. **Website:** livingwordliterary.wordpress.com. **Contact:** Kimberly Shumate, agent. Estab. 2009. Member Evangelical Christian Publishers Association

◒ Kimberly began her employment with Harvest House Publishers as the assistant to the National Sales Manager as well as the International Sales Director, continued into the editorial department.

REPRESENTS Considers these nonfiction areas: health, parenting, self-help, relationships. **Considers these fiction areas:** inspirational, adult fiction, Christian living.

8—➤ Does not want to receive YA fiction, cookbooks, children's books, science fiction or fantasy, memoirs, screenplays or poetry.

HOW TO CONTACT Submit a query with short synopsis and first chapter via Word document. Agency only responds if interested.

● LOWENSTEIN ASSOCIATES INC.

121 W. 27th St., Suite 501, New York NY 10001. (212)206-1630. **Fax:** (212)727-0280. **E-mail:** assistant@bookhaven.com. **Website:** www.lowensteinassociates.com. **Contact:** Barbara Lowenstein. Member of AAR. Represents 150 clients. 20% of clients are

new/unpublished writers. Currently handles: nonfiction books 60%, novels 40%.

MEMBER AGENTS Barbara Lowenstein, president (nonfiction interests include narrative nonfiction, health, money, finance, travel, multicultural, popular culture, and memoir; fiction interests include literary fiction and women's fiction); Emily Gref (young adult, middle grade, adult fantasy and science fiction, as well as literary and commercial women's fiction; also nonfiction in the areas of popular science, linguistics, anthropology, and history); Connor Goldsmith (literary fiction, speculative fiction (scifi/fantasy/urban fantast/mag realism), and psychological thrillers).

REPRESENTS Nonfiction books, novels. **Considers these nonfiction areas:** animals, anthropology, archeology, autobiography, biography, business, child guidance, current affairs, education, ethnic, film, government, health, history, how-to, language, literature, medicine, memoirs, money, multicultural, parenting, popular culture, psychology, science, sociology, travel, music; narrative nonfiction; science; film. **Considers these fiction areas:** crime, detective, erotica, ethnic, fantasy, feminist, historical, literary, mainstream, mystery, police, romance, suspense, thriller, young adult.

HOW TO CONTACT Please send us a one-page query letter, along with the first 10 pages pasted in the body of the message (if fiction; for nonfiction, please send only a query letter), by e-mail. Please put the word QUERY and the title of your project in the subject field of your e-mail and address it to the agent of your choice. Please do not send an attachment. We reply to all queries and generally send a response within 2-4 weeks. By mail: For fiction: Mail a query letter, short synopsis, first chapter and a SASE. For nonfiction: Mail a query letter, proposal, if available, or else a project overview and a SASE. Responds in 4 weeks to queries. Obtains most new clients through recommendations from others, solicitations, conferences.

TERMS Agent receives 15% commission on domestic sales. Agent receives 20% commission on foreign sales. Offers written contract. Charges for large photocopy batches, messenger service, international postage.

WRITERS CONFERENCES Malice Domestic.

TIPS "Know the genre you are working in and read! Also, please see our website for details on which agent to query for your project."

ANDREW LOWNIE LITERARY AGENCY, LTD.

36 Great Smith St., London SW1P 3BU England. (44)(207)222-7574. **Fax:** (44)(207)222-7576. **E-mail:** lownie@globalnet.co.uk; david.haviland@andrewlownie.co.uk. **Website:** www.andrewlownie.co.uk. **Contact:** Andrew Lownie (nonfiction); David Haviland (fiction, especially crime, thrillers and historical fiction). Member of AAA. Represents 130 clients. 20% of clients are new/unpublished writers. Currently handles: nonfiction books 90%, novels 10%.

○ Prior to becoming an agent, Mr. Lownie was a journalist, bookseller, publisher, author of 12 books, and director of the Curtis Brown Agency. Mr. Haviland is a writer and has worked in advertising, script development, and was co-founder of Sirius Television.

REPRESENTS Nonfiction books and novels. **Considers these nonfiction areas:** autobiography, biography, current affairs, government, history, investigative, law, memoirs, military, popular culture, politics, true crime, war. **Considers these fiction areas:** adventure, crime, thriller.

○— This agent has wide publishing experience, extensive journalistic contacts, and a specialty in showbiz/celebrity memoir. Seeking showbiz memoirs, narrative histories, and biographies. No poetry, short stories, children's fiction, academic or scripts.

HOW TO CONTACT Query with by e-mail only. Submit outline, 1 sample chapter. Accepts simultaneous submissions. Responds in 1 week to queries. Responds in 1 month to mss. Obtains most new clients through recommendations from others and unsolicited through website.

TERMS Agent receives 15% commission on domestic sales. Agent receives 20% commission on foreign sales. Offers written contract; 30-day notice must be given to terminate contract.

LYONS LITERARY, LLC

In Association with Curtis Brown, Ltd., 10 Astor Place, 3rd Floor, New York NY 10003. (212)255-5472. **Fax:** (212)851-8405. **E-mail:** info@lyonsliterary.com. **Website:** www.lyonsliterary.com. **Contact:** Jonathan Lyons. Member of AAR. Other memberships include the Author's Guild, American Bar Association, New York State Bar Associaton, New York State Intellectual Property Law Section. Represents 37 clients. 15% of clients are new/unpublished writers. Currently handles: nonfiction books 60%, novels 40%.

REPRESENTS Nonfiction books, novels. **Considers these nonfiction areas:** animals, autobiography, biography, cooking, crafts, cultural interests, current affairs, diet/nutrition, ethnic, foods, gay/lesbian, government, health, history, hobbies, how-to, humor, law, medicine, memoirs, military, money, multicultural, popular culture, politics, psychology, science, sociology, sports, technology, translation, travel, true crime, women's issues, women's studies. **Considers these fiction areas:** contemporary issues, crime, detective, fantasy, feminist, gay, historical, humor, lesbian, literary, mainstream, mystery, police, psychic, regional, satire, science fiction, sports, supernatural, suspense, thriller, women's, chick lit.

☞ "With my legal expertise and experience selling domestic and foreign language book rights, paperback reprint rights, audio rights, film/TV rights and permissions, I am able to provide substantive and personal guidance to my clients in all areas relating to their projects. In addition, with the advent of new publishing technology, Lyons Literary, LLC is situated to address the changing nature of the industry while concurrently handling authors' more traditional needs."

HOW TO CONTACT Only accepts queries through online submission form. Accepts simultaneous submissions. Responds in 8 weeks to queries. Responds in 12 weeks to mss. Obtains most new clients through recommendations from others.

TERMS Agent receives 15% commission on domestic sales. Agent receives 20% commission on foreign sales. Offers written contract.

WRITERS CONFERENCES Agents and Editors Conference.

TIPS "Please submit electronic queries through our website submission form."

● DONALD MAASS LITERARY AGENCY

121 W. 27th St., Suite 801, New York NY 10001. (212)727-8383. **E-mail:** info@maassagency.com. **Website:** www.maassagency.com. Member of AAR. Other memberships include SFWA, MWA, RWA. Represents more than 100 clients. 5% of clients are new/unpublished writers. Currently handles: novels 100%.

◯ Prior to opening his agency, Mr. Maass served as an editor at Dell Publishing (New York)

and as a reader at Gollancz (London). He also served as the president of AAR.

MEMBER AGENTS Donald Maass (mainstream, literary, mystery/suspense, science fiction, romance); Jennifer Jackson (commercial fiction, romance, science fiction, fantasy, mystery/suspense); Cameron McClure (literary, mystery/suspense, urban, fantasy, narrative nonfiction and projects with multicultural, international, and environmental themes, gay/lesbian); Stacia Decker (fiction, memoir, narrative nonfiction, pop-culture [cooking, fashion, style, music, art], smart humor, upscale erotica/erotic memoir and multicultural fiction/nonfiction); Amy Boggs (fantasy and science fiction, especially urban fantasy, paranormal romance, steampunk, YA/children's, and alternate history. historical fiction, multicultural fiction, westerns); Jennifer Udden (speculative fiction, urban fantasy, and mysteries, as well as historical, contemporary, and paranormal romance); Katie Shea (fiction and memoir, especially women's fiction and commercial-scale literary fiction. She is also seeking memoir, narrative nonfiction, food, pop culture, health and lifestyle, and realistic YA).

REPRESENTS Novels. **Considers these fiction areas:** crime, detective, fantasy, historical, horror, literary, mainstream, mystery, police, psychic, science fiction, supernatural, suspense, thriller, women's, romance (historical, paranormal, and time travel).

☞ This agency specializes in commercial fiction, especially science fiction, fantasy, mystery and suspense. Actively seeking to expand in literary fiction and women's fiction. We are fiction specialists. All genres are welcome. Does not want to receive nonfiction, picture books, prescriptive nonfiction, or poetry.

HOW TO CONTACT Query with SASE. Returns material only with SASE. Accepts simultaneous submissions. Responds in 2 weeks to queries. Responds in 3 months to mss.

TERMS Agent receives 15% commission on domestic sales. Agent receives 20% commission on foreign sales.

RECENT SALES *Codex Alera 5: Princep's Fury*, by Jim Butcher (Ace); *Fonseca 6: Bright Futures*, by Stuart Kaimsky (Forge): *Fathom*, by Cherie Priest (Tor); *Gospel Grrls 3: Be Strong and Curvaceous*, by Shelly Adina (Faith Words); *Ariane 1: Peacekeeper*, by Laura Reeve (Roc); *Execution Dock*, by Anne Perry (Random House).

NEW AGENT SPOTLIGHT

ANNA SPROUL-LATIMER (ROSS YOON AGENCY)

Rossyoon.com
@annasproul

ABOUT ANNA: "Like Howard Yoon before me, I've been working for Gail Ross my entire professional life. However, I've managed to get a tour of all aspects of the industry along the way: slinging customer service at Barnes & Noble in my teens; mailing press releases at an NYC house in college; and today, in my spare time, editing and ghostwriting books already sold for publication. In addition to scouting, editing, and producing book proposals, I've spent the past four years managing our agency's foreign rights list. One particular strength I bring to the domestic rights game, therefore, is my understanding of international markets: how and whether your book will sell around the world. I have a BA from Columbia and a master's degree from Oxford, both in English literature."

SHE IS SEEKING: "In two words, adult nonfiction. In six: nonfiction by and for the curious. I represent authors who explore new frontiers, uncover hidden histories, and embed themselves in unusual places. Their energy is so contagious, and their ideas so important, that they've already begun to attract media coverage and a national audience." She is *not* looking for fiction or children's books. "I also do not want self-help that's more about the messenger than the message. (If your work makes use of either of these phrases—'patented method,' 'paradigm shift'—we probably won't get along.) Political screeds, liberal and conservative. Authors who don't understand the value of collaborative editorial process: at one extreme, those who want to 'build their brand' with a book, any book; at the other, artistes. Finally, 'everything you know is wrong' Gladwelly-type books about mind, brain, and behavior. There might be room left in the market for these, but I'm tired of reading them."

HOW TO SUBMIT: "Please e-mail me (anna@rossyoon.com) a short pitch, detailing who you are and what you'd like to write, along with a chapter outline and a couple of sample chapters (if you have them). If you're an expert with an idea but no sample material yet, that's fine too; just be ready to explain your idea in some detail."

WRITERS CONFERENCES Donald Maass: World Science Fiction Convention; Frankfurt Book Fair; Pacific Northwest Writers Conference; Bouchercon. Jennifer Jackson: World Science Fiction Convention; RWA National Conference.

TIPS We are fiction specialists, also noted for our innovative approach to career planning. Few new clients are accepted, but interested authors should query with a SASE. Works with subagents in all principle foreign countries and Hollywood. No prescriptive nonfiction, picture books, or poetry will be considered.

● **GINA MACCOBY LITERARY AGENCY**

P.O. Box 60, Chappaqua NY 10514. (914)238-5630. **E-mail:** query@maccobylit.com; gmaccoby@aol.com. **Contact:** Gina Maccoby. Member of AAR. Ethics and Contracts subcommittee; Authors Guild.

MEMBER AGENTS Gina Maccoby.

REPRESENTS Nonfiction books, novels, juvenile. **Considers these nonfiction areas:** autobiography, biography, cultural interests, current affairs, ethnic, history, juvenile nonfiction, popular culture, women's issues, women's studies. **Considers these fiction areas:** juvenile, literary, mainstream, mystery, thriller, young adult.

HOW TO CONTACT Query with SASE. If querying by email, put "query" in subject line. Accepts simultaneous submissions. Responds in 3 months to queries. Obtains most new clients through recommendations from clients and publishers.

TERMS Agent receives 15% commission on domestic sales. Agent receives 25% commission on foreign sales. Charges clients for photocopying. May recover certain costs, such as legal fees or the cost of shipping books by air to Europe or Japan.

RECENT SALES This agency sold 21 titles last year.

● **MACGREGOR LITERARY INC.**

2373 N.W. 185th Ave., Suite 165, Hillsboro OR 97124. (503)277-8308. **E-mail:** submissions@macgregorliterary.com. **Website:** www.macgregorliterary.com. **Contact:** Chip MacGregor. Signatory of WGA. Represents 40 clients. 10% of clients are new/unpublished writers. Currently handles: nonfiction books 40%, novels 60%.

○ Prior to his current position, Mr. MacGregor was the senior agent with Alive Communications. Most recently, he was associate publisher for Time-Warner Book Group's Faith Division, and helped put together their Center Street imprint.

MEMBER AGENTS Chip MacGregor, Sandra Bishop, Amanda Luedeke; Erin Buterbaugh; Shannon Potelicki.

REPRESENTS Nonfiction books, novels. **Considers these nonfiction areas:** business, current affairs, economics, history, how-to, humor, inspirational, parenting, popular culture, satire, self-help, sports, marriage. **Considers these fiction areas:** crime, detective, historical, inspirational, mainstream, mystery, police, religious, romance, suspense, thriller, women's, chick lit.

8—➤ "My specialty has been in career planning with authors—finding commercial ideas, then helping authors bring them to market, and in the midst of that assisting the authors as they get firmly established in their writing careers. I'm probably best known for my work with Christian books over the years, but I've done a fair amount of general market projects as well." Actively seeking authors with a Christian worldview and a growing platform. Does not want to receive fantasy, sci-fi, children's books, poetry or screenplays.

HOW TO CONTACT Query with SASE. Accepts simultaneous submissions. Responds in 3 weeks to queries. Obtains most new clients through recommendations from others. Not looking to add unpublished authors except through referrals from current clients.

TERMS Agent receives 15% commission on domestic sales. Agent receives 15% commission on foreign sales. Offers written contract; 30-day notice must be given to terminate contract. Charges for exceptional fees after receiving authors' permission.

WRITERS CONFERENCES Blue Ridge Christian Writers' Conference; Write to Publish.

TIPS "Seriously consider attending a good writers' conference. It will give you the chance to be face-to-face with people in the industry. Also, if you're a novelist, consider joining one of the national writers' organizations. The American Christian Fiction Writers (ACFW) is a wonderful group for new as well as established writers. And if you're a Christian writer of any kind, check into The Writers View, an online writing group. All of these have proven helpful to writers."

① **RICIA MAINHARDT AGENCY (RMA)**

612 Argyle Rd, #L5, Brooklyn NY 11230. (718)434-1893. **Fax:** (718)434-2157. **E-mail:** ricia@ricia.com. **Website:** www.ricia.com. **Contact:** Ricia Mainhardt. Represents 10 clients. 50% of clients are new/unpub-

lished writers. Currently handles: nonfiction books 40%, novella 50%, juvenile books 10%.

REPRESENTS Nonfiction books, novels, juvenile. **Considers these fiction areas:** action, adventure, confession, crime, detective, erotica, ethnic, family saga, fantasy, feminist, frontier, gay, glitz, historical, horror, humor, juvenile, lesbian, literary, mainstream, mystery, police, psychic, regional, romance, satire, science fiction, sports, supernatural, suspense, thriller, Westerns, women's, young adult.

8—🔑 "We are a small boutique agency that provides hands-on service and attention to clients." Actively seeking adult and young adult fiction, nonfiction, picture books for early readers. Does not want to receive poetry, children's books or screenplays.

HOW TO CONTACT Query with SASE or by e-mail. See guidelines on website depending on type of ms. No attachments or diskettes. Accepts simultaneous submissions. Responds in 1 month to queries. Responds in 4 months to mss. Obtains most new clients through recommendations from others, solicitations.

TERMS Agent receives 15% commission on domestic sales. Offers written contract; 90-day notice must be given to terminate contract.

WRITERS CONFERENCES Science Fiction Worldcon, Lunacon, World Fantasy, RWA.

TIPS "Be professional; be patient. It takes a long time for me to evaluate all the submissions that come through the door. Pestering phone calls and e-mails are not appreciated. Write the best book you can in your own style and keep an active narrative voice."

① KIRSTEN MANGES LITERARY AGENCY

115 W. 29th St., Third Floor, New York NY 10001. **E-mail:** kirsten@mangeslit.com. **Website:** www.mangeslit.com. **Contact:** Kirsten Manges.

○ Prior to her current position, Ms. Manges was an agent at Curtis Brown.

REPRESENTS Nonfiction books, novels. **Considers these nonfiction areas:** cooking, diet/nutrition, foods, history, memoirs, multicultural, psychology, science, spirituality, sports, technology, travel, women's issues, women's studies, journalism, narrative. **Considers these fiction areas:** commercial, women's, chick lit.

8—🔑 This agency has a focus on women's issues. "Actively seeking high quality fiction and nonfiction. I'm looking for strong credentials, an original point of view and excellent writing

skills. With fiction, I'm looking for well written commercial novels, as well as compelling and provocative literary works."

HOW TO CONTACT Query with SASE. Obtains most new clients through recommendations from others, solicitations.

① CAROL MANN AGENCY

55 Fifth Ave., New York NY 10003. (212)206-5635. **Fax:** (212)675-4809. **E-mail:** submissions@carolmannagency.com. **Website:** www.carolmannagency.com. **Contact:** Eliza Dreier. Member of AAR. Represents roughly 200 clients. 15% of clients are new/unpublished writers. Currently handles: nonfiction books 90%, novels 10%.

MEMBER AGENTS Carol Mann (health/medical, religion, spirituality, self-help, parenting, narrative nonfiction, current affairs); Laura Yorke; Gareth Esersky; Myrsini Stephanides (nonfiction areas of interest: pop culture and music, humor, narrative nonfiction and memoir, cookbooks; fiction areas of interest: offbeat literary fiction, graphic works, and edgy YA fiction). Joanne Wyckoff (nonfiction areas of interest: memoir, narrative nonfiction, personal narrative, psychology, women's issues, education, health and wellness, parenting, serious self-help, natural history); fiction.

REPRESENTS Nonfiction books, novels. **Considers these nonfiction areas:** anthropology, archeology, architecture, art, autobiography, biography, business, child guidance, cultural interests, current affairs, design, ethnic, government, health, history, law, medicine, money, music, parenting, popular culture, politics, psychology, self-help, sociology, sports, women's issues, women's studies. **Considers these fiction areas:** commercial, literary.

8—🔑 This agency specializes in current affairs, self-help, popular culture, psychology, parenting, and history. Does not want to receive genre fiction (romance, mystery, etc.).

HOW TO CONTACT Please see website for submission guidelines. Responds in 4 weeks to queries.

TERMS Agent receives 15% commission on domestic sales. Agent receives 20% commission on foreign sales. Offers written contract.

MANSION STREET LITERARY MANAGEMENT

E-mail: mansionstreet@gmail.com. **E-mail:** query mansionstreet@gmail.com; querymichelle@man

sionstreet.com. **Website:** http://mansionstreet.com. **Contact:** Jean Sagendorph; Michelle Witte.
MEMBER AGENTS Jean Sagendorph, Michelle Witte.

🔑 Jean is interested in: Children's picture books (CURRENTLY CLOSED TO SUBMISSIONS), pop culture, cookbooks, gift books, general nonfiction, brand extensions. Michelle is interested in: Young adult, middle grade, children's nonfiction.

HOW TO CONTACT Submit query letter, no more than 10 pages of ms in body of e-mail. No attachments. Include "QUERY," name, title, and genre in subject line of e-mail. Responds in up to 6 weeks.

RECENT SALES Authors: Paul Thurlby, Steve Ouch, Steve Seabury, Gina Hyams, Sam Pocker, Kim Siebold, Jean Sagendorph, Heidi Antman, Shannon O'Malley, Meg Bartholomy, Dawn Sokol, Hollister Hovey, Porter Hovey, Robb Pearlman.

◑ MANUS & ASSOCIATES LITERARY AGENCY, INC.

425 Sherman Ave., Suite 200, Palo Alto CA 94306. (650)470-5151. **Fax:** (650)470-5159. **E-mail:** manuslit@manuslit.com. **Website:** www.manuslit. com. **Contact:** Jillian Manus, Jandy Nelson, Penny Nelson. Member of AAR. Represents 75 clients. 30% of clients are new/unpublished writers. Currently handles: nonfiction books 70%, novels 30%.

◐ Prior to becoming an agent, Ms. Manus was associate publisher of two national magazines and director of development at Warner Bros. and Universal Studios; she has been a literary agent for 20 years.

MEMBER AGENTS Jandy Nelson, jandy@manuslit. com (self-help, health, memoirs, narrative nonfiction, women's fiction, literary fiction, multicultural fiction, thrillers). Nelson is currently on sabbatical and not taking on new clients. Jillian Manus, jillian@ manuslit.com (political, memoirs, self-help, history, sports, women's issues, Latin fiction and nonfiction, thrillers); Penny Nelson, penny@manuslit.com (memoirs, self-help, sports, nonfiction); Dena Fischer (literary fiction, mainstream/commercial fiction, chick lit, women's fiction, historical fiction, ethnic/cultural fiction, narrative nonfiction, parenting, relationships, pop culture, health, sociology, psychology); Janet Wilkens Manus (narrative fact-based crime books, religion, pop psychology, inspiration, mem-

oirs, cookbooks); Stephanie Lee (not currently taking on new clients).

REPRESENTS Nonfiction books, novels. **Considers these nonfiction areas:** autobiography, biography, business, child guidance, cultural interests, current affairs, economics, environment, ethnic, health, how-to, medicine, memoirs, money, parenting, popular culture, psychology, science, self-help, technology, women's issues, women's studies, Gen X and Gen Y issues; creative nonfiction. **Considers these fiction areas:** literary, mainstream, multicultural, mystery, suspense, thriller, women's, quirky/edgy fiction.

🔑 "Our agency is unique in the way that we not only sell the material, but we edit, develop concepts, and participate in the marketing effort. We specialize in large, conceptual fiction and nonfiction, and always value a project that can be sold in the TV/feature film market." Actively seeking high-concept thrillers, commercial literary fiction, women's fiction, celebrity biographies, memoirs, multicultural fiction, popular health, women's empowerment and mysteries. No horror, romance, science fiction, fantasy, western, young adult, children's, poetry, cookbooks, or magazine articles.

HOW TO CONTACT Consult website for specific fiction and nonfiction guidelines. Accepts simultaneous submissions. Responds in 3 months to queries. Responds in 3 months to mss. Obtains most new clients through recommendations from others, solicitations, conferences.

TERMS Agent receives 15% commission on domestic sales. Agent receives 20-25% commission on foreign sales. Offers written contract, binding for 2 years; 60-day notice must be given to terminate contract. Charges for photocopying and postage/UPS.

RECENT SALES *Nothing Down for the 2000s* and *Multiple Streams of Income for the 2000s*, by Robert Allen; *Missed Fortune 101*, by Doug Andrew; *Cracking the Millionaire Code*, by Mark Victor Hansen and Robert Allen; *Stress Free for Good*, by Dr. Fred Luskin and Dr. Ken Pelletier; *The Mercy of Thin Air*, by Ronlyn Domangue; *The Fine Art of Small Talk*, by Debra Fine; *Bone Men of Bonares*, by Terry Tamoff.

WRITERS CONFERENCES Maui Writers' Conference; San Diego State University Writers' Conference; Willamette Writers' Conference; BookExpo America; MEGA Book Marketing University.

TIPS "Research agents using a variety of sources."

MARCH TENTH, INC.

24 Hillside Terrace, Montvale NJ 07645. (201)387-6551. **Fax:** (201)387-6552. **E-mail:** hchoron@aol.com; schoron@aol.com. **Website:** www.marchtenthinc.com. **Contact:** Harry Choron, vice president. Represents 40 clients. 30% of clients are new/unpublished writers. Currently handles: nonfiction books 100%.

REPRESENTS Nonfiction books. **Considers these nonfiction areas:** autobiography, biography, current affairs, film, health, history, humor, language, literature, medicine, music, popular culture, satire, theater.

8→ "We prefer to work with published/established writers." Does not want to receive children's or young adult novels, plays, screenplays or poetry.

HOW TO CONTACT "Query with SASE. Include your proposal, a short bio, and contact information." Accepts simultaneous submissions. Responds in 1 month to queries.

TERMS Agent receives 15% commission on domestic sales. Agent receives 20% commission on foreign sales. Agent receives 20% commission on film sales. Does not require expense money upfront.

THE DENISE MARCIL LITERARY AGENCY, INC.

110 William St., Suite 2202, New York NY 10038. (212)337-3402. **Fax:** (212)727-2688. **E-mail:** dmla@DeniseMarcilAgency.com. **Website:** www.denisemarcilagency.com. **Contact:** Denise Marcil, Anne Marie O'Farrell. Member of AAR.

○ Prior to opening her agency, Ms. Marcil served as an editorial assistant with Avon Books and as an assistant editor with Simon & Schuster.

MEMBER AGENTS Denise Marcil (women's commercial fiction, thrillers, suspense, popular reference, how-to, self-help, health, business, and parenting); Anne Marie O'Farrell.

8→ This agency is currently not taking on new authors. We are currently seeking self-help and popular reference books, including parenting, business, spirituality, and biographies. We are looking for authors with national platforms such as national seminars, columns, television and radio shows. We do not represent science fiction, children's books, or political nonfiction.

HOW TO CONTACT The best way to query is with a well-written and compelling one-page query letter and SASE. (**Do not send a query by fax or email.**) **Query letters for Denise Marcil should be sent to 156 Fifth Ave., Suite 823, New York, NY 10010. Query letters for Anne Marie O'Farrell should be sent to 86 Dennis St., Manhasset, NY 11030. We do not respond to unsolicited email queries.**

TERMS Agent receives 15% commission on domestic sales. Agent receives 20% commission on foreign sales. Offers written contract, binding for 2 years. Charges $100/year for postage, photocopying, long-distance calls, etc.

RECENT SALES For Denise Marcil: *A Chesapeake Shores Christmas*, by Sherryl Woods; *Prime Time Health*, by William Sears, M.D. and Martha Sears, R.N.; *The Autism Book*, by Robert W. Sears, M.D.; *The Yellow House and The Linen Queen* by Patricia Falvey; *The 10-Minute Total Body Breakthrough*, by Sean Foy. For Anne Marie O'Farrell: *Think Confident, Be Confident*, by Leslie Sokol Ph.d and Marci G. Fox, Ph.d; *Hell Yes*, by Elizabeth Baskin; *Breaking Into the Boys Club*, by Molly Shepard, Jane K. Stimmler, and Peter Dean.

MARIA CARVAINIS AGENCY, INC.

Rockefeller Center, 1270 Avenue of the Americas, Suite 2320, New York NY 10020. (212)245-6365. **Fax:** (212)245-7196. **E-mail:** mca@mariacarvainisagency.com. **Website:** http://mariacarvainisagency.com. **Contact:** Maria Carvainis, Chelsea Gilmore. Member of AAR. Signatory of WGA. Other memberships include Authors Guild, Women's Media Group, ABA, MWA, RWA. Represents 75 clients. 10% of clients are new/unpublished writers. Currently handles: nonfiction books 35%, novels 65%.

○ Prior to opening her agency, Ms. Carvainis spent more than 10 years in the publishing industry as a senior editor with Macmillan Publishing, Basic Books, Avon Books, and Crown Publishers. Ms. Carvainis has served as a member of the AAR Board of Directors and AAR Treasurer, as well as serving as chair of the AAR Contracts Committee. She presently serves on the AAR Royalty Committee. Ms. Gilmore started her publishing career at Oxford University Press, in the Higher Education Group. She then worked at Avalon Books as associate editor. She is most interested in women's fiction, literary fiction, young adult, pop culture, and mystery/suspense.

MEMBER AGENTS Maria Carvainis, president/literary agent; Chelsea Gilmore, literary agent.
REPRESENTS Nonfiction books, novels. **Considers these nonfiction areas:** autobiography, biography, business, economics, history, memoirs, science, technology, women's issues, women's studies. **Considers these fiction areas:** contemporary issues, historical, literary, mainstream, mystery, suspense, thriller, women's, young adult, middle-grade.

8—� Does not want to receive science fiction or children's picture books.

HOW TO CONTACT Query with SASE. No e-mail accepted. Responds in up to 3 months to mss and to queries 1 month. Obtains most new clients through recommendations from others, conferences, query letters.
TERMS Agent receives 15% commission on domestic sales. Agent receives 20% commission on foreign sales. Offers written contract. Charges clients for foreign postage and bulk copying.
RECENT SALES *A Secret Affair*, by Mary Balogh (Delacorte); *Tough Customer*, by Sandra Brown (Simon & Schuster); *A Lady Never Tells*, by Candace Camp (Pocket Books); *The King James Conspiracy*, by Phillip Depoy (St. Martin's Press).
WRITERS CONFERENCES BookExpo America; Frankfurt Book Fair; London Book Fair; Mystery Writers of America; Thrillerfest; Romance Writers of America.

MARIE BROWN ASSOCIATES, INC.

412 W. 154th St., New York NY 10032. (212)939-9725. **Fax:** (212)939-9728. **E-mail:** mbrownlit@aol.com. **Contact:** Marie Brown. Estab. 1984. Represents 60 clients. Currently handles: nonfiction books 75%, juvenile books 10%, other 15% other.
MEMBER AGENTS Janell Walden Agyeman (Miami).
REPRESENTS Nonfiction books, juvenile. **Considers these nonfiction areas:** juvenile, biography, business, ethnic, history, music, religion, womens. **Considers these fiction areas:** ethnic, juvenile, literary, mainstream.

8—ᴙ This agency specializes in multicultural and African-American writers.

HOW TO CONTACT Query with SASE. Prefers to read materials exclusively. Reports in 6-10 weeks on queries. Obtains most new clients through recommendations from others.

TERMS Agent receives 15% commission on domestic sales. Agent receives 20% commission on foreign sales. Offers written contract.

MARSAL LYON LITERARY AGENCY, LLC

PMB 121, 665 San Rodolfo Dr. 124, Solana Beach CA 92075. (858)492-8009. **Website:** www.marsallyonliteraryagency.com. **Contact:** Kevan Lyon, Jill Marsal.
MEMBER AGENTS Kevan Lyon; Jill Marsal; Kathleen Rushall; and Deborah Ritchken.
REPRESENTS Nonfiction books, novels. **Considers these nonfiction areas:** animals, biography, business, cooking, current affairs, diet/nutrition, foods, health, history, investigative, memoirs, music, parenting, popular culture, politics, psychology, science, self-help, sports, women's issues, relationships, advice. **Considers these fiction areas:** commercial, mainstream, multicultural, mystery, romance, suspense, thriller, women's, young adult.
HOW TO CONTACT Query by e-mail to either Jill Marsal at jill@marsallyonliteraryagency.com, Kevan Lyon at kevan@marsallyonliteraryagency.com or Kathleen Rushall at Kathleen@MarsalLyonLiteraryAgency.com. "Please visit our website to determine who is best suited for your work. Write 'query' in the subject line of your e-mail. Please allow up to several weeks to hear back on your query."
TIPS "Our agency's mission is to help writers achieve their publishing dreams. We want to work with authors not just for a book but for a career; we are dedicated to building long-term relationships with our authors and publishing partners. Our goal is to help find homes for books that engage, entertain, and make a difference."

⚫ THE MARSH AGENCY, LTD

50 Albemarle St., London England W1S 4BD United Kingdom. (44)(207)493-4361. **Fax:** (44)(207)496-8961. **Website:** www.marsh-agency.co.uk. Estab. 1994.
MEMBER AGENTS Jessica Woollard, Stephanie Ebdon, Charlotte Bruton, Hannah Ferguson.
REPRESENTS Nonfiction books, novels.

8—ᴙ "This agency was founded as an international rights specialist for literary agents and publishers in the United Kingdom, the U.S., Canada and New Zealand, for whom we sell foreign rights on a commission basis. We work directly with publishers in all the major territories and in the majority of the smaller ones; sometimes in conjunction with local representatives." Actively seeking crime novels.

HOW TO CONTACT Query with SASE or use online submission form. Incluce a brief cover letter with your contact details and any relevant information, including any previously published work and any experience which relates to the book's subject matter; a short synopsis. Fiction: outline the plot and main characters. Nonfiction: a summary of the work and chapter outlines. First three chapters (no more than 100 pages) double spaced with all pages numbered. Obtains most new clients through recommendations from others, solicitations.

RECENT SALES A full list of clients and sales is available online.

TIPS "Use this agency's online form to send a generic e-mail message."

● THE EVAN MARSHALL AGENCY

6 Tristam Place, Pine Brook NJ 07058-9445. (973)882-1122. **Fax:** (973)882-3099. **E-mail:** evanmarshall@thenovelist.com. **Contact:** Evan Marshall. Member of AAR. Other memberships include MWA, Sisters in Crime. Currently handles: novels 100%.

REPRESENTS Novels. **Considers these fiction areas:** action, adventure, erotica, ethnic, frontier, historical, horror, humor, inspirational, literary, mainstream, mystery, religious, satire, science fiction, suspense, western, romance (contemporary, gothic, historical, regency).

HOW TO CONTACT Do not query. Currently accepting clients only by referal from editors and our own clients. Responds in 1 week to queries. Responds in 3 months to mss. Obtains most new clients through recommendations from others.

TERMS Agent receives 15% commission on domestic sales. Agent receives 20% commission on foreign sales. Offers written contract.

RECENT SALES *Watch Me Die,* by Erica Spindler (St. Martin's Press); *The First Day of the Rest of My Life,* by Cathy Lamb (Kensington); *Highland Protector,* by Hannah Howell (Zebra); *Devoured by Darkness,* by Alexandra Ivy (Kensington).

● THE MARTELL AGENCY

1350 Avenue of the Americas, Suite 1205, New York NY 10019. **Fax:** (212)317-2676. **E-mail:** afmartell@aol.com. **E-mail:** submissions@themartellagency.com. **Website:** www.themartellagency.com. **Contact:** Alice Martell.

REPRESENTS Nonfiction, novels. **Considers these nonfiction areas:** business, economics, health, history, medicine, memoirs, multicultural, psychology, self-help, women's issues, women's studies,. **Considers these fiction areas:** commercial, mystery, suspense, thriller.

HOW TO CONTACT Query with SASE. Submit sample chapters. "Please send a query first to Alice Martell, by e-mail or mail." Consult website for complete submission guidelines.

RECENT SALES *Peddling Peril: The Secret Nuclear Arms Trade* by David Albright and Joel Wit (Five Press); *America's Women: Four Hundred Years of Dolls, Drudges, Helpmates, and Heroines,* by Gail Collins (William Morrow). Other clients include Serena Bass, Janice Erlbaum, David Cay Johnston, Mark Derr, Barbara Rolls, PhD.

① MARTIN LITERARY MANAGEMENT

7683 SE 27th St., #307, Mercer Island WA 98040. (206)486-1773. **E-mail:** sharlene@martinliterarymanagement.com. **Website:** www.MartinLiteraryManagement.com. **Contact:** Sharlene Martin.

Prior to becoming an agent, Ms. Martin worked in film/TV production and acquisitions.

MEMBER AGENTS Sharlene Martin (nonfiction).

REPRESENTS Considers these nonfiction areas: autobiography, biography, business, child guidance, current affairs, economics, health, history, how-to, humor, inspirational, investigative, medicine, memoirs, parenting, popular culture, psychology, satire, self-help, true crime, women's issues, women's studies.

This agency has strong ties to film/TV. Actively seeking nonfiction that is highly commercial and that can be adapted to film. "We are being inundated with queries and submissions that are wrongfully being submitted to us, which only results in more frustration for the writers."

HOW TO CONTACT Query via e-mail with MS Word only. No attachments on queries; place letter in body of e-mail. Accepts simultaneous submissions. Responds in 2 weeks to queries. Responds in 3-4 weeks to mss. Obtains most new clients through recommendations from others.

TERMS Agent receives 15% commission on domestic sales. Agent receives 25% commission on foreign sales. Offers written contract, binding for 1 year; 1-month notice must be given to terminate contract. Charges author for postage and copying if material is not sent electronically. 99% of materials are sent electronically to minimize charges to author for postage and copying.

RECENT SALES *Honor Bound: My Journey to Hell and Back with Amanda Knox*, by Raffaele Sollecito; *Impossible Odds: The Kidnapping of Jessica Buchanan and Dramatic Rescue by SEAL Team Six*, by Jessica Buchanan, Erik Landemalm and Anthony Flacco; *Walking on Eggshells*, by Lisa Chapman; *Publish Your Nonfiction*, by Sharlene Martin and Anthony Flacco.

TIPS "Have a strong platform for nonfiction. Please don't call. I welcome e-mail. I'm very responsive when I'm interested in a query and work hard to get my clients' materials in the best possible shape before submissions. Do your homework prior to submission and only submit your best efforts. Please review our website carefully to make sure we're a good match for your work. If you read my book, *Publish Your Nonfiction Book: Strategies For Learning the Industry, Selling Your Book and Building a Successful Career* (Writer's Digest Books) you'll know exactly how to charm me."

MARGRET MCBRIDE LITERARY AGENCY

P.O. Box 9128, La Jolla CA 92038. (858)454-1550. **Fax:** (858)454-2156. **E-mail:** staff@mcbridelit.com. **Website:** www.mcbrideliterary.com. **Contact:** Michael Daley, submissions manager. Member of AAR. Other memberships include Authors Guild.

○ Prior to opening her agency, Ms. McBride worked at Random House, Ballantine Books, and Warner Books.

REPRESENTS Nonfiction books, novels. **Considers these nonfiction areas:** autobiography, biography, business, cooking, cultural interests, current affairs, economics, ethnic, foods, government, health, history, how-to, law, medicine, money, popular culture, politics, psychology, science, self-help, sociology, technology, women's issues, style. **Considers these fiction areas:** action, adventure, crime, detective, historical, humor, literary, mainstream, mystery, police, satire, suspense, thriller.

⚯ This agency specializes in mainstream fiction and nonfiction. PLEASE DO NOT SEND: screenplays, romance, poetry, or children's.

HOW TO CONTACT The agency is only accepting new clients by referral at this time. Query with synopsis, bio, SASE. Do not fax queries. Accepts simultaneous submissions. Responds in 4-6 weeks to queries. Responds in 6-8 weeks to mss.

TERMS Agent receives 15% commission on domestic sales. Agent receives 25% commission on foreign sales. Charges for overnight delivery and photocopying.

TIPS "Our office does not accept e-mail queries!"

THE MCCARTHY AGENCY, LLC

7 Allen St., Rumson NJ 07660. Phone/**Fax:** (732)741-3065. **E-mail:** McCarthylit@aol.com; ntfrost@hotmail.com. **Contact:** Shawna McCarthy. Member of AAR. Currently handles: nonfiction books 25%, novels 75%.

MEMBER AGENTS Shawna McCarthy, Nahvae Frost.

REPRESENTS Nonfiction books, novels. **Considers these nonfiction areas:** biography, history, philosophy, science. **Considers these fiction areas:** fantasy, juvenile, mystery, romance, science, womens.

HOW TO CONTACT Query via e-mail or regular mail to The McCarthy Agency, c/o Nahvae Frost, 101 Clinton Avenue, Apartment #2, Brooklyn, NY 11205 Accepts simultaneous submissions.

MCCARTHY CREATIVE SERVICES

625 Main St., Suite 834, New York NY 10044-0035. (212)832-3428. **Fax:** (212)829-9610. **E-mail:** paulmccarthy@mccarthycreative.com. **Website:** www.mccarthycreative.com. **Contact:** Paul D. McCarthy. Other memberships include the Authors Guild, American Society of Journalists & Authors, National Book Critics Circle, Authors League of America. Represents 5 clients. 0% of clients are new/unpublished writers. Currently handles: nonfiction books 95%, novels 5%.

○ Prior to his current position, Mr. McCarthy was a professional writer, literary agent at the Scott Meredith Literary Agency, senior editor at publishing companies (Simon & Schuster, HarperCollins and Doubleday) and a public speaker. Learn much more about Mr. McCarthy by visiting his website.

MEMBER AGENTS Paul D. McCarthy.

REPRESENTS Nonfiction books, novels. **Considers these nonfiction areas:** animals, anthropology, art, biography, business, child, current affairs, education, ethnic, gay, government, health, history, how to, humor, language, memoirs, military, money, music, nature, popular culture, psychology, religion, science, self help, sociology, sports, translation, true crime, women's. **Considers these fiction areas:** glitz, adventure, confession, detective, erotica, ethnic, family, fantasy, feminist, gay, historical, horror, humor, literary, mainstream, mystery, regional, romance, science, sports, thriller, western, young, women's.

⊶ "I deliberately founded my company to be unlimited in its range. That's what I offer, and the world has responded. My agency was founded so that I could maximize and build on the value of my combined experience for my authors and other clients, in all of my capacities and more. I think it's very important for authors to know that because I'm so exclusive as an agent, I may not be able to offer representation on the basis of the manuscript they submit. However, if they decide to invest in their book and lifetime career as authors, by engaging my professional, near-unique editorial services, there is the possibility that at the end of the process, when they've achieved the very best, most salable and competitive book they can write, I may see sufficient potential in the book and their next books, that I do offer to be their agent. Representation is never guaranteed." Established authors of serious and popular nonfiction, who want the value of being one of MCS's very exclusive authors who receive special attention, and of being represented by a literary agent who brings such a rich diversity and depth of publishing/creative/professorial experience, and distinguished reputation. No first novels. "Novels by established novelists will be considered very selectively."

HOW TO CONTACT Submit outline, one chapter (either first or best). Queries and submissions by e-mail only. Send as e-mail attachment. Responds in 3-4 weeks to queries. Obtains most new clients through recommendations from others.

TERMS Agent receives 15% commission on domestic sales. Agent receives 20% commission on foreign sales. Offers written contract; 30-day notice must be given to terminate contract. "All reading done in deciding whether or not to offer representation is free. Editorial services are available. Mailing and postage expenses that incurred on the author's behalf are always approved by them in advance."

TIPS "Always keep in mind that your query letter/proposal is only one of hundreds and thousands that are competing for the agent's attention. Therefore, your presentation of your book and yourself as author has

to be immediate, intense, compelling, and concise. Make the query letter one-page, and after short, introductory paragraph, write a 150-word KEYNOTE description of your manuscript."

◐ THE MCGILL AGENCY, INC.

10000 N. Central Expressway, Suite 400, Dallas TX 75231. (214)390-5970. **E-mail:** info.mcgillagency@gmail.com. **Contact:** Jack Bollinger. Estab. 2009. Represents 10 clients. 50% of clients are new/unpublished writers.

MEMBER AGENTS Jack Bollinger (eclectic tastes in nonfiction and fiction); Amy Cohn (nonfiction interests include women's issues, gay/lesbian, ethnic/cultural, memoirs, true crime; fiction interests include mystery, suspense and thriller).

REPRESENTS **Considers these nonfiction areas:** biography, business, child guidance, current affairs, education, ethnic, gay, health, history, how-to, memoirs, military, psychology, self-help, true crime, women's issues. **Considers these fiction areas:** historical, mainstream, mystery, romance, thriller.

HOW TO CONTACT Query via e-mail. Responds in 2 weeks to queries and 6 weeks to mss. Obtains new clients through conferences.

TERMS Agent receives 15% commission.

MCINTOSH & OTIS, INC.

353 Lexington Ave., New York NY 10016. (212)687-7400. **Fax:** (212)687-6894. **E-mail:** info@mcintoshandotis.com. **Website:** www.mcintoshandotis.com. **Contact:** Eugene H. Winick, Esq. Estab. 1927. Member of AAR. SCBWI 30% of clients are new/unpublished writers. Currently handles: juvenile books.

⊶ Actively seeking "books with memorable characters, distinctive voices, and great plots." Not looking for educational, activity books, coloring books. New agent Christa Heschke reps young adult, middle grade and picture books.

HOW TO CONTACT Query with SASE. Responds to queries within 6-8 weeks. Obtains clients through recommendations from others, editors, conferences and queries.

TERMS Agent receives 15% commission on domestic sales; 20% on foreign sales.

WRITERS CONFERENCES Attends Bologna Book Fair, in Bologna Italy in April, SCBWI Conference in New York in February, and regularly attends other conferences and industry conventions.

SALLY HILL MCMILLAN & ASSOCIATES, INC.

429 E. Kingston Ave., Charlotte NC 28203. (704)334-0897. **Contact:** Sally Hill McMillan. Member of AAR.

☞ "We are not seeking new clients at this time. Agency specializes in Southern fiction, women's fiction, mystery and practical nonfiction."

HOW TO CONTACT *No unsolicited submissions.*

BOB MECOY LITERARY AGENCY

66 Grand St., Suite 1, New York NY 10013. (212)226-1398. **E-mail:** mecoy@aol.com. **Website:** www.grand streetliterary.com. **Contact:** Bob Mecoy.

MEMBER AGENTS Bob Mecoy.

☞ Fiction (literary, crime, romance); nonfiction (true crime, finance, memoir, literary, prescriptive self-help & graphic novelists). No Westerns.

HOW TO CONTACT Query with sample chapters and synopsis.

● MENDEL MEDIA GROUP, LLC

115 W. 30th St., Suite 800, New York NY 10001. (646)239-9896. **Fax:** (212)685-4717. **E-mail:** scott@mendelmedia.com. **Website:** www.mendelmedia.com. Member of AAR. Represents 40-60 clients.

○ Prior to becoming an agent, Mr. Mendel was an academic. "I taught American literature, Yiddish, Jewish studies, and literary theory at the University of Chicago and the University of Illinois at Chicago while working on my PhD in English. I also worked as a freelance technical writer and as the managing editor of a healthcare magazine. In 1998, I began working for the late Jane Jordan Browne, a long-time agent in the book publishing world."

REPRESENTS Nonfiction books, novels, scholarly, with potential for broad/popular appeal. **Considers these nonfiction areas:** Americana, animals, anthropology, architecture, art, biography, business, child guidance, cooking, current affairs, dance, diet/nutrition, education, environment, ethnic, foods, gardening, gay/lesbian, government, health, history, how-to, humor, investigative, language, medicine, memoirs, military, money, multicultural, music, parenting, philosophy, popular culture, psychology, recreation, regional, religious, science, self-help, sex, sociology, software, spirituality, sports, true crime, war, women's issues, women's studies, Jewish topics; creative nonfiction. **Considers these fiction areas:** action, adventure, contemporary issues, crime, detective, erotica, ethnic, feminist, gay, glitz, historical, humor, inspirational, juvenile, lesbian, literary, mainstream, mystery, picture books, police, religious, romance, satire, sports, thriller, young adult, Jewish fiction.

☞ "I am interested in major works of history, current affairs, biography, business, politics, economics, science, major memoirs, narrative nonfiction, and other sorts of general nonfiction." Actively seeking new, major or definitive work on a subject of broad interest, or a controversial, but authoritative, new book on a subject that affects many people's lives. I also represent more light-hearted nonfiction projects, such as gift or novelty books, when they suit the market particularly well." Does not want "queries about projects written years ago that were unsuccessfully shopped to a long list of trade publishers by either the author or another agent. I am specifically not interested in reading short, category romances (regency, time travel, paranormal, etc.), horror novels, supernatural stories, poetry, original plays, or film scripts."

HOW TO CONTACT Query with SASE. Do not e-mail or fax queries. For nonfiction, include a complete, fully edited book proposal with sample chapters. For fiction, include a complete synopsis and no more than 20 pages of sample text. Responds in 2 weeks to queries. Responds in 4-6 weeks to mss. Obtains most new clients through recommendations from others.

TERMS Agent receives 15% commission on domestic sales. Agent receives 20% commission on foreign sales.

WRITERS CONFERENCES BookExpo America; Frankfurt Book Fair; London Book Fair; RWA National Conference; Modern Language Association Convention; Jerusalem Book Fair.

TIPS "While I am not interested in being flattered by a prospective client, it does matter to me that she knows why she is writing to me in the first place. Is one of my clients a colleague of hers? Has she read a book by one of my clients that led her to believe I might be interested in her work? Authors of descriptive nonfiction should have real credentials and expertise in their subject areas, either as academics, journalists, or policy experts, and authors of prescriptive nonfiction should have legitimate expertise and considerable experience communicating their ideas in semi-

NEW AGENT SPOTLIGHT

THAO LE (SANDRA DIJKSTRA LITERARY AGENCY)

dijkstraagency.com
@ThaoLe8

ABOUT THAO: She is a graduate of the University of California, San Diego with a double major in Econ-Management Science and Chinese Studies. While interning at the agency during college, she realized where her true love lies—books—and joined the Sandra Dijkstra Literary Agency full-time in 2011.

SHE IS SEEKING: Thao is currently building her list and is specifically interested in middle grade and YA, as well as adult science-fiction and fantasy. She's particularly drawn to smart, strong and sassy characters (whether they be robots, fairies, demons or of the human variety) and twisty plots with a compelling narrative. She's always on the lookout for the type of stories that make you stay curled up in bed, turning page after page even after the sun has come up. Please note that Thao is specifically *not* interested in: biographies, business books, cookbooks, picture books, poetry, religious/spiritual books, screenplays, self-help, short stories, travel books

HOW TO CONTACT: thao@dijkstraagency.com. "We only accept electronic submissions. Any hardcopy submissions received by mail will be recycled unopened. Please send a query letter, a 1-page synopsis, a brief bio (including a description of your publishing history), and the first 10-15 pages of your manuscript. Please send all items in the body of the e-mail, not as an attachment."

nars and workshops, in a successful business, through the media, etc."

● **SCOTT MEREDITH LITERARY AGENCY**
200 W. 57th St., Suite 904, New York NY 10019. (646)274-1970. **Fax:** (212)977-5997. **E-mail:** info@scottmeredith.com. **Website:** www.scottmeredith.com. **Contact:** Arthur Klebanoff, CEO. Adheres to the AAR canon of ethics. Represents 20 clients. 5% of clients are new/unpublished writers. Currently handles: nonfiction books 85%, novels 5%, textbooks 5%.

○ Prior to becoming an agent, Mr. Klebanoff was a lawyer.

REPRESENTS Nonfiction books, textbooks.

⟞ This agency's specialty lies in category nonfiction publishing programs. Actively seeking category leading nonfiction. Does not want to receive first fiction projects.

HOW TO CONTACT Query with SASE. Submit proposal package, author bio. Accepts simultaneous submissions. Responds in 1 week to queries. Responds in 2 weeks to mss. Obtains most new clients through recommendations from others.

TERMS Agent receives 15% commission on domestic sales. Offers written contract.

RECENT SALES *The Conscience of a Liberal*, by Paul Krugman; *The King of Oil: The Secret Lives of Marc Rich*, by Daniel Ammann; *Ten*, by Sheila Lukins; *Peterson Field Guide to Birds of North America*.

DORIS S. MICHAELS LITERARY AGENCY, INC.

1841 Broadway, Suite 903, New York NY 10023. (212)265-9474. **Fax:** (212)265-9480. **E-mail:** query@ dsmagency.com. **Website:** www.dsmagency.com. **Contact:** Doris S. Michaels, President. Member of AAR. Other memberships include WNBA.

REPRESENTS Novels. **Considers these nonfiction areas:** specialties are business and self-help books from top professionals in their fields of expertise. We are also looking for books in categories such as current affairs, narrative, biography and memoir, lifestyle, social sciences, gender, history, health, classical music, sports, and women's issues. In the fiction camp, we are currently interested in representing literary fiction that has commercial appeal and strong screen potential. Go to our biography section to find out more. **Considers these fiction areas:** literary, with commercial appeal and strong screen potential. "Go to our biography section online to find out more.".

⌐ "Our specialties are business and self-help books from top professionals in their fields of expertise. We are also looking for books in categories such as current affairs, narrative, biography and memoir, lifestyle, social sciences, gender, history, health, classical music, sports, and women's issues." No romance, coffee table books, art books, trivia, pop culture, humor, westerns, occult and supernatural, horror, poetry, textbooks, children's books, picture books, film scripts, articles, cartoons, and professional manuals.

HOW TO CONTACT "We no longer accept query letters through regular mail." Query by e-mail; synopsis of your project in one page or less, and include a short paragraph that details your credentials. Do not send attachments or URL links. See submission guidelines on website. Obtains most new clients through recommendations from others, conferences.

TERMS Agent receives 15% commission on domestic sales. Agent receives 20% commission on foreign sales. Offers written contract, binding for 1 year; 1-month notice must be given to terminate contract. Charges clients for office expenses, not to exceed $150 without written permission.

WRITERS CONFERENCES BookExpo America; Frankfurt Book Fair; London Book Fair; Maui Writers Conference.

MARTHA MILLARD LITERARY AGENCY

50 W.67th St., #1G, New York NY 10023. **Contact:** Martha Millard. Estab. 1980. Member of AAR. Other memberships include SFWA. Represents 50 clients. Currently handles: nonfiction books 25%, novels 65%, story collections 10%.

⌐ Prior to becoming an agent, Ms. Millard worked in editorial departments of several publishers and was vice president at another agency for more than four years.

REPRESENTS Nonfiction books, novels. **Considers these nonfiction areas:** architecture, art, autobiography, biography, business, child guidance, cooking, cultural interests, current affairs, design, economics, education, ethnic, film, health, history, how-to, memoirs, metaphysics, money, music, New Age, parenting, photography, popular culture, psychology, self-help, theater, true crime, women's issues, women's studies. **Considers these fiction areas:** fantasy, mystery, romance, science fiction, suspense.

HOW TO CONTACT No unsolicited queries. **Referrals only**. Obtains most new clients through recommendations from others.

TERMS Agent receives 15% commission on domestic sales. Agent receives 20% commission on foreign sales. Offers written contract.

THE MILLER AGENCY

Film Center, 630 Ninth Ave., Suite 1102, New York NY 10036. (212) 206-0913. **Fax:** (212) 206-1473. **E-mail:** angela@milleragency.net. **Website:** www.mille ragency.net. **Contact:** Angela Miller, Sharon Bowers, Jennifer Griffin. Represents 100 clients. 5% of clients are new/unpublished writers.

REPRESENTS Nonfiction books. **Considers these nonfiction areas:** child guidance, cooking, design, foods, health, parenting.

⌐ This agency specializes in nonfiction, multicultural arts, psychology, self-help, cookbooks, biography, travel, memoir, and sports. Fiction is considered selectively. This agency specializes in cookbooks.

HOW TO CONTACT Accepts simultaneous submissions. Obtains most new clients through referrals.

TERMS Agent receives 15% commission on domestic sales. Agent receives 20-25% commission on foreign sales. Offers written contract, binding for 2 years; 2-month notice must be given to terminate contract. Charges clients for postage (express mail or messenger services) and photocopying.

⊘ MARK B. MILLER MANAGEMENT

PO Box 2442, Warminster PA 18974. (267)988-4226. **Contact:** Mark B. Miller.

TIPS "Inquiries welcome, no unsolicited manuscripts accepted."

MOORE LITERARY AGENCY

10 State St., #309, Newburyport MA 01950. (978)465-9015. **Fax:** (978)465-8817. **E-mail:** cmoore@moorelit.com. **Contact:** Claudette Moore. Estab. 1989. 10% of clients are new/unpublished writers. Currently handles: nonfiction books 100%.

REPRESENTS Nonfiction books. **Considers these nonfiction areas:** computers, technology.

➣ This agency specializes in trade computer books (90% of titles).

HOW TO CONTACT Query with SASE. Submit proposal package. Query by e-mail. Send proposals by snail mail. Obtains most new clients through recommendations from others, conferences.

TERMS Agent receives 15% commission on domestic sales. Agent receives 15% commission on foreign sales. Agent receives 15% commission on film sales. Offers written contract.

● HOWARD MORHAIM LITERARY AGENCY

30 Pierrepont St., Brooklyn NY 11201. (718)222-8400. **Fax:** (718)222-5056. **Website:** www.morhaimliterary.com. Member of AAR.

MEMBER AGENTS Howard Morhaim, Kate McKean, Katie Menick.

➣ Actively seeking fiction, nonfiction, and young adult novels.

HOW TO CONTACT Query via e-mail with cover letter and three sample chapters. See each agent's listing for specifics.

● WILLIAM MORRIS AGENCY, INC.

1325 Avenue of the Americas, New York NY 10019. (212)586-5100. **Fax:** (212)246-3583. **Website:** www.wma.com. **Contact:** Literary Department Coordinator. Alternate address: One William Morris Place, Beverly Hills CA 90212. (310)285-9000. **Fax:** (310)859-4462. Member of AAR.

MEMBER AGENTS Owen Laster; Jennifer Rudolph Walsh; Suzanne Gluck; Joni Evans; Tracy Fisher; Mel Berger; Jay Mandel; Peter Franklin; Jonathan Pecursky.

REPRESENTS Nonfiction books, novels, TV, movie scripts, feature film.

➣ Does not want to receive screenplays.

HOW TO CONTACT Query with synopsis, publication history, SASE. Send book queries to the NYC address. Accepts simultaneous submissions.

TERMS Agent receives 15% commission on domestic sales. Agent receives 20% commission on foreign sales.

TIPS "If you are a prospective writer interested in submitting to the William Morris Agency in **London**, please follow these guidelines: For all queries, please send a cover letter, synopsis, and the first three chapters (up to 50 pages) by e-mail only to: dkar@wmeentertainment.com."

● MOVEABLE TYPE MANAGEMENT

610 Fifth Ave., #1220, New York NY 10185. (917)289-1089. **Fax:** (646)810-5757. **Website:** www.mtmgmt.net.

MEMBER AGENTS Jason Allen Ashlock, Michele Matrisciani, Mary Kole, Adam Chromy.

➣ "Movable Type Management provides inventive and expansive management services, working with authors in a wide variety of categories and genres to develop properties for distribution across platforms, devices, and territories. A bicoastal management company, MTM performs in-house film, television, and digital development, leveraging our relationships with digital start-ups and veteran producers to add value to an author's work at every opportunity."

HOW TO CONTACT Consult website. "Please get to know our team, read the guidelines provided by each member."

RECENT SALES *The Sacred Thread*, by Adrienne Arieff (Crown); *A Game of Groans*, by George R.R. Washington (St. Martin's Griffin); *Complication*, by Isaac Adamson (Soft Skull Press); *The Riot Within*, by Rodney King (HarperOne).

● DEE MURA LITERARY

P.O. Box 131, Massapequa NY 11762. (516)795-1616. **Fax:** (516)795-8797. **E-mail:** query@deemuraliterary.com. **Website:** www.deemuraliterary.com. **Contact:**

Dee Mura. Signatory of WGA. 50% of clients are new/ unpublished writers.

○ Prior to opening her agency, Mura was a public relations executive with a roster of film and entertainment clients. She is the president and CEO of both Dee Mura Literary and Dee Mura Entertainment.

MEMBER AGENTS Dee Mura, Kimiko Nakamura, Kaylee Davis.

REPRESENTS Considers these nonfiction areas: animals, anthropology, archeology, art, biography, business, cooking, current affairs, health, history, inspirational, medicine, memoirs, New Age, photography, popular culture, psychology, science, sports, technology, travel, comedy/humor, conservation/ environmental issues, entertainment, gender studies, home/garden, mind/body, outdoors/nature, parenting/families, religion/spirituality, self-help/motivational. **Considers these fiction areas:** action, adventure, erotica, ethnic, experimental, fantasy, gay, historical, lesbian, mystery, romance, satire, science fiction, women's, young adult, chick lit, contemporary fiction, Jewish, middle-grade, paranormal, paranormal romance, teens, thriller/espionage.

☛ Fiction with crossover film potential. "No children's books please."

HOW TO CONTACT Query with SASE or e-mail query@deemuraliterary.com (e-mail queries are preferred). Please include first 25 pages in the body of the e-mail as well as a short author bio and synopsis of the work. Accepts multiple submissions. Accepts simultaneous submissions. Responds to queries in 3-4 weeks. Responds to mss in 8 weeks. Obtains new clients through recommendations, solicitation, and conferences.

TERMS Agent receives 15% commission on domestic sales. Agent receives 20% commission on foreign sales. Offers written contract. Charges clients for photocopying, mailing expenses, overseas/long-distance phone calls.

WRITERS CONFERENCES BEA Expo, San Francisco Writers Conference.

TIPS "Please include a short author bio even if you have no literary background, and a brief synopsis of the project."

● MUSE LITERARY MANAGEMENT

189 Waverly Place., #4, New York NY 10014. (212)925-3721. **E-mail:** museliterarymgmt@museliterary.com.

Website: www.museliterary.com. **Contact:** Deborah Carter. Associations: NAWE, International Thriller Writers, Historical Novel Society, Association of Booksellers for Children, The Authors Guild, Children's Literature Network, and American Folklore Society. Represents 10 clients. 90% of clients are new/ unpublished writers.

○ Prior to starting her agency, Ms. Carter trained with an AAR literary agent and in the music business as a talent scout for record companies and in artist management. She has a BA in English and music from the College of Arts & Sciences at NYU.

REPRESENTS Considers these nonfiction areas: art, biography, history, memoirs, music, lifestyle, places, children's and teen nonfiction. **Considers these fiction areas:** historical, literary, mystery, thriller, Literary fiction, multicultural and international fiction that's relatable to American readers, children's and teen fiction.

☛ Specializes in development of book manuscripts and associated journalism, the sale and administration of print, performance, and foreign rights. Actively seeking "writers with formal training who bring a unique outlook to their manuscripts. Those who submit should be receptive to editorial feedback and willing to revise during the submission process to remain competitive." Does not want romance, chick lit, sci-fi, fantasy, horror, stories about pets, vampires or serial killers, fiction or nonfiction with religious or spiritual subject matter.

HOW TO CONTACT Query with SASE. Query via e-mail (no attachments). Discards unwanted queries. Responds in 1-2 weeks to queries; 2-3 weeks to mss. Obtains most new clients through referrals and conferences.

TERMS Agent receives 15% commission on gross domestic sales, 20% on gross foreign sales. One-year contract offered when writer and agent agree that the manuscript is ready for submission. All expenses are preapproved by the client.

TIPS "Since we all look for books by familiar names, new writers need a plan for building an audience through their professional affiliations and in freelance journalism. All agreements are signed by the writers. Reimbursement for expenses is subject to client's approval, limited to photocopying and postage."

JEAN V. NAGGAR LITERARY AGENCY, INC.

216 E. 75th St., Suite 1E, New York NY 10021. (212)794-1082. **E-mail:** jweltz@jvnla.com; jvnla@jvnla.com. **E-mail:** jweltz@jvnla.com; jregel@jvnla.com; atasman@jvnla.com; atasman@jvnla.com. **Website:** www.jvnla.com. **Contact:** Jean Naggar. Member of AAR. Other memberships include PEN, Women's Media Group, Women's Forum, SCBWI. Represents 450 clients. 20% of clients are new/unpublished writers. Currently handles: nonfiction books 35%, novels 45%, juvenile books 15%, scholarly books 5%.

Ms. Naggar has served as president of AAR.

MEMBER AGENTS Jennifer Weltz (subrights, children's, adults); Jessica Regel (young adult, adult, subrights); Jean Naggar (taking no new clients); Alice Tasman (adult, children's); Elizabeth Evans (adult nonfiction, some fiction and YA); Laura Biagi (literary fiction, magical realism, cultural themes, young adult, middle grade and picture books).

REPRESENTS Nonfiction books, novels. **Considers these nonfiction areas:** biography, child guidance, current affairs, government, health, history, juvenile nonfiction, law, medicine, memoirs, New Age, parenting, politics, psychology, self-help, sociology, travel, women's issues, women's studies. **Considers these fiction areas:** action, adventure, crime, detective, ethnic, family saga, feminist, historical, literary, mainstream, mystery, police, psychic, supernatural, suspense, thriller.

This agency specializes in mainstream fiction and nonfiction and literary fiction with commercial potential.

HOW TO CONTACT Query via e-mail. Prefers to read materials exclusively. No fax queries. Consult website for specific guidelines for each agent. Responds in 1 day to queries. Responds in 2 months to mss. Obtains most new clients through recommendations from others.

TERMS Agent receives 15% commission on domestic sales. Agent receives 20% commission on foreign sales. Offers written contract. Charges for overseas mailing, messenger services, book purchases, long-distance telephone, photocopying—all deductible from royalties received.

RECENT SALES *Night Navigation*, by Ginnah Howard; *After Hours at the Almost Home*, by Tara Yelen; *An Entirely Synthetic Fish: A Biography of Rainbow Trout*, by Anders Halverson; *The Patron Saint of Butterflies*, by Cecilia Galante; *Wondrous Strange*, by Lesley Livingston; *6 Sick Hipsters*, by Rayo Casablanca; *The Last Bridge*, by Teri Coyne; *Gypsy Goodbye*, by Nancy Springer; *Commuters*, by Emily Tedrowe; *The Language of Secrets*, by Dianne Dixon; *Smiling to Freedom*, by Martin Benoit Stiles; *The Tale of Halcyon Crane*, by Wendy Webb; *Fugitive*, by Phillip Margolin; *BlackBerry Girl*, by Aidan Donnelley Rowley; *Wild Girls*, by Pat Murphy.

WRITERS CONFERENCES Willamette Writers Conference; Pacific Northwest Writers Conference; Bread Loaf Writers Conference; Marymount Manhattan Writers Conference; SEAK Medical & Legal Fiction Writing Conference.

TIPS "Use a professional presentation. Because of the avalanche of unsolicited queries that flood the agency every week, we have had to modify our policy. We will now only guarantee to read and respond to queries from writers who come recommended by someone we know. Our areas are general fiction and nonfiction—no children's books by unpublished writers, no multimedia, no screenplays, no formula fiction, and no mysteries by unpublished writers. We recommend patience and fortitude: the courage to be true to your own vision, the fortitude to finish a novel and polish it again and again before sending it out, and the patience to accept rejection gracefully and wait for the stars to align themselves appropriately for success."

NELSON LITERARY AGENCY

1732 Wazee St., Suite 207, Denver CO 80202. (303)292-2805. **E-mail:** query@nelsonagency.com. **Website:** www.nelsonagency.com. **Contact:** Kristin Nelson, president and senior literary agent; Sara Megibow, associate literary agent. Member of AAR. RWA, SCBWI, SFWA.

Prior to opening her own agency, Ms. Nelson worked as a literary scout and subrights agent for agent Jody Rein.

REPRESENTS Novels, select nonfiction. **Considers these nonfiction areas:** memoirs. **Considers these fiction areas:** commercial, literary, mainstream, romance (includes fantasy with romantic elements, science fiction, fantasy, young adult).

NLA specializes in representing commercial fiction and high-caliber literary fiction. Actively seeking stories with multicultural elements. Does not want short story collections, mysteries, thrillers, Christian, horror, children's picture books, or screenplays.

HOW TO CONTACT Query by e-mail only.

RECENT SALES *Prodigy*, by Marie Lu (young adult); *Wool*, by Hugh Howey (science fiction); *The Peculiar*, by Stefan Bachmann (middle grade); *Catching Jordan*, by Miranda Kenneally (young adult); *Broken Like This*, by Monica Trasandes (debut literary fiction); *The Darwin Elevator*, by Jason Hough (debut science fiction).

KIRSTEN NEUHAUS LITERARY AGENCY

21 W. 38th St., 11th Floor, New York NY 10018. (646)839-6899. **E-mail:** submissions@kirstenneuhausliterary.com. **Contact:** Kirsten Neuhaus.

Prior to becoming an agent, Kirsten Neuhaus worked at Elaine Markson Agency, Sanford J. Greenburger Associates and Vigliano Associates, developing her own client list as well as handling foreign rights. She began her publishing career as an intern at Where Books Begin, a freelance editing company.

REPRESENTS Considers these nonfiction areas: Kirsten Neuhaus Literary is a full-service boutique agency specializing in nonfiction, particularly current events, business, science, biographies, international affairs, pop cultural studies, and narratives with strong female voices, as well as upmarket, commercial fiction.

HOW TO CONTACT "Our preferred method for receiving queries is via e-mail. Please send a query letter, including a bio, and approximately 10 sample pages. Paste copy into the e-mail body. No attachments."

NEW LEAF LITERARY & MEDIA, INC.

110 W. 40th St., Suite 410, New York NY 10018. (646)248-7989. **Fax:** (646)861-4654. **E-mail:** assist@newleafliterary.com. **Contact:** Joanna Volpe; Kathleen Ortiz; Suzie Townsend; Pouya Shahbazian.

MEMBER AGENTS Joanna Volpe (women's fiction, thriller, horror, speculative fiction, literary fiction and historical fiction.); Kathleen Ortiz; Suzie Townsend (In adult, she's specifically looking for romance (historical and paranormal), and fantasy (urban fantasy, science fiction, steampunk, epic fantasy). In children's, she loves YA (all subgenres) and is dying to find great middle grade projects); Pouya Shahbazian, film and television agent.

HOW TO CONTACT E-mail queries only. "The word QUERY must be in subject line, plus the agent's name." No attachments. Responds only if interested.

RECENT SALES *Hunted*, by Holly McDowell; Divergent series, by Veronica Roth

WRITERS CONFERENCES Pennwriters Conference, Writer's Digest Conference (NYC).

DANA NEWMAN LITERARY

9720 Wilshire Blvd., 5th Floor, Beverly Hills CA 90212. (323)974-4334. **Fax:** (866)636-7585. **E-mail:** dananewmanliterary@gmail.com. **Website:** www.about.me/dananewman. **Contact:** Dana Newman. Estab. 2009. Author's Guild Represents 15 clients. 50% of clients are new/unpublished writers. Currently handles: 85% nonfiction books, 15% novels.

Prior to being an agent, Ms. Newman was an attorney in the entertainment industry for 14 years.

MEMBER AGENTS Dana Newman (narrative nonfiction, business, memoir, pop culture, health, literary, and upmarket fiction).

REPRESENTS Nonfiction, fiction. **Considers these nonfiction areas:** architecture, art, autobiography, biography, business, child guidance, cooking, cultural interests, current affairs, design, education, ethnic, film, foods, gay/lesbian, government, health, history, how-to, language, law, literature, medicine, memoirs, metaphysics, music, New Age, popular culture, politics, science, self-help, sociology, sports, technology, theater, women's issues, women's studies. **Considers these fiction areas:** historical, literary, women's, chick lit.

Ms. Newman has a background in contracts, licensing, and intellectual property law. She is experienced in digital content creation and distribution and embraces the changing publishing environment. Actively seeking nonfiction, historical, or upmarket fiction. Does not want religious, children's, poetry, horror, mystery, science fiction.

HOW TO CONTACT Submit query letter, outline, synopsis, 2 sample chapters, biography, and proposal. Accepts simultaneous submissions. Responds to queries/proposals in 2 weeks; mss in 1 month. Obtains new clients through recommendations from others, queries, submissions.

TERMS Obtains 15% commission on domestic sales; 20% on foreign sales. Offers 1 year written contract.

Notice must be given 30 days prior to terminate a contract. No reading fee.

RECENT SALES *How to Read a Client*, by Brandy Mychals (McGraw-Hill); *The King of Style*, by Michael Bush (Insight Editions); *An Atomic Love Story*, by Shirley Streshinsky (Turner Publishing); *Combined Destinies*, by Ann Todd Jealous (Potomac Books).

WRITERS CONFERENCES Tools of Change (New York, February); Writer's Digest Conference (L.A., October); Santa Barbara Writers Conference (Santa Barbara, June).

NINE MUSES AND APOLLO, INC.

525 Broadway, Suite 201, New York NY 10012. (212)431-2665. **Contact:** Ling Lucas. Represents 50 clients. 10% of clients are new/unpublished writers. Currently handles: nonfiction books 100%.

○ Prior to her current position, Ms. Lucas served as vice president, sales/marketing director and associate publisher of Warner Books.

REPRESENTS Nonfiction books.

⚷ This agency specializes in nonfiction. Does not want to receive children's or young adult material.

HOW TO CONTACT Submit outline, 2 sample chapters, SASE. Prefers to read materials exclusively.

TERMS Agent receives 15% commission on domestic sales. Agent receives 20-25% commission on foreign sales. Offers written contract. Charges clients for photocopying, postage.

TIPS "Your outline should already be well developed, cogent, and reveal clarity of thought about the general structure and direction of your project."

◑ NORTHERN LIGHTS LITERARY SERVICES, LLC

2323 State Rd. 252, Martinsville IN 46151. (888)558-4354. **Fax:** (208)265-1948. **E-mail:** queries@northernlightsls.com. **Website:** www.northernlightsls.com. **Contact:** Sammie Justesen. Represents 25 clients. 35% of clients are new/unpublished writers. Currently handles: nonfiction books 90%, novels 10%.

MEMBER AGENTS Sammie Justesen (fiction and nonfiction); Vorris Dee Justesen (business and current affairs).

REPRESENTS Nonfiction books, novels. **Considers these nonfiction areas:** animals, autobiography, biography, business, child guidance, cooking, crafts, current affairs, diet/nutrition, economics, environment, ethnic, foods, health, inspirational, investigative, memoirs, metaphysics, New Age, parenting, popular culture, psychology, religious, self-help, sports, true crime, women's issues, women's studies. **Considers these fiction areas:** action, adventure, crime, detective, ethnic, family saga, feminist, glitz, historical, inspirational, mainstream, mystery, police, psychic, regional, religious, romance, supernatural, suspense, thriller, women's.

⚷ "Our goal is to provide personalized service to clients and create a bond that will endure throughout the writer's career. We seriously consider each query we receive and will accept hardworking new authors who are willing to develop their talents and skills. We enjoy working with healthcare professionals and writers who clearly understand their market and have a platform." Actively seeking general nonfiction—especially if the writer has a platform. Does not want to receive fantasy, horror, erotica, children's books, screenplays, poetry, or short stories.

HOW TO CONTACT Query with SASE. Submit outline/proposal, synopsis, 3 sample chapters, author bio. E-queries preferred. No phone queries. All queries considered, but the agency only replies if interested. If you've completed and polished a novel, send a query letter, a one-or-two page synopsis of the plot, and the first chapter. Also include your biography as it relates to your writing experience. Do not send an entire mss unless requested. If you'd like to submit a nonfiction book, send a query letter, along with the book proposal. Include a bio showing the background that will enable you to write the book. Consult website for complete submission guidelines. Accepts simultaneous submissions. Responds in 2 months to queries. Responds in 2 months to mss. Obtains most new clients through solicitations, conferences.

TERMS Agent receives 15% commission on domestic sales. Agent receives 20% commission on foreign sales. Offers written contract; 30-day notice must be given to terminate contract.

RECENT SALES *Intuitive Parenting*, by Debra Snyder, PhD (Beyond Words); *The Confidence Trap* by Russ Harris (Penguin); *The Never Cold Call Again Toolkit* by Frank Rumbauskas Jr. (Wiley); *Thank You for Firing Me*, by Candace Reed and Kitty Martini (Sterling); *The Wal-Mart Cure: Ten Lifesaving Supplements for Under $10* (Sourcebooks).

TIPS "If you're fortunate enough to find an agent who answers your query and asks for a printed manuscript, always include a letter and cover page containing your name, physical address, e-mail address and phone number. Be professional!"

HAROLD OBER ASSOCIATES

425 Madison Ave., New York NY 10017. (212)759-8600. **Fax:** (212)759-9428. **Website:** www.haroldober.com. **Contact:** Appropriate agent. Member of AAR. Represents 250 clients. 10% of clients are new/unpublished writers. Currently handles: nonfiction books 35%, novels 50%, juvenile books 15%.

○ Mr. Elwell was previously with Elwell & Weiser.

MEMBER AGENTS Phyllis Westberg; Pamela Malpas; Craig Tenney (few new clients, mostly Ober backlist); Jake Elwell (previously with Elwell & Weiser); Kathleen Zakhar (YA, adult science fiction, fantasy in all its varieties, historical fiction, and horror novels, quirky middle grade, picture books, sweeping love stories, magical realism, inventive world-building, repurposed folklore, dark comedy, and genre-bending novels).

HOW TO CONTACT Submit concise query letter addressed to a specific agent with the first 5 pages of the ms or proposal and SASE. No fax or e-mail. Does not handle film scripts or plays. Responds as promptly as possible. Obtains most new clients through recommendations from others.

TERMS Agent receives 15% commission on domestic sales. Agent receives 20% commission on foreign sales. Charges clients for express mail/package services.

FIFI OSCARD AGENCY, INC.

110 W. 40th St., 16th Floor, New York NY 10018. (212)764-1100. **Fax:** (212)840-5019. **E-mail:** agency@fifioscard.com. **Website:** www.fifioscard.com. **Contact:** Literary Department. Signatory of WGA.

MEMBER AGENTS Peter Sawyer; Carmen La Via; Kevin McShane; Carolyn French.

REPRESENTS Nonfiction books, novels, stage plays. **Considers these nonfiction areas:** biography, business, cooking, economics, health, history, inspirational, religious, science, sports, technology, women's issues, women's studies, African American, body/mind/spirit, lifestyle, cookbooks.

HOW TO CONTACT Query through online submission form preferred, though snail mail queries are acceptable. *No unsolicited mss.* Responds in 2 weeks to queries.

TERMS Agent receives 15% commission on domestic sales. Agent receives 20% commission on foreign sales. Agent receives 10% commission on film sales. Charges clients for photocopying expenses.

PARAVIEW, INC.

A Division of Cosimo, Inc., P.O. Box 416, Old Chelsea Station, New York NY 10011-0416. (212)989-3616. **Fax:** (212)989-3662. **E-mail:** lhagan@paraview.com; info@cosimobooks.com. **Website:** www.paraview.com; www.cosimobooks.com. **Contact:** Lisa Hagan. Represents 75 clients. 15% of clients are new/unpublished writers. Currently handles: nonfiction books 100%.

REPRESENTS Nonfiction books. **Considers these nonfiction areas:** agriculture horticulture, New Age, animals, anthropology, art, biography, business, cooking, current affairs, education, ethnic, gay, government, health, history, how to, humor, language, memoirs, military, money, multicultural, nature, philosophy, popular culture, psychology, recreation, regional, religion, science, self help, sex, sociology, spirituality, travel, true crime, women's, Americana; creative nonfiction.

☛ This agency specializes in business, science, gay/lesbian, spiritual, New Age, and self-help nonfiction.

HOW TO CONTACT Submit query, synopsis, author bio via e-mail. Consult website for more detailed guidelines. Responds in 1 month to queries. Responds in 3 months to mss. Obtains most new clients through recommendations from editors and current clients.

TERMS Agent receives 15% commission on domestic sales. Agent receives 20% commission on foreign sales.

WRITERS CONFERENCES BookExpo America; London Book Fair; E3—Electronic Entertainment Exposition.

TIPS "New writers should have their work edited, critiqued, and carefully reworked prior to submission. First contact should be via e-mail."

PARK LITERARY GROUP, LLC

270 Lafayette St., Suite 1504, New York NY 10012. (212)691-3500. **Fax:** (212)691-3540. **E-mail:** info@parkliterary.com. **Website:** www.parkliterary.com.

○ Prior to their current positions, Ms. Park and Ms. O'Keefe were literary agents at Sanford J. Greenburger Associates. Prior to 1994, Ms. Park was a practicing attorney.

MEMBER AGENTS Theresa Park (plot-driven fiction and serious nonfiction); Abigail Koons (quirky, edgy and commercial fiction, as well as superb thrillers and mysteries; adventure and travel narrative nonfiction, exceptional memoirs, popular science, history, politics and art); Amanda Cardinale (commercial fiction and nonfiction); Emily Sweet (not an agent—liaison to film and media industries).

REPRESENTS Nonfiction books, novels.

☛ The Park Literary Group represents fiction and nonfiction with a boutique approach: an emphasis on servicing a relatively small number of clients, with the highest professional standards and focused personal attention. Does not want to receive poetry or screenplays.

HOW TO CONTACT Query by email at queries@parkliterary.com. Submit synopsis, 1-3 sample chapters in body of e-mail. Does not open attachments. Responds in 4-6 weeks to queries.

● THE RICHARD PARKS AGENCY

P.O. Box 693, Salem NY 12865. (518)854-9466. **Fax:** (518)854-9466. **E-mail:** rp@richardparksagency.com. **Website:** www.richardparksagency.com. **Contact:** Richard Parks. Member of AAR. Currently handles: nonfiction books 55%, novels 40%, story collections 5%.

REPRESENTS Nonfiction books, novels. **Considers these nonfiction areas:** animals, anthropology, archeology, art, autobiography, biography, business, child guidance, cooking, crafts, cultural interests, current affairs, dance, diet/nutrition, economics, environment, ethnic, film, foods, gardening, gay/lesbian, government, health, history, hobbies, how-to, humor, language, law, memoirs, military, money, music, parenting, popular culture, politics, psychology, science, self-help, sociology, technology, theater, travel, women's issues, women's studies.

☛ Actively seeking nonfiction. Considers fiction by referral only. Does not want to receive unsolicited material.

HOW TO CONTACT Query with SASE. Does not accept queries by e-mail or fax. Other Responds in 2 weeks to queries. Obtains most new clients through recommendations/referrals.

TERMS Agent receives 15% commission on domestic sales. Agent receives 20% commission on foreign sales. Charges clients for photocopying or any unusual expense incurred at the writer's request.

● KATHI J. PATON LITERARY AGENCY

P.O. Box 2236 Radio City Station, New York NY 10101. (212)265-6586. **E-mail:** KJPLitBiz@optonline.net. **Website:** www.PatonLiterary.com. **Contact:** Kathi Paton. Currently handles: nonfiction books 85%, novels 15%.

REPRESENTS Nonfiction books, novels, short story collections, book-based film rights. **Considers these nonfiction areas:** business, child guidance, economics, environment, humor, investigative, money, parenting, psychology, religious, satire, personal investing. **Considers these fiction areas:** literary, mainstream, multicultural, short stories.

☛ This agency specializes in adult nonfiction.

HOW TO CONTACT Accepts e-mail queries only. Accepts simultaneous submissions. Accepts new clients through recommendations from current clients.

TERMS Agent receives 15% commission on domestic sales. Agent receives 20% commission on foreign sales. Offers written contract. Charges clients for photocopying.

WRITERS CONFERENCES Attends major regional panels, seminars, and conferences.

◎ PAVILION LITERARY MANAGEMENT

660 Massachusetts Ave., Suite 4, Boston MA 02118. (617)792-5218. **E-mail:** jeff@pavilionliterary.com. **Website:** www.pavilionliterary.com. **Contact:** Jeff Kellogg.

○ Prior to his current position, Mr. Kellogg was a literary agent with The Stuart Agency, and an acquiring editor with HarperCollins.

REPRESENTS Nonfiction books, novels, memoir. **Considers these nonfiction areas:** , narrative nonfiction (topical and historical) and cutting-edge popular science from experts in their respective fields. **Considers these fiction areas:** adventure, fantasy, juvenile, mystery, thriller, general fiction, genre-blending fiction.

☛ "We are presently accepting fiction submissions only from previously published authors and/or by client referral. Nonfiction projects, specifically narrative nonfiction and cutting-edge popular science from experts in their respective fields, are most welcome."

HOW TO CONTACT Query first by e-mail (no attachments). The subject line should specify fiction or nonfiction and include the title of the work. If submitting nonfiction, include a book proposal (no longer than 75 pages), with sample chapters.

PEARSON, MORRIS & BELT

3000 Connecticut Ave., NW, Suite 317, Washington DC 20008. (202)723-6088. **E-mail:** dpm@morrisbelt. com; llb@morrisbelt.com. **Website:** www.morrisbelt. com.

○ Prior to their current positions, Ms. Belt and Ms. Morris were agents with Adler & Robin Books, Inc.

MEMBER AGENTS Laura Belt (nonfiction and computer books); Djana Pearson Morris (fiction, nonfiction, and computer books. Her favorite subjects are self-help, narrative nonfiction, African-American fiction and nonfiction, health and fitness, women's fiction, technology, and parenting).

REPRESENTS Nonfiction books, novels, computer books.

○── This agency specializes in nonfiction, computer books and exceptional fiction. Does not want to receive poetry, children's literature or screenplays. Regarding fiction, this agency does not accept science fiction, thrillers or mysteries.

HOW TO CONTACT Query with SASE. Submit proposal (nonfiction); detailed synopsis and 2-3 sample chapters (fiction). Only query with a finished ms. Accepts e-mail queries but no attachments. Responds in 6-8 weeks to queries. Obtains most new clients through recommendations from others, solicitations.

TIPS "Many of our books come from ideas and proposals we generate in-house. We retain a proprietary interest in and control of all ideas we create and proposals we write."

PEMA BROWNE LTD.

71 Pine Rd., Woodbourne NY 12788. (845)268-0029. **E-mail:** ppbltd@optonline.net. **Website:** www.pem abrowneltd.com. **Contact:** Pema Browne. Estab. 1966.

○── Specializes in general commercial.

HOW TO CONTACT For first contact, send query letter, direct mail flier/brochure, and SASE. If interested will ask to mail appropriate materials for review. Portfolios should include tearsheets and transparencies or good color photocopies, plus SASE. Accepts queries by mail only. Obtains new talent through recommendations and interviews (portfolio review). Current clients include HarperCollins, Holiday House, Bantam

Doubleday Dell, Nelson/Word, Hyperion, Putnam. Client list available upon request.

TERMS Rep receives 30% illustration commission; 20% author commission. Exclusive area representation is required. For promotional purposes, talent must provide color mailers to distribute. Representative pays mailing costs on promotion mailings.

RECENT SALES *The Daring Miss Quimby*, by Suzanne Whitaker, illustrated by Catherine Stock (Holiday House).

TIPS "We are doing more publishing—all types—less advertising." Looks for "continuity of illustration and dedication to work."

L. PERKINS AGENCY

5800 Arlington Ave., Riverdale NY 10471. (718)543-5344. **Fax:** (718)543-5354. **E-mail:** submissions@lperkinsagency.com. **Website:** http://lperkinsagency.com. **Contact:** Sandy Lu, sandy@lperkinsagency.com; Louise Fury, lfury@lperkinsagency.com. Member of AAR. Represents 90 clients. 10% of clients are new/unpublished writers.

○ Ms. Perkins has been an agent for 20 years. She is also the author of *The Insider's Guide to Getting an Agent* (Writer's Digest Books), as well as three other nonfiction books. She has also edited 12 erotic anthologies, and is also the editorial director of Ravenousromance.com, an e-publisher.

MEMBER AGENTS Lori Perkins (no longer takes submissions, but maintains her client list and blog); Sandy Lu (fiction areas of interest: literary and commercial fiction, upscale women's fiction, mystery, thriller, psychological horror, and historical fiction. She is especially interested in edgy, contemporary urban fiction. Nonfiction areas of interest: narrative nonfiction, history, biography, memoir, science, psychology, pop culture, and food writing. She also has a particular interest in Asian or Asian-American writing, both original and in translation, fiction and nonfiction); Emily Keyes (emily@lperkinsagency.com, teen and middle grade novels); Louise Fury (YA, teen, romance, nonfiction); Julia Bannon (e-books ONLY -- young adult, romance, chick lit, women's).

REPRESENTS Nonfiction books, novels. **Considers these nonfiction areas:** how-to, law, memoirs, parenting, popular culture, science, self-help. **Considers these fiction areas:** erotica, fantasy, horror, literary, science fiction, women's, young adult.

NEW AGENT SPOTLIGHT

PAM VAN HYLCKAMA VLIEG
(FOREWORD LITERARY)

lforewordliterary.com
@BookaliciousPam

ABOUT PAM: Associate agent Pam van Hylckama Vlieg joined Larsen Pomada Literary Agents as an Associate Literary Agent in 2012 before joining newly created Foreword Literary in 2013. Over the past four years, Pam has become one of the top YA book bloggers in the country at Bookalicious. org. She also partners her blog with Hicklebee's, a children's bookstore in San Jose, Calif. Pam writes supernatural young adult and middle grade fiction and is represented by Laurie McLean, also of Foreword Literary. She lives in the Bay Area of California with her Dutch husband, two children—a boy and a girl, the perfect set—a Jack Russell terrier, a bull dog puppy, and a small guinea pig. It is her greatest dream to own a menagerie.

SHE IS SEEKING: young adult and middle grade children's book authors, and adult romance authors.

HOW TO CONTACT: To query please e-mail querypam@forewordliterary.com with your query, first 10 pages, and synopsis pasted into the body of the e-mail.

"Most of my clients write both fiction and non-fiction. This combination keeps my clients publishing for years. I am also a published author, so I know what it takes to write a good book." Actively seeking a Latino *Gone With the Wind* and *Waiting to Exhale*, and urban ethnic horror. Does not want to receive anything outside of the above categories (westerns, romance, etc.).

HOW TO CONTACT E-queries only. Consult website for more details on submitting. Accepts simultaneous submissions. Responds in 12 weeks to queries. Responds in 3–6 months to mss. Obtains most new clients through recommendations from others, solicitations, conferences.

TERMS Agent receives 15% commission on domestic sales. Agent receives 20% commission on foreign sales. No written contract. Charges clients for photocopying.

WRITERS CONFERENCES NECON; Killercon; BookExpo America; World Fantasy Convention, RWA, Romantic Times.

TIPS "Research your field and contact professional writers' organizations to see who is looking for what. Finish your novel before querying agents. Read my book, *An Insider's Guide to Getting an Agent*, to get a sense of how agents operate. Read agent blogs-agentinthemiddle.blogspot.com and ravenousromance. blogspot.com."

ALISON J. PICARD, LITERARY AGENT

P.O. Box 2000, Cotuit MA 02635. Phone/**Fax:** (508)477-7192. **E-mail:** ajpicard@aol.com. **Contact:**

Alison Picard. Represents 48 clients. 30% of clients are new/unpublished writers. Currently handles: nonfiction books 40%, novels 40%, juvenile books 20%.

○ Prior to becoming an agent, Ms. Picard was an assistant at a literary agency in New York.

REPRESENTS Nonfiction books, novels, juvenile. **Considers these nonfiction areas:** animals, autobiography, biography, business, child guidance, cooking, cultural interests, current affairs, diet/nutrition, economics, education, environment, ethnic, foods, gay/lesbian, government, health, history, how-to, humor, inspirational, juvenile nonfiction, law, medicine, memoirs, metaphysics, military, money, multicultural, New Age, parenting, popular culture, politics, psychology, religious, science, self-help, technology, travel, true crime, war, women's issues, women's studies, young adult. **Considers these fiction areas:** action, adventure, contemporary issues, crime, detective, erotica, ethnic, family saga, feminist, gay, glitz, historical, horror, humor, juvenile, lesbian, literary, mainstream, multicultural, mystery, New Age, picture books, police, psychic, romance, sports, supernatural, thriller, young adult.

⚷ "Many of my clients have come to me from big agencies, where they felt overlooked or ignored. I communicate freely with my clients and offer a lot of career advice, suggestions for revising manuscripts, etc. If I believe in a project, I will submit it to a dozen or more publishers, unlike some agents who give up after four or five rejections." No science fiction/fantasy, westerns, poetry, plays or articles.

HOW TO CONTACT Query with SASE. Accepts simultaneous submissions. Responds in 2 weeks to queries; 4 months to mss. Obtains most new clients through recommendations from others, solicitations.

TERMS Agent receives 15% commission on domestic sales. Agent receives 20% commission on foreign sales. Offers written contract, binding for 1 year; 1-week notice must be given to terminate contract.

RECENT SALES *Zitface*, by Emily Ormand (Marshall Cavendish); *Totally Together*, by Stephanie O'Dea (Running Press); *The Ultimate Slow Cooker Cookbook*, by Stephanie O'Dea (Hyperion); Two Untitled Cookingbooks, by Erin Chase (St. Martin's Press); *A Journal of the Flood Year*, by David Ely (Portobello Books-United Kingdom, L'Ancora, — Italy); *A Mighty Wall*, by John Foley (Llewellyn/Flux); *Jelly's Gold*, by David Housewright (St. Martin's Press).

TIPS "Please don't send material without sending a query first via mail or e-mail. I don't accept phone or fax queries. Always enclose an SASE with a query."

● **PINDER LANE & GARON-BROOKE ASSOCIATES, LTD.**

159 W. 53rd St., Suite 14C, New York NY 10019. **Website:** www.pinderlane.com. Member of AAR. Signatory of WGA.

MEMBER AGENTS Robert Thixton, pinderl@rcn.com; Dick Duane, pinderl@rcn.com.

⚷ This agency specializes in mainstream fiction and nonfiction. Does not want to receive screenplays, TV series teleplays, or dramatic plays.

HOW TO CONTACT Query with SASE. *No unsolicited mss.* Obtains most new clients through referrals.

TERMS Agent receives 15% commission on domestic sales. Agent receives 30% commission on foreign sales. Offers written contract.

◉ **PIPPIN PROPERTIES, INC.**

155 E. 38th St., Suite 2H, New York NY 10016. (212)338-9310. **Fax:** (212)338-9579. **E-mail:** info@pippinproperties.com. **Website:** www.pippinproperties.com. **Contact:** Holly McGhee. Represents 52 clients. Currently handles: juvenile books 100%.

○ Prior to becoming an agent, Ms. McGhee was an editor for 7 years and in book marketing for 4 years. Prior to becoming an agent, Ms. van Beek worked in children's book editorial for 4 years.

MEMBER AGENTS Holly McGhee, Emily van Beek, Elena Mechlin.

REPRESENTS Juvenile.

⚷ "We are strictly a children's literary agency devoted to the management of authors and artists in all media. We are small and discerning in choosing our clientele." Actively seeking middle-grade and young-adult novels.

HOW TO CONTACT Query via e-mail. Include a synopsis of the work(s), your background and/or publishing history, and anything else you think is relevant. Accepts simultaneous submissions. Responds in 3 weeks to queries if interested. Responds in 10 weeks to mss. Obtains most new clients through recommendations from others.

TERMS Agent receives 15% commission on domestic sales. Agent receives 25% commission on foreign sales. Offers written contract; 30-day notice must be given to terminate contract. Charges for color copying and UPS/FedEx.

TIPS "Please do not start calling after sending a submission."

◑ ALIČKA PISTEK LITERARY AGENCY, LLC

302A W. 12th St., #124, New York NY 10014. **E-mail:** alicka@apliterary.com. **E-mail:** info@apliterary.com. **Website:** www.apliterary.com. **Contact:** Alička Pistek. Represents 15 clients. 50% of clients are new/unpublished writers. Currently handles: nonfiction books 60%, novels 40%.

◒   Prior to opening her agency, Ms. Pistek worked at ICM and as an agent at Nicholas Ellison, Inc. Alička has an M.A. in German Translation and a B.A. in Linguistics from the University of California, San Diego. She has studied and worked in the UK, Germany and Prague, Czech Republic.

MEMBER AGENTS Alička Pistek.

REPRESENTS Nonfiction books, novels. **Considers these nonfiction areas:** animals, anthropology, autobiography, biography, child guidance, current affairs, environment, government, health, history, how-to, language, law, literature, medicine, memoirs, military, money, parenting, politics, psychology, science, self-help, technology, travel, war, creative nonfiction. **Considers these fiction areas:** crime, detective, ethnic, family saga, historical, literary, mainstream, mystery, police, romance, suspense, thriller.

⊶   Does not want to receive fantasy, science fiction or Western's.

HOW TO CONTACT Agency only accepts queries via e-mail. Send e-query to info@apliterary.com. Include name, address, e-mail, and phone number, title, word count, genre of book, a brief synopsis, and relevant biographical information. Accepts simultaneous submissions. Responds in 2 months to queries. Will only respond if interested. Responds in 8 weeks to mss.

TERMS Agent receives 15% commission on domestic sales. Agent receives 20% commission on foreign sales. Offers written contract. This agency charges for photocopying more than 40 pages and international postage.

TIPS "Be sure you are familiar with the genre you are writing in and learn standard procedures for submitting your work. A good query will go a long way."

LINN PRENTIS LITERARY

155 East 116th St., #2F, New York NY 10029. **Fax:** (212)875-5565. **E-mail:** ahayden@linnprentis.com; linn@linnprentis.com. **Website:** www.linnprentis. com. **Contact:** Amy Hayden, acquisitions director; Linn Prentis, agent; Jordana Frankel assistant. Represents 18-20 clients. 25% of clients are new/unpublished writers. Currently handles: nonfiction books 5%, novels 65%, story collections 7%, novella 10%, juvenile books 10%, scholarly books 3%.

◒   Prior to becoming an agent, Ms. Prentis was a nonfiction writer and editor, primarily in magazines. She also worked in book promotion in New York. Ms. Prentis then worked for and later ran the Virginia Kidd Agency. She is known particularly for her assistance with manuscript development.

REPRESENTS Nonfiction books, novels, short story collections, novellas (from authors whose novels I already represent), juvenile (for older juveniles), scholarly, anthology. **Considers these nonfiction areas:** juvenile, animals, art, biography, current affairs, education, ethnic, government, how to, humor, language, memoirs, music, photography, popular culture, sociology, womens. **Considers these fiction areas:** adventure, ethnic, fantasy, feminist, gay, glitz, historical, horror, humor, juvenile, lesbian, literary, mainstream, mystery, thriller.

⊶   "Because of the Virginia Kidd connection and the clients I brought with me at the start, I have a special interest in sci-fi and fantasy, but, really, fiction is what interests me. As for my nonfiction projects, they are books I just couldn't resist." Actively seeking hard science fiction, family saga, mystery, memoir, mainstream, literary, women's. Does not want to "receive books for little kids."

HOW TO CONTACT Query with SASE. Submit synopsis. No phone or fax queries. No snail mail. E-mail queries to ahayden@linnprentis.com. Include first ten pages and synopsis as either attachment or as text in the e-mail. Accepts simultaneous submissions. Obtains most new clients through recommendations from others, solicitations.

TERMS Agent receives 15% commission on domestic sales. Agent receives 20% commission on foreign sales. Offers written contract; 60-day notice must be given to terminate contract.

RECENT SALES Sold 15 titles in the last year. *The Sons of Heaven*, *The Empress of Mars*, and *The House of the Stag*, by Kage Baker (Tor); the last has also been sold to Dabel Brothers to be published as a comic book/graphic novel; *Indigo Springs* and a sequel, by A.M. Dellamonica (Tor); Wayne Arthurson's debut mystery plus a second series book; *Bone Crossed* and *Cry Wolf* for *New York Times* #1 best-selling author Patricia Briggs (Ace/Penguin). "The latter is the start of a new series."

TIPS "Consider query letters and synopses as writing assignments. Spell names correctly."

➊ AARON M. PRIEST LITERARY AGENCY

708 3rd Ave., 23rd Floor, New York NY 10017. (212)818-0344. **Fax:** (212)573-9417. **E-mail:** info@aaronpriest.com. **Website:** www.aaronpriest.com. Estab. 1974. Member of AAR. Currently handles: nonfiction books 25%, novels 75%.

MEMBER AGENTS Aaron Priest, querypriest@aaronpriest.com (thrillers, commercial fiction, biographies); Lisa Erbach Vance, queryvance@aaronpriest.com (general fiction, international fiction, thrillers, upmarket women's fiction, historical fiction, narrative nonfiction, memoir); Lucy Childs Baker, querychilds@aaronpriest.com (literary and commercial fiction, memoir, edgy women's fiction); Nicole James, queryjames@aaronpriest.com (young adult fiction, narrative nonfiction, gay and lesbian fiction, political, and pop-culture, literary and commercial fiction, specifically dealing with social and cultural issues).

➤ Does not want to receive poetry, screenplays or sci-fi.

HOW TO CONTACT Query one of the agents using the appropriate e-mail listed on the website. "Please do not submit to more than 1 agent at this agency. We urge you to check our website and consider each agent's emphasis before submitting. Your query letter should be about one page long and describe your work as well as your background. You may also paste the first chapter of your work in the body of the e-mail. Do not send attachments." Accepts simultaneous submissions. Responds in 4 weeks, only if interested.

TERMS Agent receives 15% commission on domestic sales.

RECENT SALES *The Hit*, by David Baldacci; *Six Years*, by Harlan Coben; *Suspect*, by Robert Crais; *Permanent Record*, by Leslie Stella; *Eye for an Eye*, by Ben Coes.

PROSPECT AGENCY

551 Valley Road, PMB 377, Upper Montclair NJ 07043. (718)788-3217. **Fax:** (718)360-9582. **E-mail:** esk@prospectagency.com. **Website:** www.prospectagency.com. **Contact:** Emily Sylvan Kim, Becca Stumpf, Rachel Orr, Teresa Keitlinski. Estab. 2005. Member of AAR. Represents 80 (and growing) clients. 70% of clients are new/unpublished writers. Currently handles: 60% of material handled is books for young readers.

◯ "For some of us, it's all we've ever known. Others have worked in various facets of publishing and law."

MEMBER AGENTS "Staff includes agents Emily Sylvan, Becca Stumpf, and Rachel Orr. Emily handles YA, tween, and middle-grade literary and commercial fiction, with a special interest in edgy books and books for boys. Becca Stumpf handles YA and middle-grade literary and commercial fiction, with a special interest in fantasy and science fiction with cross-genre appeal. Rachel Orr handles picture books, beginning readers, chapter books, middle-grade/YA novels, children's nonfiction, and children's illustrators. Teresa Kietlinski hadles picture books authors and illustrators, as well as middle-grade and YA books.".

➤ "We're looking for strong, unique voices and unforgettable stories and characters."

HOW TO CONTACT Send outline and 3 sample chapters. Accepts queries through website only. "We do not accept submissions to multiple Prospect agents (please submit to only 1 agent at Prospect Agency). Manuscripts and queries that are not a good fit for our agency are rejected via e-mail." Consult website for complete submission guidelines. Responds in 1 week to 3 months following an initial query; 1 week to 2 months after a ms has been requested. Obtains new clients through conferences, recommendations, queries, and some scouting.

TERMS Agent receives 15% on domestic sales, 20% on foreign sales sold directly and 25% on sales using a subagent. Offers written contract.

RECENT SALES Sold 15 books for young readers in the last year. (Also represents adult fiction.) Recent sales include: *Ollie and Claire* (Philomel), *Vicious* (Bloomsbury), *Temptest Rising* (Walker Books), *Where do Diggers Sleep at Night* (Random House Children's), *A DJ Called Tomorrow* (Little, Brown), *The Princesses of Iowa* (Candlewick).

P.S. LITERARY AGENCY

20033 - 520 Kerr St., Oakville ON L6K 3C7 Canada. **E-mail:** query@psliterary.com. **Website:** http://www.psliterary.com. **Contact:** Curtis Russell, principal agent; Carly Watters, agent. Estab. 2005. Currently handles: nonfiction books 50%, novels 50%.

REPRESENTS Nonfiction, novels, juvenile books. **Considers these nonfiction areas:** autobiography, biography, business, child guidance, cooking, current affairs, diet/nutrition, economics, environment, foods, government, health, history, how-to, humor, law, memoirs, military, money, parenting, popular culture, politics, science, self-help, sports, technology, true crime, war, women's issues, women's studies. **Considers these fiction areas:** action, adventure, detective, erotica, ethnic, family saga, historical, horror, humor, juvenile, literary, mainstream, mystery, picture books, romance, sports, thriller, women's, young adult, biography/autobiography, business, child guidance/parenting, cooking/food/nutrition, current affairs, government/politics/law, health/medicine, history, how-to, humor, memoirs, military/war, money/finance/economics, nature/environment, popular culture, science/technology, self-help/personal improvement, sports, true crime/investigative, women's issues/women's studies.

⚷ "What makes our agency distinct: We take on a small number of clients per year in order to provide focused, hands-on representation. We pride ourselves in providing industry-leading client service." Actively seeking both fiction and nonfiction. Seeking both new and established writers. Does not want to receive poetry or screenplays.

HOW TO CONTACT Queries by e-mail only. Submit query, synopsis, and bio. "Please limit your query to one page." Accepts simultaneous submissions. Responds in 4-6 weeks to queries/proposals; mss 4-8 weeks. Obtains most new clients through solicitations.

TERMS Agent receives 15% commission on domestic sales. Agent receives 25% commission on foreign sales. We offer a written contract, with 30-days notice terminate. Fees for postage/messenger services only if project is sold. "This agency charges for postage/messenger services only if a project is sold."

TIPS "Please review our website for the most up-to-date submission guidelines. We do not charge reading fees. We do not offer a critique service."

QUEEN LITERARY AGENCY

420 W. End Ave., Suite 8A, New York NY 10024. (212)974-8333. **Fax:** (212)974-8347. **E-mail:** lqueen@queenliterary.com. **E-mail:** submissions@queenliterary.com. **Website:** www.queenliterary.com. **Contact:** Lisa Queen.

○ Prior to her current position, Ms. Queen was a former publishing executive and most recently head of IMG Worldwide's literary division.

REPRESENTS Nonfiction books, novels.

⚷ Ms. Queen's specialties: "While our agency represents a wide range of nonfiction titles, we have a particular interest in business books, food writing, science and popular psychology, as well as books by well-known chefs, radio and television personalities, and sports figures."

HOW TO CONTACT Query with SASE.

RECENT SALES *The Female Brain*, by Louann Brizendine; *Does the Noise in My Head Bother You?* by Steven Tyler; *What I Cannot Change*, by LeAnn Rimes and Darrell Brown.

SUSAN RABINER LITERARY AGENCY, INC., THE

315 W. 39th St., Suite 1501, New York NY 10018. (212)279-0316. **Fax:** (212)279-0932. **E-mail:** susan@rabiner.net. **Website:** www.rabinerlit.com. **Contact:** Susan Rabiner.

○ Prior to becoming an agent, Ms. Rabiner was editorial director of Basic Books. She is also the co-author of *Thinking Like Your Editor: How to Write Great Serious Nonfiction and Get it Published* (W.W. Norton).

MEMBER AGENTS Susan Rabiner, Sydelle Kramer, Helena Schwarz, Holly Bemiss. See the website for individual agent e-mails.

REPRESENTS Nonfiction books, novels, textbooks. **Considers these nonfiction areas:** autobiography, biography, business, economics, education, government, health, history, inspirational, law, medicine, philosophy, politics, psychology, religious, science, sociology, sports, technology.

⚷ "Representing narrative nonfiction and big-idea books—work that illuminates the past and the present. I look for well-researched, topical books written by fully credentialed academics, journalists, and recognized public intellectuals with the power to stimulate public debate on a broad range of issues including the state of our economy, political discourse, history, science, and the arts."

HOW TO CONTACT Query by e-mail only, with cover letter and proposal for nonfiction. Accepts simultaneous submissions. Responds in 2 weeks if your project fits the profile of the agency. Obtains most new clients through recommendations from others.

TERMS Agent receives 15% commission on domestic sales. Agent receives 20% commission on foreign sales. Offers written contract; 1-month notice must be given to terminate contract.

◐ LYNNE RABINOFF AGENCY

72-11 Austin St., No. 201, Forest Hills NY 11375. (718)459-6894. **E-mail:** Lynne@lynnerabinoff.com. **Contact:** Lynne Rabinoff. Represents 50 clients. 50% of clients are new/unpublished writers. Currently handles: nonfiction books 99%, novels 1%.

○   Prior to becoming an agent, Ms. Rabinoff was in publishing and dealt with foreign rights.

REPRESENTS Nonfiction books. **Considers these nonfiction areas:** anthropology, archeology, autobiography, biography, business, cultural interests, current affairs, economics, ethnic, government, history, inspirational, law, memoirs, military, popular culture, politics, psychology, religious, science, technology, women's issues, women's studies.

➤━━ "This agency specializes in history, political issues, current affairs and religion."

HOW TO CONTACT Query with SASE or e-mail. Submit proposal package, synopsis, 1 sample chapter, author bio. Responds in 3 weeks to queries. Responds in 1 month to mss. Obtains most new clients through recommendations from others.

TERMS Agent receives 15% commission on domestic sales. Agent receives 20% commission on foreign sales. Offers written contract; 60-day notice must be given to terminate contract. This agency charges for postage.

RECENT SALES *The Confrontation*, by Walid Phares (Palgrave); *Flying Solo*, by Robert Vaughn (Thomas Dunne); *Thugs*, by Micah Halpern (Thomas Nelson); *Size Sexy*, by Stella Ellis (Adams Media); *Cruel and Usual*, by Nonie Darwish (Thomas Nelson); *Now They Call Me Infidel*, by Nonie Darwish (Sentinel/Penguin); *34 Days*, by Avid Issacharoff (Palgrave).

◐ RAINES & RAINES

103 Kenyon Rd., Medusa NY 12120. (518)239-8311. **Fax:** (518)239-6029. **Contact:** Theron Raines (member of AAR); Joan Raines; Keith Korman. Member of AAR. Represents 100 clients.

REPRESENTS Nonfiction books, novels. **Considers these nonfiction areas:** action/adventure, autobiography/biography, finance/investing, history, military/war, narrative psychology, All subjects. **Considers these fiction areas:** action, adventure, crime, detective, fantasy, frontier, historical, mystery, picture books, police, science fiction, suspense, thriller, Westerns, whimsical.

HOW TO CONTACT Query with SASE. Responds in 2 weeks to queries.

TERMS Agent receives 15% commission on domestic sales. Agent receives 20% commission on foreign sales. Charges for photocopying.

◐ ◎ RED SOFA LITERARY

2163 Grand Ave., #2, St. Paul MN 55105. (651)224-6670. **E-mail:** dawn@redsofaliterary.com; jennie@redsofaliterary.com. **Website:** www.redsofaliterary.com. **Contact:** Dawn Frederick, literary agent and owner; Jennie Goloboy, associate agent. Red Sofa is a member of the Authors Guild and the MN Publishers Round Table Represents 20 clients. 80% of clients are new/unpublished writers. Currently handles: nonfiction books 97%, novels 2%, story collections 1%.

○   Dawn Frederick: Prior to her current position, Ms. Frederick spent 5 years at Sebastian Literary Agency. In addition, Ms. Frederick worked more than 10 years in indie and chain book stores, and at an independent children's book publisher. Ms. Frederick has a master's degree in library and information sciences from an ALA-accredited institution. Jennie Goloboy: In Fall 2011, Jennie Goloboy joined Red Sofa Literary as an Associate Agent. Jennie Goloboy has a PhD in the History of American Civilization from Harvard. She is also a published author of both history and fiction, and a member of SFWA, RWA, SHEAR, OAH, the AHA, and Codex Writer's Group. Her funny, spec-fic short stories appear under her pen name, Nora Fleischer.

REPRESENTS Nonfiction, fiction, juvenile books. **Considers these nonfiction areas:** animals, anthropology, archeology, crafts, cultural interests, current affairs, gay/lesbian, government, health, history, hobbies, humor, investigative, law, popular culture, politics, satire, sociology, true crime, women's issues, women's studies, extreme sports.

HOW TO CONTACT Query by e-mail or mail with SASE. No attachments, please. Submit full proposal plus 3 sample chapters and any other pertinent writing samples. Accepts simultaneous submissions. Responds in 3 weeks to queries; 6 weeks to mss. Obtains most new clients through recommendations from others, solicitations.

TERMS Agent receives 15% commission on domestic sales. Agent receives 20% commission on foreign sales. Offers written contract. May charge a one-time $100 fee for partial reimbursement of postage and phone expenses incurred if the advance is below $15,000.

WRITERS CONFERENCES Madison Writers' Institute; Novel-in-Progress Bookcamp; OWFI Conference; SDSU Writers' Conference; Florida Writer's Association Conference; The Loft Literary Center; DFW Writers' Conference; MN SCBWI Conference, Bloomington Writers' Festival and Book Fair; Women of Words Retreat; ISD 196; First Pages (Hennepin County); Writer's Digest Webinar.

TIPS "Always remember the benefits of building an author platform, and the accessibility of accomplishing this task in today's industry. Most importantly, research the agents queried. Avoid contacting every literary agent about a book idea. Due to the large volume of queries received, the process of reading queries for unrepresented categories (by the agency) becomes quite the arduous task. Investigate online directories, printed guides (like *Writer's Market*), individual agent websites, and more, before beginning the query process. It's good to remember that each agent has a vision of what s/he wants to represent and will communicate this information accordingly. We're simply waiting for those specific book ideas to come in our direction."

RED TREE LITERARY AGENCY

320 7th Ave., #183, Brooklyn NY 11215. **E-mail:** elana@redtreeliterary.com. **Website:** www.redtreeliterary.com. **Contact:** Elana Roth.

Elana is a graduate of Barnard College and the Jewish Theological Seminary, where she earned degrees in English literature and Bible.

HOW TO CONTACT E-mail only.

RECENT SALES *Doug-Dennis and the Flyaway Fib*, by Darren Farrel; *Juniper Berry*, by M.P. Kozlowsky;

The Selection, by Kiera Cass; *Unison Spark*, by Andy Marino.

THE REDWOOD AGENCY

474 Wellesley Ave., Mill Valley CA 94941. (415)381-2269, ext. 2. **E-mail:** info@redwoodagency.com. **E-mail:** query@redwoodagency.com. **Website:** www.redwoodagency.home.comcast.net. **Contact:** Catherine Fowler, founder. Adheres to AAR canon of ethics. Currently handles: nonfiction books 100%.

Prior to becoming an agent, Ms. Fowler was an editor, subsidiary rights director and associate publisher for Doubleday, Simon & Schuster and Random House for her 20 years in New York Publishing. Content exec for web startups Excite and WebMD.

REPRESENTS Nonfiction books, novels. **Considers these nonfiction areas:** business, cooking, diet/nutrition, environment, gardening, health, humor, medicine, memoirs, parenting, popular culture, psychology, satire, self-help, women's issues, women's studies, narrative, parenting, aging, reference, lifestyle, cultural technology. **Considers these fiction areas:** literary, mainstream, suspense, women's, quirky.

"Along with our love of books and publishing, we have the desire and commitment to work with fun, interesting and creative people, to do so with respect and professionalism, but also with a sense of humor." Actively seeking high-quality, nonfiction works created for the general consumer market, as well as projects with the potential to become book series. Does not want to receive fiction. Do not send packages that require signature for delivery.

HOW TO CONTACT Query via e-mail only. While we redesign website, submit "quick query" to: query@redwoodagency.com. See all guidelines online. Obtains most new clients through recommendations from others, solicitations.

TERMS Offers written contract. Charges for copying and delivery charges, if any, as specified in author/agency agreement.

RED WRITING HOOD INK

2075 Attala Road 1990, Kosciusko MS 39090. (662)582-1191. **Fax:** (662)796-3095. **E-mail:** redwritinghoodink@gmail.com. **Website:** www.redwritinghoodink.net. **Contact:** Sheri Ables. Other memberships include adheres to AAR canon. Currently handles: nonfiction books 100%.

Prior to her current position, Ms. Ables was an agent of the Williams Agency. In addition, she worked for an agency in Oregon from 1996-1997. Collectively, the staff of RWHI has more than 25 years of experience in the publishing industry.

MEMBER AGENTS Sheri Ables, agent; Terri Dunlap, literary assistant (terri@redwritinghoodink.net).

REPRESENTS Nonfiction books.

Biography, children's, crime and thrillers, entertainment, general fiction, health, history, inspirational, mystery/suspense, romantic fiction, general nonfiction, self-help.

HOW TO CONTACT Send cover letter and 2-page synopsis by e-mail. No longer accepting postal queries or submissions by mail.

TERMS Agent receives 15% commission on domestic sales. Agent receives 20% commission on foreign sales.

TIPS Writers: View submission guidelines prior to making contact.

HELEN REES LITERARY AGENCY

14 Beacon St., Suite 710, Boston MA 02108. (617)227-9014. **Fax:** (617)227-8762. **E-mail:** reesagency@reesagency.com. **Website:** http://reesagency.com. **Contact:** Joan Mazmanian, Ann Collette, Helen Rees, Lorin Rees. Estab. 1983. Member of AAR. Other memberships include PEN. Represents more than 100 clients. 50% of clients are new/unpublished writers. Currently handles: nonfiction books 60%, novels 40%.

MEMBER AGENTS Ann Collette (literary, mystery, thrillers, suspense, vampire, and women's fiction; in nonfiction, she prefers true crime, narrative nonfiction, military and war, work to do with race and class, and work set in or about Southeast Asia. Ann can be reached at: Agent10702@aol.com). Lorin Rees (literary fiction, memoirs, business books, self-help, science, history, psychology, and narrative nonfiction. lorin@reesagency.com).

REPRESENTS Nonfiction books, novels. **Considers these nonfiction areas:** autobiography, biography, business, current affairs, economics, government, health, history, law, medicine, money, politics, women's issues, women's studies. **Considers these fiction areas:** historical, literary, mainstream, mystery, suspense, thriller.

HOW TO CONTACT Query with SASE, outline, 2 sample chapters. No unsolicited e-mail submissions. No multiple submissions. Consult website for each agent's submission guidelines. Responds in 3-4 weeks to queries. Obtains most new clients through recommendations from others, conferences, submissions.

TERMS Agent receives 15% commission on domestic sales. Agent receives 20% commission on foreign sales.

RECENT SALES Sold more than 35 titles in the last year. *Get Your Ship Together*, by Capt. D. Michael Abrashoff; *Overpromise and Overdeliver*, by Rick Barrera; *Opacity*, by Joel Kurtzman; *America the Broke*, by Gerald Swanson; *Murder at the B-School*, by Jeffrey Cruikshank; *Bone Factory*, by Steven Sidor; *Father Said*, by Hal Sirowitz; *Winning*, by Jack Welch; *The Case for Israel*, by Alan Dershowitz; *As the Future Catches You*, by Juan Enriquez; *Blood Makes the Grass Grow Green*, by Johnny Rico; *DVD Movie Guide*, by Mick Martin and Marsha Porter; *Words That Work*, by Frank Luntz; *Stirring It Up*, by Gary Hirshberg; *Hot Spots*, by Martin Fletcher; *Andy Grove: The Life and Times of an American*, by Richard Tedlow; *Girls Most Likely To*, by Poonam Sharma.

REGAL LITERARY AGENCY

236 W. 26th St., #801, New York NY 10001. (212)684-7900. **Fax:** (212)684-7906. **E-mail:** info@regal-literary.com. **E-mail:** submissions@regal-literary.com. **Website:** www.regal-literary.com. **Contact:** Barbara Marshall. London Office: 36 Gloucester Ave., Primrose Hill, London NW1 7BB, United Kingdom, uk@regal-literary.com Estab. 2002. Member of AAR. Represents 70 clients. 20% of clients are new/unpublished writers.

MEMBER AGENTS Markus Hoffmann joined Regal Literary in 2006. He had been a literary scout and foreign rights agent on both sides of the Atlantic, most recently as Foreign Rights Manager at Aitken Alexander Associates in London and then Director of International Scouting at Maria Campbell Associates in New York. His main interests are international and literary fiction, crime, (pop) cultural studies, current affairs, economics, history, music, popular science, and travel literature. He also looks after foreign rights for the agency and the London and Frankfurt Book Fairs every year. He's the trumpeter of Half on Signature, the finest R&B band on the international publishing circuit. Lauren Pearson started her career at the Russell & Volkening Literary Agency, and after stints at Tina Brown's *Talk* magazine and the Chicago-based *Modern Luxury* magazine group, she joined Regal Literary in 2004. In 2007, she moved across the pond to set up our London office. In addition to handling UK rights for the agency, she is looking to represent European-based writers of literary and commercial fiction, memoir, narrative nonfiction, and young adult and children's books. If it makes sense for your primary agent to be based in London, she's your gal. She likes anything pop-culture or crime-related, and is an avid late-night watcher of *Law & Order* reruns and the British detective drama *Dalziel and Pascoe*. She is a graduate of Duke University and the Radcliffe Publishing Course. With more than a decade of experience in the book publishing industry, Michael Psaltis is a partner in The Culinary Cooperative, as well as the head of his own agency, Psaltis Literary. Michael began his book publishing career working with an independent book marketing company, then with a book publicist and then at a small press before becoming an agent at a boutique literary agency. For nine years he worked with the Book Industry Study Group (BISG), a non-profit organization that studies and reports on all aspects of the book industry. Joseph Regal got his first job in publishing at the Russell & Volkening Literary Agency in 1991. There he worked with Pulitzer Prize-winning best-selling authors Anne Tyler, Eudora Welty, Annie Dillard, Howell Raines, and Peter Taylor, as well as Tony Award-winner Ntozake Shange, Nobel Prize-winner Nadine Gordimer, and TV anchorman and novelist Jim Lehrer. After leaving music for publishing, he founded Regal Literary Inc. in 2002. He graduated from Columbia College magna cum laude. His primary interests are literary fiction, international thrillers, history, science, photography, music, culture, and whimsy. After graduating from Middlebury College, Michael Strong was a sailing instructor at the Hurricane Island Outward Bound School, a carpenter in Berkeley, California, an English teacher at a school for dyslexic students, and a graduate student in English at UNC-Chapel Hill, where he read for Carolina Quarterly. He was a PhD candidate at the Program in Comparative Literature and Literary Theory at the University of Pennsylvania, where he taught classes on technology and ethics, wrote a dissertation on FINNEGANS WAKE, and was Assistant Director of the Penn National Commission. After 7 years in digital marketing at Sotheby's, he now handles marketing and publicity at Regal Literary. He yearns for fine literary fiction and ambitious thrillers, and for nonfiction about art, politics, science, business, sports, and he loves boats and the oceans.

⊶ Actively seeking literary fiction and narrative nonfiction. Does not want romance, science fiction, horror, screenplays.

HOW TO CONTACT "Query with SASE or via e-mail. No phone calls. Submissions should consist of a 1-page query letter detailing the book in question, as well as the qualifications of the author. For fiction, submissions may also include the first 10 pages of the novel or one short story from a collection. We do not consider romance, science fiction, poetry, or screenplays." Accepts simultaneous submissions. Responds in 2-3 weeks to queries. Responds in 4-6 weeks to mss.

TERMS Agent receives 15% commission on domestic sales. Agent receives 20% commission on foreign sales. "We charge no reading fees."

RECENT SALES Audrey Niffenegger's *The Time Traveler's Wife* (Mariner) and *Her Fearful Symmetry* (Scribner), Gregory David Roberts' *Shantaram* (St. Martin's), Josh Bazell's *Beat the Reaper* (Little, Brown), John Twelve Hawks' *The Fourth Realm Trilogy* (Doubleday), James Reston, Jr.'s *The Conviction of Richard Nixon* (Three Rivers) and *Defenders of the Faith* (Penguin), Michael Psilakis' *How to Roast a Lamb: New Greek Classic Cooking* (Little, Brown), Colman Andrews' *Country Cooking of Ireland* (Chronicle) and *Reinventing Food: Ferran Adria and How He Changed the Way We Eat* (Phaidon).

TIPS "We are deeply committed to every aspect of our clients' careers, and are engaged in everything from the editorial work of developing a great book proposal or line editing a fiction manuscript to negotiating state-of-the-art book deals and working to promote and publicize the book when it's published. We are at the forefront of the effort to increase authors' rights in publishing contracts in a rapidly changing commercial environment. We deal directly with co-agents and publishers in every foreign territory and also work directly and with co-agents for feature film and television rights, with extraordinary success in both arenas. Many of our clients' works have sold in dozens of translation markets, and a high proportion of our books have been sold in Hollywood. We have strong relationships with speaking agents, who can assist in arranging author tours and other corporate and college speaking opportunities when appropriate. We also have a staff publicist and marketer to help promote our clients' and their work."

REID BOATES LITERARY AGENCY

69 Cooks Crossroad, Pittstown NJ 08867. (908)797-8087. **Fax:** (908)788-3667. **E-mail:** reid.boates@gmail.com; boatesliterary@att.net. **Contact:** Reid Boates. Represents 45 clients. 5% of clients are new/unpublished writers. Currently handles: nonfiction books 85%, novels 15%, story collections very rarely.

HOW TO CONTACT No unsolicited queries of any kind. Obtains new clients by personal referral only.

TERMS Agent receives 15% commission on domestic sales. Agent receives 20% commission on foreign sales.

RECENT SALES Sold 15 titles in the last year. New sales include placements at HarperCollins, Wiley, Random House, and other major general-interest publishers.

● THE AMY RENNERT AGENCY

98 Main St., #302, Tiburon CA 94920. **E-mail:** queries@amyrennert.com. **Contact:** Amy Rennert.

REPRESENTS Nonfiction books, novels. **Considers these nonfiction areas:** autobiography, biography, health, history, medicine, memoirs, sports, lifestyle, narrative nonfiction. **Considers these fiction areas:** literary, mystery.

8—¬ "The Amy Rennert Agency specializes in books that matter. We provide career management for established and first-time authors, and our breadth of experience in many genres enables us to meet the needs of a diverse clientele."

HOW TO CONTACT We now prefer to receive submissions by e-mail. For nonfiction, send cover letter and attach a Word file with proposal/first chapter. For fiction—and sometimes memoir—send cover letter and attach a Word file with 10-20 pages.

TIPS Due to the high volume of submissions, it is not possible to respond to each and every one. Please understand that we are only able to respond to queries that we feel may be a good fit with our agency.

◑ JODIE RHODES LITERARY AGENCY

8840 Villa La Jolla Dr., Suite 315, La Jolla CA 92037-1957. **Website:** jodierhodesliterary.com. **Contact:** Jodie Rhodes, president. Member of AAR. Represents 74 clients. 60% of clients are new/unpublished writers. Currently handles: nonfiction books 45%, novels 35%, juvenile books 20%.

◖ Prior to opening her agency, Ms. Rhodes was a university-level creative writing teacher, workshop director, published novelist, and vice president/media director at the N.W. Ayer Advertising Agency.

MEMBER AGENTS Jodie Rhodes; Clark McCutcheon (fiction); Bob McCarter (nonfiction).

REPRESENTS Nonfiction books, novels. **Considers these nonfiction areas:** autobiography, biography, child guidance, cultural interests, ethnic, government, health, history, law, medicine, memoirs, military, parenting, politics, science, technology, war, women's issues, women's studies. **Considers these fiction areas:** ethnic, family saga, historical, literary, mainstream, mystery, suspense, thriller, women's, young adult.

8—¬ "Actively seeking witty, sophisticated women's books about career ambitions and relationships; edgy/trendy young adult and teen books; narrative nonfiction on groundbreaking scientific discoveries, politics, economics, military; and important current affairs by prominent scientists and academic professors." Does not want to receive erotica, horror, fantasy, romance, science fiction, religious/inspirational, or children's books (does accept young adult/teen).

HOW TO CONTACT Query with brief synopsis, first 30-50 pages, SASE. Do not call. Do not send complete ms unless requested. This agency does not return unrequested material weighing a pound or more that requires special postage. Include e-mail address with query. Accepts simultaneous submissions. Responds in 3 weeks to queries. Obtains most new clients through recommendations from others, agent sourcebooks.

TERMS Agent receives 15% commission on domestic sales. Agent receives 20% commission on foreign sales. Offers written contract; 1-month notice must be given to terminate contract. Charges clients for fax, photocopying, phone calls, postage. Charges are itemized and approved by writers upfront.

RECENT SALES Sold 42 titles in the last year. *The Ring*, by Kavita Daswani (HarperCollins); *Train to Trieste*, by Domnica Radulescu (Knopf); *A Year with Cats and Dogs*, by Margaret Hawkins (Permanent Press); *Silence and Silhouettes*, by Ryan Smithson (HarperCollins); *Internal Affairs*, by Constance Dial (Permanent Press); *How Math Rules the World*, by James Stein (HarperCollins); *Diagnosis of Love*, by Maggie Martin (Bantam); *Lies, Damn Lies, and Science*, by Sherry Seethaler (Prentice Hall); *Freaked*, by Jeanne Dutton (HarperCollins); *The Five Second Rule*,

NEW AGENT SPOTLIGHT

LIAT JUSTIN (SERENDIPITY LITERARY AGENCY)
serendipitylit.com

ABOUT LIAT: Liat Justin is an associate agent with the Serendipity Literary Agency. Liat graduated from Boston University with a Bachelor of Science degree in Communication Studies. As an undergrad, Liat simultaneously enrolled in Boston University's Certificate Program in Book Publishing and Digital Media. Liat then moved back to New York where she began her publishing career as an intern at PMA Literary and Film Management. Soon after, Liat joined the team at Serendipity. In addition to her passion for reading, Liat has a love for film, traveling, going to concerts, and doing puzzles.

SHE IS SEEKING: Liat is actively seeking to represent a broad range of projects and is open to emerging authors. Her sweet spot genres include narrative non-fiction (especially 'big idea' books), YA, historical fiction, pop culture, humor, sports-related, and speculative fiction. While Liat is very open to a variety of genres, she is currently not interested in romance, Christian fiction, and thrillers.

HOW TO SUBMIT: Serendipity requires all submissions through a submission form on their agency website, no matter if you are querying for your adult works, nonfiction, or children's books.

by Anne Maczulak (Perseus Books); *The Intelligence Wars*, by Stephen O'Hern (Prometheus); *Seducing the Spirits*, by Louise Young (the Permanent Press), and more.

TIPS "Think your book out before you write it. Do your research, know your subject matter intimately, and write vivid specifics, not bland generalities. Care deeply about your book. Don't imitate other writers. Find your own voice. We never take on a book we don't believe in, and we go the extra mile for our writers. We welcome talented, new writers."

💬 THE LISA RICHARDS AGENCY

108 Upper Leeson St., Dublin 4 Republic of Ireland Ireland. (03)(531)637-5000. **Fax:** (03)531)667-1256. **E-mail:** info@lisarichards.ie. **Website:** www.lisarichards.ie. **Contact:** Chairman: Alan Cook; Directors: Lisa Cook (managing) Miranda Pheifer, Fergus

Cronin, Patrick Sutton; Actors' Agents: Lisa Cook, Richard Cook, Jonathan Shankey, Rose Parkinson: Comedy Agents: Jennifer Wilson, Christine Dwyer; Literary Agent: Faith O'Grady; Voice Overs: Lorraine Cummins; Corporate Bookings: Evan Kenny. Estab. 1989.

MEMBER AGENTS Faith O'Grady (literary).

REPRESENTS Movie, tv, broadcast. **Considers these nonfiction areas:** biography, current affairs, history, memoirs, popular culture, travel, politics. **Considers these script areas:** comedy, general scripts.

HOW TO CONTACT Submit proposal package, synopsis, 2-3 sample chapters, query letter with SAE.

RECENT SALES Clients include Denise Deegan, Arlene Hunt, Roisin Ingle, Declan Lynch, Jennifer McCann, Sarah O'Brien, Kevin Rafter.

THE RIGHTS FACTORY

P.O. Box 499, Station C, Toronto ON M6J 3P6 Canada. (416)966-5367. **Website:** www.therightsfactory.com. **MEMBER AGENTS** Sam Hiyate, Ali McDonald.

⚷ "The Rights Factory is an agency that deals in intellectual property rights to entertainment products, including books, comics and graphic novels, film, television, and video games. We license rights in every territory by representing 3 types of clients."

HOW TO CONTACT There is a submission form on this agency's website.

RECENT SALES *Beauty, Pure & Simple*, by Kristen Ma; *Why Mr. Right Can't Find You*, by J.M. Kearns; *Tout Sweet: Hanging Up My High Heels for a New Life in France*, by Karen Wheeler; *The Orange Code*, by Arkadi Kuhlmann and Bruce Philp.

ANGELA RINALDI LITERARY AGENCY

P.O. Box 7877, Beverly Hills CA 90212-7877. (310)842-7665. **Fax:** (310)837-8143. **E-mail:** amr@rinaldiliterary.com. **Website:** www.rinaldiliterary.com. **Contact:** Angela Rinaldi. Member of AAR. Represents 50 clients. Currently handles: nonfiction books 50%, novels 50%.

⚬ Prior to opening her agency, Ms. Rinaldi was an editor at NAL/Signet, Pocket Books and Bantam, and the manager of book development for *The Los Angeles Times*.

REPRESENTS Nonfiction books, novels, TV and motion picture rights (for clients only). **Considers these nonfiction areas:** biography, business, health books that address specific issues, career, personal finance, self help, true crime, women's issues/studies, current issues, psychology, popular reference, prescriptive and proactive self help, books by journalists, academics, doctors and therapists, based on their research, motivational. **Considers these fiction areas:** commercial/literary fiction, upmarket contemporary women's fiction, suspense, literary historical thrillers like Elizabeth Kostova's *The Historian*, gothic suspense like Diane Setterfield's *The Thirteenth Tale* and Matthew Pearl's *The Dante Club*, women's book club fiction—novels where the story lends itself to discussion like Kim Edwards' *The Memory Keeper's Daughter*.

⚷ Actively seeking commercial and literary fiction. Does not want to receive humor, techno thrillers, KGB/CIA espionage, drug thrillers, Da Vinci-code thrillers, category romances, science fiction, fantasy, horror, westerns, film scripts, poetry, category romances, magazine articles, religion, occult, supernatural.

HOW TO CONTACT For fiction send first 3 chapters, brief synopsis, SASE or brief e-mail inquiry with the first 10 pages pasted into the e-mail—no attachments unless asked for. For nonfiction, query with detailed letter or outline/proposal, SASE or e-mail—no attachments unless asked for. Do not send certified or metered mail. Other Responds in 6 weeks to queries that are posted; email queries 2-3 weeks.

TERMS Agent receives 15% commission on domestic sales. Agent receives 25% commission on foreign sales. Offers written contract.

ANN RITTENBERG LITERARY AGENCY, INC.

15 Maiden Lane, Suite 206, New York NY 10038. **Website:** www.rittlit.com. **Contact:** Ann Rittenberg, president; Penn Whaling, associate. Member of AAR. Currently handles: fiction 75%, nonfiction 25%.

REPRESENTS Considers these nonfiction areas: memoirs, women's issues, women's studies. **Considers these fiction areas:** literary, thriller, upmarket fiction.

⚷ This agent specializes in literary fiction and literary nonfiction. Does not want to receive screenplays, straight genre fiction, poetry, self-help.

HOW TO CONTACT Query with SASE. Submit outline, 3 sample chapters, SASE. Query via postal mail *only*. Accepts simultaneous submissions. Responds in 6 weeks to queries. Responds in 2 months to mss. Obtains most new clients through referrals from established writers and editors.

TERMS Agent receives 15% commission on domestic sales. Agent receives 20% commission on foreign sales. Offers written contract. This agency charges clients for photocopying only.

RECENT SALES *The Given Day*, by Dennis Lehane; *My Cat Hates You*, by Jim Edgar; *Never Wave Goodbye*, by Doug Magee; *House and Home*, by Kathleen McCleary; *Nowhere to Run*, by C.J. Box; and *Daughter of Kura*, by Debra Austin.

RIVERSIDE LITERARY AGENCY

41 Simon Keets Rd., Leyden MA 01337. (413)772-0067. **Fax:** (413)772-0969. **E-mail:** rivlit@sover.net. **Website:** www.riversideliteraryagency.com. **Contact:** Susan Lee Cohen.

8—☞ Represents adult fiction and nonfiction.

HOW TO CONTACT Query with SASE. Accepts simultaneous submissions. Responds in 2 weeks to queries. Obtains most new clients through referrals.

TERMS Agent receives 15% commission on domestic sales. Offers written contract. Charges clients for foreign postage, photocopying large mss, express mail deliveries, etc.

◑ LESLIE RIVERS, INTERNATIONAL (LRI)

P.O. Box 940772, Houston TX 77094-7772. (281)493-5822. **Fax:** (281)493-5835. **E-mail:** LRivers@LeslieRivers.com. **Website:** www.leslierivers.com. **Contact:** Judith Bruni. Adheres to AAR's canon of ethics. Represents 20 clients. 80% of clients are new/unpublished writers. Currently handles: novels 90%.

◌ Prior to becoming agents, members were in marketing, sales, project management, customer satisfaction, writers, and publishing assistants.

MEMBER AGENTS Judith Bruni, literary agent and founder; Mark Bruni, consulting editor.

REPRESENTS Novels. **Considers these fiction areas:** , All fiction genres, but no children's.

8—☞ "LRI collaborates with creative professionals and offers a customized, boutique service, based on the client's individual requirements. LRI maintains flexible hours to accommodate specific client needs. Its primary focus since 2005 is a high-end, no-fee based literary agency for authors. LRI provides high quality service, feedback, and recommendations at no charge, which include readings, proofreading, editing—including content editing, analysis, feedback, and recommendations. Send only your finest work." Actively seeking fiction/novels only—all subgenres. Does not want to receive children's books or poetry or nonfiction.

HOW TO CONTACT Query via e-mail with Microsoft Word attachments. Submit synopsis, author bio, 3 chapters or 50 pages, whichever is longer. Prefers an exclusive read, but will consider simultaneous queries. Responds in 1-2 months to queries. Responds in 4-6 months to mss. Obtains most new clients through recommendations from others or solicitations.

TERMS Agent receives 15% commission on domestic sales. Agent receives 25% commission on foreign sales. Offers written contract; 90-day notice must be given to terminate contract. This agency charges for postage, printing, copying, etc. If no sale is made, no charges are enforced.

RECENT SALES *Secrets of the Sands*, by Leona Wisoker (Mercury Retrograde Press). Other clients include Brinn Colenda, Carol Gambino, Don Armijo and Fred Stawitz: co-authors of *Homeboy's Soul: Pride, Terror & Street Justice in America*, Fletcher F. Cockrell, author of *Dismissed With Prejudice*, Kathy J. Keller, author of *The Butterfly Clinic*, Leona Wisoker, author of *Secrets of the Sands, Book 1 of The Children of the Desert*, Michael Eldrige, Patricia Forehand, RC (Ruth) White, author of *Devil's Trace*, also *The Ascension at Antioch*, Rhiannon Lynn, Skott Darlow.

◑ RLR ASSOCIATES, LTD.

Literary Department, 7 W. 51st St., New York NY 10019. (212)541-8641. **Fax:** (212)262-7084. **E-mail:** sgould@rlrassociates.net. **Website:** www.rlrassociates.net. **Contact:** Scott Gould. Member of AAR. Represents 50 clients. 25% of clients are new/unpublished writers. Currently handles: nonfiction books 70%, novels 25%, story collections 5%.

REPRESENTS Nonfiction books, novels, short-story collections, scholarly. **Considers these nonfiction areas:** animals, anthropology, archeology, art, autobiography, biography, business, child guidance, cooking, cultural interests, current affairs, decorating, diet/nutrition, economics, education, environment, ethnic, foods, gay/lesbian, government, health, history, humor, inspirational, interior design, language, law, memoirs, money, multicultural, music, parenting, photography, popular culture, politics, psychology, religious, science, self-help, sociology, sports, technology, translation, travel, true crime, women's issues, women's studies. **Considers these fiction areas:** action, adventure, cartoon, comic books, crime, detective, ethnic, experimental, family saga, feminist, gay, historical, horror, humor, lesbian, literary, mainstream, multicultural, mystery, police, satire, sports, suspense.

8—☞ "We provide a lot of editorial assistance to our clients and have connections." Actively seeking fiction, current affairs, history, art, popular culture, health and business. Does not want to receive screenplays.

HOW TO CONTACT Query by either e-mail or mail. Accepts simultaneous submissions. Responds in 4-8 weeks to queries. Obtains most new clients through recommendations from others.

TERMS Agent receives 15% commission on domestic sales. Agent receives 20% commission on foreign sales. Offers written contract.

RECENT SALES Clients include Shelby Foote, The Grief Recovery Institute, Don Wade, Don Zimmer, The Knot.com, David Plowden, PGA of America, Danny Peary, George Kalinsky, Peter Hyman, Daniel Parker, Lee Miller, Elise Miller, Nina Planck, Karyn Bosnak, Christopher Pike, Gerald Carbone, Jason Lethcoe, Andy Crouch.

TIPS "Please check out our website for more details on our agency."

◑ B.J. ROBBINS LITERARY AGENCY

5130 Bellaire Ave., North Hollywood CA 91607-2908. **E-mail:** Robbinsliterary@gmail.com. **E-mail:** amy.bjrobbinsliterary@gmail.com. **Contact:** (Ms.) B.J. Robbins, or Amy Maldonado. Member of AAR. Represents 40 clients. 50% of clients are new/unpublished writers. Currently handles: nonfiction books 50%, novels 50%.

REPRESENTS Nonfiction books, novels. **Considers these nonfiction areas:** autobiography, biography, cultural interests, current affairs, dance, ethnic, film, health, humor, investigative, medicine, memoirs, music, popular culture, psychology, self-help, sociology, sports, theater, travel, true crime, women's issues, women's studies. **Considers these fiction areas:** crime, detective, ethnic, literary, mainstream, mystery, police, sports, suspense, thriller.

HOW TO CONTACT Query with SASE. Submit outline/proposal, 3 sample chapters, SASE. Accepts e-mail queries (no attachments). Accepts simultaneous submissions. Responds in 2-6 weeks to queries. Responds in 6-8 weeks to mss. Obtains most new clients through conferences, referrals.

TERMS Agent receives 15% commission on domestic sales. Agent receives 20% commission on foreign sales. Offers written contract; 3-month notice must be given to terminate contract. This agency charges clients for postage and photocopying (only after sale of ms).

RECENT SALES Sold 15 titles in the last year. *The Sweetness of Tears*, by Nafisa Haji (William Morrow); *Paper Dollhouse: A Memoir*, by Dr. Lisa M. Masterson; *The Sinatra Club*, by Sal Polisi and Steve Dougherty (Gallery Books); *Getting Stoned with Savages*, by J. Maarten Troost (Broadway); *Hot Water*, by Kathryn

Jordan (Berkley); *Between the Bridge and the River*, by Craig Ferguson (Chronicle); *I'm Proud of You* by Tim Madigan (Gotham); *Man of the House*, by Chris Erskine (Rodale); *Bird of Another Heaven*, by James D. Houston (Knopf); *Tomorrow They Will Kiss*, by Eduardo Santiago (Little, Brown); *A Terrible Glory*, by James Donovan (Little, Brown); *The Writing on My Forehead*, by Nafisa Haji (Morrow); *Seen the Glory*, by John Hough Jr. (Simon & Schuster); *Lost on Planet China*, by J. Maarten Troost (Broadway).

WRITERS CONFERENCES Squaw Valley Writers Workshop; San Diego State University Writers' Conference.

◑ RODEEN LITERARY MANAGEMENT

3501 N. Southport #497, Chicago IL 60657. **E-mail:** info@rodeenliterary.com. **E-mail:** submissions@rodeenliterary.com. **Website:** www.rodeenliterary.com. **Contact:** Paul Rodeen. Estab. 2009.

○ Paul Rodeen established Rodeen Literary Management in 2009 after 7 years of experience with the literary agency Sterling Lord Literistic, Inc.

REPRESENTS Nonfiction books, novels, juvenile books, illustrations, graphic novels. **Considers these fiction areas:** picture books, young adult, middle grade fiction.

⚲ Actively seeking "writers and illustrators of all genres of children's literature including picture books, early readers, middle-grade fiction and nonfiction, graphic novels and comic books, as well as young adult fiction and nonfiction." This is primarily an agency devoted to children's books.

HOW TO CONTACT Unsolicited submissions are accepted by e-mail only to submissions@rodeenliterary.com. Cover letters with contact information should be included, and a maximum of 50 sample pages. Accepts simultaneous submissions. Response time varies.

● ◑ ROGERS, COLERIDGE & WHITE

20 Powis Mews, London England W11 1JN United Kingdom. (44)(207)221-3717. **Fax:** (44)(207)229-9084. **E-mail:** info@rcwlitagency.co.uk. **Website:** www.rcwlitagency.co.uk. **Contact:** David Miller, agent. Estab. 1987.

○ Prior to opening the agency, Ms. Rogers was an agent with Peter Janson-Smith; Ms. Coleridge worked at Sidgwick & Jackson, Chatto & Windus, and Anthony Sheil Associates; Ms. White was an editor and rights director for Simon & Schuster; Mr. Straus worked at Hodder and Stoughton, Hamish Hamilton, and Macmillan; Mr. Miller worked as Ms. Rogers' assistant and was treasurer of the AAA; Ms. Waldie worked with Carole Smith.

MEMBER AGENTS Deborah Rogers; Gill Coleridge; Pat White (illustrated and children's books); Peter Straus; David Miller; Zoe Waldie (fiction, biography, current affairs, narrative history); Laurence Laluyaux (foreign rights); Stephen Edwards (foreign rights); Peter Robinson; Sam Copeland; Catherine Pellegrino; Hannah Westland; Jenny Hewson.

REPRESENTS Nonfiction books, novels, juvenile. **Considers these nonfiction areas:** biography, cooking, current affairs, diet/nutrition, foods, humor, satire, sports, narrative history. **Considers these fiction areas:** most fiction categories.

O→ "YA and Children's fiction should be submitted via e-mail to clairewilson@rcwlitagency.com. We do not accept any other e-mail submissions unless by prior arrangement with individual agents." Does not want to receive plays, screenplays, technical books or educational books.

HOW TO CONTACT "Submit synopsis, proposal, sample chapters, bio, SAE by mail. Submissions should include a cover letter with brief bio and the background to the book. In the case of fiction, they should consist of the first 3 chapters or approximately the first 50 pages of the work to a natural break, and a brief synopsis. Nonfiction submissions should take the form of a proposal up to 20 pages in length explaining what the work is about and why you are best placed to write it. Material should be printed out in 12 point font, in double-spacing and on one side only of A4 paper. We cannot acknowledge receipt of material nor can we accept responsibility for anything you send us, so please retain a copy of material submitted. Material will be returned only if sent with an adequately stamped and sized SASE; if return postage is not provided the material will be recycled. We do not accept e-mail submissions unless by prior arrangement with individual agents. We will try to respond within 6-8 weeks of receipt of your material, but please appreciate that this isn't always possible as we must give priority to the authors we already represent." Responds in 6-8 weeks to queries. Obtains most new clients through recommendations from others, solicitations, conferences.

TERMS Agent receives 15% commission on domestic sales. Agent receives 20% commission on foreign sales. Offers written contract.

LINDA ROGHAAR LITERARY AGENCY, LLC

133 High Point Dr., Amherst MA 01002. (413)256-1921. **E-mail:** contact@lindaroghaar.com. **Website:** www.lindaroghaar.com. **Contact:** Linda L. Roghaar. Represents 50 clients. 10% of clients are new/unpublished writers. Currently handles: nonfiction books 100%.

O Prior to opening her agency, Ms. Roghaar worked in retail bookselling for 5 years and as a publishers' sales rep for 15 years.

REPRESENTS Nonfiction books. **Considers these nonfiction areas:** animals, anthropology, archeology, autobiography, biography, education, environment, history, inspirational, popular culture, self-help, women's issues, women's studies.

HOW TO CONTACT Query with SASE. Queries accepted by mail and e-mail. Accepts simultaneous submissions. Responds in 3 months to queries. Responds in 4 months to mss.

TERMS Agent receives 15% commission on domestic sales. Agent receives negotiable commission on foreign sales. Offers written contract.

RECENT SALES *Handmade Home*, by Amanda Soule (Shambhala); *Vintage Knits*, by Debbie Brisson (aka Stitchy McYarnpants) and Carolyn Sheridan (Wiley); *TYV Crafting for Kids*, by Jennifer Casa (Wiley); *The White Hand Society*, by Peter Conners (City Lights); *The Writing Warrior*, by Laraine Herring (Shambhala); *All Wound Up*, by Stephanie Pearl-McPhee (Andrews McMeel).

THE ROSENBERG GROUP

23 Lincoln Ave., Marblehead MA 01945. (781)990-1341. **Fax:** (781)990-1344. **Website:** www.rosenberggroup.com. **Contact:** Barbara Collins Rosenberg. Estab. 1998. Member of AAR. Recognized agent of the RWA. Represents 25 clients. 15% of clients are new/unpublished writers. Currently handles: nonfiction books 30%, novels 30%, scholarly books 10%, 30% college textbooks.

O Prior to becoming an agent, Ms. Rosenberg was a senior editor for Harcourt.

REPRESENTS Nonfiction books, novels, textbooks, college textbooks only. **Considers these nonfiction areas:** current affairs, foods, popular culture, psychology, sports, women's issues, women's studies, women's health, wine/beverages. **Considers these fiction areas:** romance, women's.

⌛ Ms. Rosenberg is well-versed in the romance market (both category and single title). She is a frequent speaker at romance conferences. Actively seeking romance category or single title in contemporary romantic suspense, and the historical subgenres. Does not want to receive inspirational, time travel, futuristic or paranormal.

HOW TO CONTACT Query with SASE. See guidelines on website. Responds in 2 weeks to queries. Responds in 4-6 weeks to mss. Obtains most new clients through recommendations from others, solicitations, conferences.

TERMS Agent receives 15% commission on domestic sales. Agent receives 15% commission on foreign sales. Offers written contract; 1-month notice must be given to terminate contract. Charges maximum of $350/year for postage and photocopying.

RECENT SALES Sold 27 titles in the last year.

WRITERS CONFERENCES RWA National Conference; BookExpo America.

ⓞ RITA ROSENKRANZ LITERARY AGENCY

440 West End Ave., #15D, New York NY 10024. (212)873-6333. **Website:** www.ritarosenkranzliteraryagency.com. **Contact:** Rita Rosenkranz. Member of AAR. Represents 35 clients. 30% of clients are new/unpublished writers. Currently handles: nonfiction books 99%, novels 1%.

⌗ Prior to opening her agency, Ms. Rosenkranz worked as an editor at major New York publishing houses.

REPRESENTS Nonfiction books. **Considers these nonfiction areas:** animals, anthropology, art, autobiography, biography, business, child guidance, computers, cooking, crafts, cultural interests, current affairs, dance, decorating, economics, ethnic, film, gay, government, health, history, hobbies, how-to, humor, inspirational, interior design, language, law, lesbian, literature, medicine, military, money, music, nature, parenting, personal improvement, photography, popular culture, politics, psychology, religious, satire, sci-

ence, self-help, sports, technology, theater, war, women's issues, women's studies.

⌛ "This agency focuses on adult nonfiction, stresses strong editorial development and refinement before submitting to publishers, and brainstorms ideas with authors." Actively seeks authors who are well paired with their subject, either for professional or personal reasons.

HOW TO CONTACT Send query letter only (no proposal) via regular mail or e-mail. Submit proposal package with SASE only on request. No fax queries. Accepts simultaneous submissions. Responds in 2 weeks to queries. Obtains most new clients through directory listings, solicitations, conferences, word of mouth.

TERMS Agent receives 15% commission on domestic sales. Agent receives 20% commission on foreign sales. Offers written contract, binding for 3 years; 3-month written notice must be given to terminate contract. Charges clients for photocopying. Makes referrals to editing services.

RECENT SALES Recently released and forthcoming books include *Replacement Child: A Memoir*, by Judy Mandel (Seal Press); *A Mind for Numbers: How to Excel at Math (Even if You Flunked Algebra)*, by Barbara Oakley (Tarcher); *A Century at Wrigley Field*, by Sam Pathy (Skyhorse); *Breakthrough Communication*, by Harrison Monarth (McGraw-Hill).

TIPS "Identify the current competition for your project to make sure the project is valid. A strong cover letter is very important."

ⓜ MERCEDES ROS LITERARY AGENCY

Castell 38, 08329 Teia, Barcelona Spain. (34)(93)540-1353. **Fax:** (34)(93)540-1346. **E-mail:** info@mercedesros.com. **E-mail:** merce@mercedesros.com. **Website:** www.mercedesros.com. **Contact:** Mercedes Ros.

MEMBER AGENTS Mercedes Ros; Mercé Segarra; Georgina Segarra.

REPRESENTS Juvenile.

⌛ "Gemser Publications publishes nonfiction and religious illustrated books for the 0-7 age group. Our products, basically aimed to convey concepts, habits, attitudes and values that are close to the child's environment, always adopt an open mentality in a globalized world. We combine excellent quality with competitive prices and good texts and beautiful illustrations to educate and inspire our young readers."

HOW TO CONTACT Accepts submissions by e-mail or on disc. Illustrations should be photocopied, ideally in colour, and also sent by e-mail.

WRITERS CONFERENCES Frankfurt Book Fair; London Book Fair; Bologna Book Fair; BookExpo of America; Tokyo Book Fair; Beijing International Book Fair; Frankfurt Book Fair 2007.

TIPS "Try to read or look at as many books a publisher has published before sending in your material, to get a feel for their list and whether your manuscript, idea or style of illustration is likely to fit."

● ANDY ROSS LITERARY AGENCY

767 Santa Ray Ave., Oakland CA 94610. (510)238-8965. **E-mail:** andyrossagency@hotmail.com. **Website:** www.andyrossagency.com. **Contact:** Andy Ross. Represents 30 clients. 20% of clients are new/unpublished writers. Currently handles: nonfiction books 100%.

REPRESENTS Nonfiction books, scholarly. **Considers these nonfiction areas:** anthropology, autobiography, biography, child guidance, cultural interests, current affairs, education, environment, ethnic, government, history, language, law, literature, military, parenting, popular culture, politics, psychology, science, sociology, technology, war.

⸻ "This agency specializes in general nonfiction, politics and current events, history, biography, journalism and contemporary culture." Actively seeking literary, commercial, and young adult fiction. Does not want to receive personal memoir, poetry.

HOW TO CONTACT Query via e-mail only. Accepts simultaneous submissions. Responds in 1 week to queries.

TERMS Agent receives 15% commission on domestic sales. Agent receives 20% commission on foreign sales through a sub-agent. Offers written contract.

● ROSS YOON AGENCY

1666 Connecticut Ave. NW, Suite 500, Washington DC 20009. (202)328-3282. **Fax:** (202)328-9162. **E-mail:** submissions@rossyoon.com. **Website:** http://rossyoon.com. **Contact:** Jennifer Manguera. Member of AAR. Represents 200 clients. 75% of clients are new/unpublished writers. Currently handles: nonfiction books 95%.

MEMBER AGENTS Gail Ross (represents important commercial nonfiction in a variety of areas and counts top doctors, CEO's, prize-winning journalists, and historians among her clients. She and her team work closely with first-time authors; gail@rossyoon.com), Howard Yoon (nonfiction topics ranging from current events and politics to culture to religion and history, to smart business; he is also looking for commercial fiction by published authors; howard@rossyoon.com); Anna Sproul-Latimer (adult nonfiction or all types).

REPRESENTS Nonfiction books. **Considers these nonfiction areas:** anthropology, archeology, autobiography, biography, business, cultural interests, economics, education, environment, ethnic, gay/lesbian, government, health, inspirational, investigative, law, medicine, money, politics, psychology, religious, science, self-help, sociology, sports, technology, true crime. **Considers these fiction areas:** occasional commercial fiction.

⸻ "This agency specializes in adult trade nonfiction."

HOW TO CONTACT "Send proposals by e-mail with a cover letter, résumé, brief synopsis of your work, and several sample chapters. We also accept query letters. No longer accepting submissions by mail." Accepts simultaneous submissions. Responds in 4-6 weeks to queries. Obtains most new clients through recommendations from others.

TERMS Agent receives 15% commission on domestic sales. Agent receives 25% commission on foreign sales. Charges for office expenses.

● JANE ROTROSEN AGENCY LLC

318 E. 51st St., New York NY 10022. (212)593-4330. **Fax:** (212)935-6985. **Website:** www.janerotrosen.com. Estab. 1974. Member of AAR. Other memberships include Authors Guild. Represents more than 100 clients. Currently handles: nonfiction books 30%, novels 70%.

MEMBER AGENTS Jane R. Berkey; Andrea Cirillo; Annelise Robey; Meg Ruley; Christina Hogrebe; Amy Tannenbaum; Peggy Gordijn, director of rights.

REPRESENTS Nonfiction books, novels. **Considers these nonfiction areas:** autobiography, biography, business, child guidance, cooking, current affairs, diet/nutrition, economics, environment, foods, health, how-to, humor, investigative, medicine, money, parenting, popular culture, psychology, satire, self-help, sports, true crime, women's issues, women's studies. **Considers these fiction areas:** crime, family saga, historical, mystery, police, romance, suspense, thriller, women's.

HOW TO CONTACT Query with SASE to the attention of "Submissions." Find appropriate agent contact/e-mail on website. Responds in 2 weeks to writers who have been referred by a client or colleague. Responds in 2 months to mss. Obtains most new clients through recommendations from others.

TERMS Agent receives 15% commission on domestic sales. Agent receives 20% commission on foreign sales. Offers written contract, binding for 3 years; 2-month notice must be given to terminate contract. Charges clients for photocopying, express mail, overseas postage, book purchase.

◐ ◉ THE RUDY AGENCY

825 Wildlife Lane, Estes Park CO 80517. (970)577-8500. **Fax:** (970)577-8600. **E-mail:** mak@rudyagency.com. **Website:** www.rudyagency.com. **Contact:** Maryann Karinch. Adheres to AAR canon of ethics. Represents 15 clients. 50% of clients are new/unpublished writers. Currently handles: nonfiction books 100%.

○ Prior to becoming an agent, Ms. Karinch was, and continues to be, an author of nonfiction books—covering the subjects of health/medicine and human behavior. Prior to that, she was in public relations and marketing: areas of expertise she also applies in her practice as an agent.

MEMBER AGENTS Maryann Karinch (nonfiction: health/medicine, culture/values, history, biography, memoir, science/technology, military/intelligence).

REPRESENTS Nonfiction books, textbooks with consumer appeal. **Considers these nonfiction areas:** anthropology, archeology, autobiography, biography, business, child guidance, computers, cultural interests, current affairs, economics, education, ethnic, gay/lesbian, government, health, history, how-to, language, law, literature, medicine, memoirs, military, money, music, parenting, popular culture, politics, psychology, science, sociology, sports, technology, true crime, war, women's issues, women's studies.

⊶ "We support authors from the proposal stage through promotion of the published work. We work in partnership with publishers to promote the published work and coach authors

in their role in the marketing and public relations campaigns for the book." Actively seeking projects with social value, projects that open minds to new ideas and interesting lives, and projects that entertain through good storytelling. Does not want to receive poetry, children's/juvenile books, screenplays/plays, art/photo books, novels/novellas, religion books, and joke books or books that fit in to the impulse buy/gift book category.

HOW TO CONTACT "Query us. If we like the query, we will invite a complete proposal. No phone queries." Accepts simultaneous submissions. Responds in 8 weeks to mss. Obtains most new clients through recommendations from others, solicitations.

TERMS Agent receives 15% commission on domestic sales. Offers written contract, binding for 1 year.

RECENT SALES Sold 11 titles in the last year. *Live from Jordan: Letters Home from My Journal Through the Middle East*, by Benjamin Orbach (Amacom); *Finding Center: Strategies to Build Strong Girls & Women*, by Maureen Mack (New Horizon Press); *Crossing Fifth Avenue to Bergdorf Goodman: An Insider's Account on the Rise of Luxury Retailing*, by Ira Neimark (SPI Books); *Hamas vs. Fatah: The Struggle for Palestine*, by Jonathan Schanzer (Palgrave Macmillan); *The New Rules of Etiquette and Entertaining*, by Curtrise Garner (Adams Media); *Comes the Darkness, Comes the Light*, by Vanessa Vega (Amacom); *Murder in Mayberry*, by Mary and Jack Branson (New Horizon Press); *Not My Turn to Die*, by Savo Heleta.

WRITERS CONFERENCES BookExpo of America; industry events.

TIPS "Present yourself professionally. I tell people all the time: Subscribe to *Writer's Digest* (I do), because you will get good advice about how to approach an agent."

● REGINA RYAN PUBLISHING ENTERPRISES, INC.

251 Central Park W., 7D, New York NY 10024. (212)787-5589. **E-mail:** queries@reginaryanbooks.com. **Website:** www.reginaryanbooks.com. **Contact:** Regina Ryan. Currently handles: nonfiction books 100%.

○ Prior to becoming an agent, Ms. Ryan was an editor at Alfred A. Knopf, editor-in-chief of Macmillan Adult Trade, and a book producer.

MEMBER AGENTS Regina Ryan; Sharona Moskowitz (for fiction queries).

REPRESENTS Nonfiction books. **Considers these nonfiction areas:** animals, architecture, gardening, government, history, law, memoirs, parenting, politics, psychology, travel, women's issues, women's studies, narrative nonfiction; natural history (especially birds and birding); popular science, adventure, lifestyle, business, sustainability, mind-body-spirit, relationships.

HOW TO CONTACT Query by e-mail or mail with SASE. No telephone queries. Does not accept queries for juvenile or fiction. Accepts simultaneous submissions. Tries to respond in 1 month to queries. Obtains most new clients through recommendations from others.

TERMS Agent receives 15% commission on domestic sales. Agent receives 15% commission on foreign sales. Offers written contract. Charges clients for all out-of-pocket expenses (e.g., long distance calls, messengers, freight, copying) if it's more than just a nominal amount.

RECENT SALES *Backyard Bird Feeding*, by Randi Minetor (Globe Pequot Press); *In Search of Sacco and Vanzetti*, by Susan Tejada (Univ. Press of New England); *Trouble Shooting the Vegetable Garden*, by David Deardorff and Kathryn Wadsworth (Timber Press); *When Johnny Comes Marching Home: What Vets Need, What They Don't Need and What All of Us Can Do to Help*, by Paula Caplan (MIT Press); *Everything Changes: The Insider's Guide to Cancer in Your 20's and 30's*, by Kairol Rosenthal (Wiley); *Angel of Death Row: My Life as a Death Penalty Defense Lawyer*, by Andrea Lyon (Kaplan Publishing).

TIPS "An analysis of why your proposed book is different and better than the competition is essential; a sample chapter is helpful."

◑ THE SAGALYN AGENCY

1250 Connecticut Ave., 7th Floor, Washington DC 20036. **E-mail:** query@sagalyn.com. **Website:** www.sagalyn.com. Estab. 1980. Member of AAR. Currently handles: nonfiction books 85%, novels 5%, scholarly books 10%.

MEMBER AGENTS Raphael Sagalyn; Shannon O'Neill.

REPRESENTS Nonfiction books. **Considers these nonfiction areas:** autobiography, biography, business, economics, history, memoirs, popular culture, science, technology, journalism.

• Does not want to receive stage plays, screenplays, poetry, science fiction, fantasy, romance, children's books, or young adult books.

HOW TO CONTACT Please send e-mail queries only (no attachments). Include 1 of these words in the subject line: query, submission, inquiry.

TIPS "We receive 1,000-1,200 queries a year, which in turn lead to 2 or 3 new clients. See our website for sales information and recent projects."

◑ SALKIND LITERARY AGENCY

Part of Studio B, 734 Indiana St., Lawrence KS 66044. (785)371-0101. **E-mail:** neil@studiob.com. **Website:** www.salkindagency.com. **Contact:** Neil Salkind. Represents 200 clients. 25% of clients are new/unpublished writers. Currently handles: nonfiction books 60%, scholarly books 20%, textbooks 20%.

• Prior to becoming an agent, Mr. Salkind authored numerous trade and textbooks.

MEMBER AGENTS Greg Aunapu, Lynn Haller, Jennifer Lawler, Malka Margolies, Neil J. Salkind.

• Greg Aunapu represents both fiction and nonfiction including true crime, technology, biography, history, narrative nonfiction, memoir (by people who have accomplished something great in their fields), finance, current affairs, politics, pop-culture, psychology, relationships, science and travel. Fiction includes suspense/thrillers, mystery, detective, adventure, humor, science-fiction and modern urban fantasy. Submission guidelines can be found at www.gregaunapu.com. Nonfiction queries should be in book-proposal format; fiction queries should include a complete book synopsis and the first 25 pages of the manuscript, and an author biography. He can be reached at greg@studiob.com. Lynn Haller represents nonfiction authors, with a special interest in business, technology, and how-to. Queries should include a book proposal, a bio, and writing samples. She can be reached at lynn@studiob.com. Jennifer Lawler represents fiction and nonfiction authors. Her nonfiction interests include narrative nonfiction, self-help and some how-to. She is interested in genre fiction, including mystery and science fiction/fantasy. She does NOT represent children's or young adult.

Please query with a book proposal (for nonfiction) and the first chapter of the manuscript (for fiction). She can be reached at jennifer@studiob.com. Malka Margolies represents predominantly nonfiction. Her interests include history, current events, cultural issues, religion/spirituality, nutrition and health, women's issues, parenting and the environment. She is not interested in science fiction, fantasy, how-to or children's books. She can be reached at malka@studiob.com. Neil J. Salkind represents these nonfiction areas: business, cooking, crafts, health, how-to, photography and visual arts, science and self-help. He also represents textbooks and scholarly books. Does not want "to receive book proposals based on ideas where potential authors have not yet researched what has been published."

HOW TO CONTACT Query electronically. Obtains most new clients through recommendations from others.

TERMS Agent receives 15% commission on domestic sales. Agent receives 15% commission on foreign sales.

SALOMONSSON AGENCY

Svartensgatan 4, 116 20 Stockholm Sweden. **E-mail:** info@salomonssonagency.com. **Website:** www.salomonssonagency.com. **Contact:** Niclas Salomonsson. Estab. 2000. Currently handles: novels 100%.

MEMBER AGENTS Niclas Salomonsson, Szilvia Monar, Leyla Belle Drake.

REPRESENTS Novels.

8—¶ "Salomonsson Agency is one of the leading literary agencies in Scandinavia. We focus on fiction from the Nordic countries."

HOW TO CONTACT This agency focuses on Scandinavian authors. "We don't consider submissions in English." Accepts submissions by regular post or e-mail.

RECENT SALES 9-book deal with Random House Canada regarding Liza Marklund; 2-book deal with HarperCollins US regarding Sissel-Jo Gazan; 8-book deal with Doubleday UK regarding Liza Marklund.

VICTORIA SANDERS & ASSOCIATES

241 Avenue of the Americas, Suite 11 H, New York NY 10014. (212)633-8811. **Fax:** (212)633-0525. **E-mail:** queriesvsa@gmail.com. **Website:** www.victoriasanders.com. **Contact:** Victoria Sanders. Estab. 1992. Member of AAR. Signatory of WGA. Represents 135 clients. 25% of clients are new/unpublished writers. Currently handles: nonfiction books 30%, novels 70%.

MEMBER AGENTS Tanya McKinnon, Victoria Sanders, Chris Kepner (open to all types of books as long as the writing is exceptional. Include the first three chapters in the body of the e-mail. At the moment, he is especially on the lookout for quality nonfiction); Bernadette Baker-Baughman (commercial adult, YA, and middle grade fiction, nonfiction, and graphic novels).

REPRESENTS Nonfiction books, novels. **Considers these nonfiction areas:** autobiography, biography, cultural interests, current affairs, dance, ethnic, film, gay/lesbian, government, history, humor, language, law, literature, music, popular culture, politics, psychology, satire, theater, translation, women's issues, women's studies. **Considers these fiction areas:** action, adventure, contemporary issues, ethnic, family saga, feminist, gay, lesbian, literary, thriller.

HOW TO CONTACT Query by e-mail only. "We will not respond to e-mails with attachments or attached files."

TERMS Agent receives 15% commission on domestic sales. Agent receives 20% commission on foreign sales. Offers written contract. Charges for photocopying, messenger, express mail. If in excess of $100, client approval is required.

RECENT SALES Sold 20+ titles in the last year.

TIPS "Limit query to letter (no calls) and give it your best shot. A good query is going to get a good response."

LENNART SANE AGENCY

Hollandareplan 9, S-374 34, Karlshamn Sweden. +46 454 123 56. **E-mail:** info@lennartsaneagency.com. **Website:** www.lennartsaneagency.com. **Contact:** Lennart Sane. Calle de Eraso 36, 1Âª planta ES-28028 Madrid, Spain +34 911 233 492 Represents 20+ clients.

MEMBER AGENTS Lennart Sane, agent; Philip Sane, agent; Lina Hammarling, agent.

REPRESENTS Nonfiction books, novels, juvenile.

8—¶ Lennart Sane Agency AB "represents the literary rights of authors, agents and publishers, in the markets of fiction, nonfiction, and film." This European agency deals in a lot of translation rights, and North American authors are best not to query this agency without a strong referral.

HOW TO CONTACT Query with SASE. "We do not accept unsolicited submissions. We accept new material by referral only."

● SCHIAVONE LITERARY AGENCY, INC.

236 Trails End, West Palm Beach FL 33413-2135. (561)966-9294. **Fax:** (561)966-9294. **E-mail:** prof schia@aol.com. **Website:** www.publishersmarket place.com/members/profschia; blog site: www.schi avoneliteraryagencyinc.blogspot.com. **Contact:** Dr. James Schiavone, CEO, corporate offices in Florida; Jennifer DuVall, president, New York office. New York office: 3671 Hudson Manor Terrace, No. 11H, Bronx, NY, 10463-1139, phone: (718)548-5332; fax: (718)548-5332; e-mail: jendu77@aol.com Other memberships include National Education Association. Represents 60+ clients. 2% of clients are new/unpublished writers. Currently handles: nonfiction books 50%, novels 49%, textbooks 1%.

○ Prior to opening his agency, Dr. Schiavone was a full professor of developmental skills at the City University of New York and author of 5 trade books and 3 textbooks. Jennifer DuVall has many years of combined experience in office management and agenting.

REPRESENTS Nonfiction books, novels, juvenile, scholarly, textbooks. **Considers these nonfiction areas:** animals, anthropology, archeology, autobiography, biography, child guidance, cultural interests, current affairs, education, environment, ethnic, gay/lesbian, government, health, history, how-to, humor, investigative, juvenile nonfiction, language, law, literature, medicine, military, parenting, popular culture, politics, psychology, satire, science, sociology, spirituality, true crime. **Considers these fiction areas:** ethnic, family saga, historical, horror, humor, juvenile, literary, mainstream, science fiction, young adult.

⚷ This agency specializes in celebrity biography and autobiography and memoirs. Does not want to receive poetry.

HOW TO CONTACT Query with SASE. Do not send unsolicited materials or parcels requiring a signature. Send no e-attachments. Accepts simultaneous submissions. Responds in 2 weeks to queries. Responds in 6 weeks to mss. Obtains most new clients through recommendations from others, solicitations, conferences.

TERMS Agent receives 15% commission on domestic sales. Agent receives 20% commission on foreign

sales. Offers written contract. Charges clients for postage only.

WRITERS CONFERENCES Key West Literary Seminar; South Florida Writers' Conference; Tallahassee Writers' Conference, Million Dollar Writers' Conference; Alaska Writers Conference.

TIPS "We prefer to work with established authors published by major houses in New York. We will consider marketable proposals from new/previously unpublished writers."

WENDY SCHMALZ AGENCY

402 Union St., #831, Hudson NY 12534. (518)672-7697. **E-mail:** wendy@schmalzagency.com. **Website:** www.schmalzagency.com. **Contact:** Wendy Schmalz. Estab. 2002. Member of AAR. Represents 35 clients. 10% of clients are new/unpublished writers.

⚷ Actively seeking young adult novels, middle grade novels. Obtains clients through recommendations from others. Not looking for picture books, science fiction or fantasy.

HOW TO CONTACT Accepts only e-mail queries. Do not attach the ms or sample chapters. Replies to queries only if they want to read the ms. Responds in 4 weeks to queries; 4-6 weeks to mss. Obtains clients through recommendations from others.

TERMS Agent receives 15% commission on domestic sales; 20% on foreign sales; 25% for Asian sales.

◐ ◉ SUSAN SCHULMAN LITERARY AGENCY

454 W. 44th St., New York NY 10036. (212)713-1633. **Fax:** (212)581-8830. **E-mail:** schulmanqueries@yahoo.com. **Contact:** Susan Schulman. Estab. 1980. Member of AAR. Signatory of WGA. Other memberships include Dramatists Guild. 10% of clients are new/unpublished writers. Currently handles: nonfiction books 50%, novels 25%, juvenile books 15%, stage plays 10%.

MEMBER AGENTS Linda Kiss, director of foreign rights; Katherine Stones, theater; Emily Uhry, submissions editor.

REPRESENTS **Considers these nonfiction areas:** anthropology, archeology, autobiography, biography, business, child guidance, cooking, cultural interests, current affairs, dance, diet/nutrition, economics, education, environment, ethnic, foods, gay/lesbian, government, health, history, how-to, inspirational, investigative, language, law, literature, medicine, memoirs, money, music, parenting, popular culture, politics, psychology, religious, self-help, sociology, sports, true crime, women's issues, women's studies. **Considers these fiction areas:** action, adventure, crime, detective, feminist, historical, humor, inspirational, juvenile, literary, mainstream, mystery, picture books, police, religious, suspense, women's, young adult.

☞ "We specialize in books for, by and about women and women's issues including nonfiction self-help books, fiction and theater projects. We also handle the film, television and allied rights for several agencies as well as foreign rights for several publishing houses." Actively seeking new nonfiction. Considers plays. Does not want to receive poetry, television scripts or concepts for television.

HOW TO CONTACT Query with SASE. Submit outline, synopsis, author bio, 3 sample chapters. Accepts simultaneous submissions. Responds in 6 weeks to queries/mss. Obtains most new clients through recommendations from others, solicitations, conferences.

TERMS Agent receives 15% commission on domestic sales. Agent receives 20% commission on foreign sales. Offers written contract; 30-day notice must be given to terminate contract.

RECENT SALES Sold 50 titles in the last year; hundred of subsidiary rights deals.

WRITERS CONFERENCES Geneva Writers' Conference (Switzerland); Columbus Writers' Conference; Skidmore Conference of the Independent Women's Writers Group.

TIPS "Keep writing!" Schulman describes her agency as "professional boutique, long-standing, eclectic."

● SCRIBBLERS HOUSE, LLC LITERARY AGENCY

P.O. Box 1007, Cooper Station, New York NY 10276-1007. (212)714-7744. **E-mail:** query@scribblershouse. net. **Website:** www.scribblershouse.net. **Contact:** Stedman Mays, Garrett Gambino. 25% of clients are new/unpublished writers.

MEMBER AGENTS Stedman Mays, Garrett Gambino.

REPRESENTS Nonfiction books, occasionally novels. **Considers these nonfiction areas:** biography, business, diet/nutrition, economics, health, history, how-to, language, literature, medicine, memoirs, money, parenting, popular culture, politics, psychology, self-help, sex, spirituality, the brain; personal finance; writing books; relationships; gender issues. **Consid-**

ers these fiction areas: crime, historical, literary, suspense, thriller, women's.

HOW TO CONTACT "Query via e-mail. Put 'nonfiction query' or 'fiction query' in the subject line followed by the title of your project (send to our submissions e-mail on our website). Do not send attachments or downloadable materials of any kind with query. We will request more materials if we are interested. Usually respond in 2 weeks to 2 months to e-mail queries if we are interested (if we are not interested, we will not respond due to the overwhelming amount of queries we receive). We are only accepting e-mail queries at the present time." Accepts simultaneous submissions.

TERMS Agent receives 15% commission on domestic sales. Charges clients for postage, shipping and copying.

TIPS "If you must send by snail mail, we will return material or respond to a U.S. Postal Service-accepted SASE. (No international coupons or outdated mail strips, please.) Presentation means a lot. A well-written query letter with a brief author bio and your credentials is important. For query letter models, go to the bookstore or online and look at the cover copy and flap copy on other books in your general area of interest. Emulate what's best. Have an idea of other notable books that will be perceived as being in the same vein as yours. Know what's fresh about your project and articulate it in as few words as possible. Consult our website for the most up-to-date information on submitting."

○ SCRIBE AGENCY, LLC

5508 Joylynne Dr., Madison WI 53716. **E-mail:** what theshizzle@scribeagency.com. **E-mail:** submissions@ scribeagency.com. **Website:** www.scribeagency.com. **Contact:** Kristopher O'Higgins. Represents 11 clients. 18% of clients are new/unpublished writers. Currently handles: novels 98%, story collections 2%.

○ "With more than 15 years experience in publishing, with time spent on both the agency and editorial sides, with marketing experience to boot, Scribe Agency is a full-service literary agency, working hands-on with its authors on their projects. Check the website (www. scribeagency.com) to make sure your work matches the Scribe aesthetic."

MEMBER AGENTS Kristopher O'Higgins.

NEW AGENT SPOTLIGHT

JENNIE GOLOBOY (RED SOFA LITERARY)

redsofaliterary.com
@JennieGoloboy

ABOUT JENNIE: Jennie Goloboy is an associate agent with Red Sofa Literary. Jennie has a PhD in the History of American Civilization from Harvard. She is also a published author of both history and fiction, and a member of SFWA, RWA, SHEAR, OAH, the AHA, and Codex Writer's Group. Her funny, specific short stories appear under her pen name, Nora Fleischer.

SHE IS SEEKING: History—must have a commercial (non-academic) focus; early American history is preferred, but will consider all projects. Biography—no personal memoirs. Genre fiction—science fiction/fantasy or paranormal, especially with a literary flair. Young adult and middle grade fiction, especially science fiction/fantasy.

HOW TO SUBMIT: jennie@redsofaliterary.com. "We highly encourage everyone to send an email and/or query letter initially, before attempting to send a full book proposal or sample chapters. Ultimately, it will save postage and time. If there is an interest, we will directly contact the author. Once these materials are received, there is usually response time of 4-6 weeks, sometimes sooner. If querying via e-mail, please only put the contents of your query in the e-mail. We will not open attachments unless they have been requested in advance."

REPRESENTS Novels, short story collections, novellas, anthologies. **Considers these fiction areas:** experimental, fantasy, feminist, gay, horror, lesbian, literary, mainstream, science fiction, thriller.

☞ Actively seeking excellent writers with ideas and stories to tell.

HOW TO CONTACT E-queries only: submissions@scribeagency.com. See the website for submission info, as it may change. Responds in 3-4 weeks to queries. Responds in 5 months to mss.

TERMS Agent receives 15% commission on domestic sales. Agent receives 20% commission on foreign sales. Offers written contract. Charges for postage and photocopying.

RECENT SALES Sold 3 titles in the last year.

WRITERS CONFERENCES BookExpo America; WisCon; Wisconsin Book Festival; World Fantasy Convention; WorldCon.

SECRET AGENT MAN

P.O. Box 1078, Lake Forest CA 92609. (949)698-6987. **E-mail:** query@secretagentman.net. **Website:** www.secretagentman.net. **Contact:** Scott Mortenson.

☞ Selective mystery, thriller, suspense and detective fiction. Does not want to receive scripts or screenplays.

HOW TO CONTACT Query via e-mail only; include sample chapter(s), synopsis and/or outline. Prefers to read the real thing rather than a description of it. Obtains most new clients through recommendations from others.

LYNN SELIGMAN, LITERARY AGENT

400 Highland Ave., Upper Montclair NJ 07043. (973)783-3631. **Contact:** Lynn Seligman. Other memberships include Women's Media Group. Represents 32 clients. 15% of clients are new/unpublished writers. Currently handles: nonfiction books 60%, novels 40%.

○ Prior to opening her agency, Ms. Seligman worked in the subsidiary rights department of Doubleday and Simon & Schuster, and served as an agent with Julian Bach Literary Agency (which became IMG Literary Agency). Foreign rights are represented by Books Crossing Borders, Inc.

REPRESENTS Nonfiction books, novels. **Considers these nonfiction areas:** interior, anthropology, art, biography, business, child guidance, cooking, current affairs, education, ethnic, government, health, history, how-to, humor, language, money, music, nature, photography, popular culture, psychology, science, self-help, sociology, film, true crime, women's. **Considers these fiction areas:** detective, ethnic, fantasy, feminist, historical, horror, humor, literary, mainstream, mystery, romance, contemporary, gothic, historical, regency, science fiction.

8— "This agency specializes in general nonfiction and fiction. I also do illustrated and photography books and have represented several photographers for books."

HOW TO CONTACT Query with SASE. Prefers to read materials exclusively. Accepts simultaneous submissions. Responds in 2 weeks to queries. Responds in 2 months to mss. Obtains most new clients through referrals from other writers and editors.

TERMS Agent receives 15% commission on domestic sales. Agent receives 25% commission on foreign sales. Charges clients for photocopying, unusual postage, express mail, telephone expenses (checks with author first).

RECENT SALES Sold 15 titles in the last year. Lords of Vice series, by Barbara Pierce; Untitled series, by Deborah Leblanc.

● SERENDIPITY LITERARY AGENCY, LLC

305 Gates Ave., Brooklyn NY 11216. (718)230-7689. **Fax:** (718)230-7829. **E-mail:** rbrooks@serendipitylit.com; info@serendipitylit.com. **Website:** www.serendipitylit.com; facebook.com/serendipitylit. **Contact:** Regina Brooks. Represents 50 clients. 50% of clients are new/unpublished writers. Currently handles: nonfiction books 50%, other 50% fiction.

○ Prior to becoming an agent, Ms. Brooks was an acquisitions editor for John Wiley & Sons, Inc. and McGraw-Hill Companies.

MEMBER AGENTS Regina Brooks; Dawn M. Hardy (dawn@serendipitylit.com), Karen Thomas (karen@serendipitylit.com), John Weber (john@serendipitylit.com); Ayanna Coleman (ayanna@serendipitylit.com); Chelcee Johns (chelcee@serendipitylit.com).

REPRESENTS Nonfiction books, novels, juvenile, scholarly, children's books. **Considers these nonfiction areas:** biography, business, christian, cooking, crafts, cultural interests, current affairs, design, economics, education, ethnic, foods, health, history, inspirational, juvenile nonfiction, medicine, memoirs, metaphysics, money, multicultural, New Age, popular culture, politics, psychology, religious, science, self-help, sports, technology, women's issues, women's studies, narrative; popular science, contemporary culture. **Considers these fiction areas:** action, adventure, confession, ethnic, historical, juvenile, literary, multicultural, mystery, romance, suspense, thriller, Christian fiction, spiritual, commercial fiction, young adult novels.

8— African-American nonfiction, commercial fiction, young adult novels with an urban flair and juvenile books. No stage plays, screenplays or poetry.

HOW TO CONTACT Only accepts electronic submissions. "For nonfiction, submit proposal, query, 1 sample chapter (electronically). For adult fiction, please send a query letter that includes basic information that describes your project. Your query letter should include the title, premise, and length of the manuscript. See our guidelines and submission form online. Based on your initial query letter and synopsis, our office may request sample chapters, or your ms in its entirety. Responds in 4-6 weeks to queries; 2 months to mss. Obtains most new clients through conferences, referrals.

TERMS Agent receives 15% commission on domestic sales. Agent receives 20% commission on foreign sales. Offers written contract; 2-month notice must be given to terminate contract. Charges clients for office fees, which are taken from any advance.

RECENT SALES *Putting Makeup on the Fat Boy,* by Bil Wright; *You Should Really Write a Book: How to Write Sell, and Market Your Memoir,* by Regina Brooks; *Living Color,* by Nina Jablonski; *Swirling,* by Christelyn D. Kazarin and Janice R. Littlejohn; *Red Thread Sisters,* by Carol Peacock; *Nicki Minaj: Hop Pop Moments 4 Life,* by Isoul Harris; *Forgotten Burial,* by Jodi Foster.

TIPS "See the book *Writing Great Books for Young Adults.* Looking for high concept ideas with big hooks."

☼ ● SEVENTH AVENUE LITERARY AGENCY

2052-124th St., South Surrey BC Canada. (604)538-7252. **Fax:** (604)538-7252. **E-mail:** info@seventhavenuelit.com. **Website:** www.seventhavenuelit.com. **Contact:** Robert Mackwood, director. Currently handles: nonfiction books 100%.

REPRESENTS Nonfiction books. **Considers these nonfiction areas:** autobiography, biography, business, computers, economics, health, history, medicine, science, sports, technology, travel, lifestyle.

☞ Seventh Avenue Literary Agency is both a literary agency and personal management agency. (The agency was originally called Contemporary Management.) Actively seeking nonfiction. Does not want to receive fiction, poetry, screenplays, children's books, young adult titles, or genre writing such as science fiction, fantasy or erotica.

HOW TO CONTACT Query with SASE. Submit outline, synopsis, 1 sample chapters (nonfiction), publishing history, author bio, table of contents with proposal or query. Send 1-2 chapters and submission history if sending fiction. No e-mail attachments. Provide full contact information. For fiction queries only contact Gloria Goodman: hettyphil@sympatico.ca. Send short query via e-mail. Obtains most new clients through recommendations from others, some solicitations. Does not add many new clients.

TIPS "If you want your material returned, please include an SASE with adequate postage; otherwise, material will be recycled. (U.S. stamps are not adequate; they do not work in Canada.)"

◑ THE SEYMOUR AGENCY

475 Miner St., Canton NY 13617. (315)386-1831. **E-mail:** marysue@twcny.rr.com; nicole@theseymouragency.com. **Website:** www.theseymouragency.com. **Contact:** Mary Sue Seymour, Nicole Resciniti. Member of AAR. Signatory of WGA. Other memberships include RWA, Authors Guild. Represents 50 clients. 5% of clients are new/unpublished writers. Currently handles: nonfiction books 50%, other 50% fiction.

○ Ms. Seymour is a retired New York State certified teacher.

MEMBER AGENTS Mary Sue Seymour (accepts queries in Christian, inspirational, romance, and nonfiction); Nicole Resciniti (accepts queries in same categories as Ms. Seymour in addition to action/suspense/thriller, mystery, sci-fi, fantasy, and YA/children's); Marisa Cleveland (specialty in middle grade fiction).

REPRESENTS Nonfiction books, novels. **Considers these nonfiction areas:** business, health, how-to, self help, Christian books; cookbooks; any well-written nonfiction that includes a proposal in standard format and 1 sample chapter. **Considers these fiction areas:** action, fantasy, mystery, religious, romance, science fiction, suspense, thriller, young adult, middle grade.

HOW TO CONTACT Query with SASE, synopsis, first 50 pages for romance. Accepts e-mail queries. Accepts simultaneous submissions. Responds in 1 month to queries. Responds in 3 months to mss.

TERMS Agent receives 12-15% commission on domestic sales.

RECENT SALES Dinah Bucholz's *The Harry Potter Cookbook* to Adams Media.com; Vannetta Chapman's *A Simple Amish Christmas* to Abingdon Press; Shelley Shepard Gray's current book deal to Harper Collins; Shelley Galloway's multibook deal to Zondervan; Beth Wiseman's Christmas two novellas and multibook deal to Thomas Nelson; Mary Ellis's multibook deal to Harvest House, Barbara Cameron's novellas to Thomas Nelson and multibook deal to Abingdon Press.

DENISE SHANNON LITERARY AGENCY, INC.

20 W. 22nd St., Suite 1603, New York NY 10010. (212)414-2911. **Fax:** (212)414-2930. **E-mail:** info@deniseshannonagency.com. **E-mail:** submissions@deniseshannonagency.com. **Website:** www.deniseshannonagency.com. **Contact:** Denise Shannon. Estab. 2002. Member of AAR.

Prior to opening her agency, Ms. Shannon worked for 16 years with Georges Borchardt and International Creative Management.

REPRESENTS Nonfiction books, novels. **Considers these nonfiction areas:** biography, business, health, narrative nonfiction; politics; journalism; memoir; social history. **Considers these fiction areas:** literary.

8→ "We are a boutique agency with a distinguished list of fiction and nonfiction authors."

HOW TO CONTACT Query by e-mail to: submissions@deniseshannonagency.com, or mail with SASE. Submit query with description of project, bio, SASE. See guidelines online.

TIPS "Please do not send queries regarding fiction projects until a complete manuscript is available for review. We request that you inform us if you are submitting material simultaneously to other agencies."

THE ROBERT E. SHEPARD AGENCY

4804 Laurel Canyon Blvd., Box 592, Valley Village CA 91607-3717. (818)508-0056. **E-mail:** mail@shepardagency.com. **Website:** www.shepardagency.com. **Contact:** Robert Shepard. Other memberships include Authors Guild. Represents 70 clients. 15% of clients are new/unpublished writers. Currently handles: nonfiction books 90%, scholarly books 10%.

Prior to opening his agency, Mr. Shepard was an editor and a sales and marketing manager in book publishing; he now writes, teaches courses for nonfiction authors, and speaks at many writers' conferences.

REPRESENTS Nonfiction books, scholarly, appropriate for trade publishers. **Considers these nonfiction areas:** business, cultural interests, current affairs, economics, gay/lesbian, government, health, history, law, parenting, popular culture, politics, psychology, sports, Judaica; narrative nonfiction; science for laypeople.

8→ This agency specializes in nonfiction, particularly key issues facing society and culture. Actively seeking works by experts recognized in their fields whether or not they're well-known to the general public, and books that offer fresh perspectives or new information even when the subject is familiar. Does not want to receive autobiographies, art books, memoir, spirituality or fiction.

HOW TO CONTACT Query either by e-mail or by regular mail with SASE (if you want material to be returned). Accepts simultaneous submissions. Responds in 4-6 weeks to queries; 6 weeks to proposals. Do not sent ms unless specifically requested to do so. Obtains most new clients through recommendations from others, solicitations.

TERMS Agent receives 15% commission on domestic sales. Agent receives 20% commission on foreign sales. Offers written contract, binding for term of project or until canceled; 30-day notice must be given to terminate contract. Charges clients for phone/fax, photocopying, postage (if and when the project sells).

RECENT SALES Sold 10 titles in the last year. *A Few Seconds of Panic*, by Stefan Fatsis (Penguin); *Big Boy Rules*, by Steve Fainaru (Da Capo Press); *The Fois Gras Wars*, by Mark Caro (Simon & Schuster).

TIPS "We pay attention to detail. We believe in close working relationships between the author and agent, and in building better relationships between the author and editor. Please do your homework! There's no substitute for learning all you can about similar or directly competing books and presenting a well-reasoned competitive analysis in your proposal. Be sure to describe what's new and fresh about your work, why you are the best person to be writing on your subject, everything editors will need to know about your work, and how the book will serve the needs or interests of your intended readers. Don't work in a vacuum: Visit bookstores, talk to other writers about their experiences and let the information you gather inform the work that you do as an author."

SHEREE BYKOFSKY ASSOCIATES, INC.

PO Box 706, Brigantine NJ 08203. **E-mail:** shereebee@aol.com. **E-mail:** submitbee@aol.com. **Website:** www.shereebee.com. **Contact:** Sheree Bykofsky. Member of AAR. Memberships include ASJA, WNBA. Currently handles: nonfiction books 80%, novels 20%.

Prior to opening her agency, Ms. Bykofsky served as executive editor of the Stonesong Press and managing editor of Chiron Press. She is also the author or coauthor of more than 20 books, including *The Complete Idiot's Guide to Getting Published*. Ms. Bykofsky teaches publishing at NYU and SEAK, Inc.

MEMBER AGENTS Janet Rosen, associate.

REPRESENTS Nonfiction, novels. **Considers these nonfiction areas:** Americana, animals, architecture, art, autobiography, biography, business, child guidance, cooking, crafts, creative nonfiction, cultural interests, current affairs, dance, design, economics, education, environment, ethnic, film, finance, foods, gardening, gay, government, health, history, hobbies, humor, language, law, lesbian, memoirs, metaphysics, military, money, multicultural, music, nature, New Age, nutrition, parenting, philosophy, photography, popular culture, politics, psychology, recreation, regional, religious, science, sex, sociology, spirituality, sports, translation, travel, true crime, war, anthropology; creative nonfiction. **Considers these fiction areas:** contemporary issues, literary, mainstream, mystery, suspense.

⌐ This agency specializes in popular reference nonfiction, commercial fiction with a literary quality, and mysteries. "I have wide-ranging interests, but it really depends on quality of writing, originality, and how a particular project appeals to me (or not). I take on fiction when I completely love it—it doesn't matter what area or genre." Does not want to receive poetry, material for children, screenplays, Westerns, horror, science fiction, or fantasy.

HOW TO CONTACT "We only accept e-queries now and will only respond to those in which we are interested. E-mail short queries to submitbee@aol.com. Please, no attachments, snail mail, or phone calls. One-page query, one-page synopsis, and first page of ms in the body of the e-mail. Nonfiction: One-page query in the body of the e-mail. We cannot open attached Word files or any other types of attached files. These will be deleted." Accepts simultaneous submissions. Responds in 1 month to requested mss. Obtains most new clients through recommendations from others.

TERMS Agent receives 15% commission on domestic sales. Agent receives 20% commission on foreign sales. Offers written contract, binding for 1 year. Charges for postage, photocopying, fax.

RECENT SALES *Red Sheep: The Search for My Inner Latina*, by Michele Carlo (Citadel/Kensington); *Bang the Keys: Four Steps to a Lifelong Writing Practice*, by Jill Dearman (Alpha, Penguin); *Signed, Your Student: Celebrities on the Teachers Who Made Them Who They Are Today*, by Holly Holbert (Kaplan); *The Five Ways We Grieve*, by Susan Berger (Trumpeter/Shambhala).

WRITERS CONFERENCES ASJA Writers Conference; Asilomar; Florida Suncoast Writers' Conference; Whidbey Island Writers' Conference; Florida First Coast Writers' Festival; Agents and Editors Conference; Columbus Writers' Conference; Southwest Writers' Conference; Willamette Writers' Conference; Dorothy Canfield Fisher Conference; Maui Writers' Conference; Pacific Northwest Writers' Conference; IWWG.

TIPS "Read the agent listing carefully and comply with guidelines."

◑ WENDY SHERMAN ASSOCIATES, INC.
27 W. 24th St., New York NY 10010. (212)279-9027. **E-mail:** wendy@wsherman.com. **E-mail:** submissions@wsherman.com. **Website:** www.wsherman.com. **Contact:** Wendy Sherman; Kim Perel. Member of AAR. Represents 50 clients. 30% of clients are new/unpublished writers.

○ Prior to opening the agency, Ms. Sherman served as vice president, executive director, associate publisher, subsidiary rights director, and sales and marketing director for major publishers.

MEMBER AGENTS Wendy Sherman (board member of AAR), Kim Perel.

REPRESENTS Considers these nonfiction areas: memoirs, psychology, narrative nonfiction. **Considers these fiction areas:** mainstream fiction that hits the sweet spot between literary and commercial.

⌐ "We specialize in developing new writers, as well as working with more established writers. My experience as a publisher has proven to be a great asset to my clients."

HOW TO CONTACT Query via e-mail only. Accepts simultaneous submissions. Responds in 1 month to queries. Obtains most new clients through recommendations from other writers.

TERMS Agent receives standard 15% commission. Offers written contract.

RECENT SALES *Z, A Novel of Zelda Fitzgerald*, by Therese Anne Fowler; *The Silence of Bonaventure Arrow*, by Rita Leganski; *Together Tea*, by Marjan Kamali; *A Long Long Time Ago and Essentially True*, by Brigid Pasulka; *Illuminations*, by Mary Sharratt; *The Accounting*, by William Lashner; *Lunch in Paris*, by Elizabeth Bard; *The Rules of Inheritance*, by Claire Bidwell Smith; *Love in Ninety Days*, by Dr. Diana Kirschner; *The Wow Factor*, by Jacqui Stafford; *Humor Memoirs*, by Wade Rouse.

TIPS "The bottom line is: Do your homework. Be as well prepared as possible. Read the books that will help you present yourself and your work with polish. You want your submission to stand out."

● ROSALIE SIEGEL, INTERNATIONAL LITERARY AGENCY, INC.

1 Abey Dr., Pennington NJ 08534. (609)737-1007. **Fax:** (609)737-3708. **Website:** http://rosaliesiegel.com. **Contact:** Rosalie Siegel. Member of AAR. Represents 35 clients. 10% of clients are new/unpublished writers. Currently handles: nonfiction books 45%, novels 45%, 10% young adult books and short story collections for current clients.

HOW TO CONTACT Obtains most new clients through referrals from writers and friends.

TERMS Agent receives 15% commission on domestic sales. Agent receives 20% commission on foreign sales. Offers written contract; 2-month notice must be given to terminate contract. Charges clients for photocopying.

●◐ JEFFREY SIMMONS LITERARY AGENCY

15 Penn House, Mallory St., London NW8 8SX England. (44)(207)224-8917. **E-mail:** jasimmons@unicombox.co.uk. **Contact:** Jeffrey Simmons. Represents 43 clients. 40% of clients are new/unpublished writers. Currently handles: nonfiction books 65%, novels 35%.

◍ Prior to becoming an agent, Mr. Simmons was a publisher. He is also an author.

REPRESENTS Nonfiction books, novels. **Considers these nonfiction areas:** autobiography, biography, current affairs, film, government, history, language, memoirs, music, popular culture, sociology, sports, translation, true crime. **Considers these fiction areas:** action, adventure, confession, crime, detective, family saga, literary, mainstream, mystery, police, suspense, thriller.

⌐⚷ "This agency seeks to handle good books and promising young writers. My long experience in publishing and as an author and ghostwriter means I can offer an excellent service all around, especially in terms of editorial experience where appropriate." Actively seeking quality fiction, biography, autobiography, showbiz, personality books, law, crime, politics, and world affairs. Does not want to receive science fiction, horror, fantasy, juvenile, academic books, or specialist subjects (e.g., cooking, gardening, religious).

HOW TO CONTACT Submit sample chapter, outline/proposal, SASE (IRCs if necessary). Prefers to read materials exclusively. Responds in one week to queries. Responds in one month to mss. Obtains most new clients through recommendations from others, solicitations.

TERMS Agent receives 10-15% commission on domestic sales. Agent receives 15% commission on foreign sales. Offers written contract, binding for lifetime of book in question or until it becomes out of print.

TIPS "When contacting us with an outline/proposal, include a brief biographical note (listing any previous publications, with publishers and dates). Preferably tell us if the book has already been offered elsewhere."

◔● BEVERLEY SLOPEN LITERARY AGENCY

131 Bloor St. W., Suite 711, Toronto ON M5S 1S3 Canada. (416)964-9598. **E-mail:** beverly@slopenagency.ca. **Website:** www.slopenagency.ca. **Contact:** Beverley Slopen. Represents 70 clients. 20% of clients are new/unpublished writers. Currently handles: nonfiction books 60%, novels 40%.

◍ Prior to opening her agency, Ms. Slopen worked in publishing and as a journalist.

REPRESENTS Nonfiction books, novels, scholarly. **Considers these nonfiction areas:** anthropology, archeology, autobiography, biography, business, current affairs, economics, investigative, psychology, sociology, true crime. **Considers these fiction areas:** literary, mystery, suspense.

⌐⚷ "This agency has a strong bent toward Canadian writers." Actively seeking serious nonfiction that is accessible and appealing to the general reader. Does not want to receive fantasy, science fiction, or children's books.

HOW TO CONTACT Query by e-mail. Returns materials only with SASE (Canadian postage only). Accepts simultaneous submissions. Responds in 2 months to queries.

TERMS Agent receives 15% commission on domestic sales. Agent receives 10% commission on foreign sales. Offers written contract, binding for 2 years; 3-month notice must be given to terminate contract.

RECENT SALES *Solar Dance*, by Modris Eksteins (Knopf Canada, Harvard University Press.US); *The Novels*, by Terry Fallis; *God's Brain*, by Lionel Tiger & Michael McGuire (Prometheus Books); *What They*

Wanted, by Donna Morrissey (Penguin Canada, Premium/DTV Germany); *The Age of Persuasion*, by Terry O'Reilly & Mike Tennant (Knopf Canada, Counterpoint US); *Prisoner of Tehran*, by Marina Nemat (Penguin Canada, Free Press US, John Murray UK); *Race to the Polar Sea*, by Ken McGoogan (HarperCollins Canada, Counterpoint US); *Transgression*, by James Nichol (HarperCollins US, McArthur Canada, Goldmann Germany); *Midwife of Venice* and *The Harem Midwife*, by Roberta Rich; *Vermeer's Hat*, by Timothy Brook (HarperCollins Canada, Bloomsbury US); *Distantly Related to Freud*, by Ann Charney (Cormorant). **TIPS** "Please, no unsolicited manuscripts."

◎ SLW LITERARY AGENCY

4100 Ridgeland Ave., Northbrook IL 60062. (847)509-0999. **Fax:** (847)509-0996. **E-mail:** shariwenk@swenkagency.com. **Contact:** Shari Wenk. Currently handles: nonfiction books 100%.
REPRESENTS Nonfiction books. **Considers these nonfiction areas:** sports.
�━ "This agency specializes in representing books written by sports celebrities and sports writers."
HOW TO CONTACT Query via e-mail, but note the agency's specific specialty.

VALERIE SMITH, LITERARY AGENT

1746 Route 44-55, Box 160, Modena NY 12548. **Contact:** Valerie Smith. Represents 17 clients. Currently handles: nonfiction books 2%, novels 75%, story collections 1%, juvenile books 20%, scholarly books 1%, textbooks 1%.
REPRESENTS Nonfiction books, novels, juvenile, textbooks. **Considers these nonfiction areas:** agriculture horticulture, cooking, how to, self help. **Considers these fiction areas:** fantasy, historical, juvenile, literary, mainstream, mystery, science, young, women's/chick lit.
�━ "This is a small, personalized agency with a strong long-term commitment to clients interested in building careers. I have strong ties to science fiction, fantasy and young adult projects. I look for serious, productive writers whose work I can be passionate about." Does not want to receive unsolicited mss.
HOW TO CONTACT Query with synopsis, bio, 3 sample chapters, SASE. Contact by snail mail only. Obtains most new clients through recommendations from others.

TERMS Agent receives 15% commission on domestic sales. Agent receives 20% commission on foreign sales. Offers written contract; 6-week notice must be given to terminate contract.

● ◐ ROBERT SMITH LITERARY AGENCY, LTD.

12 Bridge Wharf, 156 Caledonian Rd., London NI 9UU England. (44)(207)278-2444. **Fax:** (44)(207)833-5680. **E-mail:** robertsmith.literaryagency@virgin.net. **Contact:** Robert Smith. Other memberships include AAA. Represents 40 clients. 10% of clients are new/unpublished writers. Currently handles: nonfiction books 80%, syndicated material 20%.
💬 Prior to becoming an agent, Mr. Smith was a book publisher (Ebury Press, Sidgwick & Jackson, Smith Gryphon).
REPRESENTS Nonfiction books, syndicated material. **Considers these nonfiction areas:** autobiography, biography, cooking, diet/nutrition, film, foods, health, investigative, medicine, memoirs, music, popular culture, self-help, sports, theater, true crime, entertainment.
�━ "This agency offers clients full management service in all media. Clients are not necessarily book authors. Our special expertise is in placing newspaper series internationally." Actively seeking autobiographies.
HOW TO CONTACT Submit outline/proposal, SASE (IRCs if necessary). Prefers to read materials exclusively. Responds in 2 weeks to queries. Obtains most new clients through recommendations from others, direct approaches to prospective authors.
TERMS Agent receives 15% commission on domestic sales. Agent receives 20% commission on foreign sales. Offers written contract, binding for 3 months; 3-month notice must be given to terminate contract. Charges clients for couriers, photocopying, overseas mailings of mss (subject to client authorization).
RECENT SALES *Old Time Variety*, by Richard Baker (Pen & Sword); *Get Fit For The Games*, by Peta Bee (Carlton); *The Food Swap Diet*, by Peta Bee (Little, Brown); *The Complete Jack The Ripper A-Z*, by Paul Begg, Martin Fido, and Keith Skinner (John Blake); *My James*, by Ralph Bulger with Rosie Dunn (Macmillan); *The Autobiography Of Jack The Ripper*, by James Carnac (Transworld); *Seven Years with Banksy*, by Robert Clarke (Michael O'mara); *Confessions Of An Essex Girl*, by Becci Fox (Macmillan); *Call The Fire*

Brigade, by Allan Grice (Mainstream); *Dressing Marilyn*, by Andrew Hansford (Carlton); *Reggie Kray's East End Stories*, by Reggie Kray with Peter Gerrard (Little, Brown); *Nothing But Trouble*, by Roberta Kray (Little, Brown); *Pigeon Guided Missiles*, by James Moore and Paul Nero (The History Press); *All Of Me*, by Kim Noble (Little, Brown); *Enter The Dragon*, by Theo Paphitis (Orion); *The Boxer's Story*, by Nathan Shapow with Bob Harris (The Robson Press).

MICHAEL SNELL LITERARY AGENCY

P.O. Box 1206, Truro MA 02666-1206. (508)349-3718. **E-mail:** patricia@michaelsnellagency.com. **Website:** http://michaelsnellagency.com. **Contact:** Michael Snell. Represents 200 clients. 25% of clients are new/unpublished writers. Currently handles: nonfiction books 90%, novels 10%.

○ Prior to opening his agency in 1978, Mr. Snell served as an editor at Wadsworth and Addison-Wesley for 13 years.

MEMBER AGENTS Michael Snell (business, leadership, entrepreneurship, pets, sports); Patricia Snell, (business, business communications, parenting, relationships, health).

REPRESENTS Nonfiction books. **Considers these nonfiction areas:** business (all categories, all levels), creative nonfiction, health, how-to, self-help, women's issues, fitness.

⚸ This agency specializes in how-to, self-help, and all types of business, business leadership, entrepreneurship, and books for small-business owners from low-level how-to to professional and reference. Especially interested in business management, strategy, culture building, performance enhancement, marketing and sales, finance and investment, marketing and sales, finance and investment, career development, executive skills, leadership, and organization development. Actively seeking strong book proposals in any area of business where a clear need exists for a new business book. Does not want to receive fiction, children's books, or complete mss (considers proposals only).

HOW TO CONTACT Query by mail with SASE, or e-mail. Visit the agency's website for Proposal Guidelines. Only considers new clients on an exclusive basis. Responds in 1 week to queries. Responds in 2 weeks to mss. Obtains most new clients through unsolicited

mss, word of mouth, *Literary Market Place*, *Guide to Literary Agents*.

TERMS Agent receives 15% commission on domestic sales. Agent receives 15% commission on foreign sales.

RECENT SALES Nonfiction: *Business at the Speed of NOW*, by John Bernard (Wiley); *The Mind of the CEO*, by Nicole Lipkin (AMACOM); *The Gentle Art of Horseback Riding*, by Gincy Bucklin (Human Kinetics); *Backfire*, by Jake Breeden (Jossey-Bass); *Success,* by Richasrd Shell (Penguin/Portfolio); *Score Big as a Financial Advisor,* by Michael Salmon (McGraw-Hill); *The Well-Balanced Leader*, by Ron Roberts (McGraw-Hill); *Now I Get It*, by Donny Ebenstien (AMACOM); *What Did You Learn at Work Today?* by Dan Tobin (McGraw-Hill); *The Power Values*, by David Gebler (Jossey-Bass); *Communities Like Ours*, by Ken Shelton (Beacon Press); *Power Phrases for Customer Service*, by Renee Evanson (AMACOM). Fiction: *Sun House*, by David James Duncan (Little-Brown); *Glorybound*, by Jessie van Eerden (Word Farm).

TIPS "Send a maximum 1-page query with SASE. Brochure on 'How to Write a Book Proposal' is available on request with SASE. We suggest prospective clients read Michael Snell's book, *From Book Idea to Bestseller* (Prima, 1997), or visit the company's website for detailed information on how to write a book proposal plus a downloadable model proposal.

◑ SPECTRUM LITERARY AGENCY

320 Central Park W., Suite 1-D, New York NY 10025. **Fax:** (212)362-4562. **Website:** www.spectrumliteraryagency.com. **Contact:** Eleanor Wood, president. Estab. 1976. SFWA Represents 90 clients. Currently handles: nonfiction books 10%, novels 90%.

MEMBER AGENTS Eleanor Wood, Justin Bell.

REPRESENTS Nonfiction books, novels. **Considers these fiction areas:** fantasy, historical, mainstream, mystery, romance, science fiction, suspense.

⚸ Mr. Bell is actively seeking submissions in mysteries and a select amount of nonfiction

HOW TO CONTACT Query with SASE. Submit author bio, publishing credits. No unsolicited mss will be read. Queries and submissions by snail mail only. Ms. Wood and other agents have different addresses—see the website for full info. Responds in 1-3 months to queries. Obtains most new clients through recommendations from authors.

TERMS Agent receives 15% commission on domestic sales. Deducts for photocopying and book orders.

TIPS "Spectrum's policy is to read only book-length manuscripts that we have specifically asked to see. Unsolicited manuscripts are not accepted. The letter should describe your book briefly and include publishing credits and background information or qualifications relating to your work, if any."

◑ SPENCERHILL ASSOCIATES

P.O. Box 374, Chatham NY 12037. (518)392-9293. **Fax:** (518)392-9554. **E-mail:** submissions@spencer hillassociates.com. **Website:** www.spencerhillassoci ates.com. **Contact:** Karen Solem or Jennifer Schober (please refer to their website for the latest information). Member of AAR. Represents 96 clients. 10% of clients are new/unpublished writers.

○ Prior to becoming an agent, Ms. Solem was editor-in-chief at HarperCollins and an associate publisher.

MEMBER AGENTS Karen Solem; Jennifer Schober.

REPRESENTS Novels. **Considers these fiction areas:** crime, detective, historical, inspirational, literary, mainstream, police, religious, romance, thriller, young adult.

⚷ "We handle mostly commercial women's fiction, historical novels, romance (historical, contemporary, paranormal, urban fantasy), thrillers, and mysteries. We also represent Christian fiction only—no nonfiction." No nonfiction, poetry, science fiction, children's picture books, or scripts.

HOW TO CONTACT Query submissions@spencer hillassociates.com with synopsis and first three chapters attached as a .doc or .rtf file. "Please note: We no longer accept queries via the mail." Responds in 6-8 weeks to queries "if we are interested in pursuing."

TERMS Agent receives 15% commission on domestic sales. Agent receives 20% commission on foreign sales. Offers written contract; 3-month notice must be given to terminate contract.

● THE SPIELER AGENCY

27 W. 20 St., Suite 305, New York NY 10011. **E-mail:** thespieleragency@gmail.com. **Contact:** Joe Spieler. Represents 160 clients. 2% of clients are new/unpublished writers.

○ Prior to opening his agency, Mr. Spieler was a magazine editor.

MEMBER AGENTS Joe Spieler, Eric Myers.

REPRESENTS Nonfiction books, novels, children's books. **Considers these nonfiction areas:** autobiography, biography, business, child guidance, current affairs, economics, environment, film, gay/lesbian, government, history, law, memoirs, money, music, parenting, politics, sociology, spirituality, theater, travel, women's issues, women's studies. **Considers these fiction areas:** feminist, gay, lesbian, literary, mystery, children's books, middle grade and young adult novels.

HOW TO CONTACT Accepts electronic submissions, or send query letter and sample chapters. Returns materials only with SASE; otherwise materials are discarded when rejected. Accepts simultaneous submissions. Cannot guarantee a personal response to all queries. Obtains most new clients through recommendations, listing in *Guide to Literary Agents*.

TERMS Agent receives 15% commission on domestic sales. Charges clients for messenger bills, photocopying, postage.

WRITERS CONFERENCES London Book Fair.

TIPS "Check www.publishersmarketplace.com/members/spielerlit/."

● PHILIP G. SPITZER LITERARY AGENCY, INC

50 Talmage Farm Lane, East Hampton NY 11937. (631)329-3650. **Fax:** (631)329-3651. **E-mail:** Luc. Hunt@spitzeragency.com. **Website:** www.spitzer agency.com. **Contact:** Luc Hunt. Member of AAR. Represents 60 clients. 10% of clients are new/unpublished writers. Currently handles: nonfiction books 35%, novels 65%.

○ Prior to opening his agency, Mr. Spitzer served at New York University Press, McGraw-Hill, and the John Cushman Associates literary agency.

REPRESENTS Nonfiction books, novels. **Considers these nonfiction areas:** biography, history, investigative, sports, travel, true crime. **Considers these fiction areas:** crime, detective, literary, mainstream, mystery, police, sports, suspense, thriller.

⚷ This agency specializes in mystery/suspense, literary fiction, sports and general nonfiction (no how-to).

HOW TO CONTACT Query with SASE. Mail physical query containing synopsis of work, a brief bio, and sample chapters. Responds in 2 weeks to queries. Responds in 6 weeks to mss. Obtains most new clients through recommendations from others.

TERMS Agent receives 15% commission on domestic sales. Agent receives 20% commission on foreign sales. Charges clients for photocopying.

WRITERS CONFERENCES London Bookfair, Frankfurt, BookExpo America.

⊘❶ P. STATHONIKOS AGENCY

146 Springbluff Heights SW, Calgary Alberta T3H 5E6 Canada. (403)245-2098. **Fax:** (403)245-2087. **E-mail:** pastath@telus.net; stathonp@cadvision.com. **Contact:** Penny Stathonikos.

- Prior to becoming an agent, Ms. Stathonikos was a bookstore owner and publisher's representative for 10 years.

REPRESENTS Nonfiction books, novels, juvenile.

- Children's literature, some young adult. Does not want to receive romance, fantasy, historical fiction, plays, movie scripts or poetry.

HOW TO CONTACT Query with SASE. Submit outline. Responds in 1 month to queries. Responds in 2 months to mss.

TERMS Agent receives 10% commission on domestic sales. Agent receives 15% commission on foreign sales. Charges for postage, telephone, copying, etc.

TIPS "Do your homework—read any of the *Writer's Digest* market books, join a writers' group and check out the local bookstore or library for similar books. Know who your competition is and why your book is different."

● NANCY STAUFFER ASSOCIATES

P.O. Box 1203, Darien CT 06820. (203)202-2500. **E-mail:** StaufferAssoc@optonline.net. **Website:** publishersmarketplace.com/members/nstauffer. **Contact:** Nancy Stauffer Cahoon. Other memberships include Authors Guild. 5% of clients are new/unpublished writers. Currently handles: nonfiction books 10%, novels 90%.

- "Over the course of my more than 20 year career, I've held positions in the editorial, marketing, business, and rights departments of The *New York Times*, McGraw-Hill, and Doubleday. Before founding Nancy Stauffer Associates, I was Director of Foreign and Performing Rights then Director, Subsidiary Rights, for Doubleday, where I was honored to have worked with a diverse range of internationally known and bestselling authors of all genres."

REPRESENTS **Considers these nonfiction areas:** cultural interests, current affairs, ethnic, creative nonfiction (narrative). **Considers these fiction areas:** contemporary, literary, regional.

HOW TO CONTACT Accepts simultaneous submissions. Obtains most new clients through referrals from existing clients.

TERMS Agent receives 15% commission on domestic sales. Agent receives 20% commission on foreign sales. Agent receives 15% commission on film sales.

RECENT SALES *Blasphemy*, by Sherman Alexi; *Benediction*, by Kent Haruf; *Bone Fire*, by Mark Spragg; *The Carry Home*, by Gary Ferguson.

❶ STEELE-PERKINS LITERARY AGENCY

26 Island Ln., Canandaigua NY 14424. (585)396-9290. **Fax:** (585)396-3579. **E-mail:** pattiesp@aol.com. **Contact:** Pattie Steele-Perkins. Member of AAR. Other memberships include RWA. Currently handles: novels 100%.

REPRESENTS Novels. **Considers these fiction areas:** romance, women's, category romance, romantic suspense, historical, contemporary, multicultural, and inspirational.

HOW TO CONTACT Submit synopsis and one chapter via e-mail (no attachments) or snail mail. Snail mail submissions require SASE. Accepts simultaneous submissions. Responds in 6 weeks to queries. Obtains most new clients through recommendations from others, queries/solicitations.

TERMS Agent receives 15% commission on domestic sales. Offers written contract, binding for 1 year; 1-month notice must be given to terminate contract.

RECENT SALES Sold 130 titles last year. This agency prefers not to share specific sales information.

WRITERS CONFERENCES RWA National Conference; BookExpo America; CBA Convention; Romance Slam Jam, Romantic Times.

TIPS "Be patient. E-mail rather than call. Make sure what you are sending is the best it can be."

● STERLING LORD LITERISTIC, INC.

65 Bleecker St., 12th Floor, New York NY 10012. (212)780-6050. **Fax:** (212)780-6095. **E-mail:** info@sll.com. **Website:** www.sll.com. Member of AAR. Signatory of WGA. Represents 600 clients. Currently handles: nonfiction books 50%, novels 50%.

MEMBER AGENTS Philippa Brophy; Laurie Liss; Sterling Lord; Peter Matson; Douglas Stewart; Neeti Madan; Robert Guinsler; George Nicholson; Jim Rutman; Celeste Fine; Judy Heiblum; Erica Rand Silverman.

HOW TO CONTACT Query with SASE via mail. Include synopsis of the work, a brief proposal or the first three chapters of the manuscript, and brief bio or resume. Does not respond to unsolicited e-mail queries. Does not represent screenplays. Responds in approximately 1 month.

TERMS Agent receives 15% commission on domestic sales; 20% commission on foreign sales. Offers written contract.

STERNIG & BYRNE LITERARY AGENCY

2370 S. 107th St., Apt. #4, Milwaukee WI 53227. (414)328-8034. **Fax:** (414)328-8034. **E-mail:** jackbyrne@hotmail.com. **Website:** www.sff.net/people/jackbyrne. **Contact:** Jack Byrne. Other memberships include SFWA, MWA. Represents 30 clients. 10% of clients are new/unpublished writers. Currently handles: nonfiction books 5%, novels 90%, juvenile books 5%.

REPRESENTS Nonfiction books, novels, juvenile. **Considers these fiction areas:** fantasy, horror, mystery, science fiction, suspense.

"Our client list is comfortably full, and our current needs are therefore quite limited." Actively seeking science fiction/fantasy and mystery by established writers. Does not want to receive romance, poetry, textbooks, or highly specialized nonfiction.

HOW TO CONTACT Query with SASE. Prefers e-mail queries (no attachments); hard copy queries also acceptable. Responds in 3 weeks to queries. Responds in 3 months to mss.

TERMS Agent receives 15% commission on domestic sales. Agent receives 20% commission on foreign sales. Offers written contract; 2-month notice must be given to terminate contract.

TIPS "Don't send first drafts, have a professional presentation (including cover letter), and know your field. Read what's been done—good and bad."

STIMOLA LITERARY STUDIO

308 Livingston Ct., Edgewater NJ 07020. **Fax:** /Phone: (201)945-9353. **E-mail:** info@stimolaliterarystudio.com. **Website:** www.stimolaliterarystudio.com. **Contact:** Rosemary B. Stimola. Estab. 1997. Member of AAR. Represents 45 clients. 15% of clients are new/unpublished writers. Currently handles: 10% novels, 90% juvenile books.

Agency is owned and operated by a former educator and children's bookseller with a Ph.D in Linguistics.

MEMBER AGENTS Rosemary B. Stimola.

Actively seeking remarkable young adult fiction and debut picture book author/illustrators. No institutional books.

HOW TO CONTACT Query via e-mail. "No attachments, please!" Accepts simultaneous submissions. Responds in 3 weeks to queries "we wish to pursue further." Responds in 2 months to requested mss. While unsolicited queries are welcome, most clients come through editor, agent, client referrals.

TERMS Agent receives 15% commission on domestic sales. Agent receives 20% (if subagents are employed) commission on foreign sales. Offers written contract, binding for all children's projects. 60 days notice must be given to terminate contract. Charges $85 one-time fee per project to cover expenses.

RECENT SALES Sold 40 books for young readers in the past 2 years. Among these, *A Touch Mortal*, by Leah Clifford (Greenwillow/Harper Collins); *Black Hole Sun*, by David Gill (Greenwillow/Harper Collins); *Dot*, by Patricia Intriago (FSG/Macmillan); *Inside Out and Back Again*, by Thanhha Lai (Harper Collins); *The Fox Inheritance*, by Mary Pearson (Henry Holt/Macmillan); *Henry Aaron's Dream*, by Matt Tavares (Candlewick Press); *Throat*, by R.A. Nelson (Knopf/RH).

WRITERS CONFERENCES Will attend: ALA Midwinter, ALA Annual, BEA, Bologna Book Fair, NTCE, SCBWI-Illinois regional conference; SCBWI Annual Winter Conference in New York, SCBWI- New York Metro.

TIPS Agent is hands-on, no-nonsense. May request revisions. Does not edit but may offer suggestions for improvement. Well-respected by clients and editors. "A firm but reasonable deal negotiator."

STONESONG

27 W. 24th St. #510, New York NY 10010. (212)929-4600. **Fax:** (212)486-9123. **E-mail:** editors@stonesong.com. **E-mail:** submissions@stonesong.com. **Website:** http://stonesong.com.

MEMBER AGENTS Alison Fargis, Ellen Scordato, Judy Linden, Emmanuelle Morgen, Sarah Passick.

Does not represent plays, screenplays, or poetry.

HOW TO CONTACT Accepts electronic queries for fiction and nonfiction. Submit query addressed to 1 agent. Include first chapter or first 10 pages of ms.

RECENT SALES *Hemlock,* by Kathleen Peacock; *Sweet Designs,* by Amy Atlas; *The DIY Bride's Affair to Remember,* by Khris Cochran; *Dating the Undead,* by Gena Showalter.

ROBIN STRAUS AGENCY, INC.

229 E. 79th St., Suite 5A, New York NY 10075. (212)472-3282. **Fax:** (212)472-3833. **E-mail:** info@robinstrausagency.com. **Website:** www.robinstraus agency.com/. **Contact:** Ms. Robin Straus. Estab. 1983. Member of AAR.

○ Prior to becoming an agent, Robin Straus served as a subsidary rights manager at Random House and Doubleday and worked in editorial at Little, Brown.

REPRESENTS Represents high-quality adult fiction and nonfiction including literary and commercial fiction, narrative nonfiction, women's fiction, memoirs, history, biographies, books on psychology, popular culture and current affairs, science, parenting, and cookbooks.

⌐ Does not represent juvenile, young adult, science fiction/fantasy, horror, romance, Westerns, poetry or screenplays.

HOW TO CONTACT If you prefer to submit your queries electronically, please note that we do not download manuscripts. All materials must be included in the body of the e-mail. We do not respond to any submissions that do not include a SASE. No metered postage.

TERMS Agent receives 15% commission on domestic sales. Agent receives 20% commission on foreign sales. Offers written contract. Charges for photocopying, express mail services, messenger and foreign postage, galleys and books for submissions, etc. as incurred.

PAM STRICKLER AUTHOR MANAGEMENT

P.O. Box 505, New Paltz NY 12561. (845)255-0061. **E-mail:** pamstrickleragency@gmail.com. **Website:** www.pamstrickler.com. **Contact:** Pamela Dean Strickler. Member of AAR. Also an associate member of the Historical Novel Society and member of RWA.

○ Prior to opening her agency, Ms. Strickler was senior editor at Ballantine Books.

REPRESENTS Novels. **Considers these fiction areas:** historical, romance, women's.

⌐ Does not want to receive nonfiction or children's books.

HOW TO CONTACT E-mail queries only, including a one-page letter with a brief description of your plot, plus the first 10 pages of your novel all pasted into the body of the e-mail. Sorry, unknown attachments will not be opened.

THE STRINGER LITERARY AGENCY, LLC

E-mail: stringerlit@comcast.net. **Website:** www.stringerlit.com. **Contact:** Marlene Stringer.

REPRESENTS Considers these nonfiction areas: history, military, music, parenting, science, sports, middle-grade. **Considers these fiction areas:** fantasy, historical, mystery, romance, science fiction, thriller, women's, young adult.

⌐ This agency specializes in fiction. Does not want to receive picture books, plays, short stories, or poetry.

HOW TO CONTACT Electronic submissions only. Accepts simultaneous submissions.

RECENT SALES *Out for Blood* and *Stolen,* by Alyxandra Harvey (Walker Books); *Change of Heart,* by Shari Maurer (WestSide Books); *I Stole Johnny Depp's Alien Girlfriend,* by Gary Ghislain (Chronicle Books); *The Land of Hope & Glory Trilogy,* by Geoffrey Wilson (Hodder); *..And On The Piano, Nicky Hopkins!,* by Julian Dawson (Plus One Press); *Poison Kissed,* by Erica Hayes (St. Martin's); *Possum Summer,* by Jen K. Blom (Holiday House).

TIPS "If your ms falls between categories, or you are not sure of the category, query and we'll let you know if we'd like to take a look. We strive to respond as quickly as possible. If you have not received a response in the time period indicated, please re-query."

REBECCA STRONG INTERNATIONAL LITERARY AGENCY

235 W. 108th St., #35, New York NY 10025. (212)865-1569. **E-mail:** info@rsila.com. **Website:** www.rsila.com. **Contact:** Rebecca Strong. Estab. 2004.

○ Prior to opening her agency, Ms. Strong was an industry executive with experience editing and licensing in the US and UK. She has worked at Crown/Random House, Harmony/Random House, Bloomsbury, and Harvill.

REPRESENTS Nonfiction books, novels. **Considers these nonfiction areas:** biography, business, health, history, memoirs, science, travel.

8— "We are a consciously small agency selectively representing authors all over the world." Does not want to receive poetry, screenplays or any unsolicited mss.

HOW TO CONTACT E-mail submissions only; subject line should indicate "submission query"; include cover letter with proposal. For fiction, include 1-2 complete chapters only. Accepts simultaneous submissions. Responds in 6-8 weeks to queries. Obtains most new clients through recommendations from others, conferences.

TERMS Agent receives 15% commission on domestic sales. Agent receives 20% commission on foreign sales. Offers written contract, binding for 10 years; 30-day notice must be given to terminate contract.

TIPS "I represent writers with prior publishing experience only: journalists, magazine writers or writers of fiction who have been published in anthologies or literary magazines. There are exceptions to this guideline, but not many."

● THE STROTHMAN AGENCY, LLC

P.O. Box 231132, Boston MA 02123. (617)742-2011. **Fax:** (617)742-2014. **E-mail:** info@strothmanagency.com. **Website:** www.strothmanagency.com. **Contact:** Wendy Strothman, Lauren MacLeod. Member of AAR. Other memberships include Authors' Guild. Represents 50 clients. Currently handles: nonfiction books 70%, novels 10%, scholarly books 20%.

○ Prior to becoming an agent, Ms. Strothman was head of Beacon Press (1983-1995) and executive vice president of Houghton Mifflin's Trade & Reference Division (1996-2002).

MEMBER AGENTS Wendy Strothman; Lauren MacLeod.

REPRESENTS Nonfiction books, novels, scholarly, young adult and middle grade. **Considers these nonfiction areas:** business, current affairs, environment, government, history, language, law, literature, politics, travel. **Considers these fiction areas:** literary, young adult, middle grade.

8— "Because we are highly selective in the clients we represent, we increase the value publishers place on our properties. We specialize in narrative nonfiction, memoir, history, science and nature, arts and culture, literary travel, current affairs, and some business. We have a highly selective practice in literary fiction, young adult

and middle grade fiction, and nonfiction. We are now opening our doors to more commercial fiction but from authors who have a platform. If you have a platform, please mention it in your query letter. The Strothman Agency seeks out scholars, journalists, and other acknowledged and emerging experts in their fields. We are now actively looking for authors of well-written young-adult fiction and nonfiction. Browse the Latest News to get an idea of the types of books that we represent. For more about what we're looking for, read Pitching an Agent: The Strothman Agency on the publishing website www.strothmanagency.com." Does not want to receive commercial fiction, romance, science fiction or self-help.

HOW TO CONTACT Accepts queries only via e-mail at strothmanagency@gmail.com. See submission guidelines online. Accepts simultaneous submissions. Responds in 4 weeks to queries. Responds in 6 weeks to mss. Obtains most new clients through recommendations from others.

TERMS Agent receives 15% commission on domestic sales. Agent receives 20% commission on foreign sales. Offers written contract; 30-day notice must be given to terminate contract.

THE STUART AGENCY

260 W. 52 St., #24C, New York NY 10019. (212)586-2711. **Fax:** (212)977-1488. **E-mail:** andrew@stuartagency.com. **Website:** http://stuartagency.com. **Contact:** Andrew Stuart. Estab. 2002.

○ Prior to his current position, Mr. Stuart was an agent with Literary Group International for five years. Prior to becoming an agent, he was an editor at Random House and Simon & Schuster.

REPRESENTS Nonfiction books, novels. **Considers these nonfiction areas:** biography, ethnic, government, history, memoirs, multicultural, psychology, science, sports, narrative nonfiction. **Considers these fiction areas:** ethnic, literary.

HOW TO CONTACT Query by e-mail or mail with SASE. Do not send any materials besides query/SASE unless requested.

◑ EMMA SWEENEY AGENCY, LLC

245 E 80th St., Suite 7E, New York NY 10075. **E-mail:** queries@emmasweeneyagency.com. **Website:** www.emmasweeneyagency.com. Member of AAR. Other

memberships include Women's Media Group. Represents 80 clients. 5% of clients are new/unpublished writers. Currently handles: nonfiction books 50%, novels 50%.

○ Prior to becoming an agent, Ms. Sweeney was director of subsidiary rights at Grove Press. Since 1990, she has been a literary agent.

MEMBER AGENTS Emma Sweeney, president; Noah Ballard, rights manager and agent (represents literary fiction, young adult novel, and narrative nonfiction. Considers these nonfiction areas: popular science, pop culture and music history, biography, memoirs, cooking, and anything relating to animals. Considers these fiction areas: literary (of the highest writing quality possible), young adult; eva@emmasweeney agency.com); Justine Wenger, junior agent/assistant (justine@emmasweeneyagency.com).

REPRESENTS Nonfiction books, novels.

⚷ "We specialize in quality fiction and nonfiction. Our primary areas of interest include literary and women's fiction, mysteries and thrillers, science, history, biography, memoir, religious studies and the natural sciences." Does not want to receive romance, Westerns or screenplays.

HOW TO CONTACT Send query letter and first 10 pages in body of e-mail (no attachments) to queries@ emmasweeneyagency.com. No snail mail queries.

TERMS Agent receives 15% commission on domestic sales. Agent receives 10% commission on foreign sales.

WRITERS CONFERENCES Nebraska Writers' Conference; Words and Music Festival in New Orleans.

◑ THE SWETKY AGENCY

2150 Balboa Way, No. 29, St. George UT 84770. (435)313-8006. **E-mail:** fayeswetky@amsaw.org. **Website:** www.amsaw.org/swetkyagency/index.html. **Contact:** Faye M. Swetky. Other memberships include American Society of Authors and Writers. Represents 20+ clients. 90% of clients are new/unpublished writers. Currently handles: nonfiction books 45%, novels 45%, movie scripts 10%, TV scripts 20%.

○ Prior to becoming an agent, Ms. Swetky was an editor and corporate manager. She has also raised and raced thoroughbred horses.

REPRESENTS Nonfiction books, novels, short story collections, juvenile, movie, TV, movie scripts, feature film, MOW, sitcom, documentary. **Considers these nonfiction areas:** All major genres. **Consid-**

ers these fiction areas: All major genres. **Considers these script areas:** action, biography, cartoon, comedy, contemporary, detective, erotica, ethnic, experimental, family, fantasy, feminist, gay, glitz, historical, horror, juvenile, mainstream, multicultural, multimedia, mystery, psychic, regional, religious, romantic comedy, romantic drama, science, sports, teen, thriller, Western.

⚷ "We handle only book-length fiction and nonfiction and feature-length movie and television scripts. Please visit our website before submitting. All agency-related information is there, including a sample contract, e-mail submission forms, policies, clients, etc." Actively seeking marketable full-length material. Do not send unprofessionally prepared mss and/ or scripts.

HOW TO CONTACT See website for submission instructions. Accepts e-mail queries only. Accepts simultaneous submissions. Response time varies. Obtains most new clients through queries.

TERMS Agent receives 15% commission on domestic sales; 20% commission on foreign sales; 20% commission on film sales. Offers written contract, binding for 6 months; 30-day notice must be given to terminate contract.

RECENT SALES *Pointman; For Men and for Gods; Boozehound; Sorry, I Thought I Loved You; Beating Bipolar; Message to My Butterfly; 101 Incredible Moments in Golf; Youth Pen; From Cocaine to Coconuts; The Last Warlord; They Call Me Doc; From Container to Kitchen.*

TIPS "Be professional. Have a professionally-prepared product."

STEPHANIE TADE LITERARY AGENCY

P.O. Box 235, Durham PA 18039. (610)346-8667. **Contact:** Stephanie Tade.

○ Prior to becoming an agent, Ms. Tade was an executive editor at Rodale Press. She was also an agent with the Jane Rotrosen Agency.

MEMBER AGENTS Stephanie Tade.

REPRESENTS Nonfiction.

⚷ "Mostly commercial nonfiction, especially in categories of health/diet, spirituality and Eastern philosophy, relationships/dating, self-improvement, psychology, science, and women's issues.

HOW TO CONTACT Query by e-mail or mail with SASE.

◑ TALCOTT NOTCH LITERARY

2 Broad St., Second Floor, Suite 10, Milford CT 06460. (203)876-4959. **Fax:** (203)876-9517. **E-mail:** editorial@talcottnotch.net. **Website:** www.talcottnotch.net. **Contact:** Gina Panettieri, President. Represents 35 clients. 25% of clients are new/unpublished writers. Currently handles: nonfiction books 50%, novels 20%, story collections 5%, juvenile books 20%, scholarly books 10%.

◐ Prior to becoming an agent, Ms. Panettieri was a freelance writer and editor.

MEMBER AGENTS Gina Panettieri (history, business, self-help, science, gardening, cookbooks, crafts, parenting, memoir, true crime, travel, women's fiction, paranormal, urban fantasy, horror, science fiction, historical, mystery, thrillers and suspense.); Paula Munier (mystery/thriller, SF/fantasy, romance, YA, memoir, humor, pop culture, health & wellness, cooking, self-help, pop psych, New Age, inspirational, technology, science, and writing); Sara D'Emic (adult and YA fantasy, sci-fi, horror, mystery, and mainstream fiction (all the sub genres those encompass), nonfiction science/technology); Rachael Dugas (young adult, middle grade, romance, and women's fiction, food memoirs); Jessica Negron (YA and Adult fiction, but lean toward science fiction and fantasy (and all the little sub-genres), steamy romance, thrillers).

REPRESENTS Nonfiction books, novels, juvenile, scholarly, textbooks. **Considers these nonfiction areas:** animals, anthropology, art, biography, business, computers, cooking, current affairs, decorating, education, environment, ethnic, gay/lesbian, government, health, history, interior design, investigative, juvenile nonfiction, memoirs, metaphysics, military, money, music, New Age, popular culture, psychology, science, sociology, sports, technology, true crime, women's issues, women's studies. **Considers these fiction areas:** action, adventure, crime, detective, fantasy, juvenile, mystery, police, romance, suspense, thriller, young adult.

HOW TO CONTACT Query via e-mail (preferred) with first 10 pages of the ms within the body of the e-mail, not as an attachment, or with SASE. Consult website for detailed submission guidelines. Accepts simultaneous submissions. Responds in 1 week to queries. Responds in 4-6 weeks to mss.

TERMS Agent receives 15% commission on domestic sales. Agent receives 20% commission on foreign sales. Offers written contract, binding for 1 year.

RECENT SALES Sold 36 titles in the last year. *Delivered From Evil*, by Ron Franscell (Fairwinds) and *Sourtoe* (Globe Pequot Press); *Hellforged*, by Nancy Holzner (Berkley Ace Science Fiction); *Welcoming Kitchen; 200 Allergen- and Gluten-Free Vegan Recipes*, by Kim Lutz and Megan Hart (Sterling); *Dr. Seteh's Love Prescription*, by Dr. Seth Meyers (Adams Media); *The Book of Ancient Bastards,* by Brian Thornton (Adams Media); *Hope in Courage*, by Beth Fehlbaum (Westside Books) and more.

TIPS "Know your market and how to reach them. A strong platform is essential in your book proposal. Can you effectively use social media? Are you a strong networker? Are you familiar with the book bloggers in your genre? Are you involved with the interest-specific groups that can help you? What can you do to break through the 'noise' and help present your book to your readers? Check our website for more tips and information on this topic."

⬤ PATRICIA TEAL LITERARY AGENCY

2036 Vista Del Rosa, Fullerton CA 92831-1336. **Phone/ Fax:** (714)738-8333. **Contact:** Patricia Teal. Member of AAR. Other memberships include RWA, Authors Guild. Represents 20 clients. Currently handles: nonfiction books 10%, 90% fiction .

REPRESENTS Nonfiction books, novels. **Considers these nonfiction areas:** animals, autobiography, biography, child guidance, health, how-to, investigative, medicine, parenting, psychology, self-help, true crime, women's issues, women's studies. **Considers these fiction areas:** glitz, mainstream, mystery, romance, suspense.

⤔ This agency specializes in women's fiction, commercial how-to, and self-help nonfiction. Does not want to receive poetry, short stories, articles, science fiction, fantasy, or regency romance.

HOW TO CONTACT Published authors only may query with SASE. Accepts simultaneous submissions. Responds in 10 days to queries. Responds in 6 weeks to mss. Obtains most new clients through conferences, recommendations from authors and editors.

TERMS Agent receives 10-15% commission on domestic sales. Agent receives 20% commission on foreign sales. Offers written contract, binding for 1 year. Charges clients for ms copies.

RECENT SALES Sold 30 titles in the last year. *Texas Rose*, by Marie Ferrarella (Silhouette); *Watch Your Language*, by Sterling Johnson (St. Martin's Press); *The Black Sheep's Baby*, by Kathleen Creighton (Silhouette); *Man With a Message*, by Muriel Jensen (Harlequin).

WRITERS CONFERENCES RWA Conferences; Asilomar; BookExpo America; Bouchercon; Maui Writers Conference.

TIPS "Include SASE with all correspondence. I am taking on published authors only."

◑ TESSLER LITERARY AGENCY, LLC

27 W. 20th St., Suite 1003, New York NY 10011. (212)242-0466. **Fax:** (212)242-2366. **Website:** www.tessleragency.com. **Contact:** Michelle Tessler. Member of AAR. Currently handles: 90% nonfiction books, 10% novels.

    ○ Prior to forming her own agency, Ms. Tessler worked at Carlisle & Co. (now a part of Inkwell Management). She has also worked at the William Morris Agency and the Elaine Markson Literary Agency.

    ☛ "Michelle Tessler is dedicated to writers of high-quality fiction and nonfiction. Clients include accomplished journalists, scientists, academics, experts in their field, as well as novelists and debut authors with unique voices and stories to tell. She values fresh, original writing that has a compelling point of view. In nonfiction, her list includes narrative, popular science, memoir, history, psychology, business, biography, food, and travel. In fiction, she represents literary, women's, and commercial. If your project is in keeping with the kind of books we take on, we want to hear from you. We do not take on genre fiction or children's books."

HOW TO CONTACT Submit query through online query form only. Accepts simultaneous submissions. New clients by queries/submissions through the website and recommendations from others.

TERMS Receives 15% commission on domestic sales; 20% on foreign sales. Offers written contract.

RECENT SALES *Underwater Dogs*, by Seth Casteel (Little, Brown); *The Bonobo and the Atheist*, by Frans de Waal (WW Norton); *The Drunken Botanist*, by Amy Stewart (Algonquin Books); *The Chemistry Between Us*, by Larry Young, Ph. D and Brian Alexander (Current/Penguin); *Close Your Eyes*, by Amanda Eyre Ward (Random House).

◑ THREE SEAS LITERARY AGENCY

P.O. Box 8571, Madison WI 53708. (608)834-9317. **E-mail:** queries@threeseaslit.com. **Website:** http://threeseasagency.com. **Contact:** Michelle Grajkowski, Cori Deyoe. Estab. 2000. Member of AAR. Other memberships include RWA (Romance Writers of America) Represents 55 clients. 10% of clients are new/unpublished writers. Currently handles: nonfiction books 5%, novels 80%, juvenile books 15%.

    ○ Since its inception, 3 Seas has sold more than 500 titles worldwide. Ms. Grajkowski's authors have appeared on all the major lists including *The New York Times* and *USA Today*. Prior to joining the agency in 2006, Ms. Deyoe was a multi-published author. She represents a wide range of authors and has sold many projects at auction.

MEMBER AGENTS Michelle Grajkowski; Cori Deyoe.

REPRESENTS Nonfiction, novels, juvenile.

    ☛ 3 Seas focuses primarily on romance (including contemporary, romantic suspense, paranormal, fantasy, historical and category), women's fiction, mysteries, nonfiction, young adult, and children's stories. "Currently, we are looking for fantastic authors with a voice of their own." 3 Seas does not represent poetry, screenplays, or novellas.

HOW TO CONTACT E-mail queries only. For fiction titles, query with first chapter and synopsis embedded in the e-mail. For nonfiction, query with complete proposal and first chapter. For picture books, query with complete text. One sample illustration may be included. Accepts simultaneous submissions. Responds in 1 month to queries. Obtains most new clients through recommendations from others, conferences.

TERMS Agent receives 15% commission on domestic sales. Agent receives 20% commission on foreign sales. Offers written contract.

RECENT SALES Clients include *New York Times* bestselling authors: Katie MacAlister, Kerrelyn

Sparks and C.L. Wilson. Other award-winning authors include: Alexis Morgan, Norah Wilson, Liz Talley, Donna MacMeans, Anna DeStefano, Laura Marie Altom, Cathy McDavid, Trish Milburn, Winnie Griggs, Carla Capshaw, Lisa Mondello, Tricia Mills, Tracy Madison, Keri Mikulski, Lori McDonald, R. Barri Flowers, Jennifer Brown, Kristi Gold and Susan Gee Heino.

🐟⭘ TOBY EADY ASSOCIATES

Third Floor, 9 Orme Court, London England W2 4RL United Kingdom. (44)(207)792-0092. **Fax:** (44)(207)792-0879. **E-mail:** zaria@tobyeadyassociates.co.uk. **E-mail:** submissions@tobyeadyassociates.co.uk. **Website:** www.tobyeadyassociates.co.uk. **Contact:** Jamie Coleman. Estab. 1968. Represents 53 clients. 13% of clients are new/unpublished writers. Currently handles: nonfiction books 50%, novels 50%.

MEMBER AGENTS Toby Eady (China, the Middle East, Africa, politics of a Swiftian nature); Laetitia Rutherford (fiction and nonfiction from around the world).

REPRESENTS Nonfiction books, novels, short story collections, novellas, anthologies. **Considers these nonfiction areas:** architecture, art, cooking, cultural interests, current affairs, diet/nutrition, design, ethnic, foods, government, health, history, law, medicine, memoirs, popular culture, politics. **Considers these fiction areas:** action, adventure, confession, historical, literary, mainstream.

⌐ "We handle fiction and nonfiction for adults and we specialize in China, the Middle East and Africa." Actively seeking "stories that demand to be heard." Does not want to receive poetry, screenplays or children's books.

HOW TO CONTACT Send the first 50 pages of your work, double-spaced and unbound, with a synopsis and a brief bio attn: Jamie Coleman. Accepts simultaneous submissions. Responds in 2 weeks to queries. Responds in 2 weeks to mss. Obtains most new clients through recommendations from others, solicitations, conferences.

TERMS Agent receives 15% commission on domestic sales. Agent receives 20% commission on foreign sales. Offers written contract; 3-month notice must be given to terminate contract.

WRITERS CONFERENCES City Lit; Winchester Writers' Festival.

TIPS "Send submissions to this address: Jamie Coleman, Third Floor, 9 Orme Court, London W2 4RL."

⭘ TRACY BROWN LITERARY AGENCY

P.O. Box 88, Scarsdale NY 10583. (914)400-4147. **Fax:** (914)931-1746. **E-mail:** tracy@brownlit.com. **Contact:** Tracy Brown. Represents 35 clients. Currently handles: nonfiction books 90%, novels 10%.

◖ Prior to becoming an agent, Mr. Brown was a book editor for 25 years.

REPRESENTS Nonfiction, novels, anthologies. **Considers these nonfiction areas:** current events, popular history, health, psychology, sports, humor, biography, travel, nature, women's issues, and literary fiction. **Considers these fiction areas:** contemporary issues, feminist, literary, mainstream, women's.

⌐ Specializes in thorough involvement with clients' books at every stage of the process from writing to proposals to publication. Actively seeking serious nonfiction and fiction. Does not want to receive YA, sci-fi or romance.

HOW TO CONTACT Submit outline/proposal, synopsis, author bio. Accepts simultaneous submissions. Responds in 2 weeks to queries. Obtains most new clients through referrals.

TERMS Agent receives 15% commission on domestic sales. Agent receives 20% commission on foreign sales. Offers written contract.

RECENT SALES *Why Have Kids?* by Jessica Valenti (HarperCollins); *Hotel Notell: A Novel,* by Daphne Uviller (Bantam); *Healing Sexual Pain,* by Deborah Coady, MD and Nancy Fish, MSW, MPH (Seal Press).

◑ ⬤ TRANSATLANTIC LITERARY AGENCY

2 Bloor St., Suite 3500, Toronto ON M4W 1A8 Canada. **E-mail:** info@tla1.com. **Website:** www.tla1.com. Represents 250 clients. 10% of clients are new/unpublished writers. Currently handles: nonfiction books 30%, novels 15%, juvenile books 50%, textbooks 5%.

MEMBER AGENTS Lynn Bennett, Lynn@tla1.com, (juvenile and young adult fiction); Shaun Bradley, Shaun@tla1.com (literary fiction and narrative nonfiction); Marie Campbell, Marie@tla1.com (literary juvenile and young adult fiction); Samantha Haywood, Sam@tla1.com (literary fiction, narrative nonfiction and graphic novels); Don Sedgwick, Don@tla1.com (literary fiction and narrative nonfiction); Fiona Kenshole (children's authors and illustrators).

REPRESENTS Nonfiction books, novels, juvenile. **Considers these nonfiction areas:** autobiography, biography, business, current affairs, economics, environment. **Considers these fiction areas:** juvenile, literary, mainstream, mystery, suspense, young adult.

> ☞ "In both children's and adult literature, we market directly into the United States, the United Kingdom and Canada." Actively seeking literary children's and adult fiction, nonfiction. Does not want to receive picture books, poetry, screenplays or stage plays.

HOW TO CONTACT Submit e-query with synopsis, 2 sample chapters, bio. Always refer to the website, as guidelines will change. Also refer to website for appropriate agent contact info to send e-query. Responds in 2 weeks to queries. Obtains most new clients through recommendations from others.

TERMS Agent receives 15% commission on domestic sales. Agent receives 20% commission on foreign sales. Offers written contract; 45-day notice must be given to terminate contract. This agency charges for photocopying and postage when it exceeds $100.

RECENT SALES Sold 250 titles in the last year.

⬤ SCOTT TREIMEL NY

434 Lafayette St., New York NY 10003. (212)505-8353. **E-mail:** general@scotttreimelny.com. **Website:** ScottTreimelNY.blogspot.com; www.ScottTreimelNY.com. Member of AAR. Other memberships include Authors Guild, SCBWI. 10% of clients are new/unpublished writers. Currently handles: other 100% juvenile/teen books.

> ◐ Prior to becoming an agent, Mr. Treimel was an assistant to Marilyn E. Marlow at Curtis Brown, a rights agent for Scholastic, a book packager and rights agent for United Feature Syndicate, a freelance editor, a rights consultant for HarperCollins Children's Books, and the founding director of Warner Bros. Worldwide Publishing.

REPRESENTS Nonfiction books, novels, juvenile, children's, picture books, young adult.

> ☞ This agency specializes in tightly focused segments of the trade and institutional markets. Seeks career clients.

HOW TO CONTACT Submissions accepted only via website.

TERMS Agent receives 15% commission on domestic sales. Agent receives 20% commission on foreign sales. Offers verbal or written contract. Charges clients for photocopying, express postage, messengers, and books needed to sell foreign, film and other rights.

RECENT SALES *The Hunchback Assignments*, by Arthur Slade (Random House, HarperCollins Canada; HarperCollins Australia); *Shotgun Serenade*, by Gail Giles (Little, Brown); *Laundry Day*, by Maurie Manning (Clarion); *The P.S. Brothers*, by Maribeth Boelts (Harcourt); *The First Five Fourths*, by Pat Hughes (Viking); *Old Robert and the Troubadour Cats*, by Barbara Joosse (Philomel); *Ends*, by David Ward (Abrams); *Dear Canada*, by Barbara Haworth-Attard (Scholastic); *Soccer Dreams*, by Maribeth Boelts (Candlewick); *Lucky Me*, by Richard Scrimger (Tundra); *Play, Louie, Play*, by Muriel Harris Weinstein (Bloomsbury).

TIPS "We look for dedicated authors and illustrators able to sustain longtime careers in our increasingly competitive field. I want fresh, not derivative story concepts with overly familiar characters. We look for gripping stories, characters, pacing, and themes. We remain mindful of an authentic (to the age) point-of-view, and look for original voices. We spend significant time hunting for the best new work, and do launch debut talent each year. It is best *not* to send manuscripts with lengthy submission histories already."

◑ TRIADA U.S. LITERARY AGENCY, INC.

P.O. Box 561, Sewickley PA 15143. (412)401-3376. **E-mail:** uwe@triadaus.com. **Website:** www.triadaus.com. **Contact:** Dr. Uwe Stender. Member of AAR. Represents 65 clients. 20% of clients are new/unpublished writers.

REPRESENTS Fiction, nonfiction. **Considers these nonfiction areas:** biography, business, cooking, diet/nutrition, economics, education, foods, health, how-to, memoirs, popular culture, science, sports, advice, relationships, lifestyle. **Considers these fiction areas:** action, adventure, crime, detective, ethnic, historical, horror, juvenile, literary, mainstream, mystery, occult, police, romance, women's, especially young adult, women's fiction, and mysteries.

> ☞ "We are looking for great writing and story platforms. Our response time is fairly unique. We recognize that neither we nor the authors have time to waste, so we guarantee a 5-day response time. We usually respond within 24 hours." Actively looking for both fiction and nonfiction in all areas.

HOW TO CONTACT E-mail queries preferred; otherwise query with SASE. "We do not respond to postal submission that aren't accompanied by SASE." Accepts simultaneous submissions. Responds in 1-5 weeks to queries. Responds in 2-6 weeks to mss. Obtains most new clients through recommendations from others, conferences.

TERMS Agent receives 15% commission on domestic sales. Agent receives 20% commission on foreign sales. Offers written contract; 30-day notice must be given to terminate contract.

RECENT SALES *The Man Whisperer*, by Samantha Brett and Donna Sozio (Adams Media); *Whatever Happened to Pudding Pops*, by Gael Fashingbauer Cooper and Brian Bellmont (Penguin/Perigee); *86'd*, by Dan Fante (Harper Perennial); *Hating Olivia*, by Mark SaFranko (Harper Perennial); *Everything I'm Not Made Me Everything I Am*, by Jeff Johnson (Smiley Books).

TIPS "I comment on all requested manuscripts that I reject."

TRIDENT MEDIA GROUP

41 Madison Ave., 36th Floor, New York NY 10010. (212)333-1511. **E-mail:** press@tridentmediagroup.com; info@tridentmediagroup.com. **E-mail:** ellen.assistant@tridentmediagroup.com. **Website:** www.tridentmediagroup.com. **Contact:** Ellen Levine. Member of AAR.

MEMBER AGENTS Kimberly Whalen, whalen.assistant@tridentmediagroup (commercial fiction and nonfiction, women's fiction, suspense, paranormal, and pop culture); Scott Miller, smiller@tridentmediagroup.com (thrillers, crime, mystery, young adult, children's, narrative nonfiction, current events, military, memoir, literary fiction, graphic novels, pop culture); Alex Glass aglass@tridentmediagroup (thrillers, literary fiction, crime, middle grade, pop culture, young adult, humor and narrative nonfiction); Melissa Flashman, mflashman@tridentmediagroup.com (narrative nonfiction, serious nonfiction, pop culture, lifstyle); Alyssa Henkin, ahenkin@tridentmediagroup.com (juvenile, children's, young adult); Don Fehr (literary and commercial novelists, narrative nonfiction, memoirs, biography, travel, science/medical/health related titles); John Silbersack (commercial and literary fiction, science fiction and fantasy, narrative nonfiction, young adult, thrillers); Mackenzie Fraser-Bub (women's fiction, romance, upmarket commercial fiction, historical fiction, literary fiction, and YA with cross-over appeal); Erica Spellman-Silverman; Ellen Levine.

REPRESENTS Nonfiction books, novels, short story collections, juvenile. **Considers these nonfiction areas:** autobiography, biography, current affairs, government, humor, law, memoirs, military, multicultural, popular culture, politics, true crime, war, women's issues, women's studies, young adult. **Considers these fiction areas:** crime, detective, humor, juvenile, literary, military, multicultural, mystery, police, short story collections, suspense, thriller, women's, young adult. ➤ Actively seeking new or established authors in a variety of fiction and nonfiction genres.

HOW TO CONTACT Query with SASE or via e-mail. Check website for more details.

TIPS "If you have any questions, please check FAQ page before e-mailing us."

UNION LITERARY

30 Vandam St., Suite 5A, New York NY 10013. (212)255-2112. **E-mail:** info@unionliterary.com. **E-mail:** submissions@unionliterary.com. Member of AAR.

"Prior to becoming an agent, Trena Keating was editor-in-chief of Dutton and associate publisher of Plume, both imprints of Penguin, senior editor at HarperCollins, and humanities assistant at Stanford University Press.

MEMBER AGENTS Trena Keating; Sally Wofford-Girand (history, memoir, women's issues, cultural studies, fiction); Jenni Ferrari-Adler (fiction, cookbook/food, young adult, narrative nonfiction); Kezia Toth (narrative nonfiction, big ideas books, American cultural history, young adult, middle grade). ➤ The agency does not represent romance, poetry, science fiction or illustrated books.

HOW TO CONTACT Nonfiction submissions: include a query letter, a proposal and a sample chapter. Fiction submissions: should include a query letter, synopsis, and either sample pages or full ms. Responds in 1 month.

RECENT SALES *The Language of Flowers*, by Vanessa Diffenbaugh (Ballantine); *The Rebel Wife*, by Taylor M. Polites (Simon & Schuster).

THE UNTER AGENCY

23 W. 73rd St., Suite 100, New York NY 10023. (212)401-4068. **E-mail:** Jennifer@theunteragency.com. **Website:** www.theunteragency.com. **Contact:** Jennifer Unter. Estab. 2008.

Ms. Unter began her book publishing career in the editorial department at Henry Holt & Co. She later worked at the Karpfinger Agency while she attended law school. She then became an associate at the entertainment firm of Cowan, DeBaets, Abrahams & Sheppard LLP where she practiced primarily in the areas of publishing and copyright law.

REPRESENTS Considers these nonfiction areas: biography, environment, foods, health, memoirs, popular culture, politics, travel, true crime, nature subjects. **Considers these fiction areas:** commercial, mainstream, picture books, young adult.

8—⚓ This agency specializes in children's and nonfiction, but does take quality fiction.

HOW TO CONTACT Send an e-query.

ⓘ UPSTART CROW LITERARY

P.O. Box 25404, Brooklyn NY 11202. **E-mail:** info@upstartcrowliterary.com. **E-mail:** danielle.submission@gmail.com; alexandra.submission@gmail.com. **Website:** www.upstartcrowliterary.com. **Contact:** Danielle Chiotti, Alexandra Penfold. Estab. 2009.
MEMBER AGENTS Michael Stearns; Chris Richman (special interest in books for boys, books with unforgettable characters, and fantasy that "doesn't take itself too seriously"); Danielle Chiotti (books ranging from contemporary women's fiction to narrative nonfiction, from romance to relationship stories, humorous tales, and YA fiction); Ted Malawer (accepting queries only through conference submissions and client referrals); Alexandra Penfold (children's—picture books, middle-grade, YA; illustrators and author/illustrators).
REPRESENTS Considers these fiction areas: picture books, women's, young adult, middle-grade.
HOW TO CONTACT Upstart Crow agents that are currently accepting submissions are Danielle Chiotti and Alexandra Penfold. See website for what they are seeking.

VAN DIEST LITERARY AGENCY

P.O. Box 1482, Sisters OR 97759. **Website:** www.christianliteraryagency.com.
MEMBER AGENTS David Van Diest, Sarah Van Diest.
8—⚓ Christian books. "We are actively looking to discover and bring to market a few authors with fresh perspectives on timely subjects."
HOW TO CONTACT "Before submitting a proposal or manuscript, we ask that you submit an online query found on the 'Contact Us' page. We will contact you if we would like to receive a full proposal."

ⓘ VENTURE LITERARY

2683 Via de la Valle, G-714, Del Mar CA 92014. (619)807-1887. **Fax:** (772)365-8321. **E-mail:** submissions@ventureliterary.com. **Website:** www.ventureliterary.com. **Contact:** Frank R. Scatoni. Represents 50 clients. 40% of clients are new/unpublished writers. Currently handles: nonfiction books 80%, novels 20%.
◯ Prior to becoming an agent, Mr. Scatoni worked as an editor at Simon & Schuster.
MEMBER AGENTS Frank R. Scatoni (general nonfiction, biography, memoir, narrative nonfiction, sports, serious nonfiction, graphic novels, narratives).
REPRESENTS Nonfiction books, novels, graphic novels, narratives. **Considers these nonfiction areas:** anthropology, biography, business, cultural interests, current affairs, dance, economics, environment, ethnic, government, history, investigative, law, memoirs, military, money, multicultural, music, popular culture, politics, psychology, science, sports, technology, true crime, women's issues, women's studies. **Considers these fiction areas:** action, adventure, crime, detective, literary, mainstream, mystery, police, sports, suspense, thriller, women's.
8—⚓ Specializes in nonfiction, sports, biography, gambling, and nonfiction narratives. Actively seeking nonfiction, graphic novels and narratives. Does not want fantasy, sci-fi, romance, children's picture books, or Westerns.
HOW TO CONTACT Considers e-mail queries only. *No unsolicited mss* and no snail mail whatsoever. See website for complete submission guidelines. Obtains most new clients through recommendations from others.
TERMS Agent receives 15% commission on domestic sales. Agent receives 20% commission on foreign sales. Offers written contract.
RECENT SALES *The 9/11 Report: A Graphic Adaptation*, by Sid Jacobson and Ernie Colon (FSG); *Having a Baby* by Cindy Margolis (Perigee/Penguin); *Phil Gordon's Little Blue Book*, by Phil Gordon (Simon & Schuster); *Atomic America*, by Todd Tucker (Free Press); *War as They Knew It*, by Michael Rosenberg (Grand Central); *Game Day*, by Craig James (Wiley); *The Blueprint* by Christopher Price (Thomas Dunne Books).

ⓘ VERITAS LITERARY AGENCY

601 Van Ness Ave., Opera Plaza, Suite E, San Francisco CA 94102. (415)647-6964. **Fax:** (415)647-6965. **E-mail:** submissions@veritasliterary.com. **Website:** www.ver-

itasliterary.com. **Contact:** Katherine Boyle. Member of AAR. Other memberships include Author's Guild.
REPRESENTS Nonfiction books, novels. **Considers these nonfiction areas:** current affairs, memoirs, popular culture, politics, true crime, women's issues, young adult, narrative nonfiction, art and music biography, natural history, health and wellness, psychology, serious religion (no New Age) and popular science. **Considers these fiction areas:** commercial, fantasy, literary, mystery, science fiction, young adult.

8—✶ Does not want to receive romance, poetry or children's books.

HOW TO CONTACT This agency accepts short queries or proposals via e-mail only. "If you are sending a proposal or a manuscript after a positive response to a query, please write 'requested material' on the subject line and include the initial query letter."

⊘ BETH VESEL LITERARY AGENCY

80 Fifth Ave., Suite 1101, New York NY 10011. (212)924-4252. **E-mail:** kezia@bvlit.com. **Contact:** Kezia Toth, assistant. Represents 65 clients. 10% of clients are new/unpublished writers. Currently handles: nonfiction books 75%, novels 10%, story collections 5%, scholarly books 10%.

💭 *Do not contact this agency. It was closing as this edition of GLA went to print.*

REPRESENTS Nonfiction books, novels. **Considers these nonfiction areas:** autobiography, biography, business, cultural interests, economics, ethnic, health, how-to, investigative, medicine, memoirs, psychology, true crime, women's issues, women's studies, cultural criticism. **Considers these fiction areas:** crime, detective, literary, police, Francophone novels.

8—✶ "My specialties include serious nonfiction, psychology, cultural criticism, memoir, and women's issues." Actively seeking cultural criticism, literary psychological thrillers, and sophisticated memoirs. No uninspired psychology or run-of-the-mill first novels.

HOW TO CONTACT Do not contact. Query with SASE. Accepts simultaneous submissions. Responds in 2 weeks to queries. Responds in 1 month to mss. Obtains most new clients through referrals, reading good magazines, contacting professionals with ideas.
TERMS Agent receives 15% commission on domestic sales. Agent receives 20% commission on foreign sales. Offers written contract.

RECENT SALES Steve Silberman, *Neurotribes* (Penguin); Vicki Robin, *Blessing the Hands That Feed Us*, (Viking); Christina Baker Kline, *Phantom Street* (William Morrow); Greg Tate, *James Browns' Body* (FSG); Lawrence Diller, *Remembering Ritalin* (Perigee Publishers); Marjorie Garber, *The Use and Abuse of Literature* (Pantheon).
WRITERS CONFERENCES Squaw Valley Writers Workshop, Iowa Summer Writing Festival.
TIPS "Try to find out if you fit on a particular agent's list by looking at his/her books and comparing yours. You can almost always find who represents a book by looking at the acknowledgements."

⊘ RALPH M. VICINANZA LTD.

303 W. 18th St., New York NY 10011. (212)924-7090. **Fax:** (212)691-9644. Member of AAR.
MEMBER AGENTS Ralph M. Vicinanza; Chris Lotts; Christopher Schelling.
HOW TO CONTACT This agency takes on new clients by professional recommendation only.
TERMS Agent receives 15% commission on domestic sales. Agent receives 20% commission on foreign sales.

● VICKY BIJUR LITERARY AGENCY

333 West End Ave., Apt. 5B, New York NY 10023. **E-mail:** queries@vickybijuragency.com. **Website:** www.vickybijuragency.com. Estab. 1988. Member of AAR.

💭 Vicky Bijur worked at Oxford University Press and with the Charlotte Sheedy Literary Agency. Books she represents have appeared on *the New York Times Bestseller List, in the New York Times Notable Books of the Year, Los Angeles Times Best Fiction of the Year, Washington Post Book World Rave Reviews of the Year.*

REPRESENTS Nonfiction books, novels. **Considers these nonfiction areas:** cooking, government, health, history, psychology, psychiatry, science, self help, sociology, biography; child care/development; environmental studies; journalism; social sciences.

8—✶ Does not want science fiction, fantasy, horror, romance, poetry, children's.

HOW TO CONTACT Accepts e-mail queries. "Fiction: query and first chapter (if e-mailed, please paste chapter into body of e-mail as I don't open attachments from unfamiliar senders). Nonfiction: query and proposal. No phone or fax queries."
RECENT SALES *Left Neglected* and *Love, Anthony*, by Lisa Genova (Pocket Books, 2011 and 2012); *I'd Know You Anywhere* and two untitled books, by Laura

Lippman (William Morrow, 2010, 2011, 2012); *The Serious Eats Guide*, by Ed Levine (Clarkson Potter, 2012); *The Cartoon Guide to Calculus*, by Larry Gonick (HarperCollins, 2012); *Relaxation Revolution*, by Herbert Benson, M.D., and William Proctor (Scribner, 2010).

WALES LITERARY AGENCY, INC.

P.O. Box 9426, Seattle WA 98109. (206)284-7114. E-mail: waleslit@waleslit.com. **Website:** www.waleslit.com. **Contact:** Elizabeth Wales; Neal Swain. Member of AAR. Other memberships include Book Publishers' Northwest, Pacific Northwest Booksellers Association, PEN. Represents 60 clients. 10% of clients are new/unpublished writers. Currently handles: nonfiction books 60%, novels 40%.

○ Prior to becoming an agent, Ms. Wales worked at Oxford University Press and Viking Penguin.

MEMBER AGENTS Elizabeth Wales; Neal Swain.

⌐ This agency specializes in quality fiction and nonfiction. Does not handle screenplays, children's picture books, genre fiction, or most category nonfiction.

HOW TO CONTACT Accepts queries sent with cover letter and SASE, and e-mail queries with no attachments. No phone or fax queries. Guidelines and client list available on website. Accepts simultaneous submissions. Responds in 2 weeks to queries, 2 months to mss.

TERMS Agent receives 15% commission on domestic sales. Agent receives 20% commission on foreign sales.

RECENT SALES *American Savage: Insights, Slights, and Fights on Faith, Sex, Love, and Politics*, by Dan Savage (Penguin, May 2013); *The Urban Bestiary*, by Lyanda Lynn Haupt; *Bad Luck Way and the Wolves of Montana*, by Bryce Andrews (Atria/Simon & Schuster, 2014); *Heat: A Natural and Unnatural History*, by Bill Streever (Little, Brown, 2012).

WRITERS CONFERENCES Pacific Northwest Writers Conference, annually; and others.

TIPS "We are especially interested in work that espouses a progressive cultural or political view, projects a new voice, or simply shares an important, compelling story. We also encourage writers living in the Pacific Northwest, West Coast, Alaska, and Pacific Rim countries, and writers from historically underrepresented groups, such as gay and lesbian writers and writers of color, to submit work (but does not discourage writers outside these areas). Most importantly, whether in fiction or nonfiction, the agency is looking for talented storytellers."

WATERSIDE PRODUCTIONS, INC.

2055 Oxford Ave., Cardiff CA 92007. (760)632-9190. **Fax:** (760)632-9295. **E-mail:** admin@waterside.com. **Website:** www.waterside.com. Estab. 1982.

MEMBER AGENTS Bill Gladstone; Margot Maley Hutchison; Carole Jelen McClendon; Lawrence Jackel; Neil Gudovitz; David Nelson; Brad Schepp; Kimberly Brabec; Zach Romano.

REPRESENTS Nonfiction books. **Considers these nonfiction areas:** architecture, art, autobiography, biography, business, child guidance, computers, cultural interests, design, economics, environment, ethnic, health, how-to, humor, medicine, money, parenting, popular culture, psychology, sociology, sports, technology, travel, cookbooks, natural health, real estate, lifestyles and more.

⌐ Specializes in computer books, how-to, business, and health titles.

HOW TO CONTACT "Please read each agent bio [on the website] to determine who you think would best represent your genre of work. When you have chosen your agent, please write his or her name in the subject line of your e-mail and send it to admin@waterside.com with your query letter in the body of the e-mail, and your proposal or sample material as an attached word document." Obtains most new clients through referrals from established client and publisher list.

TIPS "For new writers, a quality proposal and a strong knowledge of the market you're writing for goes a long way toward helping us turn you into a published author. We like to see a strong author platform. Two foreign rights agents on staff - Neil Gudovitz and Kimberly Brabec - help us with overseas sales."

WATKINS LOOMIS AGENCY, INC.

P.O. Box 20925, New York NY 10025. (212)532-0080. **Fax:** (646)383-2449. **E-mail:** assistant@watkinsloomis.com. **Website:** www.watkinsloomis.com. Estab. 1980. Represents 50+ clients.

MEMBER AGENTS Gloria Loomis, president, Julia Masnik, junior agent.

REPRESENTS Nonfiction, novels, short story collections. **Considers these nonfiction areas:** autobiography, biography, cultural interests, current affairs, environment, ethnic, history, popular culture, technology, investigative journalism. **Considers these fiction areas:** literary, short story collections.

⌐ This agency specializes in literary fiction and nonfiction.

HOW TO CONTACT *No unsolicited mss.* This agency does not guarantee a response to queries.

TERMS Agent receives 15% commission on domestic sales. Agent receives 20% commission on foreign sales.

◐ WAXMAN LEAVELL LITERARY AGENCY, INC.

443 Park Ave. S, Suite 1004, New York NY 10016. (212)675-5556. **Fax:** (212)675-1381. **E-mail:** scott submit@waxmanleavell.com; byrdsubmit@waxman leavell.com; hollysubmit@waxmanleavell.com; williamsubmit@waxmanleavell.com. **Website:** www. waxmanleavell.com. **Contact:** Scott Waxman; Byrd Leavell; Holly Root; William Callahan. Represents 60 clients. 50% of clients are new/unpublished writers. Currently handles: nonfiction books 50%, novels 50%.

○ Prior to founding the Scott Waxman Agency in 1997, Mr. Waxman was an editor at HarperCollins.

MEMBER AGENTS Scott Waxman (all categories of nonfiction, commercial fiction—specifically thriller, science fiction, and young adult), Byrd Leavell, Holly Root, William Callahan (narrative nonfiction and memoir, comedy and pop culture, American history, crime and commercial thrillers, and literary fiction).

REPRESENTS Considers these nonfiction areas: prescriptive, historical, sports, narrative, pop culture, humor, memoir, biography, celebrity. **Considers these fiction areas:** literary, contemporary, commercial, young adult.

⚮ "We're looking for new novelists with non-published works."

HOW TO CONTACT Please visit our website. Accepts simultaneous submissions.

TERMS Agent receives 15% commission on domestic sales. Agent receives 10% commission on foreign sales. Offers written contract; 2-month notice must be given to terminate contract.

➕ CK WEBBER ASSOCIATES LITERARY MANAGEMENT

Website: www.ckwebber.com. **Contact:** Carlie Webber. Estab. 2012.

○ Prior to forming her own agency, Ms. Webber was an agent with the Jane Rotrosen Agency.

REPRESENTS Fiction, novels, memoir. **Considers these fiction areas:** young adult, middle grade, women's fiction, literary and general fiction, mystery, thriller, suspense, romance, science fiction, fantasy, memoir.

HOW TO CONTACT Send a query letter, synopsis, and the first 30 pages or three chapters of your work, whichever is more, to carlie@ckwebber.com and put the word "query" in the subject line of your email. You may include your materials either in the body of your email or as a Word or PDF attachment. Blank emails that include an attachment will be deleted unread.

◐ WEED LITERARY

55 E. 65th St., Suite 4E, New York NY 10065. **E-mail:** info@weedliterary.com. **Website:** www.weedliterary. com. **Contact:** Elisabeth Weed. Estab. 2007.

○ Prior to forming her own agency, Ms. Weed was an agent at Curtis Brown and Trident Media Group.

REPRESENTS Fiction, novels. **Considers these fiction areas:** literary, women's.

⚮ This agency specializes in upmarket women's fiction. Does not want to receive picture books, YA, middle-grade, or romance.

HOW TO CONTACT Send a query letter. "Please do not send queries or submissions via snail, registered, certified mail, or by FedEx or UPS requiring signature."

RECENT SALES *Life Without Summer*, by Lynne Griffin (St. Martin's Press); *Time of My Life*, by Allison Winn Scotch (Shaye Areheart Books); and *The Last Will of Moira Leahy*, by Therese Walsh (Shaye Areheart Books).

WRITERS CONFERENCES Muse and the Marketplace (Boston, annual).

● CHERRY WEINER LITERARY AGENCY

28 Kipling Way, Manalapan NJ 07726. (732)446-2096. **Fax:** (732)792-0506. **E-mail:** cherry8486@aol.com. **Contact:** Cherry Weiner. Represents 40 clients. 10% of clients are new/unpublished writers. Currently handles: nonfiction books 10-20%, novels 80-90%.

REPRESENTS Nonfiction books, novels. **Considers these nonfiction areas:** self-help. **Considers these fiction areas:** action, adventure, contemporary issues, crime, detective, family saga, fantasy, frontier, historical, mainstream, mystery, police, psychic, romance, science fiction, supernatural, thriller, westerns.

⚮ This agency is currently not accepting new clients except by referral or by personal contact at writers' conferences. Specializes in fantasy, science fiction, westerns, mysteries (both contemporary and historical), historical novels, Native-American works, mainstream, and all genre romances.

HOW TO CONTACT Query with SASE. Prefers to read materials exclusively. Does not accept e-mail queries. Responds in 1 week to queries. Responds in 2 months to mss that I have asked for.

TERMS Agent receives 15% commission on domestic sales. Agent receives 15% commission on foreign sales. Offers written contract. Charges clients for extra copies of mss, first-class postage for author's copies of books, express mail for important documents/mss.

RECENT SALES Sold 70 titles in the last year. This agency prefers not to share information on specific sales.

TIPS "Meet agents and publishers at conferences. Establish a relationship, then get in touch with them and remind them of the meeting and conference."

● THE WEINGEL-FIDEL AGENCY

310 E. 46th St., 21E, New York NY 10017. (212)599-2959. **Contact:** Loretta Weingel-Fidel. Currently handles: nonfiction books 75%, novels 25%.

Prior to opening her agency, Ms. Weingel-Fidel was a psychoeducational diagnostician.

REPRESENTS Nonfiction books, novels. **Considers these nonfiction areas:** art, autobiography, biography, dance, memoirs, music, psychology, science, sociology, technology, women's issues, women's studies, investigative journalism. **Considers these fiction areas:** literary, mainstream.

This agency specializes in commercial and literary fiction and nonfiction. Actively seeking investigative journalism. Does not want to receive genre fiction, self-help, science fiction, or fantasy.

HOW TO CONTACT Accepts writers by referral only. *No unsolicited mss.*

TERMS Agent receives 15% commission on domestic sales. Agent receives 20% commission on foreign sales. Offers written contract, binding for 1 year with automatic renewal. Bills sent back to clients are all reasonable expenses, such as UPS, express mail, photocopying, etc.

TIPS "A very small, selective list enables me to work very closely with my clients to develop and nurture talent. I only take on projects and writers about which I am extremely enthusiastic."

● WERNICK & PRATT AGENCY

E-mail: info@wernickpratt.com. **Website:** www.wernickpratt.com. **Contact:** Marcia Wernick; Linda Pratt. Member of AAR. SCBWI.

Prior to cofounding Wernick & Pratt Agency, Ms. Wernick worked at the Sheldon Fogelman Agency, in subsidiary rights, advancing to director of subsidiary rights; Ms. Pratt also worked at the Sheldon Fogelman Agency.

MEMBER AGENTS Marcia Wernick, Linda Pratt.

"Wernick & Pratt Agency specializes in children's books of all genres, from picture books through young adult literature and everything in between. We represent both authors and illustrators. We do not represent authors of adult books." Wants people who both write and illustrate in the picture book genre; humorous young chapter books with strong voice, and which are unique and compelling; middle grade/YA novels, both literary and commercial. No picture book mss of more than 750 words, or mood pieces; work specifically targeted to the educational market; fiction about the American Revolution, Civil War, or World War II unless it is told from a very unique perspective.

HOW TO CONTACT Submit via e-mail only. "Please indicate to which agent you are submitting." Detailed submission guidelines available on website. Responds in 6 weeks.

◐● WESTWOOD CREATIVE ARTISTS, LTD.

94 Harbord St., Toronto ON M5S 1G6 Canada. (416)964-3302. **Fax:** (416)975-9209. **E-mail:** wca_office@wcaltd.com. **Website:** www.wcaltd.com. Represents 350+ clients.

MEMBER AGENTS Deborah Wood, book-to-film agent; Ahston Westwood, book-to-film agent; Linda McKnight, literary agent; Jackie Kaiser, literary agent; Hilary McMahon, literary agent; Bruce Westwood, literary agent; John Pearce, literary agent; Natasha Daneman, subsidiary rights director; Michael Levine, film and TV agent; Chris Casuccio, administrative assistant.

HOW TO CONTACT Query with SASE. Use a referral to break into this agency. Accepts electronic query letters. Accepts simultaneous submissions.

RECENT SALES *A Biography of Richard Nixon*, by Conrad Black (Public Affairs); *The New Cold War: Revolutions; Rigged Elections and Pipeline Politics in the Former Soviet Union*, by Mark MacKinnon (Carroll & Graf).

○ WHIMSY LITERARY AGENCY, LLC

310 E. 12th St., Suite 2C, New York NY 10003. (212)674-7161. **E-mail:** whimsynyc@aol.com. **Website:** http://whimsyliteraryagency.com/. **Contact:** Jackie Meyer. Other memberships include Center for Independent Publishing Advisory Board. Represents 30 clients. 20% of clients are new/unpublished writers. Currently handles: nonfiction books 100%.

> Prior to becoming an agent, Ms. Meyer was with Warner Books for 19 years; Ms. Vezeris and Ms. Legette have 30 years' experience at various book publishers.

MEMBER AGENTS Jackie Meyer; Olga Vezeris (fiction and nonfiction); Nansci LeGette, senior associate in LA.

REPRESENTS Nonfiction books. **Considers these nonfiction areas:** agriculture, art, biography, business, child guidance, cooking, education, health, history, horticulture, how-to, humor, interior design, memoirs, money, New Age, popular culture, psychology, religious, self-help, true crime, women's issues, women's studies. **Considers these fiction areas:** mainstream, religious, thriller, women's.

> "Whimsy looks for projects that are concept- and platform-driven. We seek books that educate, inspire and entertain." Actively seeking experts in their field with good platforms.

HOW TO CONTACT Send a query letter via e-mail. Send a synopsis, bio, platform, and proposal. No snail mail submissions. Responds "quickly, but only if interested" to queries. *Does not accept unsolicited mss.* Obtains most new clients through recommendations from others, solicitations.

TERMS Agent receives 15% commission on domestic sales. Agent receives 20% commission on foreign sales. Offers written contract. Charges for posting and photocopying.

● WM CLARK ASSOCIATES

186 Fifth Ave., Second Floor, New York NY 10010. (212)675-2784. **Fax:** (347)-649-9262. **E-mail:** general@wmclark.com. **Website:** www.wmclark.com. Estab. 1997. Member of AAR. 50% of clients are new/unpublished writers. Currently handles: nonfiction books 50%, novels 50%.

> Prior to opening WCA, Mr. Clark was an agent at the William Morris Agency.

REPRESENTS Nonfiction books, novels. **Considers these nonfiction areas:** architecture, art, autobiography, biography, cultural interests, current affairs, design, ethnic, film, history, inspirational, memoir, music, politics, popular culture, religious, science, sociology, technology, theater, translation, travel memoir, Eastern philosophy. **Considers these fiction areas:** contemporary issues, ethnic, historical, literary, mainstream, Southern fiction.

> William Clark represents a wide range of titles across all formats to the publishing, motion picture, television, and new media fields on behalf of authors of first fiction and award-winning, best-selling narrative nonfiction, international authors in translation, chefs, musicians, and artists. Offering individual focus and a global presence, the agency undertakes to discover, develop, and market today's most interesting content and the talent that create it, and forge sophisticated and innovative plans for self-promotion, reliable revenue streams, and an enduring creative career. Referral partners are available to provide services including editorial consultation, media training, lecture booking, marketing support, and public relations. Agency does not respond to screenplays or screenplay pitches. It is advised that before querying you become familiar with the kinds of books we handle by browsing our Book List, which is available on our website.

HOW TO CONTACT Accepts queries via online form only at www.wmclark.com/queryguidelines.html. We respond to all queries submitted via this form. Responds in 1-2 months to queries.

TERMS Agent receives 15% commission on domestic sales. Agent receives 20% commission on foreign sales. Offers written contract.

TIPS "WCA works on a reciprocal basis with Ed Victor Ltd. (UK) in representing select properties to the US market and vice versa. Translation rights are sold directly in the German, Italian, Spanish, Portuguese, Latin American, French, Dutch, and Scandinavian territories in association with Andrew Nurnberg Associates Ltd. (UK); through offices in China, Bulgaria, Czech Republic, Latvia, Poland, Hungary, and Russia; and through corresponding agents in Japan, Greece, Israel, Turkey, Korea, Taiwan, and Thailand."

○ WOLFSON LITERARY AGENCY

P.O. Box 266, New York NY 10276. **E-mail:** query@wolfsonliterary.com. **Website:** www.wolfsonliterary.com/. **Contact:** Michelle Wolfson. Estab. 2007. Adheres

...ly handles: nonfiction

...gency in December
...years with Artists
...with Ralph Vici-

...: young adult,
..., thrillers, suspense,
..., romance, practical or narrative
...ion (particularly of interest to women).

...**TO CONTACT** E-queries only! Accepts simultaneous submissions. Responds only if interested. Positive response is generally given within 2-4 weeks. Responds in 3 months to mss. Obtains most new clients through queries or recommendations from others.

TERMS Agent receives 15% commission on domestic sales. Agent receives 25% commission on foreign sales. Offers written contract; 30-day notice must be given to terminate contract.

WRITERS CONFERENCES SDSU Writers' Conference; New Jersey Romance Writers of America Writers' Conference; American Independent Writers Conference in Washington DC.

TIPS "Be persistent."

◑◉ WORDSERVE LITERARY GROUP

10152 S. Knoll Circle, Highlands Ranch CO 80130. **Website:** www.wordserveliterary.com. **Contact:** Greg Johnson. Represents 100 clients. 20% of clients are new/unpublished writers. Currently handles: nonfiction books 50%, novels 35%, juvenile books 10%, multimedia 5%.

○   Prior to becoming an agent in 1994, Mr. Johnson was a magazine editor and freelance writer of more than 20 books and 200 articles.

MEMBER AGENTS Greg Johnson, Alice Crider, Sarah Freese (contemporary romance, historical romance, historical, contemporary women's fiction, suspense, memoir, narrative nonfiction, marriage/family/parenting from bloggers with a large platform).

REPRESENTS Considers these nonfiction areas: biography, child guidance, inspirational, memoirs, parenting, self-help. **Considers these fiction areas:** historical, inspirational, mainstream, spiritual, suspense, thriller, women's.

☙➤ Materials with a faith-based angle.

HOW TO CONTACT Please address queries to: admin@wordserveliterary.com. In the subject line, include the word "query." All queries should include the following three elements: a pitch for the book, information about you and your platform (for nonfiction) or writing background (for fiction), and the first 5 (or so) pages of the manuscript pasted into the e-mail. Accepts simultaneous submissions. Responds in 4 weeks to queries. Responds in 2 months to mss. Obtains most new clients through recommendations from others.

TERMS Agent receives 15% commission on domestic sales. Agent receives 10-15% commission on foreign sales. Offers written contract; up to 60-day notice must be given to terminate contract.

RECENT SALES Sold 1,500 titles in the last 15 years. *Redemption* series, by Karen Kingsbury (Tyndale); *Loving God Up Close*, by Calvin Miller (Warner Faith); *Christmas in My Heart*, by Joe Wheeler (Tyndale). Other clients include Doug Fields, Wanda Dyson, Catherine Martin, David Murrow, Leslie Haskin, Gilbert Morris, Robert Wise, Jim Burns, Wayne Cordeiro, Denise George, Susie Shellenberger, Tim Smith, Athol Dickson, Patty Kirk, John Shore, Marcus Bretherton, Rick Johnson.

TIPS "We are looking for good proposals, great writing and authors willing to market their books, as appropriate. Also, we're only looking for projects with a faith element bent. See the website before submitting."

◑ WRITERS HOUSE

21 W. 26th St., New York NY 10010. (212)685-2400. **Fax:** (212)685-1781. **Website:** www.writershouse.com. **Contact:** Michael Mejias. Estab. 1973. Member of AAR. Represents 440 clients. 50% of clients are new/unpublished writers. Currently handles: nonfiction books 25%, novels 40%, juvenile books 35%.

MEMBER AGENTS Albert Zuckerman, Amy Berkower, Albert Zuckerman, Stephen Barr, Susan Cohen, Dan Conaway, Susan Ginsburg, Leigh Feldman, Merrilee Heifetz, Daniel Lazar, Simon Lipskar, Steven Malk, Jodi Reamer, Esq., Michele Rubin, Robin Rue, Rebecca Sherman, Geri Thoma, Lisa DiMona, Brianne Johnson, Beth Miller (junior agent).

REPRESENTS Nonfiction books, novels, juvenile. **Considers these nonfiction areas:** animals, art, autobiography, biography, business, child guidance, cooking, decorating, diet/nutrition, economics, film, foods, health, history, humor, interior design, juvenile nonfiction, medicine, military, money, music, parenting, psychology, satire, science, self-help, technology, theater, true crime, women's issues, women's studies. **Considers these fiction areas:** adventure, cartoon, contemporary issues, crime, detective, erotica, ethnic, family saga, fantasy, feminist, frontier, gay, hi-lo, historical, horror, humor, juvenile, literary, mainstream, military, multicultural, mystery, New Age, occult, picture books, police, psychic, regional, romance, spiritual, sports, thriller, translation, war, Westerns, women's, young adult, cartoon.

⚷— This agency specializes in all types of popular fiction and nonfiction. Does not want to receive scholarly, professional, poetry, plays, or screenplays.

HOW TO CONTACT Query with SASE. "Please send us a query letter of no more than 2 pages, which includes your credentials, an explanation of what makes your book unique and special, and a synopsis. (If submitting to Steven Malk: Writers House, 7660 Fay Ave., #338H, La Jolla, CA 92037). Please do not query 2 agents within our agency simultaneously." Responds in 6-8 weeks to queries. Obtains most new clients through recommendations from authors and editors.

TERMS Agent receives 15% commission on domestic sales. Agent receives 20% commission on foreign sales. Offers written contract, binding for 1 year. Agency charges fees for copying mss/proposals and overseas airmail of books.

TIPS "Do not send mss. Write a compelling letter. If you do, we'll ask to see your work. Follow submission guidelines and please do not simultaneously submit your work to more than 1 Writers House agent."

● WRITERS' REPRESENTATIVES, LLC

116 W. 14th St., 11th Floor, New York NY 10011-7305. **Fax:** (212)620-0023. **E-mail:** transom@writersreps. com. **Website:** www.writersreps.com. Represents 130 clients. 10% of clients are new/unpublished writers. Currently handles: nonfiction books 90%, novels 10%.

◯ Prior to becoming an agent, Ms. Chu was a lawyer; Mr. Hartley worked at Simon & Schuster, Harper & Row and Cornell University Press.

MEMBER AGENTS Lynn Chu, Glen Hartley, Christine Hsu.

REPRESENTS Nonfiction books, novels. **Considers these fiction areas:** literary.

⚷— Serious nonfiction and quality fiction. No motion picture or television screenplays.

HOW TO CONTACT Query with SASE. Prefers to read materials exclusively. Considers simultaneous queries, but must be informed at time of submission.

Consult website section "FAQ" for detailed submission guidelines.

TERMS Agent receives 15% commission on domestic sales. Agent receives 20% commission on foreign sales.

TIPS "Always include a SASE; it will ensure a response from the agent and the return of your submitted material."

● ZACHARY SHUSTER HARMSWORTH

1776 Broadway, Suite 1405, New York NY 10019. (212)765-6900. **Fax:** (212)765-6490. **E-mail:** kfleury@ zshliterary.com. **Website:** www.zshliterary.com. **Contact:** Kathleen Fleury. Alternate address: 535 Boylston St., 11th Floor, Boston MA 02116. (617)262-2400. **Fax:** (617)262-2468. Represents 125 clients. 20% of clients are new/unpublished writers. Currently handles: nonfiction books 45%, novels 45%, story collections 5%, scholarly books 5%.

◯ "Our principals include two former publishing and entertainment lawyers, a journalist and an editor/agent. Lane Zachary was an editor at Random House before becoming an agent."

MEMBER AGENTS Esmond Harmsworth (commercial mysteries, literary fiction, history, science, adventure, business); Todd Shuster (narrative and prescriptive nonfiction, biography, memoirs); Lane Zachary (biography, memoirs, literary fiction); Jennifer Gates (literary fiction, nonfiction), Colleen Rafferty, Mary Beth Chappell, Bridget Wagner Matzie, Andrew Paulson, Natasha Alexis, Jacob Moore, Lana Popovic. "You can e-mail any agent on the website online form."

REPRESENTS Nonfiction books, novels. **Considers these nonfiction areas:** animals, autobiography, biography, business, current affairs, economics, gay/lesbian, government, health, history, how-to, investigative, language, law, literature, memoirs, money, music, politics, psychology, science, self-help, sports, technology, true crime, women's issues, women's studies. **Considers these fiction areas:** detective, ethnic, feminist, gay, historical, lesbian, literary, mainstream, mystery, suspense, thriller.

⚷— Check the website for updated info.

HOW TO CONTACT *Cannot accept unsolicited submissions.* Query with SASE. Obtains most new clients through recommendations from others.

TERMS Agent receives 15% commission on domestic sales. Agent receives 20% commission on foreign sales. Offers written contract, binding for 1 work only; 30-day notice must be given to terminate contract.

KAREN GANTZ ZAHLER LITERARY MANAGEMENT AND ATTORNEY AT LAW

860 Fifth Ave., Suite 7J, New York NY 10065. (212)734-3619. **E-mail:** karen@karengantzlit.com. **Website:** www.karengantzlit.com. **Contact:** Karen Gantz Zahler. Currently handles: nonfiction books 95%, novels 5%, film, TV scripts.

Prior to her current position, Ms. Gantz Zahler practiced law at two law firms, wrote two cookbooks, *Taste of New York* (Addison-Wesley) and *Superchefs* (John Wiley & Sons). She also participated in a Presidential Advisory Committee on Intellectual Property, U.S. Department of Commerce. She currently chairs Literary and Media Committee at Harmone Club NYC.

REPRESENTS Nonfiction books, novels, very selective.

"We are hired for two purposes, one as lawyers to negotiate publishing agreements, option agreements and other entertainment deals, and two as literary agents to help in all aspects of the publishing field. Ms. Gantz is both a literary agent and a literary property lawyer. Thus, her firm involves themselves in all stages of a book's development, including the collaboration agreement with the writer, advice regarding the book proposal, presentations to the publisher, negotiations including the legal work for the publishing agreement and other rights to be negotiated, and work with the publisher and public relations firm so that the book gets the best possible media coverage. We do extensive manuscript reviews for a few." Actively seeking nonfiction. "We assist with speaking engagements and publicity."

HOW TO CONTACT Accepting queries and summaries by e-mail only. Check the website for complete submission information. Responds in 4 weeks to queries. Obtains most new clients through recommendations from others, solicitations.

RECENT SALES *A Promise to Ourselves* by Alec Baldwin (St. Martin's Press, 2008); *Take the Lead, Lady! Kathleen Turner's Life Lessons*, by Kathleen Turner in collaboration with Gloria Feldt (Springboard Press, 2007); *Tales of a Neo-Con*, by Benjamin Wattenberg (Tom Dunne, 2008); *Beyond Control*, by Nancy Friday (Sourcebooks, 2009); more sales can be found online.

TIPS "Our dream client is someone who is a professional writer and a great listener. What writers can do to increase the likelihood of our retainer is to write an excellent summary and provide a great marketing plan for their proposal in an excellent presentation. Any typos or grammatical mistakes do not resonate well. If we want to review your project, we will ask you to send a copy by snail mail with an envelope and return postage enclosed. We don't call people unless we have something to report."

HELEN ZIMMERMANN LITERARY AGENCY

3 Emmy Lane, New Paltz NY 12561. **E-mail:** Helen@ZimmAgency.com. **Website:** www.zimmermannliterary.com. **Contact:** Helen Zimmermann. Estab. 2003. Currently handles: nonfiction books 80%, other 20% fiction.

Prior to opening her agency, Ms. Zimmermann was the director of advertising and promotion at Random House and the events coordinator at an independent bookstore.

REPRESENTS Nonfiction books, novels. **Considers these nonfiction areas:** diet/nutrition, how-to, humor, memoirs, parenting, popular culture, sports. **Considers these fiction areas:** family saga, historical, literary, mystery, suspense.

"As an agent who has experience at both a publishing house and a bookstore, I have a keen insight for viable projects. This experience also helps me ensure every client gets published well, through the whole process." Actively seeking memoirs, pop culture, women's issues, and accessible literary fiction. Does not want to receive horror, science fiction, poetry or romance.

HOW TO CONTACT Accepts e-mail queries only. E-mail should include a short description of project and bio, whether it be fiction or nonfiction. Accepts simultaneous submissions. Responds in 2 weeks to queries. Responds in 1 month to mss. Obtains most new clients through recommendations from others, solicitations.

TERMS Agent receives 15% commission on domestic sales. Offers written contract; 30-day notice must be given to terminate contract. Charges for photocopying and postage (reimbursed if project is sold).

WRITERS CONFERENCES BEA/Writer's Digest Books Writers' Conference; Portland, ME Writers

Conference; Berkshire Writers and Readers Conference; La Jolla Writers Conference; The New School Writers Conference; Vermont Writers Conference.

RENÈE ZUCKERBROT LITERARY AGENCY

115 West 29th St., 3rd Floor, New York NY 10001. (212)967-0072. **Fax:** (212)967-0073. **E-mail:** renee@rzagency.com. **E-mail:** submissions@rzagency.com. **Website:** rzagency.com. **Contact:** Renèe Zuckerbrot. Represents 30 clients. Currently handles: 30% nonfiction and 70% fiction.

- Prior to becoming an agent, Ms. Zuckerbrot worked as an editor at Doubleday as well as in the editorial department at Putnam.

REPRESENTS Nonfiction books, novels, short-story collections.

- Literary and commercial adult and young adult fiction, short-story collections, mysteries, thrillers, women's fiction, slipstream/speculative, narrative nonfiction (focusing on science, history and pop culture). "Looking for writers with a unique voice." No business books, self-help, spirituality or romance. No screenplays.

HOW TO CONTACT Query by e-mail: submissions@rzagency.com. Include a synopsis, publication history and a brief personal bio. Include a brief personal bio. You may include a sample chapter. Query by snail mail: Please include an SASE or an email address. Responds in approximately 4 weeks.

TERMS Agent receives 15% commission on domestic sales. Agent receives 25% commission on foreign sales (10% to RZA; 15% to foreign rights co-agent).

CONFERENCES

Attending a writers' conference that includes agents gives you the opportunity to learn more about what agents do and to show an agent your work. Ideally, a conference should include a panel or two with a number of agents to give writers a sense of the variety of personalities and tastes of different agents.

Not all agents are alike: Some are more personable, and sometimes you simply click better with one agent versus another. When only one agent attends a conference, there is a tendency for every writer at that conference to think, "Ah, this is the agent I've been looking for!" When the number of agents attending is larger, you have a wider group from which to choose, and you may have less competition for the agent's time.

Besides including panels of agents discussing what representation means and how to go about securing it, many of these gatherings also include time—either scheduled or impromptu—to meet briefly with an agent to discuss your work.

If they're impressed with what they see and hear about your work, they will invite you to submit a query, a proposal, a few sample chapters, or possibly your entire manuscript. Some conferences even arrange for agents to review manuscripts in advance and schedule one-on-one sessions during which you can receive specific feedback or advice regarding your work. Such meetings often cost a small fee, but the input you receive is usually worth the price.

Ask writers who attend conferences and they'll tell you that, at the very least, you'll walk away with new knowledge about the industry. At the very best, you'll receive an invitation to send an agent your material!

Many writers try to make it to at least one conference a year, but cost and location can count as much as subject matter when determining which one to attend. There are conferences in almost every state and province that can provide answers to your questions about writing and the publishing industry. Conferences also connect you with a community of other writers. Such connections help you learn about the pros and cons of different agents, and they can also give you a renewed sense of purpose and direction in your own writing.

SUBHEADS

Each listing is divided into subheads to make locating specific information easier. In the first section, you'll find contact information for conference contacts. You'll also learn conference dates, specific focus, and the average number of attendees. Finally, names of agents who will be speaking or have spoken in the past are listed along with details about their availability during the conference. Calling or e-mailing a conference director to verify the names of agents in attendance is always a good idea.

Costs: Looking at the price of events, plus room and board, may help writers on a tight budget narrow their choices.

Accomodations: Here conferences list overnight accommodations and travel information. Often conferences held in hotels will reserve rooms at a discount rate and may provide a shuttle bus to and from the local airport.

Additional Information: This section includes information on conference-sponsored contests, individual meetings, the availability of brochures, and more.

ABROAD WRITERS CONFERENCES

17363 Sutter Creek Rd., Sutter Creek CA 95685. (209)296-4050. **E-mail:** abroadwriters@yahoo. com. **Website:** www.abroad-crwf.com/index.html. "Abroad Writers Conferences are devoted to introducing our participants to world views here in the United States and Abroad. Throughout the world we invite several authors to come join us to give readings and to participate on a panel. Our discussion groups touch upon a wide range of topics from important issues of our times to publishing abroad and in the United States. Our objective is to broaden our cultural and scientific perspectives of the world through discourse and writing." Conferences are held throughout the year in various places worldwide. See website for scheduling details. Conference duration: 7-10 days. "Instead of being lost in a crowd at a large conference, Abroad Writers' Conference prides itself on holding small group meetings where participants have personal contact with everyone. Stimulating talks, interviews, readings, Q&A's, writing workshops, film screenings, private consultations and social gatherings all take place within a week to ten days. Abroad Writers' Conference promises you true networking opportunities and full detailed feedback on your writing."

COSTS Prices start at $2,750. Discounts and upgrades may apply. Particpants must apply to program no later than 3 months before departure. To secure a place you must send in a deposit of $1000. Balance must be paid in full twelve weeks before departure. See website for pricing details.

ADDITIONAL INFORMATION Agents participate in conference. Application is online at website.

ALABAMA WRITERS' CONCLAVE

137 Sterling Dr, Hueytown AL 35023. **Website:** www. alabamawritersconclave.org. **Contact:** Richard Modlin, President. Estab. 1923. The Alabama Writers' Conclave was organized in 1923 and has been in continuing existence since. Through the years, the Conclave has moved its conferences around the state to provide writers everywhere better access to its resources.The Conclave is today one of the oldest continuing writers' organization in the United States. Writers, aspiring writers and supporters of the writing arts may join. Sharing information, developing ideas, honing skills, and receiving practical advice are hallmarks of the annual meeting. Dates: July 12-14.

COSTS Fees for conference are $150 (member)/$175 (nonmember), includes 2 meals. Critique fee $25 (member)/$30 (nonmember). Membership $25.

ACCOMMODATIONS Special conference rates.

ADDITIONAL INFORMATION "We have major speakers and faculty members who conduct intensive, energetic workshops. Our annual writing contest guidelines and all other information is available at www.alabamawritersconclave.org."

AMERICAN CHRISTIAN WRITERS CONFERENCES

P.O. Box 110390, Nashville TN 37222-0390. (800)219-7483. **Fax:** (615)834-7736. **E-mail:** acwriters@aol. com. **Website:** www.acwriters.com. **Contact:** Reg Forder, director. Estab. 1981. ACW hosts dozens of annual two-day writers conferences and mentoring retreat across America taught by editors and professional freelance writers. These events provide excellent instruction, networking opportunities, and valuable one-on-one time with editors. Annual conferences promoting all forms of Christian writing (fiction, nonfiction, scriptwriting). Conferences are held between March and November during each year.

COSTS Costs vary based on conference. Prices also depend on whether it is a conference or a mentoring retreat.

ACCOMMODATIONS Special rates are available at the host hotel (usually a major chain like Holiday Inn).

ADDITIONAL INFORMATION Send a SASE for conference brochures/guidelines.

ART WORKSHOPS IN GUATEMALA

4758 Lyndale Ave. S., Minneapolis MN 55419-5304. (612)825-0747. **E-mail:** info@artguat.org. **Website:** www.artguat.org. **Contact:** Liza Fourre, director. Estab. 1995. Annual. Workshops held year-round. Maximim class size: 10 students per class.

COSTS See website. ncludes tuition, lodging, breakfast, ground transportation.

ACCOMMODATIONS All transportation and accommodations included in price of conference.

ADDITIONAL INFORMATION Conference information available now. For brochure/guidelines visit website, e-mail or call. Accepts inquiries by e-mail, phone.

ASJA WRITERS CONFERENCE

American Society of Journalists and Authors, 1501 Broadway, Suite 403, New York NY 10036. (212)997-0947. **Fax:** (212)937-2315. **E-mail:** asjaoffice@asja.org; director@asja.org. **Website:** www.asja.org/wc. **Contact:** Alexandra Owens, executive director. Estab. 1971. Annual conference held in April. Conference duration: 3 days. Average attendance: 600. Covers nonfiction. Held at the Roosevelt in New York. Speakers have included Arianna Huffington, Kitty Kelley, Barbara Ehrenreich, Stefan Fatsis.

COSTS $200+, depending on when you sign up (includes lunch). Check website for updates.

ACCOMMODATIONS The hotel holding our conference always blocks out discounted rooms for attendees.

ADDITIONAL INFORMATION Brochures available in February. Registration form is on the website. Inquire by e-mail or fax. Sign up for conference updates on website.

ASPEN SUMMER WORDS LITERARY FESTIVAL & WRITING RETREAT

Aspen Writers' Foundation, 110 E. Hallam St., #116, Aspen CO 81611. (970)925-3122. **Fax:** (970)925-5700. **E-mail:** info@aspenwriters.org. **Website:** www.aspenwriters.org. **Contact:** Natalie Lacy, programs coordinator. Estab. 1976. ASW is one part laboratory and one part theater. It is comprised of two tracks—the Writing Retreat and the Literary Festival—which approach the written word from different, yet complementary angles. The Retreat features introductory and intensive workshops with some of the nation's most notable writing instructors and includes literature appreciation symposia and professional consultations with literary agents and editors. The Writing Retreat supports writers in developing their craft by providing a winning combination of inspiration, skills, community, and opportunity. The Literary Festival is a booklover's bliss, where the written word takes center stage. Since 2005, each edition of the Festival has celebrated a particular literary heritage and culture by honoring the stories and storytellers of a specific region. Annual conference held the fourth week of June. Conference duration: 5 days. Average attendance: 150 at writing retreat; 300+ at literary festival.

COSTS Check website each year for updates.

ACCOMMODATIONS Discount lodging at the conference site will be available. 2014 rates to be announced. Free shuttle around town.

ADDITIONAL INFORMATION Check website for details on when to buy tickets and passes. Aspen Summer Words runs in June.

ASSOCIATION OF WRITERS & WRITING PROGRAMS ANNUAL CONFERENCE

Association of Writers & Writing Programs, George Mason University, 4400 University Drive, MSN 1E3, Fairfax VA 22030-4444. (703)993-4317. **Fax:** (703)993-4302. **E-mail:** conference@awpwriter.org. **Website:** www.awpwriter.org. **Contact:** Anne Le, conference coordinator. Estab. 1992. Each year, AWP holds its Annual Conference & Bookfair in a different city to celebrate the authors, teachers, writing programs, literary centers, and independent publishers of that region. The conference typically features hundreds of readings, lectures, panel discussions, and forums, as well as hundreds of book signings, receptions, dances, and informal gatherings. More than 11,000 writers and readers attended our 2013 conference, and over 700 exhibitors were represented at our bookfair. AWP's is now the largest literary conference in North America.

ADDITIONAL INFORMATION Upcoming conference locations include Seattle (2014), Minneapolis (2015), Los Angeles (2016), and Washington, D.C. (2017).

ATLANTIC CENTER FOR THE ARTS

1414 Art Center Ave., New Smyrna Beach FL 32168. (386)427-6975. **Fax:** (386)427-5669. **E-mail:** program@atlanticcenterforthearts.org. **Website:** www.atlanticcenterforthearts.org. Internship and residency programs. A Florida artist-in-residence program in which artists of all disciplines work with current prominent artists in a supportive and creative environment.

ACCOMMODATIONS $850; $25 non-refundable application fee. Financial aid is available. Participants responsible for all meals. Accommodations available on site. See website for application schedule and materials.

AUSTIN FILM FESTIVAL & CONFERENCE

1801 Salina St., Suite 210, Austin TX 78702. (512)478-4795; (800)310-FEST. **Fax:** (512)478-6205. **Website:** www.austinfilmfestival.com. **Contact:** Erin Hallagan, conference director. Estab. 1994. "Built around one of the most prestigious screenwriting contests in the country, the Conference attracts groundbreaking producers, agents, managers, and development execs, as well as countless working screenwriters and filmmakers. The speakers converging in Austin every October range from established A-listers like Steven Zaillian, Ron Howard, Judd Apatow, Caroline Thompson, Susannah Grant and John Lee Hancock to upstart writers and filmmakers who have just broken into the industry. The Conference is famous, like its host city, for a culture of progressive ideas, big heart and zero pretensions. You won't just watch your heroes speak from a podium—we want you to get up close and personal—so panels are designed for intimacy and interaction, workshops are hands-on dream opportunities for writers and filmmakers, and parties are grand and fun without the velvet ropes. AFF's combination of high-caliber talent with access is unmatched by any other film festival or conference." Runs in the final week of October each year.

COSTS Austin Film Festival offers 4 Badge levels for entry into the October festival, which also features access to the conference, depending on the Badge level. Go online for offers, and to view the different options with available with each badge.

ACCOMMODATIONS Discounted rates on hotel accommodations are available to attendees if the reservations are made through the Austin Film Festival office.

ADDITIONAL INFORMATION The Austin Film Festival furthers the art and craft of filmmaking by inspiring and championing the work of screenwriters, filmmakers, and all artists who use the language of film to tell a story. The Austin Film Festival is considered one of the most accessible festivals, and Austin is the premier town for networking because when industry people are here, they are relaxed and friendly. The Austin Film Festival holds annual screenplay/teleplay and film competitions, as well as a Young Filmmakers Program. Check online for competition details and festival information. Inquire via e-mail or fax.

AUSTIN INTERNATIONAL POETRY FESTIVAL

P.O. Box 26455, Austin TX 78755. (512)777-1888. **E-mail:** lynn@aipf.org. **E-mail:** james@aipf.org. **Website:** www.aipf.org. **Contact:** Ashley S. Kim, festival director. Estab. 1993. Annual Austin International Poetry Festival (AIPF) April 11-14, is open to the public. This four-day citywide, all-inclusive celebration of poetry and poets has grown to become "the largest non-juried poetry festival in the U.S." The festival will include up to 20 live local readings, youth anthology read, 20 poetry workshops, 5 open mics, 5 music and poetry presentations, two anthology competions and complete readings, two poetry slams, an all-night open mic and a poetry panel symposium. API projects over 250 registered poets from the international, national, state, and local areas

ACCOMMODATIONS Includes anthology submission fee, program bio, scheduled reading at one of AIPF's 15 venues, participation in all events, 1 catered meal, workshop participation, and more.

ADDITIONAL INFORMATION Offers multiple poetry contests as part of festival. Guidelines available on website. Registration form available on website. "Largest non-juried poetry festival in the U.S.!"

BACKSPACE AGENT-AUTHOR SEMINAR

P.O. Box 454, Washington MI 48094-0454. (732)267-6449. **Fax:** (586)532-9652. **E-mail:** chrisg@bksp.org. **E-mail:** karendionne@bksp.org. **Website:** www.bksp.org. **Contact:** Karen Dionne. Estab. 2006. Main conference duration: May 23-25. Average attendance: 100. Panels and workshops designed to educate and assist authors in search of a literary agent to represent their work. Only agents will be in program. Past speakers have included Scott Hoffman, Dan Lazar, Scott Miller, Michael Bourret, Katherine Fausset, Jennifer DeChiara, Sharlene Martin and Paul Cirone.

COSTS All 3 days: May 23-25; includes Agent-Author Seminar, Conference Program, Book Signing & Cocktail Reception, Donald Maass workshop—$720. **Backspace Members Receive a $100 discount on a 3-day registration! First 2 days**: May 23-24; includes Agent-Author Seminar, Conference Program, Book Signing & Cocktail Reception—$580. **Friday only**: May 24; Two-track conference program with literary agents, editors and authors. Includes keynote address, book-signing and cocktail reception—$275. **Saturday only**: May 25; Back-to-back craft workshops with bestselling author Jonathan Maberry in the morning and literary agent Donald Maass in the afternoon—$200.

ACCOMMODATIONS Held in the Radisson Martinique, at 49 West 32nd Street, New York, NY 10001. Telephone: (212) 736-3800. Fax: (212) 277-2702. You can call to book a reservation, based on a two-person occupancy.

ADDITIONAL INFORMATION The Backspace Agent-Author Seminar offers plenty of face time with attending agents. This casual, no-pressure seminar is a terrific opportunity to network, ask questions, talk about your work informally and listen from the people who make their lives selling books.

BALTIMORE COMIC-CON

Baltimore Convention Center, One West Pratt St., Baltimore MD 21201. (410)526-7410. **E-mail:** press@baltimorecomiccon.com. **Website:** www.baltimorecomiccon.com. **Contact:** Marc Nathan. Estab. 1999. Annual. September 7-8, 2013. Conference, "promoting the wonderful world of comics to as many people as possible." The Baltimore Comic-Con welcomes the return of The Harvey Awards: "The Harvey Awards are one of the comic book industry's oldest and most respected awards. The Harveys recognize outstanding achievements in over 20 categories, ranging from Best Artist to the Jack Kirby Hall of Fame. They are the only industry awards both nominated by and selected by the full body of comic book professionals."

ACCOMMODATIONS Does not offer overnight accommodations. Provides list of area hotels or lodging options.

ADDITIONAL INFORMATION For brochure, visit website.

BLOCKBUSTER PLOT INTENSIVE WRITING WORKSHOPS (SANTA CRUZ)

Santa Cruz CA **E-mail:** contact@blockbusterplots.com. **Website:** www.blockbusterplots.com. **Contact:** Martha Alderson M.A. (also known as the Plot Whisperer), instructor. Estab. 2000. Held 4 times per year. Conference duration: 2 days. Average attendance: 20. Workshop is intended to help writers create an action, character, and thematic plotline for a screenplay, memoir, short story, novel, or creative nonfiction. Site: Conference hall.

COSTS $95 per day.

ACCOMMODATIONS Provides list of area hotels and lodging options.

ADDITIONAL INFORMATION Brochures available by e-mail or on website. Accepts inquiries by e-mail.

◎ BLOODY WORDS MYSTERY CONFERENCE

E-mail: chair@bloodywords.com. **Website:** www.bloodywords.com. **Contact:** Cheryl Freedman, chair. Estab. 1999. "This is a conference for both readers and writers of mysteries, the only one of its kind in Canada. We also run The Mystery Cafe, a chance to get to know a dozen or so authors, hear them read and ask questions (half hour each)."

COSTS $195 (includes the banquet and all panels, readings, dealers' room and workshop).

ACCOMMODATIONS Offers block of rooms in hotel; list of optional lodging available. Check website for details.

ADDITIONAL INFORMATION Sponsors short mystery story contest—5,000 word limit; judges are experienced editors of anthologies; fee is $5 (entrants must be registered). Also sponsors The Bony Blithe Award for light mysteries; see website for details. Conference information is available now. For brochure, visit website. Accepts inquiries by e-mail and phone. Agents and editors participate in conference.

BLUE RIDGE MOUNTAIN CHRISTIAN WRITERS CONFERENCE

No public address available, 1-800-588-7222. **E-mail:** ylehman@bellsouth.net. **Website:** ridgecrestconferencecenter.org/event/blueridgemountainchristianwritersconference. Annual conference held in May (May 19-May 23). Conference duration: Sunday through lunch on Thursday. Average attendance: 400. A training and networking event for both seasoned and aspiring writers that allows attendees to interact with editors, agents, professional writers, and readers. Workshops and continuing classes in a variety of creative categories are also offered.

COSTS $320, meal package is $141.50 per person (12 meals beginning with dinner Sunday and ending with lunch on Thursday).

ACCOMMODATIONS $59 per night (Standard Accomodations), and $64-69 per night (Deluxe Accomadations), depending on rooms. Located at LifeWay Ridgecrest Conference Center, 1 Ridgecrest Drive, Ridgecrest, NC 28770.

ADDITIONAL INFORMATION The event also features a contest for unpublished writers and ms critiques prior to the conference.

◎ BOOMING GROUND ONLINE WRITERS STUDIO

Buch E-462, 1866 Main Mall, UBC, Vancouver BC V6T 1Z1 Canada. **Fax:** (604)648-8848. **E-mail:** contact@boomingground.com. **Website:** www.boomingground.com. **Contact:** Robin Evans, director. Writer mentorships geared toward beginner, intermediate, and advanced levels in novel, short fiction, poetry, nonfiction, children's writing, and more. **Open to students.** Online mentorship program—students work for 6 months with a mentor by e-mail, allowing up to 120-240 pages of material to be created. Program cost: $500 (Canadian). Site: online and by e-mail.

BREAD LOAF WRITERS' CONFERENCE

Middlebury College, Middlebury College, Middlebury VT 05753. (802)443-5286. **Fax:** (802)443-2087. **E-mail:** ncargill@middlebury.edu. **E-mail:** blwc@middlebury.edu. **Website:** www.middlebury.edu/blwc. **Contact:** Michael Collier, Director. Estab. 1926. Annual conference held in late August. Conference duration: 11 days. Offers workshops for fiction, nonfiction, and poetry. Agents, editors, publicists, and grant specialists will be in attendance.

COSTS $2,714 (includes tuition, housing).

ACCOMMODATIONS Bread Loaf Campus in Ripton, Vermont.

ADDITIONAL INFORMATION Conference Date: August 14-24. Location: mountain campus of Middlebury College. Average attendance: 230.

BYRDCLIFFE ARTS COLONY

34 Tinker St., Woodstock NY 12498. (845)679-2079. **Fax:** (845)679-4529. **E-mail:** airdirector@woodstockguild.org. **Website:** www.woodstockguild.org. Estab. 1991. Offers 1-month residencies June-September. Open to composers, writers, and visual artists. Accommodates 15 at 1 time. Personal living quarters include single rooms, shared baths, and kitchen facilities. Offers separate private studio space. Composers must provide their own keyboard with headphone. Activities include open studio and readings for the Woodstock community at the end of each session. The Woodstock Guild, parent organization, offers music and dance performances and gallery exhibits.

COSTS $600/month; fellowships available. Residents are responsible for own meals and transportation.

ADDITIONAL INFORMATION Deadline: March 15. Online application; visit woodstockguild.org for submission guidelines. Download application fee and online payment from website.

CALIFORNIA CRIME WRITERS CONFERENCE

Co-sponsored by Sisters in Crime/Los Angeles and the Southern California Chapter of Mystery Writers of America, **E-mail:** sistersincrimela@gmail.com. **Website:** www.ccwconference.org. Estab. 1995. Biennial. Conference held in June. Average attendance:

200. Two-day conference on mystery and crime writing. Offers craft, forensic and career-buildings sessions, 2 keynote speakers, author, editor, and agent panels and book signings. Breakfast and lunch both days included.

ADDITIONAL INFORMATION Conference information is available at www.ccwconference.org.

CAPE COD WRITERS CENTER ANNUAL CONFERENCE

P.O. Box 408, Osterville MA 02655. **E-mail:** writers@capecodwriterscenter.org. **Website:** www.capecodwriterscenter.org. **Contact:** Nancy Rubin Stuart, executive director. Duration: 5 days; first week in August. Offers workshops in fiction, commercial fiction, nonfiction, poetry, writing for children, humor, memoir, pitching your book, screenwriting, digital communications, getting published, ms evaluation, mentoring sessions with faculty. Held at Resort and Conference Center of Hyannis, Hyannis, MA.

COSTS Vary, depending on the number of courses selected.

CAT WRITERS' ASSOCIATION ANNUAL WRITERS CONFERENCE

66 Adams St., Jamestown NY 14701. (716)484-6155. **E-mail:** dogwriter@windstream.net. **Website:** www.catwriters.org. **Contact:** Susan M. Ewing, president. The Cat Writers' Association holds an annual conference at varying locations around the U.S. The agenda for the conference is filled with seminars, editor appointments, an autograph party, networking breakfast, reception and annual awards banquet, as well as the annual meeting of the association. See website for details.

CELEBRATION OF SOUTHERN LITERATURE

Southern Lit Alliance, 3069 S. Broad St., Suite 2, Chattanooga TN 37408-3056. (423)267-1218 or (800)267-4232. **Fax:** (423)267-1018. **E-mail:** srobinson@southernlitalliance.org. **Website:** www.southernlitalliance.org. **Contact:** Susan Robinson. "The Celebration of Southern Literature stands out because of its unique collaboration with the Fellowship of Southern Writers, an organization founded by towering literary figures like Eudora Welty, Cleanth Brooks, Walker Percy, and Robert Penn Warren to recognize and encourage literature in the South. The 2013 celebration marked 24 years since the Fellowship selected Chattanooga for its headquarters and chose to collaborate with the

Celebration of Southern Literature. Up to 50 members of the Fellowship will participate in this year's event, discussing hot topics and reading from their latest works. The Fellowship will also award 11 literary prizes and induct 2 new members, making this event the place to discover up-and-coming voices in Southern literature. The Southern Lit Alliance's Celebration of Southern Literature attracts more than 1,000 readers and writers from all over the U.S. It strives to maintain an informal atmosphere where conversations will thrive, inspired by a common passion for the written word. The Southern Lit Alliance (formerly The Arts & Education Council) started as 1 of 12 pilot agencies founded by a Ford Foundation grant in 1952. The Alliance is the only organization of the 12 still in existence. The Southern Lit Alliance celebrates southern writers and readers through community education and innovative literary arts experiences."

CRESTED BUTTE WRITERS CONFERENCE

P.O. Box 1361, Crested Butte CO 81224. **E-mail:** coordinator@conf.crestedbuttewriters.org. **Website:** www.crestedbuttewriters.org/conf.php. **Contact:** Barbara Crawford or Theresa Rizzo, co-coordinators. Estab. 2006.

COSTS $330 nonmembers; $300 members; $297 Early Bird; The Sandy Writing Contest Finalist $280; and groups of 5 or more $280.

ACCOMMODATIONS The conference is held at The Elevation Hotel, located at the Crested Butte Mountain Resort at the base of the ski mountain (Mt. Crested Butte, CO). The quaint historic town lies nestled in a stunning mountain valley 3 short miles from the resort area of Mt. Crested Butte. A free bus runs frequently between the 2 towns. The closest airport is 30 miles away, in Gunnison CO. Our website lists 3 lodging options besides rooms at the Event Facility. All condos, motels and hotel options offer special conference rates. No special travel arrangements are made through the conference; however, information for car rental from Gunnison airport or the Alpine Express shuttle is listed on the conference FAQ page.

ADDITIONAL INFORMATION "Our conference workshops address a wide variety of writing craft and business. Our most popular workshop is Our First Pages Readings—with a twist. Agents and editors read opening pages volunteered by attendees-with a few best selling authors' openings mixed in. Think the A/E can identify the bestsellers? Not so much.

Each year one of our attendees has been mistaken for a bestseller and obviously garnered requests from some on the panel. Agents attending: Carlie Webber—CK Webber Associates and TBDs. The agents will be speaking and available for meetings with attendees through our Pitch and Pages system. Editors attending: Christian Trimmer, senior editor at Disney Hyperion Books, and Jessica Williams of Harper Collins. Award-winning authors: Mark Coker, CEO of Smashwords; Kristen Lamb, social media guru, Kim Killion, book cover designer; Jennifer Jakes; Sandra Kerns; and Annette Elton. Writers may request additional information by e-mail."

EAST TEXAS CHRISTIAN WRITERS CONFERENCE

The School of Humanities, Dr. Jerry L. Summers, Dean, Scarborough Hall, East Texas Baptist University, 1 Tiger Dr., Marshall TX 75670. (903)923-2083. **E-mail:** jhopkins@etbu.edu; contest@etbu.edu. **Website:** www.etbu.edu/News/CWC. **Contact:** Sally Roden, humanities secretary. Estab. 2002. Annual conference; held October 25-26, 2013. Duration: 2 days (Friday and Saturday). Average attendance: 160. Site: East Texas Baptist University. "Primarily, we are interested in promoting quality Christian writing that would be accepted in mainstream publishing." Past conference themes were Back to Basics, Getting Started in Fiction, Writers & Agents, Writing Short Stories, Writing for Newspapers, The Significance of Style, Writing Fillers and Articles, Writing Devotionals, Blogging for Writers, Christian nonfiction, Inspirational Writing, E-Publishing, Publishing on Demand, and Editor, and Author Relations. Conference offers contact, conversation, and exchange of ideas with other aspiring writers; outstanding presentations and workshop experiences with established authors, agents, editors, and publishers; potential publishing and writing opportunities; networking with other writers with related interests; promotion of both craft and faith; and one-on-one consultations with agents, editors, and publishers. Past conference speakers/workshop leaders were Marlene Bagnull, Bill Keith, Mary Lou Redding, Marie Chapian, Vickie Phelps, Michael Farris, Pamela Dowd, Donn Taylor, Terry Burns, Donna Walker-Nixon, Lexie Smith, Marv Knox, Jim Pence, Andrea Chevalier, and Cecil Murphey. Offers an advanced track, a beginner's track, and a teen track. There is a writing contest with cash awards for grand prize and 1st-, 2nd- and 3rd-place winners. Partial scholarships available for students only.

ACCOMMODATIONS Visit website for a list of local hotels offering a discounted rate.

WRITERS IN PARADISE

Eckerd College, 4200 54th Ave. South, St. Petersburg FL 33711. (727) 864-7994. **Fax:** (727) 864-7575. **E-mail:** cayacr@eckerd.edu. **Website:** www.writersin paradise.com. **Contact:** Christine Koryta, conference coordinator. Estab. 2005. Annual. January. Conference duration: 8 days. Average attendance: 84 maximum. Workshop. Offers college credit. "Writers in Paradise Conference offers workshop classes in fiction (novel and short story), poetry, and nonfiction. Working closely with our award-winning faculty, students will have stimulating opportunities to ask questions and learn valuable skills from fellow students and authors at the top of their form. Most importantly, the intimate size and secluded location of the Writers in Paradise experience allows you the time and opportunity to share your mss, critique one another's work, and discuss the craft of writing with experts and peers who can help guide you to the next level." Site: "Located on 188 acres of waterfront property in St. Petersburg, Florida, Eckerd College is a private, coeducational college of liberal arts and sciences. In 2013, lectures were given on the craft of writing by Ann Patchett, Daniel Woodrell, Michael Koryta, and Sterling Watson. Faculty also led discussions during morning sessions of informal round tables and formal panel discussions on craft. [2013] faculty and guest faculty included: Andre Dubus III (*House of Sand and Fog*), Michael Koryta (*So Cold the River*), Dennis Lehane (*The Given Day*), Laura Lippman (*I'd Know You Anywhere*), Seth Fishman (literary agent), Johnny Temple (Akashic Books), Stewart O'Nan (*The Odds*), David Yoo (*Girls for Breakfast*), Tom Franklin (*Crooked Letter, Crooked Letter*), Beth Ann Fennelly (*Unmentionables*), Josh Kendall (editor), Ann Hood (*The Red Thread*), Les Standiford (*Bringing Adam Home*), Sterling Watson (*Sweet Dream Baby*), and more."

COSTS 2013 tuition fee: 700.

ACCOMMODATIONS Block of rooms at area hotel with free shuttle to and from conference; $582.24.

ADDITIONAL INFORMATION Application materials are required of all attendees. Acceptance is based on a writing sample and a letter detailing your writing background. Submit 1 short story (25 page max) or the opening 25 pages of a novel-in-progress, plus a 2-page synopsis of the book. Deadline for application materials is December 1. "Writers in Paradise is a conference for writers of various styles and approaches. While admission is selective, the admissions committee accepts writers with early potential as well as those with strong backgrounds in writing." Information available in August. For brochure, send SASE, call, e-mail. Agents participate in conference. Editors participate in conference. "The tranquil seaside landscape sets the tone for this informal gathering of writers, teachers, editors and literary agents. After 8 days of workshopping and engagement with peers and professionals in your field, you will leave this unique opportunity with solid ideas about how to find an agent and get published, along with a new and better understanding of your craft."

FESTIVAL OF FAITH AND WRITING

Department of English, Calvin College, 1795 Knollcrest Circle SE, Grand Rapids MI 49546. (616)526-6770. **E-mail:** ffw@calvin.edu. **Website:** festival.cal vin.edu. Estab. 1990. Biennial festival held in April. Conference duration: 3 days. The festival brings together writers, editors, publishers, musicians, artists, and readers to discuss and celebrate insightful writing that explores issues of faith. Focuses on fiction, nonfiction, memoir, poetry, drama, children's, young adult, academic, film, and songwriting. Past speakers have included Joyce Carol Oates, Salman Rushdie, Patricia Hampl, Thomas Lynch, Leif Enger, Marilynne Robinson and Michael Chabon. Agents and editors attend the festival.

COSTS Consult festival website.

ACCOMMODATIONS Shuttles are available to and from local hotels. Shuttles are also available for overflow parking lots. A list of hotels with special rates for conference attendees is available on the festival website. High school and college students can arrange on-campus lodging by e-mail.

ADDITIONAL INFORMATION Online registration opens in October. Accepts inquiries by e-mail and phone. Next festival is April 10-12, 2014.

FLATHEAD RIVER WRITERS CONFERENCE

P.O. Box 7711, Kalispeil MT 59904-7711. (406)881-4066. **E-mail:** answers@authorsoftheflathead.org. **Website:** www.authorsoftheflathead.org/conference. asp. Estab. 1990. Two day conference packed with energizing speakers. After a focus on publishing the past two years, this year's focus is on writing, getting your manuscripts honed and ready for your readers. Highlights include two agents will review 12 manuscripts one-on-one with the first 24 paid attendees requesting this opportunity, a synopsis writing workshop, a screenwriting workshop, and more.

COSTS Contact for cost information, not currently listed on website.

ACCOMMODATIONS Rooms are available at a discounted rate.

ADDITIONAL INFORMATION Watch website for additional speakers and other details. Register early as seating is limited.

FLORIDA CHRISTIAN WRITERS CONFERENCE

2344 Armour Ct., Titusville FL 32780. (386)295-3902. **E-mail:** FloridaChristianWritersConf@gmail.com. **Website:** floridacwc.net. Estab. 1988. Annual conference held in March (February 26-March 2). Conference duration: 4 days. Average attendance: 275. "The Florida Christian Writers Conference 2014 meets under the stately oaks of Lake Yale Conference Center near Leesburg, Florida. The conference is designed to meet the needs of beginning writers to published authors. This is your opportunity to learn more about the publishing industry, to build your platform, and to follow God's leading to publish the message He has given you."

COSTS $575 (includes tuition, meals).

ACCOMMODATIONS We provide a shuttle from the Orlando airport. $725/double occupancy; $950/single occupancy.

ADDITIONAL INFORMATION "Each writer may submit 2 works for critique. We have specialists in every area of writing. Brochures/guidelines are available online or for a SASE."

⬤ GENEVA WRITERS CONFERENCE

Geneva Writers Group, Switzerland. **E-mail:** info@GenevaWritersGroup.org. **Website:** www.genevawritersgroup.org. Estab. 1993. Biennial conference held at Webster University in Bellevue/Geneva, Switzerland. Conference duration: 2.5 days, welcoming more than 200 writers from around the world. Speakers and presenters have included Peter Ho Davies, Jane Alison, Russell Celyn Jones, Patricia Hampl, Robert Root, Brett Lott, Dinty W. Moore, Naomi Shihab Nye,

Jo Shapcott, Wallis Wilde Menozzi, Susan Tiberghien, Jane Dystel, Laura Longrigg, and Colin Harrison.

THE GLEN WORKSHOP

Image, 3307 Third Ave. W., Seattle WA 98119. (206)281-2988. **Fax:** (206)281-2335. **E-mail:** glenworkshop@imagejournal.org. **Website:** glenworkshop.com. Estab. 1995. A pair of annual workshops. Conference duration: 1 week. Workshop focuses on fiction, poetry, spiritual writing, playwriting, screenwriting, songwriting, and mixed media. Writing classes combine general instruction and discussion with the workshop experience, in which each individual's works are read and discussed critically. Glen West held at St. John's College in Santa Fe, NM from July 28-August 4and Glen East held Mt. Holyoke College in South Hadley, MA from June 9-16. The Glen Workshop combines an intensive learning experience with a lively festival of the arts. It takes place in the stark, dramatic beauty of the Sangre de Cristo mountains and within easy reach of the rich cultural, artistic, and spiritual traditions of northern New Mexico. Lodging and meals are included with registration at affordable rates. A low-cost "commuter" rate is also available for those who wish to camp, stay with friends, or otherwise find their own food and lodging.

COSTS See costs online. A limited number of partial scholarships are available.

ACCOMMODATIONS Offers dorm rooms, dorm suites, and apartments.

ADDITIONAL INFORMATION Like *Image*, the Glen is grounded in a Christian perspective, but its tone is informal and hospitable to all spiritual wayfarers. Depending on the teacher, participants may need to submit workshop material prior to arrival (usually 10-25 pages).

GOTHAM WRITERS' WORKSHOP

WritingClasses.com, 555 Eighth Ave., Suite 1402, New York NY 10018. (212)974-8377. **Fax:** (212)307-6325. **E-mail:** dana@write.org. **Website:** www.writingclasses.com. **Contact:** Dana Miller, director of student relations. Estab. 1993. Online classes are held throughout the year. There are 4 terms of NYC classes, beginning in January, April, June/July, and September/October. Offers craft-oriented creative writing courses in general creative writing, fiction writing, screenwriting, nonfiction writing, article writing, stand-up comedy writing, humor writing, memoir writing, novel writing, children's book writing, playwriting, poetry, songwriting, mystery writing, science fiction writing, romance writing, television writing, article writing, travel writing, business writing and classes on freelancing, selling your screenplay, how to blog, nonfiction book proposal, and getting published. Also, the Workshop offers a teen program, private instruction, and mentoring program. Classes are held at various schools in New York City as well as online at www.writingclasses.com. Agents and editors participate in some workshops.

COSTS $420/10-week workshops; $159 for the four-week online selling seminars and $125 for one-day intensive courses; $299 for 6-week creative writing and business writing classes.

ADDITIONAL INFORMATION "Participants do not need to submit workshop material prior to their first class." Sponsors a contest for a free 10-week online creative writing course (valued at $420) offered each term. Students should fill out a form online at www.writingclasses.com to participate in the contest. The winner is randomly selected. For brochure send e-mail, visit website, or call. Accepts inquiries by e-mail and phone.

THE GREAT AMERICAN PITCHFEST & SCREENWRITING CONFERENCE

Twilight·Pictures, 12400 Ventura Blvd., #735, Studio City CA 91604. (877)255-2528. **E-mail:** info@pitchfest.com. **Website:** www.pitchfest.com. Conference duration: 3 days (2-day conference, 1-day pitchfest). "Our companies are all carefully screened, and only the most credible companies in the industry are invited to hear pitches. They include agents, managers, and production companies."

COSTS Saturday is free, with a full day of industry classes, workshops, and panels, all led by industry professionals. The Sunday Pitchfest is $250; Saturday is free. The Friday/Saturday master classes are $50.

ACCOMMODATIONS All activities will be held at the Burbank Marriott Hotel & Convention Center, 2500 N. Hollywood Way, Burbank, CA 91505.

ADDITIONAL INFORMATION 2013 dates: May 31-June 2.

GREATER LEHIGH VALLEY WRITERS GROUP 'THE WRITE STUFF' WRITERS CONFERENCE

3650 Nazareth Pike, PMB #136, Bethlehem PA 18020-1115. **E-mail:** writestuffchair@glvwg.org. **Website:** www.glvwg.org. **Contact:** Donna Brennan, chair. Estab. 1993.

COSTS Members: $110 (includes Friday evening session and all Saturday workshops, 2 meals, and a chance to pitch to an editor or agent); non-members: $130. Late registration: $145. Pre-conference workshops require an additional fee.

ADDITIONAL INFORMATION "The Writer's Flash contest is judged by conference participants. Write 100 words or less in fiction, creative nonfiction, or poetry. Brochures available in January by SASE, or by phone, e-mail, or on website. Accepts inquiries by SASE, e-mail or phone. Agents and editors attend conference. For updated info refer to the website. Greater Lehigh Valley Writers Group hosts a friendly conference and gives you the most for your money. Breakout rooms offer craft topics, business of publishing, editor and agent panels. Book fair with book signing by published authors and presenters."

GREEN LAKE CHRISTIAN WRITERS CONFERENCE

W2511 State Road 23, Green Lake Conference Center, Green Lake WI 54941-9599. (920)294-3323. **E-mail:** program@glcc.org. **E-mail:** janet.p.white@gmail.com. **Website:** glcc.org. **Contact:** Janet White, Conference Director. Estab. 1948. Conference duration: 1 week (August 18-23). Attendees may be well-published or beginners, may write for secular and/or Christian markets. Leaders are experienced writing teachers. Attendees can spend 11.5 contact hours in the workshop of their choice: fiction, nonfiction, poetry, inspirational/devotional. Seminars include specific skills: marketing, humor, songwriting, writing for children, self-publishing, writing for churches, interviewing, memoir writing, the magazine market. Evening: panels of experts will answer questions. Social and leisure activities included. GLCC is in south central WI, has 1,000 acres, 2.5 miles of shoreline on Wisconsin's deepest lake, and offers a resort setting.

COSTS Short Track (Two Days): $65 per person. Full Track: Writers'—$225 per person; Artists'—$40 per person.

ACCOMMODATIONS Hotels, lodges and all meeting rooms are a/c. Affordable rates, excellent meals.

ADDITIONAL INFORMATION Brochure and scholarship info from website or contact Jan White (920-294-7327). To register, call 920-294-3323.

GREEN MOUNTAIN WRITERS CONFERENCE

47 Hazel St., Rutland VT 05701. (802)236-6133. **E-mail:** ydaley@sbcglobal.net. **E-mail:** yvonnedaley@me.com. **Website:** vermontwriters.com. **Contact:** Yvonne Daley, director. Estab. 1999. "Annual conference held in the summer. Covers fiction, creative nonfiction, poetry, journalism, nature writing, essay, memoir, personal narrative, and biography. Held at an old dance pavillion on on a remote pond in Tinmouth, Vermont. Speakers have included Stephen Sandy, Grace Paley, Ruth Stone, Howard Frank Mosher, Chris Bohjalian, Joan Connor, Yvonne Daley, David Huddle, David Budbill, Jeffrey Lent, Verandah Porche, Tom Smith, and Chuck Clarino."

COSTS $600 before June 30; $650 after June 30. Partial scholarships are available.

ACCOMMODATIONS "We have made arrangements with a major hotel in nearby Rutland and two area bed and breakfast inns for special accommodations and rates for conference participants. You must make your own reservations."

ADDITIONAL INFORMATION Participants' mss can be read and commented on at a cost. Sponsors contests. Conference publishes a literary magazine featuring work of participants. Brochures available in January on website or for SASE, e-mail. Accepts inquiries by SASE, e-mail, phone. "We offer the opportunity to learn from some of the nation's best writers at a small, supportive conference in a lakeside setting that allows one-to-one feedback. Participants often continue to correspond and share work after conferences." Further information available on website, by e-mail or by phone.

⊕ HAIKU NORTH AMERICA CONFERENCE

1275 Fourth St. PMB #365, Santa Rosa CA 95404. **E-mail:** welchm@aol.com. **Website:** www.haikunorthamerica.com. **Contact:** Michael Dylan Welch. Biannual conference held August 14-18 on board the historic Queen Mary ocean liner, permanently docked in Long Beach, California. Haiku North America (HNA) is the largest and oldest gathering of haiku poets in the United States and Canada. There are no membership fees and HNA provides breaking news and interaction at the HNA blog. All haiku poets and interested parties are welcome. It is a long weekend of papers, panels, workshops, readings, performances, book sales, and much socialization with fellow poets, translators, scholars, editors, and publishers. Both established and aspiring haiku poets are welcome.

ACCOMMODATIONS Typically around $200, including a banquet and some additional meals. Accommodations at discounted hotels nearby are an additional cost. Information available on website as details are finalized closer to the conference date.

HIGHLAND RIDGE FILM FESTIVAL

150 W. Beau St., Suite 214, Washington PA 15301. (724)344-2857. **E-mail:** HRCDCevents@gmail.com. **Website:** washpaelmstreet.org/events. **Contact:** Karen Fleet, coordinator. Estab. 2012. Highland Ridge is a non-profit organization. This is a fundraiser where all monies will be used for the community. "Small independent filmmakers, grade kids, and high school kids' from our area. Encouraging script writing. See website for details."

HIGHLAND SUMMER CONFERENCE

Box 7014, Radford University, Radford VA 24142-7014. (540)831-5366. **Fax:** (540)831-5951. **E-mail:** tburriss@radford.edu; rbderrick@radford.edu. **Website:** www.radford.edu/content/cehd/home/departments/appalachian-studies.html. **Contact:** Dr. Theresa Burriss, Ruth Derrick. Estab. 1978. The Highland Summer Writers' Conference is a one-week lecture-seminar workshop combination conducted by well-known guest writers. It offers the opportunity to study and practice creative and expository writing within the context of regional culture. The course is graded on Pass/Fail basis for undergraduates and letter grades for graduate students. It may be taken twice for credit. The class runs Monday through Friday 9 a.m.-noon and 1:30-4:30 p.m., with extended hours on Wednesday, and readings and receptions by resident teachers on Tuesday and Thursday evening in McConnell Library 7:30-9:30 p.m. The evening readings are free and open to the public.

ACCOMMODATIONS "We do not have special rate arrangements with local hotels. We do offer accommodations on the Radford University campus in a recently refurbished residence hall."

ADDITIONAL INFORMATION Conference leaders typically critique work done during the one-week conference, and because of the one-week format, students will be asked to bring preliminary work when they arrive at the conference, as well as submit a portfolio following the conference. Brochures/guidelines are available in March by request.

HIGHLIGHTS FOUNDATION FOUNDERS WORKSHOPS

814 Court St., Honesdale PA 18431. (570)253-1122. **Fax:** (570)253-0179. **E-mail:** klbrown@highlights foundation.org. **E-mail:** jo.lloy@highlightsfounda tion.org. **Website:** highlightsfoundation.org. **Contact:** Kent L. Brown, Jr. Estab. 2000. Offers more than three dozen workshops per year. Conference duration: 3-7 days. Average attendance: limited to 10-14. Genre specific workshops and retreats on children's writing: fiction, nonfiction, poetry, promotions. "Our goal is to improve, over time, the quality of literature for children by educating future generations of children's authors." Highlights Founders' home in Boyds Mills, PA.

COSTS Prices vary based on workshop. Check website for details.

ACCOMMODATIONS Coordinates pickup at local airport. Offers overnight accommodations. Participants stay in guest cabins on the wooded grounds surrounding Highlights Founders' home adjacent to the house/conference center.

ADDITIONAL INFORMATION Some workshops require pre-workshop assignment. Brochure available for SASE, by e-mail, on website, by phone, by fax. Accepts inquiries by phone, fax, e-mail, SASE. Editors attend conference. "Applications will be reviewed and accepted on a first-come, first-served basis, applicants must demonstrate specific experience in writing area of workshop they are applying for—writing samples are required for many of the workshops."

HIGHLIGHTS FOUNDATION WRITERS WORKSHOP AT CHAUTAUQUA

814 Court St., Honesdale PA 18431. (570)253-1192. **Fax:** (570)253-0179. **E-mail:** klbrown@highlights foundation.org. **E-mail:** jo.lloyd@highlightsfounda tion.org. **Website:** highlightsfoundation.org. Estab. 1985. Average attendance: 100. Workshops are geared toward those who write for children at the beginner, intermediate, and advanced levels. Offers seminars, small group workshops, and one-on-one sessions with authors, editors, illustrators, critics, and publishers. Workshop site is the picturesque community of Chautauqua, New York. Speakers have included Bruce Coville, Candace Fleming, Linda Sue Park, Jane Yo-

len, Patricia Gauch, Jerry Spinelli, Eileen Spinelli, Joy Cowley and Pam Munoz Ryan.

ACCOMMODATIONS We coordinate ground transportation to and from airports, trains, and bus stations in the Erie, Pennsylvania and Jamestown/Buffalo, NY area. We also coordinate accommodations for conference attendees.

ADDITIONAL INFORMATION "We offer the opportunity for attendees to submit a ms for review at the conference. Workshop brochures/guidelines are available upon request."

HOFSTRA UNIVERSITY SUMMER WRITING WORKSHOPS

University College for Continuing Education, 250 Hofstra University, Hempstead NY 11549-2500. (516)463-7200. **Fax:** (516)463-4833. **E-mail:** ce@hof stra.edu. **Website:** hofstra.edu/academics/ce. **Contact:** Colleen Slattery, Senior Associate Dean. Estab. 1972. Hofstra University's 2-week Summer Writers Program, a cooperative endeavor of the Creative Writing Program, the English Department, and Hofstra University Continuing Education (Hofstra CE), offers 8 classes which may be taken on a noncredit or credit basis, for both graduate and undergraduate students. Led by master writers, the Summer Writing Program operates on the principle that true writing talent can be developed, nurtured and encouraged by writer-in-residence mentors. Through instruction, discussion, criticism and free exchange among the program members, writers begin to find their voice and their style. The program provides group and individual sessions for each writer. The Summer Writing Program includes a banquet, guest speakers, and exposure to authors such as Oscar Hijuelos, Robert Olen Butler (both Pulitzer Prize winners), Maurice Sendak, Cynthia Ozick, Nora Sayre, and Denise Levertov. Often agents, editors, and publishers make presentations during the conference, and authors and students read from published work and works in progress. These presentations and the conference banquet offer additional opportunities to meet informally with participants, master writers and guest speakers. Average attendance: 65. Conference offers workshops in short fiction, nonfiction, poetry, and occasionally other genres such as screenplay writing or writing for children. Site is the university campus on Long Island, 25 miles from New York City.

COSTS Check website for current fees. Credit is available for undergraduate and graduate students. Choose one of 9 writing genres and spend two intensive weeks studying and writing in that genre.

ACCOMMODATIONS Free bus operates between Hempstead Train Station and campus for those commuting from New York City on the Long Island Rail Road. Dormitory rooms are available.

ADDITIONAL INFORMATION Students entering grades 9-12 can now be part of the Summer Writers Program with a special section for high school students. Through exercises and readings, students will learn how to use their creative impulses to improve their fiction, poetry and plays and learn how to create cleaner and clearer essays. During this intensive 2-week course, students will experiment with memoir, poetry, oral history, dramatic form and the short story, and study how to use character, plot, point of view and language.

HOW TO BE PUBLISHED WORKSHOPS

P.O. Box 100031, Irondale AL 35210-3006. **E-mail:** mike@writing2sell.com. **Website:** www.writing2sell.com. **Contact:** Michael Garrett. Estab. 1986. Workshops are offered continuously year-round at various locations. Conference duration: 1 session. Average attendance: 10-15. Workshops to "move writers of category fiction closer to publication." Focus is not on how to write, but how to get published. Site: Workshops held at college campuses and universities. Themes include marketing, idea development, characterization, and ms critique. Special critique is offered, but advance submission is not required. Workshop information available on website. Accepts inquiries by e-mail.
COSTS $79-99.

INDIANA UNIVERSITY WRITERS' CONFERENCE

464 Ballantine Hall, 1020 E. Kirkwood Ave., Bloomington IN 47405-7103. (812)855-1877. **Fax:** (812)855-9535. **E-mail:** writecon@indiana.edu. **Website:** www.indiana.edu/~writecon. **Contact:** Bob Bledsoe, director. Estab. 1940. Annual. Conference/workshops held in May. Average attendance: 115. "The Indiana University Writers' Conference believes in a craft-based teaching of fiction writing. We emphasize an exploration of creativity through a variety of approaches, offering workshop-based craft discussions, classes focusing on technique, and talks about the careers and concerns of a writing life." 2013 faculty: Alix Lambert, Scott Hutchins, Nathaniel Perry, Lloyd Suh.

COSTS 2013: Workshop, $550/week; classes only, $300/week.

ACCOMMODATIONS Information on accommodations available on website.

ADDITIONAL INFORMATION Fiction workshop applicants must submit up to 25 pages of prose. Registration information available for SASE, by e-mail, or on website. Spaces still available in all workshops and classes for 2013.

INTERNATIONAL CREATIVE WRITING CAMP

111-11th Ave.SW, Minot ND 58701-6081. (701)838-8472. **Fax:** (701)838-1351. **E-mail:** info@internationalmusiccamp.com. **Website:** www.internationalmusiccamp.com. **Contact:** Joseph Alme, interim director. Writer and illustrator workshops geared toward beginner, intermediate and advanced levels. **Open to students.** Sessions offered include those covering poems, plays, mystery stories, essays. Workshop held June 23-29, 2013. Registration limited to 40. The summer camp location at the International Peace Garden on the Border between Manitoba and North Dakota is an ideal site for creative thinking. Excellent food, housing, and recreation facilities are available.

COSTS Before May 1, $375; after May 1—$390. Write for more information.

IOWA SUMMER WRITING FESTIVAL

The University of Iowa, C215 Seashore Hall, University of Iowa, Iowa City IA 52242. (319)335-4160. **Fax:** (319)335-4743. **E-mail:** iswfestival@uiowa.edu. **Website:** uiowa.edu/~iswfest. Estab. 1987. Annual festival held in June and July. Conference duration: Workshops are 1 week or a weekend. Average attendance: Limited to 12 people/class, with over 1,500 participants throughout the summer. "We offer courses across the genres: novel, short story, poetry, essay, memoir, humor, travel, playwriting, screenwriting, writing for children, and women's writing. Held at the University of Iowa campus." Speakers have included Marvin Bell, Lan Samantha Chang, John Dalton, Hope Edelman, Katie Ford, Patricia Foster, Bret Anthony Johnston, Barbara Robinette Moss, among others.

COSTS $590 for full week; $305 for weekend workshop. Housing and meals are separate.

ACCOMMODATIONS Accommodations available at area hotels. Information on overnight accommodations available by phone or on website.

ADDITIONAL INFORMATION Brochures are available in February. Inquire via e-mail or on website.

JACKSON HOLE WRITERS CONFERENCE

PO Box 1974, Jackson WY 83001. (307)413-3332. **E-mail:** nicole@jacksonholewritersconference.com. **Website:** jacksonholewritersconference.com. Estab. 1991. Annual conference held June 27-29. Conference duration: 4 days. Average attendance: 110. Covers fiction, creative nonfiction, and young adult and offers ms critiques from authors, agents, and editors. Agents in attendance will take pitches from writers. Paid manuscript critique programs are available.

COSTS $365 if registered by May 12. Accompanying teen writer: $175. Pre-Conference Writing Workshop: $150.

ADDITIONAL INFORMATION Held at the Center for the Arts in Jackson, Wyoming and online.

KENYON REVIEW WRITERS WORKSHOP

Kenyon College, Gambier OH 43022. (740)427-5207. **Fax:** (740)427-5417. **E-mail:** kenyonreview@kenyon.edu; writers@kenyonreview.org. **Website:** www.kenyonreview.org. **Contact:** Anna Duke Reach, director. Estab. 1990. Annual 8-day workshop held in June. Participants apply in poetry, fiction, or creative nonfiction, and then participate in intensive daily workshops which focus on the generation and revision of significant new work. Held on the campus of Kenyon College in the rural village of Gambier, Ohio. Workshop leaders have included David Baker, Ron Carlson, Rebecca McClanahan, Meghan O'Rourke, Linda Gregorson, Dinty Moore, Tara Ison, Jane Hamilton, Lee K. Abbott, and Nancy Zafris.

COSTS $1,995; includes tuition, room and board.

ACCOMMODATIONS The workshop operates a shuttle to and from Gambier and the airport in Columbus, Ohio. Offers overnight accommodations. Participants are housed in Kenyon College student housing. The cost is covered in the tuition.

ADDITIONAL INFORMATION Application includes a writing sample. Admission decisions are made on a rolling basis. Workshop information is available online at www.kenyonreview.org/workshops in November. For brochure send e-mail, visit website, call, fax. Accepts inquiries by SASE, e-mail, phone, fax.

KEY WEST LITERARY SEMINAR

718 Love Lane, Key West FL 33040. (888)293-9291. **E-mail:** mail@kwls.org. **Website:** www.kwls.org. "The mission of KWLS is to promote the understanding and discussion of important literary works and their authors; to recognize and support new voices in American literature; and to preserve and promote Key West's literary heritage while providing resources that strengthen literary culture." The annual seminar and writers' workshop program are held in January. Scholarships are available to teachers, librarians, and students. Awards are given to emerging writers. See website for details.

COSTS $545/seminar; $450/writers' workshops.

ACCOMMODATIONS A list of nearby lodging establishments is made available.

KILLER NASHVILLE

P.O. Box 680759, Franklin TN 37068-0686. (615)599-4032. **E-mail:** contact@killernashville.com. **Website:** www.killernashville.com. Jaden Terrell, Exec. Dir. **Contact:** Clay Stafford. Estab. 2006. Annual. Next events: Aug. 22-25. Conference duration: 3 days. Average attendance: 200+. Conference designed for writers and fans of mysteries and thrillers, including fiction and nonfiction authors, playwrights, and screenwriters. There are many opportunities for authors to sign books. Killer Nashville's 2013 writers conference will have over 60 sessions, 2 guests of honor, agent/editor/publisher roundtables, 7 distinct session tracks (general writing, genre specific writing, publishing, publicity & promotion, forensics, screenwriting, sessions for fans), 12 breakout sessions for intense study, special sessions, manuscript critiques (fiction, nonfiction, short story, screenplay, marketing, query), realistic mock crime scene for you to solve, networking with bestselling authors, agents, editors, publishers, attorneys, publicists, representatives from law and emergency services, mystery bingo, authors' bar, wine tasting event, two cocktail receptions, guest of honor dinner and awards program, prizes, free giveaways, free book signings, and more.

COSTS Early Bird Registration: $160 (February 16); Advanced Registration: $170 (May 1); $180 for three day full registration.

ACCOMMODATIONS The Hutton Hotel has all roomas available for the Killer Nashville Conference.

ADDITIONAL INFORMATION Additional information about registration is provided online.

KUNDIMAN POETRY RETREAT

P.O. Box 4248, Sunnyside NY 11104. **E-mail:** info@kundiman.org. **Website:** www.kundiman.org. **Con-**

tact: June W. Choi, executive director. Held annualy June 19-23 at Fordham University's Rose Hill campus. "Opento Asian American poets. Renowned faculty will conduct workshops and provide one-on-one mentorship sessions with fellows. Readings and informal social gatherings will also be scheduled. Fellows selected based on sample of 6-8 poems and short essay answer. Applications should be received between December 15-February 1."

COSTS $350

ACCOMMODATIONS Room and board is free to accepted Fellows.

ADDITIONAL INFORMATION Additional information, guidelines, and online application available on website.

LA JOLLA WRITERS CONFERENCE

P.O. Box 178122, San Diego CA 92177. (858)467-1978. **E-mail:** akuritz@san.rr.com. **Website:** www.lajollaw ritersconference.com. **Contact:** Jared Kuritz, director. Estab. 2001. Annual conference held in October/November. Conference duration: 3 days. Average attendance: 200. "In addition to covering nearly every genre, we also take particular pride in educating our attendees on the business aspect of the book industry by having agents, editors, publishers, publicists, and distributors teach classes. Our conference offers 2 types of classes: lecture sessions that run for 50 minutes, and workshops that run for 110 minutes. Each block period is dedicated to either workshop or lecture-style classes. During each block period, there will be 6-8 classes on various topics from which you can choose to attend. For most workshop classes, you are encouraged to bring written work for review. Literary agents from prestigious agencies such as The Andrea Brown Literary Agency, The Dijkstra Agency, The McBride Agency and Full Circle Literary Group have participated in the past. The conference creates a strong sense of community, and it has seen many of its attendees successfully published."

COSTS Information available online.

LAS VEGAS WRITERS CONFERENCE

Henderson Writers' Group, 614 Mosswood Dr., Henderson NV 89015. (702)564-2488; or, toll-free, (866)869-7842. **E-mail:** marga614@mysticpublish ers.com. **Website:** www.lasvegaswritersconference. com. Annual. Held in April. Conference duration: 3 days. Average attendance: 150 maximum. "Join writing professionals, agents, industry experts, and your colleagues for 3 days in Las Vegas as they share their knowledge on all aspects of the writer's craft. While there are formal pitch sessions, panels, workshops, and seminars, the faculty is also available throughout the conference for informal discussions and advice. Plus, you're bound to meet a few new friends, too. Workshops, seminars, and expert panels will take you through writing in many genres including fiction, creative nonfiction, screenwriting, journalism, and business and technical writing. There will be many Q&A panels for you to ask the experts all your questions." Site: Sam's Town Hotel and Gambling Hall in Las Vegas.

COSTS $400 before December 31, $450 until conference, and $500 at the door. One day registration is $275.

ADDITIONAL INFORMATION Sponsors contest. Agents and editors participate in conference.

LEAGUE OF UTAH WRITERS' ANNUAL WRITER'S CONFERENCE

Dianne Hardy, League of Utah Writers, 420 W. 750 N., Logan UT 84321. **E-mail:** writerscache435@gmail. com. **Website:** www.luwriters.org/index.html. **Contact:** Tim Keller, president; Irene Hastings, president-elect; Caroll Shreeve, secretary. The League of Utah Writers is a non-profit organization dedicated to offering friendship, education, and encouragement to the writers of Utah. New members are always welcome. Writer workshops geared toward beginner, intermediate or advanced. Annual conference.

LOVE IS MURDER

E-mail: hanleyliz@wideopenwest.com. **Website:** loveismurder.net. Annual conference held in February for readers, writers, and fans of mystery, suspense, thriller, romantic suspense, dark fiction, and true crime. Features bestselling headliners, plus ms critiques; editors/agents participate in pitch sessions. Attorneys, criminal justice experts, forensic scientists, physicians, private investigators, computer forensic experts, weapons experts, and more give demos.

COSTS Full conference including panels, discussions, entertainment and all meals: $369.

ACCOMMODATIONS Held at InterContinental Chicago O'Hare. You can register for a room through the website.

ADDITIONAL INFORMATION Banquet and Lovey Awards for best first novel, historical novel, series, crime-related nonfiction, private investigator/police procedural, paranormal/science fiction/horror, traditional/amateur sleuth, suspense thriller, romance/fantasy, and short story.

THE MACDOWELL COLONY

100 High St., Peterborough NH 03458. (603)924-3886. **Fax:** (603)924-9142. **E-mail:** admissions@macdowellcolony.org. **Website:** www.macdowellcolony.org. Estab. 1907. Open to writers, playwrights, composers, visual artists, film/video artists, interdisciplinary artists and architects. Applicants submit information and work samples for review by a panel of experts in each discipline. Application form submitted online at www.macdowellcolony.org/apply.html.

COSTS Travel reimbursement and stipends are available for participants of the residency, based on need. There are no residency fees.

MAGNA CUM MURDER

Magna Cum Murder Crime Writing Festival, The E.B. and Bertha C. Ball Center, Ball State University, Muncie IN 47306. (765)285-8975. **Fax:** (765)747-9566. **E-mail:** magnacummurder@yahoo.com; kennisonk@aol.com. **Website:** www.magnacummurder.com. Estab. 1994. Annual conference held in October. Average attendance: 300. Festival for readers and writers of crime writing. Held in The Columbia Club, Indianapolis, IN. Usually 30-40 mystery writers are in attendance and there are presentations from agents, editors and professional writers. The website has the full list of attending speakers.

COSTS Check website for updates.

MENDOCINO COAST WRITERS CONFERENCE

1211 Del Mar Dr., Fort Bragg CA 95437. (707)937-9983. **E-mail:** info@mcwc.org. **Website:** www.mcwc.org. Estab. 1988. Annual conference held in July. Average attendance: 80. Provides workshops for fiction, nonfiction, and poetry. Held at a small community college campus on the northern Pacific Coast. Workshop leaders have included Kim Addonizio, Lynne Barrett, John Dufresne, John Lescroart, Ben Percy, Luis Rodriguez, and Ellen Sussman. Agents and publishers will be speaking and available for meetings with attendees.

COSTS $525+ (includes panels, meals, 2 socials with guest readers, 4 public events, 3 morning intensive workshops in 1 of 6 subjects, and a variety of afternoon panels and lectures).

ACCOMMODATIONS Information on overnight accommodations is made available.

ADDITIONAL INFORMATION Emphasis is on writers who are also good teachers. Registration opens March 15. Send inquiries via e-mail.

MIDWEST WRITERS WORKSHOP

Ball State University, Department of Journalism, Muncie IN 47306. (765)282-1055. **E-mail:** midwestwriters@yahoo.com. **Website:** www.midwestwriters.org. **Contact:** Jama Kehoe Bigger, director. Annual workshop held in late July. Writer workshops geared toward intermediate level. Topics include most genres. Faculty/speakers have included Joyce Carol Oates, George Plimpton, Clive Cussler, Haven Kimmel, James Alexander Thom, Wiliam Zinsser, Phillip Gulley, and children's writers Rebecca Kai Dotlich, April Pulley Sayre, Peter Welling, Claire Ewert, and Michelle Medlock Adams. Workshop also includes agent pitch sessions ms evaluation and a writing contest. Registration tentatively limited to 125.

COSTS $135-360. Most meals included.

ADDITIONAL INFORMATION Offers scholarships. See website for more information.

MONTEVALLO LITERARY FESTIVAL

Sta. 6420, University of Montevallo, Montevallo AL 35115. (205)665-6420. **Fax:** (205)665-6422. **E-mail:** murphyj@montevallo.edu. **Website:** www.montevallo.edu/english. **Contact:** Dr. Jim Murphy, director. Estab. 2003. Takes place annually, April 12.

COSTS Readings are free. Readings, plus lunch, reception, and dinner is $20. Master Class only is $30. Master Class with everything else is $50.

ACCOMMODATIONS Offers overnight accommodations at Ramsay Conference Center on campus. Call (205)665-6280 for reservations. Free on-campus parking. Additional information available at www.montevallo.edu/cont_ed/ramsay.shtm.

ADDITIONAL INFORMATION To enroll in a fiction workshop, contact Bryn Chancellor (bchancellor@montevallo.edu). Information for upcoming festival available in February For brochure, visit website. Accepts inquiries by mail (with SASE), e-mail, phone, and fax. Editors participate in conference. "This is a friendly, relaxed festival dedicated to bringing literary writers and readers together on a personal scale." Poetry workshop participants submit up to 5 pages of poetry; e-mail as Word doc to Jim Murphy (murphyj@montevallo.edu) at least 2 weeks prior to festival.

MONTROSE CHRISTIAN WRITERS' CONFERENCE

218 Locust St., Montrose PA 18801. (570)278-1001 or (800)598-5030. **Fax:** (570)278-3061. **E-mail:** info@ montrosebible.org. **Website:** montrosebible.org. Estab. 1990. "Annual conference held in July. Offers workshops, editorial appointments, and professional critiques. We try to meet a cross-section of writing needs, for beginners and advanced, covering fiction, poetry, and writing for children. It is small enough to allow personal interaction between attendees and faculty. Speakers have included William Petersen, Mona Hodgson, Jim Fletcher, and Terri Gibbs." Held in Montrose, from July 21-24.

COSTS Tuition is $175.

ACCOMMODATIONS Will meet planes in Binghamton, NY and Scranton, PA. On-site accomodations: room and board $305-350/conference; $60-70/ day including food (2009 rates). RV court available.

ADDITIONAL INFORMATION "Writers can send work ahead of time and have it critiqued for a small fee." The attendees are usually church related. The writing has a Christian emphasis. Conference information available in April. For brochure send SASE, visit website, e-mail, call or fax. Accepts inquiries by SASE, e-mail, fax, phone.

JENNY MCKEAN MOORE COMMUNITY WORKSHOPS

English Department, George Washingtion University, 801 22nd St. NW, Rome Hall, Suite 760, Washington DC 20052. (202) 994-6180. **Fax:** (202) 994-7915. **E-mail:** tvmallon@gwu.edu. **Website:** www.gwu. edu/~english/creative_jennymckeanmoore.html. **Contact:** Thomas Mallon, director of creative writing. Estab. 1976. Workshop held each semester at the university. Average attendance: 15. Concentration varies depending on professor—usually fiction or poetry. The Creative Writing department brings an established poet or novelist to campus each year to teach a writing workshop for GW students and a free community workshop for adults in the larger Washington community. Details posted on website in June, with an application deadline at the end of August or in early September.

ADDITIONAL INFORMATION Admission is competitive and by ms.

MOUNT HERMON CHRISTIAN WRITERS CONFERENCE

PO Box 413, Mount Hermon CA 95041. **E-mail:** info@mounthermon.org. **Website:** mounthermon. org. Estab. 1970. Annual professional conference (always held over the Palm Sunday weekend, Friday noon through Tuesday noon). Average attendance: 450. Sponsored by and held at the 440-acre Mount Hermon Christian Conference Center near San Jose, California in the heart of the coastal redwoods, we are a broad-ranging conference for all areas of Christian writing, including fiction, nonfiction, fantasy, children's, teen, young adult, poetry, magazines, inspirational and devotional writing. This is a working, how-to conference, with Major Morning tracks in all genres (including a track especially for teen writers), and as many as 20 optional workshops each afternoon. Faculty-to-student ratio is about 1 to 6. The bulk of our more than 70 faculty members are editors and publisher representatives from major Christian publishing houses nationwide. Speakers have included T. Davis Bunn, Debbie Macomber, Jerry Jenkins, Bill Butterworth, Dick Foth and others.

COSTS Registration fees include tuition, all major morning sessions, keynote sessions, and refreshment breaks. Room and board varies depending on choice of housing options. Costs vary from $617 to $1565 based on housing rates.

ACCOMMODATIONS Registrants stay in hotel-style accommodations. Meals are buffet style, with faculty joining registrants. See website for cost updates.

ADDITIONAL INFORMATION "The residential nature of our conference makes this a unique setting for one-on-one interaction with faculty/staff. There is also a decided inspirational flavor to the conference, and general sessions with well-known speakers are a highlight. Registrants may submit 2 works for critique in advance of the conference, then have personal interviews with critiquers during the conference. All conference information is online by December 1 of each year. Send inquiries via e-mail. Tapes of past conferences are also available online."

NAPA VALLEY WRITERS' CONFERENCE

Napa Valley College, 1088 College Ave., St. Helena CA 94574. (707)967-2900. **Website:** www.napawritersconference.org. **Contact:** John Leggett and Anne Evans, program directors. Estab. 1981. Established 1981. Annual weeklong event, July 28-August 2. Location:

Upper Valley Campus in the historic town of St. Helena, 25 miles north of Napa in the heart of the valley's wine growing community. Excellent cuisine provided by Napa Valley Cooking School. Average attendance: 48 in poetry and 48 in fiction. "Serious writers of all backgrounds and experience are welcome to apply." Offers poets workshops, lectures, faculty readings, ms critiques, and meetings with editors. "Poetry session provides the opportunity to work both on generating new poems and on revising previously written ones." **COSTS** Total participation fee is $900.

ADDITIONAL INFORMATION The conference is held at the Upper Valley Campus of Napa Valley College, located in the heart of California's Wine Country. During the conference week, attendees' meals are provided by the Napa Valley Cooking School, which offers high quality, intensive training for aspiring chefs. The goal of the program is to provide each student with hands-on, quality, culinary and pastry skills required for a career in a fine-dining establishment. The disciplined and professional learning environment, availability of global externships, low student-teacher ratio and focus on sustainability make the Napa Valley Cooking School unique.

THE NEW LETTERS WEEKEND WRITERS CONFERENCE

University of Missouri-Kansas City, 5101 Rockhill Rd., Kansas City MO 64110-2499. (816)235-1168. **Fax:** (816)235-2611. **E-mail:** newletters@umkc.edu. **Website:** http://cas.umkc.edu/ce/. **Contact:** Robert Stewart, director. Estab. 1970s (as The Longboat Key Writers Conference). Annual conference held in late June. Conference duration: 3 days. Average attendance: 75. The conference brings together talented writers in many genres for seminars, readings, workshops, and individual conferences. The emphasis is on craft and the creative process in poetry, fiction, screenwriting, playwriting, and journalism, but the program also deals with matters of psychology, publications, and marketing. The conference is appropriate for both advanced and beginning writers. The conference meets at the university's beautiful Diastole Conference Center. Two- and 3-credit hour options are available by special permission from the director, Robert Stewart. **COSTS** Participants may choose to attend as a noncredit student or they may attend for 1 hour of college credit from the University of Missouri-Kansas City. Conference registration includes Friday evening reception and keynote speaker, Saturday and Sunday continental breakfast and lunch.

ACCOMMODATIONS Registrants are responsible for their own transportation, but information on area accommodations is available.

ADDITIONAL INFORMATION Those registering for college credit are required to submit a ms in advance. Ms reading and critique are included in the credit fee. Those attending the conference for noncredit also have the option of having their ms critiqued for an additional fee. Brochures are available for a SASE after March. Accepts inquiries by e-mail and fax.

NIMROD ANNUAL WRITERS' WORKSHOP

800 S. Tucker Dr., Tulsa OK 74104. (918)631-3080. **E-mail:** nimrod@utulsa.edu. **Website:** www.utulsa.edu/nimrod. **Contact:** Eilis O'Neal, managing editor. Estab. 1978. Annual conference held in October. Conference duration: 1 day. Offers one-on-one editing sessions, readings, panel discussions, and master classes in fiction, poetry, nonfiction, memoir, and fantasy writing. Speakers have included Myla Goldberg, B.H. Fairchild, Colum McCann, Molly Peacock, Peter S. Beagle, Robert Olen Butler, and Marvin Bell. Full conference details are online in August.

COSTS Approximately $50. Lunch provided. Scholarships available for students.

ADDITIONAL INFORMATION *Nimrod International Journal* sponsors *Nimrod* Literary Awards: The Katherine Anne Porter Prize for fiction and The Pablo Neruda Prize for poetry. Poetry and fiction prizes: $2,000 each and publication (1st prize); $1,000 each and publication (2nd prize). Deadline: must be postmarked no later than April 30.

NORTH CAROLINA WRITERS' NETWORK FALL CONFERENCE

P.O. Box 21591, Winston-Salem NC 27120. (336)293-8844. **E-mail:** mail@ncwriters.org. **Website:** www.ncwriters.org. Estab. 1985. Annual conference held in November in different NC venues. Average attendance: 250. This organization hosts 2 conferences: 1 in the spring and 1 in the fall. Each conference is a weekend full of workshops, panels, book signings, and readings (including open mic). There will be a keynote speaker, a variety of sessions on the craft and business of writing, and opportunities to meet with agents and editors.

COSTS Approximately $250 (includes 4 meals).

ACCOMMODATIONS Special rates are usually available at the Conference Hotel, but conferees must make their own reservations.

ADDITIONAL INFORMATION Available at www.ncwriters.org.

NORWESCON

100 Andover Park W. PMB 150-165, Tukwila WA 98188-2828. (425)243-4692. **Fax:** (520)244-0142. **E-mail:** info@norwescon.org. **Website:** www.norwescon.org. Estab. 1978. Annual conference held on Easter weekend. Average attendance: 2,800. General multi-track convention focusing on science fiction and fantasy literature with wide coverage of other media. Tracks cover science, socio-cultural, literary, publishing, editing, writing, art, and other media of a science fiction/fantasy orientation. Agents will be speaking and available for meetings with attendees.

ACCOMMODATIONS Conference is held at the Doubletree Hotel Seattle Airport.

ADDITIONAL INFORMATION Brochures are available online or for a SASE. Send inquiries via e-mail.

OKLAHOMA WRITERS' FEDERATION, INC. ANNUAL CONFERENCE

3800 Bonaire Place, Edmond OK 73013. **Website:** www.owfi.org. **Contact:** Linda Apple, president. Annual conference. Held first weekend in May each year. Writer workshops geared toward all levels. **Open to students.** "Forty seminars, with 30 speakers consisting of editors, literary agents and many best-selling authors. Topics range widely to include craft, marketing, and all genres of writing." Writing facilities available: book room, autograph party, 2 lunch workshops. "If writers would like to participate in the annual writing contest, they must become members of OWFI. You don't have to be a member to attend the conference." See website for more information.

COSTS $150 before March 15; $175 after March 15; $70 for single days; $25 for lunch workshops. Full tuition includes 2-day conference (all events except lunch workshops) and 2 dinners, plus 110-minute appointment with an attending editor or agent of your choice (must be reserved in advance).

OZARK CREATIVE WRITERS, INC. CONFERENCE

P.O. Box 424, Eureka Springs AR 72632. **E-mail:** ozarkcreativewriters@gmail.com. **Website:** www.ozarkcreativewriters.org. Open to professional and amateur writers, workshops are geared to all levels and all forms of the creative process and literary arts. Sessions sometimes include songwriting, with presentations by best-selling authors, editors, and agents. The OCW Conference promotes writing by offering competition in all genres. The annual event is held on the second full weekend in October at the Inn of the Ozarks, in the resort town of Eureka Springs, Arkansas. Approximately 200 attend each year; many also enter the creative writing competitions.

PACIFIC COAST CHILDREN'S WRITERS WHOLE-NOVEL WORKSHOP

P.O. Box 244, Aptos CA 95001. **Website:** www.childrenswritersworkshop.com. Estab. 2003. "Our seminar ofers semi-advanced through published adult writers an editor and/or agent critique on their full novel or 15-30 page partial. A concurrent workshop is open to students age 14 and up, who give adults target-reader feedback. Focus on craft as a marketing tool. Team-taught master classes (open clinics for manuscript critiques) explore such topics as "Story Architecture and Arcs." Continuous close contact with faculty, who have included Andrea Brown, agent, and Simon Boughton, currently VP/executive editor at 3 Macmillan imprints. Registration limited to 12 adults and 6 teens. For the most critique options, submit sample chapters and synopsis with e-application by mid May; open until filled. **Content:** Character-driven novels with protagonists ages 11 and older. Collegial format; 90 percent hands-on. Our faculty critiques early as well as optional later chapters, plus synopses. Our pre-workshop anthology of peer manuscripts maximizes learning and networking. Several enrollees have landed contracts as a direct result of our seminar. **Details:** visit our website and e-mail us via the contact form."

WILLIAM PATERSON UNIVERSITY SPRING WRITER'S CONFERENCE

English Department, Atrium 232, 300 Pompton Rd., Wayne NJ 07470. (973)720-3067. **Fax:** (973)720-2189. **E-mail:** liut@wpunj.edu. **Website:** wpunj.edu/cohss/departments/english/writers-conference/. Annual conference held each spring (April 13). Conference duration: 1 day. Average attendance: 100-125. Small writing workshops and panels address topics such as writing from life, getting your work in print, poetry, playwriting, fiction, creative nonfiction, and book and magazine editing. Sessions are led by William Paterson faculty members and distinguished guest writers and editors of verse and prose. Speakers have included Francine Prose, David Means, Alison Lurie, Russell Banks, Terese Svoboda, and Anthony Swofford.

COSTS $55 (includes lunch).

PHILADELPHIA WRITERS' CONFERENCE

P.O. Box 7171, Elkins Park PA 19027-0171. (215) 619-7422. **E-mail:** dresente@mc3.edu. **E-mail:** info@pwcwriters.org. **Website:** www.pwcwriters.org. **Contact:** Dana Resente. Estab. 1949. Annual. Conference held June 7-9. Average attendance: 160-200. Conference covers many forms of writing: novel, short story, genre fiction, nonfiction book, magazine writing, blogging, juvenile, poetry.

COSTS Advance registration is $205; walk-in registration is $225. The banquet and buffet are $40 each. Master classes are $50.

ACCOMMODATIONS Holiday Inn, Independence Mall, Fourth and Arch Streets, Philadelphia, PA 19106-2170. "Hotel offers discount for early registration."

ADDITIONAL INFORMATION Sponsors contest. "Length is generally 2,500 words for fiction or nonfiction. 1st Prize, in addition to cash and certificate, gets free tuition for following year." Also offers ms critique. Accepts inquiries by e-mail and SASE. Agents and editors attend conference. Visit us on the web for further agent and speaker details."

PHOTOGRAPHERS' FORMULARY

P.O. Box 950, 7079 Hwy 83 N, Condon MT 59826-0950. (800)922-5255. **Fax:** (406)754-2896. **E-mail:** lynnw@blackfoot.net; formulary@blackfoot.net. **Website:** www.photoformulary.com; www.workshopsinmt.com. **Contact:** Lynn Wilson, workshop program director. Photographers' Formulary workshops include a wide variety of alternative processes, and many focus on the traditional darkroom. Located in Montana's Swan Valley, some of the best wilderness lands in the Rocky Mountains. See website for details on costs and lodging. Open to all skill levels. Workshops held frequently throughout the year. See website for listing of dates and registration.

PIMA WRITERS' WORKSHOP

Pima College, 2202 W. Anklam Rd., Tucson AZ 85709. (520)206-6084. **Fax:** (520)206-6020. **E-mail:** mfiles@pima.edu. **Contact:** Meg Files, director. Writer conference geared toward beginner, intermediate and advanced levels. **Open to students.** The conference features presentations and writing exercises on writing

and publishing stories for children and young adults, among other genres. Annual conference. Workshop held in May. Cost: $100 (can include ms critique). Participants may attend for college credit. Meals and accommodations not included. Features a dozen authors, editors, and agents talking about writing and publishing fiction, nonfiction, poetry, and stories for children. Write for more information.

ROCKY MOUNTAIN FICTION WRITERS COLORADO GOLD

Rocky Mountain Fiction Writers, P.O. Box 735, Confier CO 80433. **E-mail:** conference@rmfw.org. **Website:** www.rmfw.org. Estab. 1982. Annual conference held in September. Conference duration: 3 days. Average attendance: 350. Themes include general novel-length fiction, genre fiction, contemporary romance, mystery, science fiction/fantasy, mainstream, young adult, and historical fiction. Speakers have included Jodi Thomas, Bernard Cornwell, Terry Brooks, Dorothy Cannell, PatriciaGardner Evans, Diane Mott Davidson, Constance O'Day, Connie Willis, Clarissa Pinkola Estes, Michael Palmer, Jennifer Unter, Margaret Marr, Ashley Krass, and Andren Barzvi. Approximately 8 editors and 5 agents attend annually.

COSTS Available online.

ACCOMMODATIONS Special rates will be available at conference hotel.

ADDITIONAL INFORMATION Editor-conducted workshops are limited to 8 participants for critique, with auditing available. Pitch appointments available at no charge. Friday morning master classes available. New as of 2013: Writers' retreat available immediately following conference; space is limited.

RT BOOKLOVERS CONVENTION

55 Bergen St., Brooklyn NY 11201. (718)237-1097 or (800)989-8816, ext. 12. **Fax:** (718)624-2526. **E-mail:** jocarol@rtconvention.com. **E-mail:** nancy@rtbookreviews.com. **Website:** rtconvention.com. Features 125 workshops, agent and editor appointments, a book fair, and more.

COSTS See website for pricing and other information.

ACCOMMODATIONS Rooms available at a nearby Sheaton and Westin. Check online to reserve a room.

☘ SAGE HILL WRITING EXPERIENCE

Box 1731, Saskatoon SK S7K 3S1 Canada. (306)652-7395. **E-mail:** sage.hill@sasktel.net. **Website:** sagehillwriting.ca. **Contact:** Philip Adams, Executive Director. Annual workshops held in late July/August and May. Conference duration: 10-14 days. Average attendance: 40/summer program; 8/spring program. Sage Hill Writing Experience offers a special working and learning opportunity to writers at different stages of development. Top-quality instruction, low instructor-student ratio, and the beautiful Sage Hill setting offer conditions ideal for the pursuit of excellence in the arts of fiction, poetry and playwriting. The Sage Hill location features individual accommodations, in-room writing areas, lounges, meeting rooms, healthy meals, walking woods, and vistas in several directions. Classes being held (may vary from year to year) include: Introduction to Writing Fiction & Poetry, Fiction Workshop, Writing Young Adult Fiction Workshop, Poetry Workshop, Poetry Colloquium, Fiction Colloquium, Novel Colloquium, Playwriting Lab, Fall Poetry Colloquium, and Spring Poetry Colloquium. Speakers have included Nicole Brossard, Steven Galloway, Robert Currie, Jeanette Lynes, Karen Solie and Colleen Murphy.

COSTS Summer program: $1,295 (includes instruction, accommodation, meals). Fall Poetry Colloquium: $1,495. Scholarships and bursaries are available.

ACCOMMODATIONS Located at Lumsden, 45 kilometers outside Regina.

ADDITIONAL INFORMATION For Introduction to Creative Writing, send a 5-page sample of your writing or a statement of your interest in creative writing and a list of courses taken. For workshop and colloquium programs, send a résumé of your writing career and a 12-page sample of your work, plus 5 pages of published work. Guidelines are available for SASE. Inquire via e-mail or fax.

SAN DIEGO STATE UNIVERSITY WRITERS' CONFERENCE

SDSU College of Extended Studies, 5250 Campanile Dr., San Diego State University, San Diego CA 92182-1920. (619)594-2517. **Fax:** (619)594-8566. **E-mail:** sdsuwritersconference@mail.sdsu.edu. **Website:** ces.sdsu.edu/writers. Estab. 1984. Annual conference held in January/February. Conference duration: 2 days. Average attendance: 375. Covers fiction, nonfiction, scriptwriting and e-books. Held at the Doubletree Hotel in Mission Valley. Each year the conference offers a variety of workshops for the beginner and advanced writers. This conference allows the individual writer to choose which workshop best suits his/her needs. In addition to the workshops, editor reading appointments and agent/editor consultation appointments are provided so attendees may meet with editors and agents one-on-one to discuss specific questions. A reception is offered Saturday immediately following the workshops, offering attendees the opportunity to socialize with the faculty in a relaxed atmosphere. Last year, approximately 60 faculty members attended.

COSTS Approximately $365-485

ACCOMMODATIONS Attendees must make their own travel arrangements.

SAN FRANCISCO WRITERS CONFERENCE

1029 Jones St., San Francisco CA 94109. (415)673-0939. **Fax:** (415)673-0367. **E-mail:** Barabara@sfwriters.org. **Website:** sfwriters.org. **Contact:** Barbara Santos, marketing director. Estab. 2003. "Annual conference held President's Day weekend in February. Average attendance: 400+. Top authors, respected literary agents, and major publishing houses are at the event so attendees can make face-to-face contact with all the right people. Writers of nonfiction, fiction, poetry, and specialty writing (children's books, cookbooks, travel, etc.) will all benefit from the event. There are important sessions on marketing, self-publishing, technology, and trends in the publishing industry. Plus, there's an optional 4-hour session called Speed Dating for Agents where attendees can meet with 20+ agents. Speakers have included Jennifer Crusie, Richard Paul Evans, Jamie Raab, Mary Roach, Jane Smiley, Debbie Macomber, Firoozeh Dumas, Zilpha Keatley Snyder, Steve Berry, Jacquelyn Mitchard. More than 20 agents and editors participate each year, many of whom will be available for meetings with attendees."

COSTS Early price (until September) is $575. Check the website for pricing on later dates.

ACCOMMODATIONS The Intercontinental Mark Hopkins Hotel is a historic landmark at the top of Nob Hill in San Francisco. The hotel is located so that everyone arriving at the Oakland or San Francisco airport can take BART to either the Embarcadero or Powell Street exits, then walk or take a cable car or taxi directly to the hotel.

ADDITIONAL INFORMATION "Present yourself in a professional manner and the contact you will make will be invaluable to your writing career. Brochures and registration are online."

SAN FRANCISCO WRITING FOR CHANGE CONFERENCE

1029 Jones St., San Francisco CA 94109. (415)673-0939. **E-mail:** Barbara@sfwriters.org. **Website:** SFWriting forChange.org. **Contact:** Barbara Santos, marketing director; MIchael Larsen, director. Estab. 2004. Biannual conference held in early fall 2014 at a location to be announced. Average attendance: 200.

COSTS TBA; early discounts available. Includes over 20 workshops, keynote address, editor, and agent consultations.

ACCOMMODATIONS Check website for event details, accommodations, directions, and parking.

ADDITIONAL INFORMATION "The limited number of attendees (150) and excellent presenter-to-attendee ratio make this a highly effective and productive conference. The presenters are major names in the publishing business, but take personal interest in the projects discovered at this event each year." Guidelines available on website, e-mail, and fax.

⊕ SANGRIA SUMMIT: A MILITARY WRITERS' CONFERENCE

23376 E. Fifth Place, Unit 204, Aurora CO 80018. (772)418-2380. **E-mail:** isaac@cubillos.com. **Website:** www.sangriasummit.com. **Contact:** Isaac Cubillos, director. Estab. 2012. Annual conference held for two days in September. "Drawing from successful writers in the military genre, the conference will connect established writers with aspiring writers seeking to develop their craft in this niche market. The format will consist of an intensive workshop led by established writers of fiction and nonfiction books—historical, biographical, memoirs, current affairs. Beyond the workshop there will be panel discussions on writing, self-publishing, traditional publishing, selling your book and author readings."

COSTS $195 before Aug. 12, 2012; $250 afterward. $35 for editor/agent critique. Special dinners with authors $25. Cost includes: workshop, author panels, all program material, special books, two lunches.

ACCOMMODATIONS "The conference will be in meeting rooms at the Denver Marriott City Place."

SANTA BARBARA WRITERS CONFERENCE

27 W. Anapamu St., Suite 305, Santa Barbara CA 93101. (805)568-1516. **E-mail:** info@sbwriters.com. **Website:** www.sbwriters.com. Estab. 1972. Annual conference held June 8-13. Average attendance: 200.

Covers fiction, nonfiction, journalism, memoir, poetry, playwriting, screenwriting, travel writing, young adult, children's literature, humor, and marketing. Speakers have included Ray Bradbury, William Styron, Eudora Welty, James Michener, Sue Grafton, Charles M. Schulz, Clive Cussler, Fannie Flagg, Elmore Leonard, and T.C. Boyle. Agents will appear on a panel; in addition, there will be an agents and editors day that allows writers to pitch their projects in one-on-one meetings.

COSTS Conference registration is $550 on or before March 16 and $625 after March 16.

ACCOMMODATIONS Hyatt Santa Barbara.

ADDITIONAL INFORMATION Register online or contact for brochure and registration forms.

☾ SASKATCHEWAN FESTIVAL OF WORDS

217 Main St. N., Moose Jaw SK S6J 0W1 Canada. **Website:** www.festivalofwords.com. Estab. 1997. Annual 4-day event, third week of July (2013 dates: July 18-21). Location: Moose Jaw Library/Art Museum complex in Crescent Park. Average attendance: about 4,000 admissions. "Canadian authors up close and personal for readers and writers of all ages inmystery, poetry, memoir, fantasy, graphic novels, history, and novel. Each summer festival includes 60 events within 2 blocks of historic Main Street. Audience favorite activities include workshops for writers, audience readings, drama,performance poetry, concerts, panels, and music."

ACCOMMODATIONS Information available at www.templegardens.sk.ca, campgrounds, and bed and breakfast establishments. Complete information about festival presenters, events, costs, and schedule also available on website.

☾ SASKATCHEWAN FESTIVAL OF WORDS AND WORKSHOPS

217 Main St. N., Moose Jaw SK S6H 0W1 Canada. **E-mail:** word.festival@sasktel.net. **Website:** www.festivalofwords.com. **Contact:** Donna Lee Howes. Writer workshops geared toward beginner and intermediate levels. **Open to students.** Readings that include a wide spectrum of genres—fiction, creative nonfiction, poetry, songwriting, screenwriting, playwriting, dramatic reading with actors, graphic novels, Great Big Book Club Discussion with author, children's writing, panels, independent film screening, panels, slam poetry, interviews and performances. Annual festival.

Workshop held third weekend in July. Cost of workshop varies from $10 for a single reading to $200 for a full pass. Trivia Night Fun ticket is extra. Visit website for more information.

SCBWI—NEW JERSEY; ANNUAL SUMMER CONFERENCE

SCBWI-New Jersey: Society of Children's Book Writers & Illustrators, New Jersey NJ **Website:** www.newjerseyscbwi.com. **Contact:** Kathy Temean, regional advisor. This weekend conference is held in the beginning of June in Princeton, NJ. Multiple one-on-one critiques; "how to" workshops for every level, first page sessions, agent pitches and interaction with the faculty of editors, agents, art director and authors are some of the highlights of the weekend. On Friday attendees can sign up for writing intensives or register for illustrators' day with the art directors. Published authors attending the conference can sign up to participate in the bookfair to sell and autograph their books; illustrators have the opportunity to display their artwork. Attendees have the option to participate in group critiques after dinner on Saturday evening and attend a mix and mingle with the faculty on Friday night. Meals are included with the cost of admission. Conference is known for its high ratio of faculty to attendees and interaction opportunities.

SCBWI—VENTURA/SANTA BARBARA; FALL CONFERENCE

Simi Valley CA 93094-1389. **E-mail:** alexisinca@aol.com. **Website:** www.scbwicencal.org. **Contact:** Alexis O'Neill, regional advisor. Estab. 1971. Writers' conference geared toward all levels. Speakers include editors, authors, illustrators and agents. Fiction and nonfiction picture books, middle grade and YA novels, and magazine submissions addressed. Annual writing contest in all genres plus illustration display. Conference held October 26, 2013 at California Lutheran University in Thousand Oaks, California in cooperation with the CLU Graduate School of Education. For fees and other information, e-mail or visit website.

SCBWI WINTER CONFERENCE ON WRITING AND ILLUSTRATING FOR CHILDREN

8271 Beverly Blvd., Los Angeles CA 90048. (323)782-1010. **Fax:** (323)782-1892. **E-mail:** scbwi@scbwi.org. **Website:** www.scbwi.org. **Contact:** Stephen Mooser. Estab. 2000. (formerly SCBWI Midyear Conference), Society of Children's book Writers and Illustrators.

Annual. Conference held in February. Average attendance: 1,000. Conference is to promote writing and illustrating for children: picture books; fiction; nonfiction; middle grade and young adult; network with professionals; financial planning for writers; marketing your book; art exhibition; etc. Site: Manhattan.
COSTS See website for current cost and conference information.
ADDITIONAL INFORMATION SCBWI also holds an annual summer conference in August in Los Angeles. See the listing in the West section or visit website for details.

SCHOOL OF THE ARTS AT RHINELANDER UW-MADISON CONTINUING STUDIES

21 N Park St., 7th Floor, Madison WI 53715-1218. (608)262-7389. **E-mail:** lkaufman@dcs.wisc.edu. **Website:** continuingstudies.wisc.edu/lsa/soa/. Estab. 1964. "Each summer for nearly 50 years, more than 250 people have gathered in northern Wisconsin for a week of study, performance, exhibits, and other creative activities. More than 50 workshops in writing, body/mind/spirit; food and fitness; art and folk art; music; and digital media are offered. Participants can choose from any and all 1-, 2-, and 5-day classes to craft their own mix for creative exploration and renewal." Dates: July 20-24. Location: James Williams Middle School and Rhineland High School, Rhinelander, WI. Average attendance: 250.
COSTS Ranges from $20-$300 based on workshops.
ACCOMMODATIONS Informational available from Rhinelander Chamber of Commerce.

SCIENCE FICTION WRITERS WORKSHOP

English Department/University of Kansas, Wesoce Hall, 1445 Jayhawk Blvd., Room 3001, Lawrence KS 66045-7590. (785)864-2508. **E-mail:** cmckit@ku.edu. **Website:** www.sfcenter.ku.edu/SFworkshop.htm. Estab. 1985. Annual. Workshop held June 2-14. The workshop is "small, informal, and aimed at writers on the edge of publication or regular publication." For writing and marketing science fiction and fantasy. Site: Workshop sessions operate informally in a university housing lounge on the University of Kansas campus where most participants also reside. Established in 1985 by James Gunn and currently led by Christopher McKitterick, with guest authors joining for the second week. Writer and editor instructors have included Lou Anders, Bradley Denton, James Gunn, Kij Johnson, John Ordover, Frederik Pohl,

Pamela Sargent, and George Zebrowski, and each year the winners of the Campbell and Sturgeon Memorial Awards participate in 1 or more days of the workshop. A novel workshop in science fiction and fantasy is also available at the same time, led by Kij Johnson.

COSTS $500, exclusive of meals and housing.

ACCOMMODATIONS Housing information is available. Several airport shuttle services offer reasonable transportation from the Kansas City International Airport to Lawrence.

ADDITIONAL INFORMATION Admission to the workshop is bysubmission of an acceptable story, usually by May. Two additional stories are submitted by the middle of June. These 3 stories are distributed to other participants for critiquing and are the basis for the first week of the workshop. One story is rewritten for the second week, when students also work with guest authors. See website for guidelines. This workshop is intended for writers who have just started to sell their work or need that extra bit of understanding or skill to become a published writer.

SEWANEE WRITERS' CONFERENCE

735 University Ave., 119 Gailor Hall, Stamler Center, Sewanee TN 37383-1000. (931) 598-1654. **E-mail:** al latham@sewanee.edu. **Website:** www.sewaneewriters.org. **Contact:** Adam Latham. Estab. 1990. Annual conference held in the date range of July 23–August 4. Average attendance: 144. "We offer genre-based workshops in fiction, poetry, and playwriting. The conference uses the facilities of Sewanee: The University of the South. The university is a collection of ivy-covered Gothic-style buildings located on the Cumberland Plateau in mid-Tennessee. Editors, publishers, and agents structure their own presentations, but there is always opportunity for questions from the audience." A score of writing professionals will visit. The Conference will offer its customary Walter E. Dakin Fellowships and Tennessee Williams Scholarships as well as awards in memory of Stanley Elkin, Donald Justice, Howard Nemerov, Father William Ralston, Peter Taylor, Mona Van Duyn, and John N. Wall. Additional scholarships have been made possible by Georges and Anne Borchardt and Gail Hochman. Each participant—whether contributor, scholar, or fellow—receives financial support.

COSTS $1,000 for tuition and $700 for room, board, and activity costs

ACCOMMODATIONS Participants are housed in single rooms in university dormitories. Bathrooms are shared by small groups. Motel or B&B housing is available, but not abundantly so.

SILKEN SANDS CONFERENCE

Gulf Coast Chapter RWA, P.O. Box 1815, Ocean Springs MS 39566. (228)875-3864. **E-mail:** info@gccrwa.com. **E-mail:** kelly@authorkellylstone.com. **Website:** www.gccrwa.com. **Contact:** Kelly Stone, president. Estab. 1995. Bi-annual conference. Next one will be held in 2014. Average attendance: 100. Focuses on romance, fiction including paranormal, inspirational, romantic suspense, category.

COSTS To be announced.

ADDITIONAL INFORMATION Brochures available for SASE, e-mail, phone or on website. Accepts inquiries by e-mail. Agents and editors participate in conference. The conference is noted for its relaxed, enjoyable atmosphere where participants can immerse themselves in the total writing experience from the moment they arrive.

SITKA CENTER FOR ART AND ECOLOGY

56605 Sitka Dr., Otis OR 97368. (541)994-5485. **Fax:** (541)994-8024. **E-mail:** info@sitkacenter.org. **Website:** www.sitkacenter.org. **Contact:** Caroline Brooks, program manager. Estab. 1970. Workshop program is open to all levels and is held annually from late May until early October. There is also a residency program October-May. Average attendance: 10-14/workshop. A variety of workshops in the creative process, including book arts and other media. Site: The Center borders a Nature Conservancy Preserve, the Siuslaw National Experimental Forest and the Salmon River Estuary, located just north of Lincoln City, OR.

COSTS Workshops are generally $65-500; they do not include meals or lodging.

ACCOMMODATIONS Does not offer overnight accommodations. Provides a list of area hotels or lodging options.

ADDITIONAL INFORMATION Brochure available in February of each year; request a copy by e-mail or phone, or visit website for listing. Accepts inquiries in-person or by e-mail, phone, fax.

SOCIETY OF CHILDREN'S BOOK WRITERS & ILLUSTRATORS ANNUAL SUMMER CONFERENCE ON WRITING AND ILLUSTRATING FOR CHILDREN

8271 Beverly Blvd., Los Angeles CA 90048-4515. (323)782-1010. **Fax:** (323)782-1892. **E-mail:** scbwi@ scbwi.org. **Website:** www.scbwi.org. Estab. 1972. Annual conference held in early August. Conference duration: 4 days. Average attendance: 1,000. Held at the Century Plaza Hotel in Los Angeles. Speakers have included Andrea Brown, Steven Malk, Ashley Bryan, Bruce Coville, Karen Hesse, Harry Mazer, Lucia Monfried, and Russell Freedman. Agents will be speaking and sometimes participate in ms critiques.

COSTS Approximately $450 (does not include hotel room).

ACCOMMODATIONS Information on overnight accommodations is made available.

ADDITIONAL INFORMATION Ms and illustration critiques are available. Brochure/guidelines are available in June online or for SASE.

SOUTH COAST WRITERS CONFERENCE

Southwestern Oregon Community College, P.O. Box 590, 29392 Ellensburg Ave., Gold Beach OR 97444. (541)247-2741. **Fax:** (541)247-6247. **E-mail:** scwc@ socc.edu. **Website:** www.socc.edu/scwriters. Estab. 1996. Annual conference held Presidents Day weekend in February. Conference duration: 2 days. Covers fiction, poetry, children's, nature, songwriting, and marketing. William Sullivan is the next scheduled keynote speaker, and presenters include Linda Barnes, Merritt "Biff" Barnes, Judy Cox, Bruce Holbert, Elizabeth Lyon, Carolyn J. Rose, Johnny Shaw, Lauren Sheehan, William Sullivan, and Bob Welch.

ADDITIONAL INFORMATION See website for cost and additional details.

STEAMBOAT SPRINGS WRITERS CONFERENCE

Steamboat Springs Arts Council, Eleanor Bliss Center for the Arts at the Depot, 1001 13th St., Steamboat Springs CO 80487. (970)879-9008. **Fax:** (970)879-8138. **E-mail:** info@steamboatwriters.com. **Website:** www. steamboatwriters.com. **Contact:** Susan de Wardt. Estab. 1982. Annual conference held in mid-July. Conference duration: 1 day. Average attendance: approximately 35. Attendance is limited. Featured areas of instruction change each year. Held at the restored train Depot. Speakers have included Carl Brandt, Jim Fer-

gus, Avi, Robert Greer, Renate Wood, Connie Willis, Margaret Coel, and Kent Nelson.

COSTS Tuition: $50 early registration, $65 after May 4.

STEAMBOAT SPRINGS WRITERS GROUP

P.O. Box 774284, Steamboat Springs CO 80477. (970)879-8079. **E-mail:** susan@steamboatwriters. com. **Website:** www.steamboatwriters.com. **Contact:** Susan de Wardt, director. Estab. 1982. Group meets year-round on Thursdays, 12-2 p.m. at Arts Depot; guests welcome. Annual conference held in July. Conference duration: 1 day. Average attendance: 35. "Our conference emphasizes instruction within the seminar format. Novices and polished professionals benefit from the individual attention and camaraderie which can be established within small groups. A pleasurable and memorable learning experience is guaranteed by the relaxed and friendly atmosphere of the old train depot. Registration is limited." Site: Restored train depot.

COSTS $50 before May 25, $60 after. Fee covers all seminars and luncheon.

ACCOMMODATIONS Lodging available at Steamboat Resorts.

ADDITIONAL INFORMATION Optional dinner and activities during evening preceding conference. Accepts inquiries by e-mail, phone, mail.

STONY BROOK SOUTHAMPTON SCREENWRITING CONFERENCE

Stony Brook Southampton, 239 Montauk Highway, Southampton NY 11968. (631)632-5030. **Fax:** (631)632-2576. **E-mail:** southamptonwriters@notes. cc.sunysb.edu. **E-mail:** Carla.Caglioti@stonybrook. edu. **Website:** www.stonybrook.edu/southampton. **Contact:** Carla Caglioti. "The Southampton Screenwriting Conference welcomes new and advanced screenwriters, as well as all writers interested in using the language of film to tell a story. The five-day residential Conference will inform, inspire, challenge, and further participants understanding of the art of the screenplay and the individual writing process. Our unique program of workshops, seminars, panel presentations, and screenings will encourage and motivate attendees under the professional guidance of accomplished screenwriters, educators, and script analysts." Held in two sessions from July 10-28.

COSTS Residential $1495, Non-Residential $1300.

ADDITIONAL INFORMATION Space is limited.

⊕ STORY WEAVERS CONFERENCE

Oklahoma Writer's Federation, (405)682-6000. E-mail: president@owfi.org. **Website:** www.OWFI.org. **Contact:** Linda Apple, president. Oklahoma Writer's Federation, Inc. is open and welcoming to writers of all genres and all skill levels. Our goal is to help writers become better and to help beginning writers understand and master the craft of writing.

COSTS Cost is $150 before April. $175 after April. Cost includes awards banquet and famous author banquet. Three extra sessions are available for an extra fee: How to Self-Publish Your Novel on Kindle, Nook, and iPad (and make more money than being published by New York), with Dan Case; When Polar Bear Wishes Came True: Understanding and Creating Meaningful Stories, with Jack Dalton; How to Create Three-Dimensional Characters, with Steven James.

ACCOMMODATIONS The site is at the Embassy Suite using their meeting halls. There are very few stairs and the rooms are close together for easy access.

ADDITIONAL INFORMATION "We have 20 speakers, five agents, and nine publisher/editors for a full list and bios, please see website."

◯ SUNSHINE COAST FESTIVAL OF THE WRITTEN ARTS

5511 Shorncliffe Ave., Rockwood Centre, Box 2299, Sechelt BC V0N 3A0 Canada. (604)885-9631 or (800)565-9631. **Fax:** (604)885-3967. **E-mail:** info@writersfestival.ca. **E-mail:** jane@writersfestival.ca. **Website:** www.writersfestival.ca. Estab. 1983. Annual festival held August 15-18. Average attendance: 3,500. The festival does not have a theme. Instead, it showcases 25 or more Canadian writers in a variety of genres each year. Held at the Rockwood Centre. Speakers have included Jane Urquhart, Sholagh Rogers, David Watmough, Zsuzsi Gartner, Gail Bowen, Charlotte Gray, Bill Richardson, P.K. Page, Richard B. Wright, Madeleine Thien, Ronald Wright, Michael Kusugak, and Bob McDonald.

COSTS Check online for prices—tickets go on sale in late May.

ACCOMMODATIONS A list of hotels is available.

ADDITIONAL INFORMATION The festival runs contests during the event. Prizes are books donated by publishers. Brochures/guidelines are available. Visit the website for current updates and details.

◯ SURREY INTERNATIONAL WRITERS' CONFERENCE

SIWC, P.O. Box 42023 RPO Guildford, Surrey BC V3R 1S5 Canada. **E-mail:** kathychung@siwc.ca. **Website:** www.siwc.ca. **Contact:** Kathy Chung, conference coordinator. Writing workshops geared toward beginner, intermediate, and advanced levels. More than 70 workshops and panels, on all topics and genres. Blue Pencil and Agent/Editor Pitch sessions included. Annual Conference held every October. Different conference price packages available. Check our website for more information.

TAOS SUMMER WRITERS' CONFERENCE

Department of English Language and Literature, MSC 03 2170, 1 University of New Mexico, Albuquerque NM 87131-0001. (505)277-5572. **Fax:** (505)277-2950. **E-mail:** taosconf@unm.edu. **Website:** www.unm.edu/~taosconf. **Contact:** Sharon Oard Warner. Estab. 1999. Annual conference held July 14-21. Offers workshops in novel writing, short story writing, screenwriting, poetry, creative nonfiction, travel writing, historical fiction, memoir, and revision. Participants may also schedule a consultation with a visiting agent/editor.

COSTS Weeklong workshop registrations are $650

ACCOMMODATIONS Held at the Sagebrush Inn and Conference Center.

◯ THE SCHOOL FOR WRITERS SUMMER WORKSHOP

The Humber School for Writers, Humber Institute of Technology & Advanced Learning, 3199 Lake Shore Blvd. W., Toronto ON M8V 1K8 Canada. (416)675-6622. **E-mail:** antanas.sileika@humber.ca; hilary.higgins@humber.ca. **Website:** www.creativeandperformingarts.humber.ca/content/writers.html. The School for Writers Summer Workshop has moved to the fall with the International Festival of Authors. Workshop the last week in October through first week in November. Conference duration: 1 week. Average attendance: 100. New writers from around the world gather to study with faculty members to work on their novels, short stories, poetry, or creative nonfiction. Agents and editors participate in conference. Include a work-in-progress with your registration. Faculty has included Martin Amis, David Mitchell, Rachel Kuschner, Peter Carey, Roddy Doyle, Tim O'Brien, Andrea Levy, Barry Unsworth, Edward Albee, Ha Jin, Julia Glass, Mavis Gallant, Bruce Jay Friedman,

Isabel Huggan, Alistair MacLeod, Lisa Moore, Kim Moritsugu, Francine Prose, Paul Quarrington, Olive Senior, and D.M. Thomas, Annabel Lyon, Mary Gaitskill, M. G. Vassanji.

COSTS around $800 (in 2013). Some limited scholarships are available.

ACCOMMODATIONS Nearby hotels are available.

ADDITIONAL INFORMATION Accepts inquiries by e-mail, phone, and fax.

THRILLERFEST

P.O. Box 311, Eureka CA 95502. **E-mail:** infocentral@thrillerwriters.org. **Website:** www.thrillerfest.com. **Contact:** Kimberley Howe, executive director. Grand Hyatt New York, 109 E. 42nd St., New York, NY 10017. Estab. 2006. Annual. July 10-13 in Manhattan. Conference duration: 4 days. Average attendance: 900. Workshop/conference/festival. "A great place to learn the craft of writing the thriller. Classes taught by NYT best-selling authors. A fabulous event for fans/readers to meet and spend a few days with their favorite authors and packed with terrific programming." Speakers have included David Morrell, James Patterson, Sandra Brown, Ken Follett, Eric Van Lustbader, David Baldacci, Brad Meltzer, Steve Martini, R.L. Stine, Steve Berry, Kathleen Antrim, Douglas Preston, Gayle Lynds, Harlan Coben, Lee Child, Lisa Scottolini, Katherine Neville, Robin Cook, Andrew Gross, Kathy Reichs, Brad Thor, Clive Cussler, Donald Maass, MJ Rose, and Al Zuckerman. Two days of the conference are CraftFest, where the focus is on the craft of writing, and 2 days are ThrillerFest, which showcase the author-fan relationship. Also featured: AgentFest—a unique event where authors can pitch their work face-to-face to 50 top literary agents, and the International Thriller Awards and Banquet.

COSTS Price will vary from $300-1,100, depending on which events are selected. Various package deals are available offering savings, and Early Bird pricing is offered beginning August of each year.

ACCOMMODATIONS Grand Hyatt in New York City.

TMCC (RENO) WRITERS' CONFERENCE

Truckee Meadows Community College, 5270 Neil Rd., Reno NV 89502. (775)829-9010. **Fax:** (775)829-9032. **E-mail:** wdce@tmcc.edu. **Website:** wdce.tmcc.edu. Estab. 1991. Annual conference held April 27. Average attendance: 150. Conference focuses on strengthening mainstream/literary fiction and nonfiction

works and how to market them to agents and publishers. Site: Truckee Meadows Community College in Reno, Nevada. "There is always an array of speakers and presenters with impressive literary credentials, including agents and editors." Speakers have included Chuck Sambuchino, Sheree Bykofsky, Andrea Brown, Dorothy Allison, Karen Joy Fowler, James D. Houston, James N. Frey, Gary Short, Jane Hirschfield, Dorrianne Laux, and Kim Addonizio

COSTS $119 for a full-day seminar; $32 for a 10-minute one-on-one appointment with an agent or editor.

ACCOMMODATIONS The Silver Legacy, in downtown Reno, offers a special rate and shuttle service to the Reno/Tahoe International Airport, which is less than 20 minutes away.

ADDITIONAL INFORMATION "The conference is open to all writers, regardless of their level of experience. Brochures are available online and mailed in January. Send inquiries via e-mail."

TONY HILLERMAN WRITER'S CONFERENCE

1063 Willow Way, Santa FE NM 87505. (505)471-1565. **E-mail:** wordharvest@wordharvest.com. **Website:** www.wordharvest.com. **Contact:** Jean Schaumberg, co-director. Estab. 2004. Annual. November 7-9, 2013. Conference duration: 3 days. Average attendance: 100. Site: Hilton Santa Fe Historic Plaza. First day: Author/teacher Margaret Coel, focuses on the art of writing to create great characters. Other programs focus on creating memorable plots and the business of writing. "We'll honor the winner of the $10,000 Tony Hillerman Prize for best first mystery at a lunch with keynote speaker Craig Johnson, a *New York Times* bestselling author. A 'flash critique' session, open to any interested attendee, will add to the fun and information. Author attendees will also have a chance to talk about their new books at teh new Book/New Author Breakfast."

COSTS Previous year's costs: $395 per-registration.

ACCOMMODATIONS Hilton Santa Fe Historic Plaza offers $119 single or double occupancy. November 6-10. Book online with the hotel.

ADDITIONAL INFORMATION Sponsors a $10,000 first mystery novel contest with St. Marttin's Press. Brochures available in July for SASE, by phone, e-mail, and on website. Accepts inquiries by SASE, phone, e-mail. Deadline for the Hillerman Mystery Competition is June 1.

UCLA EXTENSION WRITERS' PROGRAM

10995 Le Conte Ave., #440, Los Angeles CA 90024. (310)825-9415 or (800)388-UCLA. **Fax:** (310)206-7382. **E-mail:** writers@uclaextension.edu. **Website:** www. uclaextension.org/writers. Estab. 1891. "As America's largest and most comprehensive continuing education creative writing and screenwriting program, the UCLA Extension Writers' Program welcomes and trains writers at all levels of development whose aspirations range from personal enrichment to professional publication and production. Taught by an instructor corps of 250 professional writers, the Writers' Program curriculum features 530 annual open-enrollment courses onsite and online in novel writing, short fiction, personal essay, memoir, poetry, playwriting, writing for the youth market, publishing, feature film writing, and television writing, and is designed to accommodate your individual writing needs, ambitions, and lifestyle. Special programs and services include certificate programs in creative writing, feature film writing, and television writing; a four-day Writers Studio which attracts a national and international audience; nine-month master classes in novel writing and feature film writing; an online screenwriting mentorship program; one-on-one script and manuscript consultation services; literary and screenplay competitions; advisors who help you determine how best to achieve your personal writing goals; and free annual public events such as Writers Faire and Publication Party which allow you to extend your writing education and network with the literary and entertainment communities."

COSTS Depends on length of the course.

ACCOMMODATIONS Students make their own arrangements. Out-of-town students are encouraged to take online courses.

ADDITIONAL INFORMATION Some advanced-level classes have ms submittal requirements; see the UCLA Extension catalog or see website.

UMKC WRITERS WORKSHOPS

5300 Rockhill Rd., Kansas City MO 64110. (816)235-2736. **Fax:** (816)235-5279. **E-mail:** wittfeldk@umkc. edu. **Website:** www.newletters.org/writingConferences.asp. **Contact:** Kathi Wittfeld. Mark Twain Workshop will not be held in 2013. New Letters Weekend Writing Conference was held on Friday, Saturday and Sunday, June 28-30, 2013 at Diastole. New Letters Writer's Conference and Mark Twain Writer's Work-

shop are geared toward intermediate, advanced and professional levels. Workshops open to students and community. Annual workshops. Workshops held in Summer. Cost of workshop varies. Write for more information.

UNIVERSITY OF NORTH DAKOTA WRITERS CONFERENCE

Department of English, 110 Merrifield Hall, 276 Centennial Drive, Stop 7209, Grand Forks ND 58202. (701)777-3321. **E-mail:** writersconference@und.nodak.edu. **Website:** www.undwritersconference.org. Estab. 1970. Annual conference held March 19-23. Offers panels, readings, and films focused around a specific theme. Almost all events take place in the UND Memorial Union, which has a variety of small rooms and a 1,000-seat main hall. Past speakers include Art Spiegelman, Truman Capote, Sir Salman Rushdie, Allen Ginsberg, Alice Walker, and Louise Erdrich.

COSTS All events are free and open to the public. Donations accepted.

ACCOMMODATIONS All events are free and open to the public. Accommodations available at area hotels. Information on overnight accommodations available on website.

ADDITIONAL INFORMATION Schedule and other information available on website.

UNIVERSITY OF NORTH FLORIDA WRITERS CONFERENCE

12000 Alumni Dr., Jacksonville FL 32224-2678. (904)620-4200. **E-mail:** sharon.y.cobb@unf.edu. **Website:** www.unfwritersconference.com. **Contact:** Sharon Y. Cobb, conference director. Estab. 2009.

COSTS See website for current registration fees. Full conference attendees receive: workshops, critiques by faculty and fellow students, lunches, Friday wine/cheese reception, and book signings.

ACCOMMODATIONS Nearby accommodations are listed on website. There is free parking provided at the University Center.

☼ THE VANCOUVER INTERNATIONAL WRITERS & READERS FESTIVAL

202-1398 Cartwright St., Vancouver BC V6H 3R8 Canada. (604)681-6330. **Fax:** (604)681-8400. **E-mail:** info@writersfest.bc.ca. **E-mail:** hwake@writersfest. bc.ca. **Website:** www.writersfest.bc.ca. Estab. 1988. Annual festival held October 22-27. Average attendance: 11,000. The program of events is diverse and includes readings, panel discussions, and seminars.

There are lots of opportunities to interact with the writers who attend. Held on Granville Island in the heart of Vancouver. Speakers have included Margaret Atwood, Maeve Binchy, and J.K. Rowling.

ACCOMMODATIONS Local tourist information can be provided upon request.

ADDITIONAL INFORMATION Remember—this is a festival and a celebration, not a conference or workshop. Brochures are available after August for a SASE. Inquire via e-mail or fax, or go online for updates.

VERMONT COLLEGE OF FINE ARTS POSTGRADUATE WRITERS' CONFERENCE

36 College St., Montpelier VT 05602. (802)828-8835. **Fax:** (802)828-8649. **E-mail:** pgconference@vcfa.edu. **Website:** www.vcfa.edu/writing/pwc. Estab. 1996. Annual conference for writers with MFAs or equivalent preparation on the historic campus of Vermont College of Fine Arts. August 12-18. Features intensive small-group workshops taught by an award-winning faculty, plus readings, craft talks, writing exercise sessions and individual consultations. Conference size: 70 participants. Workshops in creative nonfiction, novel, short story, poetry, poetry manuscript and writing for young people.

COSTS Costs: $875 or $995 (Poetry Ms.)/tuition, $330/private room, $180/shared room, $185/meals. Limited scholarships are available.

ACCOMMODATIONS Single or double rooms are available in the VCFA campus dormitories.

VERMONT STUDIO CENTER

P.O. Box 613, 80 Pearl Street, Johnson VT 05656. (802)635-2727. **Fax:** (802)635-2730. **E-mail:** info@vermontstudiocenter.org. **Website:** www.vermontstudiocenter.org. **Contact:** Gary Clark, Writing Program Director. Estab. 1984. Founded by artists in 1984, the Vermont Studio Center is the largest international artists' and writers' Residency Program in the United States, hosting 50 visual artists and writers each month from across the country and around the world. The Studio Center provides 4-12 week studio residencies on an historic 30-building campus along the Gihon River in Johnson, Vermont, a village in the heart of the northern Green Mountains.

ACCOMMODATIONS "The cost of a 4-week residency is $3,750. Generous fellowship and grant assistance available. "Accommodations available on site. "Residents live in single rooms in ten modest, comfortable houses adjacent to the Red Mill Building. Rooms are simply furnished and have shared baths. Complete linen service is provided. The Studio Center is unable to accommodate guests at meals, overnight guests, spouses, children or pets."

ADDITIONAL INFORMATION Fellowships application deadlines are February 15, June 15 and October 1. Writers encouraged to visit website for more information. May also e-mail, call, fax.

VIRGINIA FESTIVAL OF THE BOOK

Virginia Festival of the Book Foundation for the Humanities, 145 Ednam Dr., Charlottesville VA 22903-4629. (434)924-3296. **Fax:** (434)296-4714. **E-mail:** vabook@virginia.edu; spcoleman@virginia.edu. **Website:** www.vabook.org. **Contact:** Nancy Damon, program director. Estab. 1995. Annual. Held March 20-24. Average attendance: 22,000. Festival held to celebrate books and promote reading and literacy. Open to Students. Readings, panel discussions, presentations and workshops by author, and book-related professionals for children and adults. Most programs are free and open to the public. See website for more information. Applications available online from May through September.

COSTS Most events are free and open to the public. Two luncheons, a breakfast, and a reception require tickets.

ACCOMMODATIONS Overnight accommodations available.

ADDITIONAL INFORMATION "The festival is a 5-day event featuring authors, illustrators, and publishing professionals. Authors must apply to the festival to be included on a panel. Applications accepted only online.

WESLEYAN WRITERS CONFERENCE

Wesleyan University, 294 High St., Room 207, Middletown CT 06459. (860)685-3604. **Fax:** (860)685-2441. **E-mail:** agreene@wesleyan.edu. **Website:** www.wesleyan.edu/writing/conference. Estab. 1956. Annual conference held June 12-16. Average attendance: 100. Focuses on the novel, fiction techniques, short stories, poetry, screenwriting, nonfiction, literary journalism, memoir, mixed media work and publishing. The conference is held on the campus of Wesleyan University, in the hills overlooking the Connecticut River. Features a faculty of award-winning writers, seminars and readings of new fiction, poetry, nonfiction and mixed media forms—as well as guest lectures on a range of topics including publishing. Both new and experienced writers are welcome. Participants may attend seminars in all genres. Speakers have included Esmond Harmsworth (Zachary Schuster Agency), Daniel Mandel (Sanford J. Greenburger Associates), Dorian Karchmar, Amy Williams (ICM and Collins McCormick), Mary Sue Rucci (Simon & Schuster), Denise Roy (Simon & Schuster), John Kulka (Harvard University Press), Julie Barer (Barer Literary) and many others. Agents will be speaking and available for meetings with attendees. Participants are often successful in finding agents and publishers for their mss. Wesleyan participants are also frequently featured in the anthology *Best New American Voices*.

ACCOMMODATIONS Meals are provided on campus. Lodging is available on campus or in town.

ADDITIONAL INFORMATION Ms critiques are available, but not required. Scholarships and teaching fellowships are available, including the Joan Jakobson Awards for fiction writers and poets; and the Jon Davidoff Scholarships for nonfiction writers and journalists. Inquire via e-mail, fax, or phone.

WESTERN RESERVE WRITERS & FREELANCE CONFERENCE

7700 Clocktower Dr., Kirtland OH 44094. (440) 525-7812. **E-mail:** deencr@aol.com. **Website:** www.dean naadams.com. **Contact:** Deanna Adams, director/conference coordinator. Estab. 1983. Biannual. Last conference held September 28, 2013. Conference duration: 1 day or half-day. Average attendance: 120. "The Western Reserve Writers Conferences are designed for all writers, aspiring and professional, and offer presentations in all genres—nonfiction, fiction, poetry, essays, creative nonfiction, and the business of writing, including Web writing and successful freelance writing." Site: "Located in the main building of Lakeland Community College, the conference is easy to find and just off the I-90 freeway. The Fall 2013 conference featured top-notch presenters from newspapers and magazines, along with published authors, freelance writers, and professional editors. Presentations included developing issues in today's publishing and publishing options, turning writing into a lifelong vocation, as well as workshops on plotting, creating credible characters, writing mysteries, romance writing, and tips on submissions, getting books into stores, and storytelling for both fiction and nonfiction writers. Included throughout the day are one-on-one editing consults, Q&A panel, and book sale/author signings."

COSTS Fall all-day conference includes lunch: $95. Spring half-day conference, no lunch: $69.

ADDITIONAL INFORMATION Brochures for the conferences are available by January (for spring conference) and July (for fall). Also accepts inquiries by e-mail and phone. Check Deanna Adams' website for all updates. Editors and agents often attend the conferences.

WILDACRES WRITERS WORKSHOP

233 S. Elm St., Greensboro NC 27401. (336)255-8210. **E-mail:** judihill78@yahoo.com. **Website:** www.wil dacreswriters.com. **Contact:** Judi Hill, Director. Estab. 1985. Annual residential workshop held July 6-13. Conference duration: 1 week. Average attendance: 100. Workshop focuses on novel, short story, flash fiction, poetry, and nonfiction. 10 on faculty include Ron Rash, Carrie Brown, Dr. Janice Fuller, Phillip Gerard, Luke Whisnant, Dr. Joe Clark, John Gregory Brown, Dr. Phebe Davidson, Lee Zacharias, and Vicki Lane.

COSTS The total price for seven days is $690. This price includes workshop fees, one manuscript critique, programs, parties, room, and meals.

ADDITIONAL INFORMATION Include a 1-page writing sample with your registration. See the website for information.

WILLAMETTE WRITERS CONFERENCE

2108 Buck St., Portland OR 97068. (503)305-6729. **Fax:** (503)344-6174. **E-mail:** wilwrite@willamette writers.com. **Website:** www.willamettewriters.com. Estab. 1981. Annual conference held in August. Conference duration: 3 days. Average attendance: 600. "Williamette Writers is open to all writers, and we plan our conference accordingly. We offer workshops on all aspects of fiction, nonfiction, marketing, the creative process, screenwriting, etc. Also we invite top-notch inspirational speakers for keynote addresses. Recent theme was 'Fresh Brewed.' We always include at least 1 agent or editor panel and offer a variety of topics of interest to both fiction and nonfiction writers and screenwriters." Agents will be speaking and available for meetings with attendees. Recent editors, agents, and film producers in attendance have included April Eberhardt, Katheryn Flynn, Robert Guinsler, Laura Mclean, Tooschis Morin.

COSTS Pricing schedule available online.

ACCOMMODATIONS If necessary, arrangements can be made on an individual basis through the conference hotel. Special rates may be available.

ADDITIONAL INFORMATION Brochure/guidelines are available for a catalog-sized SASE.

🌏 WINCHESTER WRITERS' CONFERENCE, FESTIVAL AND BOOKFAIR, AND IN-DEPTH WRITING WORKSHOPS

University of Winchester, Winchester Hampshire WA S022 4NR United Kingdom. 44 (0) 1962 827238. **E-mail:** Barbara.Large@winchester.ac.uk. **Website:** www.writersconference.co.uk. **Contact:** Barbara Large. "The 33rd Winchester Writers' Conference, Festival, and Bookfair will be launched by Lord Julian Fellowes, author/scriptwriter, internationally famous for many works, including *Downton Abbey*, in-depth writing workshops June 24-25, 2-13, at the University of Winchester, Winchester, Hampshire S022 4NR. Lord Felloews will give the Keynote Address and will lead an outstanding team of 65 professional writers who will offer during 14 masters' courses, 16 Friday evening-Sunday morning, 55 lectures, and 500 one-to-one appointments to help writers harness their creative ideas into marketable work. Participate by entering some of the 17 writing competitions, even if you can't attend. Over 120 writers have now reported major publishing successes as a direct result of their attendance at past conferences. This leading international literary event offers a magnificent source of information and network of support from tutors who are published writers and industry specialists, a support that continues throughout the year with additional short courses. Enjoy a creative writing holiday in Winchester, the oldest city in England, yet within an hour of London. Tours planned to Jane Austen's home and the Chawton Study Centre for Women's Literature, the haunts of Keats and the 12th century illuminated Winchester Bible. To receive the 66-page conference programme, including all the competition details please contact us:sara.gangai@winchester.ac.uk, 44(0)1962-826367; barbara.large@winchester.ac.uk, 44(0)1962-827238; or write to us at University of Winchester, Winchester, Hampshire SO22 4NR, United Kingdom."

WISCONSIN BOOK FESTIVAL

Wisconsin Humanities Council, 222 S. Bedford St., Suite F, Madison WI 53703. (608)262-0706. **Fax:** (608)263-7970. **E-mail:** atjoneschaim@wisc.edu. **Website:** www.wisconsinbookfestival.org. Estab. 2002. Annual festival held November 7-11. Conference duration: 5 days. The festival features readings, lectures, book discussions, writing workshops, live interviews, children's events, and more. Speakers have included Michael Cunningham, Grace Paley, TC Boyle, Marjane Satrapi, Phillip Gourevitch, Myla Goldberg, Audrey Niffenegger, Harvey Pekar, Billy Collins, Tim O'Brien and Isabel Allende. **COSTS** All festival events are free.

WISCONSIN REGIONAL WRITERS' ASSOCIATION CONFERENCES

PO Box 085270, Racine Wisconsin 53408-5270. **E-mail:** cfreg@wiwrite.org. **Website:** www.wiwrite.org. Estab. 1948. Annual conferences are held in May 10 and 11 and September. Conference duration: 2-3 days. Provides presentations for all genres, including fiction, nonfiction, scriptwriting, and poetry. Presenters include authors, agents, editors, and publishers. Speakers have included Jack Byrne, Michelle Grajkowski, Benjamin Leroy, Richard Lederer, and Philip Martin. **COSTS** $40-75.

ACCOMMODATIONS Provides a list of area hotels or lodging options. "We negotiate special rates at each facility. A block of rooms is set aside for a specific time period."

ADDITIONAL INFORMATION Award winners receive a certificate and a cash prize. First place winners of the Jade Ring contest receive a jade ring. Must be a member to enter contests. For brochure, call, e-mail or visit website in March/July.

WOMEN WRITERS WINTER RETREAT

Homestead House B&B, 38111 West Spaulding, Willoughby OH 44094. (440)946-1902. **E-mail:** deencr@aol.com. **Website:** www.deannaadams.com. Estab. 2007. Annual. Conference duration: 3 days. Average attendance: 35-40. Retreat. "The Women Writers' Winter Retreat was designed for aspiring and professional women writers who cannot seem to find enough time to devote to honing their craft. Each retreat offers class time and workshops facilitated by successful women writers, as well as allows time to do some actual writing, alone or in a group. A Friday night dinner and keynote kick-starts the weekend, followed by Saturday workshops, free time, meals, and an open mic to read your works. Sunday wraps up with 1 more workshop and fellowship. All genres welcome. Choice of overnight stay or commuting." Site: Located in the heart of downtown Willoughby, this warm and attractive bed and breakfast is easy to find, around the corner from the main street, Erie

Street, and behind a popular Arabica coffee house. Door prizes and book sale/author signings throughout the weekend.

COSTS Single room: $315; shared room: $235 (includes complete weekend package, with B&B stay and all meals and workshops); weekend commute: $165; Saturday only: $125 (prices include lunch and dinner).

ADDITIONAL INFORMATION Brochures for the writers retreat are available by December. Accepts inquiries and reservations by e-mail or phone. See Deanna's website for additional information and updates.

WOMEN WRITING THE WEST

8547 E. Araphoe Rd., Box J-541, Greenwood Village CO 80112-1436. **E-mail:** conference@women writingthewest.org. **Website:** www.womenwrit ingthewest.org. Held October 11-13 in Kansas City, Missouri. "Women Writing the West is a nonprofit association of writers, editors, publishers, agents, booksellers, and other professionals writing and promoting the women's West. As such, women writing their stories in the American West in a way that illuminates them authentically. In addition, the organization provides support, encouragement, and inspiration to all women writing about any facet of the American West. Membership is open to all interested persons worldwide. Open to students. Cost of membership: Annual membership dues $60. Publisher dues are $60. International dues are $70. In addition to the annual dues, there is an option to become a sustaining member for $100. Sustaining members receive a WWW enamel logo pin, prominent listing in WWW publications, and the knowledge that they are assisting the organization. Members actively exchange ideas on a list e-bulletin board. WWW membership also allows the choice of participation in our marketing marvel, the annual WWW Catalog of Author'sBooks. An annual conference is held every fall. Our WWW newsletter is current WWW activities; features market research, and experience articles of interest pertaining to American West literature and member news. Sponsors annual WILLA Literary Award, which is given in several categories foroutstanding literature featuring women's stories, set in the West. The winner of a WILLA literary Award receives a cash award and a trophy at the annualconference. Contest open to non-members. Annual conference held in third weekend in October. Covers re-

search, writing techniques, multiple genres, marketing/promotion, and more. Agents and editors will be speaking and available for one-on-one meetings with attendees. Conference location changes each year."

COSTS Early Registration: $295 (June 30); Registration (after June 30): $320. Discounts available for members, and for specific days only.

ACCOMMODATIONS See website for location and accommodation details.

WORDS & MUSIC

624 Pirate's Alley, New Orleans LA 70116. (504)586-1609. **Fax:** (504)522-9725. **E-mail:** info@wordsand music.org. **Website:** www.wordsandmusic.org. Estab. 1997. Annual conference held November 20-24. Conference duration: 5 days. Average attendance: 300. Presenters include authors, agents, editors and publishers. Past speakers included agents Deborah Grosvenor, Judith Weber, Stuart Bernstein, Nat Sobel, Jeff Kleinman, Emma Sweeney, Liza Dawson and Michael Murphy; editors Lauren Marino, Webster Younce, Ann Patty, Will Murphy, Jofie Ferrari-Adler, Elizabeth Stein; critics Marie Arana, Jonathan Yardley, and Michael Dirda; fiction writers Oscar Hijuelos, Robert Olen Butler, Shirley Ann Grau, Mayra Montero, Ana Castillo, H.G. Carrillo. Agents and editors critique manuscripts in advance; meet with them one-on-one during the conference.

COSTS See website for a costs and additional information on accommodations. Website will update closer to date of conference.

ACCOMMODATIONS Hotel Monteleone in New Orleans.

WRITE-BY-THE-LAKE WRITER'S WORKSHOP & RETREAT

21 N. Park St., 7th Floor, Madison WI 53715. (608)262-3447. **E-mail:** cdesmet@dcs.wisc.edu. **Website:** www. dcs.wisc.edu/lsa/writing. **Contact:** Christine DeSmet, director. Open to all writers and students; 12 workshops for all levels. Includes 2 Master Classes for full-novel critique. Held the third week of June on UW-Madison campus. Registration limited to 15; fewer in Master Classes. Writing facilities available; computer labs, wi-fi in all buildings and on the outdoor lakeside terrace.

COSTS $345 before May 20; $395 after May 20. Additional cost for Master Classes and college credits. Cost includes instruction, welcome luncheon, and pastry/coffee each day.

ADDITIONAL INFORMATION E-mail for more information. "Registration opens every December for following June. See web pages online."

○ WRITE! CANADA

The Word Guild, P.O. Box 1243, Trenton ON K8V 5R9 Canada. **E-mail:** info@thewordguild.com. **E-mail:** writecanada@rogers.com. **Website:** www.writecanada.org. Conference duration: 3 days. Annual conference June 14-16 in Guelph, Ontario for writers who are Christian of all types and at all stages. Offers solid instruction, stimulating interaction, exciting challenges, and worshipful community.

WRITE ON THE SOUND WRITERS' CONFERENCE

Edmonds Arts Commission, 700 Main St., Edmonds WA 98020. (425)771-0228. **Fax:** (425)771-0253. **E-mail:** sarah.cocker@edmondswa.gov. **Website:** www.writeonthesound.com. Estab. 1985. Annual conference held October 4-6. Conference duration: 2.5 days. Average attendance: 200. Features over 30 presenters, a literary contest, ms critiques, a reception and book signing, onsite bookstore, and a variety of evening activities. Held at the Frances Anderson Center in Edmonds, just north of Seattle on the Puget Sound. Speakers have included Elizabeth George, Dan Hurley, Marcia Woodard, Holly Hughes, Greg Bear, Timothy Egan, Joe McHugh, Frances Wood, Garth Stein and Max Grover.

COSTS See website for more information on applying to view costs.

ADDITIONAL INFORMATION Brochures are available in July. Accepts inquiries via phone, e-mail, and fax.

WRITERS@WORK CONFERENCE

P.O. Box 711191, Salt Lake City UT 84171-1191. (801)996-3313. **E-mail:** jennifer@writersatwork.org. **Website:** www.writersatwork.org. Estab. 1985. Annual conference held June 5-9. Conference duration: 5 days. Average attendance: 250. Morning workshops (3-hours/day) focus on novel, advanced fiction, generative fiction, nonfiction, poetry, and young adult fiction. Afternoon sessions will include craft lectures, discussions, and directed interviews with authors, agents, and editors. In addition to the traditional, one-on-one manuscript consultations, there will be many opportunities to mingle informally with agents/editors. Held at the Alta Lodge in Alta Lodge, Utah. Speakers have included Steve Almond, Bret Lott,

Shannon Hale, Emily Forland (Wendy Weil Agency), Julie Culver (Folio Literary Management, Chuck Adams (Algonquin Press), and Mark A. Taylor (Juniper Press).

COSTS $675-965, based on housing type and consultations.

ACCOMMODATIONS Onsite housing available. Additional lodging and meal information is on the website.

WRITERS' CONFERENCE AT OCEAN PARK

14 Temple Ave., P.O. Box 7296, Ocean Park ME 04063-7296. (207)934-9068. **Fax:** (207)934-2823. **E-mail:** opa@oceanpark.org. **Website:** www.oceanpark.org. Other addresses: P.O. Box 7146, Ocean Park, ME 04063-7146; P.O. Box 172, Assonet, MA 02702 (mailing address for conference). Estab. 1941. Annual conference held in mid-August. Conference duration: 4 days. Average attendance: 50. "We try to present a balanced and eclectic conference. In addition to time and attention given to poetry, we also have children's literature, mystery writing, travel, fiction, nonfiction, journalism, and other issues of interest to writers. Our speakers are editors, writers, and other professionals. Our concentration is, by intention, a general view of writing to publish with supportive encouragement. We are located in Ocean Park, a small seashore village 14 miles south of Portland. Ours is a summer assembly center with many buildings from the Victorian age. The conference meets in Porter Hall, one of the assembly buildings which is listed in the National Register of Historic Places. Speakers have included Michael C. White (novelist/short story writer), Betsy Shool (poet), Suzanne Strempek Shea (novelist), John Perrault (poet), Josh Williamson (newspaper editor), Dawn Potter (poet), Bruce Pratt (fiction writer), Amy McDonald (children's author), Anne Wescott Dodd (nonfiction writer), Kate Chadbourne (singer/songwriter), Wesley McNair (poet/Maine faculty member), and others. We usually have about 8 guest presenters each year." Publishes writers/editors will be speaking, leading workshops, and available for meetings with attendees.

COSTS $200. The fee does not include housing or meals, which must be arranged separately by conferees.

ACCOMMODATIONS "An accommodations list is available. We are in a summer resort area where motels, guest houses, and restaurants abound."

ADDITIONAL INFORMATION Official summer hours begin in late June, check then for specific dates for 2013 conference. "We have 6 contests for various genres. An announcement is available in the spring. The prizes (all modest) are awarded at the end of the conference and only to those who are registered. Send SASE in June for the conference program."

WRITER'S DIGEST CONFERENCE (EAST IN NYC, AND WEST IN LA)

F+W Media, Inc., 10151 Carver Road, Suite 200, Blue Ash OH 45242. **E-mail:** jill.ruesch@fwmedia.com. **Website:** www.writersdigestconference.com. The Writer's Digest Conferences happen twice a year -- a spring event in New York City and a fall event (2013 dates = Sept. 27-29) in Los Angeles. They feature an amazing line up of speakers to help writers with the craft and business of writing. The most popular feature of this conference is the agent pitch slam, in which potential authors are given the ability to pitch their books directly to agents. For the 2014 conference, there will be more than 60 agents in attendance..

WRITERS' LEAGUE OF TEXAS AGENTS & EDITORS CONFERENCE

Writers' League of Texas, 611 S. Congress Ave., Suite 505, Austin TX 78704. (512)499-8914. **Fax:** (512)499-0441. **E-mail:** wlt@writersleague.org. **E-mail:** jennifer@writersleague.org. **Website:** www.writersleague.org. Estab. 1982. Established in 1981, the Writers' League of Texas is a nonprofit professional organization whose primary purpose is to provide a forum for information, support, and sharing among writers, to help members improve and market their writing skills, and to promote the interests of writers and the writing community. The Writers' League of Texas Agents & Editors Conference is for writers at every stage of their career. Beginners can learn more about this mystifying industry and prepare themselves for the journey ahead. Those with completed manuscripts can pitch to agents and get feedback on their manuscripts from professional editors. Published writers can learn about market trends and network with rising stars in the world of writing. No matter what your market, genre, or level, our conference can benefit you.

COSTS Rates vary based on membership and the date of registration. The starting rate (registration through December 15) is $309 for members and $369 for non-members. Rate increases by through later dates. See website for details.

ACCOMMODATIONS 2013 event is at the Hyatt Regency Austin, 208 Barton Springs Road, Austin, TX 78704. Check back often for new information.

ADDITIONAL INFORMATION Event held from June 21-23, 2013. Contests and awards programs are offered separately. Brochures are available upon request.

WRITERS' LEAGUE OF TEXAS WORKSHOPS AND SUMMER WRITING RETREAT

611 S. Congress Ave., Suite 130, Austin TX 78704. (512)499-8914. **Fax:** (512)499-0441. **E-mail:** wlt@writersleague.org. **Website:** www.writersleague.org. **Contact:** Sara Kocek, program coordinator. "Classes and workshops provide practical advice and guidance on the craft of writing for writers at all stages of their career." Retreat: Annual Summer Writing Academy in Alpine, TX, is a weeklong writing intensive with five tracks. Special presentations: "The Secrets of the Agents" series of workshops with visiting literary agents. Classes and Workshops: Topics: E-publishing; creative nonfiction; screenwriting; novel writing; short fiction; journaling; manuscript revision; memoir writing; poetry; essays; freelance writing; publicity; author/book websites; and blogging. Instructors include Carol Dawson, Karleen Koen, Kirsten Cappy, Eric Butterman, Cyndi Hughes, Scott Wiggerman, Debra Monroe, Jennifer Ziegler, W.K. Stratton.

WRITERS OMI AT LEDIG HOUSE

55 Fifth Ave., 15th Floor, New York NY 10003. (212)206-6114. **E-mail:** writers@artomi.org. **Website:** www.artomi.org. Residency duration: 2 weeks to 2 months. Average attendance and site: "Up to 20 writers per session—10 at a given time—live and write on the stunning 300 acre grounds and sculpture park that overlooks the Catskill Mountains." Deadline: October 20.

ACCOMMODATIONS Residents provide their own transportation. Offers overnight accommodations.

ADDITIONAL INFORMATION "Agents and editors from the New York publishing community are invited for dinner and discussion. Bicycles, a swimming pool, and nearby tennis court are available for use."

WRITERS RETREAT WORKSHOP

P.O. Box 4236, Louisville KY 40204. **E-mail:** wrw04@netscape.net. **Website:** www.writersretreatworkshop.

com. Estab. 1987. Annual workshop held June 14-23 at the Villa Maria Retreat and Conference Center in Frontenac, Minnesota. Conference duration: 10 days. Focuses on fiction and narrative nonfiction books in progress (all genres). This is an intensive learning experience for small groups of serious-minded writers. Founded by the late Gary Provost (one of the country's leading writing instructors) and his wife Gail (an award-winning author). The goal is for students to leave with a solid understanding of the marketplace, as well as the craft of writing a novel. Speakers have included Becky Motew, Donald Maass, Jennifer Crusie, Michael Palmer, Nancy Pickard, Elizabeth Lyon, Lauren Mosko (Writer's Digest Books), Adam Marsh (Reece Halsey North), and Peter H. McGuigan (Sanford J. Greenburger Literary Agency).

COSTS $1,750 for returning students and $1,825 for new students. Tuition includes private room, three meals daily, all 1-1 meetings with staff and agents, and classes.

WRITERS WEEKEND AT THE BEACH

P.O. Box 877, Ocean Park WA 98640. (360)262-0160. **E-mail:** bhansen6@juno.com. **E-mail:** bobtracie@hotmail.com. **Contact:** John Pelkey. Estab. 1992. Annual conference held in March. Conference duration: 2 days. Average attendance: 60. A retreat for writers with an emphasis on poetry, fiction, and nonfiction. Held at the Ocean Park Methodist Retreat Center & Camp. Speakers have included Wayne Holmes, Miralee Ferrell, Jim Whiting, Birdie Etchison, Colette Tennant, Gail Dunham, Linda Clare and Marion Duckworth.

COSTS $199 for full registration before February 17 and $209 after February 17.

ACCOMMODATIONS Offers on-site overnight lodging.

WRITE-TO-PUBLISH CONFERENCE

WordPro Communication Services, 9118 W. Elmwood Dr., Suite 1G, Niles IL 60714-5820. (847)296-3964. **Fax:** (847)296-0754. **E-mail:** lin@writetopublish.com. **Website:** www.writetopublish.com. **Contact:** Lin Johnson, director. Estab. 1971. Annual. Conference held June 4-7, 2013. Average attendance: 250. Conference is focused for the Christian market and includes classes on writing for children. Writer workshops geared toward all levels. Open to students. Site: Wheaton College, Wheaton, IL (Chicago).

COSTS approximately $485; includes conference and banquet.

ACCOMMODATIONS In campus residence halls. Cost is approximately $280-360.

ADDITIONAL INFORMATION Optional ms evaluation available. College credit available. Conference information available in January. For details, visit website, or e-mail brochure@writetopublish.com. Accepts inquiries by e-mail, fax, phone.

WRITING FOR THE SOUL

Jerry B. Jenkins Christian Writers Guild, 5525 N. Union Blvd., Suite 101, Colorado Springs CO 80918. (866)495-5177. **Fax:** (719)495-5181. **E-mail:** contactus@christianwritersguild.com. **Website:** www.christianwritersguild.com/conference. Annual conference held in February. Workshops and continuing classes cover fiction, nonfiction and magazine writing, children's books, and teen writing. The keynote speakers are nationally known, leading authors. The conference is hosted by Jerry B. Jenkins.

COSTS See website for pricing.

ACCOMMODATIONS The Broadmoor in Colorado Springs.

AGENTS INDEX

LITERARY AGENTS SPECIALTIES INDEX

ANTHROPOLOGY

ARCHITECTURE

ART

BIOGRAPHY

NONFICTION

ANIMALS

RELIGIOUS

SATIRE

SCIENCE